Artificial Int

Artificial Intelligence
Building Intelligent Systems

PARAG KULKARNI
CEO and Chief Scientist
EKLaT Research
Pune

PRACHI JOSHI
Associate Professor
MIT College of Engineering
Pune

PHI Learning Private Limited

Delhi-110092

2015

₹425.00

ARTIFICIAL INTELLIGENCE: Building Intelligent Systems
Parag Kulkarni and Prachi Joshi

ISBN-978-81-203-5046-5

Published by Asoke K. Ghosh, PHI Learning Private Limited, Rimjhim House, 111, Patparganj Industrial Estate, Delhi-110092 and Printed by Rajkamal Electric Press, Plot No. 2, Phase IV, HSIDC, Kundli-131028, Sonepat, Haryana.

Contents

Preface

There has been movement for years to build intelligent systems and make machines intelligent, which can be autonomous, flexible and holistically intelligent. This movement has taken impetus during computer era. Simple intelligence based on memorisation was the beginning of this movement. Event-based intelligence, pattern-based intelligence and selection-driven intelligence have been incorporated in different appliances. While building the intelligent system, human being was at the centre and the objective was to build the system that could behave like human beings.

Slowly, simple event-based learning, anomaly detection, exception handling with computers and pattern analysis became a part of many intelligent systems. The expectation from intelligent systems kept on increasing. We started expecting more from our intelligent systems, and hence, last few decades are marked by more sophisticated intelligent system building.

The handling of different complex decision scenarios and inabilities of machines to learn in these complex scenarios raised many questions on the intelligence of machine. In this process, many efforts have been made to make machines behave like human being to handle uncertain scenarios in real life. They should be able to smell, handle gestures, classify and take decisions. While making this happen, well-defined paradigms and architecture of intelligent systems were evolved. Paradigms kept changing, but the fundamentals of intelligent systems were evolved like the process to build intelligent systems. A machine, therefore, should be able to plan, search, sense the environment and act accordingly. Further, it should have different capabilities like processing text and natural language, handling scenarios with fuzzy logic, selecting the most appropriate action with an ability to make decisions.

The broad view of intelligent systems can represent it as a system that can sense environment, analyse data, learn and select the most appropriate techniques based on learning. It should take decisions, act accordingly, and even keep learning based on the outcome of its own action and feedback from the environment. It should have an ability to handle new scenarios and even similar scenarios in the most efficient manner. It has been and is going to be a long, but very interesting journey. This book is about building intelligent systems and learning different aspects of intelligent systems with reference to recent advances.

The book is intended to put all the concepts related to intelligent system in front of readers in the most simplified way so that while understanding the basic concepts of intelligent systems, they will develop thought process that can contribute to the building of advanced intelligent systems. Though this book is intended for the undergraduate and postgraduate students, we believe that it will be very useful as a reference book for the researchers and professionals working in the field of intelligent systems and allied areas. This book tries to provide more insights into the research opportunities while providing numerous questions and pointers to build problem-solving abilities.

Intelligent system tries to solve problem intelligently and optimally. The real-life problems are not static. These problems change with time, environment, and the solution even depends on the context of the problem. This book discusses different facets of intelligent systems. The book can also be used as a reference book for specialised research, and it can help the readers and researchers to appreciate a systematic way to build the intelligent systems.

Book Organisation

The book is organised in 21 chapters, each chapter covering the basic concepts along with the examples of real-world scenarios for the readers to understand and grasp the essentialities and the background needed to take up AI. The connectivity between the topics is highlighted in the following diagram:

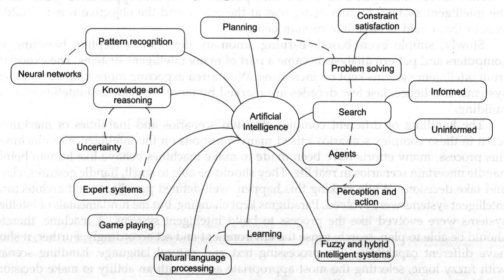

The details of the chapters are given below:

Chapter 1 provides an overview of AI along with the history and foundation of the subject. The importance and role of AI in the current scenarios and the recent developments along with advance topics are also highlighted. Chapter 2 discusses about problem solving and its representations. In AI, these representations are very critical. These representations along with the role of search and the types of problems are discussed in detail in the chapter. Chapter 3 presents methods and algorithms with simple examples of exploring search techniques in uninformed way to solve problems. Chapter 4 discusses heuristic-based search techniques. The chapter presents a detailed study of algorithms and their applications in game playing, and advanced search methods as well. Chapter 5 deals with the intelligent agents. The agent types, their percept, the impact of environment on the actions along with their applications in real-life scenarios are discussed in the chapter. Chapter 6 discusses constraint satisfaction problems. The problem formulation with constraints, its structural representation along with the use of search and the role of heuristic are elaborated in it. Chapter 7 handles the critical concept of knowledge representation and reasoning. Reasoning needs to be concrete to support the next move and infer. Every move is impacted with the logic that forms the basis of knowledge representation. All these aspects are detailed with examples in the chapter. Chapter 8 extends the knowledge representation in uncertain conditions. Decision-making with simple and complex scenarios is included in it. Chapter 9 handles the concept of planning, starting from a simple planning agent to the approaches for planning, partial order planning and the graphs. Chapter 10 deals with machine learning concepts. Today, tremendous research is diverted towards classification and data mining. The chapter details the introductory techniques as well as the advanced ones along with their applications in the current environment from the mining perspective. Chapter 11 discusses expert system building. Its need, system architecture and the rules along with case studies are detailed in the chapter. Chapter 12 provides an overview of natural language processing. The models and the importance of syntax and semantic analysis are explained. Their use in machine translation and the current applications are also covered in it. Chapter 13 handles decision theory concepts. It details the role of risks in decisions along with probabilistic reasoning. Semi-constrained influence diagrams are also introduced here. Chapter 14 details about pattern recognition. The chapter covers techniques of feature extraction and object identification along with the discussion of speech recognition. Chapter 15 provides an insight into the game playing. From the basic concepts to the knowledge structure and search strategies, the chapter covers many popular games, together with the techniques and algorithms used for them. Chapter 16 deals with image processing aspect. It details methods involved in perception and action. Image formulation, processing techniques for removal of noise and enlargement with edge detection approaches are detailed. Acting in the environment based on the percept is also discussed. Chapter 17 contains techniques with regard to hybrid and fuzzy systems. Recent trends in research with evolutionary approaches and neuro-fuzzy systems are discussed. Chapter 18 is dedicated to neural network-based learning. Representation of neural network, its types and application as a pattern recognition technique are detailed in the chapter. Chapter 19 discusses industrial applications of AI. With several case studies and model building steps, the chapter captures the gist of all the techniques previously studied in the book and presents the overall system development cycle with AI. Chapter 20 discusses the concurrency aspect as well as the role of AI in big data analytics and cloud, sentiment analysis, and elaborates different aspects of AI with reference to new technology trends. Chapter 21 concludes the series of the chapters, with a special mention of the future work and trends in AI.

Parag Kulkarni
Prachi Joshi

Acknowledgements

This book is the outcome of queries from the students, lecture notes and research in the field of Artificial Intelligence (AI) while teaching AI, intelligent systems and machine learning (ML) for more than one decade. We would like to thank all the students who opted for these courses. We are also thankful to the institutes for giving us opportunities to teach these subjects.

Since the last two decades, we have been working with various organisations, institutes, researchers, professionals and scientists. Everyone has contributed and motivated us to write a book on AI. We have, thus, utilised the opportunity to teach at many reputed institutes and universities, including IIM, Masaryk University, COEP, PICT and MITCOE. We have received opportunities to deliver more than hundred speeches at different places, which have created numerous avenues for interactions and helped in presenting this book in a better way. We are thankful to business, engineering, and research students, who gave us opportunities to build research interactions.

We have also been associated with various management, decision-making, and AI-based IT product companies. We are thankful to different organisations/institutes we are/were associated with, including Siemens, IDeaS and Capsilon. We are also thankful to the academic institutes in Pune, PCCOE, DY Patil College of Engineering, Bharati Vidyapeeth and Raisoni group of institutes, which gave us opportunity to interact with the students. We also thank Dr. V.D. Karad and Dr. Mangesh Karad of MIT group of institutions. We would also acknowledge the support given by our friends and co-workers.

We would like to express our thanks to Dr. Sarang Joshi, Sudarshan Deshmukh and P.R. Joshi. We are thankful to the team and innovators we have worked with such as Dr. Ravi, Dr. Omar and Santosh. They are always ready to work on new ideas and have contributed through collective learning. We are also thankful to young enthusiastic team at Anomaly. We are grateful to Professor Vashek, Professor Kharadkar, Dr. P.K. Sinha, Dr. Chande, Professor Hector, Dr. P. Kulkarni, Dr. Shah, Dr. Milind Pande, Dr. M. Nagmode, Dr. R. Pujeri and Professor R. Bedi for their support in this journey.

We wish to thank Dr. Sahasrabudhe (Director, COEP) and Professor Sawant, Professor M.A. Joshi (COEP) for their help during this journey. We also take opportunity to thank Sunita Jahirabadkar, Yashodhara Haribhakta, Vinod Pachghare, Nitin Pise, Pramod Patil, Deepak Vidhate, Vaibhav Khatavkar, Sheetal Sonawane and Mousami Munot.

We would like to grasp this opportunity to thank our mentors and teachers for motivating us during this journey. Also, we are grateful to our parents for everything they did for us. Most importantly, we would like to thank our family members, Manisha Kulkarni, Dr. Mrudula Kulkarni, Hrishikesh, Manoj Joshi, Preeti, Malhar, Meena Thite, Meena Joshi, and Manohar Joshi for their firm belief in our ideas as well as support, motivation, and help throughout this knowledgeable journey.

Finally, we wish to thank Malaya and the entire PHI editing team for their great work. We would like to thank all the reviewers of this book as well as the reviewers of our research papers, who helped us through their critical comments and creative suggestions to greatly improve the text.

Parag Kulkarni
Prachi Joshi

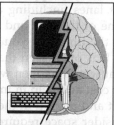

CHAPTER 1

Introduction to Artificial Intelligence

INTRODUCTION

Suppose you are on the way to some trip and travelling by road. With a large number of toll collection booths and endless multiple queues in front of you, you possibly ask your friend—"Hey which lane do we line up?" and judgmentally a friend suggests one of them. (But possibly other queue would have made your car pass by faster. Is it not dependent on the people working at the booths?) Can we have artificial intelligence (AI) to resolve this?

Imagine you pass through the booth and the toll is auto-deducted by means of in-vehicle unit specially designed for your car. Sensors capture the vehicle number and deduct the pre-deposited amount from the in-built chip. Such electronic toll collection system is found at Ahmedabad–Mumbai highway and a couple of other places in India. This system needs to be made more intelligent to make it work in Indian context across the various roads and highways in India. Certain changes can make it highly effective in terms of time and manpower utilisation in Indian context. The improved system can help the government by means of analysis of the records of the amount collection on week days and other statistics. At present, there are semi-automatic toll collection systems at Bangkok. Just imagine a toll system that is intelligent and vehicle-based. Such a system can direct the vehicle to proper lane and will be able to keep a track record of regularity of payments. In case, some very regular payee misses, the detection on one of the occasion can be possible. This can be possible with a prepaid card-based toll collection, where a prepaid card is used or even there can be a vehicle number-based toll collection, where it is connected to the bank account of vehicle owner. It can be different for interior roads and expressways. Hence, intelligent system can revolutionise the simple application of toll collection and different intelligent system applications right from planning to decision-making, and thus, can help in building a better system.

1

A simple sub-application is discussed here. At present, it is possible to suggest you to line up at a particular lane. The moment you approach a toll booth, the AI system would analyse the vehicles at the different lanes (including analysis of density and the size or even detection of some failure at one of the lane and so on) and intimate you about the lane number you should go in and the time that you would take.

Let us take one more example. It is often seen that the loading of material in trucks for transport is done manually. What would happen when a robot is employed? A simple robot can assist in saving the labour cost and help in improving the efficiency of the work. Such a robot is tuned to lift an object and place it in the truck. But is there any intelligence involved in it? Does this robot consider space requirements? No, but an intelligent one will definitely do it. An intelligent robot would take up the object and place it efficiently such that the space of the truck is utilised to the fullest. Thus, an intelligent robot would overcome space and time complexities. To add further, a robot without intelligence would fail to operate if the road/path is full of obstacles, but an intelligent one would perceive this and take a different route and carry out the task. Moreover, such an intelligent system can consider weight, size, material of which the articles in the box are composed (whether articles in box are brittle and to be kept in a particular way). Also, it can scan size of box, determine other properties of the box and load different boxes optimally.

And the last but not the least, all of us have heard the story of 'Snow White'. Her stepmother asked to the magical mirror "Who is the most beautiful lady among all?" and she got a reply. We know that it is a fairy tale. But what would happen if we have something of this sort in real? An intelligent app that would suggest some outfit that we can wear! Adding to this, a talking mirror-cum-dresser that would show how an outfit would look on us! Is this all feasible?—Definitely. With AI, we can have all these options and it is not just about dressing, but it can involve suggesting a suitable costume based on your mood, occasion, profession and so on. There are a few garment and fashion designing companies that give some sort of these facilities to recommend the best dress for you. These systems are at very rudimentary stage at present. They analyse the person's parameters, as said earlier and suggest the best garments, colours and combinations for you. Thus, intelligent systems have potential to change the way we have been using our resources resulting in more efficient, smart and friendly systems. These systems can adapt to the requirement and needs of daily operations as well as some of the very specific tasks.

So, artificial intelligence can help in making our life simple not only for taking decisions but also for the other aspects. Thus, artificial intelligence is slowly becoming a part of our day-to-day life and an essential part of all modern equipment as well. It is required for automated climate control in a car or an automated manufacturing unit in industry—Whether it is a washing machine or microwave oven—artificial intelligence is everywhere. These AI-based tools and techniques have not only improved accuracy but also made it possible to perform tasks, which were otherwise impossible without AI.

If we think about AI in holistic way, then it includes learning, searching and problem solving. The purpose of AI is to empower machine to solve the problems by making the machine intelligent. Whenever the term *intelligence* is referred, it is always referred in relevance with the human intelligence. In some cases, it is referred with reference to the reasonability in decision-making or the action taken. *AI* is defined by Rich and Knight as follows:

"AI is the study of how to make computers do things which, at the moment, people do better."

This definition catches the crux of AI and defines its purpose. This definition has its own limitations and covers one of the basic aspects of AI. It is not an easy task to define AI and all the books have done decent efforts to define AI based on some of its important facets. AI can be defined as follows:

It deals with the science that is about the efforts of making a machine behave intelligently and respond in a way as human would have responded and in due process, deliver reasonable answers. In other words, a branch of science and engineering that focuses on making machine intelligent is widely known as *AI*.

The scientists such as George Boole have led the foundation of AI logic years ago. Then, for last five decades many scientists were part of the movement of making machine intelligent. A broad categorisation of AI functions and objectives includes reasonable decision-making, demonstration of intelligence like humans and computational modelling to solve decision problems. In context with the above broad categorisation, AI can be defined in different ways as follows:

1. Machines which can think and have a capability to react like human beings
2. Systems that respond intelligently in the same way as the humans do
3. Computational models to solve various complex decision-making problems
4. Study of intelligent agents

The approaches followed while studying and representing AI include various empirical approaches—one coming from the philosophy of comparison with human and human reactions in case of different situations, while another is about use of mathematics and models for optimisation with reference to the desired outcome.

The horizon of AI includes techniques for knowledge transmission, knowledge representation, automated reasoning, and this is used to empower machines to behave intelligently. The purpose of overall data analysis and knowledge augmentation is to make machines learn and solve complex real-life, problems. AI is actually an ensemble of technologies, interactions and allied platforms which takes part in helping machine to demonstrate intelligence and reasonability. The human way of thinking, responding and decision-making is the only expectations and reference in this process.

Cognitive models deal with the computer knowledge-based models for AI. Various experimental techniques and theories about working and representation of human mind are part of the cognitive models. The study of human psychology and psychological analysis with reference to decision process is studied in these cognitive models. The fields of cognitive science and AI go hand in hand and have their application in natural language processing.

Further, for any action, there is an expected response from the aspect of rationality. Intelligent machines need to demonstrate the rational behaviour. We expect a human to react in a particular way to a given situation or respond to a particular decision scenario. Similarly, there is also an expectation from an intelligent machine to react rationally.

1.1 ARTIFICIAL INTELLIGENCE—HISTORY AND FOUNDATION

AI has been a part of mainstream research since last 60 years. But AI philosophy is as old as one thousand years. Statistics, analysis of patterns, use of formal systems have been parts of research for many years. Many philosophers including the great Aristotle tried to describe and represent human process of thinking and decision-making using symbols. In 20th century, the ideas in fiction started to realise in the form of computer. Indian and Greek philosophers developed various methods for formal reasoning. This was a structured approach towards problem solving. In the 1940s, Zuse devised high-level programming language and wrote the first chess program that could demonstrate chess playing. Before that chess playing was considered an intelligent activity that was not possible for machine. Later on, Leibniz envisioned and formulated a language of reasoning, where he mapped symbols for reasoning. When mathematical logic came to help in twentieth century, it assured that AI is very much possible.

Allan Turing devised a simple test of intelligence in 1950, where the response of machine is expected to be intelligent enough so that it is difficult to find out whether it is machine or human sitting on the other side. Since then, there is a quest for intelligent algorithm to build AI-based system to meet the expectations.

In 1956, John McCarthy insisted and made AI as a topic for conference at Dartmouth. In 1958, he (MIT) invented the Lisp language, which later became popular for AI-related programming.

Initially, AI was focussed on common sense reasoning and obvious reaction. In this common sense reasoning, AI was expected to perform some sort of general problem solving. The problem solving and decision-making was based on set of simple hypothesis. The problems were simple and did not require large knowledge base.

Slowly research began to handle large amount of knowledge and more complex relationships. It included domains like speech recognition and analysis, image processing and medical diagnosis. The complexity of the tasks and inferring mechanism kept on increasing. In case of noisy data and large information base for extraction of information, there were more challenges for the researchers. They slowly started developing intelligent systems to handle these complex research problems.

1.2   BIRTH OF ARTIFICIAL INTELLIGENCE

John McCarthy at Dartmouth College worked on research in the areas of automata theory, neural nets and study of intelligence. McCarthy gave a new term for AI, i.e., 'computational rationality'. Dartmouth is a place where formal workshop and conference on AI took place. This helped in exploring the field of AI, and the research in this field started to gain momentum. This further helped in realising the AI-related thoughts and ideas. The various concepts like intelligence, knowledge, reasoning, thoughts, cognition and learning started to formulate a platform for AI research. These concepts were further explored from the perspective of applying knowledge to perform a desired activity. These activities range from the normal activities to complex activities. This started a movement of building intelligent systems.

AI is one of the major components of intelligent systems. Let us take an example of simple mechanical intelligent system.

Figure 1.1 depicts a small example of a traditional mechanical intelligent system. Here, once the water reaches to a certain level, the water tap is closed to avoid overflow. In washing machines, these systems were replaced with the sensor-based level detector. Later, fuzzy logic came into the picture that allowed deciding the level of water dynamically based on the quantity of clothes. So, we are now having machines, with fuzzy logic included.

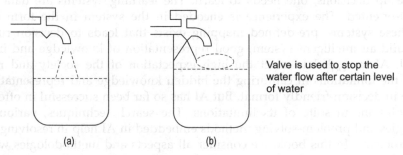

Valve is used to stop the water flow after certain level of water

(a) (b)

Figure 1.1 Mechanical intelligent system.

Traditional intelligent systems are the examples, wherein the knowledge acquired in past is programmed in the system. These systems were later replaced by electronic systems, which used some static historical knowledge to take decisions in future.

Let us consider an example related to traffic management to understand how the growth and evolution of AI can help in making things simple and manageable. We are aware of the growing traffic scenario and how much difficult it is to commute.

1. First, we begin with the history of the signals to control the traffic traditionally. They were based on some historic information. The switching time was static and independent of the road conditions, which did not account for the peak hours. This would have been sufficient if there had not been any change in the traffic.

2. The increase in the traffic resulted in total chaos. Gradually, there was a need for a tuner system that could change the signal timings with respect to the peak hours of the traffic. Was AI involved here? It could be just a simple decision-making system with a little intelligence to have the control of the signal or even manual setting could be done with no intelligence at all.

3. Gradually, the need for an intelligent system arised. A traffic jam at one road crossing could impact many roads. So, an observer with sensors like a camera to detect the current traffic conditions evolved an intelligent traffic monitor and controller that would tune the signal timing with this jam. This could be set up at every signal in operation. AI techniques, thus, can help us in solving problems in a better way.

4. At present, there is a need for an intelligent signal controller, wherein all the signals are synchronised and they can be controlled with a centralised controller. An AI-based system (that can consider events such as election rallies, major accidents, construction of road) can help in capturing the current scene at a particular route, and accordingly, dynamically change the signals timings. This information can even include the analysis and statistics of the traffic density to help in deciding the timings. The same should be reflected and transferred to the signals in proximity. It would, in turn, suggest the route too intelligently that would turn off some signals owing to some environment conditions. Such a system would need complex and advanced techniques of AI and is indeed a challenge to have one in country like India.

Thus, there is a need for AI-based systems, which are expected to react in dynamic situation and even when some information is absent.

To take up decisions, one needs to learn. The learning systems are data as well as experiment-oriented. The experience is encoded in the system in the form of data or rules. In these systems, pre-defined mapping exists that leads to decision rules. So, in order to build an intelligent system, good representation of knowledge and information is essential. AI struggled to meet the high expectation of the society and researchers because of the limitations in capturing the hidden knowledge and representation of that knowledge in decision-friendly format. But AI has so far been successful in offering many practical solutions in spite of its limitations. The search techniques, various learning methodologies and problem-solving methods embedded in AI help in resolving important practical problems. In this book, we consider all aspects and methodologies which come under AI. The purpose of this book is to realise and understand the practical aspects of AI. This book also covers the advanced and allied aspects of AI like pattern analytics, intelligent system modelling, concurrency aspects and applications of intelligent systems with reference to big data.

1.3   AI TECHNIQUES

AI deals with a large spectrum of problems. The spectrum of AI applications is spread across the domains, and even across the complexities of problems. This includes the following:

1. Various day-to-day practical problems
2. Different identification and authentication problems with their applications in security
3. Various classification problems resulting in decision-making
4. Interdependent and cross-domain problems

The generalisation may become very difficult in case of these problems, as there is a very little commonality among these different problems. But most of these problems are complex and hard to resolve. The very reason of the complexity is the dynamic nature of these problems unlike some routine mathematical problems. AI techniques need to look at these problems from analysis perspective and from the perspective of research initiatives to resolve them.

AI techniques need to be built from the problem-solving perspectives. The points raising need for AI technique are discussed below:

1. Need for analysis of voluminous and large amount of data. This data may not be confined to a single domain but may spread across the domains.
2. The analysis should be followed by the characterisation of miscellaneous data, then mapping of this data with reference to built-in knowledge, and then, building the knowledge further in this process.
3. Dealing with the constantly changing scenarios and situations, and the dynamic nature of data, the system and technique should react to the new scenario and situation. The situations are dynamic in nature, and static handling may not be useful.

4. The way in which data appears, the way it is used, the way it is organised and the way it should be used are different. Blindly using the data as it comes may result in wrong decisions.

5. Though in some cases, the huge data is available, but the relevant data is limited. Identification of relevant data, irrelevant data and outliers, and further, effective knowledge building based on limited relevant data are the challenges in front of AI techniques.

The main objective of AI techniques is to capture knowledge based on the data and information. There are different scenarios and the relevant data is captured. The AI techniques need to handle different problems. The broad categorisation of these problems can be as follows:

1. Structured problems
2. Unstructured problems
3. Linear problems
4. Non-linear problems

1.4 PROBLEM SOLVING WITH AI

AI has been very well used to solve structured problems. The *well-structured problems* are some of the very commonly faced problems during day-to-day life. These problems yield a right answer or right inference when an appropriate algorithm is applied. While *ill-structured problems* are the problems which do not yield a particular answer. In this case, there is possibility of more than one answer, and even a particular situation decides the correctness of the answer. Interestingly, ill-structured problems represent many of the real-world problems.

Some of the well-structured problems are given below:

1. Solving a quadratic equation to find out the value of X
2. Calculating path of the trajectory when a missile is fired
3. Calculating speed of ball when it reaches to batsman
4. Network flow analysis problems

Some examples of the ill-structured problems are given below:

1. Predicting how to dispose wet waste safely
2. Analysis of theoretical prepositions and adequacy of the same in a particular scenario
3. Identifying the security threats in big social gatherings

Solving ill-structured problems is challenging, since no list of specific and ordered operations or steps exists for them. Further, there is no well-defined criterion to evaluate the correctness of the outcome.

The behaviour of a typical well-structured problem is depicted in Figure 1.2, while the same for a ill-structured problem is depicted in Figure 1.3.

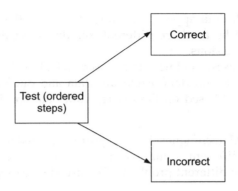

Figure 1.2 A typical well-structured problem analysis.

Figure 1.3 A typical ill-structured problem analysis.

Generally, abstracting the problem is possible in case of structured problems. The similarities and well-defined steps even allow some sort of generalisation in case of well-structured problems. The well-defined steps and well-defined way to measure accuracy allow to head systematically towards the goal state. In case of ill-structured problems, the uniqueness of problems and solution demands high level of problem-specific intelligence and makes it difficult to generalise.

EXAMPLES: A typical well-structured problem is the tic-tac-toe, shown in Figure 1.4.

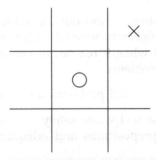

Figure 1.4 Tic-tac-toe.

Here, the final decision will depend on the value associated with all nine positions of tic-tac-toe. The legal values will be player 1 marked, player 2 marked and not marked. In this well-structured problem, solution will try to optimise chances of player 1 while minimising player 2 chances.

On the other hand unstructured problems are difficult to represent and model. There are possibilities of more than one goal states in case of unstructured problems. In most of the cases, exact goal state is not known. For example, systems to improve life expectancy of human being, expanding the business.

Linear problems are the ones which definitely have a solution or there will not be any solution. Speaking with respect to AI problem solving, these problems are the ones that typically fall under the classification category. Whereas, the problems that are not linear have to undergo some transformation for getting solution.

In case of non-linear problems, the relationship between input and output is not linear. Further decisions cannot be separated by simple linear classification function.

1.5 AI MODELS

One important aspect of building AI solutions is modelling the problem. Dunker introduced 'maze hypothesis' as a part of the psychological theory. In this particular hypothesis, the creative and intelligent tasks handled by human beings are modelled like a set of maze of paths from an initial node to a certain or resultant node. Human at any point of time analyses maze; for choices, he could find those which can lead to goal. These choices and maze-based approach can help in solving many multialternative solution problems.

Slowly, it became evident that all problems cannot be solved using maze models or the approach described above. This brought more focus on logic theory machines. Effective application of logic theory machines is found very useful in general problem solving, even this is found very useful for a wide spectrum of problems like chess problem. Chess can be viewed as a controlled environment in which computer is given a situation and a goal.

Figure 1.5 depicts the complexity of model building with reference to data and knowledge mapping.

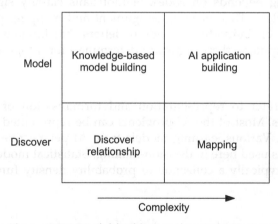

Figure 1.5 Model building and complexity.

A typical chess scenario is given in Figure 1.6. This is a much complex scenario than tic-tac-toe, but is still constrained. The chess program provided a sort of background for AI research. Two aspects that could be viewed from chess program were knowledge-based search and knowledge acquisition and representation. Models used for applications like chess programs were not effective for the other applications.

The advent of natural language processing and the need for man-machine dialogue made it more evident that the models used so far had their own limitations. Then, the formal models were proposed to solve AI problems. The requirement of complex problem solving gave birth to dynamic inductive models. Human behaviour and psychological study-based inductive dynamic models for creative problem solving slowly became popular.

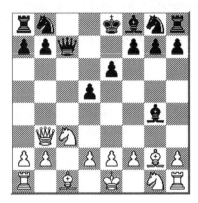

Figure 1.6   Chess: A complex scenario.

Let us have a look at the models.

Semiotic Models

These models are based on sign processes or signification and communication. The process of carrying meaning depends on codes. Semioticians classify signs or sign systems in relation to the problem. This meaning assignment and mapping process depends on the use of codes based on individual sounds or letters that humans use to form words or movements. In computers, these signs are determined for a logical sequence.

Statistical Models

Statistical models refer to representation and formalisation of relationships through statistical techniques. Most of the AI problems can be represented as statistical or pattern matching problems. Various learning models from AI perspective are based on statistics. The historical data is used here in decision-making. Statistical model employs probabilistic approaches and is typically a collection of probability density functions and distribution functions.

1.6   DATA ACQUISITION AND LEARNING ASPECTS IN AI

This section will introduce various AI-related topics on data acquisition and machine learning.

1. *Knowledge discovery—Data mining and machine learning*:   We start with some simple terms, i.e., information and data. Information can be referred to as pattern underlying the data, whereas the data refers to recorded facts. So, we define *data mining* or *knowledge discovery* as the extraction of meaningful information that is previously unknown and can be useful potentially ahead. It is more concerned with data analysis and use of some techniques to identify and recognise the patterns that would yield good predictions. The mining process includes data cleaning, preprocessing, identifying and interpreting the patterns, understanding the application and generating the target data with the consolidated patterns.

Machine learning, as described by Tom Mitchell, is a field concerned with the study of algorithms that will improve its performance with experience. It is all about making machine behave intelligently based on the past experience.

Let us have a look at the relation between knowledge discovery and machine learning. *Knowledge discovery* is about finding understandable knowledge, while *machine learning* is more focussed on improving performance of an agent. Machine learning can be thought of as a broader concept, which has mining playing an implicit part. There is actually a very fuzzy distinction between them.

That is all about the concepts' part, but what about the applications? Data mining is a tool and holds core part in business intelligence (BI). Data mining plays a critical role in case of accurate and complex decision-making. Consider a simple example of a bank which wants to access credit risk of customers. Let us say Ram applies for loan. Should the loan be approved? Data about past credit history, timely payments, security, age, salary are some of the factors that are looked upon. Bank generally develops models using machine learning methods, with the parameters mentioned. The results predict whether Ram would default on loan or not.

2. *Computational learning theory (COLT)*:   Currently, a lot of research is done to study and analyse algorithms. In COLT, formal mathematical models are defined. These models help in analyzing the efficiency and complexity in terms of computation, prediction and feasibility of the algorithms. The analysis done provides a framework to take appropriate decisions for building better algorithms that would be effective in terms of data and time.

The computational learning theory finds its importance in the field of machine learning, pattern recognition, statistics and many more. With regard to machine learning, the goal of COLT is to inductively learn the target function. Learning theories help in understanding the explicit relevant aspects of the learner and the environment to classify easy and hard learning problems and in turn guiding the design learning systems. There are two frameworks for analysing the patterns—one is Probably Approximately Correct (PAC) and the other is mistake bound. The former identifies the classes of hypothesis that possibly can/cannot be learnt, whereas the latter tries to learn target function to series of trials.

3. *Neural and evolutionary computation*:   A new technique in computation, i.e., neural and evolutionary computation is enabled to speed up the mining of data. Computation techniques that are based on biological properties fall under the category of evolutionary computing. Evolutionary computing is related to the study and use of these properties, consisting of evolutionary algorithms (of which genetic algorithm has been the most popular) that are basically used to solve multidimensional problem. The evolutionary computing finds its applications from the telecom domain to the financial decision-making, with optimisation as the base criterion.

In case of neural computing, the neural behaviour of human beings is stimulated to enable machine to learn. An artificial neural network is formed or configured for some specific application like pattern recognition or classification.

4. *Intelligent agents and multi-agent systems:* Intelligent agents and multi-agent systems (MAS) is a core part of intelligent systems, which allows timely decision-making in complex scenarios. An *agent* in simple terms, is a software program that assists user. An *intelligent agent* is the one which is flexible in terms of its action to get the desired outcome. It is goal-directed, reacts with the environment and acts accordingly. Consider an example of a student, who is pursuing a course in web designing. He uses search engine to get some notes for the subject. An intelligent agent will observe that he accesses the sites, which give him the detailed examples of the topics. So, each time he fires some query, the agent will give up sites that he is likely to refer based on the past experience. After some days, when he refers to the sites with illustrations, then the agent would need to change its behaviour pattern and act accordingly.

The capacity of an intelligent agent is restricted, and is dependent on the knowledge it has, the available resources and the different perspectives. The percept of individual agent is always limited. Complex tasks and decision-making demand combination of more than one percept of different intelligent agents. Hence, in many cases group of intelligent agents are required to solve the problems. This is a scenario of multi-agent system. So, in MAS, every agent's capability and its computation efficiency is exploited so that the overall performance is improved.

5. *Multi-perspective integrated intelligence:* For any problem to solve, each and every individual can have his own perspective. Some information might be present in some perspective, while it could be missing in other perspective, which could be effective in terms of decision-making. Utilising and exploiting this knowledge from different perspectives to build up an intelligent system giving accurate results, builds the Multi-perspective Intelligence (MPI) framework. Consider a scenario, where you want to apply for a job in a renowned company. You tend to seek feedback from some employees. Each will have his own perspective in relation to management, working environment, appraisals and so on. Some friend of yours might not be working, but is acquainted with the company. He would also have a different perspective. Based on this knowledge, possibly you could land upon a decision whether to take up the job or not. Information collected from different perspectives is used for final decision-making. This information collection can be continuous or discrete.

These learning approaches work in association with respect to the application they would be suited for. As said earlier, there is a very fuzzy line of distinction between them. And a good understanding of requirements and domain will result into accurate predictions and decision-making for solving a problem. The topics introduced here are just to make you aware of the type of work done with AI, though we will be discussing most them in detail in further chapters.

SUMMARY

Artificial intelligence has been a part of active scientific and engineering research for the last six decades. AI has gone through various stages of research during this period. Slowly, AI has become a part of the mainstream research, and many existing products and technologies are based on AI. The machines and equipment we use in our day-to-day life in some way or other use AI. Selection of model, analysis of data and building knowledge are some of the important aspects of building AI system. A large number of applications of AI need to be studied along with the practical aspects of AI to build a real-life AI solution. We want every appliance and every activity performed by machine to be intelligent. This intelligence is about understanding the problem at hand as well as the scenario and acting reasonably. (Intelligence is multi-faceted entity and this book tries to look at these facets more pragmatically).

 KEYWORDS

1. **Semiotic models:** The models which are based on sign processes or signification and communication.

2. **Formal system:** It is a system based on assignment of meanings to the symbols.

3. **Natural language processing:** A computer science and linguistic branch dealing with the interactions between human being and machines/computers is known as natural language processing.

4. **Maze models:** Creative and intelligent tasks handled by human being are modelled like a set of maze of paths from an initial node to a certain or resultant node.

5. **Well-structured problems:** These problems yield a right answer or right inference when an appropriate algorithm is applied.

6. **Ill-structured problems:** These are the problems which do not yield a particular answer. In this case, there is possibility of more than one answer, and even a particular situation decides the correctness of the answer.

7. **Linear problem:** It is the problem which can be solved or where decision can be obtained by linear solution.

8. **Non-linear problem:** It is the problem which cannot be solved or separated by linear equations.

CONCEPT REVIEW QUESTIONS

1. Give example of one ill-structured problem with description and elaborate the method for solving that problem.

2. Describe various AI models.

3. Explain the model building concepts in AI.

4. What are the statistical models?

5. List various equipment in day-to-day life, where AI is used.

6. List milestones in AI evolution.

CRITICAL THINKING EXERCISE

1. Analyse knowledge-based complexity for the AI application for chess and tic-tac-toe.
2. Try to map different AI models with AI products.
3. List applications where formal systems are used.
4. Associate evolutionary systems with traditional one from technology aspects.

PROJECT WORK

1. Program a simple intelligent system for tic-tac-toe.
2. Draw a flow diagram where you use evolutionary system for washing machine.

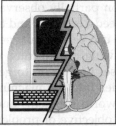

CHAPTER 2

Problem Solving

INTRODUCTION

The field of AI comprises many fascinating areas but problem solving is fundamental to many of the AI-based applications. *Problem solving*, as the name suggests, is an area to deal with finding answer for some unknown situations. It involves understanding, representation, formulation and solving. This simple definition encapsulates two types of problems—simple and complex. The simple type of problems are the ones that are or can be solved by a deterministic procedure. There is a guarantee of a solution. For example solving a quadratic equation. So, when we say that the example falls under simple category, we are aware that there is a way to have this problem mapped into an algorithm that can be executed by the computer.

In the real world, the problems are complex. Most often the data that we have is partial. In other words, we are not fully aware of the scenario. There is lack of full information. So, the problems with such a data are complex problems. Let us take a simple example of a robot. For the robot, it is complex to carry out some specific tasks like searching some object or loading boxes in trucks. It is because of the movements (that it needs to carry out), which are dependent on the information at that particular instance. Since the information available at that instance is based on partially observable environment, it is incomplete.

Solving complex problems is indeed a complex and tricky task. For us, solving a problem at hand is not so difficult since we can reason out, perceive, learn, but for a machine, it is actually very difficult. While drawing conclusions, we can use the statistical methods, the mathematical modelling processes and so on to get the best solutions. AI focuses on mapping of these intellectual abilities into the machine to get the best solutions. In this chapter, we discuss about the real-world problems and their solutions.

So, what is the main job or the objective of problem solving? The objective is to find out set of actions so as to reach the set goal. Do we mean to say that we are having some sort of search? Search is, of course, a method for problem solving, but its details are given in the subsequent chapters. This chapter is focussed on the details of problem solving, the processes and the representations, with an overview of the search method that is applied in the process of solving.

Coming back to the point of discussion, where the important approach of problem solving is search in an action space. Action space comprises a set of actions that leads to some specific goal. The methods of problem solving can be categorised as follows:

1. General purpose
2. Special purpose

The general purpose method is applicable to a wide variety of problems and it is means-ends analysis. In means-ends analysis, the present situation is compared with the goal to detect the difference. It searches in action space to select an action that will reduce the difference. Say for example, if a person wants to cover 50 km distance, the problem solving process will search from memory for auto-rickshaws, buses, bicycles and so on for the means of transport. It would then discard walking and flying so as to reduce the search space for the next step. In case of special purpose, a particular problem is modelled with various assumptions, which are specific to that problem. Specific features of the situation are used in this method. For example: classifying legal documents with reference to a particular criminal case.

Sometimes, problem solving system behaves like an expert, who has gathered knowledge on a specific area over a period of time. Then, the expert uses his knowledge to relate to the current situation and derives analogy to find out the best possible solution. In AI approach, algorithm using historical knowledge can be treated as expert. Say for example: during diagnosis of a disease the doctors feed the diagnosis process and the disease-related symptoms. This helps in building the knowledge base of diagnosis and symptoms. The knowledge base of diagnosis and symptoms helps in diagnosing in future for similar scenarios. In case of new symptom, the doctor can update knowledge base based on new observations. This can help in diagnosis process, as it can provide pointers to arrive at conclusion.

Problem solving can also assist in planning and decision-making. Planning and decisions are the key parts of an intelligent system. Managers need efficient problem-solving methods for assisting and helping them with optimised decisions. An effective step-by-step sequence of actions that has low cost and reasonably less number of steps is important in case of planning. Planning is optimal ordering of actions to reach the solution in a given scenario, environment and constraints. Even it may be effective in manufacturing units, where assembling of goods needs to be done in a specific time and specific order so as to reduce the other overheads.

In many situations, the pattern of information is used to retrieve the right information from the search space. A chess player can make use of the pattern of moves to decide the next move. Problem solving, thus, tries to make optimal use of information and knowledge at hand to select a set of actions to reach the goal state.

2.1 PROBLEM-SOLVING PROCESS

The term *problem* is used in a situation, when the desired objective is not obvious. Arriving to an objective from initial situation is unknown initially and it consists of sequence of intermediate objectives. This process of solving a problem may vary from individual to individual. An individual's acumen, knowledge and skills—all put together to generate a solution.

Problem-solving is a process of generating solutions for a given situation. Figure 2.1 shows problem-solving process applied to achieve goal state. This process consists of sequence of well-defined methods that can handle doubts or inconsistency issues, uncertainty, ambiguity and help in achieving the desired goal.

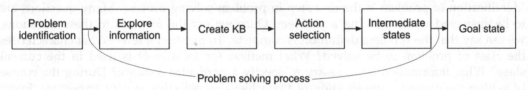

Figure 2.1 Problem-solving process.

The word *problem* encompasses computational tasks also. When we talk about problems like matrix inverse or solving quadratic or simultaneous equations, then the process involves computation to arrive at a solution. But in case of AI, the problem is formulated and solved by searching for a solution in space of possible solutions. Gradually, the problem-solving horizon is widened to include the other techniques of natural language processing, machine learning, game playing and so on. The problems may also include sophisticated information storage, retrieval, information extraction, decision-making and so on.

The term *problem* can be defined with following conditions:

1. Every problem is defined in a context. In this context, it has certain assumptions under initial conditions.
2. Every problem has a well-defined objective.
3. Solution to every problem consists of a set of activities. Each activity changes the state of problem, i.e., from the present state to the new state. This new state is closer to the solution state. Finally, initial state approaches the goal situation.
4. Previous knowledge and domain knowledge both are used as the resources during different states in the solution process.

So, the primary objective in solution process is the problem identification. Problem identification marks the problem space boundary. This precisely tells us what the achievable goal is and what information is to be used during the solution process. In case of an operational research, the objective is to optimise the operation cost of an item under boundary conditions. If they are not defined properly, number of operations and resources required may increase substantially. Hence, the solution may become complex, and sometimes, it may not be achievable. There are many real-world problems that cannot be solved if they are open for generic solution. But if it is limited to certain environment, it is solvable. Every problem needs different treatment depending on the goal, initial information and assumptions. General problem-solving techniques involve the following:

1. Problem definition
2. Problem analysis and representation
3. Planning
4. Execution
5. Evaluating solution
6. Consolidating gains

Let us take our discussion ahead to the formulation of the problems.

2.2 FORMULATING PROBLEMS

Identification of problem is the first step in problem-solving process. Many questions are to be answered while defining a problem. Once we get the answers to these questions, we can say that the problem definition is complete. To mention a few—What characterises the class of problem to be solved? What method (or technique) is used in the current stage? What information is necessary to specify a particular instance? During the course of getting the answers, specification of the achievable objective is very important. Every problem has certain initial conditions from which different actions are initiated. Finally, a set of actions or methods to be defined that cause the transitions are also important. A problem statement can have description of the data, method, procedures and algorithms that are used to solve it.

Once the problem is identified, we need to be very precise and specific with respect to the problem space along with the target that we need to achieve. At this stage, the assumptions or limitations of solution (if any) are also specified so that the solution quality is measured against the defined problem objectives and requirements.

The next important step here is the analysis and representation of the task knowledge. Usually, we understand the problem in terms of diagram, description and so on. But in AI, the target is to use machine to solve a problem, once the solution is planned and fed to it. This is done using state-space diagram. So, the problem is defined in terms of state. Each state is the abstraction of all available information. *Solution* to any problem is the collection of such different states and set of operations. This collection of states is termed as *state space*. Each of these states is achieved using the application of actions/operations to the previous state. During problem-solving process, an operator is applied to a state to move it to the next state. Then, another operator is applied and so on till the final state is achieved. This approach of generating a solution is called *state-space method*.

Figure 2.2 represents the steps involved in formulating problems.

Let us begin with the state-space approach for problem solving using a very well-known puzzle.

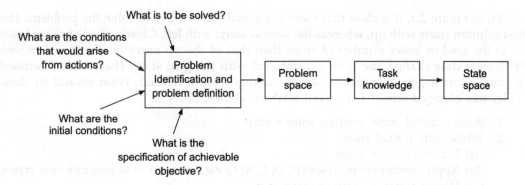

Figure 2.2 Problem formulating steps.

EXAMPLE: Consider a problem where three cells in the four-cell board are filled with single digits and one cell is left blank. The game is to change positions of the digit and blank cell of the board to arrive at new board positions. The rule of the game is blank cell can change the position with a digit by horizontal or vertical movement. Figure 2.3 represents the initial and the final states of this game.

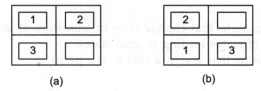

(a)   (b)

Figure 2.3 Initial and final state of the puzzle: (a) Initial state and (b) Final state.

PROBLEM: To reach from the initial state to the final state, with the minimum number of moves.

Solution: We now define the state space, and the operation and action space. Action space has the operations on the blank cell. Blank cell can move up (U), down (D), left (L) and right (R). Different board positions constitute the elements of state space. We designate every state by a symbol S_i. i represents the ith state. S_0 is the initial state and S_n is the final one. Figure 2.4 illustrates the states along with the operations. Here, in Figure 2.4, $S_n = S_3$.

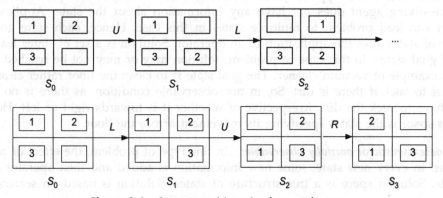

Figure 2.4 State transitions in the puzzle game.

From Figure 2.4, it is clear that there are actually two ways to solve the problem. The first solution starts with up, whereas the second starts with left. Clearly, the left move leads us to the goal in lesser number of steps than that of the up move (as the initial move). With each state change, the state is compared with the goal state. The puzzle discussed is simple, but it gets complicated when the digits are increased. What should be done under this changed scene? Let us put forth an algorithm for it.

1. State = initial state; existing state = state
2. While state $\neq$ final state
    (i) Existing state = state
    (ii) Apply operations from set $\{U, D, L, R\}$ to each state so as to generate new states.
    (iii) If new states $\cap$ existing states $\neq \varphi$
        * Existing state = existing state $\cup$ new states
        * State = new state
   End while

A well defined problem, hence, is described in terms of

1. Initial state
2. Goal state
3. List of states
4. Operators or functions that change state or transition of state
5. Path (sequence of states leading to goal state)
6. Path cost (functions that assign a cost to the path)

2.3   PROBLEM TYPES AND CHARACTERISTICS

Problems can be categorised into different types. Let us look at these types.

1. *Deterministic or observable:* This type of problem is also termed as *single-state problem*. Each state is fully observable and it goes to one definite state after any action. Here, the goal state is reachable in one single action or sequence of actions. For example, vacuum cleaner with sensor. Here next state can be found using current state and action.

2. *Non-observable:* This type of problem comes under multiple-state problems. So, the problem-solving agent does not have any information about the state. Application of operator can lead problem to multiple states in this case. Hence, each state goes to a number of states after the application of an operator. Solution is a set of states leading to a set of goal states. In this type of problem, solution may or may not be reached. Let us take an example of vacuum cleaner. The goal state is to clean the floor rather clean floor. Action is to suck if there is dirt. So, in non-observable condition, as there is no sensor, it will have to suck the dirt, irrespective of whether it is towards right or left. Here, the solution space is the states specifying its movement across the floor.

3. *Non-deterministic or partially observable:* In this type of problem, the effect of action is not clear. In every new state, some new information is added and then operator acts on the state. Solution space is a tree structure of states. Solution is based on searching the tree and finding out the path for solution. If we take the same example, and now assume that the sensor is attached to it, then it will suck if there is dirt. Movement of the cleaner will be a tree that would be based on its current percept.

4. *Unknown state space:* Unknown state space problems are typically exploration problems. States and impact of actions are not known. There is a need to discover to understand the outcomes of actions. For example, online search that involves acting without complete knowledge of the next state or searching address without map.

2.4 PROBLEM ANALYSIS AND REPRESENTATION

Performance of a solution depends on the problem representation, as discussed earlier. This task can be simple or complex depending on the way it is described. A problem representation is a complete view of the problem and approach to solve it. Determining computational complexity for the solution is not possible until a formal representation of the problem is generated.

The performance of any intelligent system depends on the problem representation and formulation. A representation is a complete view of a problem or set of problems and an approach to solve these problems.

The problem representation is an important step to understand before we start solving the problem. The quality of solution and the appropriateness of solution mechanism rely on completeness of the problem definition.

Problem definition should satisfy the following criteria:

1. Compactness (must be able to restrict and define boundaries clearly)
2. Utility (must be compatible with good solution algorithms)
3. Soundness (should not report false positive or false negative)
4. Completeness (should not loose any information)
5. Generality (should be able to capture all or maximum instance of the problem)
6. Transparency (reasoning with the representation efficiently)

Let us take an example of 'Smart home' to understand these properties. The objective of the smart home can be:

To provide a secured home, with 24 hours surveillance, together with facilities of intruder detection system, detection of anomalies like fire, earthquake, etc. along with efficient communication and alarming system. Let us elaborate the criteria for this example.

- **Compactness:** It needs to define clearly the solution space.
- **Utility:** It needs to be compatible with the existing systems, say for example, social security systems available in the city and systems at government organisations like police stations.
- **Soundness:** It should not raise false alarm for intrusion or fire.
- **Completeness:** It should not loose information about the visitors or the historical information of previous instances and should use these instances to learn and handle similar future events.

- **Generality:** It should be able to handle all similar events irrespective of changing environment. For example, the alarming system should be able to work properly irrespective of the season and day of the time.
- **Transparency:** The reasoning behind the action taken should be visible to the user.

Problem representation with different aspects

Problem representation is very critical and important in problem solving. Many different opinions and views should be investigated and explored in this representation. First and foremost, it needs machine language so as to describe the logic and specific encoding rules for the problems. Further, the problem needs to be mapped into a solution space that is actually expanded during the solution process or it can be in the form of a state space that has all the feasible states and transitions. A representation comprising data structures and programs executing on them to derive inference can also be a different view in the representation.

Researchers in 1950's worked extensively on human problem-solving process, where they encoded different tasks in the problem space through state diagrams. In these diagrams, initial situation, desired goal and various intermediate states or concepts are used.

So, problem space consists of partial solutions, which finally determine the complete solution. This approach is further extended for AI, where problems are different in many ways. The moves in case of AI can be abstracted from the real-world states. The steps of problem solving can be modelled into a system such that a machine can execute these well-defined steps and find out the solution. This automatic problem-solving system is termed as *problem solver.*

So, a *problem solver* is an algorithm or a methodology that accepts problem description, domain description and boundary conditions as input, and then, searches for a solution. The solver terminates when it finds a solution or when its solution space is exhausted or it meets the boundary condition that is defined in input. The boundary condition may include time boundary or solution boundary. When the solution space does not converge, then termination takes place either due to time or tolerance as the acceptable output variation is reached.

Coming towards the point of problem description, a problem description contains domain description and problem instances. Domain description includes properties of simulated world. For example, in case of tower of Hanoi in which possible states and moves are the description of the problem domain. Problem instances are the initial states and the goal states of the problem. So, for tower of Hanoi, problem instance may be the initial position of the disk and final goal is the desired position.

Figure 2.5 shows the problem instances for initial and goal states and possible states in the process of solving.

Problem representation consists of domain description and solver algorithm that operates on this description. The starting point for a complete problem representation is the determination of typical knowledge structure and interdependency among knowledge at different layers. A typical knowledge structure is depicted in Figure 2.6. Design knowledge plays an important role in the problem-solving process and it is at the root level in the diagram. This design knowledge actually controls and establishes the flow of information

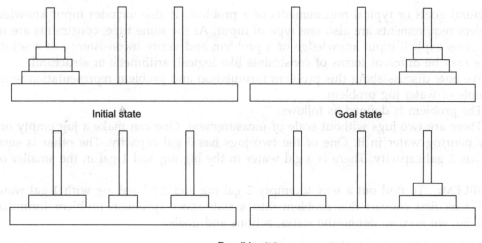

Initial state

Goal state

Possible state

Figure 2.5 Tower of Hanoi: States.

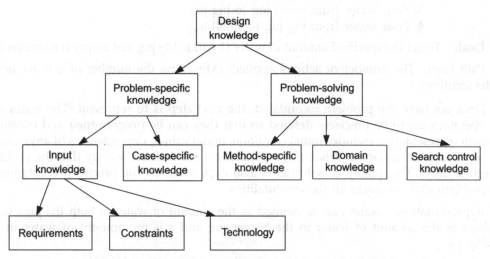

Figure 2.6 Knowledge involved in problem-solving process.

from different knowledge layers to execute the operations in order to reach the desired goal. Basically, design knowledge is used to encapsulate solution strategy by formulating the problem. So, it directly makes use of the problem-solving knowledge and problem-specific knowledge. Problem-solving knowledge is a generative way of problem-solving. In AI paradigm, problem-solving deals with the searching of solutions under a pre-defined boundary. So, search techniques come under the pre-requisite knowledge for devising a solution. Domain knowledge is a definitional knowledge, which is related to the problem domain. Whereas, problem-specific knowledge includes explicit representations of all objects, classes, their relations, constraints, etc. This can include case-specific knowledge also. This specific knowledge is required to solve a particular problem. It may comprise functions, structural goals or typical requirements of a problem. It also includes input knowledge. Problem requirements are also one type of input. At the same time, constraints are used to express explicit input knowledge of a problem and verify inconsistency of a solution. There may be different forms of constraints like logical, arithmetic or structural.

We now discuss about this problem formulation and problem representation with an example of water jug problem.

The problem is defined as follows:

There are two jugs without scale of measurement. One can make a jug empty or fill it by pouring water in it. One of the two jugs has 5 gal capacity. The other is smaller and has 2 gal capacity. There is 3 gal water in the big jug and 1 gal in the smaller one.

PROBLEM: To find out a way to empty 2 gal jug and fill 5 gal jug with 1 gal water.

Let us first convert this problem into a state-space (problem problem formulation step). So, we need to define the states, actions and goals.

States: Amount of water in the jugs

Actions: 1. Empty the big jug.
2. Empty the small jug.
3. Pour water from small jug to big jug.
4. Pour water from big jug to small jug.

Goal: To get the specified amount of water (1 gal) in big jug and empty the smaller jug.

Path cost: The number of actions applied. (Minimum the number of actions, better is the solution).

Once we have the problem formulated, the next step is to represent. The states and the operators are to be precisely defined so that they can be programmed and executed. Problem representation includes initial condition, initial values, dependencies (if any) among the states and the variables. When these parameters are defined, we say that the problem is well-defined. The quality of solution is also dependent on the precise presentation of the problem that considers all the essentialities.

Representation: States can be defined as the amount of water in both the jugs (b, s), where b is the amount of water in the bigger jug and s is the amount of water in the smaller jug.

Initial state: (5, 2)

Goal state: (1, 0)

Operators: Let us discuss about the selection of operators for this problem. At this stage, operators are to be defined carefully with all possible constraints. Applicable operators are to (i) empty the jug or (ii) fill the jug. We need to apply constraints or pre-conditions for these operators. So, the pre-condition to empty jug is the jug was not emptied earlier.

One situation is when one of the jugs is not empty, then there are two alternatives— (i) Empty big (initially, big jug is not empty and it is emptied to fill in the small jug) and (ii) Empty small (initially, small jug is not empty and then it is emptied to fill in the big jug).

Other situation is when one of the jugs is empty. Again, there are two options—big jug is empty and small jug is not empty. For small to be emptied, the states will be $(s, 0)$. That means the big jug has the contents of small and small jug has nil. Similarly, it can be (*b*, 0). The next state after this can have possibilities that (*b* – 2, 2) since small is empty so, it will have 2 gal and 2 are reduced from big (this is if *b* >= 2). But if *b* < 2, then the next state will be (0, *b*), where big will be empty and *s* will have *b* contents.

Not making things complicated, we will solve it and have a path cost calculation. The sequence of operations to be performed on the two jugs is shown in Figure 2.7. The solution is found by searching through the action space defined as operators 1 to 4.

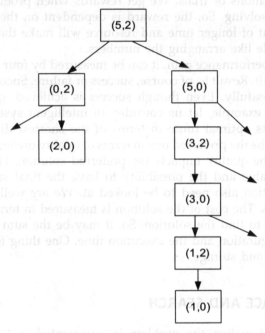

Figure 2.7 Water jug problem.

In Figure 2.7, the initial state, the intermediate state and the final states have been presented in the form of tree structure. The initial and final states are marked bold, while the intermediate states are marked by the application of the operators. So, searching for solution is same as searching for the tree. Let us look at the details of it.

Initial state: (5, 2)
Goal state: (1, 0)
Operators: These are as follows:
1. Empty big (remove the water from big jug).
2. Empty small (remove the water from small jug).
3. Big is empty (water in small jug to be poured in big jug).
4. Small is empty (water in big jug is to be poured in small jug).

Figure 2.7 shows that the goal state is achieved with the action of sequences 2, 4, 2, 4, and 2. Thus, the precise operator definitions along with the goal and the initial states representations assist in solving the problem. So, we have discussed about the basic representations to solve the problem, but on what basis is the performance accounted? Let us consider the same in the next section.

2.5 PERFORMANCE MEASURING

There are various factors that are to be considered when it comes to problem solving. The performance is governed on different things. Let us begin with the factors.

There are three outcomes of a problem solver—finding a solution, terminating with failure after search space is exhausted and hitting a time bound like terminating after certain number of iterations or trials. We get rewards when problem is solved, but pay for time required for solving. So, the reward is dependent on the specific problem and its solution. Investment of longer time and resource will make the result negative if the problem is quite simple like arranging the numbers.

When it comes to performance gain, it can be measured by four parameters—problem, time, resource and result. Result is, of course, success or failure. Success means the problem has been solved successfully. Even though success is achieved, quality of the solution is also important. For example, let us consider an intelligent system providing driving assistance that suggests optimal route in terms of the shortest distance. The suggested shortest route may not be the preferred one in terms of quality owing to the road conditions on that route. Thus, the quality impacts the preferred solution. How close the solution is to the real-world value and the possibility to have the final state to be achieved in every course of execution also need to be looked at. We are well-versed with the time and space complexities. The cost of the solution is measured in terms of the time and the resource cost required to find the solution. So, it may be the sum of the storage (space) or the hardware configuration and the execution time. One thing to mention is that gain reduces with the time and storage.

2.6 PROBLEM SPACE AND SEARCH

As we have discussed earlier, the problem is represented as the state space. Let us understand the role of search in detail here.

Search is a general algorithm that helps in finding the path in the state space. Every problem (as said before) can be solved with the help of search. It considers one or more path. The path may lead to the solution or might be dead end. In case of dead end, backtrack should occur. The search algorithm, makes use of control strategy like that of forward or backward search. Further, it needs to identify and adopt a strategy to explore the states. In broader sense, there are two types of strategies—informed search and uninformed search.

Informed search does not guarantee a solution, but there is high probability of getting a solution. In this approach, a heuristic that is specific to the problem is used to control the flow of solution path. Heuristic is a skill-based technique used to solve the problem. It is based on common sense, rule of thumb, educated guesses or intuitive judgment. It is high order cognitive process. A heuristic function is used in search algorithm to rank the alternatives at each multiple selection path in order to take decision about which path should be followed. When speedy process is required, informed search is preferred over the uninformed.

In case of uninformed strategy, it does not consider specific nature of the problem. This strategy is very simple and can be generalised to any problem. Uninformed strategy generates all possible states in the state space and checks for the goal state. Hence, it always finds a solution if it exists. But the approach is time consuming, as the search space is large. The strategy is preferred in applications where any error in the algorithm has serious consequences. This method is also used to benchmark results of the other algorithms.

The search methods are evaluated on the basis of completeness (if there exists a solution, it needs to find it), optimality (the obtained solution is the best one), time complexity and space complexity.

This was an overview of the problem solving and the search relationship. We will have a detailed study of these methods and strategies in next two chapters dealing with search in detail.

2.6.1 Defining the Problem as a State-Space Search

The problem at hand can be solved by searching the state space to find out the path that leads to a final state from the initial state. The basic notion behind the state-space search is that we can solve the given problem by checking the steps considering the fact that they might lead us towards the solution. So, each action takes a step ahead to a different state.

While defining the problem as a state-space search, we mean to say that the goal should be properly formulated. As said earlier, the states and the operators should be clearly indicated. There should be transparency in describing the rules and they should be as generalised as possible.

2.6.2 Issues in Design of Search Programs

In problems solving, we apply search. The search leads us to goal state. So, can we say the result or the solution we have obtained is dependent on the search process? Yes, indeed it is. Search techniques guide to reach a solution in the space. The way we have obtained the solution for the jug problem by applying the rules, the entire path is said to be the solution path, starting from the state (5, 2) to the goal.

We, as human beings, can analyse the state space and identify the solution. This happens because of the cognitive skills that we possess. But while searching, the state space is traversed. If an error occurs, backtrack should occur so as to evaluate the alternative path. So, there is a need of a systemic procedure for forward and backward movement at the same time systematic method for traversing states in the state space.

When we are having a search program implemented to solve the problems along with the direction of search, the other factor that needs to be highlighted is the selection of the rules. Which rules should be applied so as to reach the goal state is equally important. Further, the representation, as discussed earlier, is also a significant issue. This representation is about the knowledge that maps the node in the search process.

To summarise, the following issues are observed while designing search problems:

1. State representation and identifying relationships among states
2. Proper selection of forward and backward movement to determine optimal path to goal state
3. Rule selection

2.7 TOY PROBLEMS

Toy problems are not real-world problems. They are generated for fun. These problems are played on board or paper. Hence, the problem environment is controlled. The problem formulation is, thus, possible. All boundary conditions and the constraints are known. Hence, it is very much possible to convert them to computer programs. Many games like 8-puzzle, tic-tac-toe, backgammon are toy problems. Let us understand these problems as a problem-solving venture.

2.7.1 Tic-tac-toe Problem

It is a very well known pencil and paper game for two players 'x' and 'o'. (In fact, we have grown up playing this). Each player marks a 3*3 grid by 'x' and 'o' in turn. The game starts with 'x' and ends with win or loss or draw. The player who puts respective mark in a horizontal, vertical or diagonal line wins the game. If played without a fault, it leads to draw.

We begin now with the formulation of the game as a problem that can be solved by search strategy. By this, it is possible to convert it to a computer program. Let us consider the rules, say the rule of the game is to put 'x' and 'o' in the cell. Game gets over when either 'x' or 'o' are at the diagonal positions, as indicated in Figure 2.8.

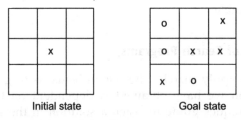

Initial state   Goal state

Figure 2.8 Tic-tac-toe game.

Formulating the problem in state-space search, we get

Initial state: State in Figure 2.8.
States: Figure 2.9 with different, 'x' and 'o' positions constitutes the states in the space. The generation of states in the state space is shown in Figure 2.9.
Operators: Adding 'x' or 'o' in cells one by one
Goal: To reach the final/winning position
Path cost: Each step costs 1 so that the path cost is the length of the path.

2.7.2 Missionaries and Cannibals

The missionaries and cannibals problem is the one, where three missionaries and three cannibals are on one side of a river. There is a boat that can hold one or two people. We need to find a way to get everyone to the other side of the river without ever leaving a group of missionaries in one place outnumbered by cannibals in that place. A maximum of two objects (missionaries/cannibals) can travel to other side and minimum of one has to be there in the boat for the boat to come back.

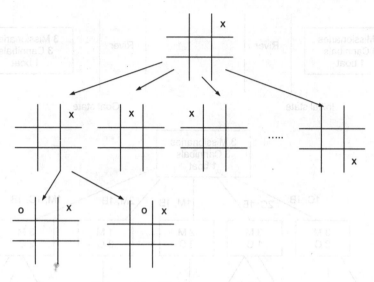

Figure 2.9 Tic-tac-toe state space.

The first step towards solving the problem is to find out the operators that involve taking one or two people from one side to another in the boat. A state represents the time when missionaries and cannibals are in the boat or on the other side. Because boat can hold only two people, there is no question of outnumbering. But the crossings are important. So, there are constraints while applying the operators.

States: Let the state consists of sequence of three numbers representing the number of missionaries, cannibals and boat. So, the initial state is (3, 3, 1).

Operators: They carry one missionary, one cannibal, two missionaries, two cannibals or one of each across in the boat.

Let us formulate the problem.

Goal state: It is the state, where missionaries and cannibals have reached the other side of the river. So, the final state is (0,0,0).

Initial state: (3, 3, 1)

Operator: Putting missionary and cannibal in boat such that the cannibal does not outnumber missionary and there may be one/two people in the boat at a time.

Path cost: Number of crossings

This is a simple problem for a computer to solve if it is represented rightly as state-space problem.

Figure 2.10 represents the initial and goal states and the snapshot of slate space diagram. The diagram begins with initial state where the boat, missionaries and cannibals are on one side of the river. It can be represented in other ways as well, where the final state can also be added in the representation with values as 0, 0, 0 for the missionaries, cannibals and the boat; and changing them with every transition from one end of river to other.

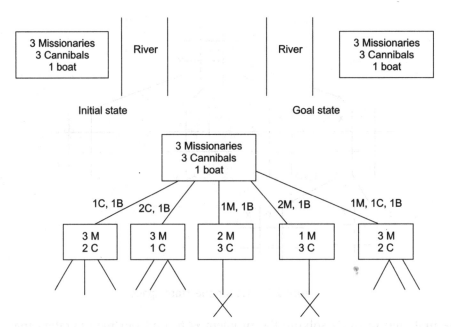

Figure 2.10 Missionaries and cannibals problem: Initial and goal states and state space.

2.8 REAL-WORLD PROBLEMS

Toy problems are used to illustrate different problem-solving methods and compare the performances of the algorithms. These problems are given concise and exact description. But the real-world problems, tend to have a single agreed upon description. The research on problem solving actually focuses on capturing properties of real-world problems. The cognitive processes of researchers attempt to solve these problems. Couple of day-to-day real-life problems are discussed below.

Route Finding

Route finding is defined in terms of specified locations and transition along links between them. Route finding algorithms are used widely in a variety of applications like automated travel advisory system, airline travel planning, car systems that provide directions and so on. The other applications can be video stream in computer network.

Let us consider airline travel planning problems that is solved by an automated travel advisory system. The objective is to arrive to a destination with the minimum cost. Each state comprises airport location and the current time. Let us formulate the problem.

Initial state: Starting point of the journey
Goal state: Final destination
Operators/Actions: Flight from current location to reach the next location in such a way so that there is enough time difference in the next flight and in transfer within the airport if there is a connecting flight.

Path cost: Total of travel fare, travel time, waiting time, time of the day, type of airline and can include special package, mileage awards, etc.

Most often, the commercial travel systems use a problem formulation of this kind, with many additional complications such as backup reservations on alternative flights. This is done to the extent that these are justified by the cost and likelihood of the original plan.

Travelling Salesman Problem

Travelling salesman is the most famous touring problem, where the objective is to find a tour—the shortest one. So, given number of cities and a starting city, the problem solving needs to cover all the cities, where each city is traversed just once minimising the tour cost and returning back to the starting city. There are many variants to this problem. Let us understand the representation of the standard one from Figure 2.11 below, where C_1 is the starting city.

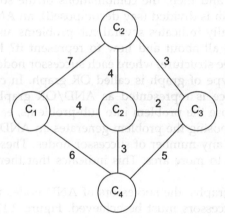

Figure 2.11 Travelling salesman: Cities and distances.

The problem can be formulated as

Initial state: The starting city for the tour is C_1.

Goal state: The complete trip ends at C_1.

Operator: Travel from one city to another with the constraint that the city is not visited before.

Path cost: Travelling time

2.9 PROBLEM REDUCTION METHODS

Problem reduction is a strategic approach to reduce complexity of a problem. A general approach for solving a large and complex problem is to decompose it into some smaller problems. Further apply this decomposition process to each of these problems iteratively till they get solved easily or they cannot be split. This paradigm of problem solving is called *problem reduction*. This approach of problem reduction can be applied to the applications of any domain in which top-down decision-making strategy is applicable.

Many a times, a problem seems to be hard to solve. These types of problem are reduced to a number of small sub-problems. Once the sub-problems are solved, the solution to the hard problems can be achieved. This is the core concept of the reduction methods.

We are well-versed with the representation in state-space search and sequences of actions that are to be followed with the search so as to reach the goal. Other approach is to decompose the goal. In the sense, more simple sub-goals are formed. As an example, when a trip is to be planned from city A to city B, which involves a sequence of actions like travel by air, travel by train and so on then, the trip can be split into many parts. The parts may be reach the station, get a train and reach city B. There can be many alternatives parts for this trip too, which could be go to airport, fly to city B. So, each of these alternatives has some travel cost and time associated with it. The best plan needs to be taken into account.

When the problem is divided into, a set of sub-problems, each of these sub-problems can be solved separately, and then, the combinations of the solutions generate the final solution. When the problem is divided (say decomposed), an AND arc is generated in the graph. This graph essentially indicates several sub-problems and solutions.

So, what the graph is all about and how to represent it? Here a simple state-space search is presented as a tree structure, where each successor node represents an alternative action to be taken. This type of graph is called OR graph. In case of problem reduction process, the problem space is represented as AND/OR graph of states. As discussed earlier, when we decompose the problem into sub-problems, each of the sub-problems is solved separately. Decomposing the problem generates an AND arc in the graph. Each of the AND arc can point to any number of successor nodes. These nodes should be solved so that the arcs may lead to more arcs. This indicates that there are more sub-problems and solutions.

In case of AND/OR graphs, the successors of AND nodes must be achieved and for OR nodes, one of the successors must be achieved. Figure 2.12 shows AND/OR graph for travel plan from city A to city B. Assume C to be intermediate city to reach B. The problem is divided into two sub-problems—travel by train and travel by air. The AND arc shows the states in each sub-problem. The child nodes or the leaf nodes can be further expanded. The travel cost at each node can be computed and shown in the graph. Thus, the best plan can be obtained with the graph traversal.

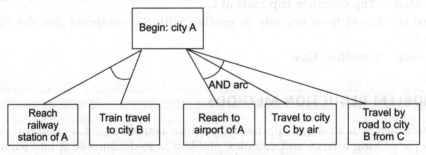

Figure 2.12   AND/OR graph.

Most often, the problems can be formulated as state space or problem reduction. State-space search is preferred when the solution can be expressed as the final state or as a path from the initial state to the final one. The set of actions can be defined so as to transform the states, whereas problem reduction will be useful when a problem can be decomposed into independent sub-problems. So, in short, the selection of approach is dependent on the type of the problem.

SUMMARY

Problem solving is an important topic in AI. We face problems at every point of time and look upon solutions for them. But the thing which is important here is how to solve a problem and what actually the problem is. Problem solving deals with the formulation of problem in terms of state and operators so that the goal is achieved. There are various ways to solve the problem, but a solution is acceptable only when it matches the required cost and time constraints or rather when it is cost-effective along with the quality. Problem solving is not just reaching the goal state, but it is rather reaching the solution optimally and following the constraints and rules defined in the problem.

While solving problems, heuristic and other advanced search techniques can be used to reach the goal. The use of AND/OR graphs helps in the evaluation of options to solve the complex problems by reduction method. Appropriate mapping and state representations help in finding out the solutions, with understanding of the problems and consideration of different paths.

 KEYWORDS

1. **Problem solving:** It is the process of generating solutions for given complex and difficult situations or problems.

2. **Simple problems:** These are the problems that can be solved by deterministic procedure, where the solution is guaranteed.

3. **Complex problems:** The problems that lack information and have partial data are complex problems. The scenario is also not fully available here.

4. **General-purpose method of problem solving:** It is a means-ends analysis method, where a comparison of the current state with the goal state takes place to find out the difference and search is carried out to decide the states to reduce the difference.

5. **Special purpose method of problem solving:** In this, a particular problem is modelled with various assumptions, which are specific to that problem.

6. **Deterministic or observable problems:** Single-state problems where each state is fully observable and it goes to one definite state under operator. The goal state is reachable in one single action or sequence of actions.

7. **Non-observable problems:** These are multiple state problems. The problem solving agent does not have any information about the state. So, each state can be transformed to a number of states after the application of operator.

8. **Non-deterministic or partially observable problems:** In every new state, some new information is added and then operator acts on the state. Some information is available here.

9. **Unknown state-space problems:** These are most often known as exploration problem. States and actions are not known here.

10. **State space:** A problem is defined in terms of state. A state represents the status of solution at a given step of solution procedure. A solution to any problem is the collection of such different states and set of operations. This collection of states is termed as state space.

11. **Informed search strategy:** It is a search that does not guarantee a solution, but there is high probability of getting a solution. It makes use of heuristic.

12. **Uninformed search strategy:** It is a strategy that generates all possible states in the state space and checks for the goal state. It always finds a solution if it exists.

13. **Problem reduction:** It is a strategic approach to solve a problem so as to reduce the complexity, where the problem is decomposed into sub-parts.

MULTIPLE CHOICE QUESTIONS

1. There are four letters a, b, c, d available for registration number to be placed on number plate of any car. Number plate can contain only 3 letters and the letters can be used in any order. How many different numbers can be generated?
   (a) 10   (b) 12   (c) 20   (d) 24

2. Ten teams are playing in a cricket tournament. The winning team of each match progresses to the next round and the loosing team is out of the game. In the 2nd round, each team plays with the other teams, after which a final round is played. How many matches will be played?
   (a) 12   (b) 15   (c) 11   (d) 16

3. In problem reduction, state space is given by
   (a) AND graph   (b) OR graph   (c) AND/OR graph (d) Tree diagram

4. A problem is reduced to 5 sub-problems. How many AND arc will be there in the graph?
   (a) 5   (b) 10   (c) 2   (d) Cannot say

5. A problem is always represented as
   (a) State search   (b) State space   (c) Search space   (d) Problem space

6. A fully observable problem belongs to the category of
   (a) Multi-state problem   (b) Two-state problem
   (c) Single-state problem   (d) Cannot say

7. Which of the following can be used in problem solving as the structure of state space?
   (i) Graphs   (ii) Trees   (iii) Queues
   (a) (i) only   (b) (i) and (ii)   (c) (ii) only   (d) (ii) and (iii)

8. The solution quality in problem solving is measured on the basis of (most appropriate)
   (a) Number of states
   (b) Time factor
   (c) Optimality
   (d) Space factor

9. Consider the word *Dealing*. In how many ways can the letters be arranged such that the vowels always remain together?
   (a) 120
   (b) 720
   (c) 420
   (d) 620

10. For a traffic alerting problem-solving agent, the type of problem category it is likely to fall is
    (a) Fully observable
    (b) Partially observable
    (c) Non-observable
    (d) Unknown state space

CONCEPT REVIEW QUESTIONS

1. Describe the problem formulation steps with example.

2. How many problem types exist? Explain each type with an example.

3. Describe how search techniques are useful for finding solution to a problem.

CRITICAL THINKING EXERCISE

1. Consider a TV channel that is to telecast six shows, viz., 'Friends', 'KBC', 'Indian Idol', 'Dancing Star', 'Big Boss', 'Sailaab'. The following constraints are to be satisfied:

   (a) 'Friends' must be shown before 'KBC' and 'Indian Idol'.
   (b) 'KBC' should be telecasted before 'Dancing Star'.
   (c) 'Big Boss' must be telecasted after 'Indian Idol' and 'Sailaab'.

   Solve the problem to telecast the shows. Discuss and argue on the state representations.

2. Suppose there are four candidates contesting for party ticket for assembly elections. The party wants to select the best candidate. Formulate a problem for this situation with possible approach to find out the solution. (Assume data as required.)

PROJECT WORK

1. Write a program to implement the first assignment of critical thinking exercise.
2. Write a program to represent the same assignment using AND/OR graph.

CHAPTER 3

Uninformed Search

Learning Objectives

- ❑ To understand searching and problem solving
- ❑ To study basics of search techniques and their types
- ❑ To understand the importance and applications of search
- ❑ To study different uniformed search techniques and their applications
- ❑ To understand the performance and quality of different search methodologies
- ❑ To know variations in basic uninformed search techniques to overcome practical limitations
- ❑ To understand the control strategy and its use
- ❑ To understand the various methods of search with reference to complexity of problems

INTRODUCTION

For every problem, we are in search of solution. Solution is typically a state, where all requirements are fulfilled. It can be referred to as the *goal state*. These problems vary from simple selection of place with the best view, selection of flat that can meet our requirements or even reaching a certain destination in time. The goal state, hence, exhibits attributes and fulfils the requirements of user. In case of a product building, the goal state could be a product that can perform necessary functionalities.

To solve problems in real life, we tend to perform certain actions to achieve some predefined goal. Consider a scenario where you want to go to a particular hotel X that serves all kinds of Indian delicacies. But unfortunately, you are not aware of the exact route leading to your goal. You try out the different routes available and finally reach the hotel.

(You are hungry enough!). What you have done is looking out for the solution, inspecting some sequences or approaches. So, search is inspecting the several sequences and choosing the one that achieves the goal. Search, hence, is nothing but the search of goal state. The search begins from the initial state and ends up at the goal state, if any (here, goal state is the state that meets certain criterion). It is equally necessary to consider the time and cost factors during the search process. Generally, everyone prefers to reach to the goal state at the earliest and in less complicated manner. There can be one or more goal states and that would make the problem even more interesting. For example, suppose there are various hotels and you are hungry and you would like to reach to the hotel that serves delicious vegetarian food.

In the above case, the problem is that you are hungry and the solution is food. There can be a number of food joints, but you are looking for good quality of food and also specific type of food you like. This restricts a number of goal states. Hence, out of all possible goal states, we are keen to reach to an optimal goal state, where healthy, tasty and vegetarian food is served, and the place is not far from your initial state. Here, initial state is hungry and a particular location. As we proceed in this chapter, we will discuss the search methods in more detail and define the goal state in more clear way.

It is obvious from the discussion so far that any problem can be treated as a search problem. Here, search is for the goal state. AI problem focuses on the use of intelligence to reach an optimal goal state. Search techniques are the core of AI problems. The problems that can be addressed by the search techniques fall under the categories of agent-based pathfinding problems, two-player games and constraint satisfaction problems. In football, the goal state is typically ball reaching to the goal post. With every pass and kick, there is a state transition. But there are many constraints, which can be rules of game or can be even due to positioning of the players of opposition team. The classic example of pathfinding problem is 3×3 (Eight digits puzzle), as shown in Fig. 3.1 and its variants. This puzzle comprises 8 tiles numbered from 1 to 8 and a blank tile space. Here, the objective is to arrange the numbers by sliding the tiles to get the desired goal. Here, it is not the actual distance, but the search is constrained by legal moves defined by the game rules.

Figure 3.1 Initial state and the goal states of 8 number problem.

Even the travelling salesman problem falls under this category of problems. The example of two-player problems is chess, whereas the constraint satisfaction example is of eight queens. The 8-queen problem involves placing 8-queens on the 8×8 board such that no queen is attacked by the other in horizontal, vertical or diagonal direction when a new queen is placed. A solution is depicted below in Figure 3.2, where no queen attacks another queen on the board:

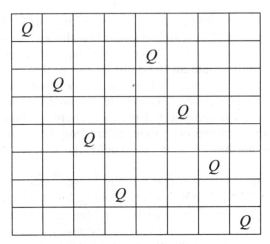

Figure 3.2   8-queens solution.

The search is about the possible legal moves allowed for the next transition and then, it helps in deciding and selecting from the various possible options, where the opponents move is also considered. Though the complexities involved are large, the addition of evaluation (often called *heuristic*) helps further in solving the problem or deciding the appropriate move. Hence, while searching, we should prefer to make optimal use of all the available information. This information builds some sort of guidelines for searching, and hence, reduces the complexity of search.

For the problem domains discussed, a search technique is the one that helps in reaching the solution or a desired goal. Even in real-life scenarios, we face various problems, where there are many possibilities and the optimal solution is generally not known. We need to inspect all the alternatives with reference to legality in this case. We can, thus, say that we are looking out or searching for the solutions. Hence, search is inspecting the various options or the sequences and choosing the one that is the most suitable and helps in achieving the goal. Thus, the expected outcome of search is typically an optimal route from the initial state to the goal state. So, to solve any problem, we need to get a solution or achieve a goal. Mapping the goal to be achieved by the search technique, leads to building a goal-based agent.

We start with the basic concepts along with the definition of the search. We can rightly define *search* as finding an appropriate option, which is provided with some directions. Search explores and evaluates the available options. It examines the states in search of goal. It generates or expands the different states while proceeding towards the solution. Sometimes, it has also cost associated with it. By adding some criteria, the search can also be restricted. So, search is an algorithm that discovers or locates a path to the solution. It makes use of typically called *control strategy* for the search process and posseses some knowledge to get the outcome.

In a broader sense, the search technique is considered to be informed and uninformed. This differentiation is on the basis of how the search actually takes place and what knowledge or information it uses during the search. Informed search, which is also called *heuristic search* is discussed in Chapter 4. In this chapter, we discuss about the uninformed search strategies (many times referred to as *blind search* or *non-heuristic search*) in detail. Let us begin our discussion with the general search algorithm.

3.1 GENERAL SEARCH ALGORITHM

What do we intend to do while searching is finally to give or to find an appropriate option. The basic or the generalised method to do so is discussed here.

Before we start with the discussion on search algorithms and its techniques, let us discuss problem solving and searching for the solutions.

3.1.1 Searching for Solutions

Searching for solution is typically finding out a path or route to goal state. While doing so, we enter into the various states. It can be referred to as an *intermediate step* during the course of search. Let us start with the basic terminologies, including state space and state-space search.

In generalised terms, a *state space* is defined as a collection of all possible configurations of the system. In short, it is a set of all states that can be reached from the initial states with all possible legal actions. A state space is represented as [*S*, *A*, *I*, *G*].

Here, *S* is the set of nodes or the states for a given problem to reach the solution; *A* is the set of arcs; *I* is the set of initial states and *G* comprises goal states. Set *A* corresponds to the steps required for problem solving; it might have some cost associated with it. One or more nodes can be a part of *I* set and every node has a set of successor nodes. A solution path is a path through the graph from *I* to *G*.

A *state-space search* is the process of searching the state space for a solution to reach the goal. Remember that every node represents a partial path. Now, let us try to develop a generalised search algorithm.

For any problem *P*, we have a set of initial states, say *I*, and a set of goal states, say *G*. We start with the first state and proceed till either we get a solution or return to failure.

Let us assume that the list *L* comprises the nodes or the states from *I*. The algorithm is described as follows:

While list *L* is not empty or has a solution

{

    Remove the state *X* from *L*.
    Take the next decision for the successor.
    Generate a new state for each possible choice for the decision.
    Merge/re-order the new states with *L*.

}

If *L* not empty (has a solution), return success.
Else return failure.

Generation of new states or the expansion mode is dependent on the search strategy used. We will discuss about the various search strategies ahead. It should be noted that in order to simplify the search techniques, it is convenient to represent the problem space as a tree.

3.1.2   Problem-solving Agents

Agent is the most common heard term in AI. What is it? An *agent* can be termed as an entity that can perceive the environment and act on it. So, an agent has an ability to perceive environment and act according to the situation to produce the required results. Hence, when we mention about the goal states and problem formulation, the thing that comes to our mind is agent. An agent, as we are familiar, acts and tries to improve its performance based on the outcome. To achieve so, it adapts to a goal. We can always say that the problem-solving agents are special type of goal-based agents. (Refer to the initial discussion on the problem solving in Chapter 2, to understand how a problem-solving agent works with search).

An agent formulates the goal as well as the problem. These are the basic steps that are required for solving any problem. Then, the actual search method comes into picture. What does the agent do in search once this is done? In search, the agent determines the possible set or rather sequence of actions. This process is carried out so that it can help the agent itself in reaching the states that can ultimately lead to the goal state. So, a search algorithm takes the input of the problem and outputs a solution, which here is an action sequence, that the agent executes finally.

The following steps describe the process:

1. Formulate goal.
2. Formulate the problem which has the goal and the initial states → problem.
3. Now search with the given problem → sequence of actions.
4. Action on the sequence → Act according to the sequence of actions.

Let us proceed towards how control strategies help and play a role in the search techniques.

3.1.3   Control Strategies

Addressing the question, i.e., how to reach or what way to follow while searching for a solution is still remaining. Control strategies are the ones that define this way. So, the rules play an important role in the decision-making; where and which rule is to be applied is decided based on the search strategy. In short, search strategy deals with the overall rules and approach towards searching.

The most common strategies used are discussed below:

Forward search: The strategy here is to explore towards a solution. The main aim is to reach a solution starting from initial state. The methods employing this strategy are often referred to as *data-directed ones*. In this case, your search expedition begins from current position. For example, locating a city from current location in map.

Backward search: In this case, the strategy proceeds, from goal to a solvable initial state. It could be to a solvable sub-problem or a state. Here, the methods employing this strategy are referred to as *goal-directed ones*. Unlike in forward search, if your search begins from target city, it can be termed as *backward search*.

There can also be a combination of these strategies as well, where both the techniques are incorporated. These are as follows:

Systematic search: A systematic strategy is used when the search space is small and systematic, but blind. We call it blind because this is the case where the search has no information about its domain. The only thing it can do is just distinguishing between the goal and non-goal states. For example, you are to locate a particular book in a library, where the books are not indexed and arranged properly. Then, there would be no option but to go blindly and check every book rack. So, systematically, you try to cover all book racks.

Depth first search and *breadth first search* are the two most common methods falling in this category. They also belong to the category of uninformed search. We will discuss these methods in detail further in the chapter.

Heuristic search: *Heuristic* is typically a technique based on the previous experience and provides guidelines to solve the problems. It is a technique that improves the efficiency of a search process. It is exploratory in nature. Imagine a teacher assisting a student in developing some layout of a document. In this process, the teacher may give some important hints to help the student in doing it in the best possible way or may miss some of them. The function of the teacher can be said to have a heuristic approach. Remember that heuristic search may not find out the best solution, but it guarantees to find a good solution in a reasonable amount of time. It uses some measure of relative merits, which can guide the search. For example, if you are locating a city, air distance of the city from current location can guide you to select the direction. This approach is most commonly used where the systems have time or space constraints, and where the dependency is on the knowledge of the problem domain. So, they rely on the promising lines of development to proceed.

This is all about the control strategies that are used in search techniques. But with every search strategy that is used, there are some parameters that measure the effectiveness of the search strategy.

Parameters for Search Evaluation

The main parameters that are used in the evaluation of search are completeness, time complexity, space complexity and optimality. Let us brief on what they mean.

1. **Completeness:** By completeness, we mean that the algorithm finds an answer in some finite time. So, the algorithm is said to be complete if it is guaranteed to find a solution, if there is one.
2. **Space and time complexity:** With space and time complexity, we address the memory required and the time factor in terms of operations carried out.
3. **Optimality and admissibility:** Optimality actually tells us how good the solution is. So, an algorithm or a search process is said to be optimal, if it gives the best solution.

Let us now proceed with the methods and the different types of uninformed search methods.

3.2 UNINFORMED SEARCH METHODS

Uninformed search methods, as discussed earlier, belong to the category of methods that have no prior knowledge of the problem. They are generally exhaustive methods that are brute force, searching all possible paths. Since these methods work in the absence of any information, they are also referred to as *blind search methods*. These methods can be understood by a very simple example. If we would like to search a boy named Ram in a school, with the number of classes from 1 to 10 and each class having two divisions, then the search would involve going to each and every class till the student named Ram, we are looking for, is found. Since no information is available, we need to select certain strategy and expand the nodes (here, the classes) in some predefined order. *Breadth first search* and *depth first search* are the two basic approaches of expanding and visiting nodes in the absence of any heuristic. These are discussed along with some other techniques in the subsequent sections.

3.2.1 Breadth First Search (BFS)

The search technique in BFS follows the shallow node approach. Here, the basic idea is that across the level of the tree, all the nodes are searched. So, it is a search technique, where from the root node, all the successors are searched across the level and expanded. Queue data structure is used to carry out the search, where things happen on first in first out basis (FIFO).

The BFS approach is shown in Figure 3.3. Here, the dotted arrows indicate the search method. With reference to the diagram, the search proceeds with the processing of all the nodes at a particular level and then proceeds to the next one.

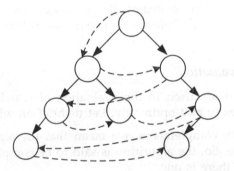

Figure 3.3 Breadth first search tree.

Let us take an example of BFS for better understanding.

Consider that *A* is the start state and *D* is the goal state (Figure 3.4). With the help of a queue, the example is demonstrated.

In BFS, the step-wise working is as follows:

Queue	Check
A	—
	Removed A, is it goal? No, add children. So, B and E are added.
BE	
E	Removed B, is it goal? No, add children. So, C is added at the end of queue.
EC	
C	Removed E, is it goal? No, add children. So, F and G are added.
CFG	
FG	Removed C, is it goal? No, add children. So, D is added.
FGD	
GD	Removed F, is it goal? No, add children. Cannot be added, leaf node, so remove the next node.
D	Removed G, is it goal? No, add children. Cannot be added, leaf node, so remove the next node.
Empty	Removed D, is it goal? YES!

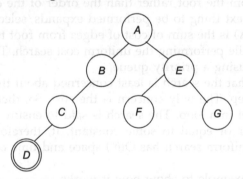

Figure 3.4 Sample tree input for BFS.

From the example discussed here, it is clear that each time you add a node, its children are to be added at the end of the queue as it proceeds level-wise. Since in the example, the goal state lies at the last level, each and every node or state is traversed and added to the queue.

The breadth first search algorithm is summarised as follows:

1. Create a node-list (queue) that initially contains the first node.
2. Do till a goal state is found
   - Remove X from node-list. If node-list is empty, then exit.
   - Check if this is goal state.
   - If yes, return the state.
   - If not, get the next level nodes, i.e., nodes reachable from the parent and add to node-list.

If for a given problem, there exists a solution, then BFS is guaranteed to find it out. Hence, we can say that it has the completeness property. It also possesses the property of optimality for the shortest path. Here, the cost of every edge is same, i.e., the cost to reach from one node to another is same. What about the space and time complexities? Let us assume that b is a branching factor or rather the number of successors at every level and d is the depth. Then, the time complexity will be $O(b^d)$—exponential in the depth of the solution. Let us map it mathematically. We start from the root and proceed towards the next level, then the nodes generated at each level are as follows:

$$b + b^2 + b^3 + \dots + b^d + (b^{d+1} - b)$$

This equals to $O(b^{d+1})$, and hence, it comes to $O(b^d)$ and the space complexity is $O(b^d)$, as every node is saved in the memory. Hence, this search is not feasible when you have a large search space.

3.2.2 Uniform Cost Search

Generally, in the search method, with every edge that we traverse, there is a cost associated with it. With BFS, we are assuming that every edge is having the same cost. Now speaking about the uniform cost search, if all the edges do not have the same cost, the breadth first search generalises to uniform cost search. So, the expansion takes place in the order of costs of the edges from the root rather than the order of the depth.

At every step, the next thing to be performed expands/selects a node X, whose cost $c(X)$ is lowest, where $c(X)$ is the sum of cost of edges from root to the node. It is the core step that is followed while performing the uniform cost search. This search technique can be easily implemented using a priority queue.

It is quiet obvious that the search is least concerned about the steps it needs to carry out to reach the goal step. The only concern is the cost. So, there could be a possibility that the search could get in a loop. The search is said to ensure completeness if the cost at every edge is greater or equal to some constant. It, therefore, satisfies the optimal property as well. The uniform search has $O(b^d)$ space and time complexities, as it mostly explores large trees.

Let us consider an example to show how it works.

Consider the following tree given in Figure 3.5, where the uniform cost search is to be applied from the start, i.e., node A to the goal node G. We will use a frontier and an expanded list while generating the solution. (An explored list can also be maintained to keep track of the explored nodes. This list is not considered in this example to avoid confusion.)

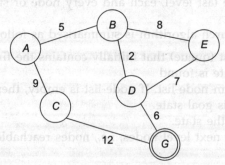

Figure 3.5 Input tree for uniform cost search.

Let us discuss how the uniform cost search proceeds step-wise.

Step 1: Start from *A*   Expanded none

Step 2: Frontier   Expanded none

Step 3: Frontier: *B* and *C*   Expanded *A*

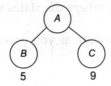

Select the lowest, i.e., *B*

Step 4: Frontier: *D, C, E* (priority queue)   Expanded *A, B*

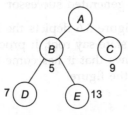

Note: Remember the costs are added from the root till the node in consideration. Select the lowest, i.e., *D*.

Step 5: Frontier (*C, E, E, G*)   Expanded *A, B, D*

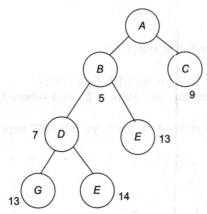

In step 5, we have considered *E*, as its parent is different. Since we have reached the goal state, from the tree, we can see that we have found a path. The path is *A-B-D-G*. With the frontiers and the tree generation process, we can easily have the solution to the problem in uninformed search. Dijkstra's approach is often considered to be variant of this uniform cost search.

3.2.3 Depth First Search (DFS)

Unlike BFS, in this method, a single branch of the tree is considered at a time. Taking the same example of finding a route to the hotel, you start with one route and continue it till you come to know that you are at the hotel or you have to change the path, as it will not lead you to the hotel or it is a dead end. While doing so you can think of going back at some point and taking up some other lane/road that can lead you to the place and this is very much possible. This is called *backtracking*. It is the stack data structure that is most commonly used in the implementation of DFS, where the states or the nodes are in operation on first in last out basis.

Speaking in terms of states, you always generate a new state as you proceed through the way.

In search, the same can be formulated as follows:

1. If initial state is the final state (You are just in front of the hotel) → success, exit
2. Do it till you get success or failure.
   Generate a successor, if no more successors can be generated → failure
   Go to step 1 with initial state to be the current generated successor.

The algorithm just discussed above does a DFS. Figure 3.6 depicts the DFS process. As described, the search starts with the initial node or state say root. It proceeds with its successor and follows the path ahead till either is knows that it has come to a solution or has to go back and seek new solution as shown in the figure.

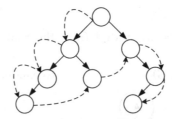

Figure 3.6 Depth first search tree.

Let us take the same example that we had for breadth first search.

Here, we will discuss two cases—where the goal state is *D*, and where the goal state is *F* (Figure 3.7).

With the start node of *A* and the goal state of *D*, we have the DFS approach carried out as follows:

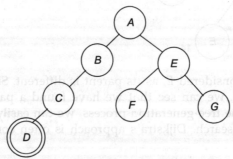

Figure 3.7 Sample tree input for DFS.

Stack

Step 1:	$A \leftarrow$ top $B \leftarrow$ top E	Pop A, is it goal? No, push its children on the stack. A's successor is pushed.
Step 2:	$B \leftarrow$ top E $C \leftarrow$ top E	Pop B, is it goal? No, push its children on the stack. B's successor is pushed.
Step 3:	$C \leftarrow$ top $D \leftarrow$ top E	Pop C, is it goal? No, push its children on the stack. C's successor is pushed.
Step 4:	$D \leftarrow$ top E	Pop D, is it goal?? YES!

Pop all the contents. Path found!

So, by traversing from one path in one direction of depth, we lead to the goal state. In this case, no backtracking is required. Consider the second case, where we want to reach to F.

The initial working is same as the way we had to reach to D. The example below shows that after having reached till D state, the next step needs backtracking and hence it starts with E. So, we will start from that point. Thus, the stack contents are as follows:

Stack

Step 1:	$E \leftarrow$ top	After having traversed the steps till D, stack will have E. So, pop E, is it goal? No, push its children.
Step 2:	$F \leftarrow$ top G	E's successor is added.
Step 3:	$F \leftarrow$ top G $G \leftarrow$ top	Pop F, is it goal?? YES!

Pop the contents. Path found! So, the path A-E-F is found.

With respect to the completeness of DFS, we cannot say that it will converge. The reason is we go through the selected path and keep on generating the successors and proceed. The search is not optimal. Always remember never use DFS if you suspect a big tree depth. In the worst case, DFS visits all the nodes before getting a solution. The time complexity of DFS, hence, results in $O(b^d)$. At any point of time, we have to keep the path from the root to the current node that is in consideration. This is clear from the example. Hence, considering the depth and the branching factor, the space complexity is $O(bd)$. This is the only good part of DFS. The advantages and disadvantages of DFS and BFS are depicted in Tables 3.1 and 3.2, respectively.

TABLE 3.1 Advantages of Depth First Search and Breadth First Search

Advantages of Depth First Search	*Advantages of Breadth First Search*
1. Simple to implement 2. Needs relatively small memory for storing the state-space	1. Guaranteed to find a solution (if one exists) 2. Depending on the problem, can be guaranteed to find an optimal solution

TABLE 3.2 Disadvantages of Depth First Search and Breadth First Search

Disadvantages of Depth First Search	Disadvantages of Breadth First Search
1. Cannot find solution in all cases, and hence, can sometimes fail to find a solution	1. Memory management along with allocation is the key factor, and hence, more complex to implement
2. Not guaranteed to find an optimal solution can take a lot of time to find a solution	2. Needs a lot of memory for storing the state space if the search space has a high branching factor

3.2.4 Depth Limited Search (DLS)

After dealing with the depth first search, we are aware that though it has desirable properties, the probabilities of it getting terminated with wrong expansion cannot be eliminated. Thus, the notion of depth limit comes. The basic idea is not allowing expansion after the certain depth. This process proves to be the most useful if one is aware of the maximum depth of the solution. Imagine that you are out for purchase of a mobile and in a particular area. For convenience, you set 3 streets as depth limit in that area. You begin with street 1. If your budget requirements and features required are available in the first shop itself, then you would stop and purchase there or else go to the next shop on that street. So, possibly at depth of that street, i.e., 1, you have explored all the shops. If the requirements are not satisfied, you would go to the next level, i.e., street 2 and then street 3. (Assumption is that you are not doing a survey!)

The following algorithm summarises the working of depth limited search:

1. Set the depth limit to the maxdepth to search.
2. Initial node = current node
   If initial node = goal, return
3. If depth(initial node) > depth limit
      return
   else
      Expand(initial node)
      Save(successors) using stack
      Go to step 2

Since depth limited search does not find solutions in all cases, it is not complete. The only reason behind it is that if the depth of the solution lies beyond the one, then it is selected. But if the depth limit is greater than that of solution's depth, then it is complete. The search method is not an optimal one. There is no guarantee that the search will give a solution that will be optimal, as it finds the one which is within its limits. With respect to the space and time complexities, the space complexity is same as that of DFS, i.e., $O(bl)$. But with respect to time complexity, it now comes till the order of l, i.e., $O(b^l)$, where l is the depth limit.

3.2.5 Iterative Deepening Search (IDS)

Iterative deepening is an enhanced version of the depth limited search. In some cases, depth limit restricts DLS from finding solution, since solution may exist beyond prescribed depth limit. Iterative deepening helps in addressing such problems. It further continues the DLS for the next level by extending the depth limit as limit = limit + 1 and so on till we are guaranteed of a solution. We can say that iterative deepening combines the benefits of BFS and DFS. If we look from a broader perspective, breadth first search is a special case of iterative deepening search, with the deepening factor equal to 1 and initial depth equal to 1. Considering the same example of mobile shopping, one can think of some limit, say 3 (number of streets), and possibly, there are 7 streets with the mobile shops. The iterative deepening, as discussed earlier, continues ahead of 3, provided the solution is not achieved till the street number 3. Figure 3.8 depicts the basic concept of iterative deepening.

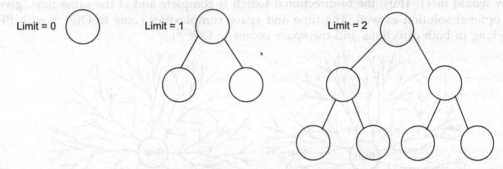

Figure 3.8 Iterative deepening.

The algorithm for IDS is as follows:

1. Set depth-limit ← 0
2. Do
   Solution = DLS(depth-limit, initial node)
   If(solution= goal state) then return
   else
   Depth-limit = depth-limit + 1
   continue

Though the algorithm is complete, the major factor of concern here is the regeneration of tree for every depth searched. That is, at every time we set up a new depth, the previous search results are discarded and we start from the scratch. So, there is a trade-off between the space and the time. With regard to completeness and optimality of this approach, the algorithm is complete and optimal. The time complexity comes to $O(b^d)$ due to the iterative calls. In the sense, higher the branching factor, lesser is the overhead of expanding the states. The space complexity of IDS comes to $O(bd)$. When the search space is large and there is unavailability of the depth factor or rather when the depth factor is not known, then in such cases, IDS method is preferred.

3.2.6 Bi-directional Search

Another variant of this type of search technique is bi-directional search. The search is carried out form both the ends and we are unsure of getting a solution. The search needs to be explicitly specified with the goal state. It comprises forward search from initial stage and a backward one from the goal state. At some point, they possibly can intersect, and if they do, then we have a solution or else there is no solution. The search is done by expanding the tree with the branching factor b and the distance from start to goal, i.e., d. We can relate this again to BFS that is carried out from both the ends. It is not the case that the bi-directional search always uses BFS as a path to search; it could be with the best first or the other method too. Bi-directional search can also be a part of heuristic.

Figure 3.9 depicts a typical bi-directional search, where search begins from both initial state and goal state. Consider a problem with the depth as 4. Here, if we have the search paths working in both the directions, one at a time, then in the worst case at depth of 2, they would meet. Thus, the bi-directional search is complete and at the same time, gives an optimal solution as well. The time and space complexities come to $O(b^{d/2})$ with BFS working in both directions and the space comes to $O(b^{d/2})$.

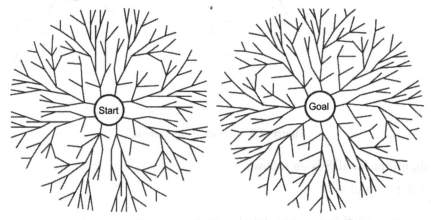

Figure 3.9 Bi-directional search.

Bi-directional search is not that easy to implement as one would think of. The implementation approach needs to be very efficient such that the intersection of the two approaches is possible.

3.2.7 Comparison of the Uninformed Techniques

Table 3.3 summarises the complexities, optimality and completeness about the search techniques.

TABLE 3.3 Comparison of Uninformed Search Techniques

Search techniques	Complete	Optimal	Time complexity	Space complexity
Breadth first search	Yes	Yes	$O(b^d)$	$O(b^d)$
Uniform cost	Yes	Yes	$O(b^d)$	$O(b^d)$
Depth first	No	No	$O(b^d)$	$O(bd)$
Depth limited	No	No	$O(b^l)$	$O(bl)$
Iterative deepening	Yes	Yes	$O(b^d)$	$O(bd)$
Bi-directional	Yes	Yes	$O(b^{d/2})$	$O(b^{d/2})$

SUMMARY

In this chapter, we have discussed about the basic search approach and the problem domains handled by the search techniques. The control strategies that help in defining the way to reach the solution have also been discussed.

In search techniques, an agent plays a critical role. It is the agent that has to formulate the goal and the problem prior to the start of the search process. An agent takes appropriate action with reference to the scenario to lead to the goal state. The different techniques of search are then applied to reach the solution. With the existence of different strategies, the search techniques are classified in a broader sense into informed and uninformed. Uninformed search are blind search techniques with restricted information availability. The effectiveness of the search is often measured in terms of the parameters of completeness, optimality, and time and space complexities. With every approach having its own flavour, there is always a trade-off between the selections of any search method and is totally dependent on the type of problem that is to be solved. In some cases, it is the problem space size that has to be considered, while in some cases, it is the efficiency that matters. Breadth first search and depth first search are the two major approaches in uninformed search. Further, there are variants like depth limited search, iterative deepening search and bi-directional search.

If any additional information other than the costs is available for the search, then it would be more effective. This is what a heuristic search does. So, by providing the guidelines, a heuristic search, which is also called informed search, helps in making it more effective.

 KEYWORDS

1. **Search technique:** It is a technique that provides with some appropriate option in reaching the solution or a desired goal.

2. **State space:** A state space is defined as a collection of all possible configurations of the system.

3. **State-space search:** A state-space search is the process of searching the state space for a solution to reach the goal.

4. **Control strategy:** It is a strategy that defines a way to follow while searching for the solution.

5. **Forward search:** It is a strategy that proceeds from the initial state towards the solution.

6. **Backward search:** It is strategy that proceeds from the goal state to the solvable initial state.

7. **Systemic search:** It is a blind search technique that is systemic in nature and is applied for small problem space.

8. **Uninformed search:** It is a search technique that is blind and does not make use of the information about the problem. It simply distinguishes between the goal and non-goal states. Also, it is systemic in nature.

9. **Heuristic search:** It is a technique that improves the efficiency of search technique by providing guidelines.

10. **Optimality:** A search is optimal when the best solution is generated by the approach.

11. **Completeness:** Completeness defines that the algorithm/approach will give the solution if there is one.

12. **Breadth first search:** This refers to a shallow approach where nodes are searched all across the levels.

13. **Uniform cost search:** It is a breadth first search, where the search takes place with respect to the cost of the edges unlike the normal BFS.

14. **Depth first search:** It is a search technique where path from one node to its children on the same line is continued. So, it is a search which goes first deeper and then across branches.

15. **Depth limited search:** This refers to a version of depth first search, where the expansion is limited to a specified depth limit.

16. **Iterative deepening search:** It is an extension of depth limited search, where if the solution is not found at the specified depth limit, it carries the search to further levels of depth.

17. **Bi-directional search:** It is a search technique, where the search is carried in both the directions—forward and backward.

MULTIPLE CHOICE QUESTIONS

1. Your friend is in a building that has 9 floors and you want to locate him. Which search technique would you use?
   (a) Depth first search   (b) Breadth first search
   (c) Depth limited search   (d) Iterative deepening.

2. In uninformed search
   (a) Heuristic plays a very critical role in the decision of next successor
   (b) There is no information about the nodes
   (c) The best path is selected
   (d) None of the above

3. A parent wants to put his child in a good school. There are many schools in the city, but the parent's preference is to the one that is nearby his house. Which of the following search technique(s) would the parent use in the selection of the school?
   (a) Depth first search   (b) Uniform cost search
   (c) Depth limited search   (d) All of the above

4. If any search algorithm is able to generate a solution, then the search is called
   (a) Efficient   (b) Optimal   (c) Complete   (d) Informed

5. Which of the following search technique uses a priority queue?
   (a) Breadth first search
   (b) Depth limited search
   (c) Iterative deepening
   (d) Uniform cost search

6. The time complexity of iterative deepening comes to
   (a) $O(bd)$
   (b) $O(d^b)$
   (c) $O(b^d)$
   (d) $O(b^l)$

7. Which search technique can be considered as the special case of iterative deepening?
   (a) DFS
   (b) BFS
   (c) Bi-directional
   (d) None of these

8. Which search is effective in the easy detection of cycles?
   (a) DFS
   (b) BFS
   (c) Both (a) and (b)
   (d) None can detect

9. In searching techniques, a node/state is marked to be visited when
   (a) It is pruned
   (b) Its successors are traversed
   (c) It is expanded
   (d) Both (b) and (a)

10. The branching factor determines
    (a) The cost for the search
    (b) The number of operators that can be applied
    (c) How close the path is to the solution
    (d) All of the above

CONCEPT REVIEW QUESTIONS

1. What is a problem-solving agent?

2. Distinguish between depth first search and breadth first search.

3. Discuss about the time and space complexities of the uninformed search techniques.

4. In which search techniques it is necessary to maintain the previous states?

5. What is the difference between completeness and optimality?

6. Show with an example that the time complexity of DFS is $O(b^d)$.

CRITICAL THINKING EXERCISE

1. For $b = 10$ and $d = 5$, compute the overhead between the depth limited search and the iterative deepening search.

2. Can you map a greedy approach to any of the search methods discussed? Discuss with an example.

3. Is it possible to relate any of the searching techniques in a case when any Bluetooth-enabled device is looking for the other Bluetooth-enabled devices?

4. Can you think of different possible combinations of DFS and BFS?

⟨**PROJECT WORK**⟩

1. Develop a program to solve the eight queens problem. Which strategy would you use for the same? Discuss about its complexity parameters.
2. Consider the graph given in Figure 3.10.

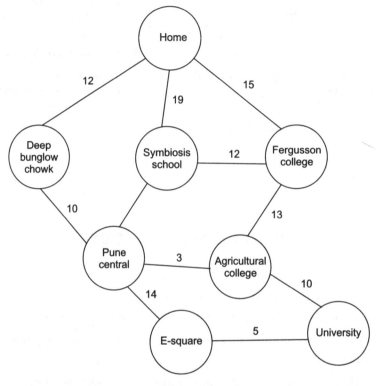

Figure 3.10

Apply the following methods to the above graph:
   (i) Implement uniform cost search, where start node is Home and goal is E-square.
  (ii) In the absence of the distance parameter, implement DFS and show step-wise how the goal state is reached.
 (iii) In the absence of the distance parameter, implement BFS and show step-wise how the goal state is reached.
  (iv) In the absence of the distance parameter, implement DLS and show step-wise how the goal state is reached, where the limit is 3.
   (v) In the absence of the distance parameter, implement IDS and show step-wise how the goal state is reached, where the limit is 3.

CHAPTER **4**

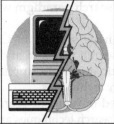

Informed Search

INTRODUCTION

As we have discussed in Chapter 3, search is one of the most important topics in AI. Any problem can be presented as a search problem. In all the cases, we are in search of a solution. This solution could be a particular destination, particular medicine, or even can be a particular person or a document. The search complexity increases with the complexity of the problem. A very simple search method may work for very simple problems, but may fail to handle a few tricky situations and may end up by getting trapped some times in the local minima, and sometimes, it returns a solution which is not optimal, and in most of the cases, it takes a lot of time to arrive at a solution.

These applications (where search methods can be employed) may vary from simple selection of an object from a stack of objects to the complex problems like route selection,

55

forecasting scenarios, and even to the search of the best strategic position. This chapter provides reader more insight into the search techniques and equips them to solve different class and complexity problems with search paradigm while elaborating the heuristic search methods in a greater detail.

Uninformed searches (that we have studied in Chapter 3) lead to higher time and memory complexity. Optimising a search problem and optimisation of the whole process are challenging tasks. Right heuristic and right application of heuristic are some of the important aspects of efficient search techniques.

Thus, there is a need for informed or heuristic search. Let us begin the discussion with informed search techniques. Informed search techniques are also called *heuristic search techniques/strategies*. These strategies use the information about the domain, or knowledge about the problem and scenario to move towards the goal nodes. Heuristic methods do not always find the best solution, but they guarantee to find a good solution in reasonable amount of time. For this, they sacrifice the completeness, but then try to increase the efficiency. We are aware that many search problems are NP-complete, so in the worst case, they can have exponential time complexity, but a good heuristic can find a solution for a problem efficiently. Hence, these methods are useful in solving tough problems, i.e., the problems that take longer time to compute solution. A very classic example of heuristic method is travelling salesman problem.

Heuristic Function

A *heuristic function* is the one that guides the decision of selection of a path. A heuristic function $h(n)$ provides an estimate of the cost of the path from the given node to reach to the closest goal node. Let us discuss the various methods in heuristic.

4.1   GENERATE AND TEST

The most easiest and obvious way to solve any problem is to generate a solution and check if this is the real one. The algorithm for the method is discussed below:

1. Generate a possible solution, which can be a node in the problem space or it can be a path from the initial state.
2. Test if the possible solution is the real one, i.e., compare with the goal states.
3. Check solution, if true, return the solution, else go to step 1.

Now you would be feeling as if you are studying depth first search, but here complete solutions are generated before testing. It is often called the *British Museum method*. Now, from where does heuristic come into picture? Heuristic is needed to sharpen the search. While generating the solutions, we can have an intermediate option between the generation of complete solutions and random solutions. This approach proceeds systematically and does not consider the paths that are unlikely to lead to the solution. Now, this evaluation of which path should be considered is done by the heuristic function.

4.2   BEST FIRST SEARCH

Best first search is a combination of depth first search and breadth first search. Each of the methods—depth first and breadth first have their own positive aspects that are exploited in the best first search. The positive aspect of DFS is that the goal can be reached without any need to compute all the states, whereas with BFS, it does not get halted or trapped in dead paths. The best first search allows us to switch between the paths, and thus, gets the benefit of both. To do so, the selection of the most promising node is done. So, it analyses and checks if the selected node is better than the previous one. If not found so, it reverts back to the previous path and proceeds. So, backtracking occurs. In order to achieve this, even though a move is selected, other options are kept so that they can be revisited.

Before we proceed to the algorithm and example of best first search, we will brief on OR graphs.

OR Graph

The notion of OR graphs is required in order to avoid the revisiting of paths and for propagating back to the successor, in case it is required. In this case, for the algorithm to proceed, a node contains the following information:

1. Description of the state it represents.
2. Indication how promising it is.
3. Parent link that points to the best node it has reached from.
4. List of nodes that are generated from it.

A graph employing these descriptions is called *OR graph*.

To have this type of graph search, we describe further two lists of nodes, viz., open and closed.

1. Open list: It consists of list of nodes that have been generated and on whom the heuristic function has already been applied, but yet not examined. We can map them to a priority queue. This queue consists of the nodes or the elements with highest priority. This is dependent on the heuristic function that associates the cost with the node, and hence, prioritises them.

2. Closed list: It contains the nodes that have already been examined. When a node is generated, then this is required to check that whether it has already been generated.

So, what is heuristic and the function evaluation procedure, $f(n)$? $f(n)$ is the function that can be defined as the sum of two elements, i.e., the cost of reaching from the initial node to the current node, $g(n)$ and the additional cost of getting from the current node to the goal state, $h(n)$. So, $g(n) + h(n)$ defines the function.

Now, let us discuss the *best first search algorithm*.

1. Open list ← initial state/node.
2. Do (till goal is found) or (no nodes in the open list).
   (i) Select the best node (since priority queue is used, this is possible) from open list. Add to closed list.
   (ii) Generate the successors.
   (iii) For every successor, do
       (a) If the successor is already generated, change the parent if this new path is better than the earlier one. Accordingly, update the costs to this node as well as to the previous successors, if any.

(b) If the successor is not generated previously, then evaluate it on the basis of heuristic, add it to the open list and make a note of its parent as well.

Consider the following graph given in Figure 4.1:

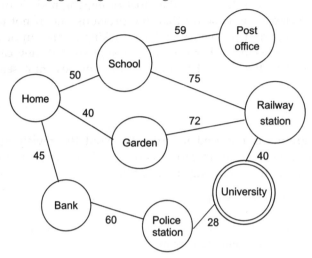

Figure 4.1   Graph sample example with sample graph.

The above graph is an example that is referred in the chapter to show the working of the methods. The values on the edges represent the distances or the costs. For the above graph, it is shown further that how a best first search finds a solution from Home (as the initial state/node) to University (as the goal state). As discussed earlier, the best first search is about using heuristic, which is used to calculate the cost. Consider the following hypothetical h values, which are straight line distances that are available from the states to reach to University (goal state).

So, here $f(n) = h(n)$. This example explains the states to proceed towards the goal of University. The values in the example represent the heuristic (you cannot actually compute the values; they are assumed to be computed on the basis of some previous experience), and hence, as the name suggests, the search proceeds in a greedy fashion.

Home 120
Bank 80
Garden 100
School 70
Railway Station 20
Post office 110
Police station 26

The approach proceeds by selecting the node that is closest to the goal state. It starts with Home, selecting the lowest heuristic, it goes to School (see Figure 4.2). From School, it proceeds towards Railway station and then to University. In this course of search, the node or the state of Police station is not considered as the part of evaluation process.

Let us come to the discussion of the properties of this algorithm. The best first search is not complete. The only reason is that heuristic puts every option or path to be the

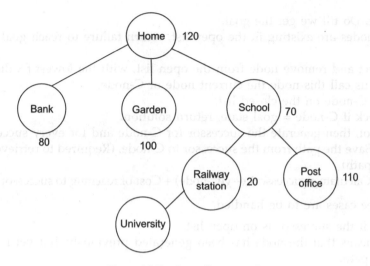

Figure 4.2 Best first search.

best one. But broadly speaking, heuristic that works reasonably will lead to a reasonable solution, and hence, will not get trapped into this problem. About optimality, it is neither optimal. The reason behind this is the selection of minimum value h. The search could also lead to dead ends. Time and space complexities of this algorithm are $O(b^m)$, where m represents the maximum depth. Since we require maintaining a queue for the successors that are not generated, the space complexity is $O(b^m)$.

4.3 GREEDY SEARCH

There is a long debate as to whether the best first search and the greedy search are same. So, we need to first understand the relationship among A*, best first and greedy. The best first is said to be the simplified version of A*. Now speaking about the greedy and best first, it is the best first search that is named as greedy best first search only. Also, a point that is worth a mention is that there is a family of best first search algorithms, which have different evaluation function. In some cases, it could be mapped as $f(n) = h(n)$ as well.

4.4 A* SEARCH

The best first search that we have learnt is a simplification of the A* approach. This algorithm was presented by Hart. A* is the most widely used approach for pathfinding. It is the A* approach that now makes use of the function $g(n)$ along with h. Evaluation function $f(n)$ represents the total cost. Here $f(n) = g(n) + h(n)$, where $g(n)$ is the cost so far to reach n, while $h(n)$ is the estimated cost from n to the goal state. The best first search is a special case of A*, where $f(n) = h(n)$. Let us discuss the algorithm in detail.

1. We begin with the open list containing only the initial state.
   (a) Let $g(n) = 0$ and $h(n) = $ value whatever it is.
   (b) So, $f(n) = h(n)$ as $g(n) = 0$.

2. Repeat: Do till we get the goal.
   If no nodes are existing in the open list, return failure to reach goal.
   Else
   1. Select and remove node from the open list, with the lowest f value.
   2. Let us call this node the current node or C-node.
   3. Put C-node on the closed list.
   4. Check if C-node = goal state, return solution.
   5. If not, then generate the successor for C-node and for every successor,
      (i) Save the path from the successor to C-node. (Required to retrieve the solution path)
      (ii) Calculate g(successor) $\leftarrow$ g(C-node) + Cost of reaching to successor from C-node.

Now, three cases are to be handled.

1. Check if the successor is on open list.
   This means that the node has been generated previously, but yet not considered in the path.
   (a) If so, throw this node (let us call this as Pnode) and add it to C-node's successor list.
   (b) Now, a decision is to be made whether the connect path between the Pnode's parent is set to C-node. This is dependent on the cost. If this cost is cheaper, then it should be. (This is true as successor and the P-node are same). This is done by comparing the g values. If g(successor) is less, reset P-node's link and update f(P-node) considering the value of g(P-node).
2. Check if the successor is on only closed list.
   If the node is present on the closed list, let us call this node as P-node.
   Add this node to the C-node's successors. Again check the costs as we have done in the previous step. Accordingly, update the g and f values.
   If this path is better, this needs to be rectified and informed to the P-node's successors. But how to inform the successors, as every successor is divided into further successors and so on. But remember, there is a stage when you get a node that is still on the open list and is a part of this successor family or does not have successor at all. To accomplish this, we have DFS that changes the g values, and in turn, f values as well. This is done for each branch till it terminates or a node to which a better path or the same value path has already been found.
   Let us make things simple. We are aware that every node's parent link points awards the best parent. As we propagate, we need to keep a track of whether the nodes' parents also point to this best parent; this is the same node from where we propagate. If it is, let the propagation continue, else g value specifies the better path and then the propagation may stop there. But it is quite possible that this new propagation might lead us to a path that is far better than the current. In that case, we need to compare and decide further. If the current path is better, stop propagation, else reset the parent and continue further.
3. Check if the successor is neither on the open list nor on the closed list.
   The most simple case, simply add it to the open list and the list of C-node's successors. Compute f(successor) = g(successor) + h(successor) and proceed.

Let us consider the same example as discussed for the best first search. Now, when it comes to A* approach, the function costs are updated. Consider that we need to find a solution from Home to University. It is the same case which we have discussed in the best first search. The steps of A* approach are shown below:

Initial state: Home
Goal: University

The detailed path for the search tree formation is represented here. At every point of time, the heuristic and the distance are taken into consideration.

Step 1:

Home   0 + 120 = 120

Step 2:

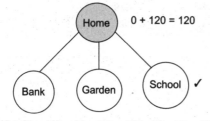

Step 3:

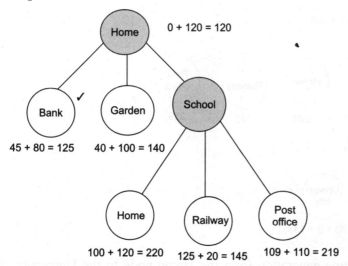

Step 4:

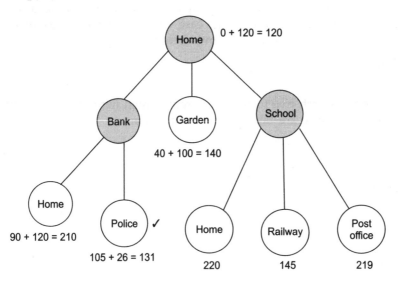

Step 5:

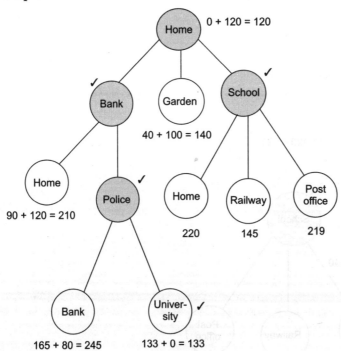

Step 5 shows the final tree generation from the Home node to the University. The ticked nodes refer to the expansion process being carried out.

4.4.1 Admissible Heuristic

Any search algorithm is admissible if it always produces an optimal solution. Here, it means that it would find the optimal solution as the first solution. So, it is required that the cost is optimal. That means for any node, say n, the heuristic, $h'(n)$ would be the cost of an optimal path from node n to the goal state. Thus, heuristic $h(n)$ is admissible if for all nodes n, $h(n) \leq h^*(n)$, where $h^*(n)$ is the actual cost to attain goal state from n.

To understand it better, let us consider Figure 4.3 showing an example related to it.

Underestimating h

Referring to Figure 4.3, it is discussed here how h' underestimates h. Let us assume that A* is applied and we are at the intermediate stage that is mentioned. Here, *Init* has been removed from the open list and the stages (where we are having the nodes/successors expanded) are represented. Now, we can see that here Q node's evaluation function $f(Q) = h(Q) + g(Q)$ is equal to 6. Since this is the lowest cost, this node is selected. Next, S is the only successor of Q. $f(S)$ is same as $f(P)$. Here we continue with our expansion, so we reach to T. Now, $f(T) = 9$, whereas $f(P) = 7$; so we go back and expand P. Thus, due to underestimation of $h'(P)$, efforts and memory are wasted.

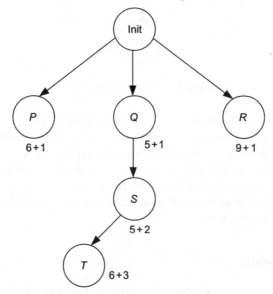

Figure 4.3 Underestimating h.

Overestimating h

Referring to Figure 4.4, now consider a scenario, where the heuristic function is overestimated. In the process of reaching to the goal state, we can see that from node Q, we move to S. $f(S) = 7$, and hence, being the lowest, it is selected. Ahead in the process, T is selected as $f(T) = 8$ and then we reach to U(say our goal state). Suppose there is direct path from P to goal state giving path length less than 3, we will not be able to find it. So, we can always say that if h' overestimates h, then, we have no assurance of getting the cheapest path.

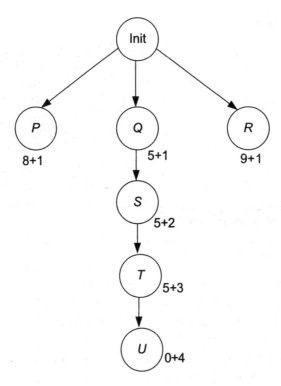

Figure 4.4 Overestimating *h*.

Then, the question is raised that if this overestimation does not occur, is the algorithm of A* admissible? We cannot guarantee whether *h'* will underestimate or overestimate A*. The only way is to set it to zero, but then this will lead to BFS.

Here, heuristic $h(n)$ is admissible, if for every node the heuristic cost $h(n)$ is always less than or equal to the actual cost required to reach the goal state from *n*, i.e., $h(n) \leq h^*(n)$, where $h^*(n)$ is actual cost to reach goal state. The heuristic that never overestimates the cost is an admissible heuristic.

4.4.2 Consistent Heuristic

Let us define what is meant by consistent heuristic. A heuristic $h(n)$ is said to be consistent, if for every node, say *n* and every successor *s* that is generated by an action *a* for *n*, the estimated cost to reach the goal state/node is not greater than the step-wise cost to reach *s* added to the cost of reaching the goal from *s*.

Mathematically we can say that for $h(n)$ to be consistent,

$$h(n) <= cost\ (n, a, s) + h(s)$$

Mapping this to the triangle inequality, we can say that each side of the triangle cannot be greater that the total of the remaining two sides.

4.4.3 Optimality of A*

Let us consider in which situation A* gives an optimal solution. Considering the algorithms, where the search is carried out from the root node, A* is said to be optimally efficient for any heuristic. By this, we mean that there exists no other algorithm or approach, which uses the same heuristic and can generate a fewer or lesser nodes than the ones generated by A*.

Time and Space Complexity

With respect to the time complexity, we always say that the time complexity depends totally on the heuristic function. In the worst case scenario, just imagine the number of nodes that would be expanded! It is exponential to the length of the solution. Mapping the sub-exponential growth mathematically, we get $log[h*(n)]$.

Here, $h*(n)$ is the true or the exact cost to reach the goal state from node n. So, the error of h now grows faster than the logarithm and it is least proportional to the cost of the path. Hence, we cannot say that it definitely results into an optimal solution. In such cases, we can use variants of A* or some other better heuristic functions.

Time complexity of A* is not the main hindrance. The main issue of concern here is the space complexity. Since all the nodes that are generated are kept in the memory, A* algorithm runs out of space. Hence, it is recommend not to use A* for large-scale problems.

4.5 MEMORY BOUNDED HEURISTIC SEARCH

Why is it necessary to have memory-bound heuristic search? Generally, we tend to run out of the memory before time! This occurs when the entire search paths are stored and the only solution to overcome this is to remember partial solutions. Thus, in order to overcome the space requirements, memory-bounded heuristic search comes into picture. Iterative deepening A* (IDA*), Recursive best first search (RBFS) and memory-bounded A*(MA*) are the algorithms that fall under this search. Let us begin our study with IDA*.

4.5.1 IDA*

We are already aware that in simple iterative deepening, the search is restricted by the depth limit, running it recursively. So, it tries to resolve the problem of breadth first search. On similar grounds, IDA* resolves the problem of A*, where the memory problem is overcome, and at the same time, optimality is also maintained.

In IDA*, at each iteration, depth first search (DFS) is applied. A track is maintained of the costs, i.e., $f(n) = g(n) + h(n)$ of each and every node that is generated. Whenever a node is generated whose cost is more or exceeding the threshold for that iteration, the path is discarded. Then, comes the backtracking method. The initial cut-off is set to be equal to the heuristic of the root node. So stepwise, the approach can be summarised as follows:

Step 1: At first, set the limit = h(root). We can call this as f-limit.

Step 2: The next step is pruning if any node does not satisfy the limit condition, i.e., prune if f(node) > f-limit.

Step 3: Set f-limit to be equal to the minimum cost of any node that is pruned.

The search terminates when the goal state is reached, whose cost does not exceed the current threshold.

From the approach, we can see that IDA* actually performs a series of depth first searches. Thus, the space constraint or the requirement is linear with respect to depth. Further things are dependent on the heuristic function as well. If an admissible heuristic exists, àn optimal solution is guaranteed. Thus, we can always conclude that IDA* is optimal in terms of time and space. Most importantly, it reduces the overhead of managing the open list and the closed list. Although in IDA*, we cannot deny the problem of excessive node generation.

4.5.2 Recursive Best First Search (RBFS)

It is the simplest recursive algorithm that performs the best first search with a linear space. The basic idea here is to remember the best path or the best alternative and backtrack if the best first gets very expensive, in the sense when the cost exceeds that of previously expanded node.

But then, tracking of the costs is required simultaneously with the backtracking. This means the *f*-value needs to be maintained. So, keeping the track of the *f*-cost or the *f*-value of the alternative paths that are available, the search process backtracks if the current path becomes expensive. As the decision to backtrack is taken, the *f*-cost of the current node (i.e., expanded) is replaced with the best *f*-cost of its children. Recording the *f*-cost enables the algorithm further to take decisions about whether there is a need to expand the tree further or not.

The algorithm for RBFS is explained below:

1. If curr_state = goal state
   Return curr_state (success!)
2. Expand(curr_node) → children
3. If empty(children) return failure
4. Do
   for each *c* (child of the curr_node)
   $f[c]$ = maximum($g(c) + h(c)$, $f[$curr_node$]$)
   best cost=lowest of *f*-cost, i.e., $f[c]$
   if(best cost >prev *f*-cost found) return failure
   consider the alternative *f*-cost
   goto step 1 with (best-cost node, min (*f*-cost, alternative *f*-cost))

The following example (Figure 4.5) shows a snapshot of how RBFS works for the same problem of Home to University.

Commenting on the optimality of RBFS, it is also optimal if the heuristic is admissible. Evaluation in terms of time complexity is very difficult, as it is totally dependent on the switching between nodes and the heuristic. The space complexity comes to O(*bd*), where *b* is branching factor and *d* is depth. The major drawback of RBFS and IDA* is the generation of same states again and again. The memory utilisation for the methods is just the *f*-cost that is required. So, if we are having more memory, why not to use it? Keeping this in mind, memory-bound variants MA* and SMA* (or Simplified Memory Bounded A*) approaches are used.

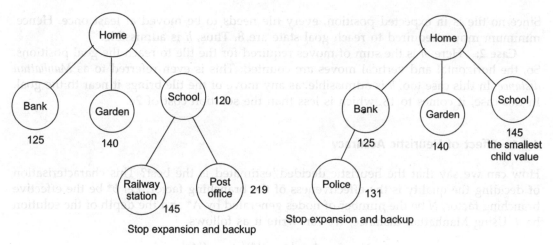

Example 4.5   RBFS snapshot.

4.6   HEURISTIC FUNCTION

We have already taken into account, in brief, the basic concept of heuristic and its function. Let us proceed further to explain the heuristic accuracy, its effect on the performance and invent admissible heuristic functions.

The discussion here is made with reference to the eight-puzzle problem. Following diagram shows initial and final states for eight-puzzle problem (Figure 4.6).

5	4	
6	1	8
7	3	2

1	2	3
8		4
7	6	5

Example 4.6   Eight-puzzle problem.

The puzzle is one of the popular heuristic search problems. The decision of heuristic is dependent on the moves taken. In the puzzle, 22 steps is the average cost required to reach goal state. The *b* value (branching factor) is set to at the most 3, but it comes to 4 only when the middle tile is empty. It also comes to 2 or 3 depending on the tile position. While solving this problem, it would require 3^{22} states generated. The state generation factor is restricted by keeping track of the repeated states. But when it comes to the increase in size of the puzzle, what can be done? So, there is a need for good heuristic function. Let us say that that we are using A*. There is need to have heuristic that will not have overestimation of *h*. With the previous efforts taken into account, the two *h*-value estimations are as follows:

Case 1:   Here, the value of h can be the number are in expected position of misplaced tiles. At the initial state, it is equal to 8, where none of the tiles are in expected positions.

Since no tile is in expected position, every tile needs to be moved at least once. Hence, minimum moves required to reach goal state are 8. Thus, *h* is admissible.

Case 2:   Here, *h* is the sum of moves required for the tile to reach the goal positions. So, the horizontal and vertical moves are counted. This is even referred to as *Manhattan distance*. In this case too, *h* is admissible, as any move of the tile brings it near to the goal. In this case, it comes to 18, which is less than the solution cost of 26.

4.6.1   Effect of Heuristic Accuracy

How can we say that the heuristic decided/estimated is the best? This characterisation of deciding the quality is the effectiveness of the branching factor. Let b^* be the effective branching factor, N be the number of nodes generated by A* and the depth of the solution be d. Using Manhattan distance, we can write it as follows:

$$N + 1 = 1 + b^* + (b^*)^2 + \dots (b^*)^d$$

This b^* can give a guideline in terms of quality of *h*. A good heuristic has b^* value near to one, and hence, can allow large problems to be solved. When we look at the two cases of *h*, then we come to know that *h* in case 2 is better. Why? Referring back to the point of admissible heuristic in A*, *h* in case 2 results in the expansion of all nodes that are expanded by *h* in case 1. But case 1 possibly expands other nodes too. So, taking up *h* with larger value is always better, but it is required to check the overestimation factor too! So, the value of *h* affects the performance.

4.6.2   Inventing Heuristic

The concept of heuristic has been crystal clear now. Things become easy when you try and relate to solve the problems on your own, but what about the heuristic that has been invented by machine?

There is a concept of relaxed problem. We have come across the word *relaxed rules*, where the criteria are somewhat less restricted or stringent. Similarly, in problem solving, if the rules are bit simplified with less restrictions on the actions, the problem is said to be a relaxed problem. Some of the constraints in the original problem are removed to convert into relaxed problem. Now, the *admissible heuristic* for the original problem is the cost of an optimal solution that is applied to a relaxed problem. This is admissible because the optimal solution of the original problem is also a solution of the relaxed problem. A simple example of relaxed problem in eight-puzzle problem is less restriction on the movement of the tiles. From these relaxed criteria, we have the mapping for the cases 1 and 2 stated earlier for *h*. But if the relaxed problem is also difficult to solve, then inventing the heuristic becomes more difficult.

ABSOLVER, a heuristic generator problem is designed by Prieditis that can generate heuristics automatically using the relaxed method approach and other methods as well.

Further, one can also think of the issues like if multiple heuristic values can be estimated, then which is to be selected? As discussed earlier, it is better to have the maximum value. So, the maximum of *h* is selected for the search.

Heuristic Building from Experience

Relaxed problem is a method for building heuristic. But there can be other possibilities also. This can be on the basis of some previous experiences. While solving the problem, you would get multiple optimal solutions. Each of these solutions can be experienced and can be used as examples to learn and build *h*. Many techniques can be used for the same. *Inductive learning* is a method that can help in building *h* function.

4.7 AO* SEARCH

A* algorithm uses open and closed lists to maintain the node status. AO* instead maintains the entire graph that has been generated till the current state. So, every node or state stores its *h*-value rather than storing the *g*-value. The algorithm is explained below:

Algorithm considers threshold value such that if *h*(start) > threshold, solution becomes impractical.

1. Initially, graph contains only start node/state. Compute *h*(start).
2. Till start is labelled as solved or *h*(start) > threshold, repeat
    (i) Generate/trace the children from start.
    (ii) Select promising node that is not yet expanded, let this be C-node.
    (iii) Generate C-nodes successors, if none, then C-node is not solvable. Hence set *h* (C-node) = threshold else for each successor, do
        Add to graph,
        if a terminal node-then label it solved and assign to it *h* = 0
        else compute its *h*-value.
    (iv) Propagate this information back. This is done as follows:
        If *X* is the set of nodes whose values are changed or is labelled as solvable, then
        (a) Select a node from *X*, whose descendents appear in the graph. If none, select any other node from *X*. Let this be select_node and remove from *X*.
        (b) Compute the cost of reaching (arcs) other nodes from select_node. This is equal to the sum of *h* values to reach there. Assign select_node the minimum of these values as its *h*.
        (c) Set the best path out of select_node that has the minimum cost computed earlier.
        (d) Label select_node as solved if all nodes connected to it are already labelled solved.
        (e) If select_node is labelled as solved, then its status must be propagated. So, add its ancestors to *X*.

It is necessary to mention that the propagation of the cost is through a long path, which impacts adversely on the efficiency of the algorithm. Along with this, we cannot forget the point that the graph may have cycles. This further increases the complexity of the algorithm.

4.8 LOCAL SEARCH ALGORITHMS AND OPTIMISATION PROBLEMS

Local search begins with one of the initial solutions and iterates, exploring the search space. Each step here is a search of solution, which is achieved through the moves associated with reference to the neighbourhood definition. Here, each step is a typical transition to one of its neighbourhood from present state. The move is based on the value of cost function. In local search algorithms, a single current state is selected and algorithm tries to improve it.

Two important parameters to be considered in local search technique are—selected initial solution and the stop criterion. Stop criterion typically defines the conditions when the search phase is over and the best solution found is returned.

Local search is based on the local view. Let us take an example of a car driver driving a car on a road with a number of curves up the hill, with possibility of multiple junctions and routes. Let us assume that he/she is driving on that road first time. He/She can see only the road close to her but cannot see the top or even beyond the next curve. His/Her decision about the route and speed depends on the local information and slope. Hence, there is only one way to check, based on the local information. The choice of the route and further selection of action among the possible actions for improving the objective function can only be made based on the local solution. It must be made by observing near or local solutions only. Though this mimics most of the real situations, the issue with the local search procedure is that no one can assure that the best solution is found. In short, it is not known whether the solution found is locally optimal or globally the best solution. There can be different ways or search strategies to deal with such situations. Local search algorithms do not guarantee an optimal solution. Generally, local search methods search non-optimally with reference to certain stop criterion. The effectiveness and widespread applicability make these techniques more appealing. There are many optimisation paradigms like evolutionary algorithms that sit on the top of simple local search techniques. In local search, larger the elements in the neighbourhood, more is the difficulty in exploring and better is the quality of local optimum.

Let us define three main entities for local search problem:

1. Search space
2. Neighbourhood relations
3. Cost function

State Space

It is a typical representation in the form of a graph, where nodes represent partial or complete solution of the problem and each of the arcs corresponds to the problem-solving process.

Neighbourhood Relations

In general, a *neighbourhood* of a point is a set or region containing the point, where one can attain that point without leaving the region. For a given state—$s(s \in S)$, a set $N(s)$ represents neighbouring solutions that can be attained in the given region. This $N(s)$ is called *neighbourhood of s*.

Cost Function

The selection of the move to be performed at each step of the search is based on the cost function. It is the cost function f that is associated with each element $s \in S$, and is represented as $f(s)$ that assesses the quality of solution.

4.8.1 Hill Climbing Search

In search methods, we continuously update the search space with reference to the goal state. In hill climbing, the search begins with a random point in search space. The basic idea of hill climbing is to always head towards a state which is better than the current state. Always move to the neighbour with a better score. Neighbour is typically a state that is reachable from the current state with any possible legal action. The neighbourhood needs to be small enough to achieve a better efficiency. The best neighbour among neighbourhood is picked. In case, there is no neighbour better than the current state, then the program stops. Since it is always moving to the node, which has a better value, it is very greedy and can easily stuck.

In steepest ascent hill climbing, the next state is always made the best successor of the current state, and it only makes a move if that successor is better than the current state. Local maxima and local optima are the major issues of this algorithm. There can be many local optima. Even there can be ridges. Figure 4.7 depicts the same.

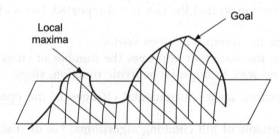

Figure 4.7 Local maxima.

Hill climbing search strategies expand the current state to evaluate children. Obviously, the best child is selected for further expansion—neither its sibling nor its parents are retained. Since it keeps no history, it cannot recover from failures of its strategy. In small settings of specific environment, though this strategy works very well, it may not be appropriate for many real-life scenarios because of the shape of the entire space. Typically, heuristic helps in deciding the direction of search.

Simple Hill Climbing

Typical steps in simple hill climbing are listed below:

1. Let *IS* be the initial state and *GS* be the goal state. At first, the initial state *IS* is evaluated.
   Check if *IS* = *GS*? If yes, then quit.
   Otherwise continue with the initial state as the current state *CS*.
2. Continue until the solution is found.
   (a) Apply an operator so far not applied to the current state and apply it to produce a new state *NS*.
   (b) Check for the goal state if *NS* = *GS*? If yes, then quit.
   Otherwise if it is better than the current state, then make *CS* = *NS*.
   (c) If *NS* is not better than the current state, then continue the loop.

Here, to determine whether the current state is better or not, an evaluation function is used. This calculation of evaluation function is based on heuristic. Generally heuristic is based on certain task-specific knowledge. Hence, this method is heuristic-based search method. This knowledge helps in building heuristic and solves some intractable problems. In this method to determine whether the state is better or not, precise evaluation is required. Hence, evaluation function-based state selection is required to make this search method work efficiently and accurately. Generally, a better state means a higher value of evaluation function.

There are a few possible issues with this algorithm. One of the most important issues is completeness. It can be a typical extension to generate and test using the knowledge that directs the search. This knowledge is based on heuristic function that detects the closeness of current state to the goal state.

EXAMPLE: Let us assume that we are solving travelling salesman problem with hill climbing.

1. Begin with the initial state (that is a city salesman has visited).
2. Move in the direction so that the city is not repeated, but additional city is visited (better state).
3. Heuristic can be the number of cities visited.
4. Keep moving in the state that improves the number of cities with legal action.
5. When there is no way to improve heuristic function, stop.

Hill climbing algorithm makes incremental changes in the optimal direction based on heuristic.

There are many variants of hill climbing algorithms. Let us discuss them.

Steepest Ascent Hill Climbing

It is a simple variant of hill climbing that considers all possible moves from the current state and selects the best current state. This method is also called *steepest ascent hill climbing* or *gradient search,* since it tries to select the state that gives the maximum gain. The algorithm works as follows:

1. Let *IS* be the initial state and *GS* be the goal state. At first, the initial state *IS* is evaluated
   Check if *IS* = *GS*? If yes, then quit.
   Otherwise continue with the initial state as the current state *CS*, i.e., *CS* = *IS*.
2. Continue until the solution is found or there is no change in the current state.
   (a) Let SS_1, SS_2, ..., SS_N be a set of successor states of *CS*. Let *SS* be any possible successor state. Apply an operator so far not applied to the current state and apply it to produce a new state *NS*.
   (b) Check for the goal state if *NS* = *GS*? If yes, then quit.
       Otherwise if it is better than all successor states, then set this state to *SS*.
   (c) If *SS* is better than current state then set *CS* to *SS*.

To apply the steepest ascent hill climbing to the travelling salesman problem, we need to consider all successor states (possible moves) to choose the best one. This algorithm has higher complexity than the basic hill climbing, since it requires selecting move from a number of possible moves.

Both basic and steepest ascent hill climbings may not able to reach the goal state, and hence, may fail to find the solution. Generally, it terminates in finding a state that does not have a better state in the vicinity or from where it is not possible to get to a better state in a single move.

Problems with Hill Climbing

We can see from the example that the process may reach a solution where no other better solution is available in percept. In short, no transition improves the situation. Typically, this happens when it reaches a local maximum, plateau or ridge.

1. **Local maximum:** This is a state better than the local region or neighbouring states, but not a global maximum. This occurs since a better solution exists which is not in the vicinity of the present state.
2. **Plateau:** This refers to a flat area or space, where neighbourhood states have the same value as the present state and hence, fails to determine the best direction to move on. This situation needs big jump in some direction or in selecting a new part or section of the search space.
3. **Ridge:** It is the search space at a higher altitude than the surroundings. It cannot be traversed by a single move. It is a special kind of local maxima. Ridges create a challenging problem, since hill climbing adjusts one element in vector at a time and keeps moving in axis-aligned direction. It may require to move in multiple directions at once to find the solution. Ridges are illustrated in Figure 4.8 and the problems are depicted in Figure 4.9.

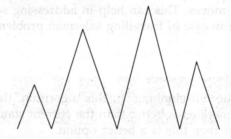

Figure 4.8 Ridges.

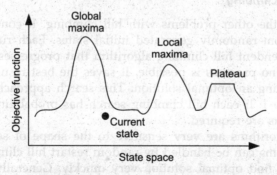

Figure 4.9 Hill climbing: Problems.

A few approaches to deal with these problems are:

1. In case, the process gets stuck at some local minima, then backtrack to some earlier node and try to move in some other direction. This is a better and acceptable option, in case, there is some other path that exists at an earlier node and looks promising. To implement this strategy, it is required to maintain earlier nodes and corresponding paths in the memory.
2. Another option is to take a big jump in case the process gets stuck. This may allow going to a different section of the search space. This is a very good option to deal with the plateau.

Variations of Hill Climbing

1. *Stochastic hill climbing* chooses randomly among the neighbours going uphill.
2. *First choice hill climbing* generates random successors until one is better. It is good for the states with high numbers of neighbours.
3. In *random restart hill climbing,* the sideway moves restart from a random state.
4. *Evolutionary hill climbing* represents potential solutions as strings and performs random mutations. It keeps the mutations that are better states. It is a particular case of first choice and the ancestor of the genetic algorithms.

Stochastic Hill Climbing

It is a variant of basic hill climbing. While the basic and steepest ascent hill climbing algorithms select the steepest uphill move, stochastic hill climbing selects at random among all possible uphill moves. This can help in addressing some issues in simple hill climbing like ridges. Even in case of travelling salesman problem, it can help in reaching an optimal solution.

First Choice Hill Climbing

It is a variant of stochastic hill climbing. In this algorithm, the successor is generated randomly until the one generated is better than the current state. When there are a large number of successor states then this is a better option.

Random Restart Hill Climbing

It tries to overcome the other problems with hill climbing. It conducts a series of hill climbing searches from randomly generated initial states. Each run from the series of runs is like an independent hill climbing algorithm that progresses until it reaches to a position from where no progress is possible. It saves the best results among all results. This can help in getting an optimal solution. This search approach is complete and its probability is close to 1. If each hill climbing search has probability p_1 to succeed, then obviously $1/p_1$ restarts are required.

Hill climbing algorithms are very sensitive to the shape of search space. A small number of local maxima can be handled by random restart hill climbing very efficiently. In such cases, it can find optimal solution very quickly. Generally, NP-hard problems have very high, rather exponential, local maxima and may get stuck. To great extent, the problem of local maxima in simple hill climbing is addressed efficiently by the random restart hill climbing.

Evolutionary Hill Climbing Search

It represents potential solutions as strings and performs random mutations. It keeps the mutations that are better states. It is a particular case of first choice and the ancestor of the genetic algorithms. This is genetic algorithm-based search.

4.8.2 Simulated Annealing

Hill climbing always moves uphill and there are no downhill moves. As a result, it can get stuck to the local minima, hence it is incomplete. A purely random walk does not care whether it is uphill or downhill and randomly selects a successor. Hence it is very expensive, though complete. One algorithm is greedy and efficient but incomplete, while the other one is very inefficient but complete. Hence, it makes sense to combine the best of both the algorithms. Simulated annealing tries to do that. It is based on metallurgy concept of annealing. This is about cooling of material in heat bath. Typically in annealing, metal or glass is heated to a very high temperature and then it is cooled gradually. This helps the molecules to settle in such a way that the material condenses to low energy crystalline state. This increases the strength of material due to proper low energy condensation. At high temperature, there is a very high energy that allows random moves. The random and bad moves that are allowed in the beginning are controlled as the temperature goes down. Figure 4.10 depicts the random jumps that can occur.

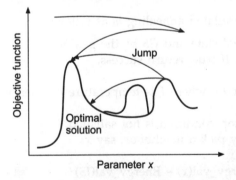

Figure 4.10 Simulated annealing.

In gradient descent model, the energy of search is increased to such an extent that it gets out of the local minima. In this process, it crosses most of the local maxima and settles at minima close to the optimal solution maxima, if the energy is reduced slowly to make it settle down. In gradient descent model, the high energy search, i.e., the random jumps are reduced slowly to get an optimal solution. Initially, the energy of a ball is increased to such a level that it is not obstructed by any of the maximas. Figure 4.10 depicts same. If the energy is then reduced slowly, it will settle near the valley of the global maxima. Next part of simulated annealing will follow algorithm very similar to hill climbing. It is not greedy as instead of best move it picks random move. In case, the move leads to a better state, it is always accepted. In case, it could not, it is accepted with lower probability *p*. The assessment of the state in terms of betterment or inferiority decides the probability. Figure 4.11 shows the basic steps.

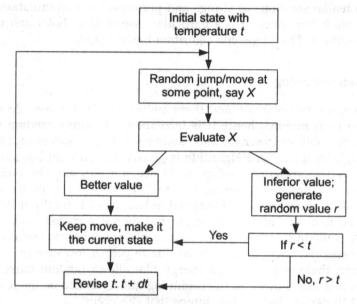

Figure 4.11 Simulated annealing: Basic steps.

The algorithm for simulated annealing is as follows:

1. Let *IS* be the initial state and *GS* be the goal state.
2. Check if *IS* = *GS*. If true, return success.
   Else
   (i) Initialise *t* for *IS*, where *t* is temperature or energy level to allow maximum movement
   (ii) Do while a stop condition is not satisfied.
       (a) Randomly pick a neighbour, say *x*.
       (b) Evaluate *x*.
       (c) ΔE = Energy_val(*x*) – Energy_val(*IS*)
       (d) If *x* = *GS*, return success.
       (e) If $\Delta E < 0$, make *x* to be *IS*. (This means new state/solution is a better one)
       (f) Else generate random number: *r*[0, 1].
           If $r < e^{-\Delta E/t}$, make *x* to be *IS*.
       (g) Revise *t* values.

Simulated annealing can be used in layout problems, arrangements, scheduling and multi-solution optimisation problems.

Let us study the example of eight-tile puzzle for better understanding. The problem solution is the one where all the tiles are in required order. The tiles need to be moved one at a time to the empty slot. From the initial condition given, it is possible to have different states. So, from every new state that is generated, different states are possible. Simulated annealing works on the principle of computing the energy. This energy is computed based on the distance measure. For example, consider it to be an absolute difference (Position where the number is – Position where the number should be). The temperature is set to some value, which is decremented or revised at every iteration.

Let us assume that the following initial and goal states are given (Figure 4.12):

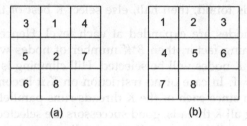

Figure 4.12 (a) Initial state, (b) Goal state.

Energy for the initial states is given as:

$(2 - 1) + (5 - 2) + (3 - 1) + (4 - 3) + (5 - 4) + (7 - 6) + (7 - 6) + (8 - 8) = 1 + 3 + 2 + 1 + 1 + 1 + 1 + 0 = 10$

We are aware that there are two different cases possible after this state. So, we have them, as shown in Figure 4.13 below.

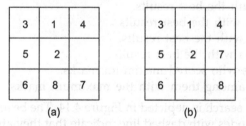

Figure 4.13 (a) Energy 12, (b) Energy 11.

Since any random neighbour is selected and in either case, the difference in the energy for the current and initial states is not less than zero, we need to consider the probabilities and select the next state. Let us assume the temperature to be 50. The probability assumes that the first state selected will be

$$e^{-(12-10)/50} = 0.96$$

So, depending on the value of r, the state can be considered to be the initial state. Do remember that since the temperature is reduced at every iteration, chances are less that it selects a worst state.

4.8.3 Local Beam Search

In hill climbing, we keep just a single node in memory. This cripples the algorithm to a great extent. *Beam search* is a heuristic search algorithm. This algorithm explores the states or graph by expanding the most promising nodes in a limited set. At any level, it expands identified best node. There can be more than one node identified at each level, say K. It is based on breadth first search to build search tree. The algorithm steps are as follows:

1. Maintain K states and not just a single state.
2. The search begins with K randomly generated states.
3. At each iteration, all possible successors of K randomly generated states are identified.
4. If the goal state is found, then halt, else select K best of the successors.

K number of best nodes are expanded at each level. Hence, K is the width of the beam. If B is the branching factor, then $B*K$ number of nodes will be evaluated at each depth. Out of that, only K nodes will be selected. Hill climbing is the special case of local beam search, where $K = 1$. In case of no restriction on K it becomes breadth first search.

In local beam search since each of the K threads runs parallel and useful information is passed/shared among all K threads, good successors are selected. The algorithm quickly stops unfruitful searches and focuses on K most leading searches. It may suffer from lack of diversity among K states and may abandon sometimes searches which could have led to an optimal outcome. Even many times, it becomes concentrated because of typical patterns in regions.

EXAMPLE: Let us assume that we want to select the best engineering students from the country, the steps are as follows:

1. First select K states from the country with the best engineering results.
2. Select K cities with the best results.
3. Select K colleges with the best results.
4. Select K courses with the best results.
5. Select K divisions with the best results.
6. Select K students who scored maximum marks.
7. Select a student among them with the maximum marks.

A typical local beam search is depicted in Figure 4.14. The beam width is of 2 nodes and the filter width is of 3. Nodes with dashed line indicate that they are pruned. Black coloured nodes are the beam nodes and the normal ones are those that are selected for evaluation.

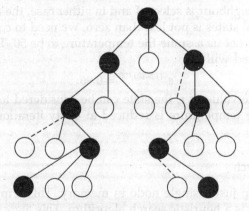

Figure 4.14 Local beam search.

Stochastic Beam Search

It is a variant of local beam search and is very similar to stochastic hill climbing. Instead of selecting *K* successors which are the best ones, stochastic beam search selects *K* successors at random. This selection is done in such a way that the probability of choosing a given successor is an increasing function of its value. This process has some similarity to genetic algorithm or natural offspring selection.

4.8.4 Tabu Search

Tabu search was created by Glover in 1986. Local searches, we have discussed so far, are focused on neighbours and have tendency to get stuck in suboptimal maxima. These methods are based on short-term memory to prevent reversal of recent moves. The idea of tabu search is very similar to the other variants, where when the searches get stuck in suboptimal region, the non-improving moves are tried to search the solution. Tracing and backtracking to previous nodes in case of local minima are prevented in tabu search with the use of list call tabulist, which is nothing but a list of recent history of search. Steepest ascent is very similar to it. Hill climbing when combined with short-term memory results into simple tabu search. Search space and neighbourhood structure are the two basic elements of tabu search heuristic.

With tabu search, one point to mention is the memory. Tabu list with long-term memory maintains history all through the exploration process, whereas short-term memory keeps the most recent ones. Tabu search flow is depicted in Figure 4.15.

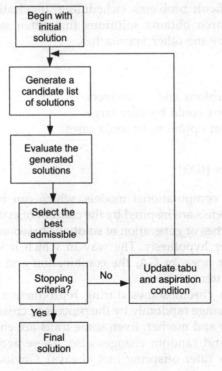

Figure 4.15 Tabu search: Flow.

The algorithm steps are as follows:

1. At any instance, the algorithm begins with some initial random solution.
2. At any iteration, find a new solution by making local movements over the current solution.
3. The next solution selected is the best among the neighbourhood.
4. During exploration, to avoid visited solutions, tabu list is maintained and updated. So, a tabu list maintains solution points that must be avoided.
5. Since the neighbourhood is changing during the course of exploration, it is dynamic unlike the previous searches.
6. A movement of tabu status is avoided for revisiting, unless it satisfies certain aspirational conditions. This overcomes the local optima issue.
7. The algorithm stops when the algorithm as a whole terminates or has a stopping criterion.

A tabu search can have stopping criteria like a number of solutions to be explored or the neighbourhood is empty. Here are the pros and cons of tabu search.

Pros

1. It allows to exit from sub-optimal regions by making non-improving solution to be accepted.
2. The use of tabu list improves efficiency.
3. It can be applied to both discrete and continuous solution spaces.
4. It can address difficult problems (scheduling, quadratic assignment and vehicle routing). Tabu search obtains solutions that often surpass the best solutions previously found by the other approaches.

Cons

1. It has higher dimensions and parameters.
2. Number of iterations could be very large.
3. It cannot find global optimum in some cases.

4.8.5 Genetic Algorithms (GAs)

Genetic algorithms are the computational models, which can be used for searching and problem solving. These models are inspired by the concept of evolution in living organisms. GA builds successive searches or generation of solutions based on the evolution. It typically begins with initial state or hypothesis. The way in which living things evolve and the fittest survives, on similar lines, in GA, the combination and changes in existing states are build to achieve the fitter solutions.

The changes occur in chromosomes during reproduction. The chromosomes from mother and father get exchange randomly by the process of crossover. Hence, the offspring has traits from both father and mother. Even some traits are changed by mutation. There can be a few accidental and random changes also. These accidents, in some cases can produce more beautiful or fitter offspring (not always). Obviously, offspring with better traits survive for longer duration, while the poor one gets extinct. So, after some period of time, offspring have genes from superior individuals. This process of fittest survival is also called *natural selection*. Figure 4.16 depicts the basic approach.

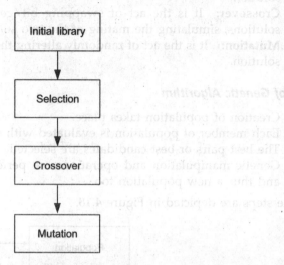

Figure 4.16 Genetic approach.

Simulated Evolution

In simulated evolution, for algorithms to be used, we need to define this process of reproduction more clear with reference to the objects or data we have. Like chromosomes, the structure here can be defined by fixed alphabets or numbers in the form of a string.

Genetic algorithms are very similar to search algorithms. In this case, search is based on natural selection that takes place in natural genetics. The natural evolution process that operates on chromosomes inspired genetic algorithms and hence, GA is developed to simulate it. Figure 4.17 shows the recombination process in genetic.

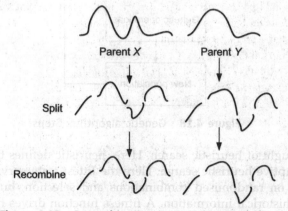

Figure 4.17 Recombination in genetic approach.

General Operations in Genetic Algorithms

1. **Reproduction:** It is the act of reproducing or making an exact copy of a potential solution
2. **Crossover:** It is the act of swapping bit/gene values between two potential solutions, simulating the mating of the two solutions.
3. **Mutation:** It is the act of randomly altering the value of a bit/gene in a potential solution.

Steps of Genetic Algorithm

1. Creation of population takes place.
2. Each member of population is evaluated with reference to fitness function.
3. The best pairs or best candidates are selected.
4. Genetic manipulation and operations are performed to produce new offsprings, and thus a new population too.

The steps are depicted in Figure 4.18.

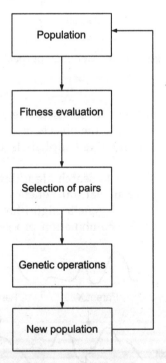

Figure 4.18   Genetic algorithm: Steps.

GA can be thought of heuristic search. Here, heuristic defines the fitness of the state. Rather, it is an adaptive heuristic search. Here the fittest state survives to get an optimal solution. It works on randomised combinations and selection, but guided by heuristic and even exploits historical information. A fitness function drives heuristic and it should return a higher value for a better state.

The selection probabilities of pairs for reproduction are directly proportional to their fitness scores.

While selecting pairs for reproduction

1. Either two pairs are selected for reproduction randomly.
2. The crossover operation recombines bits of selected candidates. There is possibility of single-point crossover as well as double-point crossover.

To solve any problem using genetic approach, a way to encode the solution is required. Generally, it is represented as bit string-chromosome.

To understand if we take simple example of generating a number, say 29, given 0–9 digits and a set of operations + and ×.

1. Represent each given data in gene. For example, let 0–0000, 1–0001 and so on till 9 and the operators be +: 1101, ×: 1010.
2. Now, let us build the chromosome. So, one solution is

$$4 \quad \times \quad 5 \quad + \quad 9$$
Represented: 0100 1010 0101 1101 1001

3. New population is generated with crossover and mutation based on fitness function. This fitness function selection can be as

$$1/(x - x')$$

where x is the desired number and x' is the one generated by chromosome.

The approach halts when it is divided by zero error.

4. Decision on selection of fitness value is dependent on the problem to be solved.

Outline of a Genetic Algorithm

1. Generate random population of n candidates.
2. Evaluate fitness of each of the candidate with fitness function $f(x)$.
3. New population is created using the following genetic operations:
   (a) Select two candidates from the population based on the fitness and other criteria.
   (b) With crossover probability from the parents, new offspring are created.
   (c) New offspring is placed in the population.
4. New population is used in the system.
5. If the goal state is reached, stop.
6. Else, go to step 2 and repeat.

As shown in Figure 4.19, the basic outline of the genetic approach is mentioned here. Let us take an example to understand how this crossover and mutation occur.

EXAMPLE: Crossover:
Parent 1: 101 | 11011
Parent 2: 100 | 10010

Child 1: 101 | 10010
Child 2: 100 | 11011

Mutation:
For the child: 10011011 → 10001011 (bit changed)

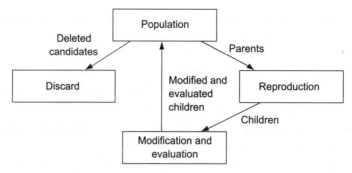

Figure 4.19 Outline: Genetic algorithm.

4.9 GRADIENT METHODS

The rationale behind the gradient methods is an assumption that if one moves in the direction, where the function is increasing most rapidly, and if the step sizes are controlled or rather kept small enough, then it is assured that the function is always being increased. Finally, it will arrive at a point, where it is at maxima and cannot be increased further.

Gradient descent is also known as *steepest descent*. The method states selection of direction with steepest slope from the present state. Let us assume that we have continuous function represented as $f(x_1, x_2, ..., x_n)$ which are to be minimised over X_1, X_2 to X_n.

The process for finding this minimum over $f(x)$ is

1. Calculate the gradients

$$\partial f(x_1, x_2, ..., x_n)/\partial x_i$$

2. Repeat until convergence for all x

$$x_i \leftarrow x_i - \eta \partial f(x_1, x_2, ..., x_n)/\partial x_i$$

(η is the learning rate that has small value, say < 0.1).

Unconstrained Optimisation and Newton's Method

As discussed earlier, the steepest descent uses only first derivative and does not yield the best result always. This is because the first derivative though detects slope, it may be advisable to consider changes in the slope. Hence, Newton's method uses the first as well as the second derivative. It performs very well, if the initial point is close to minima.

Newton–Rapson method can help in some of the problems in the first derivative usage. It helps in solving the linear equations. To find maximum or minimum of f, there is need to find x, where gradiant is zero.

$$p_k = -[\nabla^2_{xx} f(x_k)]^{-1} \nabla_x f(x_k) \tag{4.1}$$

Hessian matrix of second derivative can be used. Obviously substituting the identity matrix uses no real information from the Hessian matrix. The projection could then be derived as follows:

$$p_k = -H_k^{-1} \nabla_x f(x_k) \tag{4.2}$$

4.10 FUZZY ADAPTIVE SEARCH

Genetic algorithms have been applied to many types of optimisation problems by encoding the design variables. Genetic approaches are not always optimal considering their parameters. They also suffer from the iterations and the problem of having premature convergence. Lot of work has been undertaken to overcome these issues, where some have proposed use of dynamic control of genetic algorithms using fuzzy logic. An *adaptive fuzzy search* is the one, where the search is made efficient by the use of fuzzy rules to tune in the genetic parameters. Fuzzy adaptive techniques are most often used in parallel genetic algorithms. Average fitness and the difference between the maximum and average fitness are used while designing the fuzzy rules. Due to this, it has a quick ability to obtain a better result compared to genetic algorithms. The key aspect of this type of search is that the parameter tuning is done not only on the crossover or the mutation rate but also on the migration rate.

4.11 ADVERSARIAL SEARCH METHODS (GAME THEORY)

The searches required for game playing are bit different. Here, in this section, the typical searches required for game playing between two players, are discussed. The state space in this case can be represented as a tree. Games may give either perfect or imperfect information based on the type of game. The games generally have multi-agent environment. Further, there are different types of unpredictability, which introduce other contingencies. The environment is co-operative and competitive. Algorithms like minimax (MinMax or MM) algorithm and alpha-beta pruning are discussed under this category.

4.11.1 Minimax (MinMax or MM) Algorithm

Minimax algorithm while trying to cover the entire search space considers exhaustive possibility of state transition from the initial state. The minimax algorithm can be used in case of two-player games such as tic-tac-toe, chess, go, etc. The algorithm thus is effective for the games, which have few logical possible state transitions from the current state. Typically, these are the logic games, hence can be described by a set of rules and premises. So, it is important to know the possible moves from the present state.

A pseudocode for minimax is described below:

Minimum (node *n*, depth *d*, player *p*)

1. If depth = 0 then
   return value (node)
2. If player = 'MAX'   //for a maximizing player
   set $\alpha = -\infty$
   for every child of node
       value = minimax (child, depth–1, 'MIN')
       $\alpha = \max(\alpha, \text{value})$
   return (α)

else   //for minimizing player
set $\alpha = + \infty$
for every child of node
   value = minimax (child, depth-1, 'MAX')
   $\alpha = \min (\alpha, \text{value})$
return (α)
A maximising player would call it as minimax (start, depth, MAX).

As described above, two players are involved in this case, MAX and MIN. First starting with the current game position, a search tree is generated. That means the entire search space is expanded. Depth first can be used up to the end game position. There are two views—MIN view and MAX view. The end position is evaluated from the MAX view. The values are assigned based on the evaluation. The nodes that belong to the MAX are given the maximum value of its children. The nodes for the MIN are given the minimum value of its children. In short, if we consider Min and Max as players, MAX tries to move to a state of maximum value, while MIN tries to reach to a state of minimum value.

Let us take an example of carom game. We have situation analyser that converts the judgement about the overall positions of coins on the board into a single representative number. Let us say positive number indicates the favour to one player, while negative number indicates the favour to another player. *Static evaluation* is the process that reflects the board quality, while *static evaluator* is the procedure to determine this number. The number is evaluation score. Here, the maximiser tries to force player to move that leads to large positive score, while the minimiser tries to force to a move that leads to strong negative score. The minimax levels are depicted in Figure 4.20.

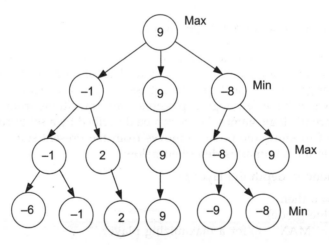

Figure 4.20   A search tree: Minimax.

There are alternate minimising and maximising levels. Eventually, the exploration limit is reached and the state evaluator helps in selecting a candidate among alternatives.

4.11.2 Optimal Decision States for Games

Generating trees for simple and not so complex games is not so time-consuming, but it is not the case when the complexity of the game increases. Hence, handling of such games demands optimisation.

One approach for optimisation could be limiting the depth of the tree. So, instead of having the entire tree generation, it is restricted by the depth. The dependency of this optimisation is on the branching factor. This results in reducing tree expansion, and hence, contributes in time optimisation. In another approach, a function for the evaluation of the game positions is used that can make use of heuristic.

4.11.3 Alpha-Beta Pruning

The minimax is an exhaustive search algorithm. It requires two-pass analysis of the search space. There can be many levels. But a question arises here—how many levels we should consider?

Minimax pursues all the branches in search space, including many branches which can be ignored or guaranteed not to lead to results. There is need for a procedure that can reduce the number of tree branches and the number of evaluations that must be done. Alpha-beta pruning uses different ideas to reduce the number of nodes we search and the overall search space. *Pruning* refers to elimination of nodes found to be unnecessary while searching and evaluation. In case, we have reached a scenario, where minimising or maximising has guaranteed certain values, and hence, pursuing certain node definitely would not take to a optimal result, then it is better to eliminate that node or path.

Note: Do not follow the idea that is surely bad.

Alpha cut-off [Refer diagram 4.21(a)],

For Max node:

1. Let us assume that we have explored branch P. The value obtained is 9. This is best value for A.
2. While exploring branch Q, at branch Q_1 we get val as 7. Since $7 < 9$, other branches, i.e., Q_2, Q_3 and Q_4 are not evaluated.
   Hence an alpha-cut takes place.
3. Thus, the best possible value at branch Q must be ≤ 9.
4. So, finally the best value obtained from branch P is returned.

Beta cut-off [Refer diagram 4.21(b)],

For Min node:

1. Let us assume that we have explored branch P_1 and obtained value 9 from it for P (i.e., ≤ 9).
2. While exploring P_2, we obtain a value of 20, where $20 > 9$.
3. Thus, other branches are not explored and a beta, cut-off takes place.
4. As the best possible value at P_2 is 20 which is greater than the best value of 9 obtained earlier. So, the value obtained from P_1 is returned.

This process for MIN and MAX is depicted in Figure 4.21 below:

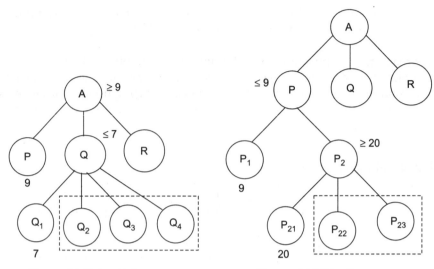

| **Figure 4.21(a)** Alpha-cut. | **Figure 4.21(b)** Beta-cut. |

α is the value of the maximum/best (i.e., the highest value) choice found so far at any choice point along the path for MAX. If any value say v is worse than α, MAX will avoid it. β is the value of the minimum/worst (i.e., the lowest value) choice found so far at any choice point along the path for MIN. If any value say v is not worse than β, MIN will avoid it.

The algorithm is similar to that of the minimax, the difference being alpha and beta values are added here. The algorithm is discussed below:

Function alpha-beta (node n, depth d, α, β, player p)

1. If depth = 0
   return value (node)
2. If player = 'MAX'
       val = $-\infty$
       for every child of the node
           val = max (val, alpha-beta (child, depth-1, α, β, MIN))
           α = max (α, val)
       if $\beta \leq \alpha$ then break //β cut-off
       return (val)
   else
       val = ∞
       for every child of the node
           val = min (val, alpha-beta (child, depth-1, α, β, MAX))
           β = min (β, val)
           if $\beta \leq \alpha$ then break //α cut-off
       return (val)

Alpha-beta cut-offs speed up the process. Using them with a good evaluation functions, makes the search much faster.

4.11.4 Refinements and Variations

In recent years, there have been many contributions towards the refinements in the alpha-beta algorithm. The main constraints were speed and efficiency. They are based on some principles such as, minimal window search, forward pruning, move ordering and so on.

Typically, you must have noticed that narrower the search window, more is the possibility that the cut-off occurs. A search window with, say $\alpha = \beta - 1$ is called a *minimal window*. As it is narrow, it is believed that using this would yield more efficiency.

Similarly, the efficiency also depends on the move of search order. For better results, it is necessary that the best move is examined at prior. Here, many ordering techniques like iterative deepening, heuristic history are used.

In case of forward pruning, the unpromising branches are discarded. This reduces the tree size. The major drawback is there is a possibility that the best move might get pruned.

4.12 ONLINE SEARCH ALGORITHMS

The offline search algorithms discussed may not able to handle the real-world scenario. In online searches and online agents, environment is observed after every action and next action is taken. This can help in handling problems in dynamic and semi-dynamic environment, and even in the case of stochastic domains and environment. Online search are typically based on exploration. In case of exploration problems, states and actions are unknown to the agent. Hence, own actions and the outcome are used to determine the next action. The typical examples where online search is required are driving a car by a robot, auto pizza delivery, robot walking on uneven surface, automatic basketball trainer. An agent knows just actions, step cost function and the goal test.

Online search problem can be solved by the agents by considering following points:

1. After each action, the agent senses environment parameter. As a result, it receives a percept telling it what state has reached.
2. An agent can build/update its map from the environment.
3. Expansion of the nodes is different for online and offline agents(search).
4. An online agent can only expand the node it is physically in.

Typically, the objective of an agent is to reach the goal state in the minimum possible cost. It can be the total path cost that is selected by the agent and travelled to reach the goal state. If the agent knows the search space in advance, then the actual shortest path can be compared with the actual cost incurred. This is also referred to as *competitive ratio*. Online DFS agent is depicted below:

```
Online_Dfs(S)
{
    If(goal(S)) then return
    If(new state) then
        Unexplored[S] = Actions(S) // set of actions
    If(!empty(S)) then
        Determine next state with respect to action
    If state is earlier explored, take similar action
    Return action
}
```

4.13 SEARCHING ALGORITHM: EXAMPLE AND APPLICATIONS

We have studied that search techniques are required for every walk of life. The problems can be of simple type, typically belonging to route finding or even game solving. It is very essential to understand the application and determine the search technique to be used. Pattern-seeking problems have important application in production planning. These can be NP-hard. The use of heuristic is proved to be very appropriate in these cases. Neighbourhood evaluation search approaches have shown substantial progress in the same.

Heuristic finds a place in decision-making approaches as well as in classification techniques. It finds place in game playing as well as in web crawlers. Text classification techniques too employ search techniques.

Let us take an example of agriculture sector, where you are to design a tool to enable a farmer to select the best crop suitable for his land. With the various parameters with regard to the land and environmental conditions, there can be different heuristic methods applied to the selection of the crop, which give final decision. Based on the earlier experiences of the crops, heuristic can be appropriately estimated and such a search method can be very much useful in assisting the farmer.

On similar grounds, let us take another example of interior designing of a room. In a hall with various objects to be placed so that it looks beautiful, an algorithm like A* would possibly give good results, considering the space occupancy of the objects to be used. It can be applied with the number of objects to be placed, considering their size, shape, dimension, weight and so on. Even an approach for appropriate colour selection from the list of available furniture can make architects and interior decorators happy by making their work easy.

The list of applications of search techniques is endless. Right from searching solution for any problem in examination to search of any destination, there are numerous problems in day-to-day life where search techniques can be used.

SUMMARY
In the chapter, we have discussed in detail the various informed search methods. These methods are used, where there is a prior domain knowledge about the problems and guidelines are provided. A heuristic function is used to guide the entire process. Estimating heuristic is the most critical aspect in these search methods. It can be based on the past experience too. We have discussed heuristic-based methods such as best first search, A* and its variants.
While selecting a search technique, one needs to keep in mind the search space to be traversed. Local search techniques that are based on local view have also been discussed in the chapter. Hill climbing, simulated annealing and other approaches that are the parts of local search methods have given a broader idea of the different search methods. Approaches to game playing are somewhat different. The minimax algorithm is discussed in this context. For better optimisation, eliminating unwanted paths that are carried out in alpha-beta pruning have also been studied.
An introduction to online algorithms and examples in terms of applications have been discussed. Finally, one has to look at the various aspects with a reasoning of 'why', one particular search is the best for the problem at hand.

 **KEYWORDS**

1. **Heuristic search:** It is a technique that improves the efficiency of search technique by providing guidelines.

2. **Heuristic function:** A heuristic function is the one that guides the decision of selection of a path.

3. **Best first search:** It is a search method that exploits DFS and BFS, switching between both to get the benefits of both using heuristic.

4. **OR graph:** It is used to avoid revisiting of paths and also for propagation to the successor. It maintains open and closed lists.

5. **Admissible:** Any search algorithm is admissible if it always produces an optimal solution.

6. **Consistent heuristic:** A heuristic $h(n)$ is said to be consistent if for every node, say n and every successor s that is generated by an action a for n, the estimated cost to reach the goal state/node is not greater that the step-wise cost to reach s added to the cost of reaching the goal from s.

7. **A*:** It is a heuristic approach that performs search to compute optimal solutions.

8. **Memory-bounded heuristic:** It is used to overcome the memory requirements of simple heuristic search. IDA*, RBFS and MA* are under this category.

9. **IDA*:** It is a memory-bounded heuristic method that employs DFS at each iteration. It maintains the f-value and applies threshold.

10. **RBFS:** It performs best first search by keeping track of the best path and backtracks when the cost exceeds.

11. **Relaxed problem:** A problem for which rules/criteria are simplified or less restricted is a relaxed problem.

12. **Admissible heuristic:** A heuristic is said to be admissible if it does not overestimate the costs.

13. **AO*:** It is a heuristic approach that maintains a graph rather than open and closed lists and performs search.

14. **Local search:** It is a search that begins with initial solutions and iterates ahead exploring the search space.

15. **Hill climbing:** It uses the notion of heading towards a state, which is better than the current state and moves to the neighbour with a better score.

16. **Local maximum:** This is a state better than the local region or neighbouring states, but not a global maximum, since a better solution exists, which is not in the vicinity of the present state.

17. **Plateau:** This refers to a flat area or space where neighbourhood states have the same value as the present state, and hence, fails to determine the best direction to move on.

18. **Ridge:** It is the search space at higher altitude than the surrounding that cannot be traversed by a single move. It is a special kind of local maxima.

19. **Stochastic hill climbing:** It is a variant of hill climbing that selects at random among all possible uphill moves.

20. **First choice hill climbing:** It is a variant of stochastic hill climbing where the successor is generated randomly until the one generated is better than the current state.

21. **Random restart hill climbing:** It conducts a series of hill climbing searches from randomly generated initial states. Each run is like an independent hill climbing algorithm.

22. **Evolutionary hill climbing:** It is a genetic algorithm-based search that performs random mutations and keeps the ones that are better.

23. **Simulated annealing:** It is an approach used for generating optimal solutions avoiding local optimas.

24. **Beam search:** It explores states or graph by expanding the most promising nodes in a limited set. At any level, it expands identified best node.

25. **Stochastic beam search:** It is a variant of local beam search and is very similar to stochastic hill climbing. Instead of selecting K successor which are the best ones, stochastic beam search selects K successors at random.

26. **Tabu search:** It is a search that tries non-improving move when gets stuck in suboptimal region. It maintains a tabu list.

27. **Genetic algorithms:** Genetic algorithms are the computational models, based on biological evolution that are used to solve optimisation problems.

28. **Reproduction:** It is the act of reproducing or making an exact copy of a potential solution that is done in genetic approach.

29. **Crossover:** It is the act of swapping bit/gene values between two potential solutions, simulating the mating of the two solutions that is used in genetic approach.

30. **Mutation:** It is the act of randomly altering the value of a bit/gene in a potential solution that is used in genetic approach.

31. **Adversarial search methods:** These are the methods used in game playing, where the environments are competitive.

32. **Minimax algorithm:** A strategy used in game playing to minimize the loss in worst cases.

33. **Alpha-beta pruning:** An approach that reduces the number of nodes evaluated by the minimax approach.

34. **Online search:** It is an algorithm, where the environment is observed and the next action is taken in real-world scenario.

MULTIPLE CHOICE QUESTIONS

1. IDA* employs
   (a) BFS at each iteration
   (b) Combination of BFS and DFS
   (c) Only DFS
   (d) None of these

2. A search algorithm is said to be admissible, if
   (a) It is informed search
   (b) It is optimal
   (c) It is uninformed search
   (d) It is efficient

3. A space where neighbourhood states have the same value as the present state and causes a problem in the hill climbing is
   (a) Plateau   (b) Global maxima   (c) Ridges   (d) Local maxima

4. Random alteration of the values in genetic algorithm is done in
   (a) Crossover   (b) Mutation   (c) Fitness function   (d) Both (b) and (c)

5. The search methods that work on one state, with an aim to improve it step-wise belong to the category of
   (a) Best first search
   (b) Depth first search
   (c) AO*
   (d) Local search methods

6. If heuristic is admissible, then A* guarantees that it will be
   (a) Complete
   (b) Optimal
   (c) Both (a) and (b)
   (d) None of the above

7. The algorithm that tries to resolve the issue of local minima with random moves is
   (a) A*
   (b) Hill climbing
   (c) Simulated annealing
   (d) Beam search

8. A search that tries a non-improving move when it gets stuck maintaining a list is
   (a) A*   (b) Hill climbing   (c) Tabu   (d) Greedy search

9. In minimax approach, the values for α, β are
   (a) $\alpha = \beta - 1$
   (b) $\alpha = \max, \beta = \min$
   (c) $\alpha = \min, \beta = \max$
   (d) $\beta = \alpha - 1$

10. A case where $f(n) = h(n)$ will be found is of
    (a) Simulated annealing
    (b) Hill climbing
    (c) Tabu
    (d) Greedy best first

CONCEPT REVIEW QUESTIONS

1. What is a heuristic function?
2. Distinguish between informed and uninformed search.
3. Explain the A* algorithm and conditions of optimality.
4. Explain the approach of alpha-beta pruning.
5. How does RBFS perform memory-bound search? Discuss.

CRITICAL THINKING EXERCISE

1. During the selection of the temperature values, which parameters should be taken into account while performing simulated annealing?

2. Can alpha-beta pruning approach fail to overcome minimax limitations? Discuss.

3. For a given problem, which parameters would you take into consideration and select a search strategy?

PROJECT WORK

1. Implement a system that performs arrangement of some set of objects in a room. Assume that you have only 5 rectangular, 4 square-shaped objects. Use A* approach for the placement of the objects in room for efficient space utilisation. Assume suitable heuristic, and dimensions of objects and rooms.

2. Implement hill climbing search to solve the following Sudoku puzzle given in Figure 4.25. Assume heuristic to be the sum of the conflicts that are identified.

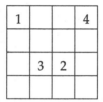

Figure 4.25

Intelligent Agent

INTRODUCTION

Information is associated with context and information resources, and hence, is not isolated. Intelligence is a cumulative manifestation of different activities resulted from learning, sensing, understanding and knowledge augmentation. Intelligence has also an association with the environment. There is need to gather the information and process it to take an appropriate action. An agent is an entity that can perceive the information and act on that information to achieve the desired outcome. *Intelligent agent* in its simplest form, is an agent that is capable of making decisions and act most logically in the scenario.

Agents, the environment and the interaction between them are very important when we study intelligent agents. Figure 5.1 depicts the general structure and working of an agent. An agent interacts with the environment through sensors and actuators. Depending on its type, it keeps a track of the goal. A *sensor* allows the agent to sense environment and perceive the present state. An *actuator* allows the agent to take actions with reference to the environment perceived. Any human being is an agent, who senses the environment

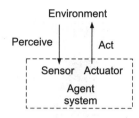

Figure 5.1 Basic structure of an agent.

through his/her eyes, ears, nose, tongue (sensory organs). He/she acts on the environment through hands, legs and other parts of the body. The sensory organs are the sensors in case of human being, while the actuators are the parts of the body which help him/her to take action. For example, consider an intelligent car, which has sensors such as cameras, ultrasonic waves and various other devices to measure distance, determine objects and calculate light and weather conditions. It has some mechanism to apply break as an actuator to act on the environment based on the perceived road, traffic and weather conditions.

5.1   WHAT IS AN INTELLIGENT AGENT?

Intelligent agent is an entity that works without assistance, interprets inputs, senses the environment, makes choices and ultimately, acts to achieve a goal. Intelligent agents have to learn and use knowledge to achieve their goals. The agents may be very simple or very complex. A reflex machine such as thermostat, a human being, community of human beings working together towards a goal are all examples of an intelligent agent. A typical relationship between the agent and the environment is depicted in Figure 5.2. It is the set of rules, (if-then) that drives the decisions of the agent towards the goal fulfilment. The rules could be domain rules that describe about the environment, inference rules for reasoning process along with the knowledge base.

An *intelligent agent* is an entity that is autonomous in nature, a good observant to detect the environmental changes, with a capacity to govern its actions in timely fashion to achieve the goals.

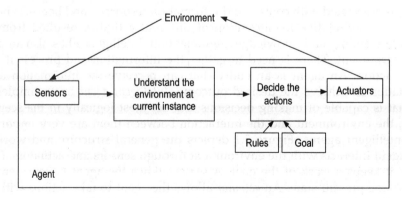

Figure 5.2 Agent-environment relationship.

EXAMPLES: Let us consider two examples. Consider an automatic attendance system. In the system, the fingerprint sensors sense the fingerprints. The actuator gives the message and the attendance is marked for the employee corresponding to the sensed fingerprint.

Other example is of auto-door opening and closing system. Here, a camera is used as sensor for sensing the existence of an object. When the camera senses that a person is standing in front of the door or close to the door, it gives this input to the agent program. The agent program gives command and then the actuator opens the door.

These two examples are discussed throughout the chapter and the need for intelligence is stressed at various stages.

5.1.1 Percept

Let us understand the concept of percept with regard to the agent's environment. Percept, in a broader sense, is the mental result or product of perceiving, as distinguished from the act of perceiving; an impression or sensation of something perceived. It can be about some view of the environment sensed and viewed by an agent. In case of intelligent agent, percept is agents' perpetual inputs at any instant. An agent, while observing has some percept at any moment of time. A percept sequence is the complete history of everything the agent has ever captured. The percept or rather the percept sequence is the window of the agent to the environment through which it observes the environment. Hence, an agent's choice of an action depends on the percept sequence.

5.1.2 Agent Function

Agent behaviour is mathematically represented by agent function. This mapping is done in various ways. One of the simple ways is tabulating actions against percept sequences. Then, this table is used for mapping and selecting the action. This agent function is generally implemented by an internal program called *agent program*. While the agent function is an abstract mathematical representation, the agent program is implementation used for this mapping. So, an agent program is based on the agent function.

An agent program uses agent function to achieve the desired goal. The agent function maps from percept histories to actions. The same is represented below:

$$f : P \to A \tag{5.1}$$

where P is percept and A is action.

The agent program acts on physical architecture along with the sensor inputs and actuators to produce f in Eq. (5.1). So, the agent consists of architecture and program. We can say that the architecture is the scenario under consideration. Hence,

Agent = Architecture + Program

The sensors get the current percept (how the environment is looking at that particular instant) or a percept sequence. The program (agent program) uses that percept sequence to decide the actions and acts with the actuators to take the decided actions.

Sensors → Agent programs → Actuators

So, we can say that an agent is completely specified by the sensors, actuators, agent function and mapping of percept sequence to the actions. The operation of the agent is dependent on the function. A program should be appropriate for architecture, in turn, the architecture should be able to support the program recommended actions.

5.1.3 Representation of Agent Function as a Subset of Agent Program

Let us take the example of auto-door opening and closing system. There is a small area on both the sides of the door identified to be under surveillance. Two cameras, one inside and other outside, cover this area. A simple agent function is that if any person is standing in that area, open the door or else close.

So, a function is like

1. If area is empty, then close the door.
2. If area is occupied, then open the door.

An agent program uses this function to achieve this complete expected behaviour. The program takes care of following activities:

1. Continuous scanning of this area
2. Opening or closing of the door or keeping it in the same position based on the output of function
3. Handling all combinations and possible issues
4. Handling the exceptions to ensure the smooth functioning
5. Ultimately achieving the results in all possible scenarios

5.2 RATIONALITY AND RATIONAL AGENT

A *rational agent* is an agent that behaves logically and does the right things. *Rationality* is a normative concept that stands for acting based on logical reasoning. In artificial intelligence and even in other disciplines like economics, game theory, decision theory, a *rational agent* is an agent that chooses to perform an action which leads to an expected optimal result. This agent has clear preferences, models uncertainty via expected values and analyses all feasible actions. Along with all sensors and actuators, the agent is provided with complete specifications of the problem and the task to be performed. Based on this information, the agent performs the most logical actions. *Rational actions* are those which can make an agent the most successful. A *rational agent* provides or makes rational rather logical decisions. Typical examples of rational agents can be a person, governing body, decision authority, firm, machine or software.

The reason behind the discussion of rationality is that it determines how an intelligent agent needs to behave/act with respect to the environment to get the expected outcomes.

A *rational agent* is expected to select an action that would maximise the performance, having the evidence on the basis of percept sequence as well as the built-in knowledge.

So, the agent takes actions and decisions on the available percept sequence. The parameters that play a role in it are as follows:

1. Priorities and the preferences of the agent

2. Information available with the agent about its environment (This information is gathered based on the experiences or may be provided in some other form)
3. Possible actions an agent can perform
4. Estimated or the actual benefits and the chances of success of the actions

The question remains what is logical, rational or correct behaviour for an agent? To decide this behaviour, we need to have the performance measure.

5.3 PERFORMANCE MEASURES

Performance measures are the criteria for success of an agent's behaviour. They are used to track the performance of an agent.

When an agent faces the environment or is thrown in the environment, it reacts with a certain sequence of actions based on the percepts or percept sequences which it receives. These sequences of actions are along with the environment, and hence, result in the change of state of the environment. So, this sequence of actions make the environment to go through a number of states. If this sequence is desirable, then we can say the agent did very well. Since there are many parameters and also there is subjectivity in measurement, it is very tricky to measure the performance. It can be measured in terms of efficiency, speed, solutions obtained, energy consumed and so on. There is a thrust on having the objective performance measures.

Note: The performance measure should more be based on what one actually wants from environment, rather than how one thinks agent should behave.

Referring to the example mentioned previously of auto-door opening and closing system, the agent's performance can be measured by timely opening and closing of the door or time delay in opening or closing the door. A rational agent is expected to optimise the performance. For instance, consider a system used in an air-conditioned shop. Then, the agent actions should make sure that the door should not remain open unnecessarily, thereby affecting the performance of the air conditioner in the shop. Neither should the open-close action occur unnecessarily. A person wanting to come inside the shop should not have a long waiting time for the door to open. So, the time factor needs to be minimal. Optimality may include minimal electricity consumption, smooth functioning, less noise and timely actions.

5.4 RATIONALITY AND PERFORMANCE

Rationality is distinct from omniscience (all knowing with infinite knowledge). *Rationality* is not absolute, but it is with reference to the knowledge available with the agent and that knowledge is derived from the percept sequence to date. Agents can perform actions in order to modify future percepts so as to obtain useful information (information gathering and exploration). We can say now that an agent is autonomous if its behaviour is determined by its own experience (with the ability to learn and adapt).

As discussed earlier, rationality maximises the expected performance and it is different from the perfection, as perfection takes actions to maximise the actual performance.

The percept sequence also needs to be informative, rather than uninformative. Consider the case of auto-door opening and closing system. If only one side percept is available, then the door will not open or close if a person is standing on the other side. So, the rational action expects proper information gathering prior to the action. Doing actions in order to modify the future percepts can also be referred to as information gathering. Exploration and gathering need to work together to maximise the outcome.

In some cases, rationality expects agent to learn from the experience. The agent may have some prior knowledge of the environment, but as it gets experience it should modify and augment the knowledge to maximise the results. So, the agent, in some cases, relies completely on prior knowledge, while in the other case, it builds knowledge as it comes across new scenarios.

If the agent relies completely on prior knowledge of its designer than its own percepts, then the agent lacks autonomy. A rational agent is expected to be autonomous. It should learn from its percepts to compensate for partial, incomplete or even incorrect prior knowledge. This autonomy may not be complete. It should be need-based with an objective to optimise the outcome. The rational agent may become independent of prior knowledge in due course of time. We can say that it is the learning agent, a part of rational agent that can adapt to multiple situations and can handle complex problems. Learning agent can succeed in a variety of environments. In short, a rational agent should possess the following properties:

1. Ability to gather information
2. Ability to learn from the experience
3. Perform knowledge augmentation
4. Autonomy

A very simple example of rationality in case of automatic car is that the car is expected to slow down when the signal is yellow and should stop if the signal is red.

5.5   FLEXIBILITY AND INTELLIGENT AGENTS

Intelligence demands flexibility. Hence, agents need to be flexible. The flexibility equips the agent to negotiate with dynamic scenarios. To exhibit the required intelligence, we expect certain properties associated with flexibility from an intelligent agent.

By flexible, we mean that the system should be able to adapt with the changing scenarios and should exhibit rational behaviour in those changing conditions. For this purpose, it needs to be

1. **Responsive:** It should respond in timely fashion to the perceived environment.
2. **Pro-active:** It should exhibit opportunistic, goal-directed behaviour and take the initiative, wherever necessary.
3. **Social:** It should be able to interact when they are deemed appropriate with the other artificial agents, or humans in order to compete problem solving.

Other properties an intelligent agent should have are as follows:

1. **Mobility:** It is recommended that an intelligent agent should be mobile to accumulate knowledge and carry out desired work/decision-making.

2. **Veracity:** Intelligent agent should be truthful. It is not expected to hide information or lie.
3. **Benevolence:** It should avoid conflict and should do what is told.
4. **Rationality:** It should act to maximise the expected performance.
5. **Learning:** Performance is increased with learning. It should have learning ability that is essential for true autonomy.

We need to keep in mind that the agent acts and responds to the environment. To act, first it needs to sense. To sense and act, it needs to have the understanding, reasoning and learning.

5.6 TASK ENVIRONMENT AND ITS PROPERTIES

Intelligence is always defined, in association with environment. The *task environment* is the environment in which the task takes place. Clearly defining task environment along with the desired behaviour and task is necessary for appropriate design of the agent program. PEAS*, that is, performance measure, environment, agent's actuators, sensors must be specified for design of an intelligent agent.

Let us again consider the example of auto-door operating mechanism. Here, the performance measures are the timeliness of operation, electricity usage, smooth operations, noise generated, and efficiency. Similarly, the environment includes both sides of the door, tiles and object belonging to it, if any. Further, the actuators are the motors which push and pull the doors as well as the indicators, if any. Sensors are the cameras on both sides, along with a mechanism deployed for sensing the obstacles. These things specify the setting for an intelligent agent design.

Let us take one more example of a washing machine. The PEAS description for it is as follows:

P: Cleanliness of clothes, time taken, electricity consumed, water used, detergent used, noise made
E: Clothes, water tap, water, detergent
A: Motor rotating the drum/spindle, time indicator, operation completion alarm
S: Water level sensor, detergent sensor, cloth weight sensor, time clock.

In this way, the four descriptors can be specified in various automated agents. Table 5.1 specifies the typical PEAS in case of various agents.

TABLE 5.1 Agent Types and their PEAS Description

Medical diagnosis system
P: Accuracy of diagnosis, time taken, recovery time, expenses E: Patient, doctors, system, equipments A: Diagnosis decision, further treatments/tests/alerts, medicines S: Sensors for different health parameters like BP measuring, blood sugar measuring, heart beat track, ECG, EEG, symptoms of patient with regard to the disease, previous reports

Artificial Intelligence: A Modern Approach, by Russel and Norvig, Pearson Education, 2003, New Delhi, India.

Auto-door operating system
P: Time taken, efficiency, idle time, response time, noise made
E: Area on both sides of the door
A: Motor closing and opening the door
S: Camera on both sides, object sensing mechanism
Face authentication system
P: Time taken, accuracy, efficiency, handling ability in case of new face
E: Face, area covered by camera
A: Command or message indicating outcome
S: Camera/Sensor sensing presence
Auto-car system
P: Time taken, accuracy, efficiency, safety
E: Streets, pedestrians, other vehicles, traffic signals
A: Steering wheel, accelerator, brake, horn
S: Cameras, GPS signals, speedometer, engine sensors

One can have more sensors and actuators based on the system structure and the complexity of the system.

Let us discuss the role and use of these specifications in case of intelligent agents.

Performance measures are more about the specifications of desirability from the type of agent. It is more like a wish list or expectations from the agent. It includes efficiency, way of functioning, handling of scenarios, usage of resources and the final outcome. Environment includes the resources, area and surroundings related to the target task in which an agent is operating. This includes other objects and systems surrounding the agent. Actuators are the ones through which the agent takes actions with reference to the environment. These actions are physical actions. The typical actions are movements, changes, switching on, displaying something, closing door, etc. Sensors are the devices through which agent senses the status or states of the environment. There is a need for continuous sensing. It refers to checking of the properties of the environment which may affect the decision-making. Generally, the sensors are temperature sensors, cameras, motion sensors, etc. So, the PEAS description plays the core part in designing an agent. Hardware agents generally work in a restricted domain, whereas software agents can work across multiple domains. In the next section, we will discuss the types of environment.

5.6.1 Environment Types

There are various ways to define the environments in which the agents operate. It is necessary to consider the types based on the way the environment appears to the agent.

Fully Observable (versus partially observable)

A *fully observable environment* is the one, where the sensors of the agent can detect all aspects that are relevant. In short, the agent sensors describe the environment fully or at each point, the environment is entirely observable. A crossword puzzle is a fully observable environment, whereas in case of automated car driving system, it is partially observable. A fully observable environment can also be termed as *accessible environment*, while the rest of the environment can be termed as *inaccessible environment*. Let us talk about Angry Birds and Temple Run games. The environment for Angry Birds can be said to be fully observable, but for Temple Run, it is partially observable.

Deterministic (*versus stochastic*)

In case of deterministic environment, the next state of the environment is described completely by the current state as well as by the action of the agent. The uncertainty factor is not an issue to be looked at in case of fully observable deterministic environment. This property, whether the environment is deterministic or stochastic, is decided from the point of view of the agent. The car system environment is clearly stochastic (as you never know about the traffic!). The environment is said to be *strategic* if it is deterministic, except for the actions of the other agents. Most of the real-life environments are non-deterministic.

Discrete (*versus continuous*)

A discrete environment has a limited/finite number of distinct and clearly defined percepts and actions. While in continuous environment those cannot be clearly defined. Chess has a finite number of discrete states, while it is not the case with football. Hence, chess environment is discrete, while that of football is continuous.

Episodic (*versus sequential*)

Think in real life, everything is in episodes. Had it been the case that the actions or the decisions taken on the previous day (considering this to be one episode) do not impact the current ones (this rarely happens, but just to understand the concept), the environment would have been episodic. One acts based on what one perceives at that instance, rather than depending on or taking into account the things that have occurred previously. In typical terms, the agent's environment is divided into atomic episodes. Each episode or the current scene consists of agent's perception and action. So, action choice in an episode, which wholly depends only on that episode. If we look at the classification problems, we will find them to be episodic, as the decision of classification depends only on that particular element and not on previous elements or previous decisions. In sequential environment, the present decision may impact future decisions unlike episodic. Chess, auto-car and football are the examples of sequential environment. Obviously, episodic environment is much simpler to model as compared to sequential environment. Let us talk about games—Angry Birds and Temple Run. Angry Birds is an example that will fall under the episodic. Think of Temple Run—is it episodic or sequential?

Static (*versus dynamic*)

We are familiar with the word *static*. As it suggests, things are at a standstill. In an agent environment, it would be static if it does not change unless the agent takes action. Things change from one state of the agent to another. So, we can say that the environment is unchanged while an agent is deliberating. In the sense, the entire scenario remains the same as it was when the agent is acting on. Just contrast is the case with dynamic environment, where the environment changes while the agent is taking action. A *semi-dynamic environment* is the one, where the environment does not change with the time slab, but the agent's performance does. In real life, many examples are dynamic. Crossword is a static environment. Car driving (traffic issue again!) is an example of dynamic environment. Chess is an example of semi-dynamic environment, whereas temple run is, of course, an example of dynamic environment.

Single (versus multi-agent)

Now, the discussion is moved to multi-agents environment. There can be a need for more than one agent in the system. So, the environment can be a single agent or multi-agent. Chess may be a two-agent environment, while football is a multi-agent environment. Similarly, an agent solving crossword is a single agent environment. The multi-agents environments can either be competitive or co-operative. Competitive means they are actually competing to come up with the goals, whereas co-operative means assisting each other. Clearly, chess is an example of competitive. Football can be categorised as multi-agent, with some co-operative and some competitive agents in picture.

Table 5.2 describes the types of the environments for some examples. The environment type largely determines the agent design. The real world is, of course, partially observable, stochastic, sequential, dynamic, continuous and multi-agent.

TABLE 5.2 Examples of Different Types of Environments

	Chess with a clock	*Chess without a clock*	*Car driving*	*Image analysis*
Fully observable	Yes	Yes	No	Yes
Deterministic	Strategic	Strategic	No	Yes
Discrete	Yes	Yes	No	Yes
Episodic	No	No	No	Yes
Static	Semi	Yes	No	Semi
Single agent	No	No	No	Yes

5.7 TYPES OF AGENT

Agents can be of many types. Agent types can be decided based on the complexity and functionality of the agent. Simple agents like table-driven agents work on the basis of simple lookup table. These agents can handle simple task like temperature control, colour selection, directing to particular location and so on. This table is the knowledge base with the agent. For any percept, the action is mapped from the table and executed. This agent can be extended to simple rule-based agents. Here, the action is based on some set of logical rules. The decision-making takes place in the form of rules that direct for right action based on the percept. These types of agent belong to simple category that are based on the knowledge built in advance and rarely modify that. So, they exploit the already known things to take the best possible action. Complex agents are expected to interact with the environment in different possible ways. These complex agents are expected to explore new routes and paths in the absence of knowledge available. These agents are expected to learn from the experience and update the knowledge base. The agent's complexity changes with respect to environment complexity and the intelligence agent is expected to exhibit. In case of dynamic environment, we expect the agent to deliberate with all intelligence and to take into account changes in the environment. These types of scenarios demand more and more intelligence. So, the complexity of environment contributes to complexity of the architecture of agent. The agent can be classified based on these complexities and expected intelligence. The five basic types of agents are as follows:

1. Table-driven agents
2. Simple reflex agents
3. Model-based reflex agents
4. Goal-based agents
5. Utility-based agents

Apart from these, we have also learning agents. We will study them in further sections.

Table-driven Agents

Table-driven agents are based on simple table. The table entries are used to determine the action with reference to percept or percept sequence. Though it is one of the easiest ways to implement the agent, it suffers from many drawbacks, which are listed below:

1. **Size of table:** As the complexity increases, the table size goes on increasing. For practical problems, it results in huge size tables.
2. **Time to build the table:** The agent works on the table that is the result of the knowledge acquired. Since knowledge acquisition is a complex task, it takes a long time to build the table.
3. **No autonomy:** All the actions are built-in. So neither flexibility, nor autonomy.
4. **Time required for learning:** Even with learning, it takes long time to learn the entries.

Simple Reflex Agents

It is one of the simple rule-based agent that takes into account only the current percept. It selects action on the basis of the current percept (ignoring the percept history and independent of the location). Based on the condition, an action is decided that is based on rules (action driven by condition). This is one of the simplest types of agent with limited intelligence. It cannot handle the complex decision scenarios, and hence, is useful only in fully observable environment. Figure 5.3 depicts simple reflex agents. An example with reference to automatic intelligent door operation is given below:

If a person is observed in the (observation area), then initiate (door opening action)—(detect and act)

General purpose interpreter for the condition detection and action-based rules is used in these types of agents. Then, the rules for specific task for environment can be

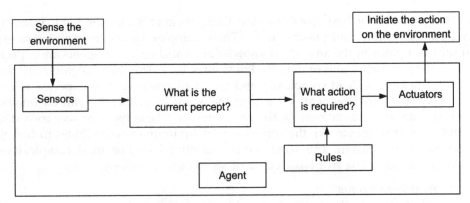

Figure 5.3 Simple reflex agents.

developed. These types of agents are very useful if the decisions can be made on only the current percept. But, as discussed earlier, due to limited intelligence, it cannot cope up with even a minor change in the system and may result in disaster. Simple reflex agents may get stuck in an infinite loop in case of unavailability of some sensors due to fix and hard coded rules. Use of randomise simple reflex agents can solve this problem to some extent. In this case, the agent randomises its action. Though randomistation can be preferred in multi-agent environment, in single agent environment, randomisation may impact rational behaviour.

Model-based Reflex Agents

In many real-life problems, the issues are faced due to partially observable environment. Without keeping track of the world and previous states, the agent cannot see a way of overcoming partially observable environment. In these types of agents, some sort of internal state, which depends on percept history, is maintained and that reflects some of the unobserved aspects of the current state. It is possible that some information is captured in the previous state and it throws light on unobserved aspects in present state. For example, if the previous frame of camera captures a vehicle that is not seen in present state, then it allows us to take decision to apply break. For this type of model, we need to know

1. How is the world evolved independent of agent?
2. How does the agent's own action affect the world?

Incorporating these two things in determining the unobserved aspects is called *model*. A model keeps track of how the world evolved and the past sequence of percept to determine the unseen part. Model-based intelligent agents have wide applications compared to simple reflex agents. Figure 5.4 depicts the model-based reflex agents.

Goal-based Agents

In many cases, only knowledge of the current state is not enough. The knowledge about how the world is evolved is definitely more useful. But it is also important to know the goal for decision-making. In some cases, absence of knowledge about the goal can make decision-making very difficult. Some description about the goal or the desirable state can

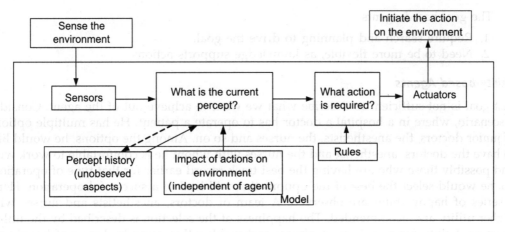

Figure 5.4 Model-based reflex agents.

always be very useful. For example, in case of car driving, knowledge about the customer destination can help in decision-making. In some cases the destination might not be the actual location, but some description about the budget, hotel near airport, or budget leisure hotel in Goa near Kolwa beach.

The goal-based action may be very complicated and may need a sequence of actions. Chapter 9 discusses about the decisions related to the sequence of actions. The decision-making scenario is different in this case than that of a simple reflex agent. Here, decision-making checks the impact of the actions with reference to the goal. The combination of how the world evolves and the understanding of the goal description makes this agent more useful in scenarios with higher complexity. Figure 5.5 depicts a goal-based agent.

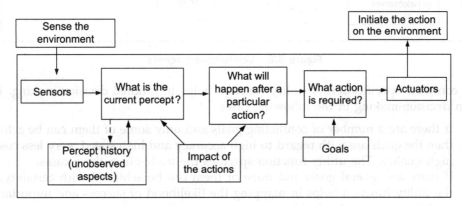

Figure 5.5 Goal-based agents.

The goal-based agents appear less efficient but more flexible. It keeps building knowledge with reference to goal, and hence, can very easily be used in different locations. We can see the resemblance to the model-based agents. But here, more amount of time is actually required for the reasoning process, as it is goal-directed.

The goal-based agents

1. Require search and planning to drive the goal.
2. Need to be more flexible, as knowledge supports actions.

Utility-based Agents

Just goal is not sufficient to describe what we want to achieve out of the agent. Consider a scenario, where in a hospital a doctor has to operate a patient. He has multiple options of junior doctors, the anesthetists, the nurses and so on. Among the options, he would like to have the doctors, anesthetist and the nurses with whom he is comfortable to work with and possibly those who are having the best track record earlier for that type of operation. So, he would select the best of the options that will lead to a successful operation. Here, a series of happy states are observed. A team of doctors, anesthetists and nurses with higher utility are recommended. The happiness of the selection is described by the utility function. Utility function is most often a real number that maps to degree of happiness. The utility-based agent structure is depicted in Figure 5.6.

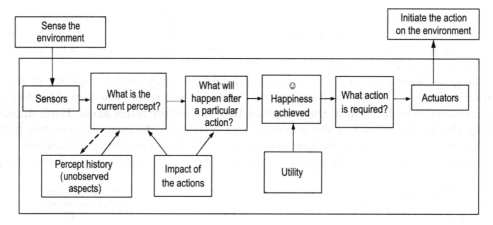

Figure 5.6 Utility-based agents.

A complete specification of utility function helps in rational decision-making. It can help in decision-making in the following cases:

1. If there are a number of conflicting goals and only some of them can be achieved, then the goals are with regard to high accuracy and high speed, very less cost and high quality. The utility function specifies the trade-off in these cases.
2. If there are several goals and none of them can be achieved with certainty, then the utility function helps in mapping the likelihood of success and importance of goal in order to take decision.
3. Problems related to route selection and modifications, if any.

So, precisely, utility-based agents are useful when:

1. Not only goals, but means are also important.
2. Some series of actions are safer, quicker and reliable.
3. Happy and unhappy states are required to be distinguished.

Learning Agents

An agent many times needs to operate individually in an unknown environment. The already provided knowledge may not allow an agent to operate in an unknown or a new situations/scenarios. This makes it necessary for the agents to have an ability to learn and explore. This ability to learn can allow an agent to respond to new or unknown scenarios in a logical way. Further, the learning can help in making improvement in behaviour as it proceeds or comes across more and more scenarios. Most importantly, it allows an agent to learn from experience. Following are the two important elements in learning agents:

1. Performance element
2. Learning element

The learning element is responsible for making improvements, while the performance element is responsible for the selection of external actions. Here, the performance element is an agent without the learning element. Any simple or complex agent when supported with learning elements forms a learning agent. The learning element needs a feedback based on the measurement of performance that how the agent is doing. It is the critic or the reviewer element that provides this feedback required for learning. Critic evaluates agent's success and gives feedback accordingly. Based on the design of performance element, many designs for learning agent are possible. The feedback may come in the form of penalty or reward. This penalty or reward helps in improving the performance of an agent and in building the knowledge base.

Another important part is the task generator or problem generator. It suggests actions that generate new examples or experiences. This, in turn, aids in training the system further. Figure 5.7 depicts the architecture of learning agent.

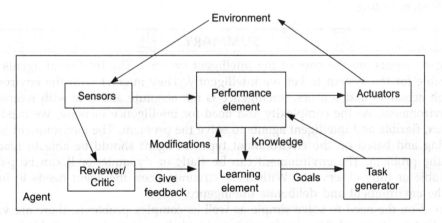

Figure 5.7 Learning agent.

Learning in an intelligent agent. It is the process of modification of each component of agent to bring the components into a closer agreement with the available feedback information, thereby improving the overall performance of the agent.

5.8 OTHER ASPECTS OF INTELLIGENT AGENTS

As the complexity of the system increases, it may require multiple agents. Applications to solve problems that are not solved or to solve already solved problems in a better way through learning can lead to the agents with dynamic learning capabilities. Some complex and practical scenarios in real life can be handled only by multi-agent systems with co-operative learning abilities. There are many applications of intelligent agents. Right from the vacuum cleaner, water purifiers to the flight control systems, intelligent agents help in various products. Some of the application domains of intelligent agents are listed below:

1. Process control
2. Manufacturing
3. Traffic control
4. Information management
5. E-commerce
6. Business process management
7. Medical domain, monitoring, etc.
8. Games

Drawbacks: Agents have been very useful, but suffer from some drawbacks like

1. No overall system controllers
2. No global perspective

While developing the agents, we need various clear specifications and problem definitions. Some of the bottlenecks in agent development are listed below:

1. Requirement specifications
2. System design
3. System implementation
4. System testing

SUMMARY

Intelligent agents are the core of the intelligent systems. The intelligent agents make it possible for the system to behave intelligently. They interact with the environment through actuators and sensors. Intelligence is not absolute and it is with reference to the environment. As the complexity and need for intelligence increase, we need more complex, flexible and intelligent agents to solve the problem. The environment is ever-changing and based on the environment type, an agent should be able to react and solve the problem. The environment can be static or dynamic, or it can be partially observable or fully observable. With these circumstances, the agent needs to interact with the environment and deliberate intelligence.

Based on the need to solve simple as well as complex problems, there are various agents that are designed. The simple reflex and table-based agents are suitable for simple applications, with less uncertainties and known environment. To deal with the other aspects of complexity, we need model-based, goal-based and utility-based agents. For high end applications, we expect the agents to learn from the experience and improve the behaviour over the time. The agent is expected to behave reasonably well in the unknown and new scenarios. There is wide range of applications of intelligent agents, and learning from experience can give an edge to the ability of intelligent agents.

 **KEYWORDS**

1. **Agent:** An agent is an entity that can perceive information and act on that information.

2. **Intelligent agent:** It is an entity that is autonomous in nature, a good observant to detect the environment changes with a capacity to govern its actions in timely fashion to achieve the goals.

3. **Percept:** It is the window of the agent to the environment.

4. **Rational agent:** It is an agent that selects an action that would maximise the performance, based on percept sequence and built-in knowledge.

5. **Fully observable environment:** It is the environment, where the sensors of the agent can detect all the relevant aspects.

6. **Deterministic environment:** It is the environment, where the next state of the environment is described completely by the current state as well as by the action of the agent.

7. **Discrete environment:** It is the environment that has limited/finite number of distinct clearly defined percepts and actions.

8. **Episodic environment:** It is the environment which is divided into atomic episodes comprising agent's perception and action.

9. **Sequential environment:** It is the environment, where the present decision impacts the future decisions.

10. **Static environment:** It is the environment that remains unchanged while the agent is deliberating.

11. **Table-driven agents:** It is based on simple table, where the entries are used to determine an action with respect to percept.

12. **Simple reflex agents:** It is a simple rule-based agent that takes into account only the current percept.

13. **Model-based reflex agents:** In these, the agent uses internal state, which depends on percept history, is maintained and reflects some of the unobserved aspects of the current state.

14. **Goal-based agent:** It keeps building knowledge with reference to goal.

15. **Utility-based agent:** On the basis of utility function, it maps the degree of happiness so that better decisions are taken.

16. **Learning agents:** These are the agents with an ability to learn and respond in unknown scenarios.

MULTIPLE CHOICE QUESTIONS

1. In what type of agent category will an internet book shopping agent fall?
   (a) Simple reflex
   (b) Model-based
   (c) Goal-based
   (d) Utility-based

2. Which of the following best defines a multi-agent environment?
   (a) Multiple intelligent agents operating in competition
   (b) Multiple intelligent agents that can share their knowledge and skills to get the solution to a complex problem
   (c) Groups of intelligent agents processing information in a fixed sequence set
   (d) Intelligent agents operating competitively as well as co-operatively

3. A rational agent is defined as
   (a) An agent that takes action according to its percept sequence
   (b) An agent that takes decision based on infinite knowledge base
   (c) An agent that tries to maximise its actual performance
   (d) An agent that thinks that it always takes correct decisions

4. If the agents are operating in distributed environment, then the agents
   (a) Are centralised
   (b) Share some common knowledge
   (c) Independently solve and get the best answer
   (d) Are decentralised

5. In what type of environment does an internet book shopping agent operate in?
   (a) Fully observable
   (b) Episodic
   (c) Discrete
   (d) Static

6. In what type of environment does a backgammon game operate in?
   (a) Fully observable
   (b) deterministic
   (c) Episodic
   (d) Discrete

7. We can say that an agent is autonomous when
   (a) Its behaviour is based on its experiences
   (b) Its behaviour is governed entirely on the current percept
   (c) It possesses social characteristics
   (d) None of the above

8. Among the domains—planning, game playing, diagnosis and internet-based systems, for which domains, intelligent agent is most suited/applicable?
   (a) All of them
   (b) Planning, game playing
   (c) Diagnosis, game playing, internet-based systems
   (d) Game playing, internet-based systems

9. Consider a scenario, where a student has a set of queries to be resolved. Among the staff members available in the college, he approaches specific staff members, who are able to solve and assist him in resolving the queries. In such a case, the staff member selection would more appropriately described/mapped to be
   (a) Goal based agent
   (b) Simple reflex agent
   (c) Utility agent
   (d) Both (a) and (c)

10. Which of the following cannot be a property of intelligent agent?
    (a) Rationality
    (b) Pro-active
    (c) Veracity
    (d) Deterministic

CONCEPT REVIEW QUESTIONS

1. What is an intelligent agent?
2. Distinguish between an agent and an intelligent agent.
3. Discuss about the rational behaviour of an intelligent agent.
4. What are the types of agents? Discuss the significance of types with reference to complex agents.

CRITICAL THINKING EXERCISE

1. Discuss with reference to agent types, buyer agents and seller agents in E-business.
2. Architect intelligent agents in network management.
3. What types of intelligent agents exist in business intelligence? Discuss about the rational behaviour of an agent.
4. Select all parameters required to develop a learning agent for collision detection of vehicles. How does your learning program deal with partially observable environment in this case?

PROJECT WORK

1. Develop an agent program for auto-door operation in a mall. Discuss about the performance measures.
2. Develop an agent architecture for football and discuss the need for learning capabilities of the agent in this scenario.
3. Implement a program for learning agent for a lift, where
    (a) The lift would halt at a particular floor based on the identity of the individual.
    (b) There would be energy optimisation through elimination of redundant operation.

Constraint Satisfaction Problems

INTRODUCTION

In the real-life problems, situations and even decisions come with constraints. The solutions demand that the goal state should satisfy a number of constraints. These constraints are not mere algebraic constraints. Rather, there is a need to satisfy a set of constraints, including logical constraints, algebraic constraints, data constraints and even resource and action constraints. Generally, for all of these problems, the search space is constrained by a set of conditions and dependencies. This class of problems where the search space is constrained, is referred to as *constraint satisfaction problems (CSP)*. For example, when someone decides to buy shoes, there are constraints like it should be of number UK 11, should not be pink, and should not be of the same colour of his brother. We deal with many such problems in everyday life. A typical example of constrained satisfaction problem can be time table scheduling problem, where you cannot have lectures of two professors scheduled at same time for same class or a case where you cannot allocate two consecutive classrooms to a particular group or division. There is a constraint on a search space and you cannot just select any division or any classroom out of the total available set. In fact, it is more or less true for all the problems. Selection of food for a patient who is advised a few dietary restrictions is another example of CSP. Selection of exercise for heart patient is also CSP. Right from the driving to the arrangement of furniture and architecting house or painting house—all are constraint satisfaction problems. While a few constraints are very evident, others are indirect.

Suppose we would like to select a team, with a constraint that every two players should have at least understanding of one common language. In this case, two parameters: (i) knowledge of language and (ii) his ability to play a particular game are considered while defining the problem. In this way, there are many CSPs we have to deal with everyday. So far, we have approached the problems for which we were trying to search the goal state. Every time state is evaluated by heuristic. Every state, from these search algorithms perspective, is a black box and there is no insight into the state at a greater depth. In CSP, the goal state has a standard, simple and structured representation. Hence, the algorithm can take the advantage of the structure and can restrict the search space. A general purpose heuristic can be used to solve large problems. To solve CSP, we need to decompose the problem and analyse the problem structure. The understanding of the structure of problem with reference to the difficulty in solving helps in solving the problem. In case of CSP, constraints are typically mathematical or logical relationships.

One interesting CSP in everyday life is loading of boxes in a truck. Here, all boxes of different shapes are to be loaded in a container. The constraints can be as follows:

1. Boxes of more weight cannot be put on that of lower weight.
2. Boxes with fragile material should always be kept on top.
3. Boxes with shape other than cubical and cuboids should not be kept at bottom.
4. A box with the largest surface area should be kept at bottom.

While dealing with the problem related to CSP, there is need to consider the following issues:

1. Are the constraints satisfiable? (whether the problem is solvable with all constraints)
2. Can the constraints be simplified by mathematical and logical equivalence?
3. Which of the other criteria need to be considered to find the optimal solution?

There are many interesting CSPs in real life. Arrangement of fielders during power play in cricket is a typical constraint satisfaction problem. Further, when a particular player with strength to hit on onside as well as offside is on strike, it becomes a bit more complicated.

Thus, almost all the problems in real world can be viewed as constraint satisfaction problems. In this chapter, we will discuss CSP and various issues in CSP. We will also discuss the ways to solve CSP.

6.1 WHAT IS CSP?

As discussed in the previous section, all problems discussed are CSPs or special cases of CSP. A hypothetical problem without CSP is a special case of CSP, where there are no constraints. Hence, any problem in the world can mathematically be represented as CSP.

To understand constraint satisfaction problem, we need to understand the constraint. In short, *constraint satisfaction problem* is finding a solution to constraint graph. The solution is typically a state that can satisfy all the constraints.

Constraint

Constraint is something that restricts movement, arrangement, possibilities and solutions. It is a sort of bottleneck. It is mathematical/logical relationship among the attributes of one or more objects. For example, if only currency notes of 2, 5 and 10 rupees are available and we need to give certain amount of money, say ₹ 111 to a salesman, and the total number of notes should be between 40 and 50. These constraints can be represented mathematically as follows:

Let n be the number of notes.

So, $40 < n < 50$

$$c_1 X_1 + c_2 X_2 + c_3 X_3 = 111$$

Here, $c_1 = 2$, $c_2 = 5$ and $c_3 = 10$

Hence,

$$\sum_{i=1}^{n} c_i X_i = 111$$

It is important to know the type of the constraint. There can be unary constraint that restricts a single variable. For example, variable value should not be greater than a certain number. Suppose we are selecting a basketball team for under 18 competition. Here, unary constraint is age of the player should not be greater than 18. Similarly, there can be binary constraint which means that the restriction is about two variables. E.g., there is a restriction that age of player 1 should not be equal to age of player 2. Similarly, the constraints can go even beyond two variables. This is typically called *higher order constraint,* i.e., the constraint involving three or more variables.

Constraints can restrict the values of variables. One simple example of constraint is a quadrilateral which is drawn inside a circle, with all four vertices on circle, as shown in Figure 6.1.

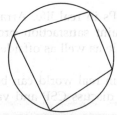

Figure 6.1 Quadrilateral with constraints.

There can be constraint on length of sides and equality of sides that can restrict the outcome further. Many times, the constraints are not absolute but interdependent. Hence, it demands analysis of constraints. As we can see, almost all real-life problems are in some way constraint satisfaction problems, but there are a few problems, which are more evident and demand special CSP techniques to get resolved. Some such problems which demand constraint satisfaction and constraint programming are listed below:

1. School, college or any time table with limited classrooms and teachers
2. Management of employees to achieve certain task
3. Course planning and scheduling
4. Bus route planning
5. Resource allocation
6. Network configuration

Before we proceed, we will just peep into cryptarithmetic puzzles that fall under the higher order CSP.

Cryptarithmetic Puzzles

Cryptarithmetic puzzles are also represented as CSP. Let take an example given below (a hypothetical one):

```
  MIKE
+ JACK
-------
  JOHN
```

Now, the problem is that we need to replace every letter in the puzzle with a single number such that the number is not repeated even once. So, the domain is {0...9}, where M and J cannot be zero. This is often represented as a ten-variable constraint problem where the constraints are as follows:

1. All the variables should have a different value.
2. The sum must work out, i.e.,

$$M * 1000 + I * 100 + K * 10 + E + J * 1000 + A * 100 + C * 10 + K$$
$$= J * 1000 + O * 100 + H * 10 + N.$$

So, we can rewrite it as constraint AllDifferent(M,I,K,E,J,A,C,O,H,N), i.e., a binary constraint implying M should not be equal to I, I should not be equal to K and so on for each of them.

Now, let us understand the constraint domain so as to get a clear idea about it in detail.

Constraint Domain

Constraint domain describes different constrainers, operators, arguments, variables and their domains. Typically, a constraint domain contains the following:

1. Legal set of operators
2. Set of variables
3. Set of all types of functions
4. Domain variables
5. Range of variables

Hence, typically, constraint domain is five-tuple and represented by

$$D = \{var, f, O, dv, rg\}$$

Here, *Var* stands for set variables while *f* for set functions, *O* stands for the set of legitimate operators to be used, *dv* is domain variable and *rg* is the range of function in the constraint.

Further, there exists a concept of primitive constraint. A constraint without conjunction is referred to as *primitive constraint*. It contains one or more constraint symbols with their arguments. A conjunction of primitive constraint is called as *non-primitive constraint* or a *generic constraint*. Typically, $x < 7$ is primitive constraint, while $x \leq 2$ and $y > 3$ is a non-primitive constraint. A person should be honest is a primitive constraint, while a person should be honest and house should be big is a non-primitive or generic constraint.

In some cases, two different constraints may represent the same information. A very simple example of equivalence is $x < 3$ and $3 > x$ are equivalent.

Hence, constraint satisfaction problem possesses the following:

1. Set of variables: $\{V_1, V_2, V_3, ..., V_n\}$
2. Set of constraints: $\{C_1, C_2, C_3, ..., C_m\}$
3. Each variable V_i has domain of possible values.
4. A state of problem is the assignment of values to the variables. The assignment that does not violate any constraint is a legal assignment. Solution to CSP is complete assignment that satisfies all the constraints. The solution needs to satisfy all the constraints, and in turn, should maximise the objective function.

Let us take another example of group assignment problem. The problem is stated as below:

There are seven groups and seven bogies.

Group 1 can speak English, Marathi and Hindi.
Group 2 can speak Tamil and Kannad.
Group 3 can speak English, Kannad and Punjabi.
Group 4 can speak Gujarati and Hindi.
Group 5 can speak Kannad and Hindi.
Group 6 can speak Marathi and Bangla.
Group 7 can speak Hindi and Bangla.

We need to put groups in bogies so that every group should be able to speak to a group in adjacent bogies (Figure 6.2).

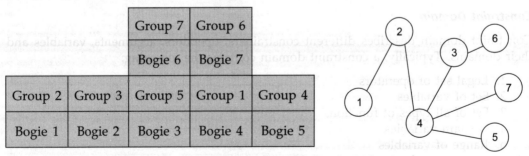

Figure 6.2 Bogie assignments with its constraint graph.

Here, the constraint is one language should be common between two adjacent groups. A simple constraint is same group cannot be present in two bogies. Here,

Variables are {Bogie 1, Bogie 2, Bogie 3, Bogie 4, Bogie 5, Bogie 6, Bogie 7}

Domain of each variable is {Group 1, Group 2, Group 3, Group 4, Group 5, Group 6, Group 7}

The constraint can be defined mathematically as follows:

(Bogie i) $\cap$ (Bogie j) $\neq \varnothing$, where Bogie i and Bogie j are adjacent bogies.

The constraint problem can be visualised as a constraint graph. Figure 6.2 represents the same. The nodes represent the groups and the arcs define the constraints in the constraint graph. The nodes connected by arcs should not be next/adjacent to each other.

There are many advantages of using graph for representing CSP. One of the prime benefits is the easier representation of problem in the form of a standard pattern. Further, generic effective heuristic can be developed. One of the commonly referred examples of constraint satisfaction problem in literature is N queens problem, a special case of the same is eight-queens problem.

6.2 CSP AS A SEARCH PROBLEM

Constraint satisfaction problem can be represented as a search problem. The initial state, successor function, goal test and path cost like any other search algorithm can be considered in such a problem. Here, the initial state can be an empty assignment, while the successor function is a non-conflicting value assigned to an unassigned variable. The goal test checks whether the current assignment is complete, while the path cost is the cost for the path to reach the goal state.

As we have discussed that almost all problems have constraints, and hence, can be represented as CSP. The representation of any problem as a constraint satisfaction problem has a number of advantages. First and foremost advantage caters with the representation of problem. The problem can be brought under a standard and known pattern. It can further allow us to develop generic heuristic, and hence, limits the need for domain-specific expertise. Some of the proven methods like constraint graph can be used to simplify the overall process to reach the goal state. In short, CSP solution leads to the final and complete assignment with no exception, which means assignment that satisfies all constraints. This can be explained with various problems like a graph colouring problem. Figure 6.3 depicts a map of all rooms (architectural view) in a house.

Here, K is kitchen, H is hall, D is dining room, Store is storeroom, B_2, B_3 are bedrooms 2 and 3, MB_1 is the master bedroom, SR is the study room, GR is the guest Room, Lib is library.

Constraints

1. All bedrooms should not be coloured in red, only one can.
2. No two adjacent rooms can have the same colour.
3. The colours available are blue, red, green and violet.
4. Kitchen should not be coloured in green.

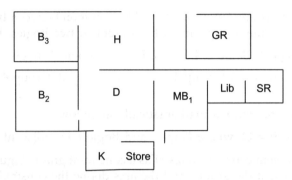

Figure 6.3 Home colouring problem.

5. It is recommended that the kitchen should be coloured blue.
6. Dining room should not have violet colour.

Representation as a Search Problem

Search can be made much simplified as and when the problem is required to satisfy the local constraints. At any point of time, we can start search of the goal state. The goal state is typically a state that satisfies all the conditions and constraints of consistency. It is possible that there can be more than one goal states. In some cases, there can be a preferred goal state. Some constraints are hard constraints, while there can be a few recommendations. We can begin search from the initial state. The pruning of branches takes place as per the constraints.

Before we represent the same problem in the form of tree, let us understand the constrained graph. Figure 6.4 shows a constrained graph. Here, all adjacent rooms are represented using connected line. When there is no adjacency but connectivity, then it is represented as a dotted line. Constraints, as discussed before, restrict the values of those which can be assigned to a particular variable.

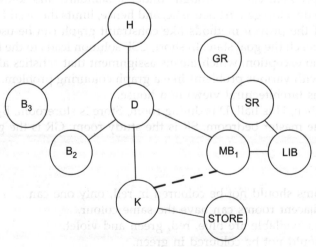

Figure 6.4 Constraint graph.

We have already discussed about unary, binary and higher order constraints. We now introduce soft constraints. These are also called *preferences*. What we mean by soft constraints is that they are cost-oriented or preferred choices. Say in house colouring problem, if white is preferred over red, then it is an example of soft constraint.

Coming back to the tree representation, Figure 6.5 shows the search tree (a sub-part of the tree) for the house colouring problem.

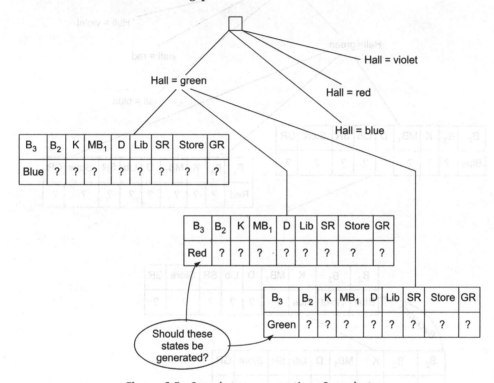

Figure 6.5 Search tree generation: Snapshot.

Figure 6.5 depicts the search tree generation. The question here is if we are aware that the bedrooms should not be coloured with red, is there a need to generate that state? or even a state, where B_3 = green that leads to constraint violation with the hall, should the tree generation be continued? So, the best option can simply not expanding the states, leading to violation of constraints further.

6.2.1 Backtracking Search for CSP

We have discussed in the previous section to represent any problem as CSP. We can assign possible values to generate different state. Assignment of value to any additional variable within constraint can generate a legal state, i.e., a simple assignment of a value to a single variable in our search algorithm generates successor state in the search tree. Here, kitchen's preferred choice is blue, but can be assigned colours blue and violet. Figure 6.6 depicts backtracking for the same example.

As it is observed in Figure 6.6, with tree generation, at a stage when a colour needs to be assigned to dining area, no options are available owing to the constraint violation. Hence, there is a need to backtrack.

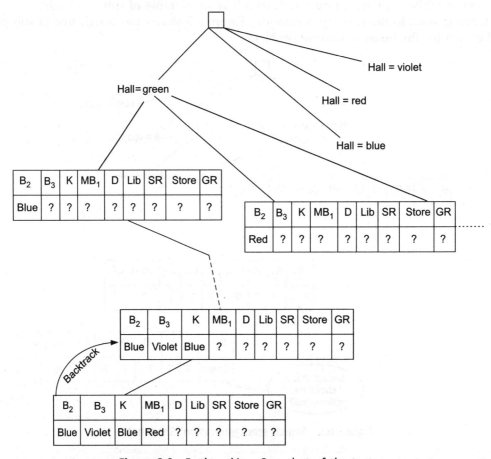

Figure 6.6   Backtracking: Snapshot of the tree.

We have seen in search algorithms that backtracking search is a simple variation of depth first search. Here, assignment of values to variables continues as per the depth, one variable at a time. When variable has no legal value left to assign, there is need to backtrack. Backtracking is the most popular way to search. Here, search continues and different constraints are checked at different stages. The next search includes a few more assignments. There is partial assignment based on alternatives available. A simple logic can be used while assigning these values based on the available options. The logic used may be based on simple random assignment or on some heuristic. Heuristic can assist in leading the goal in a better way. Many options are available in this selection. One that is most often preferred is the selection of an object/variable that has more constraints. So, with this approach, possibly for our example, we could land up selecting a bedroom. There can be many other options that are discussed in the subsequent sections. At every stage, the legality of partial assignment is checked with reference to validity of constraints. The search space continues to go to the next stage, but clearly when the constraint legality is violated by the partial assignment, backtracking comes into picture. In this scenario, backtracking helps to go to the previous decision-making node to eliminate invalid search space with reference to constraint. This algorithm is better than generate and test, since in case of inconsistency, it backtracks to the last relevant decision point.

The algorithm for backtracking is given below:

Procedure BackTracking(Var, Con), where var is variable and con is constraints

> Pick initial state
> R = set of all possible states
> Select state with var assignment
> Add to search space
> Check for con
> If satisfied
>> Continue
> Else
>> Go to last decision point-DP
>> Prune the search sub-space from DP
>> Continue with next decision option
>
> If state = Goal state
>> Return solution
> Else
>> Continue

Clearly, when we talk about backtracking, we know that pruning is going to happen till some previous decision point (DP). But is it possible to improve the backtracking approach? If we are in position to determine which variables should be assigned next, then the things can improve. Further, if we can decide up the ordering, then also the backtracking efficiency can be improved. As discussed earlier, heuristic plays a very important role here.

6.2.2 Role of Heuristic

Heuristic can help in deciding the initial state as well as in guiding for selection of subsequent states. Hence, selection of a variable with minimum number of possible values can help in simplifying search. This is also referred to as *minimum remaining values heuristic (MRV)* or *most constraint variable heuristic*. The notion behind this selection is to detect a failure at an early stage. Thus, it restricts the further searches that would possibly end up in the same variable, making the backtracking ineffective one. With reference to Figure 6.4, if B_3 is selected to be the first one, then the next selection can be H and so on.

Can just this selection help? Now, when we begin to solve the problem, selection of the first variable does not help at all. Rather in other words, MRV cannot have hold on the initial selection. Say in the colouring problem, can we decide in the beginning itself from where to start? No. So, an improvement is possible, where a variable or node with maximum constraints is selected over other unassigned variables. This is called *degree heuristics.* By this selection, the branching factor can be reduced.

Again, with reference to house colouring problem, D can be selected to be the one with constraints on other nodes to begin with, as shown in Figure 6.7. Though it is difficult to say which of the heuristic is better; but degree heuristic helps in case of ties.

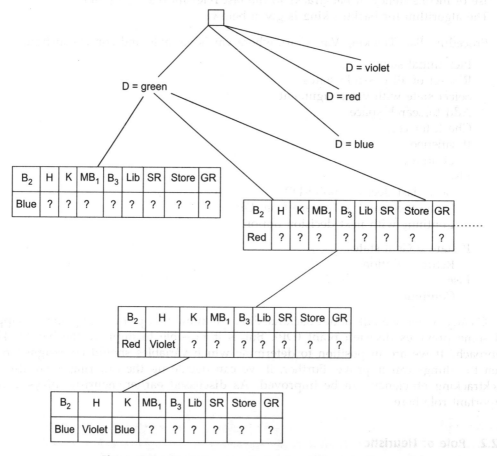

Figure 6.7 Maximum constrained variable selection.

This is about selection of the variables or the nodes, but what values it can take up is further an issue. So, the order in which the values of a particular variable can be arranged is tackled by least constraining value heuristic. Possibly, we can defend this in the example discussed (Figure 6.4) by saying that kitchen is the most eligible node to get coloured in blue.

6.2.3 Forward Checking

With the discussion on the different approaches to improve the efficiency in backtracking, we move towards forward checking. To understand this concept, let us take an example.

Consider the typical problem of four queens. If an arrangement on the board of a queen x hampers the position of queen$_{x+1}$, then this forward check ensures that the queen x should not be placed at the selected position and a new position is to be looked upon. Figure 6.8 depicts the forward checking. A snapshot for the positions of queens is discussed.

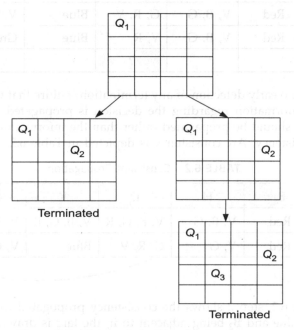

Figure 6.8 Forward checking for four-queens.

From Figure 6.8, Q_1 and Q_2 are placed in row 1 and 2 in left sub-tree, so, the search is halted, as no positions are left for Q_3 and Q_4. Similarly in the second case, Q_3 value assignment leaves no position for Q_4. Hence, it is also halted.

In short, forward checking keeps track of the next moves that are available for the unassigned variables or the nodes. The search gets terminated when there is no legal move available for the unassigned variables.

6.2.4 Constraint Propagation

Can there be any issue with the forward checking that we have discussed? Consider the case of house colouring. With the use of forward checking, we are trying to solve the problem. While solving, once a colour, say x is decided for a variable, all the adjacent nodes can take up any colour other than x. Consider an additional constraint that dining room cannot be of red colour. This can be mapped in following way:

1. At first, B_2 is selected with red (R). Accordingly, R is deleted from the adjacent nodes.
2. Then, Kitchen is assigned Blue (B). So, B is deleted from the adjacent nodes.
3. Further, as MB_1 is selected green, no color is left for D. The steps are depicted in Table 6.1.

TABLE 6.1 Decision and Information Propagation

Step number	B_3	H	D	K	MB_1	B_2
1	Red	V, B, G	V, B, G, R	V, B, G, R	V, B, G	V, B, G
2	Red	V, B, G	G, R, V	Blue	V, G	V, B, G
3	Red	V, B, G	V, R	Blue	Green	V, B
			?		?	

Hence, there is no early detection of any termination/failure that would possibly occur even though the information regarding the decision is propagated. What is required is that the constraints should be propagated rather than the information. This is possible by the use of arc consistency. Arc consistency is depicted in Table 6.2.

TABLE 6.2 Constraint Propagation

Step number	B_3	H	D	K	MB_1	B_2
1	Red	V, B, G	V, B, G, R	V, B, G, R	V, B, G	V, B, G
2	Red	V, G	G, R̶, V̶	Blue	V, G	V, B, G

From the Table 6.2, step 2 shows the consistency propogated from D to B_2. Since D can have only G value and B_2 being adjacent to it, the tarc is drawn.

It is mapped as D → B_2 or mathematically, it is represented as follow:

A → B is consistent iff for some legal value *a* of *A*, there exists non-conflicting value *b* of B.

So, if at any point of time *A*'s value is lost, the neighbour's value can be checked. Hence, the failure detection can take place at an early stage. But now, the question is when to have this arc assignment? Arc consistency can be carried out after taking decision regarding the value assignment of any unassigned variable so that early failure detection can occur.

Before we proceed to the algorithm, we need to keep in mind that the unassigned variable takes up some value from the domain values that exist. Algorithm for arc assignment is given below:

Let *X* be the variable which is being assigned at a given instance.

X will have some value from *D*{}, where *D* is the domain.

For each and every unassigned variable, that is adjacent to *X*, say *X*′

1. Perform forward check, i.e., remove the values from domain *D* that conflict the decision of the current assignment (so, removal of the inconsistent values).
2. Further, for every other variable *X*″ that are adjacent or connected to *X*′
   (i) Remove the values from *D* for *X*″ that cannot be taken as further unassigned variables.
   (ii) Repeat step (2) till no more values can be removed or discarded.

Now, from where does the propagation take place here? It is the step (2) from where the inconsistency is considered and the constraints are propagated.

Special Constraint Handling

After having the study of arc consistency approach, there is one more method for the detection of inconsistency. Consider a simple approach, where x rooms are to be coloured with y colours so that no two rooms have same colour. Now, if $x > y$, naturally this is not at all feasible. So, an improved approach for handling the constraints can be AllDifferent (discussed in Cryptarithmetics) and At most. These are most commonly used to handle the inconsistency. AllDifferent() is typically used when every node or the variable needs to have a different value. In case of house colouring problem, if all the room colours have to be different then AllDifferent (H, K, D, B_2, B_3, MB_1, S). Similarly, partial constraints are there, as all the bedrooms have to be of different colours. The inconsistency can be detected by the use of this AllDifferent, rather than going for arc consistency. Similarly, Atmost or resource constraint is used in higher order constraint, where there is a constraint on the maximum value that can be taken up. Suppose employees are to be hired for some projects P_1, P_2 and P_3. Not more than 5 employees can be taken. This representation with Atmost constraint can be done as Atmost (5, P_1, P_2, P_3). Suppose the hiring is done such that {2, 3, 4} for P_1, P_2 and P_3. Clearly, Atmost constraint cannot be satisfied. So, it would be better to delete the maximum value of the domain that leads to this inconsistency.

6.2.5 Intelligent Backtracking

Why is there a need to have backtracking to be intelligent? Typically, in backtracking, what is carried out is that a different value for preceding node or preceding variable is revisited to check consistency. In the sense, we tend to backtrack to only the previous step. Rather than doing this, won't it be an intelligent move if we backtrack to the actual node or the variable that has caused the termination of the current path? So, this means backtrack to the conflict set. A conflict set for a variable A is the set of previously assigned variables that are connected to A by the constraints. Here, comes a notion of backjumping, where backtracking is carried out to the most recent variable in the conflict set. One might feel that we are discussing forward checking itself. Things are bit different here. Let us assume an example that red colour is selected for bedroom. Then, red is deleted from all the adjacent unassigned variables with respect to bedroom. Further addition that is done here is that bedroom is added to the conflict set of all others. So, when forward checking is carried out, it is very simple to manage the conflict set. But now when does this backjumping occur? Backjumping occurs when every value in the domain is in conflict. This happens due to the current assignment that is done. In case of forward checking, the event is detected, and hence, the search is restricted from making a move towards such a node or variable. So, we can always conclude that the tree branch that is pruned by the forward checking will also be pruned by backjumping. Let us take the example of the house colouring. A condition has occurred, say hall = blue, kitchen = red, B_2 = violet, MB_1 = green (assume that they are all adjacent to dining room), then deciding the colour for dining room is a problem.

Let us consider the example of four-queens problem that we have discussed in the forward checking. From Figure 6.9, it is clear that with the conflict set, backjump occurs to Q_1 position rather that Q_2 while taking decision for Q_3. Thus, a conflict needs to be detected by the use of conflict set so that a backtrack can occur. This type of backjumping where the backtracking occurs with the use of conflict sets is referred to as *conflict-directed backjumping*.

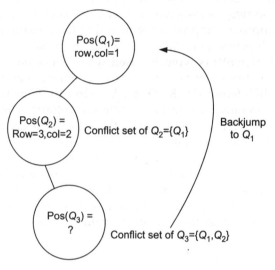

Figure 6.9 Example of backjumping.

To summarise this backtrack of the conflict, we can say that the conflict for node A is defined as conflict(A) that consists of its conflict set. Now, if there is no value left out to take on by A, then backjump to the most recent node or the variable, say B in conflict(A) and restructure the conflict set of B such that

Conflict(B) = Conflict(B) $\cup$ Conflict(A) $-$ {B}

Still this backjumping approach cannot actually restrict the earlier committed mistakes in some other branches!

6.3 LOCAL SEARCH FOR CONSTRAINT SATISFACTION PROBLEM

Local search methods have been used to solve the CSP problems to a great extent. We have already studied these methods like hill climbing, simulated annealing and so on in the previous chapters. The key point here is the usage of the complete state representation. These search methods are most applicable when there are online updates to the CSP problems. Further, there is some optimisation function that is added up to the constraints and in many cases, direct solution tends to be every effective with the use of local search techniques.

According to the working of local search, in the beginning, every variable (node) has a value assigned to it. The successor function then changes only the value at a time for one variable. Again, the question is on what basis, the variable is to be selected. In case of house colouring, it is possible that the hall is selected, which is on random basis. The value for the variable is now decided by the min-conflicts heuristics. Here, the value that would result into minimum number of conflicts is selected. This is with respect to the other variables.

The generalised approach for min-conflicts heuristic is summarised below:

1. Begin with the complete state representation.
2. Do until either a solution is found or the maximum number of iterations is exhausted.
3. Pick up randomly a variable, say X among the set of variables that are in the conflict.
4. Assign value to X such that the min-conflicts is satisfied. In the sense, it minimises the number of constraints that are violated.

It is worth to mention that min-conflicts approach has been proved very effective, especially in the case of N queens problems. Moreover, it is independent of the problem size and also shows better outcomes for hard problems too.

6.4 FORMULATING PROBLEM STRUCTURE

Can we say that the problem structure governs the solution finding process efficiently? Yes, to some extent. We have seen the constraint graphs for the given problems. What this constraint graph actually notifies us is about the constraints between the variables. Naturally, it can help in finding out solutions at a faster speed. Consider the graph shown in Figure 6.4. It is identified that the guest room is not adjacent to any of the other rooms, and hence, totally disjoint. So, it can have any colour (provided no constraints are explicitly been put up on that room). In short, we can say that excluding the guest room (GR), the entire house is one part of the problem, whereas the GR is another. So, we identify the independence property of the problems so as to reach the solutions quickly.

Which type of CSP would be simplest to solve? Assume if we have totally independent and unconnected/non-adjacent components. These problems would be the simplest ones. But in real life, we do not get things in simple form; they are rather complex with a lot of constraints! One simple scenario would be where a tree structure exists, as shown in Figure 6.10. These types of CSPs can be solved in the $O(nd^2)$, whereas in the other cases the worst case time goes to $O(d^n)$. A linear ordering of such a graph further helps in solving the problem. Let us discuss the algorithmic steps.

1. Select a variable or unassigned node as root.
2. Once selection is done, perform ordering such that the parent node precedes in the ordering.
3. For i = number of nodes(n) down to 2, perform arc consistency to remove the inconsistency.
4. For $i = 1$ to number of nodes, assign value to variable(node) X that is consistent with $Y \mid Y$ is parent of the node X.

So, here, we are actually converting or reducing the graph to tree structure. So, is it possible to convert the generalised graphs to trees? Yes. It is possible by two means—by removal of variables/nodes and by collapsing variables/nodes.

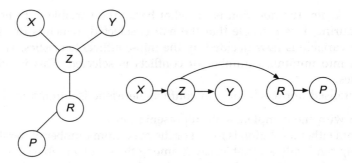

Figure 6.10 Tree structure CSP with its constraint graph and its ordering.

With the reference to house colouring problem, if removal of MB$_1$ is done, we would end up possibly in a simple tree structure that would be easier to solve considering the constraints. Figure 6.11 depicts this tree structure.

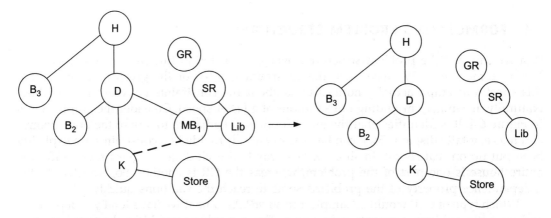

Figure 6.11 Tree structured CSP example.

A generalised algorithm for the same is given below:

1. Remove a subset from the set of variables such that after removal of this subset, the structure turns out to be a tree. Now, let us say that the subset has some set of variables, say V', whereas the other variables are V''.
2. To assign values to V' | all the constraints in subset are met or satisfied
   (a) Remove from V'' the other values that happen to be inconsistent with the ones assigned in V'.
   (b) There is a possibility that we get an answer in the V'' and return the solution with the values assigned in V'.

The above discussed approach is commonly referred to as *cutset conditioning*.

SUMMARY

All the problems that we need to complete or solve most often are bounded by constraints. Typically, CSPs are special kind of problems, where reaching a solution needs the constraints to be satisfied for the problem to be completely solved. We are already familiar that the search process helps in solving any problem, similarly in CSP, search has its role to reach the solution. Backtracking helps in resolving the constraints in reaching the solution. Heuristic helps the backtracking process and accelerates by helping in the selection of variables. Forward checking restricts the assignments of the values to the variables so as to avoid delayed termination. Constraint propagation assists in getting the inconsistency resolved. With the intelligent backtracking, making use of conflict set also helps in a better conflict handling. It is essential that the backtracking occurs to the node detection that has actually caused the termination of that particular tree, rather than just stepping down on the prior step. Local search techniques are proved to be fruitful when the online data gets added up to the problems with the use of min-conflicts heuristic in CSP. Further, a tree structure formulation helps in solving the CSP in comparatively lower time as compared to the complex ones. Hence, a problem structure also needs to be taken into account in CSPs.

 KEYWORDS

1. **CSP:** It is the problem comprising variables along with some constraints on them.
2. **Unary and binary constraints:** These restrict the value of a single variable or two variables, respectively.
3. **Constraint domain:** It describes different constrainers, operators, arguments, variables and their domains.
4. **Primitive constraint:** A constraint without conjunction is referred to as primitive constraint. It contains one or more constraint symbols with their arguments.
5. **Generic constraint:** A conjunction of primitive constraint is called as non-primitive constraint or a generic constraint.
6. **Backtracking:** It helps in going to the previous decision-making node to eliminate invalid search space with reference to constraint.
7. **Minimum remaining value (MRV) heuristic:** It helps in the selection of a variable with the minimum number of values (or moves) remaining that has an impact on the search.
8. **Least constraining value heuristic:** It helps in making the order of values which a particular variable can take up.
9. **Forward checking:** It keeps track of the next moves that are available for the unassigned variables or the nodes.
10. **Arc consistency:** It propagates the constraints rather than the information to the variables.

11. **Backjumping:** It carries out backtracking to the most recent variable in the conflict set.

12. **Min-conflict heuristic:** It is used by local search to take up value for the variables.

13. **Cutset conditioning:** It decomposes the general CSP into a tree structure.

MULTIPLE CHOICE QUESTIONS

(*Note:* There can be more than one answer)

1. Local search in CSP make use of
   - (a) Complete state representation
   - (b) Max-conflicts heuristic
   - (c) Forward checking
   - (d) None of the above

2. Constraint propagation is done by
   - (a) Min-conflicts heuristic
   - (b) Max-conflicts heuristic
   - (c) Arc consistency
   - (d) Tree structure

3. Intelligent backtracking makes use of
   - (a) Unassigned variables set to decide the values
   - (b) A conflict set to backtrack to the source
   - (c) Backjumping to detect the failure node
   - (d) Heuristic to detect the failure

4. Solution to constraint satisfaction problem
   - (a) Can be one of the feasible solutions
   - (b) Is the one that always maximises the objective function
   - (c) Is a solution that can have some relaxed constraints
   - (d) Is a solution that compulsorily has to satisfy all the constraints

5. Which of the following techniques can be used to improve the backtracking in CSP?
   - (a) Minimum remaining value heuristics
   - (b) Minimax approach
   - (c) Backward chaining
   - (d) None of the above

6. We say a problem is CSP when
   - (i) It has values from which solution that will have maximum utility is to be achieved
   - (ii) The problem consists of a set of variables with bounded conditions
   - (iii) The search space is constrained by a set of conditions and dependencies.

   Which of these are true?
   - (a) (i), (ii)
   - (b) (ii), (iii)
   - (c) (i), (iii)
   - (d) (i), (ii), (iii)

7. In CSP problems, an assignment that does not violate the constraints is said to be
   - (a) Complete
   - (b) Conflict
   - (c) Consistent
   - (d) Generic

8. In a problem, if a constraint is rose flower is better than periwinkle, then such a constraint is
   (a) Higher order constraint   (b) Lower order constraint
   (c) Hard constraint   (d) Soft constraint

CONCEPT REVIEW QUESTIONS

1. Discuss the forward checking and the constraint propagation techniques with an example of map colouring.
2. List out the benefits of having a tree structure for CSP.
3. Discuss the local search in CSP with examples and applications.
4. For the following constraint graph (Figure 6.12) for map colouring, show step-wise how constraint propagation will occur to reach the final solution.
   Assume there are 3 colours and adjacent nodes cannot take same colours.

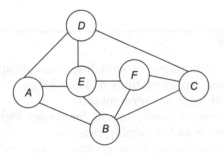

Figure 6.12

CRITICAL THINKING EXERCISE

1. Can forward checking and backjumping go together for a same problem? Discuss.
2. More complex the problem structure, more are the constraints. Is this valid? Argue on the same.

PROJECT WORK

1. Develop a program to solve the *N* queens puzzle using forward checking. Show in steps how the constraints are handled.

CHAPTER 7

Knowledge and Reasoning

Learning Objectives

❏ To understand the importance of knowledge and its approaches
❏ To study the various representations of knowledge
❏ To study the role of logic in representation
❏ To understand the use of predicate and first order logic
❏ To study the inference and reasoning process
❏ To appreciate the relationship between knowledge and reasoning

INTRODUCTION

Search techniques and intelligent agents acquire information from environment and further build the knowledge with reference to problem at hand. It is this knowledge that is exploited further with the actions and decisions. Thus, appropriate and precise representation of the knowledge becomes a critical factor in the process. With the previous study on the search techniques and the applications, the agent environment, and the problem-solving issues, we now turn towards the knowledge representation. For all the methods that have been discussed previously, we need to look at the most important aspect of how the knowledge can be represented so that it can be used effectively and applied to the process. In turn, we can say that there is a reasoning process that actually is making the use of the knowledge.

But then, a question arises what is 'knowledge' basically? It is some set of patterns and associations derived from data or information that helps in making decisions and resolves problems that may be related to any day-to-day life or some complex problems. Consider a simple example, where a teacher has to judge the performance of a student for some exam. The teacher judges on the basis of percentile the student would obtain.

The judgement could be based on the previous performances of that student or on some information given by some other teachers about that student. This can be considered as the available knowledge. So, one can arrive at some decisions based on this knowledge.

A systematic reasoning process is required when we try to relate the events to the outcomes or to arrive at judgements. Hence, *reasoning* is the way we conclude on different aspects of problems based on the available knowledge representation. Logic plays an important role in the reasoning process. So, *logic* is the one that makes the knowledge representative. In the course of representing the knowledge and utilising it, the chapter focuses on the various aspects that are essential from appropriate representations to exploit the knowledge base (KB). Though there are restrictions with the knowledge base handled here, it will be a stepping stone for us to start with the representations and understanding its use, where the knowledge is certain.

Let us begin our discussion with the knowledge representation, various issues and other aspects related to knowledge representation along with the agent environment.

7.1 KNOWLEDGE REPRESENTATION

In introduction, we have mentioned that knowledge is an important aspect of the reasoning process. Our outcomes govern the way we have the knowledge and the way we update it. Mapping it in technical terms, depending on the domain one is working on, it is very crucial to identify and create representation of the knowledge. So, can we say that knowledge representation is about representation of the facts at hand? The answer truly lies in the fact, viz. which facts at hand can be represented or to be specific, which can be manipulated. This is required from the viewpoint of specific knowledge representation that gives a broader view for problem solving. Let us proceed with the approaches and issues of knowledge representation.

7.1.1 Approaches and Issues of Knowledge Representation

Consider a case where fruits are to be arranged in a basket. This would be a simple task at present. One can easily have a knowledge representation and act accordingly. There could be multiple options that will give the desired outcome. But with the addition of more facts like the size of the fruits, the quantity, the basket size and so on, it would further narrow down the arrangements. Further, it is quiet obvious that some information gets available over a period of time. The KB representation should be able to handle this sort of environment, where limited or partial information is available in the beginning and later on, more information is evolved. We cannot say that for a particular problem, there is only a specific way of knowledge representation. But the representation definitely counts while coming to reasoning. Figure 7.1 depicts the process of deriving facts. From the diagram, it is clear that raw data, domain knowledge and, percept allow to refine internal representation iteratively to arrive at the final facts. Here, reasoning is required to establish relationships among the available data and the final facts.

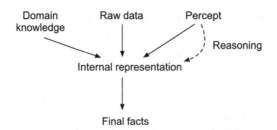

Figure 7.1 Knowledge building and representation.

Approaches

Before we start our discussion on the approaches, let us have a quick look on the properties that are required for knowledge representation in the system design. While designing a system for knowledge representation, we would always go for a system that allows representation of the entire knowledge, which is required with respect to the application or domain we work on. This is precisely the property that speaks about adequacy in terms of representation. The next property talks about adequacy in terms of inferring. Here, it is necessary that the knowledge should be represented in such a way so that there is a way to manipulate the representative data in order to derive at new ones. At the same time, it needs to be efficient in terms of inferring, where the additional data should be used in the direction of better inferring. Further, we would like to have the representation to learn; it should be adaptive and able to accommodate new additional information that would be available at any point of time. This is the property of efficiency in term of acquisition. Here, we mean to say that it should posses the property of being incremental. This could also be a simple knowledge update by the user himself.

During the course of representation, it is worth to mention that even though we expect it to possess the properties, it is not feasible that just one representation is able to fulfil them. Generally, different approaches are in use when it comes to representation of knowledge, even though it is for a specific domain.

Let us start with the basic and the simplest ways for representation. Now, when we are discussing about the representation, the obvious thing that comes to our mind is the database or files. Are they a part of knowledge representation? Are there some other methods too? Definitely, they are a part of representation. Let us understand what approaches can exist along with them with respect to the structure.

We begin with a simple *relational knowledge structure*, wherein we have the database representation. The facts can be mapped into the relations and stored in the database. This kind of representation without any additional procedure to get something out of it is a weak inference mechanism.

Table 7.1 represents a simple example of relational knowledge structure.

TABLE 7.1 Relational Knowledge Structure

Employee	Salary	Experience
Sameer	30000	3
Kavita	20000	2
Jasmin	20000	2

The next structure is *inheritable knowledge structure*. This type of representation is required as all the knowledge related to the inheritance is not mapped in the earlier case. This is critical while drawing conclusions. Hence, we need a structure that can help in inferring. So, a general hierarchy structure is used, where it is possible to have a proper mapping with inheritance. Figure 7.2 shows this type of knowledge structure.

Let us take the example of cricket. The knowledge structure for any player is based on various parameters or attributes. The player can be a batsman or a bowler. He can be a right-handed player, with some specific height. So, there exists an ISA relationship among a person, a player and a batsman or a bowler. Similarly, we can have an instance to represent the knowledge. The structure is also called *slot-filler structure*.

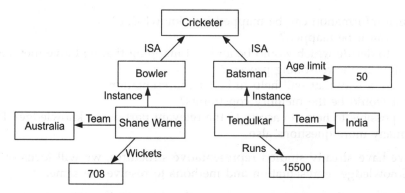

Figure 7.2 Inheritable knowledge.

Semantic network and frame collection are also related to the structure, which are discussed later in the chapter.

We are aware that finally our intention is to come out with the outcomes that will answer our queries. Now, for example, we say that we want to have a solution to a query like does Tendulkar satisfy age limit? (The diagram represents hypothetical data to understand the hierarchy). The process of seeking a solution is

1. To check if direct answer is available. In case, it is not, go to the next step
2. To check for attribute instance

Here, it will be under the category of Batsman. Had it been the case that the query was regarding the parameter like related to cricketer, we would have to move a step up in the hierarchy and got the answer. This process or the approach applies the property of inheritance. This approach actually guides the utilisation of the knowledge.

Another structure is *inferential knowledge structure*. In this type of structure, first order predicate logic is used. So, a typical example is combining the knowledge to get the outcomes. (Details of predicate logic are discussed later in the chapter.) One point to mention here is that there is a need for the inference procedure to have the utilisation of knowledge.

Procedural knowledge structure is another approach for the representation. This structure comes into picture when we need to have the knowledge in detailed form. Somewhere, it specifies steps to be followed and its details. Programming languages are used for that purpose. LISP is the most common language that finds a place in this case. Another representative structure could be in the form of rules—production rules.

We have now discussed the introduction to structures. As we will proceed through the chapter, we will have a clear picture of the other details about the knowledge representation and use of logic for the same. Let us turn towards the issues of knowledge representation.

Issues of Knowledge Representation

There are various issues of knowledge representation related to information mapping and use of structures. Most obvious questions that arise in knowledge representation are as follows:

1. Which information can be mapped into knowledge?
2. How can it be mapped?
3. How to decide which would be an ideal mapping that will give the most accurate solution to the reasoning process?
4. Is there a way that will help in better representation?
5. What would be the memory constraints?
6. Is it possible to have an access to the relevant part of the knowledge? There could be many more questions also.

Since we have already studied representative structures, we will focus on the issues related to knowledge representation and methods to resolve the same.

1. *Attributes* are the most important ones that have an impact on the representation. It is required to understand and identify the important attributes. This helps in absorbing the important parameters for the KB representation.

2. Similarly, identifying the *relationships among the attributes* in the representation is equally important. By pairing of the attributes or with ISA methods, the relationships are captured. Reasoning about values that are taken up also adds up complexities in the selection process. Hence, proper selection of the attributes impacts the relationships.

3. Handling the issue of level or upto what depth the mapping of the knowledge is to be done defines the *granularity*. This is governed by the availability of facts and the level upto which it is possible to split them and represent them. Sometimes, splitting can prove to be an option to handle the issue, making the easy accessibility, but sometimes, it adds complexities to handle the data.

4. Further, the issue is *representation of the objects as sets*. Use of logic and the inheritance that we have already studied are very well-suited to tackle this issue. Sometimes, a particular property that is applicable to the entire set has an exception. There is a need to clarify in terms of properties before we have the representations. The name that represents the set has to be precise, as this impacts the object selection, letting us know about its membership. Here, extensional definition is used, where the members are listed in the set, and the other is intensional, where rules are provided that determine the belongingness of the object. This tries to restrict the representation of the objects.

5. Finally, *selection of correct structure* is the most important part to have a proper representation. Things, here, as made clear earlier too, are dependent on the domain. Here, the issues range from how to fill in the details to when to have a new structure. Though selecting a knowledge structure that matches a particular problem is very difficult, still

to mention a few, one method can be indexing the structure with significant keywords. This can with regard to English, but then this is specific when the domain description is available in English. Other approach could be the use of pointers. Using this notion, it is possible to have intersections of the sets and to use structure that are precise. One more option could be locating and selecting a major clue in the problem. This helps in defining the structure. It is also equally important that the structure is flexible, which allows revisions as per the requirements. Getting appropriate values is the final requirement. In the sense, whenever we have structure selection, its exploitation is done by getting the results. Generally, a candidate structure is set up and then applied to the problem. But, if the outcomes are not accurate for the problem, then it is the time to change/revise the structure. This can be in terms of attribute values too.

Figure 7.3 represents the issues and their inter-relationships.

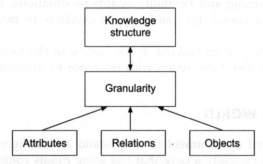

Figure 7.3 Knowledge structure hierarchy.

7.2 KNOWLEDGE-BASED AGENTS

We have already studied about intelligent agent. An *agent* is the one who acts according to the environment. To act, it needs to know the knowledge of how to act. A knowledge base (KB), hence, plays an important role in deciding the actions. This knowledge base is nothing but a representation of the information that helps an agent to act. Knowledge representation language makes use of sentences to represent facts about the world.

An agent's operating environment is based on perception and action. Depending on the current percept, it acts. So, this percept should be available with the knowledge base. Then, the action occurs. This action too needs to be updated to the knowledge base. We can say that the knowledge-based agent performs three-fold task. A typical algorithm is summarised below:

> Knowledge-based agent
> Input: Percept
> Returns: Action
>   Give-info (KB, make-percept-sentence (*p*, *t*))
>   Action ← (KB, make-query(*t*))
>   Give-info (KB, make-action-sentence (*a*, *t*))

where *p* is the current percept, *t* is the time and *a* is the action.

From the steps, it is clear that in the initial *give-info* function, it records the current percept *p* and reveals the information about the percept in the form of knowledge. This can be in the form of a sentence. In the next step, the action *a* is returned that is the result of formulation of query for the knowledge that has been received at the previous stage. The last stage is where the KB is updated about the action taken.

The basic difference between a normal agent and a knowledge-based agent is that the actions of knowledge-based agent are not arbitrary. They are dependent on the knowledge. They are described at three levels. At the knowledge level, the agent is provided with the information it should know and its targets. At the logical level knowledge is represented in logical language, while at implementation level, logical sentences are implemented. The implementation level does not hamper any of the knowledge level details.

Knowledge-based agent accepts new tasks through defined goals. They acquire knowledge through learning and flexibility adapts to situations. Before the agent starts its operation, the initial knowledge can be made available in two ways: (i) declarative and (ii) procedural.

Declarative knowledge is embedded in the system in the form of pre-defined rules, while procedural infers about the action with reference to situations.

7.3   THE WUMPUS WORLD

This is a very traditional environment to understand an intelligent agent-based system. The Wumpus World is basically a cave that has some rooms connected to each other by passways. In one of the rooms lies a wumpus (a beast) that eats anyone who enters the room. The wumpus can be shot by an agent, but the agent has only one arrow available. In some of the rooms, there are pits too. The best part of this world is that the agent might get a heap of gold. The PEAS description for this environment is as follows:

P—Performance: (i) 1000 points when gold is found
                    (ii) –1000 points when falls in pit
                    (iii) –1 for every move
                    (iv) –10 when arrow is used

E—Environment: A grid of 4*4, with pits at some squares and gold at one square and agent position at [1, 1] facing right.

A—Actuators: (i) Turn 90° left/right
              (ii) Walk one square forward
              (iii) Grab or take an object
              (iv) Shoot the arrow (agent has one arrow)

S—Sensors: There are five sensors. They capture the following:

1. In rooms adjacent to room of wumpus (excluding diagonal), the agent perceives stench.
2. In the square adjacent to pit (excluding diagonal), agent the perceives breeze.
3. In the room containing gold, the agent perceives glitter.
4. When agent walks in a wall, he perceives a bump.
5. When wumpus is killed, it screams that can be perceived anywhere in the environment.

Figure 7.4 shows the Wumpus World. (Different positions can exist for the wumpus, pits and gold and it is not the case that the room arrangement is same).

The agent in the Wumpus World draws conclusions based of the facts. If the facts are correct, naturally the conclusions will be correct and hence, its actions too. Let us understand the actions of agent in the environment.

The knowledge base of the agent contains five initial conditions that are listed in the sensors. It starts with [1,1]. It knows that this is the position, where it is safe. It needs to move ahead either to reach the room of gold or to be safe. Since at [1,1], it does not perceive a stench or breeze, the adjacent rooms are safe as concluded based on the facts. So, it can move to [2,1] or [1,2]. Let us say it goes to [2,1]. At this point, it gets a breeze. So, it concludes that at [2,2], there could be a pit or at [3,1], there could be a pit.

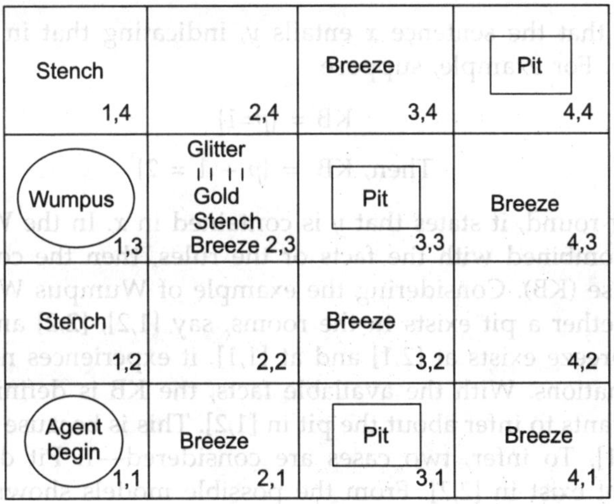

Stench 1,4	Breeze 2,4	3,4	Pit 4,4
Wumpus 1,3	Glitter | | | | Gold Stench Breeze 2,3	Pit 3,3	Breeze 4,3
Stench 1,2	2,2	Breeze 3,2	4,2
Agent begin 1,1	Breeze 2,1	Pit 3,1	Breeze 4,1

Figure 7.4 The Wumpus World.

So, it moves back. It now goes to [1,2]. It perceives a stench. This indicates the there is wumpus. The wumpus could be at [1,3] or [2,2]. But [2,2] is the position, where the agent assumes that there could be a pit. Since it does not receive a breeze in [1,2], it concludes that pit is absent in [2,2]. But then what about the wumpus? If the wumpus was present in [2,2], it would detect a stench at [2,1]. Hence, it concludes that [2,2] is safe and the wumpus is present at [1,3]. Concluding this is difficult without previous experiences. From here, the agent could go to [2,3] or [3,2]. If it selects [2,3], he will perceive glitter!

Hence, it is the reasoning that leads the agent to take correct actions and this is dependent on the correctness of the facts. So, we conclude that logical reasoning is the essence to have correct conclusions.

7.4 LOGIC

What are we actually doing by studying logic? Are we trying to understand the process of reasoning? We already know that logic basically deals with the study of principles of reasoning. So, what we are trying to put forth in this section is how logic is built, or rather how the logical representations help in the process of decisions.

So, can we say that there are syntax and semantics that are required to be handled in logical representations? Yes. Logic involves syntax, semantics as well as inference procedure. Speaking about the syntax, we know that there can be a variety of ways to represent it. It is not a concern, actually, but it is the way an agent (relating it to the Wumpus World's agent) builds the base so that the reasoning plays an important part. With respect to semantics, though it deals with the meaning, in sentential form, it can either be true or false. There is a need to define logical involvement in two sentences or facts. So, here, we are trying to model it. It can be put forth in the following way: Assume that x and y are the two sentences whose relationship is to be determined. Let us map this relationship as follows:

$$x \models y$$

This indicates that the sentence x entails y, indicating that in the model when x is true, y is also true. For example, suppose

$$KB = \{p=1\}$$

$$\text{Then, } KB \models \{p + 1 = 2\}$$

The other way round, it states that y is contained in x. In the Wumpus World, when the percepts are combined with the facts or the rules, then the combination constitutes the Knowledge base (KB). Considering the example of Wumpus World, where the agent wants to infer whether a pit exists in the rooms, say [1,2], [2,2] and [3,1] with available information that breeze exists at [2,1] and at [1,1], it experiences nothing, then there are 2^3 possible combinations. With the available facts, the KB is definitely false in the case, where the agent wants to infer about the pit in [1,2]. This is because it does not experience any breeze in [1,1]. To infer, two cases are considered—1. Pit does not exist in [1,2] and 2. Pit does not exist in [2,2]. From the possible models shown in Figure 7.5, it can be inferred that the KB $\models$ case 1. So, when every KB is true, case 1 will be true. But it cannot be judged as to whether the pit exists in [2,2]. This type of inferring is called *model checking*.

So, in logical inferring, there is a notion of truth that is to be maintained. Even it needs to have the property of completeness. Finally, the last word is if the knowledge base is true, then the sentence it derives has to be true.

7.5 PROPOSITIONAL LOGIC

After having an overview of logic part, we begin with the propositional logic; the most simple logic. Why are we studying it? The answer is—for reasoning. It is a mathematical model that provides reasoning regarding the logical value of an expression.

What is propositional logic? It is a logic that is concerned with the propositions and their relationships. Propositional logic is also called *sentential logic*. Propositions are sentences—declarative sentences, say 'Ice is cold' or 'The door is closed', and so on. But 'Is it cold?' or 'Open the door' are not propositions. Hence, they cannot be an explicit order. A declarative sentence states that it can be either true or false, but not both. Propositional logic is the fundamental logic. Let us understand the syntax and semantics first.

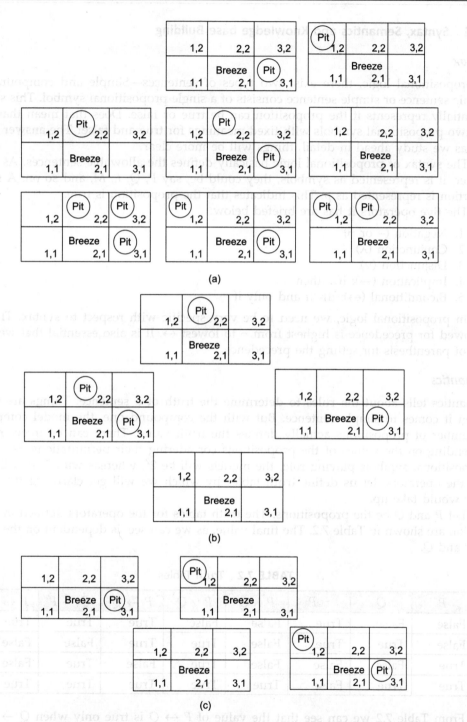

Figure 7.5 Possible (subset) cases in the Wumpus World for pits: (a) Knowledge base (KB), (b) Case 1: Subset representations, (c) Case 2: Subset representations.

7.5.1 Syntax, Semantics and Knowledge base Building

Syntax

In propositional logic, there exist two types of sentences—Simple and compound. An atomic sentence or simple sentence consists of a single propositional symbol. This symbol essentially represents if the proposition can be true or false. Does that mean that there are two propositional symbols with fixed meanings for true and false? The answer is yes. But as we study ahead in detail, things will be more clear.

The syntax of propositional logic basically defines the allowable sentences. As stated earlier, it is represented as symbols, they could be, say P, Q, L, M, and so on. A simple assertion is represented as p. This indicates that the proposition is true.

The five operators it has are briefed below:

1. Negation (~ or ¬)
2. Conjunction (∧)
3. Disjunction (∨)
4. Implication (→): If....then
5. Biconditional (↔): iff- if and only if

In propositional logic, we need to be very specific with respect to syntax. The rule followed for precedence is highest from ¬ to lowest ↔. It is also essential that we make use of parenthesis for setting the precedence.

Semantics

Semantics tells about the rules to determine the truth of a sentence. Things are simple when it comes to simple sentence. But with the compound one, the model comprising a number of propositions actually defines the truth value. There can be many models depending on the values of the propositions considering their permutations. So, with 2 propositional symbols playing role, the models will be 2^2, whereas with 3, it will be 2^3. For the operators, let us define truth tables by which we will get clarity of the values they would take up.

Let P and Q be the propositions. The truth tables for the operators defined in earlier section are shown in Table 7.2. The final value, as we can see, is dependent on the values of P and Q.

TABLE 7.2 Truth Tables

P	Q	¬ P	$P \wedge Q$	$P \vee Q$	$P \rightarrow Q$	$Q \rightarrow P$	$P \leftrightarrow Q$
False	False	True	False	False	True	True	True
False	True	True	False	True	True	False	False
True	False	False	False	True	False	True	False
True	True	False	True	True	True	True	True

From Table 7.2 we can see that the value of $P \leftrightarrow Q$ is true only when $Q \rightarrow P$ and $P \rightarrow Q$ are true. Consider the scenario of the Wumpus World again. There is a breeze in [1,1], let us represent this as B. Then, we know that a pit exists in [2,1] or [1,2]. Let P

represents pit in room [2,1] and Q represents pit in room [1,2]. Mapping it in propositional logic, we represent it as follows:

$$B \leftrightarrow (P \vee Q)$$

But we cannot have the implication operator, as it results into incompleteness of knowledge.

Building a Knowledge Base (KB)

For a subset of the Wumpus World, a knowledge base is required to be built.

To build any KB, the first step is to decide the propositions. We then construct the rules with the operators and the true/false values of propositions. Consider that i and j represent the room or the grid value. Let $P_{[i, j]}$ represents the proposition that is true if there is a pit in i, j. Similarly, let $B_{[i, j]}$ represents the proposition that is true when there is a breeze in i, j.

The KB comprises the rules now that are built with the propositions and operators. As an example one rule can be as follows:

Rule 1: $\neg P_{[1,1]}$: This rule states that there is no pit in [1,1].

Similarly, the earlier rule that we have derived in the semantics is also a KB-representing rule. We can rewrite the rule 2 as follows:

Rule 2: $B_{[1,1]} \leftrightarrow P_{[1,2]} \vee P_{[2,1]}$. In this way we can define the rules forming our KB for the Wumpus World.

Finally, the KB comprises all the rules or the sentences in the conjunction form, i.e., Rule 1 $\wedge$ Rule 2 ... $\wedge$ Rule n. This, in turn, tells that all the rules are valid and true.

7.5.2 Inference

Now, once we have our KB represented, it is the time that we decide upon the inference. With the propositions that we have discussed considering the Wumpus World, they can have different models depending on the values. By models, as said earlier, we mean the different values which the propositions take in the compound statement. So, by inferring we mean that it should be decided whether KB $\models x$. Here, x is some sentence.

So, when it comes to inference, we need to enumerate the models. Now, while doing so, the number of propositions playing part in it directly hamper the efficiency. The values where KB is true, and thus, the value of x is also true indicate inferring. As an example, assume that we have KB true for some model. Suppose you have a truth table of the values of propositions, rules and KB. A snapshot of the same is given below in Table 7.3.

TABLE 7.3 Values of Propositions—A Snapshot

$B_{[1,1]}$	$B_{[2,1]}$	$P_{[1,2]}$	...	$P_{[3,1]}$	$B_{[2,1]}$	*Rule 1*	*Rule 2*	...	*KB*
⋮									
False	True	False		True		True	True		True
False	True	False		False		True	True		True
False	True	False		True		True	True		True
⋮									

From Table 7.3, we can say that $\sim(P_{[1,2]})$ is true, so we can infer that there is no pit in [1,2]. But the same cannot be true in case of $P_{[3,1]}$, as in one case, it is false. This is just a simple case considered to understand inferring, but just image the number of models that would be generated with the increase in the propositions.

Given a sentence n, the approach for deciding entailment is based on recursive enumeration. The approach is:

Given—KB, x, list of symbols in KB and x.

Check—1. If symbols are empty then
        check if model is consistent with KB
            if true then check if x evaluates to true
        else it is inconsistent
    2. Else
        recursively construct conjunction
        for partial models with symbols in KB and x.

Some concepts: Tautology, Contradiction and satisfiability

1. Tautology: A tautology states that the sentence is true if it is true in all models. That means a proposition is always true. For example $(P \vee \sim P)$ will have true value, irrespective of the P values. Hence, it is a tautology, which is sometimes also called *validity*.

2. Contradiction: In contradiction, the proposition is always false. For example, $P \wedge \sim P$ will be always false, irrespective of the values taken by proposition P.

3. Satisfiability: A sentence or a proposition is satisfiable if it is true for some model. Let us say a sentence x is true in a model m then m satisfies x. m is a model of x.

Refutation

After studying satisfiablity, the question is how can it be determined? Can we say that we need to explore all the models and check them till we get one that satisfies the sentence? The answer is yes. To determine the satisfiability of a sentence is NP-complete problem. Now, when we talk about satisfiability, we can say that most of the problems related to computer science are satisfiable. (Constraint satisfaction and search problems have satisfiability playing a role in solving them).

Understanding the relation between the validity and satisfiability can be explained as follows:

Assume that a sentence x is valid. To prove that x is valid, we need to prove that $\sim x$ is satisfiable. Other way round, x is satisfiable iff $\sim x$ is not valid. Referring to KB representations, we can state that

$x \models y$ iff sentence $(x \wedge \sim y)$ is unsatisfiable.

Proving y from x by checking the unsatisfiability as mentioned above is *proof by refutation* or *contradiction*. This relates to the mathematical solving of problems, where by treating a value as false, we move into contradictions, and hence, carry the proof of refutation.

7.5.3 Reasoning Patterns in Propositional Logic

In reasoning patterns, we use and apply the basic rules in order to derive chains of conclusions to get the outcome or the target. These basic rules are also called *patterns of inference.*

The two most commonly used rules are *modus ponens* and *and-elimination.* Modus ponens is represented as follows:

$$\alpha \to \beta,\ \alpha \mapsto \beta$$

The rule states that when any sentence is in the form of $\alpha \to \beta$, and α is given, then we can infer β.

As an example, when we have the rule that (wumpus-ahead $\wedge$ wumpus-alive) $\to$ shoot and (wumpus-ahead $\wedge$ wumpus-alive); we can infer shoot. Considering one more example (mapping in propositional logic), suppose we have the following rule:

R: $\sim S_{[1,1]} \to \sim W_{[1,1]} \wedge \sim W_{[1,2]} \wedge \sim W_{[2,1]}$ and given that a stench is ahead

Then, with modus ponens, we get

$\sim W_{[1,1]} \wedge \sim W_{[1,2]} \wedge \sim W_{[2,1]}$, where β is inferred

In case of and-elimination, the rule is represented as follows:

$$\alpha_1 \wedge \alpha_2 \wedge \alpha_3 \wedge \alpha_n \mapsto \alpha_i$$

The rule states that from conjunctions, it is possible to infer any conjunction.

This also states that if we have wumpus-ahead $\wedge$ wumpus-alive, then we can infer wumpus-alive. From the above inference with stench, we get simply the and-elimination inference as follows:

$$\sim W_{[1,1]}\ \sim W_{[1,2]}\ \sim W_{[2,1]}$$

Now, the next question is again what is the reason behind considering these rules? These rules are actually the ones that eliminate the need for generating the models. When these rules are applied, they generate sound inferences.

Resolution

The previous point clarifies the rules being sound. We now need to discuss the completeness. Any search algorithm (we have discussed about completeness in Chapter 3) is said to be complete when it is guaranteed to go to a reachable goal. But what if the rules available are insufficient or inadequate? Can we reach the goal?

Resolution is a single inference rule that is discussed in this section, which gives a complete inference algorithm when coupled with complete search algorithm.

Coming back to the Wumpus World's example, some rules are considered here to understand the resolution. Consider the case where the agent is in [1,2], a case where he has returned from [2,1] to [1,1] and then has gone to [1,2]. Here, he perceives a stench, but no breeze. Now, we add some more rules.

Rule a: $\sim B_{[1,2]}$

Rule b: $B_{[1,2]} \leftrightarrow (P_{[1,1]} \vee P_{[2,2]} \vee P_{[1,3]})$

Rule c: $\sim(P_{[2,2]})$

Rule d: $\sim(P_{[1,3]})$

Rules c and d imply that pit is not present in [2,2] and [1,3]. Similarly, we can derive that there can exist a pit in [1,1] or [2,2] or [3,1]. Rule e represents the same as follows:

Rule e: $P_{[1,1]} \vee P_{[2,2]} \vee P_{[3,1]}$

But where is the application of resolution and how do we apply it? The resolution rule is applied in the rules c and e. By this we mean to say that $\sim P_{[2,2]}$ in rule c resolves with $P_{[2,2]}$ in rule e. By applying this, we get

Rule f: $P_{[1,1]} \vee P_{[3,1]}$

But the initial rule that we have in KB building is that $\sim P_{[1,1]}$. This again resolves with the rule f. Hence, what we get is

Rule g: $P_{[3,1]}$

This inference rule states that if there is a pit in [1,1] or [3,1] (by rule f) and there is no pit in [1,1] (by resolution), then there is definitely a pit in [3,1].

The steps applied to infer the rules f and g are called *unit resolution inference rules*.

The propositions involved in the process are also called *literals*. Resolution is actually the basis for complete inference procedures. Any search algorithm that is complete and applies the resolution rule can derive any conclusion that is entailed in KB. Suppose we know that a proposition X is true. It is not possible to have a resolution to generate $X \vee Y$, but we can determine if $X \vee Y$ is true or not. This is referred to as *refutation completeness*.

Conjunctive normal form (CNF): From the rules that are mentioned in the resolution, it is noticed that the resolution is applied only to disjunctions. But then, the rules can be in conjunction form too. What we need to do is to convert them into CNF, which is a conjunction of disjunctions. CNF is conjunction of clauses, where clauses are disjunctions of literals.

While converting, the following steps are to be carried out:

1. If a bidirectional implication exists, it has to be eliminated in following way:

   $\alpha \leftrightarrow \beta$, is replaced with $\alpha \rightarrow \beta$, $\beta \rightarrow \alpha$.

2. If an implication exists, then it has to be eliminated in the following way:

   $\alpha \rightarrow \beta$ is replaced with $\neg\,\alpha \vee \beta$.

3. Use equivalence to have $\sim$ or $\neg$.

By applying the DeMorgan's theorem, we can rewrite the rules as follows:

(i) $\neg(\neg\alpha) \equiv \alpha$
(ii) $\neg(\alpha \wedge \beta) \equiv (\neg\alpha \vee \neg\beta)$
(iii) $\neg(\alpha \vee \beta) \equiv (\neg\alpha \wedge \neg\beta)$

Once these rules are applied, we can have the resolution inference rule applied.

Let us take a simple example. Assume α and β are in CNF. Therefore, $\alpha \wedge \beta$ is also in CNF.

Now, conversion of $\alpha \lor \beta$ can be carried out as follows:

1. In a given scenario, if α and β are literals, then

$$\alpha \lor \beta \text{ is in CNF}$$

2. If $\alpha = \alpha_1 \land \alpha_2 ... \land \alpha_1$, then

$$\alpha \lor \beta = (\alpha_1 \lor \beta) \land (\alpha_2 \lor \beta) ... \land (\alpha_1 \lor \beta)$$

Assuming β is literal, then

$$(\alpha_1 \lor \beta) \land (\alpha_2 \lor \beta) ... \land (\alpha_1 \lor \beta) \text{ is in CNF}$$

Otherwise β is conjunction of β_1 to β_k and using distribution, we can convert each α_i and β_i to CNF.

Resolution algorithm: After having studied *refutation* in the previous section, we move ahead with the resolution algorithm. In refutation, proof is with contractions. For example, to prove that KB $\models y$ we need to show (KB $\land \sim y$) is unsatisfiable. While applying the resolution algorithm, we

1. Convert (KB $\land \sim y$) into CNF.
2. We get some resulting clauses.
3. The resolution rule is to be applied to each clause.
4. The complementing pairs, are resolved to generate a new rule or a clause.
5. Add this to the KB if not already present.
6. Goto step 3 till any of the following two conditions occur:
   (i) No new clauses can be added in which KB does not entail α.
   (ii) Applying the resolution yields an empty rule, indicating KB entails α.

Forward and Backward Chaining

Resolution put forth an inference mechanism that is complete. But practically speaking, in most of the cases, we do not need to have the resolution. This is because the KB comprises restricted clauses or rules (clauses where at most a single proposition or literal is positive). A clause that is disjunction of literals of which at most one is positive is a *Horn clause*.

For example, the clause has $\neg S_{[1,1]} \lor \neg$ Breeze $\lor B_{[1,1]}$ is a Horn clause ($\neg S_{[1,1]}$ is the state of the agent at 1,1). But a clause like $\neg B_{[1,4]} \lor P_{[2,1]} \lor P_{[1,2]}$ is not a Horn clause. The Horn clause containing exactly one positive literal is called *definite clause*. This literal is called *head* and other literals are said to be *body*. When there is not any negative proposition in a definite clause, it is called *fact*. A clause (for example, $\neg P_{[3,1]} \lor \neg P_{[1,3]}$ is same as writing $P_{[3,1]} \land P_{[1,3]}$) is called *integrity constraint*. It points out the errors.

Forward chaining and backward chaining are the algorithms that are used for inferring. While applying the algorithm, the knowledge base comprises the Horn clauses. What are we trying to infer in these algorithms? Let us assume we have a query that is required to be resolved. This can be resolved by going through the KB to get the answer. This query is a proposition, say whether any position in the room has a pit or not. So, we are trying to find whether this proposition is entailed in the knowledge base.

Forward chaining: In forward chaining, the process starts with the known facts. From the known facts, it adds to the conclusion. This process is carried out till we reach out the query that we have to resolve or till no inference can occur further. The approach is mapped to an AND-OR graph. Here, the constraint is that till all the conjuncts are known, it does not proceed ahead.

The steps can be summarised as follows:

1. Start with the known facts.
2. If the premise of the implication in the clauses are known, then add conclusion to the facts.
3. Go to step 2 till
    (i) We infer the value as true or false for the query, or
    (ii) No inference can occur.

This approach takes linear time. This approach is also said to be *data-driven approach*, where we try to derive considering the available facts.

Backward chaining: In backward chaining, the processing starts with the query. So, we are moving from the goal to infer the facts that would tell us about it. If the query is true, halt. (Do nothing). But if not, then find the implications that infer the query. If all the premises of these implications can be proved to be true, we infer the query to be true. This method is also called *goal-driven method*. In turn it forms a part of goal-directed reasoning.

Comparing both the approaches, the time required in this is less than the forward one. The only reason behind this is that it goes through only the relevant facts and not others. Which method should be used ideally? It is a combination of both the methods that is used by the agent during the course of inferring.

7.6   PREDICATE LOGIC

We have already studied the propositional logic—one way that helps in knowledge representation and reasoning. In this section, predicate logic is discussed. Predicate logic also known as *first order logic* is said to be more expressive. The reason of studying other form is propositional logic becomes hard and complex, when it comes to representation of the complex environments. Later, in the chapter, a comparison is made between the two logics.

Predicate logic allows to describe the objects involved and their relationships. Consider following example:

All kids are naughty.
Suzy is a kid.
Then, Suzy is naughty.

Expressing the above example in propositional logic is difficult to have valid sentences or clauses. They can be better represented in predicate. Predicate logic is powerful tool that can express and give reasoning and it is built on the top of propositional logic, making the use of ideas.

7.6.1 Representing Facts in Logic: Syntax and Semantics

The predicate logic, as the name suggests, handles the representations in the form of predicate. Any sentence has as a subject and a predicate. For example, consider a sentence—'The car is red'. Here, 'car' is the subject and 'is red' is the predicate. While representing, it would be $R(x)$, where R is red and x is any object. This is a very basic example. We now go into the details of representations. A sentence in predicate logic is built up from constants, predicates and functions. A sentence can be an atomic sentence or sentences connected to each other.

We can represent it in the following way:

Sentence → Atomic sentence |
                 Sentence connective sentence |
                 Quantifier variable_name,........ sentence |
                 ~ sentence

Further, the atomic sentence comprises predicate. The predicate has terms, which could be functions, constants or variables.

Atomic sentence → Predicate (Terms)
For example, Predicate: Blue, Academic, and so on. They express the relationships.

Term → Function(Terms) |
       Constant |
       variable_name

Constants: Mary, A, etc. They are the objects for which we want to talk about.
Variable_name: p, q, r, ..., etc.
Function: It allows to refer to the other objects indirectly. For example, father_of

The connectives and the quantifiers are used in the formulation of the sentence.

Connectives: ⇒, ∧, ∨, ⇔
Quantifiers: ∀, ∃

We need to make a note of the difference between the function and the predicate. As said earlier, a function is indirect reference to the objects. Predicate comprises the functions. It will be more clear in the example explained later. We start with the simple ones.

Simple Sentence

Sita is the mother of Rohan.
Representation: Mother(Sita, Rohan)

Complex Sentence

Reeta's uncle and Rohan's daddy booked a flat.
Representation: Booked (Uncle(Reeta), Daddy(Rohan))

Another example can be Father(Sita) = Ramesh

Connectives

Simple example of use of connectives can be:

Father(Rohan) ∧ Father(Shyam)
~ Dancer(Riya) ⇒ Dancer(Sita)

Quantifiers

There are two types of quantifiers—which are as follows:

1. ∀: Universal quantification (pronounced as 'for all')
2. ∃: Existential quantification (pronounced as 'there exists an x such that' or 'for some x')

Universe of discourse: There is a concept of universe of discourse in predicate logic. It is a set of all the things that we talk about. This is the set of objects that we can assign to a variable in a propositional function. For example, in a wide sense, it can be a set of integer that possibly defines the boundaries.

Universal quantification (∀): Syntax: ∀ x P; where P is a logical expression.

∀ x is called universal quantifier and P is the scope of the quantifier. The x is said to be bound by the scope of the quantifier.

In the example discussed earlier, we had a sentence "All kids are naughty."

It can be represented as follows:

$$\forall \ x \ \text{Kid}(x) \Rightarrow \text{Naughty}(x)$$

This says that for every x, if x is kid, then x is naughty.

Make a note that typically, the statements containing the words 'every', 'each', 'everyone' indicate universal quantifier.

Existential quantification (∃): Syntax: ∃ x P; where P is a logical expression.

This indicates that P is true for at least one value. ('There exists'.)

For example, Some people are kind.

This can be written as

$$\exists \ x \ \text{Kind}(x)$$

This says that there exists some x that is kind.

The statements containing 'some' or 'at least one' indicate existential quantifier.

These quantifiers are treated as unary connectives and have a higher precedence over the binary connectives.

7.6.2 Instance Representation and ISA Relationships

ISA and instance play a very important role in knowledge representation. These two attributes exhibit the property of inheritance. The following sentences help us in understanding these attributes:

Shyam is an engineer.
All engineers are intelligent.

Here, intelligent and engineer are the classes. ISA shows the class inclusion. ISA (engineer, intelligent) indicates that engineer class is contained in the intelligent class. Whereas, instance, as the name suggests, indicates the membership belonging to the class. Instance(Shyam, engineer) indicates the class membership.

7.6.3 Comparison of Predicate and Propositional Logic

After studying the predicate and the propositional logic in detail, let us compare them.

In terms of representation, propositional logic requires a separate unique propositional symbol. So, for representing any particular fact, it takes many symbols. (This one must have noticed in the Wumpus World). Imagine the number of symbols it would take if there were n locations and m people and you need to represent the fact of movement of some person.

Predicate logic is rich in terms of ontology. It includes the facts, relationships and the objects, whereas propositional logic is based on facts. Predicate logic also makes a compact representation available.

With respect to the complex sentences, in the introduction part of predicate logic itself, we have shown that the propositional logic cannot handle them.

7.7 UNIFICATION AND LIFTING: INFERENCE IN FOL

Unification and lifting are concerned with the inference in first order logic (FOL). It introduces the notion of logical inference. In inferring, we need to find out the results. To achieve this, quantifiers are required to be removed. This is possible by use of propositional logic. So, the basic idea is to infer in FOL; the rules of KB are converted to propositional logic and then the propositional inference is used.

We will proceed step-wise starting from the inference rules for quantifiers to the unification algorithm.

Inference Rule for Quantifiers

While inferring from quantifiers, two common rules are used—rule of universal instantiation and rule of existential instantiation.

Rule of universal instantiation (UI):   Assume that the knowledge base contains the axiom—'All students who are kind are intelligent'. This can be represented as follows:

$$\forall x \text{ Student}(x) \wedge \text{Kind}(x) \Rightarrow \text{Intelligent}(x)$$

For this example, if we want to infer for Shyam or Rohan, we would have

$$\text{Student(Shyam)} \wedge \text{Kind(Shyam)} \Rightarrow \text{Intelligent(Shyam)}$$

In the same way, it can be inferred for Rohan. What we are doing here is making the use of substitution. The rule of universal instantiation is used for substitution. The rule states that by substituting a ground term (i.e., a term without variables) for the variable, we can infer any sentence. The rule is as follows:

Let *Subs* (θ, *S*) denote the final outcome after applying the substitution, where θ is the substitution applied to the sentence *S*.

$$\frac{\forall \vee S}{Subs(\{v/t\}, S)}$$

The rule says that for any variable v of S, the substitution occurs with t, where t is ground term. It is because of this rule that we have derived the previous results. So, $Subs\{v/\text{Shyam}\}$ was used.

Rule of existential instantiation (EI): For any sentence S, and variable v, and a constant symbol c (this should not appear anywhere in the knowledge base), the rule is given below:

$$\frac{\exists \vee S}{Subs(\{v/c\}, S)}$$

Again, take a hypothetical KB having the following sentence:

$$\exists x \; \text{Car} \; (x) \wedge \text{Drive} \; (x, \text{Shyam})$$

To infer we can have Car(abc) ∧ Drive(abc,Shyam).

In this sentence, by this rule, it implies that as long as the constant abc does not appear anywhere in the KB, the inference is correct. So, a new name is to be used, this is called *Skolem constant*.

One thing to mention here is that with the application of UI, the new KB is logically equivalent to the old one. UI can be applied several times, but with EI, as it is applied once, new KB is not equivalent, but satisfiable.

Reducing to Propositional Inference

In order to reduce from predicate logic to propositional, we need to have the rules for inferring the non-quantified sentences from the quantified ones. The technique of propositionalisation is discussed here. The substitution methods mentioned in the previous section are to be used. In case of existential quantified sentence, it can be substituted by one instantiation, whereas in case of universal, it is replaced with all possible instantiations. Let us take the following KB:

∀x Student(x) ∧ Kind(x) ⇒ Intelligent(x)
Student (Shyam)
Kind (Shyam)
Friends (Shyam, Rohan)

Now, since we want to have the reduction to take place, after applying the substitution methods, we can have the representation as

Student (Shyam) ∧ Kind (Shyam) ⇒ Intelligent (Shyam)
Student (Rohan) ∧ Kind (Rohan) ⇒ Intelligent (Rohan)

The KB now has just the axioms that can be mapped as propositional symbols. The new KB would contain Student (Shyam), Kind (Shyam), Intelligent (Shyam), Student (Rohan), Kind (Rohan), Intelligent (Rohan).

Problems with propositionalisation: It is obvious to us that propositionalisation creates many irrelevant sentences. Now, we are aware of the substitution of Intelligent (Rohan).

But then is there a need to generate Kind (Rohan) if in the KB it is specified Friends (Shyam, Rohan)?

This inferring generates a lot of facts. If we are having p predicates of k-ary and n is the number of constants, then the outcome of propositionalisation would be $p * n^k$.

7.7.1 Unification

It is the process of finding the substitutions that make different logical sentences look identical, i.e., the process of finding substitutions for predicate parameters. One would think that these inferences are so simple; you look at the sentences and understand. But it is required that the machine understands them, and hence, there is need of process of substitution.

For example, $\forall x$ Student(x) $\wedge$ Kind (x) $\Rightarrow$ Intelligent (x)
Student (Shyam)
Kind (Shyam)

From this, we infer that Shyam is intelligent.

First Order Inference Rule

While inferring that Shyam is intelligent, we have applied the substitution method. First, x is found such that x is student. Then, x has to be kind and after that, we infer that x is intelligent. We have carried out the substitution of $\{x/\text{Shyam}\}$. Assume we do not have the fact of Kind (Shyam), instead we have

$$\forall y \ Kind(y)$$

Will it be possible to conclude that Shyam is intelligent? Naturally, as Shyam is student and that everyone is kind, this inference stands true.

So, we have $\{x/\text{Shyam}\}$ and $\{y/\text{Shyam}\}$.

The identicalness achieved is student(x) and Kind(x) with student(Shyam) and Kind(y). This generalised process is the rule of generalised modus ponens.

The rule states that for the atomic sentences, a_i, a'_i and q, there is a substitution θ such that $Subs(\theta, a'_i) = Subs(\theta, a_i)$ for all i.

$$\frac{a'_1, a'_2, a'_3, ..., a'_n, (a_1 \wedge a_2 \wedge a_3 \ ... \ a_n) \Rightarrow q}{Subs(\theta, q)}$$

a_1 : Student(x)
a_2 : Kind(x)
q : Intelligent(x)
a'_1 : Student(Shyam)
a'_2 : Kind(y)
θ : $\{x/\text{Shyam}\}$ and $\{y/\text{Shyam}\}$
$Subs(\theta, q)$: Intelligent(Shyam)

The generalised modus ponens is a lifted version of modus ponens. It raises the modus ponens from the propositional to FOL. This is called *lifting*.

Unification Algorithm

Now, finally coming to the discussion of unification, how do we determine the substitution of θ? The rules of inference that are lifted need to find substitutions that make different logical sentences look identical. This is called *unification process*.

The algorithm is given below:

The algorithm Unify(a, b) takes two sentences and returns a unifier for them, if there exists one. In short, we now decide the value for θ.

Unify(a,b) = θ, where $Subs(\theta,a) = Subs(\theta,b)$

Let us try to answer the query Friends(Rita,x)—who all are friends of Rita? Assume in the KB, we have the following:

Friends(Rita,Seema)
Friends(x,Maya)
Friends(y,Neha)

Applying the unification, we get:

Unify(Friends(Rita,x),Friends(Rita,Seema)) = $\{x/\text{Seema}\}$ = θ
Unify(Friends(Rita,x),Friends(x,Maya)) = Fail= θ – *
Unify(Friends(Rita,x),Friends(y,Neha)) = $\{x/\text{Neha},y/\text{Rita}\}$ = θ

The case marked as * is failed due to the use of same variable name. That is, x cannot be Rita and Maya at same time. It is required that the names should be different. To achieve this, standardising is done. The variable name is changed, and hence, we could get

Unify(Friends(Rita,x),Friends(z,Maya)) = $\{x/\text{Maya}, z/\text{Rita}\}$ = θ

The algorithm returns substitution to make x and y look identical.
Let us write a generalised algorithm for it.

1. If x and y are variables or constants,
    (i) x and y are identical return NULL
    (ii) Else, if x is variable and x occurs in y, then fail, else return $\{y/x\}$
    (iii) Else, if y is variable and y occurs in x, then fail, else return$\{x/y\}$
    (iv) Else fail
2. If the arguments mismatch, return fail.
3. If the predicates do not match, return fail.
4. Let $Subs = \{\ \}$
5. For ctr =1 to the number of arguments
    (i) Go to step 1 (call again) with ith argument of x and y and add result to Sol.
    (ii) If Sol = fail, return fail.
    (iii) If Sol! =NULL.
        Again apply Sol to the remaining part of x and y.
        Add Sol: $Subs = Sol + Subs$
6. Return $Subs$

Unification plays a very important part when it comes to natural language parsers. It has a strong mathematical concept and is important in the other AI programs as well.

7.8 REPRESENTING KNOWLEDGE USING RULES

This topic essentially covers the use of rules for the representation of knowledge. After discussing the details of propositional and predicate logic, now, the rules for encoding the knowledge are discussed. We have studied about the representation of sentences in logic formats, but the rules that actually shape the knowledge are very crucial. Let us study the representations. This section essentially covers the gist of the earlier part studied in terms of reasoning, i.e., the necessities in rule-based system with KB representation.

7.8.1 Declarative and Procedural Knowledge

The need for the representation of knowledge in terms of rules is finally to get the solution to our problem. In the previous sections, we have looked into the assertions. Here, we take them further to resolve the problem.

Two types of representations exist—declarative and procedural. In case of declarative, knowledge is specified; but extent upto which the knowledge is required to be put up is not specified. The assertions mentioned in the previous section are declarative. In order to use a declarative representation, it needs to be augmented with a program that specifies what is to be done and how it is to be done. The assertions can have resolution theorem applied. These assertions can be viewed as program. While doing so, the implication statements actually define the reasoning. In simple words, we can say that the declarative representation is of facts.

In case of procedural representation, the control information required to make use of the knowledge is embedded in the knowledge. So, here, an interpreter is required that understands the instructions in the knowledge. It can have heuristic too to have the result generated. Let us take the following example of the KB:

Bird(Parrot)
Bird(Sparrow)
Feathers(Pigeon)
$\forall x \text{ Bird}(x) \Rightarrow \text{Feathers}(x)$

Let us say we want to solve a query to find out some y that has feathers.
The query representation will be as follows:

$\exists y : \text{feathers}(y)$

What is the expected answer? It will give us the entire three—sparrow, parrot as well as pigeon. So, it is dependent on the order in which the assertions are actually being written. If some control knowledge is added to make it procedural, the answer that we might get is pigeon. This control knowledge could be the order in which the facts are to be evaluated, say depth first search.

Which representation should be selected? Generally, viewing the knowledge as procedural or declarative is not an essential characteristic for building the KB, but it is the method that permits for knowledge extraction.

7.8.2   Logic Programming

It is a programming language paradigm in which logical assertions are viewed as programs. It comprises facts and rules. The facts are the axioms and the rules determine whether the axioms are sufficient to determine the truth of the goal. We discuss about **programming logic** (Prolog) in brief to understand the paradigm. Prolog comprises Horn clauses. In Prolog, the interpreter has a fixed control strategy. The working of the control strategy is explained below:

1. It begins with the problem statement, mapping it to the final goal to be achieved.
2. Checks for assertions and rules to see if the goal can be proved.
3. For this decision to apply a rule or fact, unification process is also invoked.
4. It uses backward reasoning to get the solution.
5. It may apply depth first strategy and backtracking.
6. When it comes to the choice, consider the order while selecting the next rule or fact.

7.8.3   Forward and Backward Reasoning

In Prolog, the reasoning is backward. But in practice, there are two types of reasoning—forward and backward.

Forward Reasoning

In forward reasoning, the process starts with the starts states. A tree is built considering the different moves or intermediate steps that could be the solutions. At each point of time, the next level is generated with the selection of rule, whose left side matches with the root. The process is from left to right evaluation of a rule. This process is continued till the goal state is achieved.

Backward Reasoning

It is exactly reverse of forward reasoning, where the process starts with the goal. The rules whose right side matches with the root are considered. So, these rules define the next level that would be required for the generation. So, the process is from right to left. Once a rule is applied, its left side is then looked upon and searched in the right side again. This is continued till we reach the initial state.

Is it possible that the same rules are being used in the reasoning process? Yes. But then, which reasoning is to be applied is dependent on the topology of a problem.

In the eight-puzzle problem discussed in earlier chapters, the direction did not matter. But it does matter when

1. There are more goal/start states.
2. If new facts are likely to be evolved, then forward reasoning is better.
3. The branching factor is at the decision node.
4. Finally, the justification required may make the user to use the reasoning he/she thinks.

The two rule systems that now are taken into account are the forward and backward chaining. Prolog and MYCIN are the two systems that are under this category. A system that is directed by goals is *backward chaining*, whereas in case of *forward chaining*, it is data driven. We feel that forward chaining is very simple to process, but the rule application and matching in forward chaining are more complicated.

Is it possible to have a combination of forward and backward reasoning? The answer is yes. As an example based on some facts, if one tries to infer or conclude, especially in diagnostic cases, it is better to apply backward reasoning.

7.8.4 Matching

The question that is addressed here is how can the rules be extracted that are matched in the course of inferring a position with the current state? This needs to perform matching that is to be carried out between the current state and the preconditions of the rules. Different methods of matching are discussed below:

Indexing

A very simple thought that comes to our mind is to simply check every precondition with the current state. Are we performing linear search? Naturally, this is not the option that would be looked at because of the following two reasons—1. As discussed earlier, the large number of rules that would be existing, would end up, thereby making it the most inefficient method. 2. It is not obvious to say that whether the preconditions would be satisfied by any particular state.

The most obvious answer to this problem is the use of indexing. We need to access the appropriate rules and for that, we use index. So, an index is typically used in this case. If we have a chess board, an index is assigned to the board positions. Further, with the use of hashing technique, the key that represents the same position comprises the same rules which give a specific position. So, with the same key, all the required rules can be found. Will this method have any pitfalls? The representation has all the positions and cannot handle its generalisation. Rules can be indexed by the pieces and their positions. Though there is a drawback, indexing is a very important aspect of the matching process.

Matching with Variables

When we say that the rules are being matched, one more problem that can arise is the unmatching of the preconditions with that of the current situation. What should be done under this scenario? So, again a search is to be carried out to check whether there exists a match between the preconditions and the current state.

Generally, the unification algorithm is used to solve this, and is useful too with the single-state description scenario. Forward and backward method too can be employed here. Even unification can be applied again, but it is better to have many-many match. Here, many rules are matched against many elements. Let us discuss about an algorithm for this many-many match—RETE.

The algorithm maintains the network of the rules and it uses state descriptions to determine which rules can be applicable. This is possible, as the rules are not changed randomly and the state descriptions do not change. Structural similarity in the rules is also used. A very simple example of this is has-strips and has-spots. Actually, these predicates are structurally same. The algorithm is also persistent in case of variable binding.

The Rete algorithm is based on facts—rule pattern matching problem. It preserves information about the structure of network with matches.

The network comprises nodes that are individual condition elements. Every node has two sets.

1. Set containing all the working memory elements, where the condition node matches.
2. Combinations of working memory elements along with the bindings that generate consistent match of the conditions.

This setup helps in avoiding repetitive testing of all rules in each cycle. Thus, the nodes impacted during addition of new facts are checked.

For example, we have rule

$$\text{if } P_1(A, 5) \text{ and } P_2(A, C) \text{ then res}(A, C)$$
$$\text{if } P_1(A, 6) \text{ and } P_2(A, C) \text{ then res}(A, C)$$

It begins with the structure, as shown in Figure 7.6.

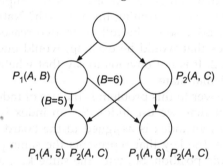

Figure 7.6 Rule pattern matching.

If a new fact $P_1(7, 5)$ is added, then it indicates mismatch in rule, as shown in Figure 7.7, where the data is propagated.

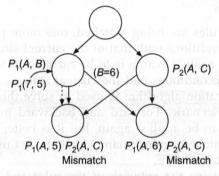

Figure 7.7 Rule propagation.

Thus, Rete algorithm performs efficient matching.

Approximate and Complex Matching

Another aspect of matching is required when the preconditions describe the properties that are not explicitly mentioned in the current state. Here, altogether a new set of rules are required to describe how only some of the properties can be inferred. There could also be a case, where we need to have the preconditions applied approximately. The most common example here is the speech. Mapping this while considering the noise and interference, it will be very difficult to approximate.

In some cases, matching the rules to the problem statement is done. ELIZA—a very old AI program that simulated the behaviour of a Rogerian therapist had used this matching. It matched the left side of rules against the last sentence a user would type. A simple dialog between ELIZA and a woman is given below:

Woman: I need your help.
ELIZA: How can I help you?

Or possibly, it would answer saying 'Tell me more about yourself', if the woman says, 'I am the only child in the family', and so on. One thing that you must have noticed is that there is a pattern matching; the patterns ask about some specific word that has been used by the woman. The entire sentence need not be matched. This approximation makes ELIZA put forth its accountability in an effective manner.

Conflict Resolution

In matching process, the rules need to be matched and it is equally necessary to decide the order in which this is to be carried out. Though it is the search method, which is responsible for matching, the decision can be built in the matching process. This stage of matching is referred to as *conflict resolution*. This preference assignment can be made on the following bases:

1. Rule that is matched
2. Objects that are matched
3. Action that the matched rule performs

7.9   SEMANTIC NETWORKS

We have already mentioned about semantic networks in the introductory section with respect to the knowledge representation. Here, we provide details of the same.

The basic idea behind semantic network is that knowledge is better understood as a set of concepts that are related. In other words, the semantic networks represent the conceptual relationships. A semantic network comprises nodes that are connected to each other by arcs. There are different variants of this network and each of them essentially does the same thing. It is noticed that the boxes or ovals are used to represent the objects or the categories of objects.

Common Semantic Relations

Though there is not a fixed set of relationships to express, we highlight the most common ones that invariably occur in every logic.

1. *Instance:* x is an instance of y, if x is a specific example of the general concept y. For example, Tendulkar is an instance of batsmen.
2. *ISA:* x ISA y if x is a subset of more general concept y. For example, batsman ISA cricketer.
3. *Haspart:* x is haspart of y, if y is part of the concept x. For example, stumps haspart bails.

Considering the same example of mapping the knowledge of some cricket domain, we can draw the semantic network. The semantic network for same is depicted in Figure 7.8.

From Figure 7.8, it is understood that the team and the runs are the values of attributes. Arrows indicate the point from object to its corresponding value. The logic for the above semantic network can be ISA(Batsman, cricketer), instance (Tendulkar, Cricketer), team (Tendulkar, India) and so on.

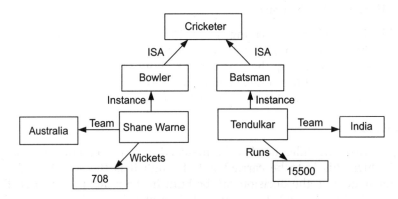

Figure 7.8 Semantic network.

ISA and instance are actually inheritable instances. Now, if we have two predicates, is it possible to map in semantic network? Definitely, we can do so. By creating the corresponding nodes and representing them with their relationships, it is possible to have a semantic network.

Inference in Semantic Network

While inferring in the semantic network, two mechanisms are followed, viz. intersection search and inheritance.

In *intersection search*, the intersection between the nodes is found, and in turn, the relationships too. This is achieved by spreading the activation and making the nodes visited. Whereas, in case of *inheritance*, the ISA and instance allow to implement this process. It provides the means for enabling default reasoning. While making the inferences, it is also required that the difference between the links (which hold values) is clearly mentioned. For example, the runs taken by players Shyam and Ram need to be explicitly differentiated, say by means of greater than link, where we need to compare them.

Figure 7.9 could be transformed into Figure 7.10. The arrow between Runs_1 and Runs_2 is the comparison of the runs.

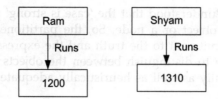

Figure 7.9 Inference with semantic network: Example.

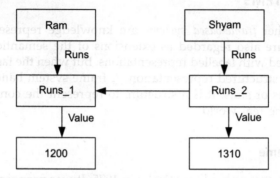

Figure 7.10 Inference with semantic network: Example.

7.9.1 Partitioned Semantic Networks

Partitioned semantic networks are the extension of semantic networks. They overcome the drawbacks of semantic networks or extend their knowledge expression. Most often, in semantic network, there exists vagueness. This occurs while finding the meaning of the tokens. The inference mechanism too is inefficient, and heuristic inadequacy exists as well. Partitioned semantic network forms a more sophisticated logical structure. Here, the network is split into spaces that consist of nodes and arcs and each space is then considered to be a node.

Consider an example, where a lawyer argues that the case is strong (Figure 7.11).

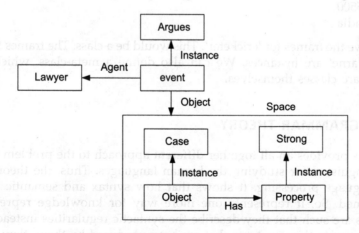

Figure 7.11 Partitioned semantic network.

From Figure 7.11, it is understood that the 'case is strong' is partitioned into a space that in turn, refers to an object or a node. So, the partitioned networks allow for the propositions, without commitment to the truth and the expressions to be quantified.

These networks enable to distinguish between the objects and to control the search space, proving them logically as well as heuristically adequate.

7.10   FRAME SYSTEMS

Frame systems or rather *frame-based systems* are knowledge representation systems that use frames. Frames are also regarded as extensions of the semantic networks. Semantic networks are concerned with labelled representations. But when the task gets more complex, what is required is a structured representation. A frame system handles this. A *frame* is a collection of attributes or slots. It is a structure to represent the concepts that have some associated value in the real world.

7.10.1   Minsky's Frame

The frame structure was proposed by Minsky in 1975. It was proposed that the knowledge should be organised into chunks, called *frames*. These frames capture the essence of the concepts by clustering relevant information. So, a large amount of procedurally expressive knowledge should be a part of the frames. Clubbing and organisation of such frames form the frame system.

Representation of Frames

Each frame has a name and slots (think of the concepts that we have studied in object-oriented programming—OOP). A simple frame is represented below (refer to Figure 7.8):

Tendulkar
    Instance: Batsman
    Runs: 15500
    Team: India

We can have the frames for 'cricketer'. This would be a class. The frames for 'Tendulkar' and 'Shane Warne' are instances. We can also define a meta-class, which contains the elements that are classes themselves.

7.11   CASE GRAMMAR THEORY

Case grammars provides an all together different approach to the problem with regard to the field of linguistics for studying the human languages. Thus, the theory plays a role in natural language processing. It shows that how syntax and semantic interpretations can be combined. So, it represents one more way for knowledge representation. The grammar rules are such that they describe the syntactic regularities instead of semantics, but when it comes to the structures that are been produced by them, they have semantic relations rather than the syntactic ones. We will discuss about this theory in detail in Chapter 12.

7.12 INFERENCE

Inference is a mechanism by which reasoning takes place. They go together and it is very much essential to have an appropriate inferring mechanism so as to carry out reasoning. This section, deals with the different categories of reasoning by which new conclusions are derived.

7.12.1 Deduction, Induction, Abduction

They are the basic types of inferences. We introduce the concept of each of them as follows:

Deduction

Deduction is the process of deriving a conclusion from the given axioms and facts. So, drawing a conclusion based on the available knowledge and observations is deduction. This conclusion can be drawn by applying the modus ponens rule.

A very simple example to explain this can be as follows:

Axiom: All kids are naughty.
Fact/Premise: Riya is a kid.
Conclusion: Riya is naughty.

Inference in deduction is also referred to as *logical inferring*. Deduction is often called *truth preserving* also. Calculus can be used for this inferring.

Induction

Induction is deriving a general rule (axiom) from the background knowledge and observations.
For the same example, we can say that
If we have the knowledge with us that

Riya is a kid.
Riya is naughty.

then we can have the general axiom that

Kids are naughty.

Abduction

A premise is derived from a known axiom and some observations. Consider the same example, but now the information available is different.
Information available:

All kids are naughty.
Riya is naughty.

We can infer that Riya must be kid.

Thus, we get the differences and understand the process of inferring. But which is to be used and at what point of time? Abduction is typically for the diagnostic and expert system, and one must have guessed that deduction is concerned with FOL to get the inferring.

7.13 TYPES OF REASONING

The type of decision-making and reasoning changes as per the application and domain involved. This section highlights some of the reasoning approaches.

7.13.1 Common Sense Reasoning

Common sense reasoning is concerned with the way we think. This is essential when we are representing the KB. Do the machines have common sense? We need to embed it. While doing so, we need to formalise the reasoning. This is possible with the use of formal logic. In humans, we relate common sense with the ability of taking good judgement. But in case of AI, this is the technical sense with the facts and understandings. This reasoning is required especially in natural language processing. Various tools are available for the common sense knowledge base like ConceptNet that is an extended version of WordNet.

7.13.2 Hypothetical Reasoning

In hypothetical reasoning, different assumptions are looked at to see what can be followed or inferred from them. It can be termed as the reasoning about different worlds. When and where is the requirement of this type of reasoning? It is applied for diagnostic system, where we can assume some hypothesis and then make predictions followed by their verification. A method of hypothetical-deductive reasoning is applied in this case.

The steps involved in the hypothetic reasoning are as follows:

1. Evaluate each of the hypothesis.
2. Hypothesis is selected and tested from which predictions are generated.
3. Using experimentation, predictions are validated for correctness. If these are correct, then the hypothesis is accurate, else the hypothesis is not valid.

7.13.3 Analogical Reasoning

It is the process of reasoning from one particular object to another. Conclusions are derived from experience or similarity-based situations or conditions. For example, P is like Q. If P contains A and B is in Q, then we can infer that A is like Q. While reasoning, we find out the analogy in the given data. This is like finding the 'like' thing. In order to use the analogy

1. One starts with a target, where a new understanding is to be created.
2. Matching domain is found and further, the matching terms as well.
3. Ahead of it, related terms are found and then attributes are transferred from matching to target.

SUMMARY

The chapter highlights the need for proper knowledge representation and reasoning. Representation of the knowledge should be such that the inference is efficient. With the different ways of representing knowledge, logic administers the overall mechanism. To have a sound inference, accurate and precise logic is a must. Propositional logic and first order logic are used in the knowledge formulation. Semantic networks help in understanding the relationships and prove to be beneficial in understanding the hierarchy structure. Further, the methods of unification and lifting make the inferring simpler. The partitioned semantic networks and the frames further help in getting the knowledge representations better. Still with the known facts, it is definitely not a complicated task to handle, but with limited and uncertain knowledge, they need to be handled in a different way. The next chapter deals with the same.

 KEYWORDS

1. **Knowledge:** It is the information that helps in taking decisions or solving problems at hand.

2. **Knowledge base:** Knowledge is stored in a structure called knowledge base, which is often referred to as KB. A KB is formed with the available facts and updated in the process of acquiring more knowledge that is used by an agent.

3. **Relational knowledge structure:** It is a knowledge structure where the facts can be mapped into the relations and stored in the database.

4. **Inheritable knowledge structure:** It is a structure that enables inheritance of the properties to improve the inference.

5. **Slot-filler structure:** It is a structure that belongs to the category of inheritable structure and allows easy accessibility and retrieval of the required information.

6. **Inferential knowledge structure:** It is a knowledge structure that makes use of logic in representation and maps the inferred facts.

7. **Procedural knowledge structure:** Procedures with the knowledge embedded in them form this type of structure.

8. **Knowledge based agent:** It is an agent whose actions are not arbitrary but are based on some valid knowledge. KB is used by the agent.

9. **Horn clause:** It is a clause that is disjunction of literals of which at most one positive literal exists.

10. **Unification:** It is the process of finding the substitutions that make different logical sentences look identical.

11. **Partitioned semantic network:** It is the extension of semantic networks, where the network is split into spaces that consist of nodes and arcs and each space is then considered to be a node.

12. **Frames:** It is also the extension of the semantic networks. It is a structure to represent the concepts that have some associated value with regard to the real world.

13. **Minsky's frames:** Early frame structure was proposed by Minsky. These frames capture the essence of the concepts by clustering some relevant information.

14. **Deduction:** It is the process of deriving a conclusion from the given axioms and facts.

15. **Induction:** It includes deriving a general rule (axiom) from the background knowledge and observations.

16. **Abduction:** In abduction, a premise is derived from a known axiom and some observations.

MULTIPLE CHOICE QUESTIONS

1. Given a fact and an axiom/premise, the reasoning falls under
   (a) Induction   (b) Deduction   (c) Abduction   (d) None of these

2. A procedure approach that produces proof by contradiction is
   (a) Abduction   (b) Refutation
   (c) Logic programming   (d) None of these

3. Which of the following is involved between the mapping of initial facts to the final facts?
   (a) Forward chaining   (b) Forward representations
   (c) Reasoning   (d) Both (b) and (d)

4. The basic difference between the normal on simple agents and the knowledge-based agents is
   (a) Knowledge-based agents can capture the entire percept, whereas the simple cannot.
   (b) Knowledge-based agents are suited for some specific tasks.
   (c) Simple agents can take arbitrary actions, whereas knowledge base do not.
   (d) All of the above

5. For a query like 'Where is my mobile?' to be resolved, which approach is appropriate?
   (a) Forward chaining   (b) Forward checking
   (c) Modus ponens   (d) Backward chaining

6. Consider the following statements:
   $S(x)$: x is a primary school student.
   $I(x)$: x likes to play games on i-pad.
   Every primary student likes to play games on i-pad' can be mapped as (where universe of discourse is a set of students)
   (a) $\forall x(S(x) \rightarrow I(x))$ (b) $\exists x(S(x) \rightarrow I(x))$
   (c) $\forall x(I(x) \rightarrow S(x))$ (d) $\exists x(S(x) \vee I(x))$

7. Which of the following clearly defines a frame system?
   (a) An inference system
   (b) A system that maps the facts and beliefs
   (c) A form of knowledge representation
   (d) A system with a set of facts and their instances

8. Which of the following best justifies the knowledge?
   (a) It is a known information   (b) It is a set of reasoning system
   (c) It is used for inferring   (d) It is a set of assumptions

CONCEPT REVIEW QUESTIONS

1. What is a knowledge base?
2. Are inferring and reasoning same? Discuss.
3. What are the different representations of the knowledge base?
4. Explain and discuss semantic networks, partitioned semantic networks and frames.
5. Write the following using first order logic
   (i) Some intelligent students study intelligent systems.
   (ii) Every student who opts for intelligent systems is a determined student.
   (iii) There is at least one student of intelligent systems, who does not like the AI assignments.

CRITICAL THINKING EXERCISE

1. For the following example, write the KB in propositional logic. Explain how the inference would occur.
   Ram is an IT professional.
   IT professionals are hardworking.
   All hardworking people are wealthy.
   All wealthy people pay heavy income tax.

PROJECT WORK

1. Develop a program to determine the state of wumpus, with the initial states and the knowledge discussed in Figure 7.4. Which type of KB representation will you use and why?
2. Using semantic network, represent different players in Indian Cricket team and their properties. Write a query to determine most prolific batsman on Australian soil using this semantic network.

CHAPTER 8

Uncertain Knowledge and Reasoning

Learning Objectives

❑ To understand the reasoning process
❑ To understand the importance of probability theory with uncertain knowledge
❑ To appreciate the role of probability with reasoning
❑ To understand the perception and its value in reasoning process
❑ To appreciate and gain knowledge of making decisions with practical applications where uncertainty exists

INTRODUCTION

Let us begin our discussion on uncertainty with a simple example. Consider a scenario where you need to go to college for a particular lecture that is scheduled at 5 p.m. Let us assume that you have to leave your place x minutes before the lecture. You have a question—will these x minutes help you reach on time? So, you are uncertain about it. You have problems like the information availability could be partial with respect to the road conditions, and you are uncertain about the traffic. Things get more complicated if it starts raining. In addition, your parents do not allow you to take the vehicle. So, the information you have from the environment is uncertain. But still you tend to rely on this incomplete information for the decisions that you need to take. Now, when it comes to decision-making, we need to deal with this uncertain knowledge efficiently and at the same time, we need to reason rationally about this information. However, the uncertainty in knowledge also introduces uncertainty in the reasoning process. To get maximum benefit from this knowledge, it is essential to represent it in a proper way so as to use it in decision-making.

The basic question that comes to our mind is how to represent or describe the knowledge. While taking decisions in our daily life, we take decision on the basis of our ability and the available uncertain knowledge or known facts. In case of a machine, we embed the intelligence. The decision-making capability of a machine is based on the intelligence, which requires sound reasoning and concise representation of the knowledge. This aids in inferring the machine to act on the environment. For this, it is necessary that the machine has a good reasoning capability and the representation of the knowledge should be such that the machine is able to deduce the inference and act with respect to the environment.

Speaking about the reasoning process in broader terms, it is an act to come to a conclusion from the premises using some methodology. In every knowledge acquisition and reasoning system, the focus lies on logic. Here, logic is the selection of particular actions or rules so as to reach the destination. Thus, we can relate reasoning to be one approach for problem solving. In the logic-building process, where there is uncertainty, it is equally essential to consider actions, where the risks involved are less. The ability to reason governs the intelligence and with uncertain knowledge, it is more complex. Let us get familiar with the terminologies and details in this uncertain environment.

8.1   UNCERTAINTY AND METHODS

We can always say that uncertainty is a fundamental feature of the real world. In order to deal with it intelligently, it is important to apply logic and take appropriate actions. Various factors result into uncertainty. It could be due to omitted data, unavailability of the entire data, and partial availability of events and so on. This uncertainty is handled using the realm of probability theory.

Uncertainty is handled by using various ways. The simplest one is the default or the monotonic logic. Relating to the example discussed in introduction, you would assume about traffic and road conditions, as well as vehicle availability to take decisions. But the assumptions are actually not reasonable. We need to handle the contradictions that arise. We can have a certainty factor that calculates the measure of belief and disbelief. Belief can be represented using probability, and hence, we can apply probability theory. We will describe the parameters and the key features involved in uncertainty before going into its details.

Dempster–Shafer theory is the one that allows for proper distinction between reasoning and decision theory. It uses the concept of belief and plausibility. Belief is referred to as all available evidences, whereas plausibility is all evidences compatible, but not consistent with the hypothesis.

Fuzzy logic and the probability theory are also the methods for representation of uncertainty. The basic idea behind fuzzy logic is that a truth value may be applied partially. Fuzzy logic uses possibilities and assigns a value between 0 and 1 to determine the degree to which it applies. A document containing information about human body definitely belongs to the class of science. But a document that has information about human body, and say the geographical area around is said to partially belong to the class of science. So, with fuzzy logic, we define degree of belongingness over here.

Probability theory assigns a probable value when you have uncertain information. Conditional probabilities capture and represent uncertainties, which involve complex relationships. Here we try to infer on the basis of Bayesian inference. Instead of rules, the relationships among variables are represented. Considering the computation and representation power, Bayesian probability is used for handling uncertainty.

8.2 BAYESIAN PROBABILITY AND BELIEF NETWORK

Probability can be interpreted from two views—subjective and objective. In objective view, it represents the physical probability of the system, whereas in case of subjective, it estimates the probability from the past experience. Hence, it calculates the degree of belief. This belief can change under new evidence. This subjective probability is called *Bayesian probability*. So, we can say that Bayesian probability is the process of using probability for predicting the likelihood of certain events occurring in the future. Since the beliefs are subjective, all the probabilities occurring in the Bayesian probability are conditional.

Bayesian probability is used in many cases. Consider a simple example, where you want to predict whether X person is likely to be selected in the cricket team. In this case, things would be dependent on number of matches he/she has played, whether he/she is an all-rounder or batsman and so on. Using Bayesian probability, we are in the position to model these relationships and infer. Under uncertain scenario, Bayesian probability has a very deep impact in the decision-making. Bayesian probability is viewed as an extension of logic that enables reasoning with uncertain statements.

Let us proceed with the discussion on the basic concepts of probability and the terminologies.

Propositions and Hypothesis

Let us understand what a proposition is. We are already familiar with the propositional logic. Propositions are typically the sentences which are either true or false but not both. Here, in probability, the notion is explained as follows:

The crucial element, here, is the random variable. A *random variable* can be an item whose status is unknown. Every random variable has a domain that determines the values it can take. The domain can fall under any of the categories like Boolean, discrete or continuous. As an example, let out be a variable, which can take value <true, false> for the statement—Is the batsman out?

Hypothesis refers to proposed explanation for an observed phenomenon. It is also referred to as *educated guess*. Typically, it is expressed in the form of if-then. For example, a hypothesis could be 'If a prisoner learns some skilled work while in prison, then he is less likely to commit crime after release'. This is typically called *testing hypothesis*. Similarly, we can have another tested hypothesis like 'A good teacher can increase the student's satisfaction'. Now, in any statement like 'If *A* occurs then *B*', *A* is called the *antecedent* and *B* is the *consequent*. *A* is also referred to as *hypothesis*.

Probability

Probability can be defined as the likelihood of some event occurring. Its value lies between 0 and 1, where 1 indicates a common event and a rare event would be close to 0. Event are said to be one or more outcomes.

There are different types of probability, which are as follows:

1. Classical probability: It can be termed as the priori theory. In the sense for an event *A*, the probability of occurence of *A* is given as follows:

Probability = Number of favourable outcomes resulting in event *A*/Total number of possible outcomes

2. *Joint probability:* It is the probability of all events occurring together. For events A and B, it can be written as $P(A, B)$.

3. *Marginal probability:* It is an unconditional probability of an event A, irrespective of the occurrence of event B. It is calculated by adding joint probabilities of A over all occurrences of event B. This gives the marginal probability of event A.

4. *Prior probability:* Prior probability or unconditional probability corresponds to belief without any observed data or before the availability of the evidence.

5. *Conditional probability:* It is the probability of some event A, given occurrence of some other event B. It is expressed as $P(A \mid B)$ and mathematically, it can be written as

$$P(A \mid B) = P(A, B)/P(B)$$

In formal definition, we say that the conditional probability of an event A is the probability that the event will occur, given the knowledge that an event B has already occurred. This is written as

$$P(A \mid B): \text{probability of } A \text{ given } B$$

In case, the events are independent, the conditional probability of A given B is simply the probability of A, i.e., $P(A)$.

But if they are not independent, then we define it as the probability of intersection of both the events. This is given as

$$P(A \text{ and } B) = P(B)P(A \mid B)$$

Now, the conditional probability is defined as follows:

$$P(A \mid B) = \frac{P(A \text{ and } B)}{P(B)}$$

6. *Posterior probability:* It is the conditional probability of an event after considering the relevant evidence.

Considering the example given in the previous section, a prior probability can be $P(\text{out})$ = true = 0.3. This is valid and used when no other information is available like 'batsman was injured or was batting against the best bowler in the world'. Whereas in conditional probability, the posterior probability can be $P(\text{out/injured})$. So, it is the probability of batsman getting out, given he/she is injured on previous ball.

Product Rule

We know that the conditional probability is written as $P(A \mid B) = P(A, B)/P(B)$. The equation can be rewritten as

$$P(A, B) = P(A \mid B)P(B) \qquad (8.1)$$

This is called *product rule*. Similarly, the equation for conditional probability for $P(B \mid A)$ will be

$$P(B \mid A) = P(A, B)/P(A) \qquad (8.2)$$

Applying the product rule to Eq. (8.1) and Eq. (8.2), we get

$$P(A \mid B) = P(B \mid A)P(A)/P(B) \tag{8.3}$$

This is called *Bayes' theorem*. It is used to infer the probability of hypothesis under observed data or evidence. This is termed as *Bayesian inference*. Let us detail it in the next section.

8.2.1 Bayesian Inference

Bayesian inference is a statistical method to infer for an unknown situation. It involves collecting the evidences that are consistent or inconsistent with a hypothesis. As more and more evidences are gathered, the degree of belief in a hypothesis changes like normal reasoning. With enough evidences, the hypothesis can become true or false. Equation (8.3) can be rewritten as follows:

$$P(H \mid E) = P(E \mid H)P(H)/P(E) \tag{8.4}$$

where E is evidence and H is hypothesis.

Here, $P(H)$ is the prior probability. $P(E)$ is the marginal probability and $P(H \mid E)$ is the conditional probability. It can also be mapped to a cause and effect problem or even to a diagnostic one.

To make it clearer, let us take an example. Let e be the proposition that 'X person has elbow pain'. Let t be the proposition that 'X has tennis elbow'. So, if we want to derive at a diagnosis, we will have the mapping as follows:

P(person having elbow pain) = $P(e)$
P(person having tennis elbow) = $P(t)$
P(person is having tennis elbow who has elbow pain) = $P(t \mid e)$ (to be found out)
P(person is having pain in elbow given that he is having tennis elbow) = $P(e \mid t)$
So, it would be

$$P(t \mid e) = P(e \mid t)P(t)/P(e)$$

So, in Bayesian inference, it uses the initial belief on the hypothesis and estimates the degree of belief as the evidences become available.

8.2.2 Belief Network

A *belief network* or a *Bayesian network* is a probabilistic graphical model that represents a set of random variables and their conditional dependencies through a directed acyclic graph (DAG). In the graph, the nodes represent random variables and the directed edges represent the conditional dependencies among the variables. The dependent node of a node is called *child node*, whereas the one on which it is dependent is the *parent node*. The directed edge points to the child node to represent the dependency. The Parent node is called *cause* and the child node is called *effect*. The nodes that are not connected are independent of each other. Every node is associated with the probability function. It takes values of the parent function and gives the probability of the variable that it represents.

A Bayesian network essentially provides the entire description of a domain. The network is seen as joint probability distribution. Each entry in this probability distribution is represented by the product of the appropriate elements of conditional probability table (CPT).

Consider a hypothetical example to understand the concept. We need to understand the probability of selection of Ram or Shyam with regard to coach. Figure 8.1 represents this in Bayesian network.

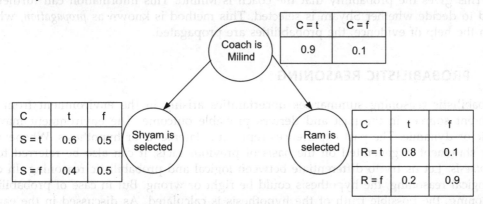

	C = t	C = f
	0.9	0.1

Coach is Milind

C	t	f
S = t	0.6	0.5
S = f	0.4	0.5

Shyam is selected

Ram is selected

C	t	f
R = t	0.8	0.1
R = f	0.2	0.9

Figure 8.1 Bayesian network.

The node 'Coach is Milind' does not have any parent node. Its value represents the prior probability. This value can be taken from the past data. Here, C = coach, S = Shyam selected, R = Ram selected. Now, we can use this example to draw the inference. In what way can Bayesian be used in this case? Let us understand.

Suppose we want to compute the probability of Ram being selected in the team, then it is computed as follows:

Let $P(C)$ = Probability that the coach is Milind

$P(no\ C)$ = Probability that the coach is not Milind

$$P(R) = P(R\,|\,C)*P(C) + P(R\,|\,no\ C)*P(no\ C)$$

$$= (0.8 * 0.9) + (0.1 * 0.1)$$

$$= 0.73$$

Similarly, we can compute the probability that Shyam is selected as follows:

$$P(S) = P(S\,|\,C)*P(C) + P(S\,|\,no\ C)*P(no\ C)$$

$$= (0.6 * 0.9) + (0.5 * 0.1)$$

$$= 0.59$$

These computations are the computations of marginal probabilities. Now, let us apply the Bayes's theorem. Suppose we know that Shyam is selected, but do not know that the coach is Milind, then the computation of the values will be based on the known evidence. Thus, it will be

$$P(C|R) = \frac{P(R|C)*P(C)}{P(R)}$$

$$= \frac{0.8 * 0.9}{0.73}$$

$$= 0.98$$

This gives the probability that the coach is Milind. This information can further be used to decide whether Shyam is selected. This method is known as *propagation*, where with the help of evidence, the probabilities are propagated.

8.3   PROBABILISTIC REASONING

Probabilistic reasoning summarises uncertainties arising in the environment from the different sources in the past and derives probable outcome. The environment may be static or dynamic. The past experiences represent statements or hypothesis. Whenever a new statement is generated on the basis of previous facts, it can also be referred to as *hypothesis*. Let us try to differentiate between logical and probabilistic reasoning. In case of logical reasoning, the hypothesis could be right or wrong. But in case of probabilistic reasoning, the possible truth of the hypothesis is calculated. As discussed in the earlier section, Bayesian inference falls under the probabilistic reasoning, or in other words Bayesian reasoning is also referred to as probabilistic reasoning, where the probability of hypothesis is modified by further data.

We have already discussed about Bayes's theorem. It is given by Eq. (8.4).

$$P(H|E) = P(E|H)P(H)/P(E)$$

where, H is hypothesis and E is evidence. H and E are the multivariate variables. Each atomic variable defines/stands for the properties or attributes in the environment. So, remember that the value of the variable remains fixed during reasoning. The prior probabilities are simplified with the use of Bayesian network. One of the biggest advantages of Bayesian network is the simplicity in calculation of the probabilities with the representation of the large variables.

So, we can always say that the Bayesian network is an important step in inferring for future. But it has some drawbacks. It is feasible in small and medium-sized network. With large and complex network, the number of variables and the relationships are increased, and on the top of it, the CPT calculations exist for each node. So, it is very essential to have these calculations through machine learning algorithms that can automate the process. (Machine learning is discussed in further chapters.) Let us brief about the various algorithms.

In connection with belief networks (BN), it involves two tasks–learning the parameters and learning the structure. In structure learning, the relationships among variables are identified from historical data on the basis of their conditional independence, with the underlying concept to maximise the posterior probability. An exhaustive search process is required to find out the possible relationship that is exponential in the number of variables. In case of parameter learning, the CPT associated with the variable are computed. In case of discrete values, probability values are used, whereas in case of continuous-valued attributes, Gaussian distributions are used as probability values.

Once the BN is built, we can infer. Since the computation is very complex with BN, there are different approaches that are used for inferring, viz. top-down and bottom-up. In top-down, effects are predicted with prior knowledge of causes, whereas in bottom-up, it is from evidence to cause. The most common algorithm that is used here is bucket elimination, where the elimination of unobserved query variables takes place by the calculation of inference equation and its elimination. Markov chain simulation—Markov Chain Monte Carlo (MCMC) algorithm uses random sampling in generation of next states to infer.

This is all about reasoning in static environment that gives us an overview of some of the approaches. But what will happen when the environment changes? Let us take an example that a person is coming late to work and there is traffic jam. Mapping it to our previous hypothesis and evidence, *H* will be 'There is traffic jam' and *E* will be 'A person is coming late to work'. The final outcome required is the prediction of 'coming late' when traffic jam exists. Here, it is assumed that the values of evidence and hypothesis are not changing. But what will happen in a dynamic scenario? This is discussed in the next section.

8.4 PROBABILISTIC REASONING OVER TIME

When we talk about agents, we cannot imagine their operation in a static environment. Consider a robot, where states of robot are its different positions at different time. When a robot is moving in a room, its next state is dependent on the previous one and its surroundings (environment) at that time. In case of reasoning for robots, it is very much essential to know the random variables at each time slice, say *t*. A dynamic environment can be imagined as a collection of small fragments taken at regular interval of time from a larger one. So, at every interval, it has a set of random variables, some of which are observed and some are not. The length of the time slice or the interval is dependent on the problem, and is discrete in nature. Mapping it symbolically, we can say X_t represents the set of unobserved variables at time *t* and E_t represents the set of observable evidence variables.

An observation at time *t* is E_t, which has some values e_t. Relating this to the example of traffic, E_t contains an evidence that the person is late and X_t contains whether there is a traffic jam. Further, we can say that X_1, X_2, X_3 are the unobserved state variables and E_1, E_2, E_3 are the evidence variables representing the case of whether the person is late or not at the different time slices. Once we have the variables defined, it is important to model the environment. We can represent the relationship graphically following the causal order. So, as cause precedes the effect, the variables can be placed in the causal order for each time slice, as it is done in BN. Hence, in dynamic environment, dynamic BN is used, where the nodes are random variables over the time *t*. Since each time slice has its own state and evidence, the relationships are more unbound and complex. Further, every variable in every time slice has its own CPT, so large CPTs could be created, where there might exist a large number of parents as well. In order to limit the CPT, it is assumed that the law which governs the process of change in environment does not change.

Markov Assumption

Let us first try to understand and resolve the problem of unbounded number of parents. Parents of every node are limited to a finite number by the Markov assumption. Markov assumption states that any state depends on the finite history of states. Processes satisfying this assumption were studied in depth by A. A. Markov and are called *Markov process* or *Markov chains*. Simplest of all is the first order Markov process. In this case the current state depends only on the previous state.

So, the state that is evolved later is contained in conditional probability distribution $P(X_t | X_{t-1})$.

This is also referred to as *transition model* for the first order process. Hence, the corresponding conditional independence assertions states that

$$P(X_t | X_{0:t-1}) = P(X_t | X_{t-1}) \tag{8.5}$$

The BN structure for first order Markov process is depicted in Figure 8.2. To add further, we also assume that the evidence E_t depends only on the current state. So, we have

$$P(E_t | X_{0:t}, E_{0:t-1}) = P(E_t | X_t) \tag{8.6}$$

This conditional distribution $P(E_t | X_t)$ is referred to as *sensor model*.

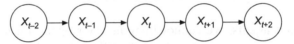

Figure 8.2   First order Markov process.

Further, the second order Markov process states that the current state depends on the previous two states. Its equivalent probability distribution is $P(X_t | X_{t-2} X_{t-1})$ and its representation is depicted in Figure 8.3.

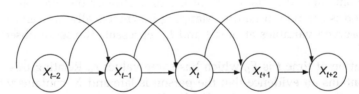

Figure 8.3   Second order Markov process.

Accordingly, for the example we have discussed, the conditional distributions are shown in Figure 8.4. $P(\text{traffic}_t | \text{traffic}_{t-1})$ represents the transition model and the sensor model is $P(\text{Late}_t | \text{traffic}_t)$. The arrows indicate the dependencies.

To summarise, the joint distribution over all the variables at any time t is given as

$$P(X_0, X_1, ..., X_t, E_0, E_1, ..., E_t) = P(X_0) \Pi_{i=1}^{t} P(X_i, X_{i-1}) P(E_i | X_i) \tag{8.7}$$

Here, $P(X_0)$ is the prior probability of state at time $t = 0$. The independent assumptions correspond to a Bayesian structure. But the selection of the Markov process is dependent on the problem. If the prediction is not accurate, the order can be changed.

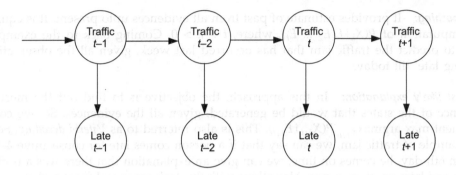

Figure 8.4 Dynamic Bayesian network.

Models

In the dynamic environment, the network model and the inference are carried out using three different models—*hidden Markov model (HMM)*, *Kalman filter* and *dynamic Bayesian network* (DBN). We have already discussed about DBN. Let us proceed with hidden Markov model. In many cases, all the variables in the problem domain are not visible or observable. In such cases, instead of DBN, HMM is used. HMM describes the temporal probabilistic model, where the state of the process is described by a single discrete structure. The example mentioned in introduction can be considered as HMM due to the presence of single-state variable that is traffic.

Kalman Filter assumes that the values of the random variable are continuous and its associated probability distribution is Gaussian. To explain it, we consider an environment, where in crowd, a familiar face is seen by you. You scratch your head to recollect where you had met that person earlier or whether you know him. You still try further to locate that face in the crowd so that you do not lose the track and are able to infer. This problem is an inference, where a noisy model exists.

Inferring

In the dynamic environment, the basic inferring tasks are described here. The computation model is selected based on the inferring required by the application.

1. Filtering: It is also referred to as *monitoring*. It is the task of computing the posterior probability of the current state or the current belief state. So, we compute $P(X_t \mid E_1E_2 \dots E_t)$. We take into consideration that evidence arrives in a stream starting at $t = 1$. The reason behind the name filtering is that the noise in the past data can be eliminated by computing the current belief state. At the same time, it is also called monitoring because in some cases, the state variables can be updated over a period of time. In the example of traffic jam mentioned in introduction, 'coming late' is monitored over a period of time. So, we are computing the probability of traffic jam.

2. Prediction: Inference is drawn here to predict the future. So, we compute the posterior probability, given all evidences for the future state. $P(X_{t+k} \mid E_1E_2 \dots E_t)$. We calculate it till some value of $k \mid k > 0$ is obtained. With respect to the example, we predict the probability of traffic jam, given some observation about 'coming late'.

3. *Smoothing:* It provides estimate of past from all evidences upto present. It is equivalent to computation of $P(X_k | E_1 E_2 \ldots E_t)$, where, $t > k > 0$. Coming back to the example, we want to predict the traffic jam that has occurred last week, given all the observations of 'coming late' till today.

4. *Most likely explanation:* In this approach, the objective is to find out the most likely sequence of the states that would be generated, given all the evidences. So, we compute argument-max $\text{argmax}_{X_{1:t}} P(X_{1:t} | E_{1:t})$. This is also referred to as *Viterbi decoding*. So, with the example of traffic jam, we can say that if a person comes late for consecutive 4–5 days and on 6th day, he comes on time, we can give an explanation that there was a traffic jam earlier and later on, there is not. Algorithms with this task are useful for speech recognition, where the most likely sequence of works can be found.

So, learning is a major task to generate any model for the problems in the dynamic environment. The goal of learning is to learn parameters along with the probability distribution. Here, the expectation maximisation (EM) method is most commonly used. In this method of learning, inferences are drawn on set of parameters to perform fixed interval smoothing, and further, these estimates are used to update the model. The updated model provides new estimates and the process of iteration continues till convergence, in the sense, till posterior probability reaches maxima. Hence, learning depends on estimation. Learning in DBN is to learn for intra-slice relationship, which is a DAG as well as inter-slice. Each node in time slice t has a parent in time slice $t-1$. As discussed earlier, we are assuming that the variables are same over all time slices. So, the problem reduces to feature selection from the set of variables as the transition occurs over time slices. When all the variables are observed, we can use the standard feature selection algorithms like forward and backward step-wise selection, and leaps and bound. In case, when the information is partially av. lable, EM is used to learn the structure of the model.

8.5   FORWARD AND BACKWARD REASONING

Consider any reasoning system. It typically constitutes of a rule base and an engine to search the rule base for appropriate rules under some available facts. We have already discussed about it in the previous chapter. The question here is how to apply it in case of uncertainty.

For many problems, it is just not possible to list out all the possible options in advance and let the system select the correct one. While discussing about uncertainty with forward and backward reasoning, make a note that the terms backward chaining/backward reasoning and forward reasoning/forward chaining are used.

Forward chaining, as the name suggests, starts searching a solution path from the initial state to the goal state. It matches with the rules and performs action. In this process, it might generate some conclusions that are not applicable. Generally, under uncertainty, if we require multiple options, then this type of reasoning is used. This reasoning has proved to be efficient when the available facts are less. Suppose we have some set of rules $A \rightarrow D$, $(C, D) \rightarrow F$, $(F, B) \rightarrow Z$ for the facts A, B, C. With forward chaining, we get the search tree as depicted in Figure 8.5. The search tree generated is an OR tree.

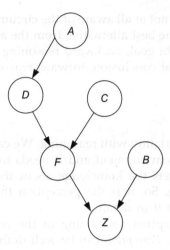

Figure 8.5 Forward chaining.

Backward chaining is goal-driven. It is the process of searching for solution path connecting goal. States are the combinations of the required conclusions or goals, whereas the transitions are defined by rules. Each rule is said to be the method of generating conclusions from the required conclusions. In this case, the inference starts with the goal state, with searching action rules to establish the sub-goals. Here, the node branches in different ways. Any rule that satisfies goal represents an alternative branch. Since more than one condition is represented, it might generate (again uncertainty) multiple sub-goals. Here, the branches from any node are divided into groups of AND branches. Again, each group is an alternative branch or an OR node. Hence, backward chaining represents AND/OR tree. For the same example, given in the case of forward chaining, the tree is shown in Figure 8.6.

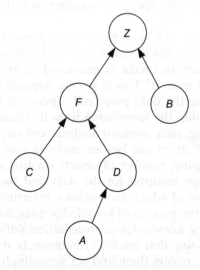

Figure 8.6 Backward chaining.

Under uncertainty, we are not at all aware of the circumstances, and things can change dynamically, yet selection of the best alternative from the available knowledge is the most efficient method. With a known goal, backward reasoning is efficient, but when it comes to number of ways to derive at conclusion, forward reasoning is useful.

8.6   PERCEPTION

We have discussed about uncertainty with reasoning. We can say that an agent's operation is governed by the uncertain environment and it needs to act upon dynamically. But to act so, it is required that it gets the knowledge about the surroundings. This is where perception comes into picture. So, it is the perception that is responsible to make this available. Let us discuss about it in detail.

Reasoning, learning, perception and acting in the complex environment form the basis for intelligent behaviour. *Perception* can be well defined as the ability to sense and interpret. Hence, it deals with the simulation of intelligent behaviour of the system. In real world, in order to automate the control of machines, it is necessary that the machine acts on the situations dynamically depending on the environment. So, real-time control is the biggest challenge of controlling systems. Hence, under this scenario, real-time decisions play a very critical role in running the automation system. The system takes decision under uncertainty as the environment changes and applies reasoning prior to the action. In case of machine, perception is the ability to sense the images, sounds and interpret their sources and properties.

Let us take an example of robot. It is an agent that operates in the environment dynamically. While moving from one place to another, it uses its vision to locate the obstacles and accordingly decides its path. Here, different sensors like the camera, microphone and so on collect the information about the obstacles. So, in turn, we are moving towards vision and speech recognition. We can now define vision or say *computer vision* as the ability to analyse visual input, whereas with speech recognition, it is the analysis of voices, speeches and interpreting them to act upon.

To begin with vision, there is a need for accurate perception systems to open broader areas of computer applications. Since, vision is all about image, let us have an idea about how things work here. When an image is generated in any state, a question comes to our mind—what is required from it? This is wholly dependent on the type of application for which one wants to have the data perceived. There are fundamental operations that one would categorise to exploit the knowledge from it. These are classification or pattern recognition, signal processing, measurement analysis and object location. Even though the problems like object identification can be decomposed into pattern matching, there are still issues like 2D–3D mapping, number of objects existing and so on. Ambiguity in the image, amount of knowledge required for the data and the presence of noise add up to more problems. Extraction of edges and regions, inferring 3D orientations along with image texture help in the entire process of knowledge gain. Still to conclude, any approach for vision is governed by the knowledge representation with respect to the application.

To summarise, we can say that *machine perception* is the ability of the machine to read input from the sensors, reason them and act accordingly. Machine interacts with the dynamic environment. It is very likely that partial information is collected, and hence, the probability theory is the best suited approach for reasoning in machine perception. As discussed in the previous sections, we can have DBN and other models used for the same. Chapter 16 discusses these concepts in elaborated form.

8.7 MAKING SIMPLE DECISIONS

Decision-making is an intelligent process of selecting an action from a set of alternatives. In this process, uncertainty about the alternatives is minimised to make a final choice. The process does not eliminate the uncertainty, but makes a decision that allows to select alternative with the highest probability from several possible alternatives.

We can always say that probabilistic reasoning is the core of the decision-making. It can handle uncertainty in the real world by means of probabilistic distribution. With Bayesian, it is quiet straightforward to calculate the probability value of any variable attached in the problem space. But a decision-maker combines the preferences that are expressed by utilities along with the probabilities to make decisions.

We begin with some basic concepts about utility and then proceed to the decisions. Utility theory has preferences. In case of our previous example of reaching on time for lecture (discussed at the beginning of the chapter), though we have many options at hand that make it possible to reach on time, you cannot go and wait outside the college for the entire day! So, the point is to have preferences. As stated in the utility theory, every state is somewhat useful or rather has a degree of usefulness, and preference is given to the ones with higher utility. Hence, a decision theory can be represented as:

Decision Theory = Probability theory + Utility theory

Details about it are discussed in Chapter 13. The basic idea of decision theory is that any agent is said to be rational iff it selects the action resulting into highest expected utility that is averaged over all possible outcomes of the action. This principle is called *maximum expected utility (MEU)*.

We proceed with the general mechanism of making rational decisions—influence diagrams. It is also referred to as decision networks that basically combines Bayesian and has additional nodes indicating utility or actions.

Influence Diagram (Decision network)

An influence diagram (ID) is a directed graphical representation of the decision-maker's preferences with respect to the real-world uncertainty and sequence of possible decisions. An ID, or more precisely, a decision network is a representation of the information regarding the agent's current state, actions and the possible outcomes. Let discuss types of node used for the representation of decision network.

Chance node: A chance node represents random variables. It is similar to the way we have in BN. It represents the uncertain variables. Each chance node has probability values that influence the decisions. It is represented in the following shape.

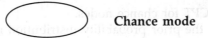

Chance mode

Decision node: It is at this node that the decision-maker has to make a choice of actions. Every decision node is attached to the chance nodes, which in turn, influence the decisions. A decision node is represented in the following shape.

Decision node

Utility node: It represents an agent's utility function. Its parents are the variables that describe the outcome that directly affects the utility. It is represented in the following shape.

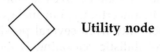

Utility node

To get more clarity, we start with the details and mapping of utility function.

Let $A = (a_1, a_2, ..., a_n)$ be the set of actions and $H = (h_1, h_2, ... h_n)$ represents the set of variables that influence the actions. $U(A, H)$ represents a utility table that holds the values for each action item and the variable that it is associated with. The decision is made by maximising the utility values associated with the action. Mathematically, it can be represented as

$$EU(a_i) = \Sigma_H U(a_i)p(H \mid a_i) \qquad (8.8)$$

$EU(a_i)$ represents the expected utility of action a_i. $p(H \mid a_i)$ is the conditional probability of variables h_i, where $h_i \in H$, given action a_i is executed. This conditional probability is calculated from CPT while traversing the BN of these variables. We explain it with the traditional example of the umbrella by Jensen. In this example, the decision-maker wants to take decision whether to carry umbrella before leaving the house. So, the decision node here is the umbrella. Uncertainty is about the weather conditions. So, we can say weather conditions and weather forecast are the uncertain variables that are represented as chance nodes. Utility is the satisfaction in carrying the umbrella. Figure 8.7 represents the decision network for the example.

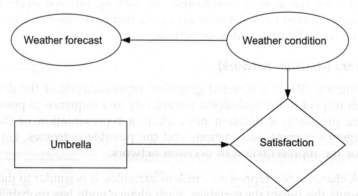

Figure 8.7 Influence diagram for umbrella example.

Let us assume typical CPT for chance nodes.

For weather condition, the prior probability distribution is shown in Table 8.1.

TABLE 8.1 Prior Probability

Weather condition	
Rain	0.7
Sun	0.3

Similarly for weather forecast, this corresponds to posterior probability, since it is influenced by weather condition, as shown in Table 8.2.

TABLE 8.2 Posterior Probability

Forecast	Weather condition	
	Rain	Sun
Good	0.6	0.2
Bad	0.4	0.8

To take decisions about taking umbrella, a utility table is to be defined. This is shown in Table 8.3.

TABLE 8.3 Utility Table

Umbrella	Weather	Satisfaction
Carry	Rain	90
Carry	Sun	20
Don't Carry	Rain	15
Don't Carry	Sun	10

Using Eq. (8.8), we compute and fill the utility and select the one that maximises it. Let us say we want to compute the expected utility (EU) for not carrying the umbrella. In such a case, the computations will be

EU (don't carry the umbrella) = (0.7 * 15) + (0.3 * 10) = 13.5

Similarly, EU(carry the umbrella) = (0.7 * 90) + (0.3 * 20) = 69

Thus, the maximum utility is the selection of an action that has greater EU. Hence, it is 'carry the umbrella'.

Further, the EU to carry the umbrella, given that the forecast is good, is computed as follows:

$$\text{EU(carry|good weather)} = \sum_{w} P(w|\text{good})U(\text{carry}, w)$$

First, let us compute P(Weather condition | Forecast = good). It is shown in table 8.4 below:

TABLE 8.4 Probability Table for Weather Condition

*Weather condition	Forecast = good*	
Rain	0.7 * 0.6 = 0.42
Sun	0.3 * 0.2 = 0.06

EU(carry the umbrella | forecast=good) = 0.42 * 90 + 0.06 * 20 = 39

Similarly, EU(don't carry the umbrella | forecast = good) = 0.42 * 15 + 0.06 * 10 = 6.9

Thus, an optimal decision is to carry the umbrella, even though the forecast is good. Selection of any action is dependent on the decision network evaluation. The algorithm for making the decisions is as follows:

1. Set the evidence variable for the current state of evaluation.
2. For every possible value of the decision node that it can take up,
   (a) Set and assign the decision node to the value.
   (b) Compute the posterior probabilities (we can compute this using Bayes's theorem).
   (c) Compute the resulting utilities—expected ones for the action.
3. Select an action with the highest utility.

8.8 MAKING COMPLEX DECISIONS

Often, decision-making becomes hard or difficult owing to the complexity of the problem. In such situations, we take up sequence of actions to accomplish the goal unlike the simple decision-making. When we talk about sequence of actions, it means that the decision-maker has to interact with the environment repeatedly for every decision. Typically, a decision-maker observes the environment in order to take decisions and then acts. Future information is also required for it. So, this process continues till the goal is achieved. The only reason to observe is to gain information for the future action.

In a simple scenario, it has one decision variable and set of action items. Whereas, in case of complex one, the set of decision variable D corresponds to $D = \{D_1, D_2, ..., D_n\}$ and each D_i has a set of alternative actions associated with it. In simple decision theory, utility is assigned to each action's outcome and in complex scenario, each of the multiple actions are associated with utility. Some of these actions may generate risk, while some may generate reward. So, the final decision is the optimal balance of the reward and the risk. There can be a possibility that single or multiple decision-makers are involved in the complex process.

The complexity of decision-making problem is dependent on the environment in which the agent is operating. We are already familiar with the different environments in which the agent operates like deterministic, dynamic, episodic and so on. In case of complex decision-making, it could be the combination of one or more of these environments. A variety of industrial applications exist, where sequences of decisions are to be made to achieve the business goal. Let us take an example of a manufacturing industry. Here, factory control, resource planning, inventory control are planned and executed to maintain the production level. In any industrial application, planning and control is a critical problem. These critical problems can be modelled as sequential decision-making problems. Problem environments for sequential decision-making are mainly of two types—competitive environments like in games, e.g. chess, checkers, etc. and co-operative like robots, portfolio management, inventory management and so on. In co-operative environment, agents ensure that the individual actions contribute to optimise the team activity, whereas in competitive environment, each agent maximises its own actions and minimises others' actions to win the game. Let us take an example of a retail shop. Assume that in a particular area, there are a number of retail shops, and each tries to improve its turnover. To achieve this, each one starts reducing the prices or gives promotional offers without knowing what others are doing. At the end, some of them gain few customers, while some loose. This is a typical competitive and non-co-operative environment. In a co-operative environment the action of agents are not hidden. Consider an example of two cars coming from opposite directions in a narrow hilly road. Here, the drivers have two options—to continue to move in the same direction, meet at some point and then take reverse, and to let the other go. The goal for the drivers is same, so they signal each other before taking any action.

Thus, we can say that simple decision-making is the application of static or dynamic decision-making, whereas sequential decision-making inherits all the problems and behaviour of static and dynamic decision-making. The static and dynamic probabilistic reasonings are used for decision-making and solving process. But if the decision theory of simple decision-making is extended to the problem of sequential one, computational complexity in the problems of real world increases substantially.

In any state, it is the agent who needs to interact with the environment prior to taking any action, and its probability to reach the outcome is governed by the previous states. This iteration makes reasoning complex and expensive one over long chain of probabilities. To make this simple, the sequential decision-making problem is solved in Markovian environment.

In general, a sequential problem is formulated as state-space model. The problem starts with initial state, say S_0. With every action, the state is changed and the goal is achieved through a set of states say, $S = \{S_0, S_1, S_2, ..., S_n\}$ that are defined over time step t. A transition model also comes into picture $T(s, a, s'):P(S_t \mid S_{t-1}, a_{t-1})$ that specifies the probability of reaching s' from the state s, where action a is performed. Each state is associated with a utility function $u(s)$ and reward $R(s)$. This value is equivalent to reward, which may be positive or negative. Negative reward can be treated as risk. An agent always tries to maximise the rewards. This formulation is also referred to as *Markov decision process* (MDP). Figure 8.8 depicts the decision network.

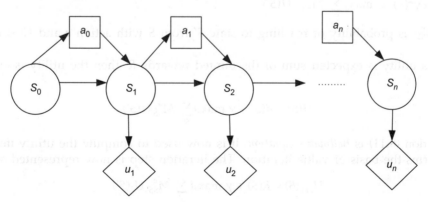

Figure 8.8 Markov decision diagram.

The action at each state is selected from a set of actions. The choice of action at time step t is called policy π and is denoted as $\pi(s)$: policy for state s.

In Markovian environment, the assumption in the state transition probability depends only on the finite number of parents. The first order Markov process is the simplest one, but in decision-making process, values for future action are also considered. There are two types of solutions here—finite horizon and infinite horizon. In *finite horizon*, the utility values are considered for n steps ahead, whereas in case of *infinite horizon*, they are considered for all the steps in the problem domain. Generally, infinite horizon is easy to deal with considering the fact that policy does not change with time and there are no stopping criteria. A utility value for future state is like ₹ 1000 is more valuable today than after a year. Then, the utility value for future states will be less. Hence, a discount factor is used while extrapolating these values. Utility over all states is

$$U(S_0, S_1, S_3, ..., S_n) = u(S_0) + \gamma u(S_1) + \gamma^2 u(S_2) + ... \tag{8.9}$$

where γ is discount factor that lies between [0, 1].

If short-term reward is considered, then low value of γ is used and for long-term, a large value is used. Further, the expected utility of all the states is given by

$$EU(S) = \sum t\gamma^t P(S_t | S_{t-1}) u(S_t) \tag{8.10}$$

To infer, a policy with the highest expected utility is the optimal policy. Once optimal policy is reached, corresponding actions at each state are selected as the best actions. Let us discuss about the algorithms for finding out these policies in the next section.

Value Iteration

In this step, the expected utility at each step is maximised and the best action is selected. This process is repeated over all the states. The decision is optimised in reverse order, i.e., from the goal state to the initial state. So, to begin, each state is initially assigned with some value and then these values are updated in reverse order.

The $U(S)$ lets selection of action that maximises the expected utility of subsequent state-policy*$(S) = \max_a \sum_{S'} M_{SS'}^a \cdot U(S')$

where $M_{SS'}^a$ is probability of reaching to state S' from S with action a and $U(S)$ is utility of S'.

If this utility is expected sum of discounted rewards R, then the utility is expressed as

$$U(S) = R(S) + \gamma \max a \sum_{S'} M_{SS'}^a U(S') \tag{8.11}$$

Equation (8.11) is *Bellman's equation*. It is now used to compute the utility iteratively, which forms the basis of value iteration. The iteration step is now represented as

$$U_{i+1}(S) = R(S) + \gamma \max a \sum_{S'} M_{SS'}^a U_i(S') \tag{8.12}$$

The algorithmic steps are as follows:

Input: M and R

$\quad\quad U$ and U' for state S initialised to zero.

do:

$\quad\quad U = U'$ and delta = 0

$\quad\quad$ for each state S:

$\quad\quad\quad\quad U'(S) = R(S) + \gamma \max_a \sum_{S'} M^a_{SS'} U(S')$

$\quad\quad\quad\quad$ if $(U'(S) - U(S)) >$ delta then

$\quad\quad\quad\quad\quad\quad$ delta $= (U'(S) - U(S))$

until delta $<$ err$(1 - \gamma)/\gamma$

return U.

So, for infinite horizon, the same best action can be chosen. Here, time is not important, so even stationary policies can be adopted. If we replace γ in the Bellman's equation by γ^k for large k, reward tends to zero or reward is insignificant. So, in Eq. (8.11), the expected utility for k number of steps is considered for value iteration. Policy found at kth iteration is used in the next steps.

The time complexities of value iteration are of the order $O(k|A||S|^2)$. Remember, the complexity increases with the number of random variables in action A and state variable S. This can be handled using dynamic decision network (DDN) with the assumption of conditional independence of random variables.

Policy Iteration

In this approach, instead of state utilities, the policy is searched at each step. This iteration is carried out in two steps. In first step, policy is evaluated for each state by calculating utility value and then policy is improved by selecting action that maximises the expected utility of that state.

The algorithm is as follows:

Input: M and R

$\quad\quad\quad U$ and U' for state S initialised to zero

Policy: initially random

$\quad\quad\quad\quad$ while (unchanged = true)

$\quad\quad\quad\quad\quad\quad U =$ evaluation policy (policy, U, M, R)

$\quad\quad\quad\quad\quad\quad\quad\quad$ unchanged = true

$\quad\quad\quad\quad\quad\quad\quad\quad$ for each state S:

$\quad\quad$ if $\max_a \sum_{S'} M^a_{SS'} U(S') > \sum_{S'} M^{\text{Policy}(s)}_{SS'} U(S')$ then

$\quad\quad$ Policy $(S) = \max_a \sum_{S'} M^a_{SS'} U(S')$

$\quad\quad$ unchanged = false

In this section, we have seen that policy optimisation is important in making complex decisions. Optimal policy has to be found through the iterations over the states and when the model of the environment is known. State transition model $T(s, a, s'): P(S_t | S_{t-1}, a_{t-1})$, utility or the reward values are integral part of the environment, but in the real world, these models may not be readily available. What is available are the states and the actions. In such scenarios, the approach of machine learning is used to generate the model of environment.

8.9   OTHER TECHNIQUES IN UNCERTAINTY AND REASONING PROCESS

We now have a look at other approaches concerned with uncertainty. With a detailed study on the decision process, the Bayesian probability and its role in uncertainty, we consider other aspects in the reasoning process and new ventures for handling the knowledge along with understanding the benefits of appropriate use of the knowledge.

8.9.1   Non-monotonic Reasoning

Before we begin with non-monotonic reasoning, let us understand what monotonic reasoning is. The predicate logic or the inferences that we work on are under the category of monotonic reasoning. In the sense, if we enlarge the set of axioms, things won't change. In simple words, we call a logic to be monotonic if the truth of the proposition does not change even when new information, i.e., axioms are available or added.

The reason to have non-monotonic reasoning is again uncertainty. The knowledge about the world is incomplete, hence it leads to non-monotonic reasoning. Monotonic reasoning falls short of the following:

1. Anticipation of outcomes.
2. Assumptions about things and
3. Drawing conclusions to plan further.

In non-monotonic reasoning, the truth of the proposition can change when new information is available. Default reasoning is the most common form of non-monotonic reasoning. We draw conclusions based on what is most likely to be true. The two approaches of non-monotonic reasoning are non-monotonic logic and default logic.

Non-monotonic Logic

The non-monotonic logic is basically an extension of first order predicate logic. This is done in order to accommodate modal operator. The reason behind this is to allow consistency.

For example, consider the following knowledge base:

Typically, engineering students can write C programs.
First year students cannot write C program.
Shyam is an engineering student.

Can we conclude that Shyam can write C program? It is plausible to conclude that. But can we say Shyam is first year student? The previous conclusion is not valid and needs to be retracted. Hence, a new conclusion holds. Remember, different interpretations give rise to different non-monotonic logics.

Assumptions: A basic understanding is that only positive information available is represented here. Negative information is not explicitly represented. If the positive fact

does not appear in the knowledge base, it is assumed that the negative one holds. This is referred to as *closed world assumption.*

So, we are proving consistency. To show that a fact X is true, attempt to prove $\neg X$. If we fail, we can conclude P is consistent.

Default Logic

Default logic basically introduces new inference rule. It extends the classical logic by non-standard inference rules.

Considering the same examples, we can say that

$$\frac{\alpha(X):\beta(X)}{\gamma(X)}$$

Here, $\alpha(X)$ is prerequisite, $\beta(X)$ is justification and $\gamma(X)$ is consequent.

This can be interpreted as if X is an engineering student and we can consistently assume that engineering students can write C programs, then we infer that X can write C programs.

8.9.2 Data Mining

Data mining in a broader sense, is about analysis of the data to extract some meaningful information. This information could be related to profits, making business investments, helping in applying new strategies and so on. A lot of data mining tools exist today in the market and have proved to be a boon. It handles the large-scale information and performs the analysis. While doing so, the knowledge representations and the warehouses have a significant impact. Uncertainty plays a key role in impacting the decision. This is affected to a great extent when forecasting is required in terms of business strategies to be employed or any other important decision is to be taken. The way knowledge is grouped, say classes or clusters influences the process. Moreover, the relationships, associations and the patterns should also be in place to prove the mining effective.

8.9.3 Fuzzy Logic

The fuzzy logic basically defines the degree of truth. Unlike Boolean values, it defines the degree of membership. It takes the values of 0 and 1 as the extreme cases of truth, but also considers in between states. Fuzzy is actually the way we think. Fuzzy logic can be viewed as the way reasoning process works. Very simple examples of fuzzy logic can be as follows: Seema is having high fever. She is slightly tall. Here, we are not exactly specifying the illness or the height. It is the notion of fuzzy that is put forth in these cases. So, there could be totally different sets which are defined for extreme fever as well as for high fever. This is discussed in detail in Chapter 10.

8.9.4 Knowledge Engineering

It is the process of structuring, formalising and operationalising the information and the knowledge contained in the problem domain. This is required so that we are able to get the desired results. It is the process of eliciting knowledge. When there is a complex knowledge, it is difficult to have proper representations. There can be difference in the sources from where the information is made available. To add further, there can be representations of varied types as well. These all things account to more complexities in the engineering process. There is a need to have proper knowledge engineering. MYCIN is an example of knowledge-based systems (KBS). For past few years, modelling frameworks that have become most popular are model-based incremental knowledge engineering (MIKE) and KADS. Figure 8.9 depicts process followed by KBS.

Figure 8.9   Process followed by KBS.

8.9.5   Ontological Engineering

Ontologies describe domain knowledge in a generic way. They provide agreed understanding of the domain. We are aware that the problem-solving methods describe the reasoning process of a KBS. Ontology defines the terms as well as the rules to combine the terms and relations. Ontological engineering basically studies the methods for building the ontologies.

Representations of the abstract concepts of the actions and time are the examples of ontological engineering. It is very closely related to KBS. In fact, the modelling framework used in KBS is influenced by ontologies.

In ontologies, organisation of the concepts takes place. They comprise the relations for the concepts with their sub-classes, and the mapping for the functions of the concepts. The instances and axioms too form the part of the ontology. But how can we build such taxonomy for the concepts? It is formed by identifying the sub-classes or the partitions with regard to the concept, whose ontology is to be built. Even the ISA sort of relations can prove to be useful in building them.

To understand the concept, let us take an example. Generally, when we use any search engine, a personalised search can be made possible by the use of ontologies. This can be used when the user enters some new concepts and a search is required on it. An already built ontology can be proved useful in this search to get the related searches. Further, the built ontology can also be refined based on the user queries.

8.9.6   Dempster–Shafer Theory

Evidential logic is based on the Dempster–Shafer theory, which is based on the beliefs. It is rather the degree of belief that is warranted when given the evidence. It comprises two propositions—plausibility and belief. To each of them, an interval is assigned in which the degree of belief lies. Belief naturally has its value between 0 (no evidence) and 1 (certain). Similarly, for plausibility, the value is also 0 to 1, indicating the extent to which the evidence favours.

Plausibility is defined as follows:

$$PL(p) = 1 - BEL(\neg p)$$

where, p is a particular statement or a set of parameters.

It is just not the belief that helps us in decisions. For some hypothesis where we have no information, we can say that the likelihood lies in the range of 0 to 1. But as information gets available, the interval becomes more precise. This is unlike the Bayes's theorem, where the prior probabilities are already determined.

Let us take an example to understand the details of this theory. Here, the set of conclusions is represented as follows:

$$\Theta = \{\theta_1, \theta_2, \theta_3, ..., \theta_n\}$$

where θ_1 to θ_n are conclusions.

This theory is concerned with the evidences that support the conclusions, rather a subset among the conclusion's set. There is a notion of power set (we have studied this in set theory). The power set comprises all possible subsets of Θ.

Let us take an example. To reach any location, many parameters are involved, representing Θ set = {traffic_jam, signal_not_working, bus_breakdown, rain}.

For some given conditions, let us assume we want to predict if we can reach on time or not. Here, Dempster–Shafer theory helps us in handling this by making the use of hypothesis. By this, we mean that using a density function that is probable helps us in making decision. Let us call this function to be m. Now, the function $m(s)$ measures the amount of belief. If theta has n elements, then there are 2^n subsets. We need to assign m values so that all the subsets equal to 1. This $m(s)$ or mass $m(s)$ represents proportion of relevant and available evidence that supports s in the power set. Let us take three parameters out of the above to form our Θ = {T, R, B} (T = Traffic, R = Rain, B = Bus breakdown). The mass or rather the probabilities are set based on some observations. Let these observations be taken from a person who has seen that the signals are not working. $P\{\} = 0$. Let the following values represent them for the said parameters (Table 8.5).

TABLE 8.5 Mass, Belief and Plausibility Values

	$m(s)$	Belief	Plausibility
{T}	0.1	0.1	0.4
{B}	0.2	0.2	0.7
{R}	0.1	0.1	0.6
{T, R}	0.1	0.4	0.8
{B, R}	0.3	0.7	0.9
{T, B}	0.1	0.4	0.9
{T, B, R}	0.1	1.0	1.0

As discussed earlier, the probabilities or the m values are based on some observations. Now let us discuss the computations of belief. For example, BEL{T, R} = $m(T)$ + $m(R)$ +

$m(T, R)$. Hence, it comes to $0.1 + 0.2 + 0.1 = 0.4$. In the same way, other computations are done. In case of plausibility computations, the value of PL(s) is computed as the sum of m values that have intersection with s. So, for PL$\{T, R\}$, it is given as $m(T) + m(R) + m(T, R) + m(B, R) + m(T, B) + m(T, B, R) = 0.8$. In the same manner, other computations are done. The gap between the belief and plausibility is regarded as uncertainty. PL(s) can also be defined as follows:

PL(s) = 1 − DISBEL(s). Hence, we can compute disbelief as DISBEL(T) = 1 − 0.4 = 0.6 and so on. Further, the theory states that we can combine the beliefs. Assume some independent probability distribution or the m value is being available. That is, new values are available for the conditions from some other person who watches a policeman controlling the traffic. Under such a scenario, the rule states that

$$m_{new} = \frac{\sum_{P \cap Q = R} m_1(P) \cdot m_2(Q)}{1 - \sum_{P \cap Q \neq \phi} m_1(P) \cdot m_2(Q)}$$

where, m_1 and m_2 are the probability functions over Θ. P and Q are the combination of pairs that are subset of Θ.

With this, we can compute new m value. Suppose you get some more set of information about T, B, R from some other source. In that case, the new values for m can be computed for the conclusions. For example, we get new information from the new source as shown below (Table 8.6).

TABLE 8.6

	$m_2(s)$
$\{T\}$	0.3
$\{B\}$	0.1
$\{R\}$	0.1
$\{T, R\}$	0.2
$\{B, R\}$	0.1
$\{T, B\}$	0.1
$\{T, B, R\}$	0.1

The computation for $m_{new}(T, R)$ is shown below. We refer to the previous observations as m_1.

$$m_{new}(T, R) = [(0.1 * 0.2) + (0.1 * 0.1) + (0.2 * 0.1)] / [1 - (0.31)]$$

$$= [0.02 + 0.01 + 0.02] / [0.69] = 0.05 / 0.69$$

Thus, we can compute new beliefs and plausibility for the new available information and the evidence that is acquired. The main advantage of using this theory is that, as we have discussed earlier, this adds to our KB, thereby giving us evidence for further inferring. The theory assists in making the beliefs more strong with the availability of the evidences.

SUMMARY

In this chapter, we have discussed about how the problem environment is captured and represented using random variables and how this information is used further to provide reason and inference for an unknown situation.

Uncertainty in the real world is best handled using probability theory. The problem environment can be static or dynamic. In dynamic environment, a set of random variables is used to represent the world at each point. Bayesian network is used to represent the dependencies and infer in the static world. It is assumed that finite previous states influence the present state of the world. With these assumptions, dynamic environment is represented with Markov models.

Once inferences are drawn for unknown situations, one can attach utility value with each state of world to take decisions. Decision-making may be simple with the choice of one action at any stage. Influence diagram is graphical approach to represent it. Things become complex when multiple actions are involved. Complex or sequential decision-making is modelled using Markov decision process, with the assumption of dynamic world. Dempster–Shafer theory helps in capturing the beliefs and is applied in inferring process.

Perception is another intelligent behaviour. It simulates intelligent behaviour in machine. A machine needs to reason and change the actions with respect to the dynamic environment. It percepts the world through sensors, reasons on accumulated knowledge and then takes action. Non-monotonic reasoning too plays a vital role in the uncertain environment with respect to the knowledge base formulation. Figure 8.10 summarises the dependency of reasoning on decision-making and how they are handled in the static and dynamic environment.

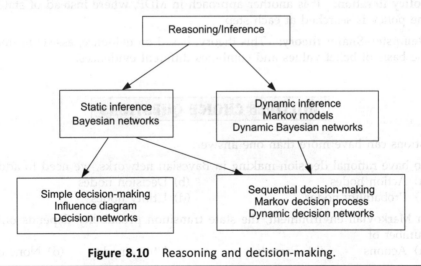

Figure 8.10 Reasoning and decision-making.

KEYWORDS

1. **Bayesian probability:** Bayesian probability provides degree of belief. It allows to reason with hypothesis.

2. **Hypothesis:** It refers to proposed explanation for an observed phenomenon.

3. **Belief network:** Bayesian network is a probabilistic graphical model that represents a set of random variables and their conditional dependencies through a directed acyclic graph (DAG).

4. **Filtering:** It is also referred to as monitoring (in Markov model context). It is the task of computing the posterior probability of the current state or the current belief state.

5. **Prediction:** Inference is drawn here to predict the future (in Markov model context). So, we compute the posterior probability, given all evidence for the future state.

6. **Smoothing:** This involves estimating past from all evidences upto present time.

7. **Influence diagram:** It is a directed graphical representation of the decision-maker's preferences with respect to the real-world uncertainty and sequence of possible decisions.

8. **Principle of maximum expected utility:** This involves selection of actions that help in maximising the expected utility.

9. **Value iteration:** It is an approach in MDP to compute the optimal policy and the value.

10. **Policy iteration:** It is another approach in MDP, where instead of state utilities, the policy is searched at each step.

11. **Dempster–Shafer theory:** This theory, based on evidence, assists in inferring on the basis of belief values and combines different evidences.

MULTIPLE CHOICE QUESTIONS

The questions can have more than one answer:

1. To have rational decision-making in Bayesian networks, we need to add
   (a) Action nodes
   (b) Decision nodes
   (c) Probability nodes
   (d) Utility nodes

2. In Markovian environment, the state transition probability depends only on the number of
   (a) Actions   (b) Parents   (c) Utility nodes   (d) None of these

3. _____ describes data mining.
   (a) Grouping of knowledge in efficient way
   (b) Extracting meaningful information by the use of techniques
   (c) Reasoning and inferring for the structured data
   (d) None of the above

4. Which of the following is true for decision networks?
   (a) Compute the decisions based on probabilities.
   (b) Compute utilities which help in decisions
   (c) Compute expected utilities and the decision node value
   (d) All of them

5. In Markov decision process (MDP), which of the following is true?
   (a) An action with the lowest discount factor is selected
   (b) An action with the minimum expected value is selected
   (c) An action with the lowest penalty is selected
   (d) An action with the maximising reward is selected

6. In MDP, the discounting factor plays a role of
   (a) Helping in converging to solution
   (b) Getting sooner rewards
   (c) Getting a lower penalty rate
   (d) All of the above

7. Dempster–Shafer theory is concerned with the evidences to support
   (a) Any single outcome
   (b) Highest reward outcome
   (c) Subsets of outcomes
   (d) None of the above

8. Uncertainty can be regarded as a gap between
   (a) Belief and disbelief
   (b) Belief and plausibility
   (c) Plausibility and belief
   (d) None of the above

CONCEPT REVIEW QUESTIONS

1. What is Markov assumption?

2. Describe the Markov process of kth order and write the corresponding transition model.

3. What are the commonalities and differences between static and dynamic Bayesian networks?

4. Referring to the Markov model for inventory management, apply value iteration and policy iteration to find out the optimal policy.

CRITICAL THINKING EXERCISE

1. Consider an example where X person has planned a trek in Himalayas. Suppose you are to assist in the decision-making of whether X should go ahead with the plan or not. Which model would you employ under the uncertainty management?

2. Assume we have some data regarding hotel booking of a hotel. How would you model the uncertainty with regard to no-shows for the hotel if the season is rainy season?

1. Develop a model for college admission process using Markov decision process.

CHAPTER 9

Planning

Learning Objectives

- ❑ To understand the concept and importance of planning
- ❑ To understand the role of planning in intelligent systems
- ❑ To understand the importance of planning in autonomous agents
- ❑ To study and understand the application and usage of planning in AI
- ❑ To acquire knowledge about the algorithms and the methods in planning
- ❑ To understand the planning systems and its impact on uncertainty and multi-agent systems

INTRODUCTION

Planning is required to convert objectives into actions. To perform any activity effectively, one needs to plan. Every morning one gets ups and decides the agenda and plans for that day. A mother has her own set of do's and for that she plans according to the timings of her kids coming from the school. Based on different constraints related to timings of other family members, she plans all her household activities including shopping, laundry visit, etc. Similarly, students plan their study based on the exam schedule and other constraints. They take into account examination schedule, time available at hand, subjects he/she is good at and a number of other factors related to this activity. Planning for the studies includes scheduling of all the subjects in such a way so that a particular subject is studied in a specified time; thus, it deals with scheduling and ordering of studies! There are dependencies like subject A is mandatory to understand subject B, so subject A should be studied prior to subject B.

You have a lot of constraints too while planning—number of days left for the exam, subject category (simple/hard), number of chapters to study, notes availability and so on. Still, you have to plan to achieve some goal. The goal could be to get distinction or just to clear all the subjects. So, planning involves the steps to be taken to reach the goal optimally. Thus, we can say that it determines how and when to do the necessary steps, given the set of goals.

Further, in the real world, without prior knowledge, one ends up in searching exhaustively for the goal state. Let us take an example of problem-solving agent. An exhaustive search is required to reach the goal. It would typically be a search that may have to traverse back and re-apply (re-think) of the actions. How nice it would be if we were to have some heuristic before taking any decisions (in real life just not possible)! If we could have the problem divided into different tasks, it would make the things simpler. Having some guidelines as to how to travel to the goal state with some intermediate states known would make it much better. Considering all these situations, there is a need to have planning to solve the problem, optimally.

What is the role of planning in case of AI? Intelligent systems need to be aware of what is to be done and how it can be done. Planning allows exploring different possibilities; it makes intelligent systems more flexible, and hence, increases their decision-making capabilities. In order to plan, the problem needs to be well-understood. Planning needs proper representation of what needs to be achieved. It involves the reasoning as well as the techniques that are applied. Planning plays a major role in various tasks like spacecrafts missions, robotics, specific military tasks and so on. Let us start a detailed study on the concepts of planning.

9.1 PLANNING PROBLEM

So, what is the basic planning problem? The *planning problem* is actually the question that how to go to the next state or the goal state from the current state. As discussed earlier, it involves two things 'how' and 'when'. It definitely involves selecting appropriate action and sequencing them so that the required action is invoked first. Let us make things more clear and more technical. The planning problem is defined with:

1. Domain model
2. Initial state
3. Goal state (next state)

The domain model defines the actions along with the objects. It is necessary to specify the operators too that actually describe the action. Along with this, information about actions and state constraints while acting should also be given. This entirely formulates the domain model. The *initial state* is the state where any action is yet to take place (the stage when the exam schedule is put up!). The *final state* or the *goal state* is the state which the plan is intended to achieve. It constitutes of the facts that will be true once your plan gets completed (getting an all clear in the subjects!).

So, we work on a strategy that actually forms the plan. The decision of the sequence in which the actions are performed too is a plan.

9.1.1 Components of Planning System

Let us refer to the same example of the planning for the exam to understand the components of planning system. A student who wants to get an all clear (i.e., to score marks above cut-off in all subjects) applies some selection criteria to begin with the study of any subject. He recognises the difficulties that he is likely to face. What he is actually doing is forming the components of the planning system. We highlight them in technical terms for planning in AI. The components are as follows:

1. Selection of the best rule/action by the use of heuristic (say selection of a simple subject—this would be based on the past experience or inputs from the seniors or lectures attended.)
2. Taking action and applying the rule (studying of the subject, so as to proceed towards the next stage)
3. Understanding and recognising when the goal is reached or the solution is found (a position is reached where he can score more than cut-off marks.)
4. Understanding and recognising the dead ends (got stuck with some difficult topic which takes him nowhere.)
5. Understanding and recognising partial solution that is correct and making efforts to make it entirely accurate. (In position to get more than cut-off marks in all subjects except mathematics and then strategise to reach the goal state.)

9.1.2 Basic Planning Representation

To plan, one should be able to represent the problem properly. Representation of the planning problem is mapping of the states, actions and the goals. For the representation, the language used should be concrete, understandable and expressive. In a broader perspective, there are different representation methods or ways that are followed like propositional, first order, state variable. Figure 9.1 depicts the high-level diagram for planning.

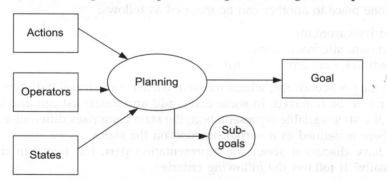

Figure 9.1 Planning.

Planning essentially needs the representation in terms of time. This is required so that we are able to reason regarding the actions that are to be taken along with the reactions that we get back. Let us proceed towards the representations of the states, goals and the actions.

State Representation

States are the representation of the facts. States are represented as conjunction. It comprises the positive literals that specify the state. We are already familiar with the first order logic and propositional logic. Any of them can be used for representation. In the state representation, while using the first order logic, the representation has to be easily understood. There has to be grounding (variables are replaced by constants) also in the representation. For example, kind(Richa) ^ hardworking(Richa) can be a state unless some actions are performed or friends(Richa, Hema) ^ friends(Seema, Meena). One more example can be On(Apple, Table) that represents some state. But we cannot have friends (x, y), as said earlier about grounding. Further, the representation also assumes that the conditions we do not specify explicitly are not accounted or rather are not considered to be true. This is also referred to as *closed world assumption*. So, the objects that are specified in the states only exist in the world. In case of propositional literals, we can have a state as kind ^ hardworking. (STRIPS representation follows the first order literals, the details of STRIPS will be discussed later.)

Goal Representation

Goal is most often a partially specified state. A state or say proposition is said to achieve or satisfy the given goal if it consists of all the objects required for the goal or may be some other too. As an example, if the goal is kind^hardworking, then a state that has kind^hardworking^pretty fulfils the goal.

Action Representation

Whenever we decide to do something, we are aware of the state we are in and what possibly the effects are. When it comes to the mapping of the actions for an agent or in case of robots, the pre and the post situations need to be specified. These can also be called as *pre-conditions* and the after effects are called *post-conditions*. For example, an action to drive from one place to another can be mapped as follows:

Action(drive(c,from,to))
Pre-condition: at(c,from)^car(c)
Post-condition: ~at(c,from)^at(c,to)

Here, in the post-condition, where we have written ~at(c,from) indicates that the state is deleted or is to be removed. In some cases, add and delete list can also be used.

In case of a state variable representation, the state comprises different state variables. The action here is defined as a partial function on the states.

So, we have discussed about the representation part, but how can the actions be applied actually? It follows the following criteria:

1. A substitution is to be identified for the variables. That is, for the current state that exists, identify the action with a pre-condition that satisfies the current state (the current state can be subset of the pre-condition).
2. Apply this substitution (for whatever part of the current state it is applicable).
3. Add the post-condition (effects) to the remaining subset of the current state if any.

9.2 SIMPLE PLANNING AGENT

We have been familiar with the agent world in the previous chapters. One would have easily guessed that the *planning agent* is the one that plans its actions. We have detailed the representation in the previous section and it helps us in understanding the planning agent and how it acts upon the environment. A planning agent is the one that makes use of knowledge and problem solving to get the goal. It performs the following steps:

1. Defining a goal (a goal is initially set by the agent).
2. Planning (a plan is built).
3. Taking action (actions are invoked as per the plan).

The process continues each time with some new goal. Things are simple to understand in the planning agent. (It is the same way we decide when we have some goal set). But since it is an agent environment, there have to be some assumptions. (Recollect the environment types an agent has). So, what does an agent assume?

1. The actions occur one at a time (no parallel execution) and that they cannot be further divided.
2. There is no uncertainty and the agent is well-versed with the outcome that is specified with the action.
3. Rules/things which are not specified are assumed to be false.
4. The agent's action causes the changes in the state and it has the knowledge about it. So, the environment is fully observable.

9.3 PLANNING LANGUAGES

After briefing about the representation, let us have a look at the different planning languages. We know that a language is the one that should be expressive. Again referring to the earlier section of representation, is this a part of the language? The answer is yes. Every planning language makes use of the representation schema so that the algorithms can be operated on it. We highlight three languages here.

1. Stanford Research Institute Problem Solver (STRIPS)
2. Action Description Language (ADL)
3. Planning Domain Description Language (PDDL)

9.3.1 Stanford Research Institute Problem Solver (STRIPS)

STRIPS is a language that is historically important. It was developed in 1970's at Stanford for the first intelligent robot. It makes use of the first order predicates. Hence, the representation structure that we have discussed earlier with the first order logic essentially belongs to the STRIPS. STRIPS allows function-free literals. We discuss one example for better understanding of STRIPS. Since the planning discussed is related to the agent's environment, we have the typical example of a robot. The example involves a robot, a cup of tea, guest and two rooms. We want the robot to get the tea and give it to the guest. The planning with STRIPS is done as follows:

Let us begin with the STRIPS representation for this example. Initial and final states are depicted in Figure 9.2.

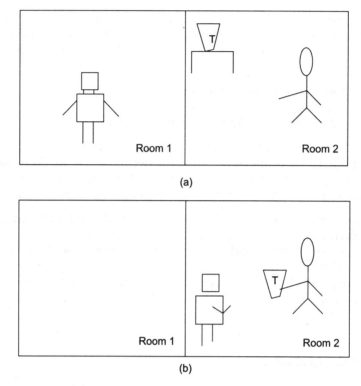

Figure 9.2   (a) Initial stage, (b) Goal state.

State Representation

The possible states can be as follows:

1. in(robot,room1)^in(tea,room2)^in(guest,room2)
2. in(robot,room1)^in(tea,room1)^in(guest,room1)
3. in(robot,room2)^in(tea,room1)^in(guest,room1) and so on.

Let the goal state be in(guest,room2)^in(robot,room2)^in(tea,room2)^have(tea,guest). Let us assume the first case in the possible states to be the initial state.

Action Representation

The operators or the actions have name, pre and post-conditions. (Post-conditions can also be represented as add-list or delete-list.)

Let us take an action.

Action 1:   move-to-room2
Pre-condition: in(robot,room1)
Post-condition: add-list: in(robot,room2)
                   delete-list: in(robot,room1)

There can be other actions like pick-tea, where the robot is in room2 and the tea as well, and the post-condition is hold(tea,robot). In such action, the delete-list can be empty, which is valid. Let us map it.

Pick-tea

Pre-condition: in(robot,room2)^in(tea,room2)
Post-condition: add-list: hold(tea,robot)
                  delete-list: NULL{empty-list}

In this manner, STRIPS makes use of lists, actions and operates.

Semantics

Whenever the pre-condition is false, the action cannot occur, as the state does not exist and it cannot be applied. But remember the order in which the add and delete lists operate is important.

From this, we can conclude that the STRIPS language is easy to understand. The use of propositional logic makes the implementation and building of the knowledge base easy. Due to this, inference and reasoning become simple. But the language is restricted. It assumes propositions in limited numbers. This can be a major drawback when considered with a different domain, where there could be more involvement of large number of propositions.

9.3.2 Action Description Language (ADL)

STRIPS language lacks the expressive power. It can be extended very well to overcome some of the limitations and ADL does that. The properties of ADL are as follows:

1. It allows negative literals.
2. It makes use of quantified variables along with the disjunctions and the conjunctions.
3. Conditional post-conditions are allowed.
4. Variables with different types at the same time are allowed and also equality property is available.

For example, consider the car driving case, with STRIPS, it will be

Action(drive(c,from,to))
    Pre-condition: at(c,from) ^ car(c)
    Post-condition: ~at(c,from) ^ at(c,to)
(Remember in STRIPS, the post-condition means remove the 1st 'at' condition and add the 2nd 'at' condition.)

With ADL, the same action is represented as follows:

Action(drive(c,from,to))
    Pre-condition: at(c,from) ^ car(c) ^(from≠to)
    Post-condition: ~at(c,from) ^ at(c,to)

ADL, thus, comes out to be more expressive language as compared to STRIPS and is looked upon for building reasoning approaches.

9.3.3 Planning Domain Description Language (PDDL)

It is a standardisation of the planning languages. It is defined by the researchers as a standard language. We can say it is a superset of STRIPS and ADL that allows features like

1. Objects can have type specifications.
2. It can have negative pre-conditions.
3. The add and delete lists can be conditional.
4. In some cases, it also allows numeric values.

PDDL is used in case of classical planning tasks. The planning tasks in PDDL are separated into domain file and problem file. A domain file consists of

```
(define (domain <Domain_name>)
    <PDDL code for the predicates>
    <PDDL code for the actions>
....)
```

A problem file comprises

```
(define (problem <problem_name>)
    (:domain <Domain_name>)
    <PDDL code for the objects>
    <PDDL code for the initial state>
    <PDDL code for the goal specification>
)
```

A domain_name identifies the planning domain, whereas a problem_name is the one that identifies the planning task. Most of the planners require this type of specification of PDDL.

9.4 BLOCKS WORLD

The blocks world is a known example that is used to demonstrate the planning using STRIPS. It is simple to understand and most important well behaved.

What is the blocks world? It consists of

1. A table or say a table top
2. Identical blocks that have unique letters on them.
3. The blocks can be put one on other to form a stack (a tower that has no height restriction).
4. This stack is built with a robot arm. The arm can perform operations of lifting a single block at a time and placing it. Operators and states are used, where logic is applied for the arm.

Let us say we have the following initial and goal states. This is a very simple example with just two blocks (Figure 9.3).

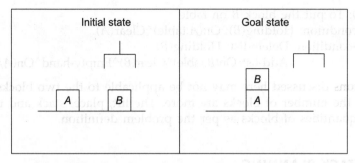

Figure 9.3 Blocks worked—Initial and goal stages.

The predicates used here are given below:

On(*A*,table): Block *A* is on the table.
On(*B*,table): Block *B* is on the table.
On(*B*,*A*): Block *B* is on block *A*.
Clear(*A*): Block *A* has nothing on it.
Clear(*B*): Block *B* has nothing on it.
Holding(*B*): Robot hand is holding *B*.
Empty-hand: The hand is not holding anything.

The state representation can be as follows:

On(*A*,table)^On(*B*,table)^Clear(*A*)^Clear(*B*)^Empty-hand
On(*A*,table)^Holding(*B*)^Clear(*A*)
On(*A*,table)^On(*B*,*A*)^Clear(*B*)^Empty-hand

The initial state is:

On(*A*,table)^On(*B*,table)^Clear(*A*)^Clear(*B*)^Empty-hand

The goal state is:

On(*A*,table)^On(*B*,*A*)^Clear(*B*)^Empty-hand

The actions that can take place are given below:

1. Unstack(*B*,*A*): To lift block *B* from *A*
      Pre-condition: Empty-hand^On(*B*,*A*)^Clear(*B*)^On(*A*,table)
      Post-condition: Delete-list: Empty-hand^On(*B*,*A*)^Clear(*B*)
                      Add-list: Holding(*B*)^Clear(*A*)^On(*A*,table)
2. Stack(*B*,*A*): to place block *B* on *A*
      Pre-condition: Holding(*B*)^Clear(*A*)^On(*A*,table)
      Post-condition: Delete-list: Holding(*B*)^Clear(*A*)
                      Add-list: On(*B*,*A*)^Clear(*B*)^Empty-hand^On(*A*,table)
3. Lift(*B*): To lift the block *B* from the table
      Pre-condition: On(*B*,table)^Clear(*B*)^Empty-hand^On(*A*,table)^Clear(*A*)
      Post-condition: Delete-list: On(*B*,table)^Clear(*B*)^Empty-hand
                      Add-list: Holding(*B*)^On(*A*,table)^Clear(*A*)

4. Place(*B*): To put the block *B* on table

      Pre-condition: Holding(*B*)^On(*A*,table)^Clear(*A*)

      Post-condition: Delete-list: Holding(*B*)

                  Add-list: On(*B*,table)^Clear(*B*)^Empty-hand^On(*A*,table)^Clear(*A*)

All the actions discussed here may not be applicable to the two blocks problem, but required when the number of blocks are more. The lift, place, stack and unstack can be with different quantities of blocks as per the problem definition.

9.5 GOAL STACK PLANNING

After studying the blocks world, we introduce the goal stack planning. This approach is used in STRIPS and is one of the very early approaches. In this approach, goal stacks are maintained to carry out the task. With the blocks world example, let us consider the initial and goal states given in Figure 9.4.

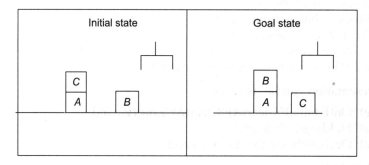

Figure 9.4 Goal stack planning—Initial and goal states.

In goal stack planning, a stack of goals is maintained. Accordingly, the corresponding actions are carried out to get the solution.

The initial state here is

On(*A*,table)^On(*B*,table)^On(*C*,*A*)^Clear(*C*)^Clear(*B*)^Empty-hand

The goal state is

On(*A*,table)^On(*B*,*A*)^On(*C*,table)^Clear(*C*)^Empty-hand^Clear(*B*)

For the goal, the following steps are carried (For simplicity, let us neglect the clear and empty-hand conditions here, as things will get more complicated.):

The refined goal will be

On(*A*,table)^On(*C*,table)^On(*B*,*A*)

The stack for the goal will be

    Stack 1

    On(*C*,table)

    On(*B*,*A*)

    On(*B*,*A*)^On(*C*,table)^On(*A*,table)

Here, the last operation leads to final goal, where *A* is already placed on the table. So, for the On(*C*,table), we need

Place(*C*) and Unstack(*C*,*A*)

So, we replace the On(*C*, table) and add this to it.

Unstack(*C*,*A*)
Place(*C*)
On(*B*,*A*)
On(*B*,*A*)^On(*C*,table)^On(*A*,table)

For unstack, the pre-conditions are to be added. This is done in the following way:

On(*A*,table)
Clear(*C*)
On(*C*,*A*)
Empty-hand
Empty-hand^On(*C*,*A*)^Clear(*C*)^On(*A*,table)
Unstack(*C*,*A*)
Place(*C*)
On(*B*,*A*)
On(*B*,*A*)^On(*C*,table)^On(*A*,table)

Since it is observed that the first state of *A* block on the table is true, hence we remove it. Further, Clear *C* is also valid, and hence, it is also removed. So, these exist for the other two conditions of On(*C*,*A*) and Empty-hand. Since all the pre-conditions are valid, so we can proceed. They are removed to move further. Finally, the stack has:

Unstack(C,A)
Place (C)
On(*B*,*A*)
On(*B*,*A*)^On(*C*,table)^On(*A*,table)

Since all pre-conditions are satisfied for the unstack operation to occur, we record this action to be the first step that is required to be carried out in the planning sequence. For Place (*C*), the pre-conditions are—the hand should be holding *C* and then only it can be placed. So, the pre-conditions are added, and since all are valid, this action is also finalised.

Unstack(C,A)
Place(C)
On(*B*,*A*)
On(*B*,*A*)^On(*C*,table)^On(*A*,table)

In this way, the sequence is continued. There could be a case, where multiple options can exist. So, there could be two or more goal stacks, where the operation has to be carried out. Once the first goal is achieved, the next goal is looked upon. Similarly, the actions and the conditions are added.

Now, consider a case, where the second goal is itself contained in the first goal, say if the order is changed, for *B* to be on *A*, the goal of *C* to be on the table becomes contained in it. So, naturally, the sub-goal is reported to be reached.

Thus, we have discussed the overview of the goal stack planning. Now, the query arises here—is this approach an efficient one? For smaller problems, it is fine, but with larger ones, it becomes complicated. The case could occur, where the action that is not required is carried out, and further, it adds to the complications. There can be options to go back and recall the step that has been done in order to undo it. Still, there can be more and better methods to design and extract a plan instead of this one.

9.6 MEANS ENDS ANALYSIS

Means-ends Analysis is one of the important concepts that is used for problem solving and planning. The notion of means-ends analysis is same as what is used in STRIPS. Means-ends analysis is dependent on a set of rules. The rules are used for the transformation from one state to another. The pre-conditions and the post-conditions are included in it. A *difference table* is used to represent the difference between the current state and the next state. The action selection is based on this difference. It also follows a backward search to locate an action that has the required pre-conditions.

The steps carried out in means-ends analysis are given below:

1. Computing the difference between the current/initial state and the goal/next state.
2. Based on the satisfaction of preconditions, recommending the action (This reduces the difference between them).
3. Checking the possibility of executing the action (If not possible, then this current state is treated as the goal state and recursive call takes place).

Let us take an example. Suppose you are new in a city and you want to purchase a laptop. You do not know where the shop is. You have a contact number of your friend, who stays in that city and can help you with the address. With means-ends analysis, the difference table can be (only some rules are shown):

1. If you want to purchase a laptop then recommended actions are visit_shop or purchase online.
2. If you do not know the address then recommended actions are call friend or use tools like Google maps to get it, and so on.

For each of the recommended action, there is a pre and post-condition.

For example, for the action visit_shop, pre-condition can be—you should know the location to the shop, and the post-condition can be—you have the laptop purchased.

This set is formed for all the actions in the difference table.

Now, assume that you are at the first state, where you want to purchase the laptop. Since the pre-condition of the location of the shop to have the rule1 executed is not satisfied, the recursive call takes place with the condition of location not known and so on.

9.7 PLANNING AS A STATE-SPACE SEARCH

There are two approaches to planning: state-space planning and plan-space planning. What we intend to do in both the cases is to find a plan.

A *state-space planning* is the one that works at the states and the operators. This is also called *planning as a state-space search*. In this case, the plan is found as a search through the search space. Here, the search takes place in both the directions—forward and backward. In case of *plan-space planning*, the search is carried out through the space of plans. So, naturally, we need to begin with some plan that might be incorrect or incomplete. The ordering in the actions is done so as to get the accurate plan. It involves additions or deletions of the steps as well.

Let us discuss the first case, i.e., planning with state-space search in detail.

As discussed earlier, the planning can be from the initial state to the goal state or in reverse way. It is called *forward state-space search* and *backward state-space search*. A forward state-space search is called *progression planning*, whereas backward state-space search is called *regression planning*.

Progression Planning

This planning starts with the initial state and proceeds with search. It follows the effects of the possible actions. So, the sequence of actions is considered till we are able build or form a sequence to reach the goal.

Figure 9.5 represents the forward search for a case in which a robot (say) is in room1, and the tea and guest are in room2 and room3.

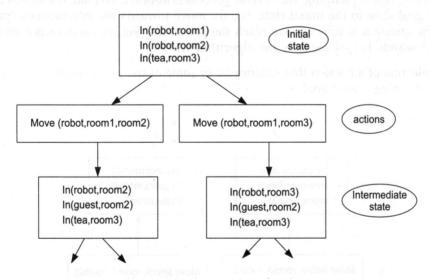

Figure 9.5 Progression planning.

The problem is formulated as below:

1. *Start state:* The start state is the initial state of the problem prior to any action applied to it. It assumes that the things not mentioned (objects not involved) are not true.

2. *Goal check:* Checking of whether the goal is achieved/reached or not reached.

3. Actions: It involves a list or sequence of actions with respect to the pre-conditions that allows moving to the next intermediate state.

4. Step cost: It is a cost associated with every action that is taken. Most often, this is 1.

Any of the search method that comes to the solution, if at all exists, is complete. Hence, a complete planning algorithm is possible to obtain. But are there any drawbacks of such a search? We can see in Figure 9.4, the scenario is simple with a limited number of propositions. But what will happen if the number of propositions is increased? It is also observed that the actions that are considered in the planning are all the possible actions. There is a possibility that irrelevant actions not leading to the goal are carried out. For understanding, let us take an example. You plan for getting 75% marks, and focus on some topics that are out of syllabus or some points are never asked. Since you are unaware of it, you study them too, and hence, they are also taken in the planning. If you have the knowledge, the plan can be made better. Here, heuristic comes in picture. Can forward planning be made more efficient with the aid of heuristic? We will discuss heuristic methods later in the chapter to clarify this. Let us begin with the backward state-space search.

Regression Planning

In case of regression planning, the reverse process is applied. To plan, the search is started from the goal state to the initial state. So, we move towards the intermediate (pre-states) states. The question is how can we reach the pre-states? Figure 9.6 depicts a snapshot of backward search. Let us see how the algorithm works.

1. Selection of an action that satisfies all or some of the propositions in the goal state.
2. Reforming a new goal.

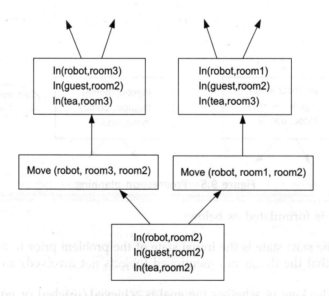

Figure 9.6 Regression planning.

Here, the goal propositions that are satisfied by invoking the actions are eliminated, whereas unsolved ones are keep intact. The pre-condition is the state prior, so this is added.

Steps 1 and 2 are repeated till the initial state or the start state is reached.

Note: The way the propositions are achieved is important here (i.e., ordering is important). The main advantage of backward search is that the relevant actions are considered.

Any of the search strategy can be made use of in the process of planning. Let us proceed towards the discussion of heuristics.

Role of Heuristics

The methods discussed above, i.e., progression and regression planning can be made efficient with the use of heuristics. Is it possible to identify the number of steps or the actions to be executed so that the goal is achieved? This comes to a NP-hard problem. Still, some solutions to it are discussed here.

So, what we intend to do is to find an admissible heuristic. This is done in the following way:

1. By converting the problem into a relaxed one (Here all the pre-conditions are removed.)
2. By assuming that the sub-goals are independent (So, the cost to solve the problem is approximated by summation of the costs, where the sub-goals are solved independently.)

To summarise, the progressive and regressive planning actions are dependent on the sequences. There is a need to have planners that can consider sub-goals, solve them independently and then the final plan can be a combinations of the sub-results obtained. Thus, we can proceed to partial order planning.

9.8   PARTIAL ORDER PLANNING

The concept of total order planner states that any planner that maintains the solution (may be partial too) as a totally ordered steps it has identified so far forms a linear planner. Whereas, if partially we are able to put up the ordering constraints (temporal), it is referred to as a *partial order planning*. With the progressive and regressive plannings that are linear in nature and are often referred to as *totally ordered*, there is a necessity to have the plannings to exploit the sub-problem structure.

Consider a case where you have to latch the door. With the use of lock and keys, the total order plan and partial order plan (POP) are depicted in Figure 9.7.

There is a notion of least commitment strategy in POP. *Least commitment strategy* is a policy, where the decisions or the choices are delayed. It simply says that 'do not make any decisions unless required'. One advantage of using this is that it avoids the re-work. The tasks might have to be undone. To understand the concept, take a simple example. Assume some assignment is given for a particular course. A student completes the assignment on the same day. But he does not get it evaluated from the course teacher till a deadline or say some grades regarding submission have been put up. (Hoping that the re-work would be avoided!)

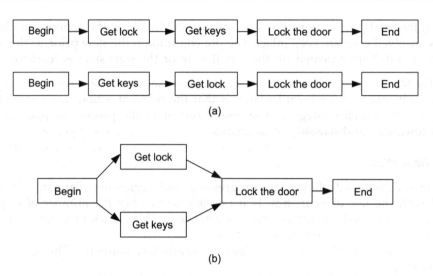

Figure 9.7 (a) Total order planning and (b) Partial order planning.

In case of partial order plans, the plans are created by making a search through plan spaces. It follows the least commitment strategy. This strategy allows to make choices relevant to current solvable part of problem. The question is how can the partial order plans be actually represented? The answer is in the form of graphs. Typical graph structure for the POP comprises temporal constraints. These constraints are the ones that specify that state x is before state y. In POP, the planning algorithm can put two or more actions into a plan, where the sequence in which the actions are to be carried out does not matter.

POP Representation

Consider a case of four states. A graphical representation for such a POP is shown in Figure 9.8. The temporal constraints are State 1 < State 2, State 1 < State 3, State 2 < State 3, State 3 < State 4.

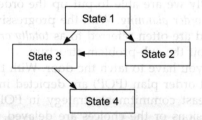

Figure 9.8 Basic graph representation for POP.

The total order plans here are (State 1, State 2, State 3, State 4) and (State 1, State 3, State 2, State 4).

We now look at the creation of the POP. We know that the plans are created by searching in the plan space. Let us create a graph. An arc shows the transition from one state to another. These arcs can be categorised into two types—where a normal transition from one state (plan) to another can occur, and where constraints indicating that a particular state has to occur before next are indicated (time factor is not accounted).

The plan is represented as follows:

1. Set of plan steps. The operators are mapped into steps.
2. It also has 'ordering constraints' for the steps. This is represented as $S \prec S'$, where S occurs before S' step.
3. Bindings on variable are also added of the form var = x, where var is variable and x could be referring to another variable on some constant.
4. The causal links are also established. It is represented as $S \rightarrow$ cl:S', where the pre-condition 'cl' for step S' is satisfied by S.

A *consistent plan* is defined as a plan that contains no cycles for ordering constraints and there are no conflicts with the causal links as well.

The partial order plan algorithm comprises

1. Begin with initial plan
   This plan consists of only start and finish steps.
2. Till a solution plan is achieved:
   (a) Select an unachieved pre-condition and achieve it.
   (b) Resolve threats by applying promotion or demotion.

Let us take an example to understand the threats, promotion and demotion. Consider a case, where you have to update on the social network sites or the professional ones like Linkedin and check office mails.

Writing it syntactically,

1. **Goal:** update(Linkedin)^update(facebook)^check(office-mails)^update(twitter)
2. **Initial step:** Login(office-email-id)
3. **Operators:** The operators can be
   (i) Checking-mails
      Pre-condition: Login(office-email-id)
      Post-condition: check(office-mails)
   (ii) Updating-social-network-sites
      Pre-condition:
      Post-condition: update(x)^~Login(office-email-id)
   (Assume you are already ready with your laptop and also the sites are on for you to update.)

Plan search: The first step is where we want to go from the initial state, i.e., to the goal state.

In the next step, as shown in Figure 9.9, a graph is generated. Here, the unsolved goals are just added. The links are established.

Moving ahead, there are some pre-conditions that we have not added like login to office email. So, add them. The next step is depicted in Figure 9.10.

The next part is to add the ordering. As we can notice from Figure 9.9, we say that the four activities can be performed at any point of time. But the steps of updating the sites do not require the office-login. So, if they are performed prior, then this pre-condition will not occur. (In the given example, this is required.) Hence, it is treated as a threat. So, this is added where it is indicated that the update operation can be performed any time after

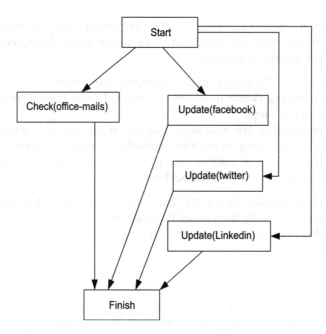

Figure 9.9 Adding unsolved goals—Step 1.

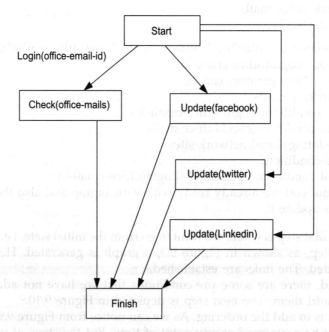

Figure 9.10 Adding pre-conditions—Step 2.

the emails are done. So, the graph now becomes different as shown in Figure 9.11. Thus, an ordering constraint is added. It is said here that the previously achieved pre-condition has been clobbered. We will discuss this once the entire plan is complete.

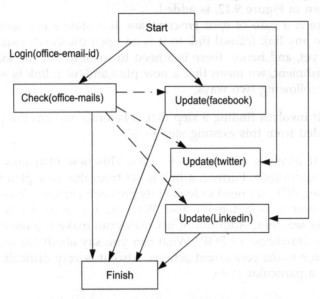

Figure 9.11   Adding pre-conditions—Step 3.

The ordering constraints are Check(office-mails)<Update(facebook), Check(office-mails)<Update(Linkedin), Check(office-mails)<Update(Twitter).

So, the solution we have obtained in step 3 is a complete plan.

Coming back to the discussion of clobbered, we have detected a threat in the previous example. The threat is fixed by promotion or demotion, i.e., declobbering.

Consider the following case of actions a_x and a_y

$$a_x \xrightarrow{\ e\ } a_y$$

where e is the effect of action a_x.

Now, there can be an action a_z that could have an effect e'. In such a case, there is a threat. This is resolved by ordering a_z after a_y or ordering a_z before a_x. The former case is promotion and the latter case is demotion. So, in promotion, the threat step is ordered after the link, whereas in demotion, it is before the causal link. In the given scenario, the threatening steps were of update. So, the threat was allowed to come after the check-mails was done. Hence, we applied a promotion to it.

Let us represent the promotion and demotion as given in Figure 9.12.

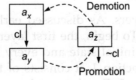

Figure 9.12   Promotion and demotion of action.

Figure 9.12 shows that a_y is generated from $a_x \cdot a_y$ has cl as pre-condition. In a POP, assume a step a_z is added, which has ~cl as the effect. If a_z occurs between a_x and a_y, then it creates issue. a_z is conflicting action. So, an ordering constraint of promotion or demotion, as shown in Figure 9.12, is added.

Similarly, there is a case of *open pre-condition*. If a state *s* has some pre-condition *p* that does not have any link (causal link to it is an open pre-condition), then we say that this is not solved yet, and hence, there is a need to solve it. For the same, establishment is done. By establishment, we mean that a new plan and/or a link is added. This can be carried out in the following two ways:

1. *Link addition:* It involves finding a step that is before *s* and has the pre-condition true. Then, a link is added from this existing step to '*s*'.

2. *Plan addition:* It involves adding a new plan. This new plan now contains the pre-conditions as post-conditions. Further, a link is set from this new plan to *s*.

While discussing POP, we need to look at its pros and cons too. It is clear that the POP is complete. Moreover, it is systematic also. With the use of least commitment strategy, it may have shorter searches. Addition of heuristics can make it more efficient. Now, can you think of some drawbacks of POP? What can you say about the search spaces? They are huge. This is due to the concurrent actions. Also, it is very difficult to state that what is actually true in a particular state.

9.9   PLANNING GRAPHS

After having an elaborated study on POP, we now come to planning graphs. The concept of planning graph was introduced by A. Blum and M. Furst in 1995. *Planning graph* is a data structure that encodes the information contained in the states regarding their reachability. The basic idea, as introduced by Blum and Furst, is to construct smaller size graphs that would contain partial information about the reachability. Reachability means an estimate about the steps required to reach a particular state from the initial state. Also the graphs can be used in heuristic estimation as well. By the use of algorithms like Graphplan, it is possible to get a direct solution from the planning graphs.

A *planning graph* is a layered graph comprising states and actions that form a layer and they appear alternately. So, it can be represented as follows:

{State 1, Action 1, State 2, Action 2, ..., State *n*, Action *n*}

For each operator *o* that belongs to action$_x$ (say), there is an edge from literal in state *x*. This literal is the pre-condition for operator *o*.

Constructing the Planning Graph

The graph is constructed in layers. As discussed earlier in STRIPS, it consists of states and actions forming one layer. To begin, the first layer of state consists of an initial state. So, every positive literal in the initial state and every negative literal not in the state are added. This forms state 1. For action 1, it consists of the operators for which the literals are the pre-conditions from state 1. For the next layer, the state 2 consists of all the post-conditions of the operators used in action 1. This process is carried out till there is a stabilisation. It means that the layer$_{n-1}$ is equal to layer$_n$.

Let us take an example of constructing a building and selling it. Let the initial state be that the building is constructed, i.e., constructed (building) and the goal state is constructed (building)^sold(building).

Let us have two actions—selling of the building and constructing it.

Action: Selling(building)
Pre-condition: constructed(building)
Post-condition: ~constructed(building)^sold(building)

Action: Constructing(building)
Pre-condition: ~constructed(building)
Post-condition: constructed(building)

The planning graph for the example is represented in Figure 9.13. Details are given below:

Layer **1:** It involves state 1 and action 1.

State 1: (All the atomic facts are in initial state) union (negation of the atomic facts is not in the state). So, state 1 has constructed(building) and ~(sold(building)).

Action 1: All the action where the pre-conditions are satisfied, so it will have only selling(building).

Layer **2:** This involves state 2 and action 2.

State 2: We map the post-conditions here. The literals that remain unaffected are carry forwarded.

Action 2: Similar to action 1, it carries the task.

Layer **3:** It involves state 3.

State 3: As it is observed that the state is similar to state 2, this is called *stabilisation*. This stage comes after *n* iterations (say), where the states remain same. Hence, there is no need to go ahead for building the layers.

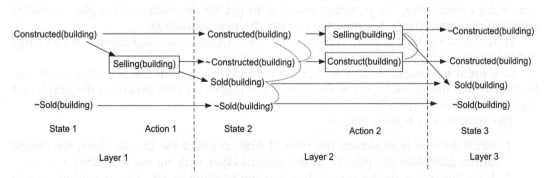

Figure 9.13 Planning graph.

One more point to address here is that we can see some dotted arcs in the states. These are called as *mutex links*. They indicate that they are mutually exclusive. This is due to the conflicts that arise. This means they cannot be selected together, or else there would be a conflict. This pair in conflict is called *mutex*. (*Note:* Only few mutexes are shown in the diagram). The mutex can exist for literals as well as for actions.

With respect to the actions, it is said that the two actions at the same layer are mutex if they show the following conditions:

1. Inconsistent effects: In the sense, say actions a_x and a_y are mutex, if a_x results in L_x and a_y results in $\sim L_x$ as post-conditions.

2. Interference: A pre-condition of a_x and post-condition of a_y are inconsistent. That is, Pre-condition = ~Post-condition.

3. Competing needs: In this case, the pre-conditions are actually the inverse. Say pre-condition p_1 in a_x and p_2 in a_y are competing, i.e., $p_1 = \sim p_2$.

In case of literals, the literals (or the states here) are mutex if

1. There exists inconsistency, i.e., if l_1 and l_2 are the literals then $l_1 = \sim l_2$ and $l_2 = \sim l_1$.
2. If there exists a pair of actions a_x and a_y such that l_1 is the post-condition of a_x and l_2 the post-condition of a_y, and a_x and a_y are mutex, then l_1 and l_2 are also mutex.

Heuristics

Planning graphs are very useful in terms for heuristic estimation. So, we want to estimate the cost. A very simple thing to understand is that suppose a literal does not exist in the final layer and it is present in the goal (This is after the planning graph has stabilised), then the goal cannot be achieved. Further, in heuristics, the numbers of levels are counted to be the cost. But will this be a better option? No. The reason being the number of actions that take place in each of the layers. But if a condition is added where only one action can occur at a particular time, then this is called *serial graph*. A serial graph also adds the mutex. The cost to get the literal in the goal is computed as the summation of cost of the number of levels it appears before.

Why is it necessary to have all this explanation regarding literals and layers? Where is it useful? With the planning graph, we are able to identify the reachable states. The reason for constructing the planning graph is to get the heuristics and a plan extracted from the planning graph. So, now we discuss the plan extraction.

How can we extract a plan? Through the use of Graphplan algorithm, we can carry out the process of plan extraction.

One point to remember here is that the plan extracted from the planning graph can be longer than the actual layers in the graph. The algorithm first generates the graph and then extracts a plan from it.

The algorithm is briefed below:

1. Since the aim is to extract the plan, it first checks if the literals (here, the states) in the goal state are present in the current layer with no mutex chains.
2. If so, there is a strong probability that the solution exists. The algorithm tries to get the plan extracted.

3. But if not, then it expands to the next level. So, it goes to the next layer. This is done with the addition of actions and states.
4. The steps 1, 2, 3 are repeated till a solution is found or it is observed that the solution will not exist.

While extracting the plan, the process is carried out from the last layer to the beginning of the graph. The actions are selected that do not have the mutex links and also there should not be any mutex links in the pre-condition as well. So, we can say that the process is backward. This process is carried out till all the required goals are reached or rather they are satisfied.

When will the algorithm terminate actually? It will be based on the mutex. For example, if in the goal, the states are mutex in the planning graph, then the solution is not going to occur. As discussed before, there exists a stabilisation constraint, where the layers become same or identical. But still, there can be further expansion of stages if the solution is not obtained; hence, the termination of the algorithm is a complicated issue.

9.10   HIERARCHICAL PLANNING

The traditional planning approaches always have to face complexity issue. They lack the ability to build a structure that can distinguish and prioritise between the important and unimportant aspects., i.e., operators and properties. Hierarchical planning overcomes this inability by providing abstraction in planning.

The abstraction is provided at two levels.

1. Situations and 2. Operators

1. Situations: Weight is assigned for each literal, where priority is given to literals with higher weights. For example, weights can be assigned as

Property: Weight
On: 3
Clear: 2 and so on.

2. Operators: In order to provide operator abstraction, any operation is viewed as operator abstraction of other operators, say for example, for 'lift' operator, we can split it as

(i) Placing the robot arm
(ii) Holding the block
(iii) Picking the block

This planning is demonstrated by ABSTRIPS. The hierarchical planning is governed by criticality value. Any operation that possesses minimum criticality is trivally achievable. This specifies operators with few or no pre-conditions, whereas one with more pre-conditions has high criticality. This type of planning is effective where pre-conditions are shown to be achievable and can be achieved independently.

9.10.1   Hierarchical Task Network (HTN)

Some recent work on hierarchical planning and co-ordinated plan executions by P. Gorniak and I. Davis discussed the need for hierarchical planning, where it put forth that the

STRIPS are turning out to be poor designers in planning. With an approach based on hierarchical task networks, the paper addressed the co-ordinations and efficiency along with planning intelligently. A complier based on JSHOP, a hierarchical planner is used. The idea presented is to write a tool that generates the specific plans. It shows its efficiency in case of generation of plans for combat situations, squad as well as in game context. Some more examples of HTN are SIPE-2 or SHOP.

What does this HTN planning actually do? The HTN planning puts to practice this abstraction making use of the operators. The operators can be abstract and primitive. But the final plan generated is only with the primitive operators.

A simple HTN is depicted in Figure 9.14.

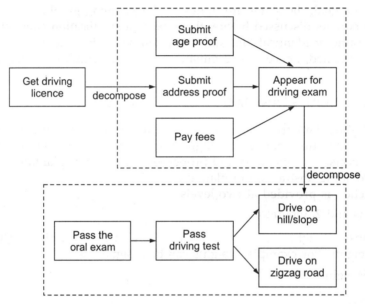

Figure 9.14 A simple HTN.

To summarise, in hierarchical planning, the actions are split into sub-tasks. The sub-tasks are specific. The actions are serialised into an abstract level. So, we are, in short, prioritising the tasks, where the operators are actually planned. Most often, HTNs are used, where the problem structure itself has some organised hierarchy. In case of HTN, rather than having the main goal set up, it comprises partially ordered tasks to take up. So, a decomposition process starts till the planner can reach the primitive tasks that can be easily carried out with the operators. Whereas, for the non-primitive tasks, further decomposition takes place.

9.11 NON-LINEAR PLANNING

A plan that consists of sub-problems, which are solved simultaneously is said to be a *non-linear plan*. In case of the goal stack planning, as discussed previously, it poses some problems. To achieve any goal, it could have an impact on the one that has been already achieved. In linear planning, the effects change according to the situations in which they are operated. So, just one goal is taken at a time and solved completely before the next one is taken is the job of linear planning.

Let us take an example. You want to take the car for servicing and have to make an important phone call. To complete these two tasks, we can have an interleaving form. Rather than completing both the tasks in a linear way, after completion of the task 1, as partial step, i.e., start the car and put on the Bluetooth, then complete the task 2 of phone call and then finally, complete the task 1 by leaving the car at the service station. This can be an example of non-linear planning. Figure 9.15 depicts a simple non-linear plan.

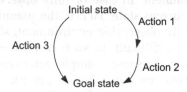

Figure 9.15   Non-linear planning.

There is a concept of constraint posting that comes with non-linear planning. The constraint posting states that the plan can be built by

1. Addition of operators or suggesting operators
2. Ordering them
3. Binding the variables to the operators

Initially, we are not aware of how the operators that are available should be worked on. So, incrementally, the constraints and the details are added. Planning systems like TWEAK and MOLGEN are non-linear in nature, which employ this constraint posting.

9.12   CONDITIONAL PLANNING

Before going into discussion of conditional planning, we look at undeterministic environment and prepare some background for the concept. The methodologies that have been studied belong to the classical planning. Here, the environment is deterministic, fully observable and static. What can happen in case of partially observed environment? For example, you have planned for studying in the preparation leave. For a particular subject, you are to go to the market to purchase the book. You decide that on a particular day, say Tuesday you would go and get the book. But on that day, all of a sudden, the shopkeepers call a strike indefinitely. Your entire planning is disturbed and so is the plan. Hence, we can say that the information available was incomplete (owing to sudden change) in the plan. In such a case, the plan generated is actually correct, but due to the circumstances, it turns out to be less strong. Take one more case, where the plan is hampered if the exam schedule is changed. In all these scenarios, there is a need to handle the incompleteness.

Now, we look at the concept of bounded indeterminacy. This governs how much concrete the environment is in which an agent has to operate. A *bounded indeterminacy* is defined as a condition in which actions can result into unpredicted outcomes, but it is possible to get the listing of the possible outcomes. For instance, if you visit a person without intimation, then there is uncertainty that the person may be at home or may not. Hence, there is unpredicted outcome from the known set. So, planning is very much possible with this bounded indeterminacy. In conditional planning, it handles this indeterminacy. A simple approach to this is to construct the plan with the possible outcomes. So, the possible alternatives are listed. So, in case of above example, you can have plan for both outcomes. In case the person is at home, you can have a meeting with him, else you can watch a movie in a theatre next to his residence. We can say that with the rules of if-then, conditional planning occurs. Further, it also makes use of AND-OR graph search for the planning. Conditional planning can occur in fully observable as well as partially observable environment. In case of fully observable environment, the agent in operation is aware of the current state. Hence, the planning becomes simple with the rule-based structure. In partially observable environment, since the entire information is not available, planning becomes difficult. In such cases, the conditional planning makes use of belief states. Considering the same example, after reaching the person's residence, you came to know that he was not there. So, as per plan, you go for the movie, but there is a possibility that movie tickets may be available or may not be. This state is the belief state. It is defined as a set of possible states an agent can be in. With the use of the belief states and AND-OR graphs, the planning in partially observable environment can occur. The major drawback of conditional planning is that they can be harder than the NP-complete problems. Still, what can you say about the space requirements of this approach? They are large enough.

Conditional planning is also referred to as *contingency planning*. So, it is a planning approach, which can handle the various contingencies that can arise. These types of planners belong to the category of non-deterministic domains, where a dependency lies on the parameters other than the current state.

9.13 REACTIVE PLANNING

Reactive planning is planning under uncertainty. Here, rather than building the plan with the branches, it makes use of the if-then rules. So, what different are they doing? The reactive planners are based on the concept that they should be able to handle an unknown situation too. So, the reaction rules are used that help them in doing so. But there is also a need to have reasoning while applying the reaction rules. The reactions rules are prioritised. A rule selection is based on the priority and a holding condition that maximises the priority. The rule which is at present in execution is said to be active whereas the ones with holding priority (we can call them possible competitors) are pre-active and the others are *inactive*. Many's the time, in reactive planning suspension can occur in the rule that is at present in execution. A B-tree structure is used in reactive planning, where the algorithm selects the rule. Sometimes, no rule can be selected. In such a case, things are dependent on the algorithm implementation for rule selection.

9.14 KNOWLEDGE-BASED PLANNING

The planning methods (like HTN) actually belong to the category of knowledge-based planning. Early in 1998, Kautz and Selman identified the planning knowledge categories as follows:

1. Knowledge regarding the domain.
2. Knowledge regarding the good plans
3. Explicit search control knowledge.

It is not just this knowledge, but today, it is also about interacting with the user and getting the preferences. Some of the features of a knowledge-based planner are mentioned below:

1. *Expressive:* It should be able to express the types of goals and constraints, to look at the additional resources, and so on.

2. *Correct:* The HTN planners have proved to be effective in terms of correctness. The property of correctness tells that though the real-world domain cannot be modelled, system can be verified with the effectiveness of some properties.

3. *User interaction:* A planning model can be made more effective, if it allows for user interactions. This allows the necessary changes to be made in the plan as per the requirements and provides guidance in the search too.

4. *Constraints:* With ontology, it is possible to encode the knowledge, and thus, reason about the system. This proves the method to be more effective, as it is able to reason that the relations set earlier cannot be changed. Further, temporal constraints that are time-based help in developing a better planner.

9.15 USING TEMPORAL LOGIC

The planning is based on the time in case of temporal logic. The rules and the propositions are governed by the time factor. It tackles conditions that would gradually be true, or dependency of one condition to be true based on some other, and so on.

Temporal logic essentially provides a mathematical framework that can be made use of in the reasoning process during the planning. The requirements of the system can be represented in a better way by the use of temporal logic. This results in the correctness of the process. After studying the knowledge-based planning, do you think that there could be a way to use temporal logic here also? Yes, it is very much possible. Moreover, domain dependent search control knowledge can also be represented with the use of temporal logic. This is further exploited and used in forward chaining planner. TLPlan is an example of such a system, where the temporal logic is used. Currently, it is put to practice in the motion planning.

9.16 EXECUTION MONITORING AND RE-PLANNING

As the name suggests, *execution monitoring* is the process of checking the current state and its percepts, and ensuring that the things are moving ahead as per the plan. When things are not going as per the plan, re-planning is done.

Let us take the example of a robot serving tea to the guest (refer to Figure 9.2). We have a plan, according to which the robot has to move to room 2 to give the tea to the guest. Now, while executing the plan what will happen if the guest moves to room 1 in the mean time? Here, comes the execution monitoring that performs the check on the current percept. So, the pre-conditions are checked. This check indicates that the guest is not in room 2. This is handled at the time of execution. Hence, re-planning for the set of actions is done next to some point in the plan. With the agent scenario in picture, this type of planning involves two types of agents to control the execution process—Action-check agent and re-planning agent.

It is the action-check agent that checks if it is possible to execute the next action. If so, it, in turn can direct some work to the plan-check agent that would verify the plan remaining. The job of the re-planning agent is to maintain a track of the plan completed till the current state and the one remaining. It is the re-planning agent that actually calls the action-check agent, and further, based on discrepancies, re-planning of the actions takes place.

The algorithm for this is summarised below:

1. Observe the current percept.
2. Check for the pre-conditions.
   If satisfy, proceed.
   Else report a failure state and re-plan.
   (i) Find a state in the plan such that the failure state is repaired.
   (ii) Create a new plan with this new state added and continue.

9.17 CONTINUOUS PLANNING

Continuous planning can be thought of as a planning, wherein the monitoring and the re-planning activities are clubbed together. In case of these planners, the operation is incremental in nature. By incremental, we mean that the plan formulation is dependent on the current percept, and the continuous planning agent always begins with this percept and generates a plan. So, at each point of time, the percept is observed and the plan is generated. Thus, the methodology is incremental.

Considering the same scenario of the agent and the guest, if the plan for the next action is selected based on the current percept available, it would prove to be a better option. So, if the agent has planned to execute the action of 'give tea', with pre-conditions as guest and robot both are in room 2, the continuous planning agent sees the change, whether the guest has moved to room 1. If so, the plan is changed. The agent in this scenario detects that the pre-condition has turned out to be false. Hence, the other actions are required to be worked out. These types of planners are similar to that of POP, yet they need to carry out a lot of activities like detecting conflicts in case of action execution, detecting unwanted actions, updating the new actions, building and identifying the plans, and so on.

9.18 MULTI-AGENT PLANNING

The multi-agent planning involves use of multiple agents to carry out the planning tasks. The background behind this is that a teamwork can prove to be better when an individual cannot accomplish the task. We are already familiar with what planning does and what a single agent can do. If the task is extended to multiple agents, it would be easier. The multi-agent planning generally is of two types, i.e., by and for multiple agents. The planning in case of agent environment obviously needs the interactions between them; hence, there should be co-ordination and communication. This is necessary from the goal achievement perspective. What would happen if the agent would work with only his available set of environment? Can the goal achieved be efficient? Can an agent depend on the other agents actions? The answer to all these questions is yes. Hence, there is a need to have proper co-ordination between them. At the next level, it could even be distributed.

Can there be any issues that are required to handle in this planning? The answer is definitely yes. There are things that need attention like robustness of the plans, the costs involved in the interactions along with the scalability issues.

Where is this required? The multi-agent planning is most commonly used in the industries associated with assembling of components, in case of electronic devices or vehicle assembling and not to forget, the gaming part as well.

The tasks involved in multi-agent planning technique are summarised below:

1. Setting goals and assigning to individual agents
2. Refining the goals and further decomposing them into sub-goals
3. Converting sub-goals into achievable tasks
4. Scheduling the tasks (This includes resource allocation to agents and timing deadlines, if applicable, for the task)
5. Co-ordinating and communicating to avoid conflicts
6. Executing the plan

9.19 JOB SHOP SCHEDULING PROBLEM

It is a problem that needs to handle the time constraints, the scheduling, and at the same time, has to perform check on the availability of resources. Let us understand how it is resolved with planning.

The job shop problem consists of jobs j_1 to j_n that are to be completed. To complete them, machines m_1 to m_n are used. For the jobs to complete, there is a sequence of actions, say a_1 to a_n that is required to take place on the machines. Every action has a specific duration and it might make use of some resources also. The problem is to minimise the time required for the completion of the jobs, and at the same time, handle the resource constraint, if any. (Remember that there are some variants for the job shop problem.)

So, is it a scheduling problem in planning? Yes. The job shop scheduling problem occurs in cases of the production scheduling. There is a need to have an appropriate planning so that the constraints are taken care of. Let us take an example, where the scheduling is to occur for two vehicles to assemble the engine assembly, frame assembly and the chassis. A POP is shown in Figure 9.16. The numbers above each of the action indicate the time it needs to execute. While scheduling, there is a concept of slack. Suppose along with the time durations required to get the action completed, if early start and late start timings are provided, then this slack is identified. Let us say that the early and the late start timings for action 1 of engine assembling for both the vehicles is 0,0. Then, there is no slack. But suppose the early start time and the late start time for action 2 for vehicle A is 40,50, then there exists a slack of 10 for the action.

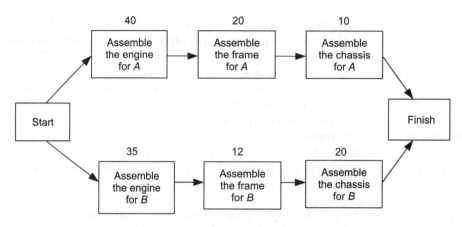

Figure 9.16 A partial order plan for the problem.

This can be very much represented in terms of Gantt chart. But we are here to talk about planning and constraints, let us take things ahead in the constraint part. Suppose for each of the action, there is a resource person, who actually evaluates and monitors whether the things have been assembled in a proper way or not, and then, there is a constraint added to it. If there are six different people to carry out the task, the constraints are nil. But if only three persons are available to carry out the fixed tasks like one working as engine checking manager, one as frame check managers and one as the chassis checking manager, things would get very much complicated. There is a need to have a proper plan for this, wherein these resource persons should be used in the planning process with the constraints that exist. The solution to this is depicted in Figure 9.17. The time required here comes to 107.

Can there be any heuristics in case of planning for the job scheduling? The greedy approach is the one that is often used. According to a simple rule that is applied here, the entire problem should be split into sub-tasks and then the planning and execution should occur. The actions can be very well-formulated using STRIPS. Yet, it is worth to mention that the constraints naturally add up the complexity of the problem, making it an NP-hard problem.

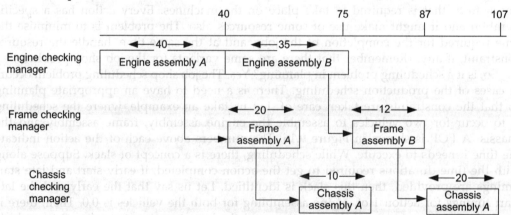

Figure 9.17 Possible solution for the problem with the resource constraint.

SUMMARY

With the necessity for the planning in AI, the chapter highlights the need and importance of planning in the fully observable environment as well as under uncertainty. A planning system comprises initial states, and goal states and actions to achieve them. The actions are represented in the form of operators to achieve the goal. Representation for a planning system has to be effective. Different languages like STRIPS, ADL are used for planning. Approaches like the goal stack planning and the means-ends analysis show their characteristics with the STRIPS. The state-space search and the forward and backward searches assist in the selection of an action. Addition of heuristics makes the planning more effective. Planning is not just concerned with the organisation of tasks, but forms the basis for reasoning. POP approaches prove to be a better option than the total ordering, helping in building partially and parallel executable plans. The least commitment strategy adds benefits to the POP.

Further, the planning graphs, helps in determining the reachability of a state and the term of mutex tackles the constraints. Hierarchical planning, conditional planning and the concepts of non-linear planning too are important when it comes to handle the real-time complex problems. HTN planning is been widely used in research at present for gaming purposes, whereas the multi-agent planning finds its place in military tasks and vehicle assembling.

 KEYWORDS

1. **Planning:** It determines how and when to do/perform the necessary steps for defined goals.
2. **STRIPS:** It is a planning language that makes use of first order predicate, allows function-free literals and has historic importance.
3. **ADL:** A planning language that is more expressive than STRIPS and used for reasoning purposes.
4. **PDDL:** A planning language that is a superset of STRIPS and ADL and used for classical planning tasks.
5. **Goal stack planning:** It is an approach used in STRIPS that maintains stacks of goals to achieve the tasks.
6. **Means-ends analysis:** It is a rule based concept used in STRIPS that makes use of difference table for the selection of an action.
7. **Progression planning:** This planning starts with the initial state and proceeds with the search. The forward state-space search approach is used here.
8. **Regression planning:** This planning works from the goal state towards the initial state. The backward state-space search is used here.
9. **Total order planning:** Progression and regression planning belong to this category of planning. They operate linearly and exploit sub-problems that can be solved independently.

10. **Partial order planning:** It is a planning approach where the actions in the plan can occur without the rule that specific action has to come prior. It makes the use of temporal constraints and least commitment strategy.

11. **Planning graph:** It is a data structure that encodes the information contained in the states regarding their reachability.

12. **Hierarchical planning:** It sets priorities in planning. Actions are split into sub-tasks.

13. **Hierarchical task networks:** They comprise partially ordered tasks and are used where the problem structure itself has some organised hierarchy.

14. **Non-linear planning:** It is a planning that consists of sub-problems, which are solved simultaneously.

15. **Conditional planning:** It is a planning approach that handles incomplete information, bounded indeterminacy and gives the plan.

16. **Reactive planning:** It is somewhat similar to conditional planning, but the reactive planning handles uncertainty in a better way considering unknown situations too.

17. **Knowledge-based planning:** HTN belongs to this category of planning. It is not based on the available knowledge, but considers the user preferences and interacts with them.

18. **Temporal logic:** It provides a mathematical framework that can be used in the reasoning process during the planning.

19. **Re-planning:** It occurs when in the course of execution, action cannot take place owing to the state change or pre-conditional changes.

20. **Continuous planning:** It is a planning that considers and builds a plan incrementally. This clubs execution monitoring and re-planning.

21. **Multi-agent planning:** This involves use of multiple agents to carry out the planning tasks through co-ordination and co-operation.

MULTIPLE CHOICE QUESTIONS

1. The statement that 'hierarchical task network generates a plan with primitive operators' is subjective. The statement is
   (a) Always valid
   (b) Invaild
   (c) Sometimes valid
   (d) None of these

2. In non-linear planning,
   (a) Parallel action executions can occur
   (b) Partial execution of an action can occur
   (c) Only one action can occur and that too sequentially
   (d) An ordered form is required

3. STRIPS make use of
   (i) Goal stack planning
   (ii) Equality property
   (iii) First order logic
   Which of them is true?
   (a) Both (i) and (iii)   (b) Both (i) and (ii)
   (c) Both (ii) and (iii)   (d) All of the above

4. In POP, a plan is said to be consistent if it
   (i) Is ordered
   (ii) Has no cycles
   (iii) Is linear
   (iv) Has no conflicts
   Which of them is true?
   (a) (i), (ii), and (iii)   (b) (i), (ii), and (iv)
   (c) (ii), (iii), and (iv)   (d) Only (ii) and and (iv)

5. What defines an empty plan in POP?
   (a) Null states in it   (b) A plan without any solution
   (c) A plan with start and end states   (d) None of these

6. _____ makes use of domain file and problem file.
   (a) STRIPS   (b) ADL   (c) PDDL   (d) None of these

7. Mutex are used to indicate
   (a) Linearly occurring events/actions   (b) Parallel occurring events/actions
   (c) Actions in conflicts   (d) None of these

8. In POP, which of the following is true?
   (a) There is a strict ordering constraint
   (b) Least commitment strategy is employed
   (c) Occurrence of action execution does not matter
   (d) All of the above

9. Conditional planning is used when the
   (a) Information is incomplete   (b) Environment is changing
   (c) Environment is partially observable (d) None of these

10. Regression planners belong to the category of
    (a) Partial ordered planners
    (b) Totally ordered planners
    (c) Forward state-space search planning
    (d) Backward state-space search planning

CONCEPT REVIEW QUESTIONS

1. Is planning and scheduling same? Discuss.

2. Consider a scenario where a robot is in room 1, and room 2 is unclean. Room 2 needs to be cleaned. What possible actions will you consider? Represent the actions in STRIPS.

3. Consider a concept is explained on page number 35, which you need to understand to answer important question in exam. This concept could not be understood unless you read concept on page number 5 or page number 6. Concept on page number 6 is based on page number 5. Draw POP and full order plan to answer the question in examination.

CRITICAL THINKING EXERCISE

1. Can a planning be related to problem solving? Discuss with example.
2. Can one use temporal planning in multi-agent planning? Give justification for the answer.

PROJECT WORK

1. Develop a plan that would allow user interaction for planning for a vacation from Mumbai to Goa with a flight. Is this plan a feasible one? Assume suitable data that is necessary. Which language representation would you use? Can this involve hierarchical planning?

2. A robot has to paint 2 walls for the 3 rooms that are in the following fashion as shown in Figure 9.18. Develop a plan for the same. Is it possible to have multiple plans? On what basis one would decide the optimal one? Assume the actions to be right, left, enter (to enter a room and paint). Formulise the problem.

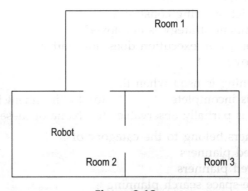

Figure 9.18

CHAPTER 10

Learning

Learning Objectives

- ❑ To understand the concepts of machine learning and its importance in AI
- ❑ To understand the various learning paradigms
- ❑ To study supervised, semi-supervised and unsupervised learning methodologies
- ❑ To understand and briefly study the various learning methods
- ❑ To acquire knowledge about reinforcement learning
- ❑ To appreciate the role of learning methods with reference to various applications
- ❑ To analyse and identify the importance of various learning approaches in the real world

INTRODUCTION

One of the most important aspects of intelligence is learning. Learning is manifested in different ways and includes various outcomes like ability to adapt to the changing environment, dealing with new scenarios and surroundings. Learning covers various things like understanding new concepts, refining skills, reacting in a better way in case of re-occurrence of similar scenario, and so on.

Primarily, learning consists of various activities like understanding, memorisation, knowledge acquisition and inference. It can range from simple memorisation of experiences that is rote learning to the incremental inference and decision-making in case of complex and new scenarios to the development of new theories. Machine learning is one of the most important components of artificial intelligence. The performance of a system and its decision-making capabilities improve with learning. Learning has different facets. The systems learn from examples, while in some other cases, the systems learn based on inferences. Learning can be based on observations too. The learning can be guided in some cases, while in the other cases, it is not guided. The learning ability without constraints is one of the greatest strengths of human being. The kid, while learning to walk, goes through various experiences and each experience makes it richer and richer in terms of knowledge and experience.

So, learning is not just knowledge acquisition, but rather knowledge acquisition, knowledge augmentation and knowledge management along with essential inference. Knowledge deals with the significance of information and learning deals with building knowledge.

How can a machine be made to learn? This research question has been chased for more than six decades by the researchers. The outcome of this research has built a platform for this chapter. Learning is involved in every activity.

Consider scenario 1. While going to office yesterday, Ram found some road repair work being carried out on route 1. So, he followed route 2 today. Thus, Ram learnt something yesterday.

Now in scenario 2, if Ram finds that

1. Road repair work is in progress on route 1
2. Announcement is done that in case of rain, route 2 will be closed
3. He needs to visit a shop *X* while going to office
4. He is running out of petrol

This means his decision is going to be much more complex as compared to scenario 1. The complexity of any learning increases as the number of parameters, and time dimensions start playing role in decision-making. The scenario can be well-tackled by Ram based on his previous experiences.

All this, sets the background to study the details as to how and in what way, the learning can be carried out. Thus, the data and information used for learning are very important. The data cannot be used as it is for learning. It may contain unessential information or outliers. Often, the most frequent patterns are used for learning. There can be learning based on exceptions. It can even take place based on similarities as well as differences. The positive as well as negative examples help in effective learning. Various models are built for learning, with the objective of exploiting the knowledge.

Thus, learning is a continuous process. The new scenarios are observed and new situations arise, which need to be used for learning. Learning from observation is required to construct meaningful classification of observed objects and situations. It is the most commonly used method by the human beings. While taking decisions, we may come across the scenarios and objects, which we have not used or come across during learning phase. The inference allows us to handle these scenarios. Further, we need to learn in different new scenarios, and even while taking decisions, the learning continues. Let us explore this learning for machines.

10.1 WHAT IS MACHINE LEARNING?

Before going through the machine learning, let us understand the activities of learning, which are active in humans. There are three fundamental continuously active learning mechanisms—perceptual learning (learning of new objects, categories, relations), episodic learning (learning of events like what, where and when) and procedural learning (actions and their sequences to accomplish a task). Implementation of this human cognition can impart intelligence to a machine. So, a unified methodology around intelligent behaviour is the need of the hour.

Interestingly, psychologists have played a major role in the development of machine learning techniques. It has been a movement taken by the computer researchers and psychologists together to make machines intelligent for more than two decades. The application areas are growing and research done in the last two decades makes us believe that it is one of the most interesting areas to make machines learn. A very common definition for machine learning is given as follows:

Machine learning is building and exploring of methods for programming computers to make them learn.

We, as humans, take decisions based on our past experiences. The same should be inculcated in machines. So, the machines need to be intelligent to carry out tasks. The tasks could be related to the automation industry or even to the scenarios, where high degree of accuracy is required. The most important characteristic of the intelligence would be the ability to forecast.

Typically, a machine learning system has its knowledge base built. It has prediction rules to assist in the decision-making. Many's the time, it is observed that even we are not actually able to relate and explain how our brain understands the natural language and processes it. But for the machines, things could be mapped and made available to them. The algorithms designed for machine learning essentially understand this mapping and help in giving appropriate decisions.

10.1.1 Concept

An approach of machine learning is depicted in Figure 10.1 (showing an approach of supervised learning). As it is observed, the input to the learning algorithm is actually a training data. It is clear from Figure 10.1 that some model for predictions is built based on the available information and then further used to infer/predict unknown data.

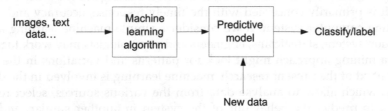

Figure 10.1 Machine learning approach.

Let us understand what it is all about. We might, for instance, be interested in learning to complete a task, to make accurate predictions, to react in certain situations or to behave intelligently. The learning that is being done is always based on some sort of observations or data such as examples (the most common case in this course), direct experience, or instruction. So, in general, machine learning is about learning to do better in the future based on what was experienced in the past.

So, for making the machine intelligent, there has to be some algorithm/approach. Coming back to Figure 10.1, the approach depicted forms a method of supervised learning. The input data here forms the training data. Training data/set comprises a set of examples (known samples) from which the algorithm is capable of generating or building sufficient knowledge, which is used/applied for inferring a new example. In this case, known data is available, whereas in case of unknown data, it is all about unsupervised learning approach. Why do we need all this? The answer is—for inferring. This inference could be related to classification, grouping used for prediction and so on. We study about it in detail in further sections.

10.1.2 Scope of Machine Learning

Traditional machine learning approaches are susceptible to dynamic continual changes in the environment. However, perceptual learning in humans does not have such restrictions. Learning in humans is selectively incremental, so it does not need large number of known examples (training set), and simultaneously, it is not biased by already learnt but outdated facts. Learning and knowledge extraction in human being are dynamic and the human brain adapts to the changes occurring in the environment continuously. Let us discuss some cases and problems, in which one would prefer to go with machine learning.

A dynamic environment is one such aspect that demands the use of machine learning. Generally, issues are raised when the environment is unstable. In principle, the scenarios are continuously varying. Considering the changes in the environment, if we have to build a program for prediction purpose, then the changes would be required to be accommodated each and every time. But a learning algorithm can make things hassle-free by self tuning the knowledge and the prediction set it has.

Applications demanding customisation form another aspect, where machine learning finds its place. The learning algorithm that addresses the requirements and the priorities of the customer would definitely be a boon. Thus, the algorithm would be customer-specific that has capability to adapt to the maximum satisfaction of the customers.

What could be the other reasons for opting machine learning as a potential methodology? Quick response and accurate decision making are the other factors that add value to it. It is primarily concerned with the timely response, accuracy and effectiveness of the resulting computer system. If we consider a simple machine learning approach for face recognition system, statisticians, engineers and psychologists may work together on this front. A data mining approach might look for patterns and variations in the image data.

In the context of the present research, machine learning is involved in the development of programs, which allow to analyse data from the various sources, select relevant data, use that data to predict the behaviour of the system in another similar, and if possible, different scenarios, classify objects and behaviours to finally impart the decisions for new input scenarios. The interesting part is that more learning and intelligence is required to deal with more uncertain situation. Machine learning has become an inevitable part of data mining today.

Typically, problems like character recognition, face authentication, document classification, spam filtering, speech recognition, fraud detection, weather forecasting, occupancy forecasting are some of the examples of machine learning problems.

10.1.3 Goals of Machine Learning

The primary goal of learning/machine learning is to produce some learning algorithm with practical value. The goal of machine learning is the development and enhancement of computer algorithms and models to meet the decision-making requirements in practical scenarios. Interestingly, it has achieved the set goal in many applications. Right from the washing machines and microwave ovens to the automated landing of aircraft machine, learning is playing a major role. The era of machine learning has introduced methods from simple data analysis and pattern matching to fuzzy logic and inferring.

In machine learning, the inferring mechanism is data-driven. The sources of data are limited, and many times, there is difficulty in identifying the useful data. It may be possible that the source contains large piles of data and the data contains important relationships and correlations among them. Machine learning can extract these relationships, which is an area of data mining application. The goal of machine learning is to facilitate in building intelligent systems (IS) that can be used in solving real-life problems.

10.1.4 Challenges of Machine Learning

One of the major aspects of learning is the selection of learning data. All the information available for learning cannot be used as it is. It may contain a lot of data that may not be relevant or captured from a completely different perspective. Every bit of data cannot be used with the same importance and priority. The prioritisation of this data is done based on scenarios, system significance and relevance. The determination of relevance of this data is one of the most difficult parts of the process.

There are a number of challenges in making the machines learn and take suitable decisions at right time. The challenges start from the availability of limited learning data and unknown perspectives. For example, a machine is expected to prescribe medicine to a patient. The learning set may include samples of patients, their histories, their test reports and the symptoms reported by them. Further, the data for learning may also include other information like family history, habits, etc. In case of a new patient, there is a need to infer. This inference is based on the available limited information, as the manifestation of the same disease may be different in his case.

When we look at the way human being learns, we find many interesting aspects. Generally, learning takes place with understanding. The learning progresses whenever new knowledge is acquired. The knowledge often is organised with reference to important concepts and principles. During learning, either some principles are already there or developed in the process, which work as a guideline for learning. All these tasks account to challenges in developing efficient machine learning approaches. Moreover, the learning also needs prior knowledge. Application of pre-learnt knowledge is what the learners do to construct new understandings. This is more like building knowledge. Hence, accurate, compact and precise knowledge building too comes out to be a difficult and complex task for the learning process in machines. Further, there are different perspectives and metacognition. This adds up complexities too.

10.2 LEARNING PARADIGMS

An empirical learning method has three different approaches of modelling problem based on the observation, data and partial knowledge about the problem domain. These are generative modelling, discriminative modelling and Imitative modelling. Each of these models has its own pros and cons and is best suited for different application areas depending on the training samples and prior knowledge.

In *generative modelling approach,* statistics provide a formal method for determining the non-deterministic models. This is done by estimating joint probability over variables of problem domain. Bayesian networks are used to capture dependencies among domain variables as well as distributions among them. This partial domain knowledge combined with observations enhances probability density function. Generative density function is then used to generate samples of different configurations of the system and draw inference on unknown situations. The traditional rule-based expert systems are giving way to the statistical generative approaches due to visualisation of interdependencies among variables, which yields better prediction than heuristic approaches. Natural language processing, speech recognition, topic modelling among different speakers are some of the application areas of generative modelling. This probabilistic approach of learning can be used for computer vision, motion tracking, object recognition and face recognition. In a nutshell, learning with generative modelling can be applied to the domains of perception, temporal modelling and autonomous agents.

Discriminative modelling approach models the posterior probability or discriminant functions with less domain-specific or prior knowledge. This technique directly optimises target task-related criteria. For example, support vector machine maximises a margin of a hyperplane between two sets of variables in n dimension. This approach can be widely used for document classification, character recognition and other numerous areas, where interdependency among problem variables does not play any role or play minimum role in observation variables so that prediction is not influenced by the inherent problem structure and also by domain knowledge.

The third approach is *Imitative learning.* Autonomous agents, which exhibit interactive behaviour, are trained through imitative learning model. The objective of imitative learning is to learn agent's behaviour by providing real example of agents' interaction with the world and generalise. Figure 10.2 depicts the learning model that is based on passively perceiving

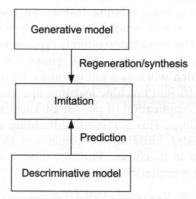

Figure 10.2 Imitative learning model.

real-world behaviour and learning from it. Interactive agents perceive the environment using generative model to regenerate/synthesise virtual characters/interaction and use discriminative approach on temporal learning to focus on prediction task necessary for the selection of an action. An agent tries to imitate the real-world situations with intelligence so that if the exact behaviour is not available through the use of learnt hypothesis, then the agent can take some action based on synthesis.

10.3 LEARNING CONCEPTS, METHODS AND MODELS

What is to be learnt and how? It is one of the important questions about machine learning. Different computational structures are used for learning in different scenarios. Computational structures may be

1. Functions
2. Logic programs and rule sets
3. Finite state machines
4. Grammars
5. Problem-solving system

We will see in due course that machine learns these structures from the samples provided to its learning technique. As a result, machine's intelligence and learning ability is largely dependent on the input sample also.

Let us understand some concepts related to the same. Labelled data and unlabelled data are the terms very commonly used in learning. By labelled data, we mean that we are aware of the output for a specific set of inputs. It could be group of students (say) amongst which subsets are labelled or categorised with respect to the university in which they are studying. The samples labelled can be positive or negative. A positive sample means it provides information that it belongs to a particular category, whereas a negative sample states it does not. A set of positive as well as negative samples forms the *training set*. A *test set* is the one, which measures the accuracy of the classifier or the learning approach. It consists of just the input instances, where the labelled class is absent (is known to us) and check is done to see whether an appropriate output is generated. Table 10.1 shows the sample labelled data.

TABLE 10.1 Labelled Data Set

Input	Feature 1	Feature 2		Feature n	Belongs to class X
1	1.55	10	...	35.8	Yes
2	1.9	13	...	22.7	Yes
3	6.8	2	...	1.5	No
–					
–					
–					

Training sample instances may be labelled with the expected result (generally by some expert who knows the classes/labels). It is possible that there are some samples that are not labelled with the output due to difficulty in getting the information or due to amount of effort required to label the output. This is referred to as *unlabelled data*, where the category or the possible outcome is absent. Even the training instances may be the combination of both labelled and unlabelled outputs.

Learning with the labelled samples is like a supervisor telling an agent whether it is correct or not and the process of learning is termed as *supervised learning*. Let us take an example to understand the concept of supervised learning. Assume you are given a set of documents (labelled ones) comprising history, geography and science as different classes. Then, you are provided with a new document and asked to put in the correct category. Precisely, your task is what a supervised algorithm/learning does. Based on the known data, it analyses and builds a model for the classes it knows. Then, for a new data, it classifies to the ones it belongs. In case of unlabelled samples, learning is harder without trainer and the machine adapts its parameters autonomously. This is called *unsupervised learning*. There is an approach that combines both the labelled and unlabelled data. This is called *semi-supervised learning*. Another approach of learning with unlabeled data, called as *reinforcement learning*, bridges gap between supervised and unsupervised learning. A learner does not explicitly know input-output sequence, but gets reward or punishment from the environment as feedback. If the training instances are the combination of both labelled and unlabelled data, then the learner makes use of both the instances to maximise his intelligence. Details about the different types of learning along with their applications are discussed in the next section.

Notations

Let an input instance be x and an output label or class or category be y.

The labelled data is $(X_n, Y_n) = \{(x_1{:}n, y_1{:}n)\}$

The unlabelled data is $X_u = \{x_1{:}n\}$

Learning function f learns from the set of $X \rightarrow Y$, and maps the input to a predictive function.

10.3.1 Rote Learning

Let us start with the traditional paradigm of learning—Rote learning. *Rote learning* is a rudimentary form of learning, which focusses on memorisation. This is one of the important forms, when it comes to repetitive actions. Here, the values are stored so that these are not re-computed. The storing or memorising some of the results improves the performance of a system, when in future, we go for similar computations. When computations are more expensive than re-computing from scratch, this strategy can save a significant amount of time. Selective paging and caching are some of the examples of rote learning.

10.3.2 Learning from Observations

This type of learning includes the following:

1. Learning from agents

2. Inductive learning
3. Decision tree learning

Let us discuss them.

Learning from Agents

An *agent* is defined as a computational entity, which is capable of perceiving the environment and can act based on the situation. So, we can say that in the agent-based learning, the behaviour pattern is observed typically and the actions are taken accordingly. We are already familiar with the intelligent agent. Let us understand the learning process here again. Consider a scenario, in which a woman has gone for purchase of some outfits. A salesgirl (intelligent agent) considering the customer's colour choice, pattern of the outfit and budget, suggests different designs to the customer. So, the agent has to act with respect to the environment and give the best performance that it can. A typical learning pattern for an agent-based system is depicted in Figure 10.3. We can say that the agent is composed of learning element, performance element and a curiosity element. Based on the co-ordination between these elements, the outcome of the agents behaviour is measured.

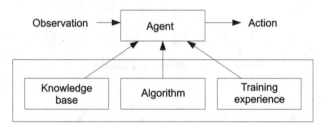

Figure 10.3   Typical agent structure.

Inductive Learning

Inductive learning offers the ability to establish connection between the pieces of information. The critical information is used, and conceptualisation and generalisation takes place. Sequence and patterns are also used as a part of inductive learning. Examination of data and interpretation of the same is the first step of learning process. The data is synthesised and analysed for the learning. Inductive learning can be observed when a small kid learns a new thing. While learning about the bird, say parrot, it goes through multiple examples of parrot. After going through numerous examples, it takes an inductive leap that is beyond the data observed. Based on that, it tries to tell whether the new bird it comes across is a parrot or not. In case of inductive learning, structured knowledge and statistical inference work together.

Inductive theory uses various related concepts like set of causal laws, structured information and all these are used for the process of inductive inference. Generally, in case of inductive learning, you arrive at a conclusion after observing a few samples. Let us consider a very simple example, say you are in Paris. You observed for two days in Paris that it was raining in the evening and you concluded that it rains in the evening in Paris. The conclusion is based on limited information and may be wrong in some cases. Most important part about this learning is it can allow you to take major decision based on limited cognitive effort.

Inductive learning may not be completely superficial and is guided by the background information and has much more to offer than the unpredicted search. This works on the principle of induction. You observe that *A* possesses property *P*. Let *X* belongs to *A* then *X* also possesses property *P*. The success of learning in this way has led to research in this area. Such learning is more commonly referred to as *learning from observations*. There are a few cases in which relatively weak inductive paradigm offers a great value to the decision-making. Many traditional artificial intelligence systems use inductive learning.

Decision Tree Learning

Decision tree method is widely used a inductive learning inferencing method. In this method, the learned function is represented by a decision tree. In terms of programming, it is also represented as if-then rules. Figure 10.4 depicts a typical decision tree for the decision whether to play cricket. In case of sunny weather and temperature below 37°, it is yes, while for above 37° it is no. Similarly, decision is no in case of rainy weather and poor light conditions.

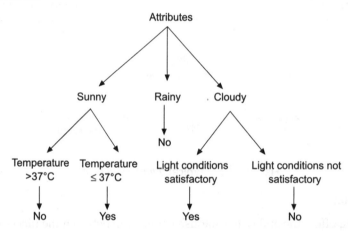

Figure 10.4   Decision tree.

This representation is suitable for the problems in which instances are represented by attribute values. Here, the actual attribute directly derives instance. Further, when the target function has discrete output values and disjunctive description is required, then decision tree learning can be used.

The decision tree depicts the simple learning from the observation method. Based on the observation, at every node, decision is taken. Learning is not necessarily goal or task-driven.

10.3.3   Supervised Learning

This is one of the most common and frequently used learning methods.

If we take an example of document classification, the classification problem consists of various entities playing role in it. First, there is a labelled data set. By labelled data, we mean it has some available documents and their classes. Second there is a classifier—a program that performs mapping of the input documents to appropriate classes. Essentially, a classifier learns and is tuned with the labelled data set. Typically it understands the properties and features of labelled data and based on that, builds ability to classify similar documents in future. On receiving a new data or document, the classifier categorises the document accurately.

As discussed earlier, supervised learning is based on the labelled examples. Thus, labelled examples are used for training here. They form a set often referred to as *training samples* that is used in the initial learning process.

So, the basic job of supervised learning is building up the classifier, given a set of (labelled) training examples. It is basically the learning algorithm that is provided with the set of training data and the algorithm further induces the classifier to classify the unseen or new data.

A typical classification is depicted in Figure 10.5 which represents a line (hyperplane), which is generated after learning, separating two classes—class *A* and class *B* in two parts. Each input point presents input-output instance from sample space. In case of document classification, these points are documents. Learning computes separating line among documents. An unknown document type is decided by its position with respect to separator.

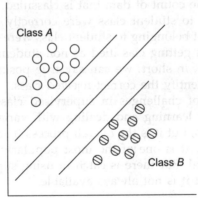

Figure 10.5 Hyperplane separating two classes.

The classifier, and of course, the decision-making engine should minimise false positives and false negatives. Here, *false positive* stands for the result yes, i.e., classified in a particular group wrongly. *False negative* is the case where it should have been accepted as a class, but got rejected. For example, let us assume we have two classes—one is that a person is culprit and other class represents that a person is not culprit. Now, a classifier is trained on some examples so that it can distinguish between them. Assume for a new sample input (some person) if the classifier says that he is a culprit, though he is not in actual, then this is regarded as *false positive*. But if a person is actually a culprit and he is considered to be not, then it is *false negative*. False negative is the one that proves to be fatal, and a classifier that makes very few false negatives is often preferred, irrespective of the amount of false positives it detects. This is so because false negative takes away the identity of the objects or elements which are classified correctly.

We introduce the concept of confusion matrix here. A *confusion matrix,* also called error matrix, represents the performance of any classifier. Since we have discussed about false positive and false negative, we will introduce here true positive and true positive as well. These four values form the confusion matrix.

Let us take some example of determining a student (class) for some set of data that is to be classified. The confusion matrix after classification is shown in Figure 10.6.

Predicted class

		Student	Not student
Actual class	Student	True positive	False positive
	Not student	False negative	True negative

Figure 10.6 Confusion matrix.

The matrix contains the count of data that is classified, where true positives indicate students (data) belonging to student class were correctly predicted and true negatives indicate students (data) not belonging to student class were also predicted correctly. False positives indicate students getting classified as non-students and the opposite is true in case of false negatives. So, in short, we can say true positives identify the correct class and three negatives too identify the correct-rejected class.

There are a number of challenges in supervised classification like generalisation, selection of right data for learning and dealing with variations. Supervised learning is not just about classification, but it is the overall process that has guidelines to map to the most appropriate decision. It is one of the most popularly used ways of learning, as it is very simple and practical. But there is catch in using supervised learning. Supervised data is very expensive and it is not always available.

10.3.4 Unsupervised Learning

It is not possible to learn in supervised way in the absence of proper labelled data. Huge unlabelled data is available and there is a need to use unlabelled data during the training. The method used for learning based on unlabelled data is referred to as *unsupervised learning*. Here, the learning is more based on similarities and differences which are visible. These differences and similarities are mathematically represented in unsupervised learning.

Understanding and Visualisation

As humans, our learning is based on the understanding of the relationship of the entities. When we are exposed to a set of objects, we intend to understand their similarities and have a visualisation of their relations. As an example, a child is able to separate cars from boats or ships. This is based on the basic point of dissimilarity measure that the cars have wheels, whereas the vehicles running on water do not. This learning at the initial point provides with the most visible aspects. Based on the visualisation, it is very much possible to perform grouping to have a categorisation of the objects visible for a better understanding of relationships. To have the same, hierarchical structures are built up to get the final grouping.

The unsupervised learning methods perform this hierarchical grouping. The objective of *hierarchical clustering* is arranging the set of objects into a hierarchical structure in such a way so that similar objects are grouped together. Another approach for grouping is *non-hierarchical clustering*. This approach of clustering partitions the data set into disjoint clusters. The basic clustering approach is shown in Figure 10.7. In this type of learning environment, the learner is provided with some scattered data sets. Figure 10.7 shows the outcome of the learning process, where two clusters are being formed. Clustering mechanism, thus, results in grouping of the points based on the similarities and differences between them.

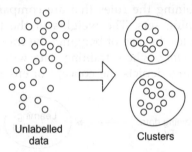

Unlabelled
data

Clusters

Figure 10.7 Clustering of data.

Information Retrieval

The most important unsupervised learning task is to retrieve relevant objects (documents, images, etc.) from a large collection of objects. Information retrieval systems are typically given a partial description of an object, and they use this partial description to identify the K most similar objects in the collection. In other cases, a few examples of complete objects may be given, and again, the goal is to retrieve the K objects that are likely to possess similar properties.

Clustering approach suit these types of problem. Given partial or complete descriptions of the objects, the most similar cluster can be identified.

10.3.5 Semi-supervised Learning

Semi-supervised learning is developed to cope up with the issues of learning in supervised or unsupervised mode in isolation. In real-life scenarios, we need to learn both from labelled and unlabelled data. Further, there are other aspects like learning simultaneously based on all available information. As we have discussed, in supervised learning, labelled data is used. Labelled data is expensive and also difficult to get. But many times, unlabelled data is available and semi-supervised learning tries to learn from the labelled as well as unlabelled data.

One simple semi-supervised learning method is described below:

Let U be a set of unlabelled data and L be a set of labelled data. As the learning progresses, the learning approach identifies the unlabelled data U with reference to labelled data L and keeps on labelling the unlabelled data. This unlabelled data also takes part now in the learning process. This method is also called *self-training in semi-supervised learning.*

10.3.6 Ensemble Learning

Ensemble learning method is the one where multiple learners/learning algorithms are trained. In most of the learning algorithms, a single hypothesis drives the learning. In ensemble learning method, the whole collection or ensemble of hypothesis is selected from the hypothesis space and their predictions are combined. In this approach, the learners are referred to as *base learners.* The most commonly used ensemble learning methods are boosting and bagging. Boosting can broadly be defined as the method for generating accurate predictions by combining the rules that are comparatively inaccurate. Boosting works on the weighted training sets. The weights of the training example reflect the importance of training examples. In case of bagging, the training data is re-sampled. This is referred to as *bootstrap sampling,* where training data with replacement is taken in the learning approaches. Figure 10.8 depicts the concept of ensemble methods.

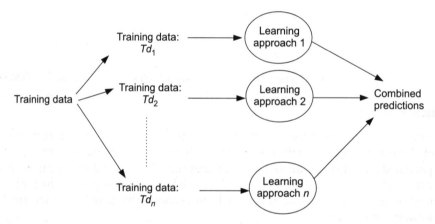

Figure 10.8 Ensemble method: The concept.

10.3.7 Discovery-based Learning

In supervised learning, there is a supervisor who guides the outcome. In case of discovery learning the learning, takes place without any help of teacher or supervisor. It is called unsupervised. It can be said to be inquiry-based learning, where the learner on the basis of past experience and knowledge tries to discover the outcomes.

10.3.8 Learning by Problem Solving

It is like unsupervised learning. In learning from problem solving, various parameters related to solution and problem are considered. These parameters are used and effectively desirability of a particular outcome or decision is determined. It is typically based on the way a problem is solved and the outcomes at every step. Even in pattern-based decision-making, the correct category is determined based on the previous results.

10.4 STATISTICAL LEARNING METHODS

Uncertainty is handled by the method of probability and decision theory. Statistical learning methods are suited for problems in which the outcome is uncertain. Some statistical methods are discussed here.

10.4.1 Bayesian Learning

In Chapter 8, basics of Bayesion network have been introduced. Here, we will discuss important aspects of Bayesian network from learning perspective. Bayesian forms an important approach in learning methods of AI. As we are familiar, in Bayesian learning, each training sample can increase or decrease the estimated probability supporting the hypothesis. Prior knowledge is combined with the observed data to determine the probability of hypothesis from the space, say H, and this is done using observed training data D. Popularly, this is done by finding out the most probable hypothesis with reference to the observed data and knowledge about initial probabilities. Conditional probability helps us in calculating the probabilities to determine the best hypothesis.

EXAMPLE: In a particular school, the student distribution is as follows:

10% Mexican students, 20% Indian students, 30% Spanish students and 40% Canadian students.

The probability of student getting job in ABCD Inc. is 30%. If we are to find the probability that any Canadian student can get job in ABCD Inc., then to solve these types of problems, we use Bayes's theorem.

Bayes's theorem is used to calculate probability of hypothesis based on known-prior probabilities.

Consider $P(h)$ to be the initial probability that hypothesis holds; $P(D)$ as the probability of D (training data), given no knowledge of hypothesis; $P(D \mid h)$ as the probability of observing D with some given hypothesis h. (Probability of D given h); $P(h \mid D)$ as the probability that hypothesis h holds, given the training data D observed (posterior probability of h).

Bayesian theorem provides a method for calculating the posterior probability, given the prior probability.

$$P(h \mid D) = (P(D \mid h) * P(h)) / P(D)$$

Bayesian learning calculates the probability of different hypotheses based on the observed and given data, and predicts all hypotheses. Weighted probabilities are used rather than relying on single best hypothesis.

EXAMPLE: To illustrate Bayesian learning, a medical diagnosis problem is given below:

Hypothesis 1: Patient has an ischemic heart disease (IHD).
Hypothesis 2: Patient does not have ischemic heart disease.

Laboratory tests or a set of tests lead to two outcomes—positive and negative.

1. We have a prior knowledge that 0.011 people have IHD.
2. The test returns 97.5% correct positive results in case the disease is present actually.
3. The test returns correct negative result in 96% cases when the disease is not there.

$$P(\text{IHD}) = 0.011$$
$$P(\neg\,\text{IHD}) = 0.89$$
$$P(\text{Positive} \mid \text{IHD}) = 0.975$$
$$P(\text{Negative} \mid \text{IHD}) = 0.025$$
$$P(\text{Positive} \mid \neg\text{IHD}) = 0.04$$
$$P(\text{Negative} \mid \neg\text{IHD}) = 0.96$$

Suppose we have a new patient for whom laboratory test is positive. Shall we diagnose that he has IHD?

$$P(\text{Negative} \mid \text{IHD})^*P(\text{IHD})$$
$$= 0.96 \times 0.011$$
$$= 0.01056$$

$$P(\text{Positive} \mid \text{IHD})^*P(\neg\text{IHD})$$
$$= 0.04 \times 0.89$$
$$= 0.0356$$

Thus, the maximum post-priori

$$P(\text{IHD} \mid \text{Positive})$$
$$= 0.01056/(0.01056 + 0.0356)$$
$$= 0.2287$$

The post-priori calculations, hence, can be used to calculate the probability of hypothesis with the given training data.

To minimise the complexities arising through a large number of hypotheses, assumption of uniform prior probabilities over the space of hypothesis is to be considered. The maximum post-priori learning is reduced to selection of hypothesis that maximises $P(D/h)$. This is called *maximum likelihood hypothesis*.

10.4.2 Learning with Hidden Variables—The EM Algorithm

Real-world problems contain hidden variables. They are also called *latent variables*. In many practical problems, we treat symptoms rather than actually observing the event. This is very common in many applications like medical treatments. The hidden variables reduce the number of parameters one needs to specify using Bayesian.

Expectation maximisation (EM) algorithm simplifies difficult maximum likelihood problems. The EM algorithm can be used even for the variables whose value is not observable. Each iteration of the EM algorithm consists of two processes—the E-step, and the M-step. In the expectation or E-step, the intention is to determine the missing values. The missing data is estimated based on the observed data. This is done given the observed data and the current estimate of the model parameters. For this estimation the conditional expectation explaining the choice of terminology is used. In M-step, the likelihood function is maximised under the assumption that the missing data is known. In place of missing data, the estimated data in E-step is used. Convergence is assured, since the algorithm is guaranteed to increase the likelihood during each iteration.

10.5 ARTIFICIAL NEURAL NETWORK-BASED LEARNING

Artificial neural network (ANN) is a computational model that performs simulation of the human biological neurons. The simulation is concerned with the functioning of neurons. The complexity of real neurons is very high. Hence, this complexity is highly abstracted while modelling the artificial neurons. It has different inputs (like synapses); these inputs are weighted as per the strength of signal and then computed by a mathematical function, which determines the activation of the neuron. ANNs are nothing but non-linear mathematical functions. ANNs combine artificial neurons in order to process information. A typical ANN structure is depicted in Figure 10.9. The hidden layer is the one that learns to recode for the inputs.

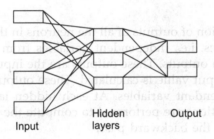

Input   Hidden   Output
           layers

Figure 10.9   Artificial neural network.

An important concept in neural network is the firing rule that determines whether a neuron should fire for an input pattern. This rule gives the neuron a sense of similarity so that it can respond to the unseen patterns.

10.5.1 Backpropagation Algorithm

The backpropagation algorithm (Rumelhart and McClelland, 1986) is used in layered feed-forward ANNs. As shown in Figure 10.10, the artificial neurons are organised in layers, and send their signals forward, and then the errors are propagated backwards. The network receives inputs by neurons in the input layer, and the output of the network is given by the neurons on an output layer. The hidden layers (typically, one or two) may be present in these networks. The backpropagation algorithm is supervised, and hence, error can be calculated. A user provides the algorithm with the examples of inputs and outputs we want the network to compute, and then the difference between the actual output and the expected output is calculated. This is referred to as *error*. The purpose of the backpropagation algorithm is to adjust the weights in order to reduce this error, until the ANN learns based on the training data. Generally, learning begins with some default or random weights, and the goal is to adjust them so that the error is minimal.

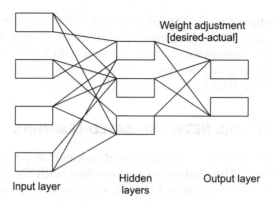

Figure 10.10   Error adjustment in backpropagation.

There are two passes in backward propagation algorithm. Forward pass is followed by backward pass. The algorithm goes through these passes multiple times. The training data is scanned several times.

Forward Pass

In forward pass, computation of outputs of all the neurons in the network is done. Hidden layer uses the input values, i.e., independent variables from the training data. Hidden layer computes the neuron outputs. These outputs are the input for the next hidden layer and so on. Finally, the output value is calculated. These outputs constitute the prediction of the values for the dependant variables. At each hidden layer, the relevant sum and activation function calculations are performed to compute the outputs. These weights are adjusted to new values in the backward pass.

Backward Pass

Error propagation and calculation of weights.

The error is computed in the output layer at each neuron. These errors are used to adjust weights. Low values give slow but steady learning and high values give erratic learning that may lead to an unstable network. The process is repeated for the connections between nodes.

Another layer can be added by calculating how the error depends on the inputs and weights of the first layer. One should just be careful with the indices, since each layer can have a different number of neurons, and complexity and confusion may increase many folds. For practical reasons, it is recommended that ANNs implementing the backpropagation algorithm do not have too many layers. The higher number of layers may result in higher complexity and the time for training the networks grows exponentially. Chapter 17 discusses in detail about the methods and algorithms for NN.

10.6   SUPPORT VECTOR MACHINES (SVM)

Let us say that we have a set of training examples, where each example belongs to category/class 1 or 2. SVM approach builds a model that determines the class of new unlabelled data. To perform this, mapping of training examples in feature space is done such that they are separated with a maximum margin or gap. Accordingly, new examples are mapped with respect to the space and are classified. To achieve this, SVM generates hyperplanes. While classifying data there are many hyperplanes which can classify data. Figure 10.11 depicts same.

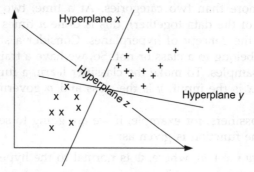

Figure 10.11 Hyperplanes separating the data sets.

The goal of SVM modelling is to determine

1. The optimal hyperplane that separates clusters (of vector) so that it separates one class of the target variable from the other category of variables. The vectors near the hyperplane are the support vectors.
2. The support vectors are determined so that they separate two classes optimally.

Figure 10.12 shows that H_3 is the optimal hyperplane that maximises the gap between the classes.

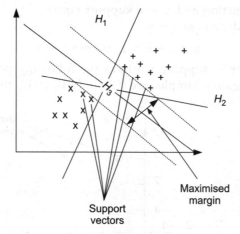

Figure 10.12 Support vectors with optimal hyperplane.

There is possibility that target variables are separated by non-linear plane. SVM works on the principle that separation may be easier in higher dimension. The concept of kernel mapping function is very powerful in SVM. This kernel is a mathematical function that performs this mapping or re-arranging of the objects. There are many kernel functions, but some of them work very well across all the problems. One of such popularly used kernel functions is radial basis function (RBF). Ideally, the objective of SVM is to find out the hyperplane to separate target variables into two non-overlapping groups. But it may not be possible in all cases, and in some cases, when there are non-separable training sets, it may result in overfitting.

SVM can handle more than two categories. At a time, two categories are handled (one category and rest of the data together), this is done n times to handle n categories.

Let us understand the concept of hyperplanes. Consider a simple case in which we have set of points that belong to a class or not. So, we have a training set that consists of positive and negative samples. To make the classifier learn, a function exists as

$y = f(x, \alpha)$, where, x is the input, y is the class and α governs the parameters of the functions.

In case of linear classifiers, for example, if we are going to select a model from a set of hyperplanes, then the function is given as:

$f(x, \{w, b\}) = \text{sign}(w \bullet x + b)$, where, w is normal to the hyperplane.

So, the points that lie on the hyperplane satisfy $w \bullet x + b = 0$
Whereas, for the support vectors, they will be:

$$w \bullet x + b = \pm 1$$

So, x_i would be a positive sample that would have $w \bullet x_i + b \geq 1$,
Whereas, negative sample would be

$$w \bullet x_i + b \leq -1$$

Now, to determine the maximising hyperplane boundary,

$$w = \sum_i \alpha_i y_i x_i \text{ and } b = y_i - w x_i$$

where α_i is a learned function and x_i is a support vector.

Here, decision boundary is given as

$$w \bullet x + b = \sum_i \alpha_i y_i x_i \bullet x + b$$

Let us take an example, suppose we have the following points as positive samples $\{(3,0), (3,3), (4,1)\}$ and negative samples are $\{(-1,0), (1,1), (1,3)\}$, then from Figure 10.13, we can identify the support vectors.

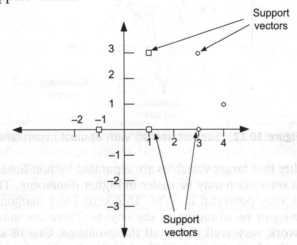

Example 10.13   Support vectors.

10.7 REINFORCEMENT LEARNING

The main objective of machine learning problem is to produce intelligent programs or intelligent agents through the process of learning and adapting to the changed environment. Reinforcement learning is one such machine learning process. In this approach, learner or software agents learn from direct interaction with the environment. This mimics the way human being learns. The agent can also learn even if the complete model or information about environment is not available. An agent gets feedback about its actions as reward or punishment. During learning process, these situations are mapped to actions in an environment. Reinforcement learning algorithms maximises rewards received during interactions with the environment and establishes mapping of states to actions as decision-making policy. The policy can be decided at once or it can adapt with the changes in environment also.

Reinforcement learning differs from the traditional approach of supervised learning. We are familiar that in case of supervised learning, the labelled data set is provided. Training is provided so that the unlabelled data can be accurately classified by the classifier. But in this approach of learning, interactions cannot occur. By this, we mean to say that in problems, wherein interactions are involved, the availability of correct and precise labelled data set cannot be possible. Acting in such a scenario becomes complex. It is desirable that under these situations, the agent should act upon based on the past experience, and at the same time, from the environmental parameters. Hence, in case of reinforcement learning, there exists a combination of supervised learning along with the dynamic programming to build an learning approach that would work in the same way as humans would be acting on.

Reinforcement learning is not an easy approach. It has to tackle many issues. One of the problems that arise here is whether the agent should go into exploring the new ways to gain benefits or exploit the previously learnt knowledge. To achieve rewards, a safe action is to select an action which has proved to be effective so as to get the rewards. But at the same time, unless new ways are explored, how can an action be selected that would reap more benefits? Thus, the complexity of the agent in reinforcement learning lies in the exploitation to obtain reward and exploration so as to have a better selection of the actions. Hence, the dilemma occurs with the perusal of exploration and exploitation. The fact is that this dilemma cannot get resolved unless either of the events occurs. Thus, there is a possibility that a failure at any task would enable to sort out the dilemma. For the same, it is appropriate for the agent to try out a variety of actions and then progressively favour the ones that seem to be the best. Practically, there is a need to perform and evaluate every action multiple times to have a proper estimate of the rewards that it would gain. As one must have a noticed, this dilemma does not exist in supervised learning, as everything is well-defined there.

One important feature of reinforcement learning is that it takes into account the problem to be solved as a goal-directed one, with the existence of uncertain environment.

Now, it is possible for us to point out the differences between the supervised learning and reinforcement learning. Out of these, the already known is the absence of the labelled data set. In reinforcement learning, once the agent takes up an action, it gets rewards. But the agent is not made aware of as to which action would have given him more rewards that would be effective in a longer run. The agent has to be active all the time and based on the experience, the current state and the possible states, and the rewards it is likely to get, it has to decide the next action. One more point of difference is that here, the system evaluation is based on the active learning.

In case of reinforcement learning, as said before, the learning methodology is goal-centric. Hence, in this learning scenario, the agents have their goals specified. Based on the environment, selection of the action occurs. Further, it is expected that the agent needs to work under each and every circumstance even though there is a high degree of uncertainty. Also, if there is an involvement of planning activity in this learning, it has to tackle the shift between both planning as well as learning, in the real time. At the same time, observing, acquiring and improving the learning models too need to be handled. There is a possibility that the learning could rely on supervised learning in some cases to resolve issues in the decision process. Hence, hybrid learning is very much possible.

From the concepts that we have studied so far about reinforcement learning, you must have noticed that there exists some properties that are similar to the search and planning techniques of AI. It is well known that search techniques traverse through the states giving routes. In planning, it is concerned with the 'when' and 'how' to reach the states where the representations take up expression forms for the state and the actions. These approaches are said to be less generalised as compared to what reinforcement learning tends to build. Often, the approaches are characterised by pre-compiled model representing the transitions. On contrary, in reinforcement, it is presumed that the whole state space can be enumerated. This is never accounted in the traditional approaches involving search.

Reinforcement learning is the problem of agent to learn from the environment by interactions with the dynamic environment. In reinforcement learning, the agent gets response from critic as opposed to supervisor in supervised learning. The interactions are trial and error in nature because critic does not tell that the agent actions are right or wrong unlike in supervised learning. There are mainly two main strategies to solve this problem. The first one is to search the behavioural space to identify the action-behaviour pair that would give positive rewards. Whereas, in the other case, statistical methods and dynamic programming strategies can be looked upon to have an estimate, which in turn, would assist in determining the action utility to reach the goal.

10.7.1 Learning Model

From the detailed explanation about reinforcement learning, we now come to the actual learning model. A standard reinforcement learning model comprising an agent connected to its environment via perception and action, is depicted in Figure 10.14.

The process can be explained as follows:

At every interaction that occurs, the agent would get some input i. This i gives a brief detail about the current state. The action a is determined by the agent based on this input acquired. Every action that is executed results in the transition to a new state and a value associated to this transition is conveyed to the agent by means of a signal known as *reinforcement signal*, represented as r. This r is nothing, but the reward factor. The agent's behaviour should necessarily select actions that would increase the final summation for the r values. This can be achieved by means of trial and error versions in a systematic way (with the help of some algorithms). This process is modelled in Figure 10.14.

Figure 10.14 Agent—environment interaction.

More technically, the model comprises discrete set of environment states S; a discrete set of agent actions A; and a set of scalar reinforcement signals, typically {0,1} or the real numbers. A model is depicted in Figure 10.15.

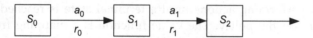

Figure 10.15 Reinforcement learning model.

Now, the goal is to learn to choose actions that maximise Eq. 10.1.

$$r_0 + \gamma r_1 + \gamma r_2 + \dots \qquad (10.1)$$

where $0 \leq \gamma \leq 1$ (discount factor).

There are three different fundamental parts of a reinforcement learning model which are as follows:

1. Environment
2. Reinforcement function
3. Value function

The agent learns a mapping from states to actions by interaction with the dynamic environment and the environment is at least partially visible to learner. The goal of learning is to find a mapping from states to actions so that the reinforcements or rewards are maximised. After performing an action, learner receives reward as scalar value. The agent learns to perform actions that maximise sum of rewards received from starting to the final state. This mapping is called *reinforcement function*. The reinforcement function is defined using three basic strategies so that the objective of learning is achieved. These are pure delayed reward, avoidance problems, and minimum time to goal and games.

In pure delayed reward strategy, all rewards are set to zero, except at the final state. The sign of reinforcement value is +1 for the goal state. For example, if learning agent tries to learn moves for the game of backgammon, the learning model can be defined as follows:

The moves at different stages represent actions, and the stages of game are equivalent to states. The reinforcement values for different moves are all zeros. If any move leads to win, then reinforcement value for that move is +1 and reinforcement value is −1 if the move leads to loss.

Reinforcement function for the type 'minimum time to goal' causes a learner to learn actions that leads to goal state through the shortest path. The reinforcement value in this case is −1 for all states, except the goal state. Since an agent tries to maximise the reinforcement, it will learn to choose actions to avoid penalty, and thus will reduce time to reach the goal state. In doing so, it will learn optimal strategy to reach the goal state.

The other reinforcement function is in the context of a game environment, where two or more players are involved with opposite goals. Each player wants to maximise his own chance of winning and minimise the chance of opponent. A learning agent learns to generate optimal behaviour for the players involved by maximising, minimising or saddle point of reinforcement function. The actions for each player is chosen independently, but executed in parallel. The goal of learning here is to choose actions for each player such that this action generates the best outcome for the player in the worst scenario.

A learning agent must be able to choose good actions, i.e., utility of agent's action should be measured. A policy determines which action should be performed in each state. A policy is a mapping from states to actions and the value of a state is defined as the sum of the reinforcements received. The optimal policy would, therefore, be the mapping from states to actions that maximises the sum of the reinforcements when starting in an arbitrary state and performing actions until a terminal state is reached. So, the value of a state is dependent on the policy. The value function is a mapping from states to state values, and this value function is approximated using function approximators. Generally, multi-layered perceptron, memory-based system, radial basis functions, lookup table, etc. are used to approximate value function.

Reinforcement learning is a complex learning system because there may not be reward/penalty involved in each action among the set of actions needed to reach the goal state. In this case, the learner does not know what to do with these types of intermediate states. This problem is solved using the concept of dynamic programming. This involves two basic principles, which are as follows:

1. If an action under some situation leads to something bad, then the learner should not select that action in that situation again.
2. If all actions in a certain situation lead to unfavourable outcome, then that situation should be avoided always.

If $V(x_t)$ is approximated value function, $V^*(x_t)$ is optimal value function, where x_i is state vector, and γ is discount factor in the range [0,1], then according to dynamic programming theory,

$$V(x_t) = e(x_i) + \gamma V^*(x_t) \qquad (10.2)$$

Equivalently, in reinforcement learning, limiting error approximation is replaced by reinforcement function and Eq. (10.2) becomes

$$V(x_t) = r(x_i) + \gamma V^*(x_t) \qquad (10.3)$$

So, an optimal value function can be defined using function approximator. It can be assumed that function approximator forms a lookup table for values of different states. The lookup table is traversed to find the condition in which the state values converge. Thus, this approximation function is generated through learning. There are various algorithms to perform search in state value space.

Maze problem are used here to discuss the scope and applicability of reinforcement learning.

Figure 10.16 is an example of maze problem. In Figure 10.16, one has to reach the goal state from start. The circles show different stages/states and arrows are the directions to move to the next state. The objective of learner is to learn states that lead to the goal state with minimum attempts.

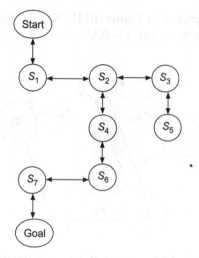

Figure 10.16 Maze problem.

Start state leads to S_1 only. At S_1, choices are start/S_2. Suppose state S_2 is selected randomly from the possible states. At S_2, choices are S_1, S_4, S_3. S_3 is selected randomly. Since all these paths are not leading to the goal state, these actions of path change will be associated with less reward, and if any path leads back to the previous state then the negative reward will be associated with that action. If S_4 is selected at S_2 as the next state, then it can lead to S_6, S_7 and then the goal state. Further, since S_7 leads to the goal state, these three actions are to be associated with the maximum reward. Maze is started again. This time S_4–S_6–S_7 is strengthened. After a few iterations, all the states leading to goal are associated with the reward and then the learner is able to identify the minimum path to reach the goal.

10.7.2 Q-Learning

Specific type of reinforcement learning, Q-learning helps in selecting an optimal action. It is most useful in Markov decision process. Let us understand this. In Q-learning, Q-function (quality function) helps in computing the maximum discounted reward. Mapping it, $Q(s,a)$ specifies the reward that can be achieved from state s with an action a.

So, the Q-matrix is generated and updated at every episode action that takes place. A typical Q-learning algorithm is given below:

1. Determine and set the parameter for γ (the discount factor).
2. Set the reward matrix.
3. For every episode (where the goal state is reached)
    (i) Select an action from the current state (random current state selection).
    (ii) For that action, check the immediate rewards and update the Q-entry:

$$Q(s, a) = r(s, a) + \gamma \max_a (Q(s', a'))$$

    (iii) Set the next state to be the current state

The algorithm is said to be *value iteration*, where it converges at some point of time, where every state-action pair is visited. $Q(s', a')$ considers the next state and all the actions.

A simple example is depicted in Figure 10.17. For the goal state S_5, the reward is 50 or else it is considered to be zero. Let $\gamma = 0.3$.

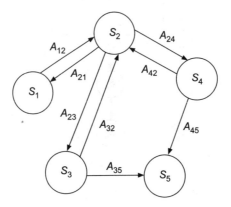

Figure 10.17 Example for value iteration.

The Q-computations are discussed as follows:
Let us say we are at state S_1. The action selection is A_{12}. For this,

$$Q(S_1, A_{12}) = r(S_1, A_{12}) + 0.3*\max(Q(S_2, A_{21}), Q(S_2, A_{24}), Q(S_2, A_{23}))$$

$$= 0 + 0.3*0$$

This is because initially the Q-values are zero. Let the next state selection be S_2 with the action selection as A_{24}. Now the Q-values would be computed as follows:

$$Q(S_2, A_{24}) = r(S_2, A_{24}) + 0.3*\max(Q(S_4, A_{42}), Q(S_4, A_{45})) = 0$$

Further, on S_4 with A_{45} action, the Q-value would be $Q(S_4, A_{45}) = 50$. Thus, the final state is reached.

Similarly, the computations take place with the different action selections along with updation of Q-values. When the matrix converges, we can say that the optimal paths to reach the goal are learnt. Can there be any drawbacks of using this method? What would happen in case of more number of states?

10.8 MULTI-AGENT-BASED LEARNING

Let us move our discussion to multi-agent learning. A single agent cannot handle learning in case of complex applications. A team or group of agents possesses the potential to overcome the limitation of single agent and work in co-ordination to accomplish a task. There can be two cases in multi-agent-based learning—one where the agent tries to maximise its own utility and other, where they work in collaboration to achieve some common goal. Consider a manufacturing industry domain. The tasks are split and assigned where each agent works in co-operation to build the end product. This is the case to achieve a common goal. Let us consider one more example. A simple example of multi-agent-based learning is game playing. Assume that in a particular gaming environment, multiple agents are in operation to select the best strategy. Now this can be related with the reinforcement learning, where for each strategy of the agent, some reward is achieved. This is where each agent tries to maximise his own utility function.

10.9 DISTRIBUTED LEARNING

In distributed learning, the task of learning is distributed. The need of distributed learning arises due to large data sets and time constraints. In this case, more than one agent works on different parts of data set. There will be distributed learning algorithms taken part in each partition to get the desired outcome, which would then be combined. The efficiency of distributed learning is a factor to look at. It is extremely important that the outcome of distributed learning matches with the ones achieved under the absence of distributed environment. After reading this, you must be wondering that it is similar to multi-agent system or you might have a feel that there is relation between them. The answer is obviously yes; multi-agent systems can be thought of as a subset of distributed learning.

10.10 ADAPTIVE LEARNING

No learning method is complete in itself and there is need to select the learning method based on the requirement. Further, there is need to develop a combination of some of the existing methods based on need. *Adaptive machine learning algorithms* are the machine learning models, where the changes in the environment help in selecting the algorithm or learning method. As per the scenario, most suitable algorithm is selected. Moreover, the development of especially fast-adapting algorithms poses many different issues like selection of choices, handling equilibrium states and so on. The adaptive learning solves some of the complex problems for which a single learning method is not enough. This method is even more appropriate when the environment is continuously changing and real-time response is expected.

10.11 LEARNING FOR DECISION-MAKING

What is observed in different learning mechanisms is that with the learnt concepts, the capability to take decisions in increased. Speaking about the supervised or unsupervised methodologies, the decisions taken are not sequential in nature. That is, if the system makes a mistake on one decision, this has no bearing on the subsequent decisions. To cope up with this dynamic situation, there is a need to understand the perspective of decision-making. Another aspect is environment and system learning, which also needs to be looked upon during decision-making. Hence while taking decisions, one specific learning approach may not be suitable. The learning approach is dependent on decision scenario.

10.12 SPEEDUP LEARNING

Speedup learning typically deals with speeding up problem solving by effective use of problem solving experience. Hence, prior problem solving experience is an input for speedup learning.

In this learning,

1. There is no interaction with the environment.
2. New problems cannot be solved.

So, speedup learning accelerates the process based on the previous experiences and prior observations.

The process of speedup learning is depicted in Figure 10.18.

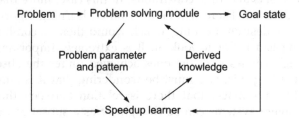

Figure 10.18 Speedup learning modules.

Another dimension to the speedup learning is generalised caching. This is also known as *explanation-based learning*. There are a number of issues with explanation-based learning, as it is implemented and embedded in system to solve real-life problem and is suitable for a particular set of problems, where the sequential processes once developed can be used again and again. But this is not the case in many real-life problems, where dynamic change in environment demands the improvement in the established scenarios and even there is a need to keep on learning based on the new findings.

10.13 ANALYTICAL AND EMPIRICAL LEARNING TASKS

Learning tasks has many facets and numerous dimensions. One important dimension is the distinction between empirical and analytical learning. This even includes the presentation of the experience in the format that can allow machine to learn. Empirical learning is a learning that relies on some form of external experience, while analytical learning requires no external inputs. Consider, any game with limited possibilities and combinations. Then, analytical learning can make a strong case and there is actually no need for empirical learning. This is true in the case of games like tic-tac-toe and chess. Analytical learning can be proved very effective when the actual experience-based learning is not required and analytically, it is possible to represent the possible scenarios.

For example, let us consider a problem of learning to play tic-tac-toe (noughts and crosses). Suppose a programmer has provided an encoding of the rules for the game in the form of a function that indicates whether the proposed moves are legal or illegal and another function that indicates whether the game is won, lost, or tied. If these set of details are available, then developing an analytical learning-based program becomes an easy task. Such a program would play as opponent to itself. This case of learning is not based on any form of external inputs and has the ability to improve its accuracy by analysing the problem instance. Here, the problem analysis allows representing all possible scenarios and outcomes of those scenarios.

Even if we are discussing two different learning methods, you would find an overlap between the approaches. This is because there is a very thin boundary to distinguish between these two methodologies. Human beings use a combination of various methods for learning and selectively choose the best one based on the demand.

In short, given the rules, learning chess may look like an analytical problem. But in real-life scenarios, where analytical rules may work as a guideline (but there is learning with every move and every new scenario), there is need of analytical and empirical learning and that too simultaneously.

There is a sort of computational infeasibility in some of the problems. This computational infeasibility leads to different assumptions. These assumptions may lead to learning inabilities in certain scenarios. These assumptions are necessary, but should not become a hurdle in building truly intelligent system.

From a cognitive science perspective, the difference between different methods and mapping of certain learning task based on the method is also very important. People frequently confront learning tasks, which could be solved analytically, but they cannot (or choose not to) solve them in this way. Instead, they rely on empirical methods. In short, analytical method is the strength of machine learning and it enables the system to learn selectively and efficiently when real empirical learning is not required.

Analytical learning method does not rely on external source of data; it does not gather knowledge with new additional training data. This approach of learning is used to accelerate learning process and increase reliability on the inferences drawn. On the other hand, empirical method learns from observation and generalises hypothesis to draw inference. But there has to be a trade-off between algorithm complexity, size of observation data and generalisation accuracy on new data. Normally, generalisation accuracy increases as the size of training increases. As the learning algorithm complexity increases, generalisation accuracy increases first, but after certain size, this values goes down.

10.14 LEARNING ALGORITHM: PERFORMANCE MATTERS

Performance of learning algorithm is governed by the input instances, the training and the test data, the hypothesis, the noise as well as the application it is meant for. These issues are looked upon in the subsequent sections.

10.14.1 Prior Knowledge and Bias

Traditional learning approaches, say supervised learning methods are dependent on the training data at large. The assumptions taken up by the classifier regarding the properties of training data are not concrete. Hence, continuous knowledge building does not occur. All this creates a necessity to have large amount of training data for learning and to produce accurate classification results. But unfortunately, a large amount of data does not solve the problem at hand. There is a way of building prior knowledge and using it. The algorithms which allow the use of prior knowledge are generally weak and based on heuristics. However, there is a risk in introducing prior knowledge. Building the right and the required prior knowledge and using it appropriately is a challenge in building machine learning algorithm that works in an incremental way.

So, a question arises—what is prior knowledge and how can it be gathered? Learning process generates hypothesis, which satisfies input data. So, more than one equation may qualify as a hypothesis. But it is required to limit the complexity of equation. For example, in a learning application, hypothesis is limited to quadratic equation. This kind of priori information is called *bias* and learning is useful with bias. Two types of bias have been identified—absolute and preference. In *absolute bias*, hypothesis is limited to definite set of functions. In *preference bias*, hypothesis that is minimal according to some ordering scheme across all hypothesis is selected. For example, if the complexity of hypothesis is measured by some means, then the one with minimal complexity among a set of hypothesis performing satisfactorily over a sample will be selected.

10.14.2 Noise

Sometimes, the sample space might contain outlier or noise. Noise may be due to wrong data selection. It may also be due to wrong attributes in the sample. Noisy sample might deviate from the output values even for training samples.

10.14.3 Performance Evaluation

Once learning algorithm is used for different applications, it is important to evaluate the performance of learning algorithm to decide the suitability of the approach to the applied problem. In case of supervised learning, hypothesis learnt is applied on test set and close fit of the solution in unknown situation is the measure of performance. Normally, mean square error and the total number of errors are common measures.

10.15 MULTI-PERSPECTIVE DECISION-MAKING

Decisions are the result of analysis of information and situation. Most of the times, it is based on the analysis of situation, historical information and presentation of problem blended with decision-maker's perspective. It is not necessary that decision-makers' perspective is always correct. In the absence of information of one or more important perspectives, the decision sequence may result in wrong decision or even incomplete decisions. For any problem, there are thousands of perspectives and capturing all of them and prioritising them for decision-making is one of the major challenges at our hand. Further, the problem scenario demands a particular perspective or prioritisation of perspectives in a particular way. This prioritisation is very specific to a particular scenario and prioritisation based on historical information may not of any use.

So, multi-perspective decision-making deals with these issues by capturing most of the perspectives, and dynamically, decide the priority based on the analysis of scenarios and problems.

10.16 ACTIVE LEARNING

We are already familiar with the supervised and unsupervised learning. In these types of traditional learning approaches, the learner is passive one. By passive, we mean that the learner takes input of the data sets that are randomly sampled from the previously collected data set and needs a prior data collection. There are a few issues in this learning. First, it relies on the collection and gathering of the data set, where it is labelled or unlabelled, the data needs to be made available. Data evolved at later stages is not accounted. Further, the selection of random samples in the learning scenario is assumed to be independent, which may not be the case. An approach that would have this selection mechanism based on some queries to have specific set of input data(specially training data) can impart better learning capabilities. This type of learning is active, where based on the outcomes of one query, desired outputs can be obtained for new data. It is a form of semi-supervised learning. Moreover, an improvement is very much possible in active learning that resolves the data collection issue at later stages. With this approach, subsequent queries can be triggered to make the selective approach to consider the data evolved later. The subsequent query to be fired is based on the previous results and accommodates the new data, selectively improving the overall learning process. Figure 10.19 shows the active learner model.

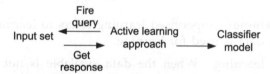

Figure 10.19 Active learner.

10.17 LEARNING BASED ON LIMITED INFORMATION

In practical scenarios, the information or data available for learning does not cover all the possible scenarios. In short, machine needs to learn based on the limited available information and the learning continues as new scenarios come in the picture. There is a need for learning on limited information and in process, understanding the relevant data and separating outliers. The next important aspect is inferencing and taking decision in new scenarios and incrementally, learning based on new experiences. This is referred to as *knowledge augmentation*. The knowledge augmentation not just builds knowledge based on already available knowledge, but selectively builds and discards, prioritises and re-prioritises the information, knowledge and perspectives.

SUMMARY
Machine learning is about making machine to learn and take appropriate decisions in complex and dynamic scenarios in the real life. There are various learning methods like supervised, unsupervised and semi-supervised methods. With labelled data, supervised learning takes place, whereas in its absence, unsupervised learning occurs. Effective combinations of both the methods perform semi-supervised learning. Further, as no learning method is complete in itself, there is a need for adaptive learning. There is a need for capturing perspectives and prioritising them. Thus, there comes the role of multi-perspective learning.

Statistical methods have a vital role in the learning approaches. Uncertainty while learning is handled using probabilities. Learning with some prior probabilities at hand helps in improving the classification. Conditional probability is used for Bayes's theory. With neural networks, it is very much possible to have an efficient supervised classifier built that suits the patternmatching problems. SVM proves to be a boon for classification and regression. Reinforcement learning adds a feather to the learning methodologies, where with the rewards, accurate decision-making is possible. Further, the different types of learning approaches that combine different perspectives, work with uncertain environment, are active and selective, thus contributing in making the learning an efficient one. These different learning methods are the core of artificial intelligence.

 KEYWORDS

1. **Supervised learning:** Supervised learning refers to learning under supervision, where labelled data is used for learning.

2. **Unsupervised learning:** When the data available is not labelled but learning takes place based on generic properties like similarity, closeness, etc., the learning is referred to as unsupervised learning. Clustering is one of the very popular techniques of unsupervised learning.

3. **Semi-supervised learning:** When labelled and unlabelled data are used in tandem for learning then the learning is termed as semi-supervised learning.

4. **Inductive leaning:** It is a learning approach that is based on observations. It could also be based on some experimental analysis.

5. **Reinforcement learning:** Reinforcement learning algorithm maximises rewards received during interactions with the environment and establishes mapping of states to actions as decision-making policy.

6. **Rote learning:** Rote learning is a rudimentary form of learning which is focussed on memorisation. This is one of the important forms when it comes to repetitive actions. Here, the values are stored so that these are not recomputed.

7. **Ensemble learning:** In ensemble learning method, the whole collection or ensemble of hypothesis is selected from the hypothesis space and their predictions are combined.

8. **Adaptive learning:** Adaptive machine learning algorithms are the machine learning models where the changes in the environment help in selecting the algorithm or learning method. Even for similar problem but in different scenario, suitable algorithm is chosen.

LEARNING EXERCISES

For each problem/scenario given below, identify the type of learning used:

1. You are provided with some documents. Some related to lawsuits under the category of divorce, civil, criminal and some are unknown. After some time, you are given a single new document. You categorise it properly. What learning did you use?

2. Sameer wants to book a flat in X area. His wife says that it is too far. His friend has an opinion that rates will inflate in the next couple of years. His parents like the area. Which type of learning will govern his decision?

3. Every evening Riya's mother takes her study books. One evening, Riya herself takes her notebooks and goes to her mother. Which learning has been used by her?

4. Mohit wants to watch a movie. He has three options of theatres. One of the theatre shows are for small children. Timings of the other theatre are not suitable for him, but show casts the movie he wants to watch. The third one is a bit far from his place. Which learning forms the basis of taking the decision?

5. You are taught some chemical formulae. Now, you are building up a chemical equation. Which learning are you using?

6. Consider a scenario in which you are going out for some work. While on the way, you get an alert at a particular road that you need to drop a cheque in the bank that is on the road. Some time later, at some other road, you are alerted about collecting clothes from the laundry that is nearby. What type of learning has been used in the scenario?

7. Indian cricket captain wins the toss and decides to bat first. What type of learning makes him take this decision?

8. In your house, to prepare tea, your mother keeps at hand small bottles filled with sugar and tea instead of making use of the big ones each time. Which learning is working behind your mother's out?

9. You are playing the game of table tennis. Is it the case that only one learning is used in the entire process? Explain.

MULTIPLE CHOICE QUESTIONS

1. Which type of learning best describes the problem of learning to ride a bicycle?
   (a) Supervised   (b) Unsupervised   (c) Reinforcement   (d) Inductive

2. Which approach would you use to address the problem of character recognition?
   (a) PCA   (b) EM
   (c) SVM   (d) All of them

3. A survey of cancer suffering patients and their relatives was conducted by some students with the aim to give them better environment to minimise the critical pain. This was conducted in three phases, with a gap of four months. At each

phase, some new information was available to them. You would relate this entire process to what type of learning?

(a) Inductive   (b) Multi-perspective
(c) Learning on limited information   (d) Reinforcement

4. Why would you prefer to use neural network for the problem of speech recognition?
(a) It is a task of supervised learning   (b) Intensity of speech can be well-detected
(c) It is a pattern recognition problem   (d) Fast and accurate results are obtained

5. A company forms groups of people to manufacture T-shirts of small, medium and big sizes. The learning used is
(a) Supervised   (b) Unsupervised
(c) Decision tree-based   (d) Reinforcement

6. Which type of learning will be best suited for forecasting in financial market?
(a) Supervised   (b) Semi-supervised   (c) Reinforcement   (d) Agent

7. Consider the statement 'I can decide about the document by considering its properties incrementally'. I am trying to refer to the learning called
(a) Supervised   (b) Reinforcement   (c) Decision tree-based
(d) Agent   (e) Multi-perspective

CONCEPT REVIEW QUESTIONS

1. Describe two supervised, semi-supervised and unsupervised learning methods and also give practical scenarios where these methods are most appropriate.

2. Elaborate the difference between supervised and reinforcement learning.

3. What is boosting?

4. Discuss the need for semi-supervised learning and multi-perspective learning.

CRITICAL THINKING EXERCISE

1. Discuss subtle differences between adaptive learning and ensemble learning.

2. Using the concept of ensemble learning, describe the learning by kids.

3. In computers, in many cases, rote learning is used. Give five such examples of rote learning.

PROJECT WORK

1. Develop a learning model for chess. With each game, it will use experiences to come up with a better strategy next time.

2. You want to decide signal times at road crossing based on the traffic density in each direction. Describe the learning algorithm to set the optimal time.

CHAPTER 11

Expert Systems

Learning Objectives

- ❏ To understand the relationship between an expert system and AI
- ❏ To understand the concept of expert system and the process of building the same
- ❏ To study the importance of knowledge representation for expert systems
- ❏ To study the role of reasoning
- ❏ To identify the impact of uncertainty in expert systems
- ❏ To gain knowledge about inferring and various types of expert systems in practice

INTRODUCTION

Consider the bidding process of Indian Premier League. The owners of participating teams look upon the experts to assist them in the selection of a player during the bidding process. Similarly, a newly joined employee in a company looks upon a financial adviser to give him an idea of investments and so on. So, everyone in some or the other way relies on the expert to get some sort of recommendations, suggestions or guidelines to assist in taking decisions.

So, what is an expert system? An *expert system*, as the name suggests, is a computer system that possesses or emulates all the decision-making capabilities like that of human expert. When we say so, do we mean to say that any program can be called an expert system when it has these capabilities? Almost all the problems discussed so far have been exploited in some or other expert system. What matters the most is the representation and the mapping mechanism of the knowledge with a strong reasoning and inferring process. Now, you would feel we are going back to the chapter of knowledge representation, and yes, you are right; it affects the overall mechanism of an expert system.

Expert systems (ES) have their roots in cognitive science, where the study of human mind exists with the combination of artificial intelligence and psychology. Expert systems are said to be the first successful applications of AI to have real-world problem solving. A few of the areas of its applications are medicine, finance, space research and so on.

Let us go through the history of ES. A rule-based system was the first one that was proposed by E. Post in 1943. Its typical example is a system based on the if-then rules. Then in 1961, a General Problem Solver was proposed by A. Newell and H. Simon. Later, it was the DENDRAL and MYCIN, which are the most representative examples of ES studied till today. These systems are described further in detail.

Precisely, we can say that an expert system is the one that finds its place in problem solving domains and gives a reasonable solution. Thus, it comprises knowledge base and a strong inferring mechanism. It is a system that is capable to reason out the actions and the outcomes it suggests. Hence, the ES can be classified into the areas of application for prediction, planning, monitoring, diagnosis and so on. Let us begin with the architecture of expert system.

11.1   ARCHITECTURE OF EXPERT SYSTEM

With reference to our introduction, we are already familiar that an expert system needs to have a strong knowledge base along with an inference mechanism. Figure 11.1 depicts the ES in operation.

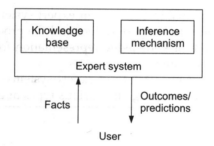

Figure 11.1   Expert system: Working.

What forms the knowledge base (KB) for the ES is the knowledge that it has attained from humans or some sort of information that may be in text or other form. This forms the factual knowledge—the knowledge that is generally agreed upon. The other type of knowledge that KB can contain is the heuristic—the knowledge that is based on experience and that helps in good predictions. The inference mechanism is responsible for getting the conclusions with the help of KB. The user tells the facts and asks the expert to give a solution. The ES accordingly processes the rules and gives the outcomes.

Further, in an expert system, we can relate two types of knowledge—one is problem knowledge that is specific to the type of problem at hand and the other is domain knowledge, where an expert knowledge persists with the know-how about solving specific problems. So, the domain knowledge forms the subset of problem knowledge. Hence, both of them are influential in the formulation of KB. This knowledge can be represented in many ways.

How can the expert system be designed? There is need to convert knowledge so that it can be initialised by the expert system. Building the KB is a two-phase process. In the first phase, the knowledge engineer sets up communication with the human expert. This is essential to get the maximum of the knowledge that can help in inferring. In the next phase, the knowledge engineer codes in the knowledge for KB explicitly. The evaluation for such a system is then again carried out by the expert. The expert here acts as a critic whose inputs would help in refining and building a better system. Figure 11.2 shows the development process.

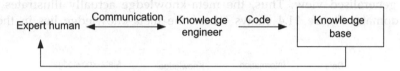

Figure 11.2   ES: Building process.

11.1.1   Parameters in Building an Expert System

After describing the architecture of the ES, we move to the basic parameters in building the system. The parameters described here essentially tell the activities required to be undertaken during the building process. The three basic parameters are described here briefly, viz. *domain exploration, expertise transfer* and *meta knowledge*.

Domain Exploration

Domain exploration is concerned with the exploration of the knowledge about the domain in which the system is operational. This knowledge is valid and can be directly applied and made use of. Various experts or specialists are in picture for this domain exploration. Here, the objects and their relationships to the domain are identified along with the other relevant information essential from the KB building perspective.

Expertise Transfer

Expertise transfer is the transfer of expertise from one system to another. In ES, this expertise transfer takes place from acquiring the knowledge from the expert to the transfer of it to the user. This takes place during data acquisition phase. Once the knowledge is obtained, there is a transfer to represent it for the system to understand. At later stage, the transfer takes place to build an interface and finally, to have the outcomes transferred back to the user. So, at every stage, it is understood that some expertise is transferred. Figure 11.3 shows the stages, where the expertise is transferred in the form of knowledge.

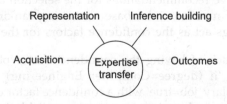

Figure 11.3   Expertise knowledge transfer stages.

Meta-knowledge

We know that *meta-knowledge* is a knowledge about available knowledge. But how is it used as a parameter block for building an expert system? We have already discussed about domain knowledge and problem knowledge. Meta-knowledge is systematic as well as domain independent knowledge. This actually helps in performing or building an expert system that is less dependent on a particular domain, thereby helping in keeping a generalised view. Thus, the meta-knowledge actually illustrates everything about the domain. Figure 11.4 shows where the meta-knowledge lies in the hierarchy structure.

Figure 11.4   Meta-knowledge: Hierarchy structure.

11.2   CONFIDENCE FACTORS

There is a notion of confidence factors in expert system. This is like an expert suggesting a student some college to join, but at the same time, gives another option of some specific course not offered in that college that could be beneficial. So, there is some uncertainty in this scenario because at the same time, the expert gives multiple options on the basis of some confidence factors. *Confidence factors* are the values associated with a particular variable. They indicate the degree of truth for that particular variable. So, there is a fuzzy notion here.

Obtaining the Confidence Factor

Based on the confidence factor, an expert system can give guidelines or recommendations. But from where can we obtain this factor? It can be made available in various ways, which are as follows:

1. *User input:* A user specifies the confidence level for some specific variable. This could be direct or indirect. For direct, let us take an example. Suppose there is a question like 'Do you plan to appear for IIT entrance exam?' and a possible answer from the user is 'Yes, 50% chances are there that I will appear for the exam.' Here, this 50% provided by the user is the confidence factor. In indirect form, a database is used by ES to determine confidence factor. This is based on the inputs obtained from the user. Consider a scenario in which the ES is used to give recommendations for the selection of a mobile. Let us assume that for different types of mobiles, a database containing rankings obtained from user is maintained. These rankings act as the confidence factors for the ES to give suggestions.

2. *Rule set:* Other approach of having the confidence factor obtained is simply the use of rules. Assume a rule 'if (degree=Computer Engineering) and (Masters=Computer Engineering) then High_salary_job=true' with a confidence factor of 75. Such rules associated with confidence factors can be based on previously available information and heuristics. Further, these rules can propagate these confidence factors to the subsequent rules.

Moreover, probabilistic approaches can assist in developing these confidence factors based on the previous available probable values for any variable. A simple probability value can be treated as the confidence factor. Yet in many cases, we cannot say that the probability value can prove to be effective in giving judgments, as there might be next level testing requirement, where the earlier value fails.

11.3 EXISTING EXPERT SYSTEMS

In this section, we discuss early expert systems—MYCIN and DENDRAL.

MYCIN

MYCIN is an early expert system developed in 1970's at Stanford University to provide users with an explanation of its reasoning. It was developed to aid the physicians in diagnosis and treatment of meningitis and bacterial infections. So, it used to provide a consultative advice about the infections. The diseases handled by MYCIN are observed to be developed during a recovery from some other disease. Physicians need to act fast in case of such complications. Taking samples of the patient and getting results from laboratories generally takes too much time. It is essential that the treatment should be started prior; even though the entire laboratory results are not available. Under this scenario, MYCIN is useful.

MYCIN is a computer program that takes inputs form the physician and gives advice. For this purpose, it invokes a dialogue. The physician answers the questions and on the basis of the knowledge MYCIN has, it provides diagnosis and detailed drug recommendations. It reasons about the data. It also takes into account the characteristics of the patient and the available laboratory results. Working in two phases, it performs the diagnosis in the first phase and drug recommendation in the second phase. MYCIN also considers the certainty factor based on the doctors confidence that assist in decisions.

Reasoning being a very important characteristic of the expert system, the physician can ask 'why' in between the process. At this instance, MYCIN explains the hypothesis that is under consideration. At the end, it is also possible to trace the entire reasoning process.

A snapshot (hypothetical) of the dialogue between MYCIN and the physician is given below:

The initial input consists of the following:

Patient's name: Mohan
Age: 30
Sex: Male

Q: Which type of test is it?
A: Blood
Q: How many days ago the blood test was obtained?
A: 3

Here, if any of the questions asked are not known, then the physician can type 'unknown'.

Q: Was Mohan a diabetic patient?

A: Why?

At this instance, the hypothesis is stated by MYCIN. For example, MYCIN puts forth the following hypothesis:

It is known that the test is of blood. The platelets count is on higher side. Then, with the rule, if the platelets of the patient are on higher side and the patient is diabetic, then with certainty of 0.5, identity of the disease is thrombocytosis.

From such a dialogue, it makes some prescriptions; a sample is given below:

1. XYZ medicine
   Dose: 770 mg (calculated on the basis of 15 mg/kg)
   Comments: Repeat blood test after 2 weeks.
2. .... and so on.

The above discussion gives an overview of the system. But it is obvious that the entire accuracy is based on the rules. For every input provided, MYCIN takes decisions from the set rules with reference to the certainty factor and further proceeds to the next action. For example, it can have rules that conclude likelihood of the infection. For every rule, a unique number is applied. So, rule 333 could have 0.8 likelihood for some disease with an answer, yes, the infection is likely to occur' or in some other rule, say 366 could have 0.45 likelihood with an answer 'no', indicating the disease is less likely to occur.

Thus, MYCIN has displayed the use of expert system in medical domain. The expert systems developed after MYCIN have actually set MYCIN as a benchmark. Accuracy of MYCIN is based on various factors. One of them is it assumes that the physicians are familiar with the terms it makes use of. Other factor is even though it has showed great ability and usefulness in its applications, its operation and reasoning process are restricted with the available knowledge it has. A physician cannot ask 'why' for a particular rule. So, the existing rules cannot be questioned.

To summarise, MYCIN represents the first of the new generation expert systems having an ability to reason. MYCIN's evolvement has actually set up a trademark in the research field of AI. Even today also, it is used for other research purposes with some modifications. Allowing rules, to be added incrementally and using them further have made the expert system a strong one, helping for better justifications and decisions.

DENDRAL

AI researcher, Edward Feigenbaum and geneticist, Joshua Ledeberg started work on heuristic DENDRAL in 1965. It was later called DENDRAL. The intention of this work was to have an expert system for chemical analysis. DENDRAL analyses the organic compounds so as to determine their structure. This was one of the early examples of the AI program.

DENDRAL infers the structures of the organic compounds. For this, a strategy, called *plan-generate-test* is used. The strategy comprises three sub-programs—the generator, the planning program and the testing and ranking programs. The generator forms the core of the heuristic approach. It comes out with potential solutions that are further generated into larger graphs of chemical atoms. In order to restrict the structure generation, CONGEN technique is employed that further assists the chemist in determining the chemical structure. Even though CONGEN has made things simple and is a standalone package, further assistance in inferring occurs with the planning programs. A large amount of knowledge is put to use in planning programs. The planning programs analyse the data and infer the constraints. It could come out with solutions revealing that an unknown molecule is a ketone, but not a methylketone. The planning information is actually provided with the list of good or bad features to the generator module. The last module actually ranks them. Programs like MSPRUNE and MSRANK are used here for making testable predictions from the plausible candidate module. This includes the analysis of the solution and discarding the scenarios that are not satisfying specific criteria.

To summarise, the stages of DENDRAL are initial stage of planning and to have hypothesis formation that helps the generator to have potential solutions and further tester to have predictions.

DENDRAL programs have been very much in practice for the problems related to structure determination of organic acids in human urine, antibiotics, and impurities in manufactured chemicals and so on.

One of the major problems faced by DENDRAL was the extraction of domain specific rules from experts. To overcome the same, Meta-DENDRAL was initiated. It is an automatic rule formulation program that has been structured for building a strong knowledge base. This has further resulted in higher accuracy in the prediction of correct spectra of new molecules.

With the success of MYCIN and DENDRAL, there has been a rapid growth in the development of new and better expert systems. At present, many expert systems have been developed with the baseline of these existing ones.

11.4 KNOWLEDGE ACQUISITION

Generally, in expert system, the knowledge engineer takes inputs from the domain expert to build the KB. Things get more complex when the expert is unwilling to co-operate to give in the fullest information. Further, the KB that is built needs to be refined so as to match the required performance. The process of acquiring expert knowledge, hence, becomes a complex task. Thus, to construct a good KB, acquisition has to be at its best.

Most often, a set of programs is compiled to extract the expert knowledge effectively. These programs called *knowledge acquisition systems*, though not fully automatic, assist in building effective KB. These systems provide support for different activities and are most effective when confined to specific problem-solving task. The tasks they carry out are input of the knowledge, maintaining the consistency and finally, making it richer. With respect to the specificity of the given problem for which the expert system is to be designed, the acquisition process should work in that direction. As an example, if we are to design a system that is meant for diagnosis purpose only, then the knowledge acquisition should be concentrated more on the hypothesis and the possible cause-and-effects. This helps in the identification of different causes for one hypothesis. Thus, the acquisition system is able to get maximum benefit by getting inputs on unknown causes (more knowledge) from the expert. Moreover, the decisions to be taken in case of conflict are resolved when appropriate inputs are made available from the expert.

There are various knowledge acquisition systems, viz., MORE, MOLE, SALT, LEAP, OPAL, TIMM, Meta-DENDRAL and so on. We discuss a few of them.

MORE is basically a tool that assists in eliciting knowledge from the experts and is most commonly used for diagnostic inferring. It refines the domain model with newly available information that can form hypothesis. Once a rule set is developed, the expert is asked to put in more knowledge for better rules set development. It makes use of qualitative model of causal relations to have the diagnosis.

MOLE is an extension of MORE. MOLE helps the experts in building a heuristic problem solver. It has the capability to disambiguate the under-specified knowledge and refine the KB that is incomplete. MOLE develops a KB that is called *MOLE-p(performance)*. It carries out various tasks that include formation of the initial KB and its refinement. It begins with getting an initial knowledge regarding the symptoms and the other details from the expert. It prompts the expert for explanations of the symptoms till it comes to the precise and ultimate set of causes. Determining correct explanations in case of conflict is also resolved by MOLE. Inferring anticipatory knowledge is also handled. In refinement stage, it identifies the weak slots and tries to fill them with more explanations from the experts. Finally, it is able to extract the knowledge intelligently to build a reasonable KB. MOLE has been used for different diagnostic purposes like diagnostic problems in car engines and others.

SALT is a knowledge acquisition system that works on the principle of propose and revise. This is useful for design tasks. SALT was developed for an elevator system configurer. It incrementally constructs designs by proposing values for design parameters. At the same time, constraints are noted and in case of violation, domain expert is used to revise the past decisions. In the beginning of knowledge acquisition, the user is provided with a menu, which operates for three different types of cases—procedures for proposing values, constraint identification on individual parameter values, and suggestions to revise the design, if the constraints are not met. Once this information is available, SALT stores the knowledge in dependency network.

Despite the tremendous growth in different knowledge acquisition techniques, there is still a necessity to have efficient ways for acquisition for more efficient expert systems.

11.5 SHELLS AND EXPLANATIONS

Shells are the interpreters that are used for building the ES, whereas *explanations* allow the system to express itself when it applies some reasoning. Let us discuss in detail.

Shells

Imagine you have to develop an expert system—a system that has to perform some predictions with regard to the weather. First and foremost, you would collect the information. Rules would be encoded with the formation of KB. Then, you would have an interpreter for it. Here, the data is all about the weather conditions and related information. Now, if you have to develop a new system for predicting traffic conditions, you would start from scratch. Instead if you have a shell, then by adding just the problem knowledge, things would get solved. So, as said earlier, for the ES, where the rules and the interpreter are combined together, the interpreter can be separated from the domain-specific knowledge, enabling to build new systems. These interpreters are shells. Sometimes, they are also called *AI tools or skeletons*.

EMYCIN (empty MYCIN) is an example of such shell. Building the shell has many advantages and one of the biggest one is that is simple and you need to enter only task knowledge. The inference mechanism that exploits the knowledge is built into the shell. Further, if the problems are not very complicated, the expert too can have the knowledge entered in. Figure 11.5 shows the shell structure.

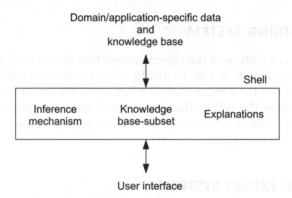

Figure 11.5 Shell structure.

At present, a large number of shells are available in the market. They tend to give a better flexibility in terms of knowledge representations and reasoning with the support of rules or frames or other mechanisms. Some shells also have mechanisms for the representation of knowledge as well as for reasoning and explanations. But remember though shells help in the building systems with simplicity, they do not help in knowledge acquisition. But to mention—some shells also have tools that help in better knowledge acquisition. Finally, the power of an expert system lies in the knowledge; more the knowledge, more will be its efficiency.

Explanations

Explanation is an important feature of the ES, which shows the ability of the system to express itself. In general, there is a necessity to have explanations for any action that is being taken. We do not accept things unless they are clarified and we are convinced about them. Similarly, for making the ES effective, it should be interactive. By this, we mean that the explanations as to how a particular conclusion has been drawn upon should be made available. For example, suppose an ES suggests a course to a student; it should be able to explain why that course is beneficial to him/her.

The explanations are based on the rules that are used for the inference process. So, these rules are the ones that help in reasoning. They are very important from the knowledge engineer perspective too, as they give the path in which the inference has been drawn.

Are the explanations really required? Depending on the system, say in case of bird identification system, the explanations could just be obvious, but in some cases, they are really vital, say in case of medical diagnosis.

In the course of explanations, the ES asks you some questions to infer. The question that comes to your mind is 'why?'; why is there a need for the system to ask? To arrive at a conclusion based on a particular rule, it asks the questions. With the backward reasoning and the previously answered questions, the ES is capable of giving these explanations as well.

So, we can say that two things are covered in explanations. One is when the ES is asking you questions, you need an answer as to why these questions are asked, and second is when a conclusion is derived, then an answer is needed as to how it has been drawn?

11.6 SELF-EXPLAINING SYSTEM

Self-explaining system is a feature of the expert system that shows its ability to explain itself. Self-explanation means that it is able to justify why a particular question is being asked and how it has arrived to the conclusions. We have just discussed about the explanations and it precisely specifies the self-explaining system. In some systems, there could be a self-explaining module inbuilt, typically in medical diagnosis, where there is a requirement of reasoning for diagnosis purpose.

11.7 RULE-BASED EXPERT SYSTEMS

Rule-based systems consist of rules (if-then), set of facts and an interpreter. The rules are the ones that constitute the complete KB. Rule-based systems are essentially designed so that they can have heuristic reasoning and proper explanations. They can separate the knowledge from the reasoning and facts. Figure 11.6 depicts a rule-based system. The inference mechanism, often referred to as *inference engine*, seeks the necessary information and the relationships from the KB to answer. It is also responsible to find the right facts. Two types of inference mechanisms are used—forward chaining and backward chaining. Explanations make the user understand how a particular conclusion has been derived. So, they trace the rules in the inference chain and provide user with the facts/rules used in the process.

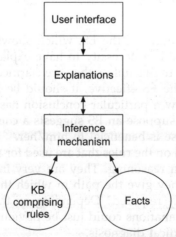

Figure 11.6 Rule-based expert system.

A simple example of if-then rule for a rule-based system that is in the form of if antecedent, then consequent, is given below:

If the number is divisible by 2, then it is even.

This is a very simple rule, but the rules can be complex, where multiple antecedents and consequents can exist. Multiple antecedents are often connected with 'and' or 'or', i.e., conjunctions or disjunctions. For example, if the students are absent or the students have not done the submission, then there will be no class.

Even there can be multiple consequents, which can be connected with conjunctions.

From the discussed example, it can be noticed that the rules fall under certain semantics. The semantics tells us that the production rules have some meanings. The semantics can also be overlapping rather that explicitly belonging to a particular category. They are broadly classified as follows:

1. *Relation:* Here, the relationship between the antecedent and the consequent is specified. For example, if the water is boiling, then the water is hot.

2. *Recommendation:* A rule that directs or gives some advice. For example, if the water in glass is hot, then advice not to touch the glass.

3. *Strategy:* A strategy tells what needs to be checked. These types of semantics advice regarding actions for betterment. For example, if road 1 is blocked, then try road 2.

4. *Directive:* It refers to an implication or indication of some action that needs to be carried out. It is a part of directive semantics. For example, if the light is green, then you can proceed.

5. *Heuristic:* It states guidelines-based rule. For example, if there is severe pain in chest and difficult to breathe, then the diagnosis might be as heart attack.

With the above discussion on the rule-based expert systems, we can say it is just matching of the rule to come to a conclusion, but there can be cases of conflicts also. Conflict can arise with regard to the selection of rule, or there could be conflicts with respect to the consequent mapping too. There can be different approaches to handle this. One way is to apply explicit ranking to the rules. This means prioritising them. Another approach can be to have a sequential way to trigger the rule. Firing of the rule can also occur on the basis of the current data that is treated having higher ranking or is found to be potential. Sometimes, an approach of triggering the longest rule is also taken up in case of conflict.

Let us proceed towards the pros and cons of the rule-based expert system. The major advantage of a rule-based expert system is the way the knowledge is represented. It resembles the human reasoning process, and hence, becomes effective. It can handle uncertain knowledge as well. When the ES deals with huge amount of data, managing and updating the KB get complex. Further, the conflict resolution gets more complicated with the growing size. Another problem is the rigid behaviour of the system that makes it useless outside the scope of the domain.

11.8   FORWARD AND BACKWARD CHAINING

In the rule-based expert systems, we have mentioned about the inference mechanisms that were used in the processes, viz. forward chaining and backward chaining. In forward chaining, as the name suggests, the facts are processed first. It keeps on looking out for the next rule till it is fired and proceeds. So, a rule is fired where the antecedent is matched, else it halts. Forward chaining is also called *data-driven approach*. Let us take an example that has the following rules:

Rule 1:   If P and Q, then A.
Rule 2:   If P and R, then B.
Rule 3:   If S, then R.
Rule 4:   If B, then C.

To prove: C is true given the facts that P and S are true.

Here, the forward chaining will work in the same way as explained above. It starts from the first rule till a match is found. The antecedent match is found at rule 3. From this, it is concluded that R is also true. So, addition of a new fact states that we have R, P and S as true. The next rule that is fired is rule 2 (as P and R are true). This adds that B is also true. This helps in triggering rule 4, where C is true; hence it is proved.

Considering the same example for backward chaining, it begins in the reverse way. The approach is commonly referred to as *goal-driven*. Here, from the goal/conclusion, it moves to find out evidence to prove it. (The way police traces the culprit once any crime has occurred.) Given to prove C is true, it will now proceed for matching the consequent rather than the antecedent. Starting from rule 4, it keeps moving till the given facts are found to be true. The antecedents are now made new sub-goals.

A question that comes to our mind—what should be used and when? Forward chaining is used when data collection is an expensive task and the size is limited. Backward chaining is useful when the data to be handled is substantially large. It is also a common practice to use backward chaining, where specific characteristics are looked upon by the expert system.

11.9   FRAME-BASED EXPERT SYSTEMS

With the study of rule-based expert systems and the forward and backward chaining methods, let us begin with the frame-based systems. The expert systems which make use of frames for the knowledge are called *frame-based expert systems*.

But what is a frame? A *frame* is a data structure with a typical knowledge about the object or the concept. We are already familiar with Minsky's frame. So, a frame has its name and a set of attributes. For example, a car frame can have make, type, colour and so on as the slots/attributes in the frame. Each of the slot or the attribute has a unique value associated with it. So, we can say that the frame gives a concise representation. Hence, a frame-based representation is suited for object-oriented programming techniques.

In AI terms, a knowledge engineer actually calls the object as the frame. The slots can contain a default value, or a pointer to another frame, or a set of rules or procedures so as to obtain the slot value. To detail it more, we can have the following things included in the slot:

1. Frame name
2. Relationship with other frames
3. Values or ranges
4. Procedural information

By relationship, we mean that the hierarchy, or to be specific, the inheritance is depicted. Value and ranges, as discussed earlier, represent the actual/default values or the specified ranges. In case of procedural information, the slot is attached to a procedure that is executed when any event is triggered such as change in the value of the slot. Generally, an instance-frame refers to an object and a class-frame refers to a group. So, car, person, bird can be referred to as class-frames. Figure 11.7 represents the frame structure for class and instance.

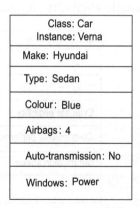

Class: Car
Make:
Type:
Colour:
Airbags:
Auto-transmission:
Windows:

Class: Car Instance: i10
Make: Hyundai
Type: Small car
Colour: Red
Airbags: 2
Auto-transmission: No
Windows: Power

Class: Car Instance: Verna
Make: Hyundai
Type: Sedan
Colour: Blue
Airbags: 4
Auto-transmission: No
Windows: Power

Figure 11.7   Frames: Class and instance.

Since we have been discussing that frames are most useful in object-oriented approach, the generalisation and aggregation concepts apply here as well. For example, engine and chassis can be the parts of a class car. Similarly, car is a kind of a vehicle. So, both the concepts are applicable here. Can there be any association? Yes. An association can exist between the classes, say a book class may belong to a person or in other words, the book is owned by a person.

Till now, we have concentrated only on the knowledge part, but as we know that an expert system needs to have some methods too, so, methods and demons are added to the frames. A *method* is a procedure that is executed when requested. It is associated with the frame. Sometimes, we want a specific event or an action to occur when any value changes. Based on these facts, the methods are categorised into two categories when changed, and when needed.

A *when changed method* is executed when the value changes, whereas a *when needed method* is used to obtain the value for the attribute. This happens in course of problem solving that the value is required. We have discussed about the demons too. What is the difference between a method and demon? A demon makes use of if-then structure, whereas methods are used for more complex things.

Working of a Frame-based Expert System

After having understood the concept of frames, slots, methods, let us study its working. We know that in rule-based expert system, it is the chaining mechanism in the inference that fires the rules so as to reach the goal. In case of frames that have the knowledge representation, the methods or the demons essentially add actions to them. The goal, hence, is set in the methods or the demons.

For example, the process for an expert system to check the eligibility of a student appearing for an exam is explained (refer to Figure 11.8). We have a set of slots/attributes as well as methods and demons for the frames of check eligibility, request, actions and so on. A when changed method is invoked when the expert system is asked for the evaluation status, whereas when needed method is, in turn, invoked by the system to check the submission status of that particular student. So, there can be a flow from a staff to get the details of the student for evaluation. Let us assume that this frame has an attribute, i.e., evaluate eligibility. A sample view of the same is depicted in Figure 11.8.

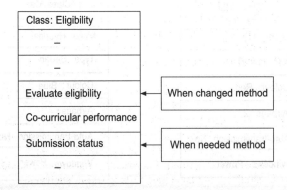

Figure 11.8 When needed and when required methods: Snapshot.

Guidelines to Build a Frame-based Expert System

1. The first step that is involved in designing any expert system is the scope and the specificity of the problem at hand. There has to be utmost clarity about these two factors.
2. The next step is the identification of classes, instances and the attributes.

3. Since the events or to be specific, the methods are the key role players in evaluation, the display of the system has to be presented in the most simple and transparent manner.
4. The next task is to have the methods of when changed and when needed. This is dependent to the design in step 3, where the events are decided.
5. Rules are to be also defined along with the methods.
6. Finally, a full-proof evaluation of the built system, and if required, expansion should be handled.

A detailed example is handled in the case study for the frame-based expert system, provided further in the chapter.

11.10 FUZZY EXPERT SYSTEMS

Many things are uncertain and most often, we face a dilemma with respect to determination of belongingness of a particular thing. Still, as humans, we are in position to handle the reasoning in such cases. A *fuzzy logic* is the one that provides mapping for this uncertainty. To put it in simple words, a *fuzzy expert system* is the one that makes use of fuzzy membership functions. In fuzzy logic, as we are aware, approximation exists rather than exactness. The same concept is put to practice in these expert systems.

The most common rule that is found in the fuzzy expert system is in the form of If X is low and Y is high, then Z is medium.

Here, X, Y are the inputs and Z is the output. Z is the one whose value is to be computed. Low, high and medium define the degree of membership. The expert systems based on fuzzy can have multiple conclusions per rule. So, the set of fuzzy rules comprises its KB.

Figure 11.9 depicts the fuzzy expert system. Every expert system has an inference mechanism, but the way in which the mechanism derives the conclusions is different. In this case, the four processes that are commonly used are as follows:

1. Fuzzification
2. Inference
3. Composition
4. Defuzzification

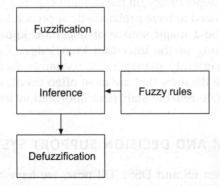

Figure 11.9 Basic architecture of fuzzy expert system.

In *fuzzification* process, the membership functions are defined on the variables. Input variables are applied to the actual values. This helps in determining the degree of truth for each rule premise. This degree of truth for the premise is called as *alpha*.

In the *inference process*, the truth value for the premise is calculated. The inference mechanisms that are applied are min and product. In case of *min*, the output membership is cut off at a specific height that maps to the computed degree of truth of the premise. In *product*, the output is scaled by the computed degree of truth of the premise.

In *composition process*, the fuzzy subsets are combined to form a single fuzzy subset for output variable. Composition process consists of max and sum compositions. In *sum* compositions, point-wise sum over the fuzzy sets is considered. Whereas, in case of *max* composition, point-wise maximum value over the fuzzy sets is taken.

In *defuzzification process*, the fuzzy value is converted to a crisp value. The most common methods are centroid and maximum methods. In case of centroid approach, a fuzzy centroid is calculated, while in *maximum* methods, average-maximum is the one that returns average value where maximum truth value occurs. (Detailed example is covered in Chapter 18.)

Fuzzy expert systems are most effectively used in the category of pattern recognition. There are many advantages of fuzzy systems. To mention a few, the KB has limited number of rules, and hence, is efficient. Since the knowledge is structurally shallow, the run-time chaining for the inferences are not required. They exhibit less maintenance costs and can be built at a faster rate. The KB is semantically rich, and hence, the fuzzy experts systems can be well-suited for decision-making.

11.11 UNCERTAINTY MANAGEMENT IN EXPERT SYSTEMS

Uncertainty exists in every aspect. It means lack of exact knowledge that allows us to come to an exact conclusion. So, can we say that the information we have is partial? Yes, the information can be incomplete and uncertain.

There are many reasons of this uncertain knowledge. Even in writing, we use the terms—often, hardly, may be, sometimes. While using these terms, we are uncertain about some factors. Uncertainty can arise when we get different opinions possibly from different sources. Even in some cases, the data values are actually missing too. For expert systems, to build concrete rules, the dependency on the domain expert adds up more complications.

So, the experts systems need to have probabilistic approach for handling the uncertainty. The KB is also treated to be a major source of uncertain knowledge. Rule-based expert systems are good at handling of the uncertain knowledge. Though numerous methods are worked on for the uncertainty management (certainty factors, Bayesian probability, Dempster–Shafer theory are the ones that are most often used), yet the selection of method is dependent on the available reliable statistical information for the application.

11.12 EXPERT SYSTEM AND DECISION SUPPORT SYSTEM (DSS)

What is the relation between ES and DSS? Till now, we have discussed about ES which assists in taking decisions. The fact is that the ES is used in DSS. So, it is basically an expert system technology that is embedded in DSS. On a broader scale, DSS is categorised into data-oriented DSS, model-oriented DSS and process-oriented DSS. Data-oriented DSS focusses on data warehouse, model-oriented DSS handles small databases, whereas process-oriented DSS deals with the question-oriented models. Thus, ES falls under this category of DSS. Though the distinguishing factor between the two is a thin line, we can always say that ES too, of course, will be making the use of these models, where the facts will be made available through the databases.

Often it is observed that ES face the problem of lack of deep knowledge. By this, we mean that in-depth knowledge will always aid in giving improved decisions. Further, system models along with ES can help in providing the support components for computations in the decision process. So, DSS is not built by just ES, but includes other components too that support decisions. DSSs are used at a higher level of business intelligence to avail strategic decisions. DSS, where the data sets are structured, could wholly rely on ES. In case of complex and unstructured data, it uses other methods. Moreover, it is actually the nature of output that is expected from the DSS that will, in turn, determine the way ES is to be used in it.

11.13   PROS AND CONS OF EXPERT SYSTEMS

What can be the possible benefits of having an expert system as machine rather than a human? They are many! A few of them are listed below:

1. A consistent output
2. Quick and fast response
3. Location/date/day/time independent
4. Can be made generalised. (A change in application would result in looking out for a human expert related to that field if we are not relying on expert systems. But with expert systems, having generalisation, the process gets less complicated.)
5. Efficient utilisation of the knowledge (Human experts may forget some aspects, whereas expert systems consider all the rules and scenarios.)
6. Simple future enhancements with additional information of the knowledge and the rules (but with humans, it is difficult)
7. Easy maintenance of system.

The disadvantages of expert systems are mentioned below:

1. They cannot handle new dynamic situation.
2. The systems cannot be adaptive based on the decisions taken earlier.
3. Limited set of knowledge will leave them with limited set of decision outcomes.
4. Development cost could be high depending on the purpose they are used for.

Still, with the listed advantages and disadvantages, whether to have an expert system or not is wholly dependent on the purpose of use.

11.14 CASE STUDY

There has been a substantial growth in the need and development of expert systems for the increasing application domains. With a lot of expert systems to handle the predictions, diagnosis, classifications like that of Buy Smart (a frame-based expert system) that addresses the housing needs or an audit-based system to tackle the compliance norms, there is much to study and discuss. Here, we discuss Prospector—an expert system in geology domain.

Aim of the Expert System

The aim of this expert system is to evaluate the mineral potential of a geological region. It handles the geological settings, structural controls and different types of rocks as well as minerals.

Target Users

The target users for this system are the geologists who are at an early stage of investigating the site to be a drilling site.

Key Points

Prospector can handle uncertain data and incomplete data. It is also a domain independent system. Data is matched to the models to check the presence of ore so as to identify the site to be a drilling site.

KB

The KB of Prospector is divided into two parts—general and special purpose. As discussed earlier, the system is domain independent, so the general KB maintains background information that can be used for other applications as well. The special purpose KB contains knowledge that is relevant to the domain and is in the form of inference network.

Methodology

Prospector makes use of production rules and semantic networks. It makes use of backward chaining inference strategy.

Representation

The representation used by the developers is the inference network. *Inference network* is a collection of evidence and hypothesis. There exists a linkage between the evidences. In short, it explains the factors which actually affect each other. It is in the form of if E, then H, where E is the evidence and H is the hypothesis. The hypothesis has some degree that is pre-stored or ranged. This degree specifies the likelihood of sufficiency and necessity. Also, the values of E and H (probabilities) are changed with the use of Bayes's theorem in the course of execution. So, the inference network actually provides with a way to compute the probabilities of the influential factors. It also makes use of semantic network. It is a network of nodes that is used to represent relevant knowledge like taxonomy relations. It represents the associative memory model.

Inference Mechanism

Since it has to handle uncertainty, probability has to come in picture. It makes use of Bayesian, certainty factors and fuzzy sets. A form of Bayes's theorem that is referred to as *odds-theorem* is used in Prospector. As discussed earlier, there is a measure of sufficiency that is used when the evidence E is known to be existing, whereas measure of necessity is used when E is not known to be existing.

Some of the sample models used in the Prospector are shown below in Figure 11.10.

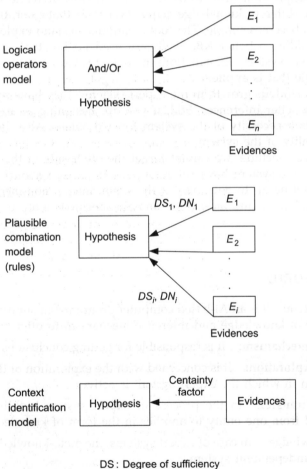

DS : Degree of sufficiency

DN : Degree of necessity

Figure 11.10 Prospector models.

SUMMARY

Expert systems are the ones that help in problem solving. With an efficient expert system, the diagnosis and predictions have become simple. One of the important aspects of expert system is the inference mechanism. Forward and backward chaining are used for inferencing in case of a rule-based expert system. Handling uncertainty is the most critical task and is better tackled by the rule-based expert system. Frame-based expert systems are most suited for object-oriented approach. Fuzzy systems use fuzzy logic and have proved to be better in pattern analysis problems. Expert systems, in a broader sense, are used for prediction, classification, diagnosis, monitoring and control, and many more. MYCIN and DENDRAL are the early expert systems that are now used as benchmark in developing the new ones.

Knowledge acquisition also needs to be taken care of while building an expert system. With the different knowledge acquisition tools that exist, the task of building an expert system becomes simple. The tool communicates and exploits the information that helps in building a better KB. Shells are used further that act as a skeleton for building an expert system. Explanations help in providing information to the user regarding the rule that is applied.

With the tremendous growth in the expert systems, they have proved to be a boon in assisting with better inferences. Still, if you are designing an expert system, make sure that there is a necessity of the system for a problem. Also, be specific with the design and usability of the system.

But before we conclude, we cannot forget the other side of the expert system, the drawbacks! Does the system have common sense to reason about? The answer is no. The system cannot be up to date, and at the same time, is non-incremental in nature. It is not always adaptive and most often domain-specific. On top of it, it needs experts for its maintenance.

 KEYWORDS

1. **Expert system:** It is an AI-based computer program that simulates expert judgment by the use of knowledge and inference mechanism to offer an advice or infer.

2. **Inference mechanism:** It is responsible for getting conclusions with the help of KB.

3. **Domain exploration:** It is concerned with the exploration of the knowledge about the domain in which the expert system is active.

4. **Expertise transfer:** In the process of expert system building, the expertise is transferred from one entity to another in the form of knowledge to build KB.

5. **Meta-knowledge:** In case of expert systems, the meta-knowledge helps in building a domain independent system.

6. **MYCIN:** It is an early expert system that was developed to aid the physicians in diagnosis and treatment of meningitis and bacterial infections.

7. **DENDRAL:** It is also an early expert system that analyses the organic compounds so as to determine their structure.

8. **Knowledge acquisition tools:** These tools assist and help in getting the knowledge from the expert.

9. **Shells:** These are the interpreters used for building an expert system.

10. **Explanations:** These are the features of an expert system that tell about the reasoning.

11. **Self-explaining system:** It is the ability of an expert system to justify the rules it has fired.

12. **Rule-based expert system:** It is an expert system that is based on if-then rules, facts and the inference mechanism.

13. **Frame-based expert system:** It is an expert system that makes use of the knowledge as frames.

14. **Fuzzy expert system:** It is an expert system that makes use of fuzzy logic consisting of collection of membership functions and rules to reason.

MULTIPLE CHOICE QUESTIONS

(*Note:* There can be more than one answer.)

1. MYCIN falls under the category of
   (a) Shell
   (b) Rule-based expert system
   (c) Frame-based expert system
   (d) None of these

2. A rule of 'If you are wearing a cardigan, then it is cold' falls under the semantics of
   (a) Recommendation
   (b) Heuristic
   (c) Relation
   (d) Directive

3. The core part of decision-making for the expert system lies in the
   (a) Knowledge base
   (b) Explanations
   (c) Inference mechanism
   (d) Facts

4. A when needed method is invoked in frame-based expert system
   (a) By an event in when changed
   (b) In the decision-making, as required
   (c) By any action that needs some data
   (d) All of the above

5. The interpreters in expert systems are termed as
   (a) Frames
   (b) Explanations
   (c) Shells
   (d) None of these

6. The process of coding the knowledge in expert systems is
   (a) Knowledge base
   (b) Knowledge engineering
   (c) Knowledge acquisition
   (d) None of the above

7. In fuzzy expert system, conversion to crisp value is done by
   (a) Inference mechanism
   (b) Defuzzification
   (c) Composition
   (d) Fuzzification

CONCEPT REVIEW QUESTIONS

1. Discuss the expert system framework.
2. List out the benefits of expert systems.
3. What are shells and explanations?
4. What are frame-based expert systems?

CRITICAL THINKING EXERCISE

1. Why is there a need to have efficient knowledge acquisition systems?
2. 'Better the user interface, better is the expert system.' Is this valid? Discuss.

PROJECT WORK

1. Develop an expert system for society maintenance. Discuss the knowledge representation and acquisition. Define the set of rules that would be used. The system should answer the following:
   (a) Why was there no water supply on Monday?
   (b) Why were there no lights in the common passage?

2. Develop an expert system for library that would recommend book for its project work. Assume suitable data.

CHAPTER **12**

Natural Language Processing

Learning Objectives

- ❑ To understand the concept of natural language processing
- ❑ To study the techniques involved in the processing of the text or information
- ❑ To understand the analysis of the text and its applications
- ❑ To understand the importance and necessity of effective information retrieval systems
- ❑ To identify and study the various aspects of natural language processing, with the role of grammars in the representation
- ❑ To study the applications of natural language processing in building intelligent systems

INTRODUCTION

"We are like a pre-paid card with limited validity. If we are lucky, we may last another 50 years. Do we really need to get so worked up? It is ok to bunk a few classes, goof up some interviews; we are people, not programmed devices[1]. A part of speech by Chetan Bhagat on 'keeping the spark alive in one's life.' He means to convey a message by this speech, i.e., enjoy the life and not to take it too seriously. This inference is possible because you have understood the language as well as the context and are able to read between the lines. So, you have processed the language to get something out of it.

Even while reading the text of this book or while listening to a professor, one tries to understand, correlate, analyse or possibly map the knowledge that is written or verbal. So, the brain actually performs the task of these mentioned things. But when it comes to machine, we need to provide the intelligence—the intelligence to map and understand, which would enable it to analyse the extracted knowledge the way we want. Let us make things simple more technically!

---

1. http://www.chetanbhagat.com/other-works/speeches/spark/

What is natural language? A language that is in use and has been developed naturally. It is in practice and a way for communication. So, it can be in oral or written form. What are we going to study in natural language processing (typically referred to as *NLP*)? Let us try to bring it in more clarity. We can say that there are two things—one is the source in which the language lies and the other is the destination or what the processing needs to do as a target. So, NLP involves the study of various methods and approaches. This chapter discusses about the processing tasks, which can be carried out on the input language, and represent the language in some resulting form, as required. Hope now things are getting simple. So, to have some definition, *NLP* can be defined as

A computerised mechanism involving computation techniques to analyse and represent the text (oral or written) in some form for achieving human-like processing for a variety of applications.

Representation into some other form is a processing that includes the task of converting or mapping into some other suitable form. Even when we say that the language form is oral or written, one must be clear that things get very much complicated with the use of oral form owing to the noise in the signal.

NLP: Brief History

The work related to NLP was started with machine translation (MT) in 1950s. It was Allen Turing who proposed what today is called the *Turing test* in 1950s. It is the testing ability of the machine program to have written conversation with human. This program should be written so well so that one would find it difficult to determine whether the conversation is with a machine or it is with the other person actually. During the same period of 1950s, cryptography and language translation took place. Later on, syntactic structures came up along with linguistics. Further, the sentences were considered with knowledge augmentation and semantics. In 1960s, ELIZA (the most common NLP system) was developed that gained popularity. It was the simulation of a psychotherapist. At a very later stage, it was the case grammars that came up. Now, there has been a complete revolution in the NLP, with the machine learning approaches coming up. Many NLP systems have been developed till today and a lot of competitions are being organised that are based on the Turing test. Figure 12.1 gives a few of the tasks that come under NLP.

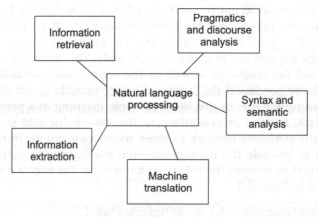

Figure 12.1   NLP: Tasks.

More than having the concept of natural language processing, natural language understanding is what that is essentially required. There is a very fundamental question— is Google or any other search engine making use of NLP, after looking at the concept discussed so far? What is your answer? Indeed, it does. Let us study about it too in the chapter.

12.1 LEVELS OF NLP

Before we go into the details of how actually the processing takes place, let us look at the different levels or the models (given below) at which NLP can take place and then study them in detail.

1. *Morphology:* It is the analysis of individual words that consist of morphemes—the smallest grammatical unit. Generally, words with 'ing', 'ed' change the meaning of the word. This analysis becomes necessary in the determination of tense as well.

2. *Syntax:* Syntax is concerned with the rules. It includes legal formulation of the sentences to check the structures. (Some aspects are covered in compiler's phase of syntax analysis that you must have studied). For example, 'Hari is good not to.' The sentence structure is totally invalid here.

3. *Semantic:* During this phase, meaning check is carried out. The way in which the meaning is conveyed is analysed. The previous example is syntactically as well as semantically wrong. Now, consider one more example, i.e., 'The table is on the ceiling.' This is syntactically correct, but semantically wrong.

4. *Discourse integration:* In communication or even in text formats, often the meaning of the current sentence is dependent on the one that is prior to it. Discourse analysis deals with the identification of discourse structure.

5. *Pragmatics:* In this phase, analysis of the response from the user with reference to what actually the language meant to convey is handled. So, it deals with the mapping for what the user has interpreted from the conveyed part and what was actually expected. For a question like 'Do you know how long it will take to complete the job?', the expected answer is the number of hours rather than a yes or no.

6. *Prosody:* It is an analysis phase that handles rhythm. This is the most difficult analysis that plays an important role in the poetry or *shlokas* (chants involving the name of God) that follow a rhythm.

7. *Phonology:* This involves analysis of the different kinds of sounds that are combined. It is concerned with speech recognition.

Can the analysis levels discussed be overlapped or interrelated? Yes. It is very much possible to have an analysis actually forming a fuzzy structure. They can work in stages, where the second level makes use of the analysis or the outcomes of the first level. We now study them in detail.

12.2 SYNTACTIC AND SEMANTIC ANALYSIS

Morphology deals with word formation from small parts. Morphological analysis finds out the pieces which have contributed for word formation.

The morphological analysis is simply separating or tokenising the words. Removal of the additional words like 's', 'ed' (as discussed earlier) and assigning them to the syntactic category are carried out in morphological analysis. So, we do not go into a detail discussion on it. (This sounds similar to the tokenisation concept in compilers!). We proceed to the next step of syntactic and semantic analysis. Let us begin with syntax analysis.

12.2.1 Syntax Analysis

Syntactic analysis is concerned with checking of the syntactic structure and its components. Once the words of a sentence are categorised into different parts of speech, the syntax analysis generates a parse tree. A parse tree is a representation for the sentence into a structure. This structure, which is hierarchical in nature, helps in identifying the sentence bits on which the next level of semantic analysis operates.

What things are essential to produce a parse tree? There exists the concept of grammar. A *grammar*, as is used in English, tells us about how the statements should be constituted, with the usage of the parts of speech at appropriate places. In NLP, grammar is the description of language. It comprises rules. There is a Chomsky hierarchy that represents the different grammars that are used. Amongst them is context-free, context-sensitive and so on. Let us discuss context-free grammar.

Context-free Grammar (CFG)

A CFG consists of terminals, non-terminals, start symbol and production rules, where left side of a production rule contains only one non-terminal. The grammar describes the language. Following are the things contained by CFG:

1. *Terminals:* Terminals are syntactic symbols that cannot be replaced further. The terminals are written in small letters.

2. *Non-terminals:* Symbols that are replaced by terminals are called *non-terminals*. They are written in capital letters.

3. *Start symbol:* It refers to starting of the sentence rules (mostly it starts with capital letter S).

4. *Production rules:* These are the rules to be applied for splitting the sentence into appropriate syntactic form for analysis. They consist of terminal, non-terminals and the start symbol.

The grammar (in technical terms) is a quadruple, represented as (V, T, P, S), where V is the set of non-terminals, T is the set of terminals, P is the set of production rules and S is the start symbol.

For example, a sample CFG is

$$S \rightarrow \alpha_1 \mid \alpha_2 \mid R$$

$$R \rightarrow \alpha_3$$

Here, S and R are the non-terminals, whereas α_1, α_2 and α_3 are the terminals. What is the purpose behind using the CFG? It is used to check if a sentence is syntactically correct. Starting from the start symbol, if we are able to derive the sentence using these rules by substitution, syntactically correct sentence can be determined. So, the grammar is nothing but the rules that are required to from the hierarchical structure. How is this grammar used? Let us take an example that is always given for an English statement.

Let S be the sentence. This sentence can have subject and predicate. The subject can be a noun phrase as generally called and a predicate comprises the verbs/adverbs and so on. The grammar representation is discussed below for an example, say 'Ram read the interesting book' or 'Ram ate the delicious cake':

Let

S : Sentence → SB VP OB

SB : Subject → PN

VP : Verb phrase → ADV V | V

OB : Object → the S_1

S_1 : Subset of S → ADJ | N

PN : Proper noun → Ram

ADJ : Adjective → interesting | delicious

N : Noun → book | cake

V : Verb → read | ate

Parsing: Once we have the grammar, parse tree is generated. One point to be noted here is there can be different sets of grammar rules depending on the text. For the above example, let us see how the parse tree is generated.

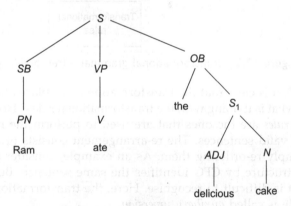

Figure 12.2 A parse tree.

In the process of generation of a parse tree, the grammar rules are compared with the input. Whenever a rule matches, it is expanded, thus generating the tree. As it is observed from Figure 12.2, at every stage, one rule is applied, thus helping in generating the entire structure.

Top-down and bottom-up parsing: Two ways of building a parse tree are top-down and bottom-up. In *top-down*, the parser begins with the main symbol or the start symbol(S) in the rules. It keeps on applying the rules till the terminals become the symbols of the sentences. Whereas, in case of *bottom-up parsing*, the reverse procedure is applied. Beginning with the sentence, the rules are applied backwards by replacing the words in the sentence with the appropriate rules till start symbol is reached.

Though top-down parser can build trees without the time factor making a constraint, it is quite possible that the trees are produced without having a look at what the next symbol or token in the sentence is to be parsed. So, may be wrong rules are selected. The branching factor is also a point of concern in both the approaches. Note that the bottom-up parsing can take place from left to right or right to left. Many's the time, a combined approach is also used.

Transformational Grammar

The transformational grammar comprises tags that are used to handle the plural or the passive sentences. This grammar is an extension to the CFG. So, the parse tree generated by the CFG is further refined with the addition of tags and re-structuring. Commonly, the tree generated by CFG is called *deep structure*, and the one with the transformational grammar is called *surface structure*. The reason behind this is that it consists of the additional tags that enable to understand the context-sensitive entities. Figure 12.3 depicts the structure of transformational grammar.

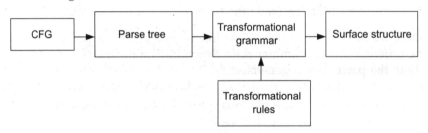

Figure 12.3   Transformational grammar—Tree building.

From Figure 12.3, it is clear that the transformation takes place after the parse tree has been generated. So, what is it doing with the transformational rules? How are they different? The *transformational rules* are the ones that are used to perform the re-arrangement. This is done so as to get valid sentences. The re-arrangement consists of addition or removal of the tokens, or simply re-ordering them. As an example, consider a statement 'Milli is dancing'. The tree structure by CFG identifies the same sentence. But if we change it to 'is Milli dancing?', it is difficult to recognise. Here, the transformation rule is applied for re-ordering. This rule is called *auxiliary inversion*.

Augmented Transition Networks (ATN)

To check the correctness of the sentence grammatically, ATNs are used. Basically, ATNs represent the grammars in NLP and parse them. But prior to its study, an introduction to *recursive transition network (RTN)* is given, which is the core concept for augmented transition networks (ATNs). RTNs are based on the finite state automata, but are equivalent to push down automata. Let us start with RTN.

An RTN is a directed graph. The graph consists of states and arcs that are labelled. It has a start state and the Final state is marked with '/F' or '/1'. What does the RTN do? It takes the input sentence and tells whether the string is acceptable or not. Hence, it performs the syntactic check. The arc indicates the labelled category or can even refer to the other networks. That is the labelled category can be a start state for another network. A sample RTN is depicted below (Figure 12.4):

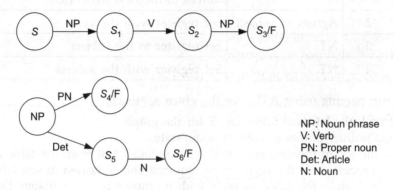

NP: Noun phrase
V: Verb
PN: Proper noun
Det: Article
N: Noun

Figure 12.4 Sample RTN.

A RTN has
1. A set of finite terminals, say T.
2. A set of non-terminals.
3. A category C and a mapping $T \rightarrow C$.
4. A start symbol S.

An ATN differs from RTN. In ATN, it is essentially an RTN that has a set of test rules, which need to be satisfied prior to the arc traversal. While doing so, it makes use of registers to save the states. So, in ATN's, we would have a table consisting of arc, test and action. A sample snapshot of a table is given Table 12.1. A sample ATN is shown in Figure 12.5. Do remember that the baseline for ATN is the transformational grammar.

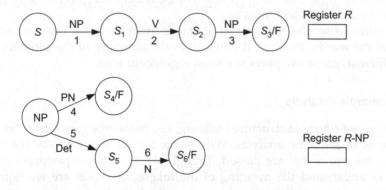

Figure 12.5 Sample ATN.

Let us take a simple example 'The cat drank the milk.'

TABLE 12.1 Table listing test conditions for arc traversals

Arc	Test	Action
1	NT	Set register to the subject, the network moves to the next network
2	Agrees to subject	Set register with the verb
3	NT	Set register to the subject
4	NT	Set register with the subject

To perform parsing using ATN, for the given sentence,

1. Start with the leftmost node, i.e., *S* for the graph.
2. Let the pointer points to current node/state.
3. Select the arc to traverse such that the associated test from the table is satisfied.
4. In the process, save the registers as required and indicated in test table.
5. If we end up in the terminal node with no inputs being available, the parsing is said to complete.

For the given example, from the first arc itself, another ATN is being referred. So, the test of subject is being registered and the ATN pointer moves to the next network. Once the tests and parsing for this subset are done, i.e., 'The cat' is accepted, it returns back to the previous states and continues to parse till no input is left. At this, the parsing is complete. At any point of time, if there is no arc left for traversal and input text is still remaining, the parsing fails.

A very recent study revealed the use of ATN's for garden path sentences. *Garden path sentences* are the ones in which parsing could result into ambiguity. This ambiguity occurs as humans tend to interpret the sentences, one word at a time. It generally happens when the entire sentence is not heard due to which one cannot predict the meaning. So, it becomes confusing. An example can be 'Because Riya exercises a half hour walk is not difficult for her.' In the initial interpretation, we think of that Riya exercises for half an hour, but actually from 'half hour', a new phrase is beginning. ATNs tend to resolve these misleading garden path sentences too.

So, to summarise, the outcome of syntactic analysis is the ordering structure or the sequence of the words. In short, it determines the structure of the sentence. To make this analysis efficient, grammar plays the most significant role.

12.2.2 Semantic Analysis

With the study of syntactic structure building, i.e., parse tree generation, let us understand the next level of semantic analysis. With semantic, we mean to say the 'meaning'. The meaning of the words that are parsed. Though syntax analysis performs the parsing, it is necessary to understand the meaning of the tokens. So, what are we doing in semantic analysis? (Remember one thing that for each of the tasks NLP is performing, there is some output that you expect.) In semantic analysis, we are having some representation that contain the meaning of the input sentence. How can we have this? Is this again some grammar? Let us understand it better. Humans have prior knowledge about the words to understand their meaning. So, when we talk about word, say table, we have some knowledge about it. Consider two sentences—'Keep the book on the table' and 'Learn the table of number 23'. The contexts in which the table is referred are different. This understanding is done in semantic analysis. How will a machine know that we are referring to physical object table or mathematics concept of table? Let us discuss the different aspects of semantic analysis.

Lexical Processing

In lexical processing, the meaning of the tokens (words in the sentences) is found out. There is a concept of word sense disambiguation here.

Understanding the meaning of a particular word in the context is called *word sense disambiguation*. So, it is concerned with the sense where it would be operational. In order to determine this, additional information about where it would be operational can be attached to the knowledge. For the example of the table, we can have additional information, called *semantic markers* that help in the identification of the meaning. So, the markers here can be physical entity or a mathematical entity. With relation to the verb 'keep', it will be physical entity, whereas with 'learn', it will be mathematical one.

Semantic Grammars

The syntax analysis performs the parsing. Don't you think even though the meaning of a sentence is wrong (like 'The pen is on the ceiling'), it would be parsed? What would happen if the parsing is done where there is no proper meaning to the sentences? This issue is handled by the semantic grammars. So, these grammars perform the semantic as well as syntactic checking tasks. ATNs are used with the semantic grammars.

This grammar has syntactic category that corresponds to the group of words. Then, it is possible to infer the meaning that is generated after the parse.

For example, the grammar can be like

$$S \rightarrow \text{Action the Food}$$
$$\text{Action} \rightarrow \text{eat} \mid \text{drink} \mid \text{shallow} \mid \text{chew}$$
$$\text{Food} \rightarrow \text{burger} \mid \text{sandwich} \mid \text{coke} \mid \text{pizza}$$

This can generate the meaning so as to perform an action task on a particular food for sentences like 'Eat the pizza' or 'Drink the coke'. Sometimes, the semantic action is written in curly braces after the rules. With this parsing, we are able to get the meaning as well. But what can you say about the rules? They would be large enough, as we are not taking into account the generalisations!

Case Grammar

Case grammar is also called as *Fillmore grammar*. The grammar introduced by Fillmore in 1968 helps in characterising the relationships between the verbs and the nouns. Here, the rules are formed that discuss the syntax instead of semantics.

Heads or the leads are defined for the verbs. These leads are linked with some particular role that they play. These roles are the cases. Some of the elements of the set cases are given below:

1. Object (thing on which it is acted)
2. Agent/actor (someone who carries out the action or the event)

3. Dative (someone/something who is affected by the event)
4. Instrument (cause of the event)
5. Location (place where the event/action occurs)
6. Time (date or time at which the action/event takes place)

So, each verb sense accepts finite cases. Some cases are compulsory, while some are optional. Let us take an example, say 'Rohit will meet Kunal at mall'.

The event here is of 'meet'. So, this becomes the head. The details of set cases are depicted in Figure 12.6 for this head.

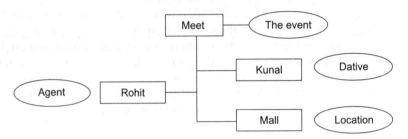

Figure 12.6   An example for case grammar.

As discussed earlier, in some events, the cases could be optional. For example, an event like 'hit'. There can be a sentence like 'Shyam hit the ball' or 'Shyam hit the ball with bat'. So, for 'hit', we can have agent, object, and (instrument).

The underlying notion for the case grammars is the *case frame generation*. These are also called *case slots*. For first sentence, the case frame is shown below:

[<hit>
[Agent: Shyam
  Object: ball]
]

One major advantage of using case grammars is their capacity to handle noisy or incomplete sentences. For example, 'Ram ran'. It is possible to represent this type of sentence with case grammar. The only issue occurs when there is a need to tackle complicated syntax. ATNs are also used for building appropriate structures to carry out parsing.

Conceptual Dependency

This is a parsing technique that explicates the meaning. Conceptual dependency (CD) makes case frame representations for the verbs that are common using conceptual dependency structures. So, small primitive actions are formed. These primitives, called *ACTS* comprise a fixed set of cases. As discussed by Shank, some of the primitives ACTS are given below:

1. *ATRANS*: It represents the transfer of some relationship for verb, say 'give'.
2. *PTRANS*: It represents the transfer of location of an object, say verb 'go'.
3. *GRASP*: This primitive occurs with verbs like 'throw'.
4. SPEAK: This primitive has some sound production, say the verb 'speak' or 'say'.

The sentence—'Kavita went for a movie' falls under the PTRANS. The CD structure for the verb is given in Figure 12.7 in which PP indicates the picture producer. In short, it is an entity that can be concrete or abstract. The bi-directional arrow indicates the conceptualisation between the ACT and Kavita. There are other concepts too like picture aider (adjective) and action aider(adverb) referred to as *PA* and *AA*, respectively. The PP, ACT, PA and AA are the conceptual categories and their relations are the dependencies.

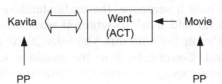

Figure 12.7 A conceptual dependency structure.

While generating a parser that employs the conceptual dependency, the most important part is the ACT primitive formulation. Same verb can exist in different environments. For example, a verb like 'want' can have different ACT. Some examples of the parsers that use CD are SAM, MARGIE.

To conclude, for the semantic parsing, it is very much essential to have an appropriate structure representation so that the meaning of the sentence is determined.

12.3 DISCOURSE AND PRAGMATIC PROCESSING

We now move towards the next level of discourse and pragmatic processing. After performing the semantic analysis, where the understanding of the sentence is clear, it is now necessary to understand and recognise the individual specific tokens. For example, a token like I could be some individual, say Danny. This involves discourse integration. In pragmatics, the context and what the user wants, needs to be analysed. So, it is more concerned with the speech acts or the conversations. This is done with the proper knowledge base. For more clarity, we can say that pragmatics and discourse analysis is concerned with the study of the meanings of the words, where they can be explained using some knowledge with reference to the context and the environment (oral or written) in which they occur. So, in short for discourse and pragmatic processing, the context is very much important and so are the relationships between the sentences. Do remember discourse analysis is often referred to as a *sub-field of pragmatics*. There are a number of relationships that exist, a few of which are mentioned below:

1. *Anaphoria:* Consider an example—Sam had a blue car. It was a big one. Here, it is understood that the word 'it' is used for car.

2. *Part of objects/entities:* Consider an example—Sam opened the door of the car. He found that the CD player was stolen. Here, the relation of understanding the CD-player as a part of the car is considered.

3. *Names of the objects/persons:* Consider a sentence—Sam went for a drive. Here, Sam as a name is identified.

4. *Planning sequences:* Consider the sentences—Hari wanted to get a mango from the tree. He got a big stick. The reason behind getting the stick was to reach the mango.

These are just a few relationships that need to be recognised. How are we going to do that? Still things are not clear what we are doing in pragmatics and discourse analysis. Let us go back to the first dialogue mentioned in the introduction of this chapter. You have inferred something from the dialogue. This inference is concerned with the pragmatic and discourse analysis. If you hear a sentence, the understanding of that sentence involves answering to questions—who said that? To whom it was addressed? Where was it said? What was it all about? and so on. So, with this, you infer. Naturally one has the knowledge and capacity to understand. Coming back to the machine level, a knowledge base is required and that too strong enough to have this understanding of the relationships as discussed when provided with the same text. We do not go into the representation part for the knowledge bases here. Let us look at what knowledge is to be used in this analysis.

1. *Dialogue focus:* This is concerned with understanding the relevance, i.e., the part which is relevant to the knowledge base. This knowledge needs to be taken care of along with ambiguity handling.

2. *Modelling the beliefs:* It involves expressing or representing the belief while participating in a dialogue. If you have a dialogue with somebody, it is necessary that you represent your belief as well as belief of the other participant too. Mapping it to the machine world, the program with which (let us assume) the communication is taking place, there is a need to have proper representation of the program's belief and the communicating person's belief too.

3. *Goal planning:* In some cases, to understand what the text is all about, we need to understand the overall meaning. As said earlier, the meaning in terms of dialogue or the beliefs is important but goal planning is more about goal and plan recognition. The example of planning sequence relationship where the goal of Hari was to get a mango and he planned to get a stick for it comes under this knowledge usage. Though the goal here was getting the mango, there can be different goals. There can be career goals like getting admission to some renowned school or achieving certain position. These would fall under the category of achievement goals.

4. *Speech acts:* What we say verbally could be an advice, a threat, a warning, a request and so on. These all come under the speech acts. A simple sentence—'Read the chapter till the end' is a speech act. Speech acts fall into the different categories mentioned above. These are modelled in a different way for understanding and play an important role in pragmatic analysis. Recent study shows the use of speech acts for message board posts, where typically, in forum, a question-answer session takes place and the categories are uniquely identified.

So, we have discussed about the different relationships and their contexts based on the knowledge that build the pragmatics and discourse analysis. But is it the only way pragmatics and discourse analysis work? Can it involve focusing on other aspects rather than just words like—gestures, expressions and so on? Yes, indeed, and this is referred to as *multi-modal discourse analysis.*

12.4 INFORMATION RETRIEVAL

Let us first understand the problem of information retrieval. So, what is it? Suppose you want to retrieve information about first players who scored 200+ runs in a single inning in ODI. So, you are in discussion with your friend who knows about cricket. First, you will get information about all players who scored 200+ runs, and then you will get years in which they scored. This simple retrieval will, conclude that Sachin Tendulkar is the first player to score 200+ runs. Similarly, we come across various scenarios in everyday life which demand information retrieval.

A very common example that we have discussed in the introduction is of the search engines. The search engine performs information retrieval (IR). We type in a query and the information required by us is retrieved. Figure 12.8 depicts the basic IR system.

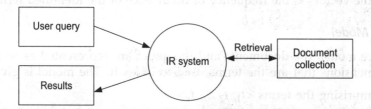

Figure 12.8 An IR system—Getting relevant documents.

We have talked about the search, but the question here is—is it possible to have an optimal way that can be exploited by the search engines for retrieval? What could it be and how would the things work here?

12.4.1 IR Models

We begin with the different models. These models are the mappings for the data that are used to retrieve the information. Let us discuss them.

Boolean Model

In Boolean model, the tokens are treated in the form of 1's and 0's. The presence or absence of a term is marked accordingly. So, the document is represented in the form of $t_1 \wedge t_2 \dots t_n$, where t_i forms a term. The query can be $t_1 \wedge \sim t_2$. The Boolean mapping is found to be the simplest one that was used in earlier systems. With the Boolean model, the requirement is to find the probability of relevance R for a document d and a query q. It is represented as follows:

$P(R \mid d, q)$, where R can be true or false.

But it has a lot of drawbacks. Since it is dependent on the bit presence, the ordering becomes an issue. (In what way the relevant ones are to be presented?). Further, matching similar words, for example, if the terms are cardigan and sweater, then it becomes another issue. Most importantly, a question raises up here—is it possible as an end user to formulate the Boolean query? Though it is pretty complex, still, many probabilistic approaches have been developed with Boolean models.

Bag of Words

The frequency of a word is taken into account instead of ordering. Consider the following texts:

Rohan drives Audi. (text 1)

Sameer drives BMW. He drives Mercedes also. (text 2)

(At a very basic level, to understand the concept, the words identified here are Rohan, drives, Audi, Sameer, he, Mercedes, also). The dictionary or the bag of words has these tokens. So, a vector for the text 1 and 2 would be

[1, 1, 1, 0, 0, 0, 0] for text 1

[0, 2, 0, 1, 1, 1, 1] for text 2

The count in the vectors is the frequency of occurrence of the identified terms in the text.

Vector Space Model

In vector space model, the documents and the query are represented as *vectors*. A vector comprises dimensions that are the terms used to index it. The model is given below:

Vector comprising the terms $<t_1, t_2 ..., t_n>$

The document and query are formed as $<p_1, p_2, p_3 ... p_n>$, where p_x represents the weight of the term x in the document. The query is represented as $<q_1, q_2, q_3, ..., q_n>$.

Relevance of a document d to the query q is computed based on the similarity between them. There are various functions to do so. The different ways to compute the similarity measures are cosine, dot product, dice, Jaccard and so on.

Let us proceed with the matrix representation in vector space model. Figure 12.9 shows the matrix.

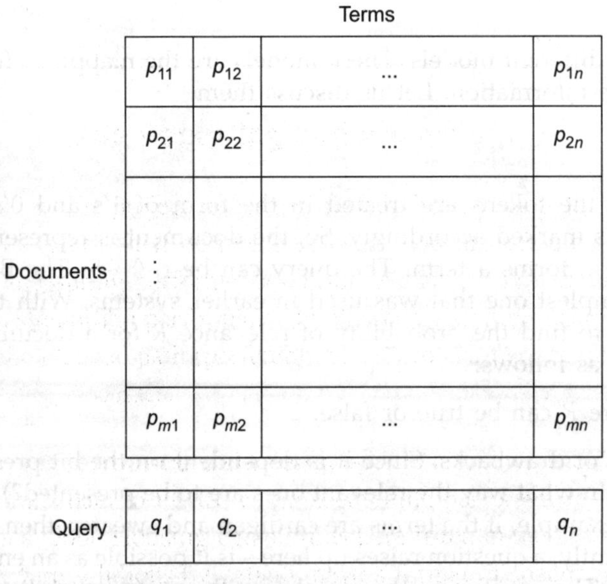

Terms

p_{11}	p_{12}	...	p_{1n}
p_{21}	p_{22}	...	p_{2n}
:			
p_{m1}	p_{m2}	...	p_{mn}

Documents

Query | q_1 | q_2 | ... | q_n |

Figure 12.9 Matrix representation.

Term-frequency, document frequency and inverse document frequency: The concept of term frequency and inverse document frequency is highlighted now. Most often what is observed is when we refer to the term, the weights are the occurrence of the terms in the matrix. So, the *term frequency* is defined as the frequency of occurrence of the term in the document. It is represented as *tf*. The document frequency tells about the number of documents that have a specific term. It is represented as *df*. Inverse document frequency determines the unevenness of the term in the distribution throughout the documents. This is represented as *idf*. The weights are now computed as follows:

P_{11} = Weight of 1st term in document 1

So, to make it more generalised, we have (Remember the term frequencies are normalised by maximum frequency count of that term.)

Weight of a term in $d = wt(t, d) = tf(t, d) * idf(t)$

where $tf(t, d)$ is the occurrence of the term t in d.

$idf(t)$ = log (Total number of documents/Documents containing t term)

Probabilistic Model

Bayesian probability is the most common mechanism that is used in probabilistic inferring. The major drawback of using the Bayesian approach is that it requires prior knowledge. But it is able to address the uncertainty factor that could occur while submitting the query. (The details of Bayesian approach are covered in Chapter 7.)

12.4.2 Pre-processing

Let us start with pre-processing tasks. Why is this pre-processing required? Are all the terms equally important during retrieval? There are terms like 'a', 'and', 'the', 'to', etc., which occur quiet frequently in the document. These terms may not be equally important as some other terms in the document; hence, to have an appropriate representation, pre-processing is essential. Some of the pre-processing tasks are as follows:

1. *Tokenisation:* It refers to separation of the tokens from the text. In simple words, it is concerned with the removal of punctuation marks or some characters that are not required. For a sentence—'Thanks for treat!', it would return 'thanks', 'for' and 'treat' as the tokens.

2. *Stemming:* In stemming, the keywords are used as they are or they can be transformed. For example, we can have words like 'playing', 'played', 'plays' which together can become 'play'. This is carried out in stemming. So, stemming reduces the distinct terms that are used to refer a word. *Porter's algorithm* is the most common one in stemming. This results in a better performance for retrieval.

3. *Lemmatisation:* Here, the base form of the word is returned. For example, in case of 'heard', it also returns 'hear'.

4. *Case folding:* This is simply conversion of the case. If a word like 'PLAY' occurs, the case folding converts it into 'play'.

5. *Stop word removal:* The words like 'the', 'on', 'after', 'an', 'it' and so on are called *stop words*. It is of limited use to assign weight to them in the retrieval part. Thus, the removal of the articles, conjunctions, prepositions is carried out in stop word removal.

6. *Normalisation:* Many times, this is also called *equivalence classing*. Here, equivalence classes are built to have correct mapping, where synonyms too could be considered.

Generally, spell checking option is also performed. (You must have noticed this while using search engine.)

12.4.3 Indexing

Remember the indexing that you have studied in the data structures. *Indexing* is a technique in which the index terms and their related information essential for retrieval are stored. So, what is indexed? The document corpus is indexed. What is related information? This related information consists of the term weights and their postings. What are these postings? The *posting list* is the document number that contains the term.

The concept is expressed with *inverted file index*. This is used to have efficient retrieval. In indexing, the following steps occur:

1. Tokenising of terms from the document corpus.
2. Performing other pre-processing tasks (where the stop word removal, case folding, etc. occur)
3. Indexing the documents with the creation of inverted index file (This file consists of dictionary and posting list. A sample snapshot of the same is given in Figure 12.10).

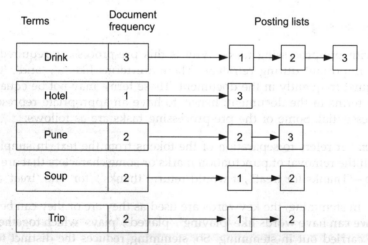

Figure 12.10 An index structure.

The left-hand side of Figure 12.10 shows the terms that are in sorted order, whereas the right-hand side has the posting lists. It might store some more information that is essential to make the retrieval better. The document along with the weight for the term (not shown in Figure 12.10) can also be maintained in the posting list. This information proves to be useful when ranking comes into picture.

Getting Right Answers

On what basis, can we say the IR system is giving us appropriate results or the ones that we actually expect? There are a few computational formulae to determine them, which are mentioned below:

1. *Precision:* It refers to measuring the proportion of retrieved documents that are actually relevant. It is given as follows:

Precision = Number of retrieved relevant documents/Total number of relevant documents

Note that precision is actually nearer to accuracy.

2. *Recall:* It refers to measuring the proportion of relevant documents that have been retrieved. It is given as follows:

Recall = Number of retrieved relevant documents/Total number of retrieved documents

Also, F-measure is used that combines the recall and precision. It is given as follows:

F-measure = (2*Precision*Recall)/(Precision + Recall)

3. *Confusion matrix:* It is a matrix that is often used in classification purposes and tells us about the accurate prediction of the classes. Coming back to the IR system, Figure 12.11 depicts a confusion matrix, showing us whether the retrieved documents are relevant or not. We can treat them as two classes and identify the misleading one. *True positives* are the relevant documents that are correctly retrieved, whereas *false positives* are non-relevant documents retrieved. Similarly, *false negatives* are the non-retrieved documents that are relevant, whereas *true negatives* are the non-relevant documents that are not retrieved.

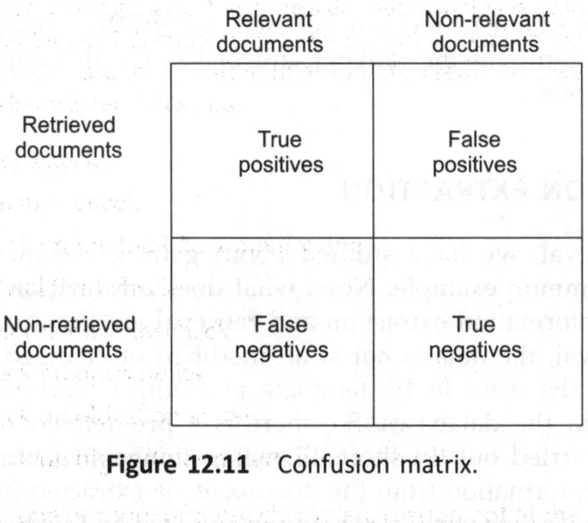

	Relevant documents	Non-relevant documents
Retrieved documents	True positives	False positives
Non-retrieved documents	False negatives	True negatives

Figure 12.11 Confusion matrix.

12.4.4 Similarity Measures

For different text documents or for computing the similarity between the two texts, we discuss different similarity measures. Let us discuss the cosine measure here. A *cosine similarity* measures the angle between the two vectors. In cosine similarity, if the value is zero, then there is no similarity, whereas with 1, they are similar. Let us say we have formed two vectors v_1 and v_2 for two sentences—'Read AI book' and 'Read AI to understand AI'. Let us use bag of words approach for vector formulation. So, the tokens are 'read', AI, 'book' and 'understand'. The vectors would be

$$v_1 = (1, 1, 1, 0) \text{ and } v_2 = (1, 2, 0, 1)$$

The cosine similarity is given by the following formula:

$$\cos \theta = \frac{v_1 \cdot v_2}{\|v_1\|\|v_2\|}$$

So, numerator $= 1 * 1 + 1 * 2 + 1 * 0 + 0 * 1 = 1 + 2 + 0 + 0 = 3$

and denominator $= \sqrt{1^2 + 1^2 + 1^2 + 0^2} \sqrt{1^2 + 2^2 + 0^2 + 1^2} = 1.73 * 2.44 = 4.2212$

$$\cos \theta = 3/4.2212 - 0.71.$$

What would be the cosine similarity between square shape and rectangular shape? Do you think they will give an exact match? Will things differ if used with *tf-idf*? Try to solve.

To summarise, IR is all about getting the required relevant information. With the various techniques in practice to find the similarity between the inputted query and the documents, search engines put to use ranking techniques too additionally. There could be clustering of relevant results, where similar sets are grouped in one group (k-means and other techniques) for providing the user with relevant data. At the back-end, prior classification too can take place. Further, depending on the user's response to the ranked results, a feedback mechanism too can be used, where the needs of the user are best served. This further improves the ranking and makes the IR system an efficient one as well as personalised one.

12.5   INFORMATION EXTRACTION

In information retrieval, we have studied about getting the information—the search engines being the common example. Now, what does information extraction (IE) do? Is it not the case that information extraction and retrieval are the same? Do remember that in information retrieval, the data is not at all modified or changed. Simply, the relevant data is presented to the user. In IE, template matching is carried out. The IE module could make entries in the databases. So, there is a pre-defined fixed format in which the text entries are carried out. In short, IE makes things structured from unstructured inputs. With IE, the information from the documents is extracted into the templates. Are you feeling like there is some similarity between retrieval and extraction? IR gets relevant documents, whereas IE gets relevant information from the documents. Though there could be an overlap between them. IE could lie between IR and text understanding. Figure 12.12 depicts the basic IE system.

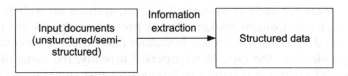

Figure 12.12 Information extraction.

Let us take an example to explain IE. An employment agency has to send mails to the clients whose profile suit some ABC company's requirements. From the CVs of these clients, only the mail-id needs to be extracted to send the date for interview. In another example, a company wants to categorise candidates based on their skill set. In this case, the information about the skills is retrieved from their CVs. Here, terms like Java, .Net etc. are used for template matching. This is also a task of IE.

There are various aspects of IE such as what is to be extracted?, what is the input data? what methods are to be used?, How is the output expected? Let us try to address them. To extract, it could be any particular entity, or any specific table or relations. Whereas, the input data could be a simple set of documents, web pages and so on, which is unstructured. The methods applied can be handwritten patterns, learning-based methods, rule-based methods or statistical methods. Figure 12.13 shows the basic modules of IE.

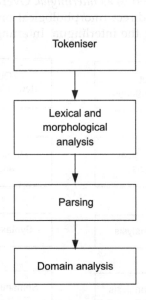

Figure 12.13 Modules of IE.

What is the job of each of them? Tokeniser, as we are already familiar, does the word separation. In *lexical and morphological analysis,* part of speech tagging is done. Identifying the parts of speech or learning the word sense is carried out here. In *parsing,* syntax analysis is done, whereas in *domain analysis,* merging the partial results or co-reference is carried out.

FRUMP, LSP were the early IE systems. Later on, systems for web-based information extraction were Crunch, Content Seeker, etc. At present, wrappers are used on a large scale. They are called *information extraction procedures* that extract some content or bits from the text. Meta-crawlers are the type of wrappers. Currently, the focus of the research is on investigating and inventing different techniques for text summarisation as well as on cross-media and language-based IE systems.

12.6 MACHINE TRANSLATION

It is the process of translating source language into target language. This has to be necessarily natural language. Why do we need this translation? Generally, you refer to a number of sites to get some sort of information. Let us say you want to have some paper related to AI, you get a link for downloading it and you find that the paper is presented by a Spanish author in Spanish! You need machine translation (MT) here. Some of the aspects it needs to know are the target language, and the source language, to have a detailed knowledge about the contents, to understand the 'context' in which things are written or said (and speech analysis as well). Figure 12.14 below depicts the basic steps required for MT. As it can be observed from Figure 12.14, there is need to perform the syntax and semantic tasks too. Then, the representations from the source to target also exist. The representation is referred to as *interlingua*. Overall in MT, three major techniques exist for this translation, one is direct (morphological one), other is transfer (syntax and semantic), and the last one being the interlingua. Interlingua is the most difficult one and

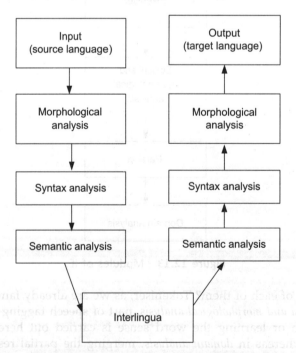

Figure 12.14 Steps of machine translation.

makes the analysis work more, thus increasing the cost. In interlingua, the dependencies and the language-specific distinctions are accounted. So, it is a single representation for the source and the target language. Today, MT systems are also looked upon as research areas. But it is very difficult to have MT systems developed. Can you think of the drawbacks that would arise in building these systems? In some source language, there is a single word that tells something. For the same thing, in another language, there could be 4–5 words that are required. Further, the meanings and mapping of the similar words add up complexity. The parts of speech are different. Hence, developing MT systems has become a challenging task.

12.7 NLP AND ITS APPLICATION

From the study of the entire concepts regarding NLP, we now move towards the applications of NLP. Let us look at one of them to understand when, where and in what way these concepts are used. In the sections discussed earlier, we have mentioned about IR with search engines. NLP techniques can enhance them to have a personalised search. Suppose a person enters 'apple' as a query to search engine. He tends to get information about Apple products, and the expected result will also include a information regarding fruit apple. So, he gets information about the fruit apple too, but often these web pages have lower ranks. What we mean to put forth here is that the results expected are dependent on the profile of the user, or it even could be decided on the basis of previously clicked/accessed data. So, in turn, this historic data of the user can form and contain potential information that can be utilised for helping the user in getting personalised results.

How can this historic data be useful? With the NLP models, weighing schemes can be put to work to have similarity factors computed. For this, search engines use previously accessed results. These weights can be refined by re-assignment on the basis of statistical methods that inform about the accessibility pattern. Each term/word captured and accessed, thus, has increased weight. Further, word and concept ranking can be employed to have re-ranking schemes. This approach can be employed with different models to have the representation of the data/text. Moreover, a feedback mechanism can add up to assist the overall personalisation techniques.

SUMMARY

This chapter discusses about NLP along with preliminaries that are needed to be understood. NLP techniques have gained a lot of importance recently, showing larger prospects for research. They are important in the perspective to understand and infer things. With the various techniques discussed in syntax and semantic analysis, today there is a need to appropriately represent the content and the context. The use of ATNs has been proved effective in the analysis of natural language with the required representation structure. The grammar and knowledge base too play a vital role in processing. With CFG and Fillmore grammar, the rule mapping can be carried out with ease. Parsing is another important task that helps in getting the syntax correct, whereas pragmatics and discourse analysis handle speech.

Further, with the wide use of search engines like Google, information retrieval has taken up a big leap. New techniques are in development phase, where efficient retrieved and ranked results are made available to the user. Information extraction too is an important aspect of handling NLP. There are learning and rule-based systems that help in the information extraction. With the increasing information, getting the precise data in a structured format is now looked at. Machine translation, yet other aspect of NLP, helps in the conversion of source languages into target language, and handles speech too.

All the steps or the topics discussed in NLP are closely related to each other and one would find an overlap among them. NLP can also be used in many applications like sentiment analysis, product recommendation system, etc. To conclude, we can say at present, NLP finds a noteworthy position in the area of research and if one is looking forward to it, he should not forget the text and the context.

 KEYWORDS

1. **Natural language:**   It is a language that is in use and has been developed naturally. It is in practice and is a way for communication that can be in oral or written form.

2. **Natural language processing:**   It is a computerised mechanism involving computation techniques to analyse and represent the text (oral or written) in some form for achieving human-like processing for a variety of applications.

3. **Information retrieval:**   It involves obtaining relevant information with respect to the need/query from the set of data collection.

4. **Parse tree:**   It is a structure tree representation for the sentence.

5. **Indexing:**   It is a technique in which the index terms and their related information essential for retrieval are stored.

6. **Precision:**   It is measuring the proportion of retrieved documents that are actually relevant.

7. **Recall:**   It is measuring the proportion of relevant documents that have been retrieved.

8. **Information extraction:**   It involves mapping of an unstructured/semi-structured data to a structured one.

9. **Wrappers:**   These are the information extraction procedures that extract some content or bits from the text.

10. **Machine translation:**   It is a process of translating an input source language to another language.

MULTIPLE CHOICE QUESTIONS

(*Note:* The questions can have more than one answer)

1. In case grammar, the agent case is always a compulsory case with any verb.
   (a) It has to be with dative
   (b) The above statement is true
   (c) The case grammar can have instrumental case too
   (d) It depends on the verb

2. Semantic analysis is based on
   (a) Transitive networks
   (b) Context-sensitive grammars
   (c) Any grammars
   (d) Knowledge representation

3. Which of the following checks the correctness of the sentence grammatically?
   (a) ATN   (b) RTN   (c) Indexing   (d) Wrappers

4. In which of the following, the context and the relations among the sentences are important?
   (a) Conceptual dependency
   (b) Case grammars
   (c) Discourse and pragmatic processing
   (d) None of the above

5. Suppose we want to identify fraud transactions in bank. Under this scenario, we would look upon
   (a) High precision
   (b) High Recall
   (c) Precision and recall = 1 value
   (d) None of the above

6. Which of the text pre-processing task would return 'learn' if the input word is 'learnt'?
   (a) Text standardisation
   (b) Term stripping
   (c) Stemming
   (d) None of these

7. Which of the following does not exist in the Boolean model?
   (a) Ranking   (b) Weighting   (c) Indexing   (d) All of these

CONCEPT REVIEW QUESTIONS

1. Can parsing be related to a search problem? Discuss.

2. Write the rules and generate a parse tree for each of the following sentences:
   (i) The book lies on the shelf.
   (ii) Ram answered the phone call while driving the car.

3. List out the possible advantages of using semantic grammar.

CRITICAL THINKING EXERCISE

1. Suppose we want to determine whether a given question is related to concept review or critical thinking. On what factors can you decide this? Using the different aspects discussed in this chapter and related topics of machine learning, discuss the model.

2. Given two sentences, each containing 15 words, we want to find out similarity between them. But we want to have the feature size to be less than or equal to 10. How would you go on deciding the terms to be included in the feature vector? Will considering a particular term/removing a particular term impact the output? Can random selection be useful? Discuss.

PROJECT WORK

1. Develop a retrieval system using indexing technique for some set of text documents.

2. Develop an application that can identify the association between the two paragraphs. The output would simply state whether the two paragraphs are associated or not.

3. Write a program to associate different news in newspaper and prioritise them with reference to your context.

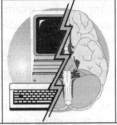

CHAPTER 13

Decision Theory

INTRODUCTION

Decision is a very important word in life. A student who has just passed 12th is worried about selection of career. A pass out student from engineering background thinks about whether to pursue masters, take up the job or start his own venture. This continues throughout the life. Simple decisions, complex decisions—whatever decisions you take, ultimately you are the one who has to accept the consequences and move ahead. Not going more into psychological aspects, but what would happen when you know that a particular decision would be a better choice which would help you further? Here, we are not talking about astrology, but statistical and probabilistic approaches, with risk associations in AI to help the machine in making decisions. Let us relate the things from the real world to understand the concepts. So, in astrology, you have your horoscope and other things that help you or rather guide you in taking decisions. Sometimes, the decisions do not give the expected results. But, still you are ready to take up risks. So, when there are more than one logical choices, you need to take decisions. Somewhere at the back of your mind, you feel that you have preferences, and accordingly, you take up the decision. Which preference is to be given a higher priority would be based on some previous experiences or some known information or some inputs. For example, some friend who has taken up a job and does well in his carrier may impact your decision to go for a job. What makes you to have this preference is some sort of utility value. This utility helps you in knowing that a particular or expected result could be achieved, thereby helping you in reaching the goal. Hence, the decisions are dependent on the goals that are to be achieved.

Are we going to talk about uncertainty here also? Yes, in real-life dynamic scenarios, we have to deal with uncertainty. So, here, we discusses that the decision theory is all about providing a framework to allow reasoning along with the preferences.

13.1 PREFERENCES

In introduction, we have discussed about the preferences. These preferences are related to some real-life examples. We have studied about the different types of agents in Chapter 5, but now we focus on the utility-based agents. How different are these agents? For an agent, to carry out the task in decision-making, it is necessary to know whether the next state is good enough to proceed. To move ahead in the states, the preferences play an important role. What is the role? When the agent decides to take any action, it gives some result (some consequence!). The agent wants that the result should be as per its expectations. Let us call the results to be the outcomes. So, the agent naturally prefers to take up that action which will provide the desired outcome. So, an agent has some preferences with respect to the outcomes. There could be cases in which unawareness exists regarding the outcomes. Coming to the technical things, how can we map the preferences.

Let us consider two outcomes—O_1 and O_2. The preferences to the outcomes can be categorised into following three cases:

1. $O_1 \succ O_2$: This preference tells that O_1 is preferred over O_2 (getting first class than pass class).
2. $O_1 \sim O_2$: The agent is actually indifferent (moderate) to both the outcomes (higher second class and second class, both seem to be ok!).
3. $O_1 \succeq O_2$: Here, preference is given to O_1 rather than O_2 (pass class better than fail). This preference is given to at least desirable outcome.

Consider that the agent is unaware of the outcomes (do not know about what will happen, whether pass class, fail or distinction. In such cases, the agent is familiar with the probability distribution over the results or the outcomes. Thus, here comes the concept of lotteries. So, the outcomes are sometimes called *lotteries*. In a lottery L, there is a set of outcomes along with their probabilities.

$$L = \{p_1, O_1; p_2, O_2; p_3, O_3 \dots p_n, O_n\}$$

There can be different or same outcomes in multiple lotteries. Taking the same example to understand the concept, in one lottery, it could be (pass, fail or second class) with some probabilities and in other, it could be (distinction, first, second).

We now proceed towards the axioms of the preferences. These axioms enable to draw the consequences (outcomes). The consequences of the actions are called *rewards*, whereas the axioms are also called *axioms of utility theory*. They can also be called *constraints* that are essential for the rational agent. They are as follows:

1. **Transitivity:** It is a very familiar property that we have always studied. In case of outcomes, the transitivity is represented as follows:

$$(O_1 \succ O_2) \wedge (O_2 \succ O_3) \Rightarrow O_1 \succ O_3$$

This can be explained with a simple example. Suppose a student's wish list includes a car, a laptop and a vacation. He has already a car. His father says to get laptop, he has to sacrifice car along with some part of his pocket money; to get vacation, he has to sacrifice laptop with some part of the pocket money; and to get a car again, he has to sacrifice the vacation with some part of the pocket money (if any is left with him!). Under this scenario, it is very difficult for him to have any of them and decide what he actually wants. This difficulty comes if the transitivity is not followed. The lack of this property leads to inadequacy in assisting for the decisions. So, necessarily, there is a need for transitivity to occur and to be followed.

2. **Orderability:** This is also called *linearity*. From the given outcomes, the axiom states that the agent can take any of the two or rate both of the outcomes to be equal. This is given as follows:

$$(O_1 \succ O_2) \vee (O_2 \succ O_1) \vee (O_1 \sim O_2)$$

3. **Continuity:** Let us say that there is some outcome O_2 which lies in between the outcomes O_1 and O_3. There is some probability p for which the agent would act indifferent in getting O_2 or O_1 (having probability p) or O_3 (with the probability $1-p$). It is represented as:

$$(O_1 \succ O_2 \succ O_3) \Rightarrow \exists p(p, O_1; 1 - p, O_3) \sim O_2$$

4. **Monotonicity:** Assume that there are two lotteries. The two lotteries have the same outcome sets. Let O_1 and O_2 be the outcomes occurring in both the lotteries, and if $O_1 \succ O_2$, then the lottery having greater value of probability for O_1 than the probability for O_2 is preferred. (To understand the concept, consider the probability for the pass/fail example, a lottery with higher probability for distinction is preferred over fail; if fail and distinction both are to appear in the lotteries). Let $O_1 \succ O_2$ and $p > q$, then it is represented as follows:

$$(p, O_1; 1 - p, O_2) \succ (q, O_1; 1 - q, O_2)$$

where p and q correspond to the probabilities of the outcomes in the lotteries.

5. **Substitutivity:** This refers to the concept that if the agent is indifferent to the outcomes O_1 than O_2, i.e., $O_1 \sim O_2$ then it will remain indifferent to the lotteries, where O_1 is substituted instead of O_2. It is mapped as follows:

$$O_1 \sim O_2 \Rightarrow (p, O_1; 1 - p, O_3) \sim (p, O_2; 1 - p, O_3)$$

6. **Decomposability:** This axiom states the reduction of compound lotteries to a single one. It can be mapped as follows:

$$(p, O_1; 1 - p (q, O_2; 1 - q, O_3)) \sim (p, O_1; (1 - p) (q), O_2; (1 - p) (1 - q), O_3)$$

So, the preferences and the axioms are important for getting the rewards as expected by the agents. Let us now proceed to the concept of utility.

13.2   UTILITIES

We have studied about the rewards. But from where do we get them? The agent wants to get to a state that is desirable from its perspective. What decides this? It is the utility that maps some value (real) to the states. It is given as follows:

$$U : S \to R$$

where S is the state and R is some real number. Typically, utility can be defined as a real value that specifies the desirability of a state. So, the utility is computed on the basis of the action of an agent. The result of this action is considered. Thus, the expected utility is computed. Utility helps in ordering of the preferences. While taking decisions in uncertain environment, the expected utility is considered. We are already aware that the probable distribution is considered in the uncertainty; hence, we can say that

$$EU(A|E) = \sum_{i=1}^{n} P(\text{State} - \text{reached}_i | A) U(\text{State} - \text{reached}_i)$$

Thus, the expected utility of an action A having evidence E is computed as the probability of state-reached or the effect after the action A is executed. (To be specific, it is the result of the particular state.) The following example shown in Figure 13.1 helps us in understanding this in a better way. *Note:* The result mentioned in the diagram is the utility of that state.

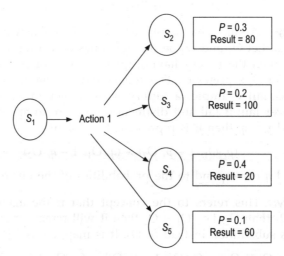

Figure 13.1   Example for utility measurement for state S_1.

Let us assume you are in state S_1, where you have not studied anything for exam. In action 1 you study from senior's notes and appear for the exam. Let us assume after the exam, the state you are in are the marks (utility of the state that you would possibly get). These are the probabilities of states after the action has taken place. (This is dependent on the difficulty of question paper!). Right now, we want to decide what action is to be taken. Before we introduce another action, let us first calculate the expected utility of this action. Since we have the probabilities and the results of the states, the utility of S_1 with action 1 will be

$$U(S_1) = (80 * 0.3) + (100 * 0.2) + (20 * 0.4) + (60 * 0.1)$$
$$= 24 + 20 + 8 + 6$$
$$= 58$$

Now, consider a case in which action 2, i.e., study from reference book, is added upon. In this case, action 2 generates three states, as depicted in Figure 13.2.

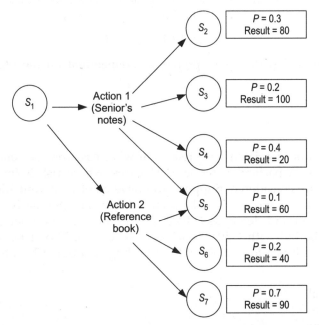

Figure 13.2 Example for utility measurement for state S_1, action 2 added.

Now, the utility of S_1 with action 2 will be

$$U(S_1) = (60 * 0.1) + (40 * 0.2) + (90 * 0.7)$$
$$= 6 + 8 + 63$$
$$= 77$$

So, Max (58, 77) = 77. Hence, $U(S_1) = 77$. (So, which action would you prefer? There is a possibility of getting 90 marks too!).

Now, imagine that there is some cost associated with the action that is to be performed. Let us assume for our understanding that it is the number of weeks you have to spend for the study. We deduct this cost from the utility values achieved. Let us assume with action 1, it is 10 and with action 2, it is 30. Now, the values that we get are with action 1, it is 48, whereas with action 2, it is 47. (Things have changed with this.) Thus, addition of the cost to carry out an action too has an impact on the decisions.

Further, the example can have an additional decision-making with the perspective of a decision regarding study from notes—yes or no. Then, the EU(decision = yes) or EU(decision = no) can be computed. But then, we need to have the utility and the probability values with both the cases of decisions.

Remember that what action is to carry out depends on the utility values of the states. What is applicable and preferred by one person may not necessarily be true for the other one. So, possibly, your friend would have different sets of utility values for the states, and thus, his preferences would be different.

There is a principle of maximum expected utility (MEU). This principle states that the decision taken to select an action under uncertainty is the one that has the highest EU and is an optimal one. The utility model based on the works of Ramsey et al. has proved to be the most beneficial one today. The MEU theorem says that

$$O_1 \succ O_2 \text{ iff } U(O_1) \geq U(O_2)$$

So, the outcomes that the agent prefers are dependent on the utilities. Let us now proceed to risk.

13.3   RISK

Any decision taken is associated with risks. On what basis do we conclude that there is less risk involved in a particular decision? In cases, where risk is involved, most often monitory benefits are considered. Suppose you have a bet with your friend for ₹ 500. But if the betting amount is above ₹ 10,000, then will you bet? Similarly, if a scheme offers to double the amount and demands ₹ 1000 (minimum) for investment, then you will go ahead and take risk, but with ₹ 50,000, will you take a risk? So, generally everyone likes to play safe. Even if it is a loss, it should not be huge enough. Thus, the risk aspects are categorised below:

1. Risk neutral
2. Risk averse
3. Risk seeking

These risks are actually the attitudes that tell us what you prefer. Let us understand them. Figure 13.3 shows a graph depicting three cases. (Lines are intentionally shown in different formats for identification.)

We can note from Figure 13.3 that we have mentioned money on the x-axis. (It could be any other thing too.) For example, a woman is generally happy if she gets more things for comparatively lower price. This is *risk averse* indicating that the people want high returns, but at the same time, the money put in should be low. *Risk neutral* indicates consistency. Whereas, in case of *risk seeking*, the curve indicates the increase in the utility. So, this concave curve indicates the high potential risk.

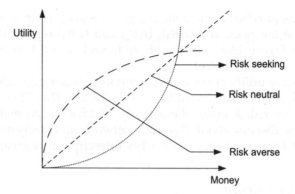

Figure 13.3 Different risk curves.

13.3.1 Risk Premium

Let us discuss further risk premium with relation to gains. So, what is risk premium? *Risk premium* is the difference between the expected amount and the amount (may be something) one would accept while taking the decisions. For example, as a student, you want to give exam of GRE. One option is to study on your own entirely. Let this be denoted as R_1 (some risk is involved). Other option is to join a coaching class by which you would get admission in a good university. Let us call this R_2. (This decision too involves some risk). Instead, if there is some intermediate option, which offers some classnotes to you without joining the coaching class so that you can study, will you prefer this? So, let us call this as R_{int}. This can be represented as follows:

$$R_{int} = R_1 + R_2/2$$

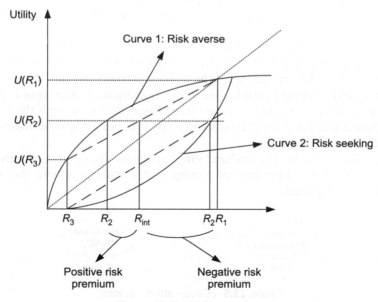

Figure 13.4 Risk premium.

Mapping in terms of returns one gets, the graph shows the risk values (Figure 13.4). Let R_1, R_2, R_3 indicate the risks, and $U(R_1)$, $U(R_2)$ and $U(R_3)$ represent the utilities. When $R_1 > R_3$ as shown in Figure 13.4, one would try to seek a mid between them (notes and study on your own—a better choice).

Whenever a concave utility curve exists, a certainty factor equivalent to R_2 also exists. This R_2 is less than R_{int} which is referred to as *risk premium*. The difference $R_{int}-R_2$ is called *positive risk premium* for risk averse, whereas it is *negative risk premium* for risk prone.

The next sections discuss about Bayesian network and decision network. Both are already detailed in Chapter 8; hence, only a brief description is given here.

13.4 BAYESIAN NETWORK

As discussed earlier, a *belief network* or a *Bayesian network* is a probabilistic graphical model that represents a set of random variables and their conditional dependencies through a directed acyclic graph (DAG). In the graph, the nodes represent random variables and the directed edges represent the conditional dependencies among the variables. It is a very compact representation that shows the distributions. The dependent node is called *child node*, whereas the one on which it is dependent is the *parent node*. The directed edge points to the child node to represent the dependency. The parent node is called *cause* and the child node is called *effect*. The nodes that are not connected are independent of each other. Every node is associated with probability function and takes values of the parent function and gives the probability of the variable that it represents. A Bayesian network essentially provides the entire description of a domain. The network is seen as a joint probability distribution. Each entry in this probability distribution is represented by the product of the appropriate elements of the conditional probability table (CPT).

The working, hence, is governed by the probable values we have. Moreover, the uncertainty factor handled by Bayesian network proves its suitability for incomplete information as well.

In addition, causal relationships too are very well-understood with Bayesian network. Let us take an example. Suppose you plan for a techfest in your college. You need to decide whether to have the marketing of the techfest through e-mails to different colleges. Possibly, this (causal relation) could yield more registrations. This could also help you in the analysis of the registration received from the colleges through the e-mails. Other important aspect is that the prior gained knowledge is exported with statistics to get better decisions in Bayesian networks.

Figure 13.5 shows the basic cause and effect relationship, whereas Figure 13.6, shows a Bayesian network for a hypothetical example of a college, where the students and teachers scenario is depicted.

Figure 13.5 Cause-effect relation.

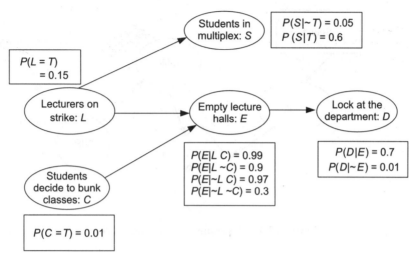

Figure 13.6 A Bayesian network—Hypothetical example.

From Figure 13.6, one can understand the cause and effect relationship in a bigger scenario. There are the prior probabilities and the posterior ones too. So, how can one use the Bayesian network in decision theory? Having understood the concept of the Bayesian network and given some evidence, is it possible to determine the effect? If we have some known things like the department is locked, but the students are not in multiplex, then what is the probability that the lecturers are on strike? This is about evaluating the network to get the answers. So, don't you think that the Bayesian network, where evidence is conquered or the cause is determined (on the basis of some observed data), helps you to know (decision) about something? Indeed, this helps in reasoning too! Do remember that the Bayesian network computation is NP-hard.

13.5 DECISION NETWORK

Decision network is a directed graphical representation of the decision-maker's preferences with respect to the real-world uncertainty and sequence of possible decisions. Based on the concept of Bayesian networks, a decision network is also called *influence diagram*. It is representative about the information regarding the agent's current state, actions and the possible outcomes. The decision network comprises the following:

1. **Circles (chance nodes):** These indicate the uncertain variables.
2. **Rectangles (decision nodes):** These are connected to the chance nodes that influence the decisions.
3. **Diamond-shaped boxes (utility nodes):** These represent the agent's utility. They tell how good the states are.

Figure 13.7 shows a simple decision network. Let us take a simple case, e.g. decide to go to office by car. The action (select car for commute or not) is given in a rectangle. There are three random variables—traffic (there will be traffic or not), car (have a car or not) and VIP (in town or not). We do not go into further details of this diagram, as it is already covered in Chapter 8.

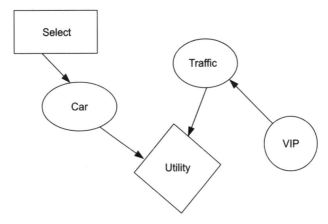

Figure 13.7 A simple decision network.

13.5.1 Semi-constrained Influence Diagram (SCID)

We would like to introduce a new concept of semi-constrained influence diagram here. *Semi-constrained influence diagram* is actually an extension of the influence diagram that we have discussed previously. The intention here is that we have to understand what is visible to a decision-maker. From the influence diagram, it is clear that it depicts the perspective of a decision-maker, letting it know about the information available. But there could be a case when the complete information is not available at the time of decision-making. So, some dependencies could remain unresolved, while some information may become gradually available. This leads to the concept of semi-constrained influence diagram (SCID). So, these diagrams are more from the perspective that is available. They could come up with the representation of fuzziness. Even some relationships that could exist are also accommodated in these diagrams.

A generalised structure and an example of SCID are shown in Figures 13.8 and 13.9, respectively.

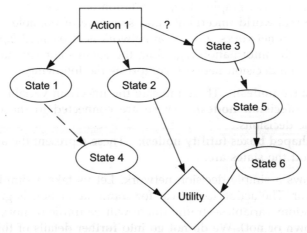

Figure 13.8 An SCID.

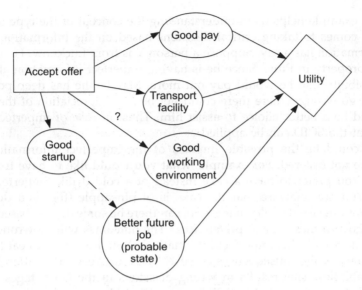

Figure 13.9 An example of SCID.

As it is visible from the diagrams, we can see that we have indicated dotted lines and question marks. The dotted lines indicate the possible relationship, whereas the question mark indicates the fuzzy relationships. These are used when one is necessarily unaware of the impact of this relation on the decision. Imagine the example given in Figure 13.9. The action is about whether to accept the given offer from the company, where you are placed. Assume that it is your first job. So, from Figure 13.9, we can say that getting a better future job could be a probable state. (You might remain in the same company with a better growth in the positions than jumping to any other company.)

So, in short, SCID is related to the fuzziness. Don't you think that further it is possible to have the different perspectives combined for better decision-making?

13.6 DECISION-MAKING AND IMPERFECT INFORMATION

We are slightly diverting from the agent and the computational perspective to the concept of imperfect information. We would like to discuss here some of the examples to study its impact on decision-making.

Till now, we have discussed about incomplete information. But don't you think that whatever information you have, whether it is incomplete or complete, could be imperfect?

Let us take a simple example.

'Tomorrow there will be a lecture on data mining by professor X in the main auditorium of the college.' This sentence is complete and perfect.

'Tomorrow there will be a lecture on data mining by professor X.' This sentence is incomplete but perfect.

'Tomorrow there will be a lecture on some subjects by professor X in the main auditorium of the college.' This sentence is complete but imperfect.

'Tomorrow there will be a lecture on some subjects by professor X.' This sentence is incomplete and imperfect.

The above example helps us in understanding the concept of the type of information. Now, when it comes to taking critical decisions based on the information we have, the imperfect information has a say. Suppose a person Y is from Lucknow. He is interested in buying some property in Pune. Since he is having imperfect information about the rates, there is a possibility that he would pay out more. May be, he has deep pockets, but the decision could go wrong, where there could not be any appreciation of the property. So, an SCID would be a better choice to assist him. Thus, in case of imperfect information, we can say that the SCID can be applied.

But what could be the possible impacts of the imperfect information? Here, the preferences, are not ordered. For example, what you would like to have from a cake and a cold drink? You prefer to have a cake instead of a cold drink (imperfect information is available). You are unaware that the cake is of pineapple (that you don't like). The preference of your decision could change! So, can there be some degree-based relationships which would govern these vague preferences? The outcomes will be wrong totally if the decisions are taken with this imperfect information. (You are forced to eat the same cake. Have you thought of the consequences of this?) The imperfect information has altogether different probabilities. This results in wrong decisions in the later stages. Altogether, a fuzzy approach (again indicated in SCID) can prove to be a good option.

Let us take an example of game playing. In case of chess, the entire environment is fully observable. You have perfect information. The entire chess board and the opponent's chess pieces are in front of you. But in case of cards, things are totally imperfect.

Where would these be applicable in real life? From the investment perspective, things are at very high risks! So, naturally the EU and risk factor are on a toss when the information is imperfect.

SUMMARY

After studying the decision theory and the different approaches of risks along with utility, it is the time that we understand the relationship of them with the already studied concepts. These are planning and searching that we have studied earlier, which are related with the decision theory. Taking help of the decision theory, with the utilities in picture, don't you think it would be possible to have a better planning and searching? The only thing that matters is the computation. In uncertainty, the expected utility has a significant impact. There are different risk attitudes that are involved while making decisions. In the chapter, we have studied about the Bayesian network that is involved in conditional probabilities and helps in understanding the decision-making in the probable environment. The decision network helps further in understanding and deciding the action, where the relationships of the states and the actions are learnt. The representation of the possible relationships among the states and/or the actions along with the fuzzy nature is captured in the semi-constrained influence diagram. Moreover, the perspectives combination can result in improved decision-making. Combining the perspectives helps in handling the decision process, whereas the imperfect information can be taken care of by having some degree definition to the preferences. SCID can prove to be beneficial in case of imperfect data.

Overall, the decision theory is the one that helps in making things simple and allows the agent to take an optimal decision.

 **KEYWORDS**

1. **Decision theory:** It is the combination of probabilistic theory and utility theory.

2. **Preferences:** This refer to the ordering or ranking of the states for decision-making.

3. **Utility:** It is a real value that specifies the desirability of a state.

4. **Expected utility:** It is a utility value for an action that is determined by the probability and the expected outcome of that action.

5. **Maximum expected utility:** It involves selecting the highest EU from the ones that are computed so that an optimal decision is taken.

6. **Risk:** This depicts the attitude of an agent, with the indication of its preferences.

7. **Bayesian network:** It is a probabilistic graphical model that represents a set of random variables and their conditional dependencies through a directed acyclic graph (DAG).

8. **Decision network:** This is a representation of the states of the agent, actions and the outcomes.

9. **Semi-constrained influence diagram:** It is an extended version of influence diagram that allows understanding the dependencies when the complete information is not available at the time of decision-making.

MULTIPLE CHOICE QUESTIONS

(*Note:* There can be more than one answer.)

1. Expected utility value is a value that is
   - (a) Pre-determined
   - (b) Based on probability
   - (c) Can be zero
   - (d) None of the above

2. A random variable in the decision network can be
   - (a) An event
   - (b) An action
   - (c) An object that agent has
   - (d) None of the above

3. In the selection process of utility value, it is based on

   (i) Maximum utility; (ii) Satisfying utility; (iii) Minimum utility

   Which of the following is true?
   - (a) (i) and (ii)
   - (b) (ii) and (iii)
   - (c) Only (i)
   - (d) Only (ii)

4. Which of the following representations would be appropriate when the data could get available gradually?
   - (a) Decision network
   - (b) Decision tree
   - (c) Influence diagram
   - (d) Semi-constrained influence diagram
   - (e) None of the above

5. Semi-constrained influence diagram would be preferred instead of decision networks when
   (a) There is imperfect information
   (b) There is partial information available that gets update later
   (c) Perspective-based information exists
   (d) Preferences are to be handled
   (e) None of the above

CONCEPT REVIEW QUESTIONS

1. List the utility theory axioms.
2. Explain the concept of decision networks with example.

CRITICAL THINKING EXERCISE

1. What are the issues that are likely to arise in case of utility computations?
2. For the following example (Figure 13.10), which option is to be selected (refer to Chapter 8)? Let us assume you have three options of electives. What would be the data required to select the appropriate one? Explain in steps how you would proceed.

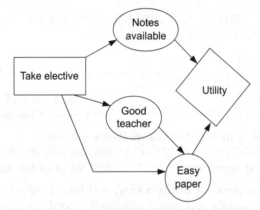

Figure 13.10

PROJECT WORK

1. Write a program that would give the desired results for the above problem. Take inputs of the random variables with their prior probabilities. Make the approach a generalised one that would suit any other problem too on similar ground.
2. In typical election scenario, represent the selection of a candidate using influence diagram. Assume suitable data.

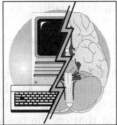

CHAPTER 14

Pattern Recognition

Learning Objectives

❑ To understand the role of pattern recognition in day-to-day applications
❑ To understand different techniques and mathematical background for pattern analysis
❑ To identify the need for pattern analysis
❑ To build knowledge about the features and selection of feature extraction methods
❑ To study the role of pattern analysis in classification
❑ To study the applications of pattern analysis

INTRODUCTION

Suppose you are busy in reading some old notes and you come across some paragraph written by someone (hand-written). You can easily identify that it is written by a particular friend. On what grounds can you take this decision? It is the writing style of the friend, who had written it. What you have recognised is a pattern. We, as humans, have an ability to perceive association and anomalies in patterns. *Pattern*, in general, is a consistent sequence showing the order of occurrence of events. It could be a written text, an image, a speech or anything else. This gives us a capability to authenticate face, recognise speech, identify hand-written characters and distinguish different objects based on shape, smell and other characteristics. That's why the concept of pattern is vague. But on what basis a pattern is selected? Is the selection based some characteristics or the features? That is right. So, in turn, patterns are typically associated with their features and occurrence.

What is the pattern recognition system supposed to do? It should not only observe the environment but should also have the abilities to learn and distinguish the occurrence of different patterns and intelligently identify the patterns of interest. But for a machine to be able to understand and recognise, it is required to make it intelligent.

Hence, *pattern recognition* is about understanding and developing the mechanism so that machines can perceive the environment, analyse it, and build an ability to distinguish between the different patterns of interest, leading to reasonable decisions about pattern categories.

So, in pattern recognition, we study about the techniques and methods for the same and different models.

Where is the pattern recognition now being applied? Suppose a person gets a phone call that he is eligible to be a gold customer, or say he will be getting a credit card for free from some bank. Why? On what basis has the bank made the selection? Again, based on some pattern! The bank has found that on the basis of his previous track record that follows a pattern, he is a potential customer for it. So, pattern recognition systems are required at a large scale for face recognition, speech, intrusion detection systems, text classification, medical disease diagnosis, forecasting and many more.

Is pattern recognition in any way related to machine learning? Of course yes, it is. After recognition of a pattern, what you do is finally the classification.

14.1 MACHINE PERCEPTION AND PATTERN RECOGNITION

So, from the introduction, we have understood the concept of pattern recognition. Let us understand what we, as humans, perceive. We interpret things on the basis of what we have learnt. It may be through physical sensing or on the basis of some background knowledge we have. Now, what is machine perception? In a layman's language, machine perception is about the capacity of a system to interpret the data the way we, as humans, do. For the same, it needs to sense. Hence, for the machines to possess this, there is an involvement of pattern recognition.

Let us start with how the entire process of pattern recognition (PR) is carried out so that the machine can perceive.

Pattern Recognition System

Typically, a pattern recognition system consists of the following modules, as shown in Figure 14.1.

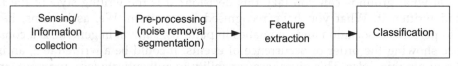

Figure 14.1 Basic steps of pattern recognition.

Before we discuss the modules, we would like to mention that here, we are giving an outline about the tasks in the statistical pattern recognition systems. Such a system operates in two modes—in training mode and in testing mode. Figure 14.1 shows the modules in testing mode, whereas in training, instead of classification, it is the learning algorithm that is trained.

1. ***Sensing/Information collection:*** This is the data acquisition step of pattern recognition. For the same, electronic devices like sensors (camera or a microphone) are used

depending on what data is required. The data could be in different forms like audio, video, text, etc.

2. **Pre-processing:** Pre-processing involves converting the data into some standard format. It is essentially bifurcation of the pattern of interest. This includes removal of the noise, normalisation and other activities like segmentation, smoothing (for image-based pattern recognition), etc.

3. **Feature extraction:** As discussed earlier, the features are the ones which are the actual representation of a pattern. So, which features are to be selected to be able to identify the pattern is an important task. Features can be like shape, colour, size, texture and so on. These are the things that identify an object. What importance does a feature make in pattern recognition? It must be noted that good feature selection helps in improving the pattern recognition. A vector, called *feature vector*, is formed of the features selected. For a labelled data (as an example), 10 objects belong to class A and 6 objects belong to class B. The feature vector (FV) is formed for every object. The FV for objects in class A will have more matching (close) values amongst themselves than the ones in class B. The extraction method has to select the relevant ones.

Feature extraction can be mathematically represented as follows:

Let $X = \{x_1, x_2, x_3, ..., x_n\}$ (All these are features)

The extraction process is

$$Y = f(X)$$

where the function f, actually transforms the vector X into vector Y. Here $Y = \{y_1, y_2, y_3, ..., y_m\}$ and $m < n$. These methods are discussed in detail later in the chapter.

4. **Classification:** This is often referred to as the main step of recognition. So, after identifying the relevant features, the process to detect that this particular pattern or the FV belongs to this class or category is the classification task. A model selection that can be taken up as a pre-step to this also exists. The classification could be supervised or unsupervised learning and we have already studied about the different supervised and unsupervised techniques in Chapter 10.

After carrying out these basic steps, PR systems also have post-processing, which involves evaluation system. This is done to improve the performance of the system. The post-processing actually measures the performance; the error rate is also accounted. Many's the time, it happens that for the same task of classification, one method gives good results but the other does not. All this evaluation is done in post-processing. Further, it also performs context exploitation.

Let us start with the feature extraction process.

14.2 FEATURE EXTRACTION

The *feature extraction process* is the one which is responsible for getting small and distinguishing features that enable to identify an object with precise quantities that are essential. For example, in case of diagnosis for cancer of multiple myloma (a type of cancer), features like the WBC count, the platelet count, haemoglobin percentage and others are taken into account to confirm the diagnosis, though height or other body features are not significant. Feature extraction considers the ones that are relevant. Now, there is a concept of feature selection too. *Feature selection* is a subset of extraction, where from the extracted features, the selection is done to form one or more subsets. We can always say that it is a transformation process. To summarise, from the set of features to the selection of relevant ones, forming subset S is *feature extraction* and from the subset S to the selection of further subset S' is *feature selection*.

In pattern recognition, there is a concept of *curse of dimensionality*, which actually states that a large number of features are harmful in the recognition process. Let us brief on it.

Curse of Dimensionality

In pattern recognition, often we classify. This classification performance is impacted by various factors. The recognition system is dependent on the feature set, the number of samples and the complexity of the classifier. Consider a simple example of labelled data—a training set. Suppose the number of samples here are t and the dimensionality of the features is d; the number of t and number of d impact the performance. If d is too large, with t being small, then we cannot deny the probability that the performance of the algorithm would degrade. This occurs as the training samples are not sufficient to have an appropriate estimation of the parameters. This is often called *overfitting*. Other factor is the complexity. If d is too large, naturally the execution time will be impacted. Further, it is also observed that if the number of features selected earlier are not sufficient in recognition, then addition of more features by increasing d, and keeping t to be same adds up more complications. It is a myth that with additional features, the performance of a system gets improved. In fact, the case is its performance could be worst! All the mentioned factors account for the curse of dimensionality.

Hence, reduction techniques are employed. Let us study the most commonly used transformations—Principal component analysis (PCA) and Linear discriminant analysis (LDA).

14.2.1   Principal Component Analysis (PCA)

This is a transformation that is done on the features. What sort of transformation is it? It is a transformation to reduce the features—a technique for compression. Let us begin with some terminologies for eigenvector and eigenvalues.

An eigenvector can be explained by taking the following example:

$$\begin{pmatrix} 2 & 3 \\ 2 & 1 \end{pmatrix} \times \begin{pmatrix} 3 \\ 2 \end{pmatrix} = \begin{pmatrix} 12 \\ 8 \end{pmatrix} = 4 \times \begin{pmatrix} 3 \\ 2 \end{pmatrix}$$

Matrix 1 × Matrix 2

What relations can be found from the example? The matrix 2, i.e., $\begin{pmatrix} 3 \\ 2 \end{pmatrix}$, which we call vector, is multiplied with a square matrix, i.e, matrix 1. The result that we get is actually a scaled result of the original vector. Matrix 1 here is now referred to as *transformational matrix*. Matrix 2 is the *eigenvector*. When we talk about eigenvectors, we must note that the transformational matrix has to be a square matrix. So, we have found out an eigenvector for the matrix. How many eigenvectors can be computed is dependent on the square matrix. For 2 * 2 matrix, 2 eigenvectors can be found and so on. Other important thing to note is that whatever eigenvectors are found, they are perpendicular to each other, irrespective of the dimensions. Remember if we draw a line from (0, 0) to (3, 2), it will be a vector. Scaling up the vector does not change its direction, and this matters a lot in vectors, i.e., the direction should not change.

Moving ahead, there is a concept of eigenvalue too. The factor '4' here is the eigenvalue. The length of the eigenvectors has to be equal to one. So, we have now understood the concept of eigenvectors and eigenvalues. Let us start with the basic steps of PCA. We assume the data is having two dimensions—X and Y. So, let us say that there are n sample of data available with us. The steps are given below:

1. ***Getting the co-variance matrix:*** Remember that the data has to be on the same scale while calculating the co-variance matrix. The co-variance is calculated as follows:

$$\text{cov}(X, Y) = \frac{\sum\limits_{i=1}^{n}(X_i - \overline{X})(Y_i - \overline{Y})}{n - 1}$$

Let the co-variance matrix obtained be $\begin{pmatrix} \text{cov}(a_{11}) & \text{cov}(a_{12}) \\ \text{cov}(a_{21}) & \text{cov}(a_{22}) \end{pmatrix}$

Remember the values at a_{11} and a_{22} will be same. $\overline{X}$ and $\overline{Y}$ represent the mean.

2. ***Getting the eigenvalues:*** The eigenvalues are obtained by solving the determinant $(A - \lambda_i)$. This is represented as follows:

$$\begin{pmatrix} \text{cov}(a_{11}) - \lambda & \text{cov}(a_{12}) \\ \text{cov}(a_{21}) & \text{cov}(a_{22}) - \lambda \end{pmatrix}$$

How can we get λ? This is done by solving the following

$$\lambda^2 - [\text{cov}(a_{11}) + \text{cov}(a_{21})] * \lambda + [\text{cov}(a_{11}) * \text{cov}(a_{21}) - (\text{cov}(1, 2)^2)]$$

So, we need to solve it to get the value of λ as follows:

$$\lambda = \frac{-b \pm \sqrt{b^2 - 4ac}}{2a}$$

The values that we get for λ are the eigenvalues. So, we get λ_1 and λ_2.

3. ***Getting the eigenvectors:*** To get the eigenvectors, we need to solve $(A - \lambda_i) * [X] = [0]$. We already have got the values for λ, that is, we have got the eigenvalues. We order them from highest to lowest (here, we will get two of them). The eigenvectors are obtained by subtracting the eigenvalue from the co-variance matrix that has been obtained in step 1. Once this is done, we will get $(A - \lambda_i)$:

$$\begin{pmatrix} \text{cov}(a_{11}) - \lambda_1 & \text{cov}(a_{12}) - \lambda_1 \\ \text{cov}(a_{21}) - \lambda_1 & \text{cov}(a_{22}) - \lambda_1 \end{pmatrix}$$

The same step is followed for λ_2. The next step is to determine eigenvector $\begin{pmatrix} \text{eig}_{11} \\ \text{eig}_{12} \end{pmatrix}$ for λ_1.

$$\begin{pmatrix} \text{cov}(a_{11}) - \lambda_1 & \text{cov}(a_{12}) - \lambda_1 \\ \text{cov}(a_{21}) - \lambda_1 & \text{cov}(a_{22}) - \lambda_1 \end{pmatrix} * \begin{pmatrix} \text{eig}_{11} \\ \text{eig}_{12} \end{pmatrix} = \begin{pmatrix} 0 \\ 0 \end{pmatrix}$$

The same step is to be carried out with λ_2 to get its corresponding eigenvector $\begin{pmatrix} \text{eig}_{21} \\ \text{eig}_{22} \end{pmatrix}$.

4. ***Getting the co-ordinates of data points:*** The next step is to get the co-ordinates of the data points in the direction of the eigenvectors. To get this, we multiply the data points that are centred, i.e., the data points are converted into

$X - \overline{X}$	$Y - \overline{Y}$	$* \begin{pmatrix} \text{eig}_{11} & \text{eig}_{21} \\ \text{eig}_{12} & \text{eig}_{22} \end{pmatrix} =$	*Projection with the first principal component*	*Projection with the second principal component*
...	...		...	...
...	...		...	...
...	...		...	...

What are eig_{11}, eig_{22} and so on? The first column indicates the first eigenvector, whereas the second column is the second eigenvector. We have actually got the projection with the two eigenvectors. It is upto us which eigenvector to consider. Most often, if for some x, eigenvalue$_x$ << eigenvalue$_y$, then all the eigenvalues above x are eliminated. So, in this entire process, a transformation can occur to a single dimension. A graphical representation of the eigenvectors is given in Figure 14.2, showing the eigenvectors.

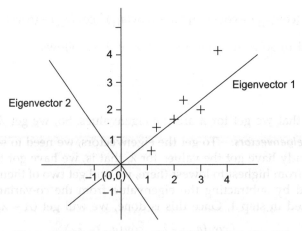

Figure 14.2 A snapshot showing the eigenvectors.

14.2.2 Linear Discriminant Analysis (LDA)

The goal of LDA is to find a transformation in which the inter-cluster distances between the classes are maximised, whereas the intra-cluster distances are minimised. Remember the major difference between the PCA and LDA is that PCA is concerned with feature classification, whereas in LDA, data is classified. LDA tries to make the classes or the clusters more separable. There are two cases—class dependent transformation and class independent transformation.

The steps that are carried out are given below:

1. *Computing the mean:* The mean for the classes is computed. Diagrammatically, it is represented in Figure 14.3 (for two classes).

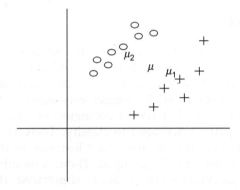

Figure 14.3 A representation for mean values for the data sets.

Let us represent it mathematically.

After calculating μ_1 and μ_2, μ is calculated. As it is clear from Figure 14.3, it is the mean of the entire data. How is it computed? It is calculated as follows:

$$\mu = p_1 \times \mu_1 + p_2 \times \mu_2$$

Here, p_1 and p_2 are the probabilities. Since it is a two-class problem, it will be 0.5. So, the d-dimensional mean vector calculations take place.

2. *Calculating the scatter:* In this step, scatter is calculated. This is done so as to determine the separation between the classes. This is given as follows:

$$S_{\text{within\_class}} = \sum_i p_i * (\text{cov}(i))$$

If there are two classes, it will be

$$S_{\text{within\_class}} = 0.5 * \text{cov(class 1)} + 0.5 * \text{cov(class 2)}$$

The scatter for between the classes is calculated as

$$S_{\text{between\_class}} = \sum_i (\mu_i - \mu) * (\mu_i - \mu)^T$$

Here, T is the transpose.

3. In the next step, the problem is solved to get the eigenvalues and eigenvectors. This is achieved by solving problem for matrix

$$S_{within\_class}^{-1} \, S_{between\_class}$$

4. Selection of linear discriminants to form new feature space occurs in this step. The sorting of eigenvectors (as in PCA) and selecting 'P' eigenvectors with largest eigenvalues to form $P \times d$ matrix.

5. The matrix obtained in step 4 is used to transform into new subspace. Thus, LDA projects d-dimensional data into a smaller subspace by maximising class separations.

14.3 CLASSIFICATION

We now have a look at the different classification methods. Though we have studied supervised and unsupervised learning earlier, a glimpse of it is provided here also. Now, once the feature extraction is done, we need to classify based on the features.

So, what is done in classification? Two cases exist here. In first case, we have a set of labelled data, i.e., prior available patterns belonging to some specific classes, and for a new unknown data or pattern, we need to classify. There is a training that occurs in this case. We have learnt about this in supervised learning. In the other case, we simply have patterns, which are required to be grouped. There is no information available about their classes. This is unsupervised learning. So, to summarise, the pattern recognition is all about classification of patterns into the classes in which any of these techniques are used. Let us have a look at them.

A very simple approach could be a lookup table. With the lookup table, the classification of the unknown pattern is done. So, template matching occurs, where similarity-based notion comes into picture. This is based on the correlation and various distance measures. There can be methods that are based on use of some search techniques as well in this category.

The other approaches include supervised learning with probabilistic approach like that of Bayesian. So, the estimation methods come under this category. Even k-nearest neighbour is one of the techniques. Branch and bound technique is also used in the classification of syntactic patterns. Markov chain model and HMM too have a role in the classification.

To discuss among other methods, neural networks (NNs) are the most common. NNs work on the principle where imitation of the way we (as humans) learn takes place. A perceptron model is built here and there are different categories for NN like feed-forward, multilayer and so on. (We will study NN in Chapter 17.) Various other methods that are in use are boosting, and today, one of the most commonly used method is the support vector machines (SVM).

After understanding the methods, we would also like to mention that many's the time, the classification techniques are grouped into syntactic and statistical models as well. In statistical, it is based on the features, whereas in syntactic, it is based on the primitives. A grammar plays an important role in the syntactic model. Let us discuss k-nearest neighbour (k-NN) here.

k-Nearest Neighbour (k-NN)

This is the simplest approach for classification and is called *lazy learner*. To explain this, let us consider we have set of labelled data. The *labelled data* is the data which belongs to a particular class. If you remember, generally in supervised learning, there is a training which occurs using the labelled data. But in this case, k-NN being lazy does nothing with the labelled data. When a new sample pattern comes, it finds k-nearest ones (k is an integer) and the ones with higher probability are selected to the final class for the new sample. Figure 14.4 represents the concept.

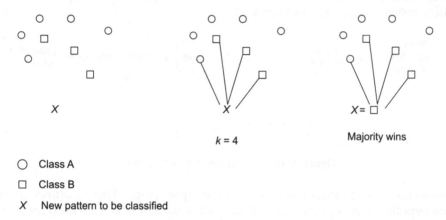

O   Class A

□   Class B

X   New pattern to be classified

Figure 14.4   k-NN example.

X is the new pattern that is to be classified. We already have class A and class B data patterns. k-NN simply have them in the pattern space maintained and do nothing till it is given a new pattern for classification. For example, the value of k is set to 4. Once, X is given, the pattern space is searched to find k-nearest ones (here 4) and the most common class among these (majority) is assigned to the X pattern. Diagrammatically, it is fine, but how can the nearest one be found? The answer is by Euclidean distance. It is given as if X and Y are two patterns, where $X = \{x_1, x_2, ..., x_n\}$ and $Y = \{y_1, y_2, ..., y_n\}$ (the features of the patterns), then the Euclidean distance is given as follows:

$$\text{dist}(X, Y) = \sqrt{\sum_{i=1}^{n} (x_i - y_i)^2}$$

Now, this has to be done between all the labelled patterns and X. Once the distances are obtained, they are sorted and the k-nearest ones are taken up along with the classes. Then, comes the majority voting among these k to determine the class for X.

Now, what would happen when k = 1? Select the nearest one as to be the class for X. How can k be decided? This is to be decided prior and mostly it is $\sqrt{m}$, where m is the total number of data patterns. What about the computations? Naturally, the number of comparisons will be O(m) for m patterns. But with the use of some other techniques, this can be reduced.

14.4 OBJECT RECOGNITION

We now proceed towards the concepts of object recognition. Here, we discuss the pattern recognition in terms of image.

An *object recognition system* is a system that identifies the objects from a percept that is available in the form of image. To do so, the system makes use of different recognition tasks and uses object models. When we say that the objects are recognised, we mean to say that they are essentially labelled.

An object recognition system consists of different components. A representative object recognition system is depicted in Figure 14.5.

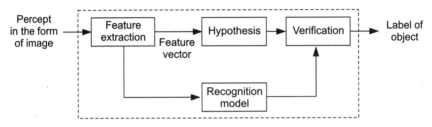

Figure 14.5 Object recognition system.

Feature extraction extracts features from the input image. These features are used to formulate hypothesis. Recognition model has a set of models which are used for hypothesis verification. Using object model, verifier assigns label to the object.

There holds some relationship between segmentation, recognition and detection. A detection process involves segmentation. After this process, we have the separated objects which are then recognised. For example, in an image, there are some trees and flowers. Identifying the flowers is object detection, whereas saying that the flower is of rose is recognition. Let us discuss in detail about some of the aspects of object recognition and matching theories.

14.4.1 Template Matching Theory

Template matching is one of the most commonly used approaches for object verification and recognition. A template is used to detect its instance in an image. A pattern matching approach is used here. In a simple layman's term, we can say that a small child going to kindergarten has a set of meccano blocks. His teacher gives him a square shape template block. He needs to recognise this among the blocks he has. What would he do? He would match it with every block. In the similar way, the template is actually compared with the input pattern with reference to different locations in the image. It requires a large memory, since all the templates are stored. Figure 14.6 depicts the template matching process. Do we detect the object in template matching? Yes, we do.

In Figure 14.6, what do you think should be the output? For all the 5 input objects, should it match and give output that appropriate match is found? Ideally yes, but to get this, it has to perform some computations. The tasks that are required to enable template matching recognise all the above patterns; it performs standardisation and normalisation.

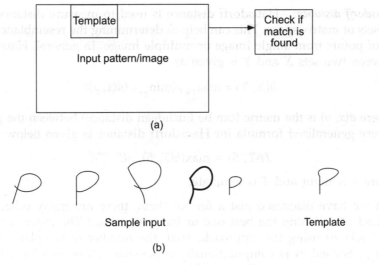

Figure 14.6 (a) Template matching and (b) Template matching example.

So, the P characters above need to be transformed into standard format to enable them to match the template. Various image transformations are included.

Template matching is performed based on similarity factor. Similarity factor is also associated with correlation. An appropriate distance-based measure is used here. The complexity can be reduced substantially using binary representation of images.

Among the different techniques used for template matching, Chamfer matching, Hausdorff distances are used commonly. Few of them are as follows:

1. **Correlation:** A correlation is basic operation that is performed to extract information from images. This operation is shift invariant and linear. A correlation rule is given below:

$$\text{Correlation} = \frac{\sum\limits_{i=0}^{n-1} (x_i - \bar{x})(y_i - \bar{y})}{\sqrt{\sum\limits_{i=0}^{n-1} (x_i - \bar{x}) \sum\limits_{i=0}^{n-1} (y_i - \bar{y})}}$$

The above formula is for a grayscale image, where x factors are with respect to the template and y are with respect to the source. The cross-correlation is computed as follows:

$$\text{COR} = \sum_{p=1}^{m} \sum_{q=1}^{n} t[p, q]\, s[i + p, j + q]$$

where t is the template, s is the input image, and i and j are the displacement factors.

2. **Sum of squared errors:** The formula for template matching is given below:

$$\text{SSD} = \sum_{p,q \in R} (t[p, q] - s[i + p, j + q])^2$$

Here, R is the region of the template.

3. ***Hausdorff distance:*** Hausdorff distance is used to measure distance between two subsets of matrix space. This can help in determining the resemblance between two set of points from single image or multiple image. In general, Hausdorff distance between two sets X and Y is given as

$$h(X, Y) = \max_{x \in X}(\min_{y \in Y}(d(x, y)))$$

where $d(x, y)$ is the metric (can be Euclidean distance) between the points x and y. A very generalised formula for Hausdorff distance is given below:

$$H(T, S) = \max\{h(T, S), h(S, T)\}$$

where S is input and T is template.

Though we have discussed just a few of them, there are many other methods too. Is this method of matching the best one or the easiest one? The latter is true. There are many drawbacks of using this approach. First, the number of templates required to be saved is large. Second, it is computationally expensive, where you have to perform the matching for the entire image. There could be many template representation for a single object. In case of rotation or size change, it is not very effective. Most importantly, will it work for a partial view of an object? Yet it is worth to mention that the approach is still in practice and many optimal improvements have been suggested for many image processing applications, including face recognition. Let us proceed with structural descriptions. One more point to discuss here is that template matching is also treated as a verification process that determines the likelihood.

14.4.2 Prototype Matching Theory

The prototype matching theory is similar to that of template, with the difference that here, the exact match is not encountered, thus allowing to get some flexibility in the matching process. A prototype is an abstract definition for an object. The major advantage of using prototype is even if somewhere the image representation is not appropriate or is somewhat blur, the prototype will still help in getting the match. Let us say we have a prototype for eyes. So, small eyes, big eyes, eyes wide open can be found similar (in some percentage, to have the object) to the prototype of simple eyes. What would happen when the eyeball is absent or when the position of the eyeball is different? Still, it will identify some similarity using this model.

14.4.3 Structural Description

A *structural description* is a symbolic description for the objects. Unlike the case of template matching, here the object recognition is given by the language of structural descriptions. They are of great importance for machine vision and they imply on the parts and the relationships. In short, we can say that the configuration of the objects is described. But it is really hard to generate a structural description. Biederman's theory is based on this, where the object are represented in terms of parts called *geons* (geometric icons). This is also called *recognition by components (RBC)*.

For example, an object and its possible geons are shown in Figure 14.7. In the matching process, the perceived object is parsed and with the structural descriptions, their relationships are identified. So, a match is done with the structural description to identify it. There are two things that exist in case of structural descriptions—first is a model for the structural description and second is the structural description itself. A simple example to show a structural description of a letter *L* is given in Figure 14.8.

Figure 14.7   An object and its geons.

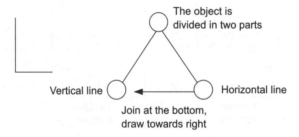

Figure 14.8   Structural description for letter *L*.

As said before, the structural description comprises structural model too. If the relation between horizontal and vertical line is represented as the horizontal line meeting the vertical line at its end, with the major portion of horizontal line towards vertical line, then an accurate letter *L* could be matched. Whereas, in Figure 14.8, the description is able to handle somewhat bifurcated character.

After understanding the concept of structural description, we now look at different aspects of having structural descriptions. Will they find out the object accurately always? If the spatial relationships and sufficient geons are used, then it would definitely. For letters *L* and *T*, they have two same geons, but the relationships make a lot of difference. Can other features like texture matter in the descriptions? These too can be added up for better perception. Will the view to capture an object make an impact on the matching process? If the structural descriptions are made available at the different viewpoints, naturally it will be able to accommodate these too.

14.4.4   Feature-Based Approach

In the chapter, we discuss about the dimensionality and the features. Now, coming back to the feature-based approach, as the name suggests, it is concerned with the matching of the features of the object rather than templates or prototypes. So, for letter *T*, instead of the lines, a set of features is represented. There is a model called *Pandemonium model* that describes this approach. It comprises feature demons and cognitive demons, and finally, there is a decision demon. The basic feature are represented by the feature demons for example, if we have to detect some letter, then the feature demon has a horizontal line, an inclined line, an angle and so on. The cognitive demon has two horizontal lines and one vertical line. For example, for a letter *I*, this would be the case. The concept is like you raise your hand if you know an answer to a particular question in the class. Similarly, here, the cognitive demon shouts (as said so) if it finds a match and the decision demon takes the final call. Figure 14.9 depicts a simple feature-based approach.

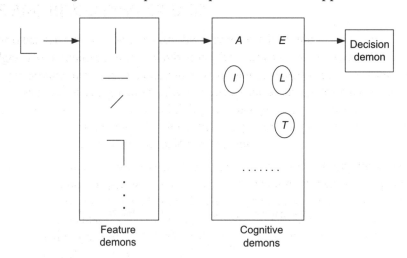

Figure 14.9   Sample Pandemonium model.

In Figure 14.9, it is observed that the letters *I*, *L* and *T* are circled. So, these are different cognitive demons which shout; and the one which shouts loud is the letter *L*. The decision demon, hence, selects this.

So, we have discussed all about the cognitive and perceptual view of pattern recognition. Let us discuss speech recognition before we conclude the chapter.

14.5   SPEECH RECOGNITION

Speech is a natural way of interaction of human beings. Hence, intelligent agents are expected to recognise speech to interact with humans intelligently. Many mobile applications have emerged which can recognise voice to search contacts, to dial numbers and open applications. These systems have some sort of voice recognition system inbuilt. Are we doing speech recognition here? Are speech and voice recognition one and the same? Though the terms are used interchangeably, we would like to put forth that there is a difference. In speech recognition system, what is intended is to recognise the data/speech and analyse it, say by converting into some text. Whereas, voice recognition involves the identification of the person. We discuss about speech recognition here. But we can always say that voice recognition is a subset of speech recognition.

Why do I need to have these systems? Suppose you want to write a letter. Then, using the speech recognition system, you can escape from hassle of typing. You have to just speak into the system and the letter would be ready. Not only that, using the system, you can give commands to your car, home appliances and they will perform the task for you.

There are different types or ways of speech recognition.

1. *Single word handling:* This is in some sort of isolation, where only one word is taken at a time for processing.

2. *Multiple words:* Unlike the first approach, the system recognises from the continuous words that are uttered.

3. *Human-like recognition (fluent):* This is the extension of the previous one, where actually the way we speak is taken and analysed.

There are two cases in speech recognition systems—response to a command and dictation. In the first case, you give a command on your mobile that places a call to Mr. X and a call is actually initiated. In the second case, it just converts the text of what is said.

Now, imagine your phone is with your mom (unlocked). (At this instance, forget about directly dialing). She can simply speak out some name and a call is placed (may be to some unwanted person). Can you stop this from happening? Your phone should recognise only your voice. So, precisely, this is speaker dependent recognition. This needs some previous training.

A basic diagram for the speech recognition system is given below in Figure 14.10.

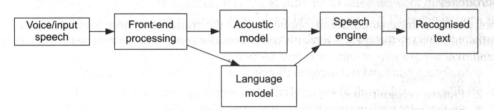

Figure 14.10 Simple speech recognition system.

Let us discuss about the speech signal. Which parameters decide the speech signal? Most of us are familiar that the speech signal has the bandwidth of more than 4 KHz, but within 4 KHz, it is possible to understand the necessary information. So, a speech signal is processed through a front-end. The activities like conversion to digital signal, noise removal take place. Thus, we can have some sort of pre-processing here. Then, the notion of acoustic model comes. An *acoustic model* is the one that describes the sounds of the words that are uttered. Let W be the set of words that could be said, and S be the acoustic signal that is observed. The goal here is to identify the utterance of particular word from W that maximises $P(W|S)$. We can put forth this with the Bayes's rule.

$$P(W|S) = \frac{P(S|W)P(W)}{P(S)}$$

As $P(S)$ is independent of W, the acoustic model is given as $P(S|W)$, whereas the language model is $P(W)$. The speech engine is the one that performs the search to get the speech into a recognised text. The acoustic model is made up with the *phonology*. It is the study of how a particular language sounds (the generic pronunciations). There exist different language sounds, which are called *phones*. Then, the concept of phoneme (that is the smallest unit for a sound) comes. A simple example of phone and a word can be 'eng' for the part of word 'swimming'.

With the clarity of the acoustic model, we move to understand more about the acoustic signal. The acoustic signal is digitised and frames are captured. A frame has the signal properties and it is taken at particular intervals. Generally, there is an overlap between the frames. In each frame, a vector consisting of features is built. This tells about the signal. A diagram for this process is given in Figure 14.11.

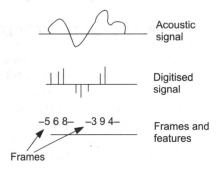

Figure 14.11 Acoustic signal to frame.

Approaches

Since we have understood about phoneme and the frames, we now look at the different approaches to have the speech recognition. In broader sense, the approaches are categorised as follows:

1. Rule-based
2. Pattern recognition
3. Statistical

We begin with *rule-based approach*. Another name for it is the *acoustic-phonetic approach*. This was the preliminary approach that was based on the rules built on the basis of the phonetics and the linguistics. This set of decision rules is used to estimate the possibilities and accordingly, the recognition occurs. The method has many issues like building the rules, difficulty in decoding, and further, the scalability of the method. Figure 14.12 shows this approach. As it is observed from Figure 14.12, the parameter measurement does the spectral representation. In the further steps, the acoustic features are identified and with the help of vocabulary, the speech is recognised.

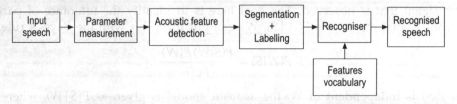

Figure 14.12 Acoustic-phonetic approach (Rule-based).

In the *pattern recognition-based approach*, which started gaining momentum in 1970s, the concepts of template matching, dynamic time warping (DTW) with a decision logic have been introduced. As we are familiar with the pattern recognition concept in supervised learning, a training is carried out on known speech samples. Figure 14.13 depicts the process of recognition in this approach. A parameter measurement block is same (as in the previous one), which performs DFT. There are some learned patterns based on which training occurs. Template matching mechanism is used next. *DTW* is a method that is used to have an optimal alignment in the two sequences. This is used in the decision logic prior to the recognition.

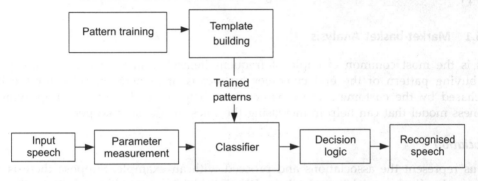

Figure 14.13 Pattern recognition-based approach.

Statistical approach includes a lot of Mathematics! It is an approach that is basically hybrid one and is also sometimes called *AI approach*. This involves the acoustic-phonetic model as well as the pattern-based approach. Hidden Markov model belongs to this category.

At present, work in speech recognition system is being carried out at a large scale, where the use of HMM with DTW is put to use. The concept of deep neural networks is widely used at present for the same. Along with this text-to-speech (TTS) systems are also in use today.

14.6 PATTERN MINING

We move towards the concept of pattern mining. Before we go into the details of what pattern mining is, first we look at the concepts of association rules, frequent patterns, frequent pattern mining and so on. Let us understand them.

1. *Frequent pattern:* It is a pattern that is observed frequently in the data. It could be sub-sequences or the subsets that are observed frequently with respect to user-specified threshold.

2. *Frequent pattern mining:* It involves identifying the recurrent patterns in the data.

3. *Frequent itemset mining:* It involves identification of associations or the correlations between the data items from huge data sets (transactional database usually). This is often found to be of interest for growth in the business, as many noteworthy relations can be identified that can help in improving the business model.

4. Association rule mining: We now know what a frequent itemset mining is. Association rule detects the common usage of the items. So, a simple association rule can be mapped as the associative relation that states the purchase of a product X when Y has also been purchased.

Now, what is pattern mining? The identification of relevant patterns that can aid in improving the business models with discovery of frequent items based on association rules for mining altogether is *pattern mining*.

When, how and where can it be used? Let us look at the application perspective and the approaches for this mining. We begin with market-basket analysis.

14.6.1 Market-basket Analysis

This is the most common example of frequent itemset mining. It involves analysis of the buying pattern of the end customer by means of association rules for the items purchased by the customer. These associations help in modifying and improving the business model that can help in increasing the sales for the shopkeepers.

Association

Let us represent the associations and proceed with an example. Suppose there is a set of items $I = \{i_1, i_2, ..., i_m\}$ in a database Db. Db consists of transactions. Thus, the Db is represented are $Db = \{t_1, t_2, ..., t_n\}$.

Each transaction t contains a set of itemset from I. Assume M is a set of items in a transaction t_x. Association rule expresses an implication $M \Rightarrow N$ in the Db transactions, where $M \subset I$ and $N \subset I$ and $M \cap N = $ Null. By establishing this association, we actually put forth the relations and association between the itemsets that can prove highly beneficial for business decision policies.

We now move towards finding the frequent itemsets that help in building the association rules. A very known approach for this is Apriori algorithm. Let us take an example and discuss the same.

14.6.2 Apriori Algorithm

Consider the following data set (Table 14.1).

TABLE 14.1 Transactions and Data Items

Transactions	Data items
t_1	I, B, L
t_2	B, U
t_3	L, U
t_4	I, M
t_5	I, B, L, U
t_6	I, B, M

Here, I is i-phone, B is Bluetooth, M is mobile cover, U is USB stick, L is laptop. Some terminologies required for the algorithm are given below:

1. *Item set:* It is the collection of one or more items. For example, $\{I, B\}$.

2. *Support count:* It is the frequency of occurrence of an itemset. For example, support count or $\sigma\{I, B, L\} = 2$.

3. *Support:* It is the fraction of transactions that contain the itemset. So, s for $\{I, B, L\} = 2/6$. Suppose we have an association rule like $\{I\} \rightarrow \{B\}$, then the support is computed as the fractions of transactions that contain them. Not to confuse, let $\{I\} = X$ and $\{B\} = Y$, then the support is given as

$$\text{Support} = \text{Support count } (X \cup Y)/N$$

Here, N is number of transactions.

Thus, it would be $3/6$.

4. *Confidence:* It is the fractions of transactions in Db containing itemset X that also contained itemset Y in an association rule $X \rightarrow Y$. So, confidence is

$$c = \text{Support count } (X \cup Y)/\text{Support count}$$

For example if $\{I, B\} \rightarrow \{M\}$, then $c = 1/3$.

Note: What do the confidence and support tell? Confidence measures the strength of the rule, whereas support tells about how often it should occur in the database.

5. *Frequent itemset:* It is an itemset whose support count is greater than the minimum threshold.

Let us proceed with the algorithm. For the data set given, we want to find out frequent itemsets. We need to set up minimum support threshold before we begin. Let us set this to 2.

Apriori Property

In generation of the frequent items sets, the property states that all the non-empty itemsets of the frequent itemset must also be frequent.

Operations

1. *Join:* This involves generation of candidate k-itemsets.

2. *Prune:* It determines itemsets that satisfy the minimum support threshold.

Algorithm

1. Scan the Db to count the number of times each individual itemset is found. With this, we generate a candidate itemset C_1 (Table 14.2).

TABLE 14.2 C_1 Obtained in Step 1

Itemset	Count of occurrence
I	4
B	4
L	3
U	2
M	2

2. Generate frequent itemsets F_1 that satisfy the minimum support value (Table 14.3). Since all of them are above 2, they are in F_1.

TABLE 14.3 F_1 Obtained in Step 2

Itemset	Count of occurrence
I	4
B	4
L	3
U	2
M	2

3. Perform join of F_1 join F_1^* to obtain C_2 (Table 14.4). No pruning takes place.

TABLE 14.4 C_2 Obtained in Step 3

Itemset
I, B
I, L
I, U
I, M
B, L
B, U
B, M
L, U
L, M
U, M

---

* This join is joining of the itemsets such that they share k-1 items

4. Traverse Db and compute the support count for the itemsets in C_2. Let the obtained table be C_2' (Table 14.5).

TABLE 14.5 C_2' Obtained in Step 4

Itemset	Support count
I, B	3
I, L	2
I, U	1
I, M	2
B, L	2
B, U	2
B, M	1
L, U	2
L, M	0
U, M	0

5. Generate F_2 that contains the frequent two itemsets that satisfy the minimum support threshold (Table 14.6).

TABLE 14.6 F_2 Obtained in Step 5

Itemset	Support count
I, B	3
I, L	2
I, M	2
B, L	2
B, U	2
L, U	2

6. (i) Generate candidate three itemsets. This involves again a join operation F_2 join F_2. The obtained C_3 is given here. Let us study step wise how C_3 is generated. While performing a join, the following itemsets are generated:

{{I,B},{I,L},{I,M},{B,L},{B,U},{L,U}} join {{I,B},{I,L},{I,M},{B,L},{B,U},{L,U}} = {{I,B,L}, {I,B,M}, {I,L,M}, {B,L,U}}

(ii) Applying the prune property stating that the frequent itemsets must also be frequent, from the join operation we get:

(a) **{I,B,L}:** The two-itemsets are {I,B}, {I,L}, {B,L}. Are these frequent in F_2? Yes. Keep in C_3.

(b) **{I,B,M}:** The two-itemsets are {I,B}, {I,M}, {B,M}. Are these frequent in F_2? No. Hence prune it.

(c) {*I*,*L*,*M*}:   The two-itemsets are {*I*,*L*}, {*I*,*M*}, {*L*,*M*}. Are these frequent in F_2? No. Hence prune it.

(d) {*B*,*L*,*U*}:   The two-itemsets are {*B*,*L*}, {*B*,*U*}, {*L*,*U*}. Are these frequent in F_2? Yes. Keep them in C_3.

Thus, the final C_3 generated is given below (Table 14.7):

TABLE 14.7 C_3 Obtained in Step 6

Itemset
I, B, L
B, L, U

7. Get the support count; generate C'_3 (Table 14.8).

TABLE 14.8 C'_3 Obtained in Step 7

Itemset	Support count
I, B, L	2
B, L, U	1

8. Generate F_3 that contains the frequent three-itemsets that satisfy the minimum support threshold (Table 14.9). Hence, F_3 will have

TABLE 14.9 F_3 obtained in Step 8

Itemset	Support count
I, B, L	2

Thus, frequent itemset is generated. (Further, four-itemset could have been generated if there are more three-itemsets satisfying the Apriori rule.)

From this frequent itemset, the association rules are generated. This generation is based on the confidence threshold. For the above example, let us understand the process. Let the frequent itemset be represented as *FI*. Let the confidence_threshold be 75%. Now the process is

1. Generate non-empty subsets of *I*. Let us call it *x*.
2. Now, for every *x*, generate the rule: $x \rightarrow FI - x$ such that the following condition is satisfied:

Support count (*FI*)/Support count (*x*) >= Confidence_threshold

Thus, we have

$$FI = \{I, B, L\}$$

x can have values {*I*,*B*}, {*B*,*L*}, {*I*,*L*}, {*I*}, {*B*}, {*L*}. Thus the association rules generated are shown in Table 14.10.

TABLE 14.10 Association Rules Generated

Rules	Confidence	Rules selected
$I \wedge B \to L$	2/3 = 67%	
$B \wedge L \to I$	2/2 = 100%	√
$I \wedge L \to B$	2/2 = 100%	√
$I \to B \wedge L$	2/4 = 50%	
$B \to I \wedge L$	2/4 = 50%	
$L \to I \wedge B$	2/3 = 67%	

The rules selected are the ones that have strong confidence levels. Thus, with frequent pattern mining, we are able to identify the association rules that can be used for the business development models.

SUMMARY

The chapter has introduced the concepts and models of pattern recognition with the preliminaries of the same. We have studied about the steps that are to be carried out for recognition. Starting from the data collection to the final classification, the pattern goes through different stages. Among the steps, feature extraction has a deep impact on the pattern recognition system and it is very much crucial that optimal number of features is used for the process of classification. PCA and LDA are most commonly used methods for the features estimation. Dimensionality issue is a key factor that needs to be handled in this process.

The chapter has also introduced object recognition and the various methods of matching theories. Some of them are still in practice, finding a place in face recognition systems. Talking about speech recognition, it is the most promising field, wherein at present, the trend is towards speech-enabled web as well as text to speech systems.

The last aspect that has been addressed is the pattern mining with a glimpse of Apriori algorithm. The algorithm proves its efficiency with the frequent set mining. Today, many extensions are been proposed for the Apriori algorithm and is often looked upon from business intelligence perspective.

To conclude, the current trend of the pattern recognition systems is towards feature ranking methods and feature weighing schemas to build better recognition systems and better learning too!

 **KEYWORDS**

1. **Pattern:** It is the typical repetitive behaviour in data, image or structure.
2. **Pattern recognition:** It involves identification of implicit objects, types and relationships, repetitive behaviour in raw data.

3. **Pre-processing:** The task of removal of noise, normalisation, smoothing, segmentation is pre-processing of the data.

4. **Feature extraction:** It is the process of selection of relevant features from the ones available.

5. **PCA:** Principal component analysis is a technique for feature extraction and dimensionality reduction.

6. **LDA:** Linear discriminant analysis is a method where transformation is done maximising the inter-distance and minimising the intra-distances for feature extraction.

7. **Pattern classification:** It is a technique that classifies the pattern into some classes. The approach can be simple lookup or probabilistic, where either supervised or unsupervised technique can be used.

8. **k-nearest neighbour:** It is a classification method, where majority voting is used to classify a new pattern among the k-selected ones.

9. **Object recognition:** It involves recognition of object in an image along with classification to a particular class.

10. **Template matching:** It is a matching technique that makes use of a template, where match is found by considering different parts of source.

11. **Prototype matching:** In this, similar to template matching, a prototype for the object (which is more abstract) is used to check the match.

12. **Structural description:** It is a method to determine the object match, where the parts and the relationships of the object are described.

13. **Feature analysis:** It is a matching method based on features rather than templates for the objects.

14. **Frequent pattern:** It is a pattern that is observed frequently in the data.

15. **Support count:** It is the frequency of occurrence of an itemset.

16. **Frequent pattern mining:** It involves identifying the recurrent patterns in the data.

17. **Pattern mining:** This involves identification of the relevant patterns that can aid in improving the business models with discovery of frequent items based on association rules for mining.

18. **Support:** It is the fraction of transactions that contain the itemset.

19. **Confidence:** It is the fraction of transactions in Db containing itemset X that also contains itemset Y in an association rule $X \rightarrow Y$.

MULTIPLE CHOICE QUESTIONS

1. What will happen in a case where $\mu_1 = \mu_2$ to PCA and LDA?
   (a) PCA will work fine, LDA will not
   (b) Both will work fine
   (c) Both will fail
   (d) LDA will work, PCA will not

2. Among the matching theories for object recognition, other than feature analysis which method would have feature playing a role in the process?
   (a) Template matching
   (b) Structural description
   (c) Prototype matching
   (d) None of the above

3. Which of the following are not the factors accounting for the curse of dimensionality?
   (a) Input sample   (b) Feature size   (c) Execution time   (d) All of these

4. Which of the following is not an advantage of Apriori algorithm?
   (a) It can be easily parallelised
   (b) It exploits the frequent itemset property
   (c) It generates huge candidate sets
   (d) None of the above

5. Which of the following is not a frequent pattern mining task?
   (a) Outputting an hypothesis or some rule
   (b) Identifying significant relationships between the itemsets
   (c) Employing support and confidence levels
   (d) None of the above

CONCEPT REVIEW QUESTIONS

1. Explain the concept of PCA.
2. Write a short note on template matching.
3. Explain the concept of pattern mining.

CRITICAL THINKING EXERCISE

1. What issues are likely to arise in case of high dimensions of the data in pattern recognition?
2. What could be the drawbacks of using structural descriptions?

PROJECT WORK

1. Write a program that would perform classification based on some features using k-nearest neighbours. Assume any data. For testing, use any one of the prior labelled data and see if it accurately recognises the class. What is the impact on the recognition process if different values of *k* are used?
2. For an automobile shop, various accessories are bought with different models of car. Using Apriori, calculate frequent itemsets. Assume suitable data.

Game Playing

INTRODUCTION

Games have always represented a means to express power and intelligence. In computer games, it is more of the intelligence which is put to test. Game playing has developed as a science, which can be adapted to analyse various scenarios in different domains. Game playing is an important aspect of a system, where two or more entities compete to achieve a state of maximum gain at the cost of other. We can identify players or entities struggling to maximise their own gains and inflict loss to the opponent. A system can be thought of as an environment, which decides the rules and permissible states. In the environment, there can be teams or an individual. A player or a team is bound by some set of rules that need to be followed for the game. Permissible moves within the framework of rules may result in gain or loss to the players. Violation of rules can be flagged as non-permissible moves and may result in negative reward as punishment.

For example, think of an ecosystem in equilibrium, where each living being struggles to survive. Nature has decided the environment and ecosystem. Depending upon the various factors, even the environment may change. We can visualise the changing environment as permissible moves by nature, and hence, nature can also be seen as a player in the ecosystem. In the ecosystem, a lion with strong muscles and jaws chases a deer, which reflects its plausible moves. A deer is equipped with highly sensitive sensors and is capable of maneuvering through the bushes to escape attack of lion. Too many wins for lion will result in the extinction of deer and amount to depletion of food stock for lion, and ultimately, it will also die out. Too many wins for deer will result in starvation of lion, and hence, it may perish. No rain will result in drought and force deer to abandon or perish in the ecosystem. This will in turn result in starvation among lions and they will tend to migrate towards greener pastures. The game between nature and players of the ecosystem goes on. Nature tries to create a balance between the players of the system by controlling the environment of ecosystem. It has also provided the power of adaptation to living beings for survival in the modified environment. The fittest survives by developing new skills. The weaker perishes for not being able to adapt. The game of struggle and survival is just an example, where multiple players survive by enhancing the chance of survival at the cost of others.

The essence of opportunistic gain appears in various fields around us. Think of a game played by police and thief in the environment called society. Society frames the rules. Police enforces the rule and a thief tries to maximise his/her gain by breaking societal norms. People from different cultures try to enforce their ideology on others; it is again an example of game playing for survival or to prove oneself as the best. Politicians try to maximise their influence base on the basis of social structure, which is again at the cost of opponent by social reengineering. There are various fields such as economy, biology, computer science, interrelations, human behaviour etc., where we find several entities struggling to enhance their gains.

Over a period of time, game theory has developed as an advance tool in mathematics and has been applied to various fields in order to have foresight before taking any decision, under a given scenario, which may be captured in the state of the game. Even before a game is played, various states, permissible moves, counter moves of opponents, gain and loss related to moves, etc. can be visualised, and hence, the best possible move can be made so as to force the opponent into a state of disadvantage. The player's behaviour in strategic problem can be modelled in proven mathematical terms, in which success of a player A depends on the move of player B. Formalisation of game theory began in 1944 through a book 'Theory of Games and Economic Behaviour', authored by John von Neumann and Oskar Morgenstern. Since then, the art of game playing has been adapted to several fields and has developed as an advanced tool in artificial intelligence because of its capability of foresight in a decision-making process carried out by a player.

Game theory has helped the economists to get insight into behaviour patterns of various organisations and their customer interactions and have an analysis of the transactional information. The focus of this analysis is on the maximisation of the utilities. Other areas where it is put to work include political sciences, other behaviour and social aspects of humans and biology too. When we say about political science, it is more about the application of the theory in fair division, political economy, public choice, war bargaining, positive political theory, and social choice theory. In regard to the biological domain, the concept of payoffs is mapped with the fitness. The main focus has been on evolutionary aspects of life. Additionally, biologists have used evolutionary strategies for the game theory that would highlight the existence of animal communication. What is the use and impact of this theory with regard to machines? Talking about logic, the theory is essential for prediction purposes. The *predictions* are the moves that possibly the opponent is likely to execute. Besides, the researchers in the domain of computers have applied this theory to the model interactive computations. Game theory provides a basis for modelling and behaviour analysis of multi-agent systems. Approaches have been developed for equilibrium in games, markets, computational auctions, peer-to-peer systems, security, etc.

15.1 IMPORTANT CONCEPTS OF GAME THEORY

A game may have several facets. Some of the important concepts related to games are set of rules, number of players, plausible strategies for players, state of the game, equilibrium, information about moves of opponent, turn to make move, probabilistic approach, finiteness of turns, etc., which are to be considered while describing a game. In this section, we discuss some of the important concepts related to the game theory such as game classes, game strategies and game equilibriums.

15.1.1 Game Classes

Diversified approach has resulted in several classes of games. Some of the important classes are as follows:

1. *Symmetric game:* In symmetric game, the gains for playing a specific strategy is dependent on the other strategies or the techniques that are in practice. It is independent of the players, thus it is possible to differ the identities without impacting the gains.

2. *Zero-sum game:* In zero-sum game, participant's gain or loss is balanced by losses or gains of other participant(s). If the total gains of all the participants add up to G, and the total losses incurred by all is L, then, $G - L = 0$. Zero-sum can be thought of as a constant sum, where the benefits and losses to all players sum to the same value. It can be thought of as a closed/constant system game with no external source or sink of resources. Contrary to this, in *non-zero-sum game*, the interacting players aggregate gains and losses, which is either less than or more than zero. The non-zero-sum game provides situations in which participants may lose or gain simultaneously. Other situations in the non-zero-sum game arise when the sum of gains G and losses L, of the players are sometimes more or less than what they began with. Thus, in non-zero-sum game we have two possibilities— $G - L < 0$ or $G - L > 0$, where, G is cumulative gain of all the participants and L is cumulative loss of all the participants.

3. *Perfect information game:* A game belongs to perfect information category, if all moves taken till any point of the game by all players are known to all players. Chess, tic-tac-toe and go are the examples of games with perfect information. On the other hand, several card games represent games with imperfect information.

4. *Simultaneous game:* In simultaneous game, the action/move selected by the player is independent of the move of the other players. Thus, the player is unaware and has no information about the other player's moves. A matrix, which is often called *Normal form* is used for the representation of the possible moves and the outcomes. Prisoners' dilemma is a classic example of simultaneous game.

5. *Sequential game:* In sequential game, one player takes the move before other players. The rest of the players get some information of the first player's choice. Extensive form representation can be used for sequential games. Most of the combinatorial games are sequential in nature and are often solved by backward induction.

6. *Repeated game:* This type of game has repetitions of some base game known as *stage game*. Stage game is a well-known two-player game. A player considers the effect of his current move on the future moves of the other players. Since a player plays the game repeatedly with the same player, possibility of retaliation exists, and hence, equilibrium strategy differs from the other popular games.

7. *Signalling game:* There are two players in signalling games—a *transmitter* or often called the *sender* and the *receiver*. In this type of game, incomplete information exists. Often one player is more informed than the other. Let us say that the sender S has to take decisions regarding some sort of signalling. Signalling is nothing, but an action. The receiver is less informed and it has to take decisions based on this, as this signalling could be strategically decided by the sender. The two players earn rewards depending upon the sender's signalling. A very simple example for this type could be the case of used cars, where a dealer could take decision whether some sort of warranty should be given or not.

8. *Large poisson game:* It is a game with a random number of players N, which is a Poisson random variable. The type t_i of each player is selected randomly, independently of other players' types from a given set T. Each player selects an action and then the gains are determined. Voting procedures can be modelled by such games.

9. *Non-transitive game:* It is possible that non-transitivity can arise, where multiple strategies are involved. Non-transitive game arises when the multiple strategies generate loops. For example, if in a non-transitive game, preference for some strategy A over strategy B is given and preference for strategy B over strategy C is also given, then it does not necessarily state that strategy A is preferred over strategy C.

10. *Global game:* This game too falls in the category of games in which complete information is not available. It is based on some sort of probabilities and signalling about the environment. Global games find their applications in the analysis of financial market crisis.

15.1.2 Game Strategies

Move is an action taken by a player at some point during the progress of a game. *Strategy* is a complete approach for playing the game. Generally, the strategy adopted by a player is the entire plan for the move to be executed for the situations. Strategy fully determines the player's behaviour. Some of the important strategies of the game are as follows:

1. *Dominant strategies:* Strategic dominance occurs when one strategy is better than another strategy for one player, irrespective of opponent's game.

2. Pure strategy: This strategy provides a complete approach for a player's game plan. It determines the move a player will make for any situation at any point of the game.

3. Mixed strategy: In mixed strategy, probability is assigned to each pure strategy. This allows for a player to randomly choose pure strategy from a set for a given situation.

4. Tit for tat: Initially, the player is co-operative. If the opponent betrays, then in the next cycle, the player chooses to betray. It is an effective strategy in iterated prisoner's dilemma. A player using this strategy initially co-operates and then responds in kind to the opponent's previous action. If the opponent has been co-operative previously, then the agent is co-operative. If not, the agent is also not co-operative.

5. Collusion: It is illegal and back door agreement between multiple parties (more/equal to two) to impose restriction with regard to the use of rights. It leads to uncertainty about behaviour of colluding entities in the mind of non-colluding entities and may throw surprises for non-colluding entities during the game, for which it may not be prepared.

6. Backward induction: It is a process that constitutes reasoning in a backward direction to identify optimal actions to be executed in the problem.

15.1.3 Game Equilibrium

Game theory attempts to find the state of equilibrium. In equilibrium, each player of the game adopts a strategy, which he is unlikely to change. Equilibrium depends on the field of application, although it may coincide. Several game equilibriums have been proposed to represent the scenario. Some of the important equilibrium concepts mentioned in literature are Nash equilibrium, Sub-game Perfection, Bayesian Nash, Perfect Bayesian, trembling hand, proper equilibrium, correlated equilibrium, sequential equilibrium, Pareto efficiency, self-confirming equilibrium, etc. Here, we discuss the most popular concept of Nash equilibrium.

Nash Equilibrium

Equilibrium is about selection of a stable state. In case of Nash equilibrium, it involves multiple players (two or more) and the following rules:

1. The participants (players) in the game are aware of the equilibrium strategies of the other participants.
2. None of the participant can gain by selecting or changing the strategy unilaterally (that would affect only one player).
3. If a participant has taken up or selected a specific strategy, then none of the other participants can get any gain by means of change in their strategy (where the other participants do not have any change in their strategy).

The situation discussed above with a set of strategy choices and their gains (payoffs) forms the Nash equilibrium.

Let us consider an example that there are two players involved in the game, say X and Y. In Nash equilibrium, X selects a strategy or a decision that is best for him considering what decision Y would be taking. Similarly, Y looks from his perspective to go for the best decision in his terms considering what X's decisions would be.

Let us take another example. Rohan and Mohan are mischievous students. They are caught by the school authorities for doing some pranks. Each of them is brought in front of the Principal separately. The Principal states that they are suspended for 2 days. This is notified to them individually. But then, the Principal feels that they are involved together in another mischief also, where a student's cycle was punctured. He speaks with them individually and tells them that if one of them confesses and the other does not, then he would suspend the one who has confessed for just 1 day, whereas the other one for 5 days. He also mentions that if both of them confess, each would be suspended for 3 days, whereas if both deny, both would be suspended for two days surely. Now, irrespective to what other's decision is, let us look from Rohan's perspective.

1. If confess, when Mohan has also confessed: 3 days of suspension
2. If confess, when Mohan has denied: 1 day of suspension
3. If deny, when Mohan has confessed: 5 days of suspension
4. If deny, when Mohan has denied: 2 days of suspension

He would like to be safe. So, he would go for confess (1 and 2), where in the worst case, he would get 3 days of suspension. The same perspective exists for Mohan. The same can be represented in the form of payoff matrix (normal form), as shown in Figure 15.1 (This matrix is detailed in the further sections).

Mohan

		Confess	Deny
Rohan	Confess	3/3	1/5
	Deny	5/1	2/2

Figure 15.1 Payoff matrix.

Thus, the confession forms Nash equilibrium. (This is the example of prisoner's dilemma that we would be studying in detail later). But do make a note that in Nash equilibrium it does not necessarily mean that the best cumulative payoff or gain is achieved for the players. Hence, it is a set of strategies in which none of the player can simply perform well by unilaterally changing the strategy. With prior knowledge of other strategies, where the others do not change the strategies but one player is able to get benefit by changing his strategy, then it is not Nash equilibrium. So, the set of strategies where the player decides not to go with the other option or perform a switch come under the Nash equilibrium. Hence, the strategy selected comes out to be the best possible response to all other strategies.

There is a concept of *Pareto optimal solutions*. These solutions are the ones in which it is not possible to make a participant, better off without dooming the other participant. An outcome is Pareto optimal, if there is no other outcome that all participants would prefer. An outcome is Pareto dominated by another outcome, say *P*, if all players would prefer the other outcome *P*.

15.2 GAME PLAYING AND KNOWLEDGE STRUCTURE

Capturing any computational problem for efficient processing has always been a challenge across various domains. The field of game playing is not an exception. Structural knowledge is basic to problem solving. It is required for creation of plans and strategies, setting conditions for different procedures, and for determining what to do when failure occurs or when a piece of information is missing. The field of game playing involves high level of planning and needs specific data structures to handle various categories of games. In this section, some of the knowledge structures are covered, with specific emphasis on game theory. Depending on the category of the game, a particular knowledge structure may suit better for a given problem. Now we are aware that any game (a problem is mapped to be a game) comprises participants or a set of players. Along with them, there are different strategies that they would be selecting and the payoffs or the gain they would achieve.

Knowledge structure is capable of capturing different aspects of the game. Some of the important structures depending upon the form of games are discussed in the subsequent sections.

15.2.1 Extensive Form Game

This form of game is used to acquire games in an order and to have the representation in the form of a game tree. The nodes in the tree inform about a decision or a choice from the player's perspective. The branches of the tree specify the strategy or the move for the player, whereas the leaf nodes represent the payoffs. A simple game tree representation is shown in Figure 15.2.

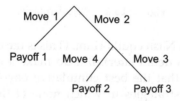

Figure 15.2 A game tree.

Let us assume that there are two players A and B. Player A is to move first. At level 0, we have the root of the game tree and first player has an option of selecting the strategy. In this case, at level 0, player A has strategy set as [Move 1 or Move 2]. Similarly, at level 1, it is B's turn to select a strategy. The leaves can be given payoff weights P_m = [Gain of A: Gain of B] for the *m* leaf node. It represents gain of respective players in case the game ends at the node *m*.

15.2.2 Strategic Form Game

As we have observed in the example of Nash equilibrium, the normal form representation is shown with the help of example of Payoff matrix. This depicts the strategies and the associated gains or the payoffs. The same can be represented in the form of some function that is able to acquire the payoffs and the corresponding strategies. Player A and B may have same or different set of strategies. The moves may be simultaneous, with each player not aware about the move of the other player.

In Figure 15.3, there are two players A and B; one player is represented across rows (say A) and other down the column (say B). Number of rows for player A will be same as the number of strategies for A and the number of columns for player B will be same as the number of strategies for player B. The payoffs are marked as pairs (G_A: Gain of A, G_B: Gain of B). For instance, if player A makes a move 'red' and player B makes a move 'black', then A scores 10 and B scores 20. On the contrary, if B makes a move 'white', then 'A' scores −10 and B scores −20. Often when the game is represented in the normal form, it is assumed that the action selected by any player is independent of the action of the other players. In the sense, the player is unaware about the next action of the other player. Whereas, if the players have knowledge about what choices others are likely to opt, the presentation of the game is in extensive form. It involves sequencing of the actions, all payoffs or gains, information available and so on. More than two players can be captured through multiple dimension representation by extending the above structures.

	Player B chooses black	Player B chooses white
Player A chooses red	G_A, G_B = [10, 20]	−10, −20
Player A chooses green	20, 10	0, 0

Figure 15.3 Payoff matrix.

15.2.3 Co-operative/Coalition Form Game

In a co-operative game, coalitions consisting of players may behave in co-operative manner to achieve the target. Hence, the game is all about having a competition between the coalitions of participants or the players. Coalition partners may agree on any aspect of the game without any restrictions. There is a transferable utility (TU), which allows side payments to be made. TU is passed to a coalition which may be distributed among players as per their agreements, which may differ from coalition to coalition. Side payments may be used as an encouragement for some players to use certain mutually beneficial strategies. There is a characteristic function to determine payoffs to each coalition. In a coalition game with $n \geq 2$ players, labelled from 1 to n, a set of players may be denoted as $P = \{1, 2, 3, ..., n\}$. A coalition C is a subset of P, $C \subset P$ and the set of all coalitions will be 2^P. The set P may be visualised as a grand coalition. Even a null coalition may be allowed for the sake of completeness. For two players, $n = 2$, four coalition, [null, {1}, {2}, {1,2}] are possible. For three players, there are 8 coalitions possible, namely, [null, {1}, {2}, {3}, {1, 2}, {1, 3}, {2, 3}, {1, 2, 3}]. Similarly, for n players, the set of coalitions, 2^P will have 2^n elements. As can be seen from the formation of coalitions, there can be members who may be shared among coalitions. However, ideally, disjoint coalition may be expected.

A coalition for game with n person can be defined as a pair (P, g), where $P = \{1, 2, 3, \ldots, n\}$ is a set of players and g is a real-valued function called *characteristic function* reflecting power of coalition of the game defined for all the coalitions such that

1. $g(\text{null}) = 0$
2. If A and B are disjoint coalitions $(A \cap B = \phi)$, A and B both belonging to 2^P, then $g(A) + g(B) \leq g(A \cup B)$. This is termed as *super additive property of coalitions*.

The function $g(C)$ reflects power of a coalition $C \in 2^P$.

15.3   GAME AS A SEARCH PROBLEM

Any intelligent game results into several possible moves from all the involved players. At any stage of the game, several options are available to a player for making the next move. Optimally correct choice in a state may result in superior gains. For this, a foresight is needed before initiating a move. In game theory, this foresight can be achieved by means of generating search trees, and comparing profit/loss function. The deeper the tree, the more is the foresight and more refined is the result. Unfortunately, a game tree may result into infinite search tree. Therefore, search algorithms have to limit the depth of the tree, and a comprehensive search approach may not be feasible in a reasonable time for the games resulting in infinite moves. Several AI search techniques such as iterative deepening, A*, DFS, secondary search, etc. have been successfully applied to different categories of games. In this section, we discuss the most popular game search technique minimax and subsequently discuss its refinement in the form of alpha-beta approach.

In order to formalise and understand the game theory, let us consider any board game with two players. Various components of the game would be the board itself. The initial state of the board reflects the starting configuration of the board and the players ready to move. It also includes a successor function which provides a list of legal moves corresponding to a state (move, state), a terminal test which finds out if the game has ended in a particular end state, and a payoff function which gives the value to the terminal gains in a state. The game can be represented as a search problem using these components.

15.3.1   Minimax Approach

Minimax is a decision rule that is used in the game theory so as to reduce the possible loss while maximising the potential gain. It can also be thought of as maximising the minimum gain (maximin). The rule was originally developed for two-player zero-sum game theory for two cases—players make simultaneous moves and players make alternate moves.

Each player minimises the maximum gain possible for the other player. Being zero-sum game, a player also maximises his own minimum gain. However, minimax and maximin are not equivalent. Maximin may be used in non-zero-sum game scenarios.

Minimax Theorem

It was given by John von Neumann. For every two-person, zero-sum game with finite strategies, there exist a value V and a mixed strategy for each player such that

1. Given player B's strategy, the best payoff possible for player A is G.
2. Given player A's strategy, the best payoff possible for player B is $-G$.

That is, player A's move assures him gain of G, irrespective of player B's move, and similarly, player B can assure himself a payoff of $-G$.

In two-player combinatorial game theory (CGT), players make alternate moves in a defined way or strategy to achieve a defined winning condition. Game position is known to both the players, and the set of available strategies is also public. Such approach can be applied to the games like chess.

The minimax game tree can be thought of as a game tree with alternatively maximising ply and minimising ply. The root is generally taken as maximising ply with respect to the first player making a move. At a MAX level, the player tries to make a move which will maximise its gain. At the MIN level, the player tries to pass on the minimum return to the opponent.

In Figure 15.4, children of node at level Z are already evaluated. Our aim is to evaluate the maximum gain that can be achieved by player A at node X_1. Node X_1 is a maximising node. Nodes Y_1, Y_2 and Y_3 at Y level are minimising nodes. Being at maximising level, node Z_1 is assigned a value of 5 and $Z_2 = 9$, $Z_3 = 8$. Trying to return a minimum gain to Player A, at Y level, Player B can select a move limiting the gain of Player A to 5. Hence,

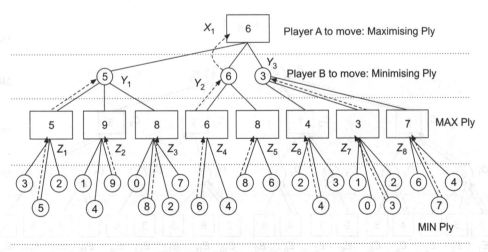

Player A and B to move alternatively,
Minimax tree evaluating value for node X_1 with respect to maximising player A

Figure 15.4 Minimax algorithm node evaluation.

Y_1 evaluates to 5. Similarly, nodes $Y_2 = 6$ and $Y_3 = 3$. Since X_1 is a maximising node, it has an option of selecting option, which will lead it to gain of 6. By increasing the depth of the game tree, more insight can be obtained; however, for infinitely large trees, this is a difficult task because of the complexity of number of plausible moves.

15.3.2   Minimax Algorithm

The regular algorithm of minimax (as presented in the above discussion) requires dealing with minimising and maximising players separately. However, an important property, i.e.,

$$MAX(x, y) = -MIN(-x, -y)$$

can help in achieving the same result with one common evaluation function, thereby reducing the programming effort. The approach results in negmax version of minimax algorithm, which is presented as below:

int minimax(node, depth) // negmax version of minimax algorithm

Step 1: if (leaf node) or (depth<=0) return(node value);
Step 2: Initiate alpha = −∞;
Step 3: for child in node{
        alpha = MAX(alpha, −minimax(child, depth−1))
        }
Step 4: return (alpha);

In Figure 15.5, a game tree is given with leaf nodes evaluated. At node A_1, a maximising player wants to evaluate its optimal gain.

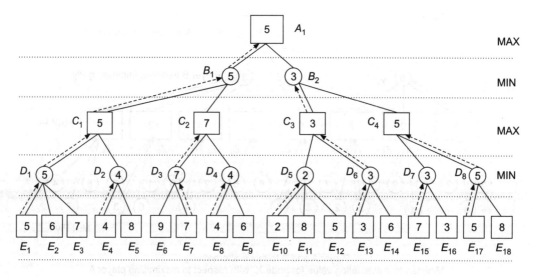

Figure 15.5 Minimax algorithm execution.

EXAMPLE: Trace the game tree to find out the optimal value for the node A_1, using minimax algorithm as given above.

Solution: Partial trace for the game tree is given in Figure 15.6. Readers are advised to traverse the complete tree for evaluating intermediate values also.

AT D_1: Minimising Node, depth = 3	
Step 1	Leaf node = false, depth==0 is false
Step 2	alpha= –15
Step 3	For(child=[E_1, E_2, E_3]){ alpha=MAX(alpha= –15, val(E_1) = –minimax(null,4–1) = –5, val(E_2)= –minimax(null,3) = –6, val(E_3)= –minimax(null,3) = –7)};hence alpha = –5
At Node D_1, we get D_1 = –5	
Similarly, at Node D_2, we get D_2 = –4	
At C_1: Maximising Node, depth = 2	
Step 1	Leaf node = false, depth==0 is false
Step 2	alpha= –15
Step 3	For(child=[D_1, D_2]){alpha=max(alpha=–15, D_1 = –(–5) = +5, D_2 = –(–4) = +4)}; hence, alpha = 5
At node C_1, we get C_1 = 5	
Similarly, at node C_2, we get C_2 = 7	
Similarly, at node B_1, we get B_1 = –5	
Similarly, at node B_2, we get B_2 = –3	
Similarly, at node A_2, we get A_2 = 5	

Figure 15.6 Trace for minimax algorithm with negmax property.

15.4 ALPHA-BETA PRUNING

Minimax approach discussed in earlier section amounts to exhaustive search of solution space. In a realistic game of even modest complexity, the search space can be extremely large. It is possible to heuristically reduce the search space for games having minimax solutions. Alpha-beta pruning algorithm provides mechanism to decrease the number of count of the nodes (thus impacting the search space) in minimax tree. Most common examples of games where this is used are chess and tic-tac-toe. Further, search is stopped once it encounters a branch where at least a single value has been found that confirms that the branch would be worst in comparison to the earlier payoffs. Thus, these actions or moves should be avoided, and hence, can be pruned. Alpha-beta pruning is a perfect optimising technique and is assured to return the same result in spite of pruning. Strength of alpha-beta pruning lies in the fact that it is possible to discard the branches of the search tree without impacting any of the decisions. This results in reduction of the search time and further, it is possible to have a deeper search allowing a greater depth of sub-tree to be scanned. The algorithm comprises two values—alpha and beta. Alpha value holds the minimum (lowest) score that the maximising player is assured of. Beta value holds the maximum score that the minimising player is guaranteed to earn. The initial condition is equal to $-\infty$ and $= +\infty$. As the search progresses, this difference becomes smaller. When beta (β) value becomes lower than alpha (α), it signifies that the search beyond the current node can be restricted.

Algorithm for Alpha-Beta Pruning

The algorithm given here is a recursive algorithm for alpha-beta pruning. Parameters passed to the algorithm are as follows:

1. Player (maximising or minimising player)
2. Position (the node being evaluated)
3. Alpha (value of alpha at the node)
4. Beta (value of beta at the node)

Depending on the nature of player, algorithm returns alpha or beta value (under cut-off situation or otherwise).

alpha_beta(player,position,alpha,beta){

Step I: if(game decided in current board position) return (Winning Player)
Step II: children = all permissible moves for a player from node
Step III: if(Maximizing Player to Play){
          for (each child){
          Step III.1: value = alpha_beta(other player, child, alpha, beta)
          Step III.2   if (value > alpha) alpha = value; // update alpha
          Step III.3   if(alpha >= beta) return (alpha); // ALPHA CUT-OFF FOUND
          }
          Step III.4: return (alpha); //Best move in alpha
          }
Step IV: else (Minimizing Player to Play){
          for (each child){
          Step IV.1: value = alpha_beta(other player, child, alpha,beta)
          Step IV.2: if (value < beta) beta = value; // update beta
          Step IV.3: if(alpha >= beta) return beta; // BETA CUT-OFF FOUND
          }
          Step IV.4: return (beta); //Opponent's best move in alpha
          }
}

Let us consider the game tree, as shown in Figure 15.7. Leaf nodes at level E reflect return values from the respective nodes and are considered to be solved. Shaded nodes are pruned using alpha-beta pruning as presented above. We trace the above algorithm to demonstrate working to achieve α-cut and β-cut.

At minimising Level D, in DFS manner, consider the node D_1. The node has received $[\alpha = -15$ and $\beta = +15]$, as infinity signifying the value of gain and/or loss is within the limit. From Step II, we get $[E_1 = 5, E_2 = 6, E_3 = 7]$. Since D_1 is a minimising level node, we use sequence in Step IV to evaluate it further.

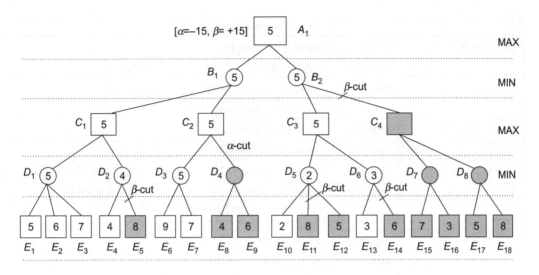

Figure 15.7 Alpha-beta pruning.

$$[\alpha = -15; \beta = +15]$$

From Step IV.1:   value = 5; //as returned by E_1.
      Step IV.2:   (value < beta) is TRUE, hence beta = 5;

$$[\alpha = -15; \beta = +5]$$

Step IV.3:   (alpha >= beta) is FALSE, hence child E_2 to be picked and Step IV continues. Step IV continues with node E_2 as next child of D_1.

Step IV.1: value = 6;

Step IV.2: (value < beta) is FALSE;

Step IV.3: (alpha >= beta) is FALSE, hence child E_3 to be picked and Step IV continues. Step IV continues with node E_3 as next child of D_1.

Step IV.1: value = 7;

Step IV.2: (value < beta) is FALSE;

Step IV.3: (alpha >= beta) is FALSE and next child is empty, hence move to Step IV.4

Step IV.4: return(beta=5)

Note IV.4: The value returned in the above step is the evaluated value at the node D_1 which has picked the minimum value returned by any of its opponent's move in the form of children E_1, E_2 and E_3. Same would have been done by minimax algorithm also as of now.

The trace moves to node C_1 (Figure 15.8) which is a maximising node with children $[D_1 = 5, D_2 = ?]$. Recursion has unwounded and hence, $[\alpha = -15; \beta = +15]$.

At C_1: Maximising Node			
$[\alpha = -15; \beta = +15]$	Step III.1	value = 5 // from D_1	
	Step III.2	value > alpha is TRUE	alpha= 5
$[\alpha = 5; \beta = +15]$	Step III.3	alpha >= beta is FALSE	Continue
At next child D_2: Minimising Node			
$[\alpha = 5; \beta = +15]$	Step IV.1	value = 4 // from E_4	
	Step IV.2	value < beta is TRUE	beta = 4
$[\alpha = 5; \beta = 4]$	Step IV.3	alpha >= beta is TRUE	beta-cut has been found
	Step IV.3	return(beta = 4) as value of D_2	returns to node C_1
At C_1: Maximising Node with $D_2 = 4$ and $[\alpha = 5; \beta = +15]$			
$[\alpha = 5; \beta = +15]$	Step III.1	value = 4 //from D_2	
	Step III.2	value > alpha is FALSE	
	Step III.3	alpha >= beta is FALSE	next child is null
	Step III.4	return(alpha = 5)	Control is transferred to B_1 with $C_1 = 5$, and $[\alpha = -15; \beta = +15]$

Figure 15.8   Trace for alpha-beta pruning.

The trace continues resulting in overall four beta-cuts and one alpha-cut. Readers are suggested to trace the remaining cuts and have a feel of working of the algorithm.

15.5   GAME THEORY PROBLEMS

In the chapter we have gone through various concepts related to gaming theory that have been put to application to create state of the art gaming software in different challenging fields. Most popular gaming programs are chess, backgammon, go, checkers, bridge, poker, tic-tac-toe, and others. Several intelligent and logical scenarios arising in real life have also been addressed using game theory. Some of the important problems are prisoner's dilemma, coordination game, chicken, centipede game, volunteer's dilemma, dollar auction, battle of the sexes, pirate game, dictator game, deadlock, diner's dilemma and Nash bargaining game. Computer programs have been designed to simulate the scenario in effective ways.

15.5.1   Prisoner's Dilemma

This is analogous to what we studied in the Nash equilibrium. In this section, we discuss prisoner's dilemma, which is capable of capturing several concepts related to game theory and thought process. It has a flavour of logical thinking. The problem of classic prisoner's dilemma (PD) is stated as follows:

Scenario

Two suspects, for example, A and B have been arrested by the police. The police is short of any conclusive evidence against them. Hence, it decides to separate both the prisoners. Individually, they are offered same deal by the police. The deal has the following points:

1. Here is a case where the suspects take up different decisions (or options). If one of the suspect, say A defects from the other suspect B where the other (B) does not speak up anything, the one who betrays (A) will be set free whereas the other (B) would get 14-year life imprisonment.
2. It is a behaviour where none of them speak up. Here, if A and B both remain silent, their sentence tenure comes to just 6 months of imprisonment. This is due to lack of evidence.
3. If each of them betrays the other (no common conclusion), each receives a 7-year sentence.

The suspects have following conditions:

1. Each of them has to select one of the two options—to betray the other or not to speak up (to remain silent).
2. Each of them is given assurance that the other suspect will not be provided with the information about the betrayal.

Since they are now prisoners and they are under the dilemma of which option to select, it is known as the *prisoners' dilemma*. So, they have to decide their action.

Since there is no communication between the prisoners (simultaneous game), in its standard form, each player feels safe to defect, thereby tries to maximise his own gain. In the classical scenario, the only possible equilibrium for the game is for all players to defect. No matter what the other player does, one player always gains a greater payoff by playing defect. Since in any situation, playing defect is more beneficial than co-operating, all rational players play defect.

If each player tries only to minimise his imprisonment, then the prisoner's dilemma is said to be a non-zero-sum game, where the players involved may co-operate with each other or defect from (betray) the other player. Although rational choice leads the two players to defect each other, however, the individual reward gets maximised if each player co-operates.

There are various variants for the prisoner's dilemma capturing various facets of the gaming theory. Iterated prisoner's dilemma can be played repeatedly with the same set of prisoners. Hence, the player gets a chance to punish the other player for the prior play that would possibly be non-co-operative. This format may have finite or infinite cycles. Applications of problems can be extended to economics, political science, law and study of human behaviour.

The prisoner's dilemma is shown below in Figure 15.9:

Prisoner A \ Prisoner B	Co-operates with A (Silent)	Defects against A (Betrays)
Co-operates with B (silent)	Each serves 6 months (imprisonment)	Prisoner A: 14 years (imprisonment) Prisoner B: Go free
Defects against B (betrays)	Prisoner A: Go free Prisoner B: 14 years (imprisonment)	Each serves 7 years (imprisonment)

Figure 15.9 Prisoner's dilemma problem.

Irrespective of what the other prisoner chooses, each player always receives a higher payoff (lower sentence) by playing betrayal. Prisoner A is sure about "No matter how prisoner B plays, I will be better by betraying rather than remaining silent". Therefore, to maximise his own reward, player A betrays. However, if the other player acts in the similar fashion, then they both defect and both end up getting 7 years imprisonment, which is lower payoff than they would get by co-operating. Rational self-motivated decisions result in each prisoner being worse than selecting an option that would reduce the other suspect's sentence, though his own sentence is increased. Ironically, if both players co-operate with each other, their term of punishment will be only 6 months, which could be optimal. However, both would tend to prefer betrayal and end up with 7 years of imprisonment. This reflects Pareto domination of betrayal by both the players.

15.5.2 Rock-Paper-Scissors

Rock-paper-scissors is a two-player zero-sum game. Let the two players be A and B. At their turn, players produce, paper, a pair of scissors, or a rock by a gesture of the hand. Rock beats scissors, since it can crush it. Rock can be covered by paper, and hence, it is beaten by paper. Scissor beats paper, as it can cut it. The round is a draw if both A and B choose the same item.

The game can be represented by payoff matrix as given in Figure 15.10.

		Player B		
	Moves	*p*	*s*	*r*
Player A	*p*	0, 0	–1, 1	1, –1
	s	1, –1	0, 0	–1, 1
	r	–1, 1	1, –1	0, 0

Figure 15.10 Payoff matrix for rock-paper-scissors.

From the payoff matrix, it is evident that if the game is played in sequential (Rock-paper-scissors is a simultaneous game, but it is not played simultaneously) form with second player knowing the choice of the first, it is the first player who will always loose. If player A chooses Paper *p*, B will respond with scissors *s*, inflicting a loss of –1 to player A. Similarly, on choice of scissors *s* by player A, player B will choose rock *r*, to inflict a loss of –1 to player A. Similarly, on choice of rock *r* by player A, player B will choose paper *p* to inflict a loss of –1 to player A. However, the game is played in simultaneous format, where on occurrence of certain event (such as countdown), each player brings the hand hidden in the back with any one gesture of the rock paper or scissors. This infuses randomness in the game, making it probabilistic. Usually, the game is played for several cycles. A player may choose a fixed strategy or a probabilistic strategy. When the same set of players play the game, then over a period of time, they tend to know the behaviour of each other. Though each move is independent, their decision may be influenced by the earlier occurrences. After several cycles of game, each player tends to learn about the behaviour of the opponent, and hence, previous moves may affect the decisions of each party.

15.5.3 Some Popular Computer Games

Game theory has been used in several computer programs to achieve a level of strategy execution comparable to that of human beings. Computer programs have been developed to play games such as backgammon, chess, draughts, bridge, scrabble, etc. It may be noted that such capability may reflect power of machine and software in defeating a human being, but in no way, it can be termed as evidence of machine intelligence, though it encompasses decision-making of very high order. Success in Turing tests would be more appropriate when it comes to the comparison of machine intelligence.

Chess

A chess playing computer program Deep Blue developed by IBM generated ripples across the world in 1997, when it defeated the then chess world grandmaster champion, Garry Kasparov. It was seen as a major achievement by any computing system in the field of artificial intelligence. Deep Blue carried out a parallel search of a chess tree. The machine has a capability of performing evaluation at the rate of nearly 200 million moves per second. Deep Blue uses α–β search with further heuristics such as singular extensions which further reduces the search space. Deep Blue was fine tuned to match with grandmaster's games.

Draughts/Checkers

The game of draughts/checkers has been automated to such an extent that it is difficult to beat the machine. Chinook was developed in 1989 by a team comprising Rob Lake, Paul Lu, Martin Bryant, and Norman Treloar led by Jonathan Schaeffer. Around 2007, it was announced that the program has mastered the game to perfection and cannot lose a game of checkers. The program uses a library of opening moves from games played by checker's grandmasters, a deep search algorithm, a move evaluation function, and terminal game database for all positions with eight or less pieces.

Go

The game is played between two players, who alternately place black and white pieces in an empty cell on a grid. The size of grid may vary. Once placed on the board, pieces cannot be moved elsewhere, unless they are surrounded and captured by the opponent's pieces. Go represents a zero-sum, perfect information, partisan, deterministic strategy game. Computer programs have been developed successfully for small board size. For large board size, the complexity becomes high and results in prohibitive search space.

SUMMARY
Aspects of game theory have introduced possibility of intelligence, planning and decision-making in machine. Various concepts have been used to enable computers play games, which were otherwise thought to be possible only by entity with intelligence level comparable to human beings. Using the concepts of game theory, several problems in real life can be visualised or solved.

Depending on the nature of game, it may fall in one or more categories such as symmetric game, zero-sum game, perfect information game, simultaneous game, sequential game, repeated game, signalling game, large poisson game, non-transitive game, global games, etc.

Players or teams in a game may have several game strategies. Some of the popular game playing strategies are dominant strategies, pure strategy, mixed strategy, tit for tat, collusion, backward induction, etc.

Strategy adopted by a participant may attain the level of stabilisation. Depending upon the state of strategies used by a player or team, a level of equilibrium may be attained. Based upon the nature of game and player strategies, several game equilibriums have been proposed—Nash equilibrium, Sub-game Perfection, Bayesian Nash, Perfect Bayesian, trembling hand, proper equilibrium, correlated equilibrium, sequential equilibrium, Pareto efficiency, self-confirming equilibrium, etc.

Games can be mapped as a move search problem to optimise the gain with respect to a team or player. Minimax approach is one popular approach to find such solution. In any reasonable gaming problem, the dimensionality of search space can rise exponentially. Alpha-beta pruning helps in reducing the search space.

 **KEYWORDS**

1. **Alpha-beta pruning:**   This returns same optimal value as returned by the minimax, but is efficient in termination because it reduces the search space.

2. **Game:**   In a game, multiple (two or more) players or teams or adversaries or agents participate with the conflicting goals, leading to search and optimisation problems taking into consideration various participating entities. The aim of search is to find a move with respect to a participant in order to optimise its gain.

3. **Game components:**   A game consists of initial state (which gives initial board position), permissible moves (a set of rules in a given state), states (reflecting progress of game at any instant), evaluation function [which gives list of pairs containing (moves, state) from any state], terminal condition (reflecting end of game with payoff awards such as won, lost or drawn or any other value).

4. **Game equilibrium:**   It is a state of game when participants stick to their strategies for optimal results.

5. **Game theory:**   It is a branch of Mathematics highly influenced by economist, which deals with strategies of finding optimal moves for the participants.

6. **Game tree:**   A data structure to capture opponents is the game tree. It gets alternate player at the next level.

7. **Imperfect information games:**   These are the games in which adversaries may not be aware of the moves made by opponents such as card games.

8. **Minimax algorithm:**   It deals with finding optimal value for gain of loss of the player at root (which is mostly the maximising player's ply).

9. **Nash equilibrium:** It is a strategic profile in which no player has an incentive to deviate from the specified strategy.

10. **Payoff matrix:** This matrix captures reward to each player for each combination of actions by all the players. Players may or may not have different sets of legal moves.

11. **Perfect information games:** These are the games in which adversaries are aware of the moves made till the current state by each players at any instant such as chess.

12. **Zero-sum game:** In this game, a participant's gain or loss is balanced by losses or gains of the other participant(s).

MULTIPLE CHOICE QUESTIONS

1. Alpha-beta search essentially performs
   (a) Reduction in the number of moves
   (b) Reduction in the MAX-MIN values for the nodes
   (c) Reduction in the gains for the opponent
   (d) None of the above

2. Consider the payoff matrix given in below for two employees to get increment in salary with regard to a proposal submission. For a simultaneous game, a single move Nash equilibrium would be

Employee 1		Employee 2	
		Submit proposal	Don't submit
	Submit proposal	50, 50	70, 10
	Don't submit	10, 70	90, 90

   (a) Both the employees submit the proposal
   (b) Employee 1 submits the proposal, employee; 2 does not
   (c) Employee 2 submits the proposal, employee; 1 does not
   (d) None of them submit the proposal

3. Which of the following constitutes the game playing model?
   (a) Equilibrium   (b) Payoffs
   (c) Strategies   (d) None of these

4. Consider the payoff matrix given below. It belongs to the category of

Player 1		Player 2	
		Accept	Decline
	Accept	50, –50	–50, 50
	Decline	–50, 50	50, –50

(a) Pure strategy

(b) Nash equilibrium

(c) Mixed strategy

(d) None of these

5. A dominant strategy is the one in which
   (a) Best payoffs are yielded, irrespective to the strategy of other players
   (b) Multiple actions are randomised to select the best one
   (c) The player deviates from his strategy to gain maximum rewards
   (d) All of the above

CONCEPT REVIEW QUESTIONS

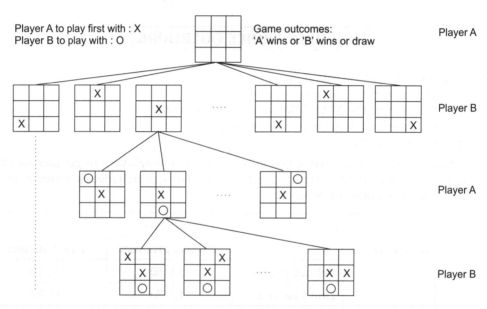

Player A to play first with : X
Player B to play with : O

Game outcomes:
'A' wins or 'B' wins or draw

Player A

Player B

Player A

Player B

Figure 15.11   Partial game tree for tic-tac-toe.

1. With reference to the game tree given in Figure 15.11 for tic-tac-toe (assuming reader is aware of the game rules), answer the following:
   (a) What is the maximum number of chances first player A may get before game terminates?
   (b) What is the maximum number of chances player B may get before game terminates?
   (c) What could be the maximum depth of the above game tree?
   (d) What is the minimum length of a branch when a game may terminate?
   (e) What are number of possible moves for player A at the first ply?
   (f) What are number of possible moves for player B at its first chance?
   (g) Reward +1 for A's win, –1 for B's win and 0 for draw. Draw complete game tree from 3rd ply by selecting any node.
   (h) Can you suggest an evaluation function for the non-terminal states?

2. Refer to Figure 15.7 some pruning values are given. Trace the alpha-beta algorithm for the respective values in the game tree.

3. Using Figure 15.4, replace the values for terminal nodes as shown below:

	E_1	E_2	E_3	E_4	E_5	E_6	E_7	E_8	E_9	E_{10}	E_{11}	E_{12}	E_{13}	E_{14}	E_{15}	E_{16}	E_{17}	E_{18}
(i)	–2	4	3	7	–10	8	6	0	–5	4	3	–11	12	14	–5	6	9	10
(ii)	12	18	5	3	–3	8	0	5	–5	10	0	0	–1	12	13	11	12	16

Two sets of randomly selected data sets are given for terminal nodes. While retaining the structure as given in Figure 15.4, work out optimal value for the player A for both the data sets using
(a) Minimax algorithm
(b) Alpha-beta pruning

CRITICAL THINKING EXERCISE

1. In case, there are more than two players (say three-player games), with each player taking its chance in a cycle. Draw a game tree for three-player game, with each player trying to maximise his own gain and putting the other two at maximum possible loss. Work out a minimax approach for such a game tree.

2. Two countries A and B have powerful army, navy and airforce. Country B is having missile shield with 30% success rate, but A does not have any missile shield. Both countries have missiles. You are planning the game for country A. As player A decides whether to attack your opponent B by land, sea or air, so B must simultaneously (ignorant of A's move) decide whether to launch an all-out air defence, an all-out sea defence or a combined air and sea defence or a land attack. If there is no defence from B for your nature of attack, you win 1000 carrots. If your attack is met by an air and coastal defence, you win only 500 carrots. If your attack is met with an attack on your land, you lose 100 carrots. If your attack is met by an all-out defence, you lose 200 carrots. Decide the nature of attack to be launched.

PROJECT WORK

1. Write a computer program to play tic-tac-toe game.
2. Implement move generators and evaluation functions for any of the following games:
   (a) Chess
   (b) Checkers
   (c) Othello

CHAPTER 16

Perception and Action

Learning Objectives

❑ To understand the concept of perception
❑ To study the techniques involved in perception with its relevance to action
❑ To study image formation from the viewpoint of vision
❑ To understand the importance of image processing and gain knowledge about the various image processing techniques
❑ To appreciate the role of perception in action and its application in robotics

INTRODUCTION

What is perception? The most common definition is the ability to identify, interpret or be aware of something, through senses, to understand the environment. We, as humans, perceive through what we see and what we hear. It can be also through smell, taste or even touch. So, we recognise and identify from what we see, or what we hear. The way we act most often depends on these two aspects. In the entire process, knowledge building takes place and it is the result of what is being observed or rather perceived.

We highlight some aspects of agent scenario in this perception. The agent's actions are dependent on what is being perceived from the environment. But when we talk about the robots, the actual action needs to be carried out in real time. There are a lot of activities involved after the perception has occurred and prior to the action that need to be completed by the robots. Overall, it is the perception and action that go hand in hand for the agent to operate. Now, let us start with perception.

Where do you think perception and action find their importance? Many groups with focus on research related to robotics and perception are formed. For example, a project called *drone project* is being developed. In case, when natural calamity occurs, a camera mounted device (robot) is able to identify the victims and locate them despite all the obstacles that exist after the calamity has taken place. This will assist in the rescue operation for the victims. A lot of AI tasks are involved in the back-end for this identification and execution.

We begin with the concept of vision in this chapter. More or less in the perception, it is the vision that is discussed. Some part of it (i.e., object recognition and speech recognition) has been detailed in Chapter 15. In this chapter, we focus on the image formation and the processing techniques with the 3D representations as well.

16.1   MACHINE VISION

Computer vision deals with getting the knowledge or analysing from what is being sensed visually. From the images, the required or the essential information needs to be made available. How is this information extracted? The answer is by processing it. The environment has objects in 3 D form, but the image is in 2 D form. Despite the loss that occurs in this 3 D to 2 D conversion, it is the task of machine vision to have image formation, processing, segmentation, pattern matching and other tasks to understand the useful information. The steps are briefed below in Figure 16.1.

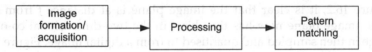

Figure 16.1   Steps of image vision.

Is it possible for the machines to understand and correlate or analyse the images as we can? Naturally, no. Which problems could arise? Basically, we, as humans, have an ability to learn in incremental fashion and our knowledge is evolved based on the previous experiences. Thus, for the perception, it has to be active. By active, we mean the learning should occur based on the response. Moving ahead, another issue is having cognitive model like humans in machine. Other point of comparison between human perception and machine is the computation aspect. Is it possible to have the same level of computation and response as in humans? But what will you say about illusions that we have? There could be some ambiguity when we perceive something. Can this happen with machines? Let us try to find out the answers, as we study it in detail. We begin with the image formation process.

16.2   IMAGE FORMATION

What is an image? An *image* is made up of pixels. It can be viewed as a grid that has light spots of varying intensities that form the pixel. But before that, let us understand the process of how this actually happens where any object/scene is captured with a camera. How is an image formed? Some scene/object from the environment is sensed. The scene is in 3 D form. The image formed is in 2 D form. The camera captures the scene to make the image. (The number of pixels perceived by a camera is much smaller than to what we perceive.) Figure 16.2 shows the image projection onto the image plane.

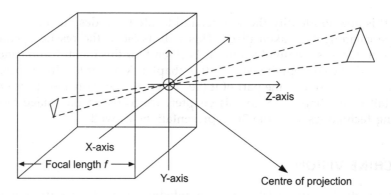

Figure 16.2 Image projection.

While forming an image with the camera, many parameters are to be accounted from the camera's perspective. These are the type of camera or to be more specific the lens and its capacity (zoom), its positioning, light reflections, and illumination. Not only these parameters, but also the depth and the surfaces of the scene/object impact the discontinuity of the image.

From Figure 16.2, it is clear that the image plane is at distance f from the centre of projection. The image plane now has the object in the two-dimensional co-ordinates. The captured image in then sampled and quantised to from a digital image. Figure 16.3(a) shows a sample image and its digital image is shown in Figure 16.3(b). The image resolution is determined by sampling, whereas it is the quantisation that tells about the intensities of the pixels. The sampling rates and the quantisation rates may affect the image formation process. Thus, the image is a grid of pixels. The *pixel* is defined as (x, y), where x is the row and y is the column. The pixel values are generally between 0–255.

Thus, image formation process is a process where a scene/object is captured by some means (image acquisition devices like cameras and scanners), which is projected onto an image plane and further digitised.

16.3 IMAGE PROCESSING

Image processing is processing the image to get something out of it. It is a transformation process that converts the image into some other form of image or extracts some attributes or information. (Though we can say that conversion of the image to digital one is also a transformation, we go into other details here after the digital image is available.) So, what sort of transformations are to be done and for what? The processing is required to identify the objects, regions from it. In the processing of the image, many operations are carried out on input image, viz., thresholding or segmentation, smoothing, image enhancement, intensity transformations, edge detection, compression and so on. These techniques assist in the task of image processing and analysis. Let us have a look at a few of these techniques.

(a)

205	195	196	186	179	177	170	163	165	162	160	160	169	162	155
204	199	197	192	178	175	175	161	162	162	164	165	165	167	156
163	201	195	194	183	173	176	165	162	163	162	172	167	163	157
117	183	196	201	189	176	174	171	163	163	158	166	176	168	164
106	127	165	189	193	180	173	171	168	168	163	163	178	177	176
109	106	106	137	192	184	179	173	166	170	167	151	148	166	156
109	108	105	114	182	184	177	181	168	173	151	106	101	105	98
108	107	102	104	137	177	177	180	168	138	108	103	101	97	91
106	107	97	103	104	115	130	123	108	100	103	101	97	96	91
108	105	97	105	107	100	99	95	97	100	101	99	94	94	91
105	99	95	103	105	100	99	97	94	99	103	99	92	89	89
104	100	93	103	106	96	97	96	93	99	101	98	93	87	85
104	100	94	105	106	97	95	93	94	101	102	97	92	85	81
103	98	95	108	104	96	93	91	96	100	99	96	91	84	80

(b)

Figure 16.3   (a) Sample image and (b) Snapshot: Digital image (a part of the image is shown).

16.3.1 Thresholding

When an image is partitioned into some groups or regions, it is called *segmentation*. These groups usually refer to objects of interest and may differ with the applications. *Thresholding* is one of the methods of segmentation to extract specific object or entity from input image. The terms *thresholding* and *segmentation* are most often used interchangeably. Mathematically, it can be represented as follows:

Let $I[x, y]$ be the image. This is to be partitioned into different regions or groups of pixels, say G_1 to G_n, where for all p_1 to p_m (the pixels in the group, say G_i) have some property that is common. (Though the adjacent regions might not satisfy this clause). These common properties of the grouped pixels may most popularly include similar intensity, texture, neighbourhood and many others.

Thresholding is used when an object, within an image has homogeneous intensity, and the intensities at the background are different than that of the object. Hence, it becomes simple to apply thresholding. An appropriate value of threshold enables the separation of desired object from the undesired background. (However, this may not be the case always. Literature reports application where background is of interest). Thus, it is the processing of threshold converting a grayscale image into a binary one.

There can be fixed threshold T or adaptive. A simple single value thresholding is given below:

$$I_T[x, y] = \begin{cases} 1 & \text{if } I[x, y] \leq T \\ 0 & \text{if } I[x, y] > T \end{cases} \tag{16.1}$$

Further, if the range of intensities is available, it can be mapped as

$$I_T[x, y] = \begin{cases} 1 & \text{if } T_2 \geq I[x, y] \geq T_1 \\ 0 & \text{else} \end{cases} \tag{16.2}$$

What is the criteria to decide value of threshold? Some algorithms consider T as the average of gray levels in an image and is considered to be initial value of threshold. The literature reports numerous algorithms to calculate the value of threshold. Histogram of image is also used to calculate the value of threshold. Figures 16.4(a), (b) and (c) show the impact on image with different values of threshold. [Figures 16.4(b) and (c) depict results of inappropriate value selection of threshold].

The histogram gives good information regarding the intensity distribution, and hence, is useful for determining T. There are other methods too like clustering-based thresholding or even entropy-based approaches. The discussion is restricted to histogram-based approach.

The approach is self-explanatory from Figure 16.5(a), which is a sample image. The values in the matrix are intensities of pixels in image 16.5(b) showing histogram. Histogram is a plot of total number of pixels having a specific gray intensity in an image. It, therefore, depicts the distribution of gray levels. As clearly seen in Figure 16.5(b), the image has two regions. One region whose gray level varies from 1 to 3 and another region with intensity value of 6 and 7. A threshold value of 4 or 5 helps in separating two regions of image.

So, we have discussed all about using single-valued threshold. At times, application demands *local thresholding*, where different thresholds for sub-images are used. So, image I, is split into I_1 to I_m, where I_x has its own threshold T_x. Thus, each image or the sub-region has its own thresholding at work.

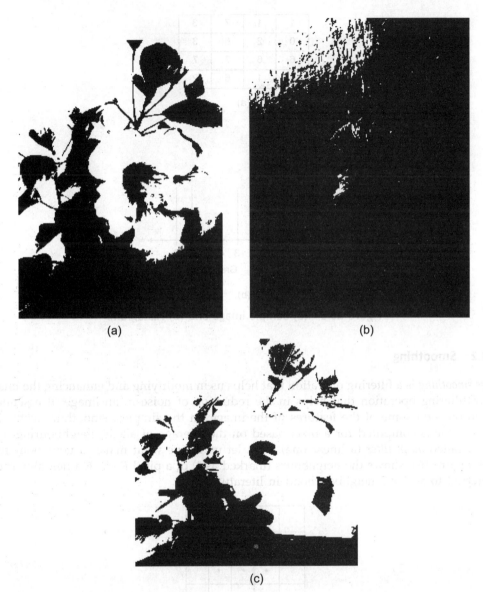

Figure 16.4 (a) Thresholding; (b) Over thresholding (high threshold value) and (c) Thresholding (low threshold value).

In case of *adaptive thresholding,* a different value is computed for each pixel in the image. A lot of techniques for having the adaptive thresholding have been proposed, one of them is *Wellner's adaptive thresholding* (1993) in which every pixel is compared to its surrounding pixels. The only problem is that this approach is based on the scanning order for the pixels of the image. Extension to the methods, where thresholding is applied to a window of pixels has also been proposed such that the illumination effect that hampers the thresholding is taken care of.

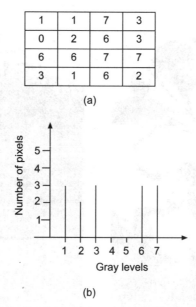

(a)

(b)

Figure 16.5 (a) Sample image and (b) Histogram.

16.3.2 Smoothing

Image smoothing is a filtering operation that helps us in modifying and enhancing the image. It is a filtering operation that helps in the reduction of noise in an image. It essentially concentrates on some of the features of the image. In the simplest smoothing technique, a new value is computed for a pixel based on the average of all the neighbouring ones. This is called *mean filter* (a linear one). First let us define what makes a neighbour for a pixel. Figure 16.6 shows the neighbours (marked as *) of a pixel *P*. Such a neighbourhood is referred to as 3×3 neighbourhood in literature.

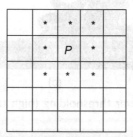

Figure 16.6 Neighbours of a pixel *P*.

So, as said earlier, new values for a pixel *P* are computed. Averaging operation includes calculation of average value of all the intensities in the highlighted 3×3 matrix. The new average value is assigned to pixel *P*. The procedure is repeated for all pixels in image. Figure 16.6 that tells about the neighbours, is actually a matrix of 3×3. This is also called *filter* or *mask*. It is an image enhancement technique, where we can say that the new brightness values are computed. It is also called *low frequency filtering technique*. Remember these filters are used with convolution. They are also called *kernels*.

Another approach to smoothing is a *median filter*, where a pixel is changed by computing the median of the neighbourhood pixels. So, among the window of 9 pixels, the value for the centre one, say X is computed by sorting the pixels in ascending or descending manner and selecting the middle value as the new one for X. This filter is non-linear. Median filter is very effective in reduction of salt and pepper noise in image.

Gaussian Smoothing

As other linear filters work, this filter too results in smoothing and removal of the noise. The difference here is in the filter values that are used or in the coefficient of mask. We are familiar with the one-dimensional Gaussian function. In two-dimensional form, it is given as

$$G(x, y) = \frac{1}{2\pi\sigma^2} \, e^{-\frac{(x^2+y^2)}{2\sigma^2}}$$

where σ is the standard deviation and x, y are pixel. With this filter, the new value for a pixel is the weighted average of the neighbourhood pixels, where more weight is given to the centre ones. Further, since they own the symmetric property, uniform smoothing occurs. How much impact do you think will the smoothing have with the value of σ? It should be noted that a high value of σ yields more smoothing. Figure 16.7 shows a smoothed image with Gaussian. So, we perform convolution with the Gaussian.

Figure 16.7 Smoothed image.

To summarise, smoothing operation effectively performs noise reduction. The filters can be square or rectangular-shaped and can be linear or non-linear. Just a point of difference is that in case of non-linear filters, they do not use weighted sum of the pixels.

16.3.3 Edge Detection

Edge is defined as a boundary where either intensity or other property of pixel changes significantly. Edge detection is very important operation in many applications like image understanding, object detection and object recognition. In *edge detection*, a line drawing is generated. It is also an approach for segmentation. For an image, the boundaries are detected for the objects present in it. This detection is based on the change in the intensity of the pixel value. Had it been the case of 1-D, the edge would have been the peak in the first derivative. In other words, derivation of a function signifies the change in quantity. In edge detection, it is used to understand change in intensity. Figure 16.8 shows a signal and its first order derivative.

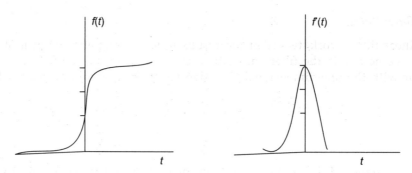

Figure 16.8   Derivative (First order).

Different methods that exist for the edge detection techniques are classified mainly into gradient-based and Laplacian-based methods. In Figure 16.8, the derivative is the gradient of the signal.

We know that identifying the change in the brightness value results in detecting the edges. Thus, we look at the locations in the image, where the magnitude of the derivative is large. To detect the edges, the image should be noise-free. The first step in this is smoothing followed by identification of the edges. Now, is it not possible to have the edges detected and smoothed in one go, i.e., simultaneously? A simple solution to this can be smoothing plus convolution with the derivative.

A simple algorithm for the same is given below:

1. Convolution of the image with the derivative.
2. Applying thresholding for the edge selection (values above the threshold considered). This eliminates the peaks that would arise.

Gradient Method

The gradient method looks at the Max or Min in the derivative and detects the edges. The vector is defined as

$$G[(f(x, y)] = \left(\frac{\partial f}{\partial x}, \frac{df}{dy}\right) \tag{16.3}$$

where, x and y are pixels.

This vector tells about the direction of increase in the intensity, whereas the magnitude tells the rate of increase in the intensity.

$$\text{Mag} = \sqrt{\left(\frac{\partial f}{\partial x}\right)^2 + \left(\frac{\partial f}{\partial y}\right)^2} \tag{16.4}$$

Equation (16.4) shows the magnitude. Since, here we deal with the digitised images, a simple gradient that is approximated is given as

$$G_x \approx f[i, j + 1] - f[i, j] \qquad (16.5)$$

$$G_y \approx f[i, j] - f[i + 1, j] \qquad (16.6)$$

The direction of the gradient is given as

$$\tan^{-1} \frac{G_y}{G_x} \qquad (16.7)$$

One point to mention over here is that the magnitude of the gradient does not depend on the edge detection.

Most often, edge detection techniques have the following steps:

1. A filtering step that helps in the reduction of the noise
2. Enhancement step (use of gradient magnitude)
3. Detection step to determine the exact points where an edge exists (Thresholding is used here)
4. Localisation (optional step) that determines the exact location of the edge

Let us discuss the operators in the detection.

Sobel Operator

The Sobel operator uses a 3*3 convolution mask or 3*3 neighbourhood (remember the smoothing). These are convolved with the input image. It determines the approximate gradient magnitude. When we say that it makes use of 3*3 mask, it has to be in pair, where one gives an estimate for the gradient in x direction and other in y. The convolution masks along with the input image are convolved to get separate gradients and later on, combined to get the absolute magnitude. The masks are given in Figure 16.9.

Figure 16.9 Convolution masks for x and y gradients.

How does it work? The mask is actually slid across the image to get the output horizontally working row-wise. Sobel operator is the simplest method for edge detection. Smoothing is inbuilt here and it possesses the property of better noise reduction. What could be the possible drawbacks? Simple techniques often lead to less efficient approaches and Sobel operator is one of them. Can the mask be placed for the uppermost left pixel? Methods of zero padding and pixel replication are used to deal with the convolution operators of the pixels on the boundary of matrix.

Prewitt Operator

A Prewitt operator is similar to Sobel; the only difference is in the masks. The masks here are shown in Figure 16.10.

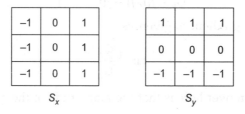

$$S_x \qquad\qquad\qquad S_y$$

Figure 16.10   Prewitt masks.

The gradient methods use smoothing and thresholding to detect the edges. Hence, the ones satisfying the threshold are detected to be the edges. One of the major problem that is encountered here is that the thick edges are identified. Figure 16.11 shows the edge detection with Sobel and Prewitt operators.

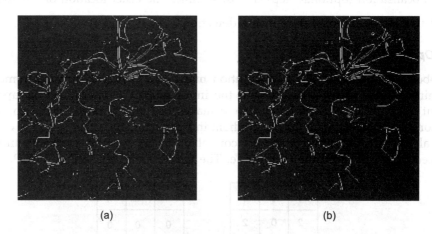

(a)   (b)

Figure 16.11   Edge detection: (a) Sobel operator and (b) Prewitt operator.

Laplacian Method

Laplacian operator: The Laplacian method makes use of second order derivative. As it can be seen from Figure 16.12, there exists a zero crossing due to the sudden intensity change. The Laplacian of function *f* is given below:

$$\nabla^2 f = \frac{\partial^2 f}{\partial x^2} + \frac{\partial^2 f}{\partial y^2} \tag{16.8}$$

The mask that is used is shown in Figure 16.13, and is equal to ∇^2.

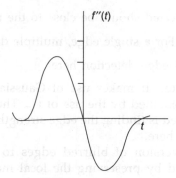

Figure 16.12 Zero crossing in second order derivative.

0	1	0
1	– 4	1
0	1	0

Figure 16.13 Standard mask for Laplacian.

Laplacian of Gaussian (LoG): One of the major drawbacks of using the second order derivative is that it is very much sensitive to the noise. Hence, it is essential that noise is removed. To have this, following steps are performed:

1. The input image needs to be smoothed with a Gaussian
2. Apply the Laplacian
3. Detect the zero crossings

When Gaussian is performed with smoothing, noise reduction occurs. In the next step, Laplacian is used. Detection of inadequate edges is handled by putting up a threshold on the first derivation. Hence, it considers the edges where zero crossing exists for this setup condition. The outputs for this are then computed as

$$h(x, y) = \nabla^2[g(x, y) * f(x, y)] \tag{16.9}$$

where
$$\nabla^2 g(x, y) = \left(\frac{x^2 + y^2 - 2\sigma^2}{\sigma^4} \right) e^{-\frac{(x^2 + y^2)}{2\sigma^2}} \tag{16.10}$$

It is also known as *Mexican hat operator*.

Here, x, y represent pixel and σ is standard deviation.

Canny edge detector: It is one of the most widely used edge detection technique. It was introduced by Canny in 1986, to have an optimal edge detection approach. The main three objectives of this detector are mentioned below:

1. *Low error rate:* If an edge exists in the image, then the detector has to detect it and if the edge does not exist, it should not detect it.

2. *Localisation:* The edges detected should be close to the real ones.

3. *Single response to an edge:* For a single edge, multiple detections should not occur.

Let us discuss the steps of edge detection here.

1. The first step is to filter. It makes use of Gaussian filter. So, for image I, the smoothed image I_f is obtained by the use of G_σ. Thus, $I_f = G_\sigma \otimes I$.

2. The second step involved is finding the edge strength by the gradient. Use of Sobel operator is considered here.

3. The next step is conversion of blurred edges to sharp ones in the gradient image. This is achieved by preserving the local maxima and discarding others. Thus, *non-maxima suppression* is performed. Here, broad ridges of gradient magnitude are thinned. This is performed by suppressing the values that are not peak along the direction of gradient.

4. Making use of thresholding is the last step. We are very well familiar that the value selection impacts the detection process. Dual thresholding is applied in this case. Two thresholds (high and low) are used for edge detection, where the edges with value greater than threshold are marked as strong. Edges below low threshold are discarded. Further, edges in between are kept if they are connected to the strong ones. This is also called *hysteresis thresholding*.

Figure 16.14 shows the Canny edge detection. What would be the performance of Canny detection? It is dependent on σ and the threshold values selected. Moreover, it is costly when compared to the other approaches. It must also be noted that the coefficients of the mask add to zero. This is of utmost importance. With the coefficients adding to zero, the filtering operation will have zero output when the intensity of all pixels in mask is same.

Figure 16.14 Canny edge detection.

16.4 ROBOTICS

We have discussed about intelligent agents already. Now, we move towards how a hardware robot operates in the environment. The operating concept here is analogous to that of intelligent agent. It needs to perceive and act; so, naturally it needs sensors and actuators. What sort of sensors would be required? A few of them are listed below:

1. **Cameras:** It senses the environment and captures the scene.

2. **Sonar sensors:** These are also sometimes referred to as *sonic sensors* and are based on sound waves transmission. The transmitted wave gets reflected back. This helps in the identification of the obstacles in the movement. These sensors are also called *ranging sensors*.

3. **Infrared light-based sensors:** These sensors make use of light pulse that is projected and reflected back again. Based on this reflection, the obstacles are detected. So, these things are essentially the part of the robots.

Now, let us turn towards the actuators. *Actuators* are the mechanisms to carry out the action. So, they include electromechanical devices that help them in the movements. Some of the examples are stepper motor, AC servo motors, synchronous motors and so on. Do not confuse between an effector and an actuator. *Effector* in a robot is the one that actually affects and acts on the environment. This includes wheels, legs, arms, fingers, etc. of the robot. Effector works on the mechanism of actuator.

One more concept to be introduced here is the *degree of freedom*. This talks about the motion space, i.e., the directions in which the effectors move and the actuators work. An actuator often controls a single degree of freedom, that is, a single motion. For simple application, robot needs x, y and z directions. In enhanced application, there can be other movements like pitch movement (up-down movement), yaw movement (side-to-side movement) and roll movement (rotation). Do remember this degree of movement adds complexities to the design of the robot, and thus, decides the configuration of the robot.

Other important aspect of the entire movement of a robot is the controller. A *controller* controls the entire operating environment by means of intelligence. The sensors pass the information to the controller. The controller processes it and commands the actuators to execute the actions.

In addition, there can be computation hardware and storage associated with the overall working of the robot. Figure 16.15 shows the basic components of a robot.

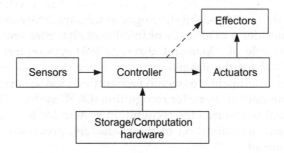

Figure 16.15 Components of a robot.

16.5 MANIPULATION AND NAVIGATION WITH PERCEPTION AND ACTION

After having a detailed study of the image-related tasks, we now turn to the robotics with the action and perception. In this topic, rather than going in a traditional way, we discuss the current trends and the work undertaken in robotics with the perceived world. We are versed with the fact that based on what is perceived, an action is taken. What do we mean by manipulation and navigation then? *Navigation* is the movement done to carry out some task. *Manipulation* is carrying out the task. From the perspective of robotics, it can be thought of 'lift something' and 'put'. Now, for this manipulation and navigation, a robot needs to perceive. The perception enables it to recognise the possible obstacles in reaching the goal and then further to perform the task. Let us discuss a few research contributions to this area.

At the beginning, let us take an example of household robots. What will happen if the robot enters in an unknown environment? If the unknown environment is similar to the one it has perceived earlier, its perception will be adaptive, and probably, it will act in an appropriate manner. A recent published work in this area has come up with a robot that can perceive the environment and open the doors in unseen environment. The idea behind this work is to enable the robot to navigate in an unknown environment, where it is not previously trained on the doors that exist in this environment. The approach obviously needs to have some perception about the objects. The approach comprises two things—perception of the object and inferring regarding its manipulation. But do remember that this perception is based on the characteristics of how well the captured image is. Definitely, the light conditions at that time too will have a deep impact on it.

Despite the advancements in this area and with simultaneous localisation and mapping (SLAM) technique that builds a map in unknown environment along with maintaining the track of current place, it is still required that the robots exhibit human-like performance and show dexterity. A survey on perception guided navigation and manipulation has recognised that this will be the next thing for robotics. Since the environment is cluttered, the perception and manipulation lag far behind, and on the top of it, it needs high level of intelligence. The current trend is towards building active systems of perception to have human-like behaviour.

16.6 INTELLIGENT CHARACTER RECOGNITION

With the detailed study of vision, object recognition, image analysis along with the action execution, we now consider a case study of intelligent character recognition (ICR) system. Let us understand the role of vision in the recognition system and which AI techniques can be proved beneficial for the usage.

An ICR involves intelligent character recognition and is often considered as the advanced version of an optical character recognition (OCR) system. The major contribution of the system at present is towards the recognition system for forms. So, it performs form processing that involves identification of the characters, processing them and compiling them into resultant output.

Process

Let us assume that we have some set of hand-written forms. In order to process and recognise them, they are scanned and an image is generated. Now, the image processing is done. A lot of pattern recognition tasks are also involved here. It can comprise border filtering, edge detection techniques and noise removal. Once this part of pre-processing is complete, it moves to the next part of template matching and identification. A neural network-based approach too is preferred for this process. So, a pattern analysis takes place here. Further, a validation factor can be involved for accurate recognition of the images being scanned. Once the entire process is complete, the data sets are compiled into the required formats. One point to mention is that this process involves acceptance, rejection or even change in the detected characters based on the percentile of the confidence levels set by the system.

SUMMARY

The chapter has introduced the basic concepts in regard to vision. Computer vision indeed plays a very important role when it comes to action according to the perceived environment. Processing activities where smoothing occurs result in the blur images, but have a significant role in noise reduction. Amongst the methods, Gaussian has proved to be the major contributor.

We have studied in the chapter about the different edge detection techniques, where threshold is the decision-maker for the final edge selection. Many extended techniques have been proposed like Canny edge detector with optimal edge selection. The techniques of perception and processing accelerate the growth in the area of robotics, where there is a necessity of high accuracy for real-time operations.

We have also looked at the various aspects of robotics and how an intelligent character system works. Definitely in both the cases, the entire outcome is based on the way the input data is sensed. So, the image processing and identification of the various aspects to have the intelligent motion or action determination define the entire density of the operation.

At present, image fusion (where multiple images and multiple sensors are used and one image is fused) has taken up a big leap in the image processing and if you are keen in taking up research ahead, the area can be looked upon. In the coming years, the robotics along with image fusion is bound to create a deep impact on the perception and action, and there is a long way to go for it!

 **KEYWORDS**

1. **Computer vision:** It involves extracting the knowledge and analysing from what is sensed visually.

2. **Image formation:** It is a process where a scene/object is captured by some means (camera) that is projected onto an image plane and further digitised.

3. **Image processing:** This involves activities/transformations on the image like segmentation, edge detection to further perform analysis of the image.

4. **Segmentation:** This is partitioning of image into groups where the groups tend to possess common property.

5. **Thresholding:** It involves conversion of a grey image to binary.

6. **Smoothing:** It is a processing technique that aims at noise reduction.

MULTIPLE CHOICE QUESTIONS

The questions can have more than one answer

1. In a single value threshold, if, the output is 1 when $I[x, y] < T$, the object we are separating be
   (a) Will be darker than the background
   (b) Will be lighter than the background
   (c) Cannot be distinguished
   (d) Will have the same intensity as the background

2. Discontinuity in the intensities is used for
   (a) Smoothing   (b) Single value thresholding
   (c) Thinning   (d) Edge detection

3. While using linear filters
   (a) The image gets sharpened   (b) The quality of the image is lost
   (c) The image gets enlarged   (d) None of these

4. What sort of intelligence can exist in the robot?
   (a) A simple Bayesian network-based approach
   (b) A hidden Markov model
   (c) A simple rule-based
   (d) All of the above

5. Which of the following is true for a mobile robot?
   (a) It replicates human activities
   (b) It is an intelligent expert system
   (c) It is used as a means for transportation
   (d) None of the above

CONCEPT REVIEW QUESTIONS

1. Explain the method of smoothing with an example.

2. Explain in detail Canny edge detection approach.

3. Compare the gradient method and LoG.

4. Compare different edge detection techniques.

CRITICAL THINKING EXERCISE

1. Given a grayscale image with three objects. A simple thresholding is applied on it. What pros and cons would occur in the processing?

2. Is it possible for an intelligent robot to distinguish between good review, bad review and average review from a set of hard copies provided to it about some movie reviews? He needs to pile them accordingly. If yes, then how and if no, then why? Explain in detail.

PROJECT WORK

Develop a program to detect edges using Sobel and Prewitt operators for different image files. Mark the difference in the outcomes. Are they same? Justify.

Neural Network-based Learning

Learning Objectives

- ❏ To understand the concept of neural network in learning scenario
- ❏ To study and gain knowledge about the use and importance of types of neural networks
- ❏ To understand the application view of neural network
- ❏ To acquire knowledge about the different algorithms and approaches in neural networks
- ❏ To learn the importance of neural network with current research
- ❏ To identify the importance of neural networks with practical applications

INTRODUCTION

While learning tables, a question may arise—'What is the value of 18*7?' What sort of question is this? Of course, you know the answer (without using calculator) because you have learnt it in your childhood; you can give a quick answer. Why? Because you have trained your brain for it. You have practised it a lot that in fraction of seconds, you are able to give the answer. Similarly, consider any game, say tennis. You practise day in, day out with the inputs given by your coach and start playing well. While training, you are corrected at different stages. At later stages, you have an expertise over it, and you too become a coach! Neural Network (NN) concept is analogous to this. Let us understand it conceptually with relation to human brain.

A human brain consists of billions of neurons. Each neuron is connected to many other neurons. They co-operate with each other to do a specific task. There is a transfer of information that occurs between them. A neuron is typically fired when it gets some input and sends signals to further neurons. For example, you perceive that a car is coming with high speed while crossing the road. The brain works telling you to make a move to avoid the accident. Things happen here simultaneously or we can say that there is a

392

parallelism. In short, in humans, there is some movement or action that is initiated by the brain after processing is done. On similar grounds, artificial neural network (ANN) process works. This is also called *information processing system*. Simple human neuron architecture is shown in Figure 17.1, where the neuron gets signals from synapse and outputs through axons. The dendrites are the membranes of the neurons.

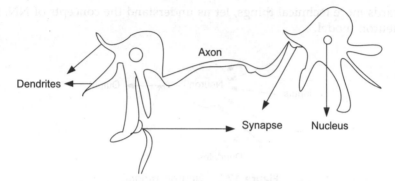

Figure 17.1 Neuron architecture.

Coming back to the concept of ANNs, the networks model the human brain structure. An ANN comprises neurons that are connected. They are trained to do some task. Unlike humans where we can forget things, the neural network does not. It becomes an expert gradually when more amount of training is provided to it.

But for what tasks an ANN is used? Remember that ANN is configured for a specific type of task only. It is often used for pattern recognition, image matching and speech recognition; in short, classification tasks and forecasting. Can it work with unlabelled data? (Remember clustering.) Let us explore and see what can be learnt with NN.

17.1 HISTORICAL DEVELOPMENTS OF NEURAL NETWORKS

Let us begin with how work started in NN till what tasks have been achieved by it today.

The first neural model was proposed by Pitts and McCulloch in 1943. The first ANN was built by them consisting of electric circuits. Later on, in 1949, Hebb put forth that the neural network can be built stronger with more amount of training. In 1950s Minsky's research contributed to the further development of NN and later on, in 1958, it was Frank Rosenblatt, a neurobiologist who came up with the model of perceptron, where the theory of McCulloch–Pitts was put to work. Additionally, learning rules with weights were also contributed to the research for neural network. In late 1960s, Minsky and Papert wrote a book, which had brought in picture the limitations of the perceptron model. Due to this, the research in the field of NN received a great setback.

Though some were still working in this area, in late 1970s and later, NN emerged and made a come back. In 1980s, Rumelhart and McClelland came up with the backpropagation network that is widely used today. This was based on the perceptron model. Around the same time, models with practical applications were developed by Hopfield, which are in use even today. In 1980s, IEEE took initiative to host up NN-based conferences to promote more research. Today, NNs have gained popularity and is taken up as a field to explore and investigate.

17.2 CONCEPTS AND TERMINOLOGIES OF ANN

Moving towards more technical things, let us understand the concepts of NN. Figure 17.2 shows the neuron model.

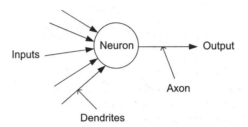

Figure 17.2   Neuron model.

The neuron model consists of many inputs and one output. Typically, it operates in two ways—first is training mode and second is application mode. In training mode, the neuron is trained to learn some specific pattern. The inputs are multiplied by some weights and then a computation is done by means of some mathematical function that determines whether the neuron should be fired or activated. This occurs when an unknown pattern is given. Further, a bias can be applied to the neuron. A more detailed diagram of the neuron is shown in Figure 17.3.

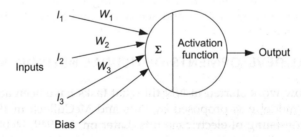

Figure 17.3   Neuron structure.

Are you confused? Let us bring in more clarity. So, we have inputs, some processing that the neuron will be doing and some output. What would be the inputs and outputs? Let us take a simple learning scenario of classifying fruits based on their properties into three distinct categories. The properties will form the inputs, and the output is category. So, we can use two variables to generate the output (say 00 indicating category 1, 01 for 2, 10 for 3). For training the network, a training set (remember the labelled data) is used to train the neurons. This tells the neurons that it needs to output specific values when specific inputs are provided. Further, this is applied to a new unknown data to determine the category (this is dependent on the firing rule). Now, let us go back to the neuron structure.

From Figure 17.3, one must have noted that output, say x is computed as the summation over the inputs and the weights, that is,

$$x = \sum_{j=1}^{n} I_j W_j + \text{Bias}$$

where n is the number of input neurons, I is the input and W is the weight.

A perceptron model makes use of the bias (optional) and a variable threshold. Do remember that the activation and the summation together are the part of the neuron. Let us understand each of the terms in detail.

1. *Inputs:* The inputs to the network depend on the model that is used. It can be {0, 1} or {–1, 1}. Even real numbers can be the inputs.

2. *Weights:* The inputs are multiplied by weights. Each input will have an associated weight that is generally between 0 and 1. They play a very important role in the training phase of an NN.

3. *Summation function:* The summation function adds up the product of weights and the inputs (along with the bias, if any). This function can have other operators (instead of just summing) like anding or oring operations or any other.

4. *Bias:* It is an optional entity that can have weight (generally 1).

5. *Activation function:* The activation function specifies the output of the neuron. It is also known as *transfer function*. The function checks whether the neuron is active or it is inactive. It can also scale the output. The activation function can be linear or non-linear. Non-linear activation function allows NN to compute solutions of complex problems using small number of nodes. If there is no change in the net summation that has been taken at the output, the activation is linear. It is also called *identity*. This is also known as *regression model*. Let the activation function be $f(x)$. (Remember that x is the output after summation.) If $f(x) = x$, then it is linear. Figure 17.4 shows the identity function.

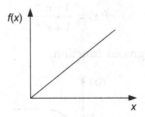

Figure 17.4   Identity function.

Further, there is a concept of *binary step activation* or *simple step activation*. Figure 17.5 shows the binary step activation. It can be represented as follows:

$$f(x) = \begin{cases} 1 & \text{if } x \geq \theta \\ 0 & \text{otherwise} \end{cases}$$

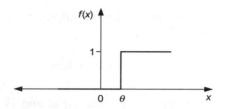

Figure 17.5   Binary step activation.

There is a threshold θ that controls the activation. This is user specified. A neuron that makes use of simple step function is also known as *Heaviside neuron*.

The most common activation function that is used is the sigmoid. There are different variants in it too. A unipolar sigmoid function is given as

$$f(x) = \frac{1}{1 + e^{-x}}$$

The following graph shown in Figure 17.6 depicts this function:

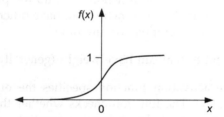

Figure 17.6   Unipolar sigmoid function.

This function outputs in the range of 0 and 1. It is most commonly used in backpropagation networks.

A bipolar sigmoid function outputs in the range of –1 and 1. It is given as follows:

$$f(x) = \frac{1 - e^{-x}}{1 + e^{-x}}$$

Figure 17.7 shows the bipolar sigmoid function.

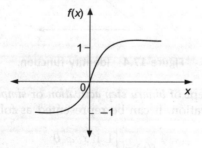

Figure 17.7   Bipolar sigmoid function.

There are other activation functions too like the hyperbolic tangent function and radial basis function. The tangent function is given as

$$\tan h(x) = \frac{e^x - e^{-x}}{e^x + e^{-x}}$$

The tangent function too outputs in the range of 1 and –1. We do not go into the details of other functions. So, we can say that these activation functions give output as (1 and 0) or (–1 and 1).

Before we go into further details of the different types of networks, let us implement a simple AND gate operation to understand how it would be used. Don't you think a simple perceptron model can suit here? Let us understand it. Logical AND truth table is given below (Table 17.1):

TABLE 17.1 Logical AND Truth Table

I_1	I_2	Y
0	0	0
0	1	0
1	0	0
1	1	1

A neural network for the logical AND is given below in Figure 17.8.

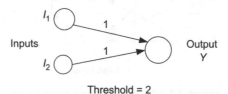

Threshold = 2

Figure 17.8   AND operation.

It makes use of a simple step function where threshold value is 2 and the weights are 1 for each input. Why is the threshold value equal to 2 here? Remember when we perform the summation at the inputs 1 and 1, we get the output as 2. Only at that time, the output expected is 1. Rest it has to be zero. Let us go through the steps. For inputs 0, 0, the computation will be $0*1+0*1 = 0$, i.e., less than 2; so, the output will be 0. Similarly, for 1, 1 it will be $1*1+1*1 = 2$, so the output will be 2. Thus, AND operation is implemented. Is it so that only these weights and threshold can work for the AND to be implemented? Can additional bias be introduced too? Think about it!

It is necessary to note that while using a perceptron model, the classes having the output are linearly separable. Linearly separable means there should be a line that can be differentiating between the output 1 for the inputs and output 0 for the inputs. So, an NN essentially defines the hyperplane, as shown in Figure 17.9. Is it possible to implement and XOR operation with this?

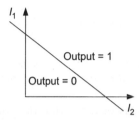

Figure 17.9 Linearly separable problem.

To solve the problem of XOR, we have to introduce additional layers into the network, as a single layer perceptron (till now we have dealt with single layer perceptron) cannot handle it. Hence, the concept of multilayer perceptron (MLP) needs to be applied. A simple diagram depicting multilayer perceptron is given in Figure 17.10 (for simplicity weights and other details are not shown). The layers in between the inputs and the output are called *hidden layers*. The advantage of having multiple layers is to resolve the problems like that of XOR. The first layer, as we have seen, can draw linear boundaries. The next layer can have combination of the boundaries (XOR), whereas the further layer is able to have complex boundaries built.

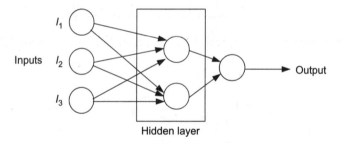

Figure 17.10 A multilayer perceptron.

Let us look at the XOR problem. The truth table is given in Table 17.2.

TABLE 17.2 Truth Table: XOR Problem

I_1	I_2	Y
0	0	0
0	1	1
1	0	1
1	1	0

A possible solution to the XOR is shown in Figure 17.11.

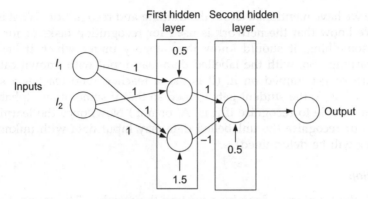

Figure 17.11 NN for XOR.

Let us understand its working. If the inputs I_1 and I_2 are 1 and 0, it should give an output 1. The first hidden layer has two neurons that get the input as $1*1+0*1 = 1$; the neuron with threshold as 1.5 will not get fired, as $1 < 1.5$, whereas the other one will get fired. So, the inputs to the second hidden layer will be 0 (this is because one with 1.5 is not triggered) and 1. So, $0 + 1 = 1$ and as $1 > 0.5$, the output will be 1. Similarly, the working can be understood for the other values, and thus, the logical XOR is resolved.

Let us know more about MLP—the layered network. It has input layers, output layer and a hidden layer (refer to Figure 17.10). The job of the input layer is to pass the input to the next hidden layer, where the processing is done, and finally, it goes to the output layer that produces the output. There is no fixed requirement of the hidden layers. There can be one, two or hundreds of them. How many inputs are required for the system? It depends on the number of attributes one would be taking for the network to perform the recognition/classification task. Similarly, how many neurons should exist in the hidden layers? This depends on the fitting of the input data with respect to the output expected; still, not a specific rule. What about the output nodes? Again, it depends on the type of the problem whether the output has a simple classification, where 1 is expected or there are different outputs.

In ANN, the neuron can be used in two ways—to train and to recognise. Still, we have not gone through the discussion of training and testing; these are discussed in the subsequent sections.

An important aspect is the different structures that exist for the neural networks. They are categorised as feed-forward and feedback. Let us study them.

17.3 FEED-FORWARD NN

What is the meaning of feed-forward? It means that the input passes in one direction. The network is simply a function of the inputs. The MLP network that we have studied in Figures 17.10 and 17.11 are actually feed-forward. They are also known as *feed-forward MLP*. They are most widely used today for the classification domain in data mining. Even the network of single layer (perceptron) belongs to this category of networks. Among the activation functions, sigmoid is used more as compared to threshold in feed-forward NN.

Just before we have mentioned about the training and recognition. What is the meaning of training? We know that the network is used for recognition tasks or for classification. To recognise something, it should know the category under which it has to recognise (supervised learning). So, with the labelled data (say input with known category), it has to initially learn or get trained on it. (It is like a teacher, who teaches a student that a letter written as A is A; the student gets trained so that if some other alphabet is given to him, he should be able to recognise if it is 'A' or not.) Now, once the learning is done, it is made to test or recognise the unlabelled data (say input data with unknown category, whose category will be determined).

Backpropagation

In case of NN, the training is done by adjusting the weights. The training is done to get the correct outputs for the given set of inputs. The network is trained iteratively where a comparison between the actual output and the desired one is done. Accordingly, the weights are adjusted. Naturally, there is an error that needs to be propagated back to do these adjustments. Again, the process is carried out. There is a concept of epoch. An *epoch* tells the number of iterations the NN has to go through. Training once for each sample of the training data forms one epoch. So, it is the number of cycles the training data goes through before it converges. We will come to what is meant by convergence soon. There is also a concept of learning rate η that is used. The *learning rate* is a parameter that controls the weight adjustments. This factor speeds up or slows down the learning process. Most often, the value of the learning rate is 0.001 or 0.01 or even 0.1(depends). Many versions have been proposed for the value selection as well as for changing this learning rate. There are other parameters too (like momentum), but here we do not go into the details. Learning rate and epoch are sufficient to understand the backpropagation.

One more aspect to mention is that there can be offline/online learning. In case of offline learning, the weight updates are carried out after the entire training sample is provided, whereas in online, after every training sample, the weights are updated. Accordingly, the offline has gradient descent approach, whereas online has stochastic gradient descent.

We discuss it on the basis of sigmoid function. We are aware that it is given as

$$f(x) = \frac{1}{1 + e^{-x}}$$

It should be noted that the entire mathematics is explained in consideration of 1 input layer, 1 hidden layer and 1 output layer, as shown in Figure 17.12.

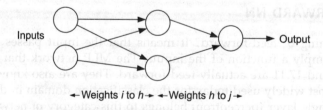

Inputs

◄─Weights *i* to *h*─► ◄─Weights *h* to *j*─►

Output

Figure 17.12 NN representation for weights.

Coming back to the computations, for a single training neuron, the squared error is given as

$$E = 1/2 \text{ (Expected – Actual)}^2$$

So, it would be

$$E = 1/2 \ (T - O)^2$$

where, T is the expected value and O is the output we are getting. Suppose we have n output nodes then, it can be given as

$$E = \frac{1}{2} \sum_{j=1}^{n} (t_j - o_j)^2$$

where t_j is the expected output and o_j is the actual output at j node.

At this instance, assume that E is the error for single training. Then, in that case, we actually want to calculate the rate of change in the error with respect to the weight and that is given as partial derivative. So, we need to compute $\partial E / \partial W_{hj}$, where, W_{hj} is the weight between h node and j node. Let us begin with the calculations between h as the hidden layer node and j as an output node.

$$\frac{\partial E}{\partial W_{hj}} = \frac{\partial}{\partial W_{hj}} \frac{1}{2} (t_j - o_j)^2$$

$$\frac{\partial E}{\partial W_{hj}} = (t_j - o_j) \frac{\partial}{\partial W_{hj}} t_j$$

$$= (t_j - o_j) \frac{\partial}{\partial W_{hj}} f(x_j) \qquad (17.1)$$

Now, we first compute the derivative of $f(x_j)$, i.e., $f'(x_j)$. This is given as

$$f'(x_j) = f(x_j) \ (1 - f(x_j)) \qquad (17.2)$$

Substituting in Eq. (17.1), we get

$$\frac{\partial E}{\partial W_{hj}} = (t_j - o_j) f(x_j)(1 - f(x_j)) \frac{\partial}{\partial W_{hj}} x_j$$

$$\frac{\partial E}{\partial W_{hj}} = (t_j - o_j) t_j (1 - t_j) t_h$$

Let

$$\partial j = (t_j - o_j) t_j (1 - t_j) \qquad (17.3)$$

So, we have $\partial E / \partial W_{hj} = t_h \partial j$.

That is for the output node. Let us turn towards the hidden node. We know that the error needs to be computed for the output and hidden nodes. The hidden node computations are given below:

Let W_{ih} shows the weight between input to hidden node. The error is calculated as

$$\frac{\partial E}{\partial W_{ih}} = \frac{\partial}{\partial W_{ih}} \frac{1}{2} \sum_{j} (t_j - o_j)^2$$

Remember j is the set of nodes belonging to the output ones. So, we have the layered network as *i-h-j*.

$$\frac{\partial E}{\partial W_{ih}} = \sum_j (t_j - o_j) \frac{\partial}{\partial W_{ih}} t_j$$

$$= \sum_j (t_j - o_j) \frac{\partial}{\partial W_{ih}} t_j$$

$$= \sum_j (t_j - o_j) \frac{\partial}{\partial W_{ih}} f(x_j)$$

We already know the derivative of $f(x_j)$, i.e., $f'(x_j)$ [Eq. (17.2)].
So, we get

$$\frac{\partial E}{\partial W_{ih}} = \sum_j (t_j - o_j) f(x_j)(1 - f(x_j)) \frac{\partial x_j}{\partial W_{ih}}$$

$$= \sum_j (t_j - o_j) t_j (1 - t_j) \frac{\partial x_j}{\partial W_{ih}}$$

$$= \sum_j (t_j - o_j) t_j (1 - t_j) \frac{\partial x_j}{\partial t_h} \frac{\partial t_h}{\partial W_{ih}}$$

$$= \frac{\partial t_h}{\partial W_{ih}} \sum_j (t_j - o_j) t_j (1 - t_j) \frac{\partial x_j}{\partial t_h}$$

$$= \frac{\partial t_h}{\partial W_{ih}} \sum_j (t_j - o_j) t_j (1 - t_j) \frac{\partial x_j}{\partial t_h}$$

$$= \frac{\partial t_h}{\partial W_{ih}} \sum_j (t_j - o_j) t_j (1 - t_j) W_{hj}$$

$$= t_h (1 - t_h) \frac{\partial x_h}{\partial W_{ih}} \sum_j (t_j - o_j) t_j (1 - t_j) W_{hj}$$

$$\frac{\partial E}{\partial W_{ih}} = t_h (1 - t_h) t_i \sum_j (t_j - o_j) t_j (1 - t_j) W_{hj}$$

You must have by now guessed the substitution for the intermediate terms with delta. Using Eq. (17.3), we get

$$\frac{\partial E}{\partial W_{ih}} = t_h (1 - t_h) t_i \sum_j \partial_j W_{hj}$$

Minimising it in terms of delta, we can have it as

$$\frac{\partial E}{\partial W_{ih}} = t_i \partial_h$$

where,

$$\partial_h = t_h (1 - t_h) \sum_j \partial_j W_{hj} \qquad (17.4)$$

That is all about the error calculations. Now, the weights are to be updated.
For output layers,

$$\Delta W_{hj} = \eta \partial_j t_h$$

$$W_{hj\_new} = W_{hj\_old} + \Delta W_{hj}$$

where W_{hj_new} is new weight calculated between h and j nodes and W_{hj_old} is old weight between h and j nodes.

Similarly, for hidden layers (i.e., weight between input to hidden),

$$\Delta W_{ih} = \eta \partial_h t_i$$

$$W_{ij\_new} = W_{ih\_old} + \Delta W_{ih}$$

Do remember that the learning rule used here is a generalised delta rule. (There are different learning rules).

Let us generalise the algorithm now.

For every example in the training,

1. Apply a simple forward pass on the network. (At the end of it, you would be getting some output.)
2. Compute the delta (errors) for the output nodes and the hidden nodes. [Refer Eqs. (17.3) and (17.4)]. Remember that for this, we are aware of what output value is expected.
3. Adjust the weights. (The learning rate η has to be pre-decided).
4. Continue this process till some stopping criterion is reached or satisfied. (It could be some permissible error value or till all the classes are identified correctly.

After having the trained network, we need to test it. Here, comes the concept of convergence and cross-validation. In order to have the convergence, validation data is used. This keeps track of the validation errors. Here, training and validation process is repeated and at a particular point, the validation error starts increasing. (We do not change the weights during validation, but keep track of the errors). Once it is found that the error for validation is getting on higher side, the weights, when it becomes low, are seized on and used for the next final level of classification.

Some of the problems of backpropagation are also discussed here. If the learning rate is too small, it may result in convergence very slowly and vice versa, if large. Similarly, there is local minima issue, where the error value actually gets increased to be a part of a process in order to decrease it further, but the backpropagation gets stuck up. In this case, resetting the weights or having momentum introduced is the solution to the problem.

17.4 FEEDBACK NETWORKS

Feedback networks receive feedback from the output. That is, there is a connection from the output to the same node or the preceding nodes. So, there can be loops. They form a complicated network. The flow is in both the directions, unlike feed-forward, where the connections are in one direction only. They are also dynamic in nature. Figure 17.13 shows a simple feedback network.

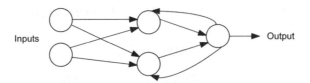

Figure 17.13 A feedback network.

Recurrent Neural Networks (RNN)

They belong to the category of feedback networks, where there are connections between the input, output and the hidden layers, and there can be interconnections between the nodes as well. Many's the time, it is seen that the feedback networks are actually referred to as *recurrent networks*. A recurrent network has at least one cyclic path. For training the network, many variants have been proposed in the recurrent networks and are in practice. Owing to the connections in backward direction also, they provide an internal memory. Figure 17.14 depicts a recurrent network. Today, it is most commonly used for speech recognition. Bayesian and RNN are also combined for time series modelling.

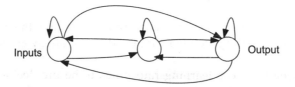

Figure 17.14 Recurrent network.

17.5 PATTERN ASSOCIATIVE NETWORKS

In case of pattern associative network, a pattern itself is generated at the output, given an input pattern. A weight matrix is used in the neural networks, which are used as associative memories. The process of learning or storing the desired patterns is actually a process to generate the weight matrix. (This is discussed further in the chapter). So, pattern associative networks have associative memory. The pattern associative networks are categorised into two tasks—auto-associative and hetero-associative.

Auto-associative

In auto-associative, the patterns are stored in the network (associative memory). The network corrects the inputs. When a new pattern is given as an input, comparison (association) is done with the ones that are stored and a nearest matching is given as an output. With an auto-associative network, a distorted image can be corrected. We can say that the noise is erased off from the pattern. A very fundamental task that is done by these networks is character recognition. Figure 17.15 shows an auto-associative network model. You must have noted by now that this learning, hence, belongs to unsupervised category.

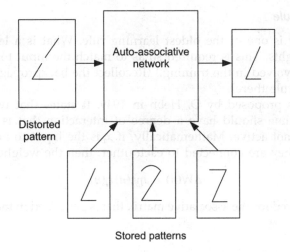

Figure 17.15   Auto-associative network model.

Hetero-associative

Unlike auto-associative where the patterns are stored in the memory, here the association is stored. It is better understood from Figure 17.16. So, the output is altogether a different pattern.

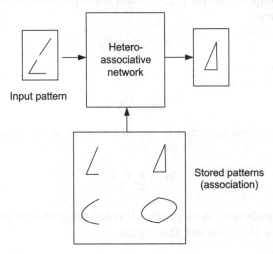

Figure 17.16   Hetero-associative network model.

Mathematically, we can say that in association, we are having X_i as the input pattern and Y_i as the output pattern. The mapping $X_i \rightarrow Y_i$ is the task to be carried out where $i \in \{1, 2, 3, ..., n\}$ that are the stored patterns. In case of auto-associative, the output and the input have same dimensionality, whereas it is not the case with hetero-associative.

Hebbian Learning Rule

Hebbian learning rule is one of the oldest learning rule. What is a learning rule? A rule that adjusts the weights. This is required so as to match the input to the target required. (Naturally this is involved in the training.) (Recollect the backpropagation; we have used a generalised delta rule there).

Hebb's rule was proposed by D. Hebb in 1949. It states that two neurons that are active at the same time should have a degree of interaction that is higher than that of the ones which are not active. Mathematically, if x_i is the input to neuron i and y_j is the output of j, where they are connected to each other, then the weight is given as:

$$\Delta W(n) = \eta y_i(n) x_i(n)$$

This rule is required for the associative matrix that is generated in the pattern association. Let us find it out.

17.5.1 Associative Memory

In case of associative memory, we are actually considering the calculations of W. We know that we want the mapping from $X \rightarrow Y$. For the association to be established, we can rewrite it as $XW = Y$. If the network is auto-associative, it can be simply written as $XW = X$.

If the output belongs to the set $\{-1, 1\}$, then a simple sign function can be applied. It can be given as follows:

$$X_j = \text{sign}(Y_j)$$

where, $j = 1$ to k (dimensions)

Now, W can be given as

$$W = YX^{-1}$$

By the Hebbian learning rule that is applied to each of the input-output neuron pair, we can have

$$W = \sum_P Y_p X_p^{-1}$$

where, P refers to the patterns. To be precise, it is the product of matrix where the columns are output vectors and the rows are the inputs.

17.5.2 Hopfield Network

It belongs to the category of auto-associative networks and is a feedback network. It consists of a single layer. The neurons in the layer are fully connected. The training stage of Hopfield network is less complicated and the network values go through state transitions. Figure 17.17 represents the Hopfield network.

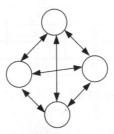

Figure 17.17 Hopfield network.

There are stored patterns in Hopfield network that help in the correction of input patterns. To correct, it should be trained (trained to store the patterns) and later on, should be used to recall the correct pattern for the given distorted pattern. The Hopfield network works as content addressable memory. Let us take an example and see how this correction occurs along with the concept of training.

Training

In training, the Hopfield network learns a pattern. For it to learn, it has to determine the weight matrix. (Just before we have discussed about the association matrix.) There are different learning rules that can be used for the determination of the matrix. The one we discuss is again inspired by Hebb's rule and is the simplest one! Two conditions that are generally fixed in training are given below:

1. The weights between the two connected nodes are same, that is, $W_{ij} = W_{ji}$
2. Self weight is zero, that is, $W_{ii} = 0$.

Hence, the simple weight rule can be $W_{ij} = x_i x_j$ where x_i is the input to ith node and x_j is the input to jth node. Suppose there are p patterns, then we can generalise it as

$$W_{ij} = \sum_{p=1}^{P} x_{ip} x_{jp}$$

Let us say that there are two patterns '–1 –1 –1' and '1 1 1' and we want them to be trained and they should be identified. The neurons are going to be 3. Let us assume x_1, x_2 and x_3 to be the inputs. So, the network should essentially correct the pattern as follows:

For pattern 1: $x_1 = -1$, $x_2 = -1$ and $x_3 = -1$

For pattern 2: $x_1 = 1$, $x_2 = 1$ and $x_3 = 1$

$W_{12} = -1*-1 + 1*1 = 2$

$W_{23} = -1* -1 + 1*1 = 2$

$W_{34} = -1* -1 + 1*1 = 2$

So, the weights here are now same, that is, all are equal to 2.

Thus, the weight matrix is given below in Figure 17.18.

	X_1	X_2	X_3
X_1	0	2	2
X_2	2	0	2
X_3	2	2	0

Figure 17.18   Weight matrix.

Recall:

Now, let us see how it would correct the input pattern '1 -1 1'. A node is selected at random for update here. Say node 2 is randomly selected for update, and then its net input is

$$W_{12} * x_1 + W_{23} * x_3 + x_2$$

So, we get

$$(2 * 1) + (2 * 1) + (-1) = 2 + 2 - 1 = 3$$

Suppose sign function is used, then sgn(3) will give us 1. Thus, the node value is changed giving us (1, 1, 1). Similarly, if node 1 is selected, then the net input will be $(2 * -1) + (2 * 1) + 1 = -2 + 2 + 1 = 1$. Then, sgn(1) = 1. Hence, it remains unchanged giving us the corrected pattern (1, 1, 1). Remember that there are various ways to select the nodes; sometimes, it is as simple as even/odd. This updation of the node takes place till it converges to the one that is present.

There is a concept of energy function. It measures the simulation that is required for a neuron to fire. This energy is required to decide upon the weight so that it is proportional to the patterns. Here, depending on the patterns that are to be stored, the weight computation is done on the correlations between the input values. Though in the example, we have used a simple weight calculation, generally the weights are computed as follows:

$$W_{ij} = \frac{1}{P} \sum_{p=1}^{P} v_{pi} v_{pj}$$

where v_{pi} and v_{pj} are the values for ith and jth parameter, respectively, in the input pattern p.

What could be the drawbacks of this network? Suppose that the network is presented with some pattern it has not learnt. Will it always repair it? If the pattern stored is too large, then there is a possibility that an altogether new spurious pattern could be generated or the case could occur that the network would not converge.

17.6   COMPETITIVE LEARNING

Competitive learning is an unsupervised learning, where the idea behind this learning is to determine weights to update during the learning. This update is done only for a winning neuron in the whole process of learning. So, the neurons compete with each other and only one wins. It is winners take it all approach. Figure 17.19 shows a simple competitive learning network.

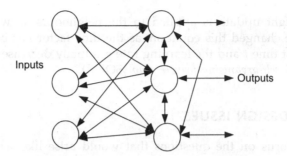

Figure 17.19 A competitive network.

For competitive learning, the competitive nodes are represented in the form of weight vectors. This means a competitive output node y will be formed by the weights connected with the input nodes and this dimension is same as that of the inputs. It is to be noted that the initial weights are randomly selected between 0 and 1. Consider a competitive node $y_a = \{w_{1y}, w_{2y}, ..., w_{ny}\}$ where n is the number of input dimensions. Assume we have m output nodes. Let i be some input pattern. When an input is presented, the distance between the input and the competitive weight vectors is computed. This is most often the Euclidean distance that is used. So, $d(i, y_a)$, where, $a = \{1, 2, ..., m\}$ and m is the number of outputs is computed. For every output competitive vector, this is calculated and the one with the lowest value wins. Suppose y_j wins. That means it is closest to the pattern. Then, the weights associated with this are updated by the rule.

$$y_{j\_new} = y_{j\_old} + \eta(i - y_{j\_old})$$

where y_{j_old} is the previous value and y_{j_new} is the new weight for y_j.

How long will it be done? Again, till the network converges. In competitive learning, it is observed that after the training is over, a clustering mechanism is found in the learning process, where the patterns are grouped.

17.7 SELF-ORGANISING MAP (SOM)

Now, come to the last point in this chapter, i.e., self-organising maps. They are unsupervised networks based on the competitive learning. They were proposed by Kohonen in 1980s and are also called *Kohonen networks*. As said, they are based on the competitive learning in which the winner is found out. But a slight change in SOM is done. Instead of updating the weights of just the winner, the neighbours are also given a share and the adjustments take place. An SOM network actually transforms the input space into a 2D feature map that maintains the topological order. Often, this property of SOM is used to visualise the high dimensional data. SOM makes use of pre-determined topology to form the neighbours in order to carry out propagation. So, the topological distance between the winner and the other nodes is the criterion for this propagation.

The initial weights are selected at random as before, and in the learning process, the weight vector actually moves towards the centroid of the subsets of an input pattern. The weight update rule is given below:

$$y_j(t + 1) = y_j(t) + \eta(t)\,(i(t) - y_j(t))$$

This rule of weight update is applied to the neighbours as well. You must have noticed that we have changed this equation, as the time factor has been added. In SOM, the weights change at time t and the learning rate gradually decreases. Do remember that SOMs are also called *self-organising feature map* (SOFM).

17.8 NETWORK DESIGN ISSUES

In this section, we focus on the questions that would arise like which neural network should be used? When? How? Though conceptually things are clear, the design parameters of the network are dependent on the expected activity or the outcome from the NN.

Consider a simple application of detecting a disease of a person based on the characteristics of chromosome. This is a simple case of feed-forward MLP. In such a scenario, the input and output configurations are based on different parameters. Let us assume that the input parameters are the features of the chromosome (say its length, shape and so on). These real values form the input parameters. The number of input nodes to be taken is based on these parameters. Specific values for the parameters indicate the presence of a particular disease. Let us assume that there are 6 diseases to be identified and 11 input parameters. In such a case, the input nodes are 11 and the output nodes are 4. The four output nodes can have binary outputs, where bit-wise setting can be performed, indicating the presence or absence of the disease. The hidden layers and the number of neurons in it (no fixed thumb rule) impact the performance of the network. Jeff Heaton said that the optimal size of the hidden layer is between the size of the input and the size of the output. (Do you think that hidden layers are required for linearly separable problem?) Once the input, output and hidden layers are fixed, we turn to weights.

With the training samples, the network needs to be trained. We need to decide upon the weight factor now. Often, this is randomly selected. Different weights are generally worked out and the network is trained multiple times. Sometimes, the user may have heuristics for deciding the weights based on the application domain.

What about bias and learning rate? *Bias* actually signifies the input neurons value. In each training step, the values can be modified depending on the requirement. Whereas, learning rate considers the overall rate at which the network can learn. The bias values are dependent on the learning rate. So, for any problem, the learning rate value is observed to be at a very lower side < 1 (often 0.001 or so). Higher the learning rate, faster is the training, but at what cost? The classification or the outcomes are then subjected to localised minimal solutions, which result in hindering the process of making the network enable to give the optimal outcomes.

SUMMARY

Neural networks are based on simulation of working of the human brain. Comprising inputs, outputs and hidden layers, they are of immense importance in classification and prediction tasks. Many open source tools are available for implementing simple single layer and multilayer NN.

The chapter has provided an insight into NN in different learning environments. The feed-forward network that employs backpropagation is the one that is most widely used for classification tasks. Recurrent networks that can be single layer, fully connected or even competitive find their place in temporal data processing. Recurrent networks with associative memory are also looked upon at present. New methods to build ANN and associative memories using genetic programming and other evolutionary algorithms are considered to be the current research areas. Today ANN is also highly looked upon even for many biomedical imaging tasks. In short, NN are non-linear mathematical models which help in mapping input and output to solve complex problems. Despite the potential and wide usage, often a concern point for researchers is the training time in the neural networks!

 KEYWORDS

1. **Artificial neural network:** It is a network comprising many neurons that work in coordination to carry out certain specific task.

2. **Multilayer perceptron:** It is a feed-forward neural network that has one or more hidden layers.

3. **Backpropagation:** It is an algorithm that adjusts the weights by considering the errors between the output and the expected value.

4. **Feedback/recurrent networks:** This is a network where the connections between the nodes are in both the directions along with loops.

5. **Pattern associative networks:** This is a network that generates output pattern itself.

6. **Auto-associative network:** It performs unsupervised task where the correction of input pattern occurs.

7. **Hetero-associative network:** In this type of network, for a given input pattern, an altogether new pattern is generated. Associations are stored here.

8. **Hopfield networks:** This is single layer fully connected network used for pattern association in auto-associative way.

9. **Competitive learning:** It is an unsupervised learning approach where the winner neuron is allowed to change the weights during the learning phase.

10. **Self-organising maps:** Based on competitive learning, it is an unsupervised network where the winner shares the weight change with the neighbours. It is often used for 2D mapping of high-dimensional data.

MULTIPLE CHOICE QUESTIONS

1. In an ANN, a bias is
   (a) Used in the activation function   (b) Used along with the inputs
   (c) Optional to use with the inputs   (d) An other term for threshold

2. Which of the following statements are true in context of NN?
   (a) The number of inputs has to be equal to the number of outputs
   (b) The number of hidden layers is always less than the number of outputs
   (c) The number of inputs can be more or less than the number of outputs
   (d) None of the above

3. A network that would have no hidden layers can be categorised as
   (a) Feed-forward MLP   (b) Recurrent network
   (c) Hopfield network   (d) All of the above
   (e) None of the above

4. Which of the following are supervised methods of NN?
   (i) Hopfield   (ii) Feed-forward MLP   (iii) SOM   (iv) Recurrent
   (a) (i) and (ii)   (b) (ii) and (iii)
   (c) (iii) and (iv)   (d) (ii) and (iv)

5. Which of the following statements are true?
   (a) Associative memories can be implemented with or without feedback
   (b) Associative networks can determine the continuity in the images
   (c) A perceptron is an associative network
   (d) All of the above

CONCEPT REVIEW QUESTIONS

1. Implement a simple logical OR using the perceptron model. What are the different possible threshold values?
2. Write a detailed note on backpropagation.
3. Explain Hopfield network with example.
4. List out the advantages of neural networks.

CRITICAL THINKING EXERCISE

1. Consider a simple case where we have trained an NN for recognising patterns X_1 to X_n belonging to some classes, say A and B. Suppose we have a new training data X_{n+1} that belongs to class C. We want this also to be trained. Will the previous training be impacted? How would it work?
2. Compare and contrast genetic algorithm and neural networks. In which scenario one would use genetic approach and an NN-based approach? Explain.

PROJECT WORK

1. Take any classification problem (two classes) and some input pattern and implement a feedforward backpropagation network. Increase the data sets and see what happens. Compare the outcomes with any other tool. What difference do you notice? Add one more training set to it that belongs to a new class. How would you now train your network? Draw a confusion matrix to show the results of data.
2. Design an NN to map different hand gestures to emotions.

CHAPTER **18**

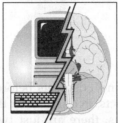

Fuzzy and Hybrid Intelligent Systems

INTRODUCTION

Fuzzy! The meaning of fuzzy is 'vague'. In fuzzy system, the system is not vague, but it talks about the vagueness. Fuzzy set theory was introduced by Zadeh in 1960s, but it started gaining momentum from 1990s, where it was looked for control systems automation. With the hardware support and design tools, it got more accelerated, and today, it has made its place with ANN, genetic approaches and machine learning under soft computing.

There are different tasks and applications' perspectives to which fuzzy systems are suited. When we discuss about washing machine or the camera with fuzzy logic, we actually discuss the fuzzy control systems. Fuzzy theory has, thus, made a strong hold on control systems. The other tasks for which it is used are pattern recognition, classification, forecasting, diagnosis and even decision support systems.

So, what is fuzzy system all about? It consists of fuzzy logic and rules, and is used for classification-related tasks. When we talk about fuzzy, we are uncertain about things. A fuzzy system uses a notion of membership to reason about the data. Fuzzy logic maps the numeric input data based on some inference mechanism. This inference mechanism makes use of degree of membership to help in reasoning about the data.

In the chapter, we introduce the concepts of fuzzy logic and its inference procedure along with neuro-fuzzy systems and other related concepts. So, let us begin with crisp sets.

18.1   CRISP SETS

We start with classical set theory and crisp sets before discussing about fuzzy sets. We know that a *set* is a collection of objects. In classical set theory, a set is determined uniquely by the elements it is made of. Thus, there are just two possibilities for an element—to belong to a set, or does not belong. More mathematically, we define X to be the universal set. For a set C if all the elements in C are subset of X, then we can represent C for all the elements $x \in X$ (where x are generic elements of X) as follows:

$$\mu_C(x) = \begin{cases} 1 & \text{if } x \in C \\ 0 & \text{otherwise} \end{cases}$$

This is a characteristic function that represents the set C. The $\mu_C(x)$ can, hence, take up the value of 0 or 1. That is, an element either belongs to a set or it does not. This is the notion of a crisp set. It is defined precisely. Suppose we have a set of natural numbers upto 100. Let this be X. It is possible to have a set of odd numbers or prime numbers, and it forms a crisp set. We are already familiar with the various operations that are performed in classical set theory and we do not go into its details.

18.2   FUZZY SETS

Unlike crisp sets where there is a concrete or clear definition of belongingness, this is absent in fuzzy sets. In fuzzy set theory, degree of belongingness or membership is defined. For example, if it is the classical set theory, we can say that a student has understood 100% of the chapter or 0%; but in fuzzy, we can say that it is 25% or 0.25. So, this 0.25 defines the degree of membership. The degree of membership can also be defined by words like 'fair understanding', 'good understanding' or 'poor understanding'. In real-life situations, things may not be defined clearly. When we say, for example, a short person, it is actually vague. In fact, we cannot have a fixed boundary to clearly distinguish a short person.

Coming to the fuzzy set theory, an element is said to belong to a set with a degree d, when $0 < d < 1$. Hence, fuzzy logic makes use of the interval between 0 to 1. Fuzzy sets have now become a membership function (which is generalisation of the characteristic function) that has been defined earlier. Now, the fuzzy membership is also $\mu_C(x)$, but there is a difference. This membership function is the one that maps an element $x \in X$ to some value of membership between 0 and 1. The membership function is represented as follows:

$$C:X \to [0, 1]$$

Thus, we can define C set as

$$C = \{(x, \mu_C(x); x \in X \quad \text{and} \quad \mu_C(x): X \to [0, 1]\}$$

Consider a simple example of box office collections for a movie. Let us say if the collection is above 50 crore, the film is a hit, else not. This forms a crisp set. But what would happen when the collection is 49 crore? Would it be categorised as a flop? Hence, a fuzzy notion can be described, as shown in Figure 18.1 below:

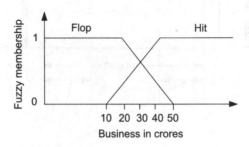

Figure 18.1   A fuzzy membership.

In Figure 18.1, two fuzzy sets are coming into picture—hit set (H) and flop set (F). So, for the hit set, if $x >= 50$, then $\mu_H(x) = 1$, indicating that the movie is hit, whereas if $x < 10$ then $\mu_H(x) = 0$, indicating it is a not a hit. But in between 10 and 50, it still belongs to hit, with some membership value between [0, 1]. So, if $x = 25$, then $\mu_H(x) = 0.4$. But for the same value of 25, $\mu_L(x) = 0.75$. Remember the membership value is also called *membership grade*.

For example, X = {Advance databases, artificial intelligence, mobile computing}, a fuzzy set P to an easier elective to study can be given as

P = {0.6/Advance databases + 0.8/Artificial intelligence +0.4/Mobile computing}

Other representation is

{(Advance databases, 0.6) (Artificial Intelligence, 0.8) (Mobile computing, 0.4)}

So, for discrete values, generally the fuzzy representation that you find is

$$P = \sum_{x \in X} \frac{\mu_P(x)}{x}$$

whereas for continuous values, it is $P = \int_X \frac{\mu_P(x)}{x}$

18.2.1   Fuzzy Sets: Characteristics and Operations

Let us look at the characteristics of the fuzzy sets (Figure 18.2).

1. *Core:*   The core of a fuzzy set P defined over X is a crisp subset of the set P, where the membership value is 1. It is represented as:

$$\text{Core}(P) = \{x \mid x \in X \quad \text{and} \quad \mu_P(x) = 1\}$$

where $\mu_P(x)$ is the membership of x belonging to P and x is element of X.

The fuzzy set P is called normalised if its core is non-empty.

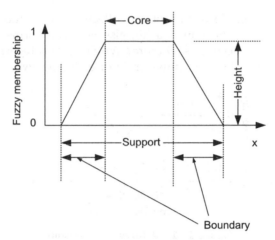

Figure 18.2   Fuzzy set characteristics.

2. *Height:* The height of a fuzzy set P is the maximum of the membership value of P. It is given as

$$\text{Height } (P) = sup\{\mu_P(x) \mid x \in X\}$$

where *sup* stands for supreme, i.e., maximum.

3. *Support:* The support set for P is defined as the set of elements with non-zero membership values.

$$Supp(P) = \{x \mid x \in X \quad \text{and} \quad \mu_P(x) > 0\}$$

where *Supp* stands for support set.

4. *Boundary:* The boundary set for P is the set consisting of the elements whose membership value is between 0 and 1. It is given as

$$Bnd(P) = \{x \mid x \in X \quad \text{and} \quad 0 < \mu_P(x) < 1\}$$

where *Bnd* stands for boundary set.

5. *Alpha-cut (α-cut):* The α-cut of P is defined to be crisp subset of P, where the membership values are at least α. It is given as

$$P_\alpha = \{x \mid x \in X \quad \text{and} \quad \mu_P(x) \geq \alpha\}$$

For example, if $X = \{a, b, c, d\}$ and $P = 0.4/a + 0.5/b + 0.7/c + 0.6/d$, then $P_{0.6} = \{c, d\}$. That means, for alpha value = 0.6, we consider the membership values greater than or equal to it. Each of the membership value can actually contribute to its alpha-cut as well. Generally, strong alpha-cuts are formed that satisfy strictly the greater than equations.

Now, let us look at the operations.

1. *Compliment:* A compliment of a fuzzy set P that is defined over X is given as

$$P' = \{(x, 1 - \mu_P(x)) \mid x \in X\}$$

where P' is compliment of P.

2. *Union:* For P and Q fuzzy sets, the union is given as

$$\mu_{P \cup Q}(x) = \max\{\mu_P(x), \mu_Q(x)\}$$

where, $\mu_Q(x)$ is membership of x for set Q, $\mu_{P \cup Q}(x)$ is membership of P union Q.

Thus, it takes up the maximum value for the elements in either of the set to form the union. It is also called *S-norm operator*.

3. *Intersection:* For P and Q fuzzy sets, the intersection is given as

$$\mu_{P \cap Q}(x) = \min\{\mu_P(x), \mu_Q(x)\}$$

It takes up the minimum value for the elements in the sets. It is also called *T-norm operator*.

18.2.2 Membership Functions

It is understood that the membership function takes the values between 0 and 1. But how can the membership be determined for an element? It can be based on the past experience of the user or on machine learning approaches, or on mathematical functions or the shapes.

A few of the shape-based functions for computing the membership are mentioned below:

1. *Triangular function:* Let i, j and k represent the co-ordinates for $\mu_P(x)$, where i and k are the ones corresponding to membership values of zero at lower and upper boundary, and j is the one with centre at membership value = 1. The triangular function is then defined as

$$\mu_P(x) = \begin{cases} 0 & \text{if } x \leq i \\ \dfrac{x-i}{j-i} & \text{if } i \leq x \leq j \\ \dfrac{k-x}{k-j} & \text{if } j \leq x \leq k \\ 0 & \text{if } x \geq k \end{cases}$$

2. *Trapezoidal membership:* It is given with four co-ordinates i, j, k and l and its function is given as

$$\mu_P(x) = \begin{cases} 0 & \text{if } x < i \text{ or } x > l \\ \dfrac{x-i}{j-i} & \text{if } i \leq x \leq j \\ 1 & \text{if } j \leq x \leq k \\ \dfrac{l-x}{l-k} & \text{if } k \leq x \leq l \end{cases}$$

3. *Gaussian function:* It is given as

$$\mu_P(x) = e^{-\frac{(x-c)^2}{2k^2}}$$

where, c is the central value and k is the deviation (greater than zero).

Let us now proceed to fuzzy inference process.

18.3   FUZZY INFERENCE PROCESS

The *fuzzy inference process* refers to the mapping of a given input to an output using fuzzy logic. Figure 18.3 shows the fuzzy inference process. There are different names given to fuzzy inference systems. They are also known as *fuzzy rule-based systems* or *fuzzy expert systems*. So, in the inference, we come up to some conclusion. To conclude something, we should have the knowledge. In the inference process, the knowledge is represented in the form of rules. For example, a rule can be—if the GRE score is high, then one can get admission in a high rank university. Getting this outcome due to the score high is what the inference does.

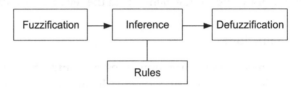

Figure 18.3   Fuzzy inference system.

The process consists of the following:

1. *Fuzzification:* Fuzzification is the conversion of the crisp set into a fuzzy set. The membership functions defined are applied to the input values. This is done to get the result of the antecedent. Hence, the degree of truth of each premise is determined.

2. *Inference:* In the inference process, truth value for premise is computed, and further applied to the consequent part of the rule. There are two methods, viz. Min and Product inference that are used. In Min inference, the output is clipped off at a value, whereas in case of Product, the output is scaled. This is also known as *implication*. Further, there is aggregation where the fuzzy subsets are combined to give a single fuzzy number. Max composition and Sum composition are used here.

3. *Defuzzification:* In defuzzification, the fuzzy value is converted back to a crisp number. Many approaches exist here like centroid methods and maxima methods.

Before we summarise the process, we highlight what is linguistic term and variable. The fuzzy logic that has been introduced is based on linguistic approach. *Linguistic variables* are the variables in the sentences which take linguistic values.

Suppose we have a set of rules (in terms of buying a flat).

Rule 1:   If the location is excellent and the builder is renowned, then the rates are high.
Rule 2:   If the location is average and the builder is unknown, then the rates are low.

Here, location, builder and rates are linguistic variables. They are quantified to take up excellent/average or renowned/unknown or high/low values. Thus, a set can be built to have decomposition for the linguistic variables, where each term is called *linguistic term*. So, excellent and average form the linguistic terms. Why is this discussed here? When the fuzzy inference system is built, things start from the linguistic approach. The rules are bound to be in this way! Now, let us summarise the process.

   1. The linguistic variables and terms are defined.
   2. Once the terms and variables are noted, a membership function has to be built.

3. The rule set is made ready.
4. Fuzzification converts the crisp input into fuzzy, based on the membership function.
5. Inference evaluates the rules and combines the results (the inferring steps).
6. Defuzzification converts the value back to crisp.

Now coming back to the rules, the terms like excellent, average define the membership of the variables in fuzzy nature. Referring to rule 1, the location will have some value based on the membership function defined for excellent. Similarly, for other terms too, there will be some membership function. Now, when we have some crisp values, the rules are to be evaluated. Figures 18.4 and 18.5 explain the steps.

Do remember in the rules, when we have 'location and builder', we apply the intersection operator (Min). Had it been the case that it was 'location or builder', we would have used union (Max) operator.

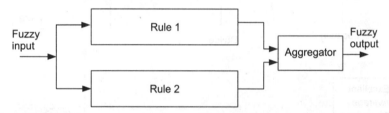

Figure 18.4   Fuzzy inference system: Block diagram.

Figure 18.4 shows a Mamdani fuzzy inference system, where the minimax inference is used, as shown in Figure 18.5. It is for the two rules, two inputs. The other approach is Sugeno approach, which makes use of weighted sum. In Figure 18.5, the line that intersects the membership function occurs as the inputs are mapped into fuzzy numbers and they are made to intersect. As it can be observed from Figure 18.5, the first rule contributes to some value of truth, which is then inferred to R_1. Similarly, the second rule gives output R_2. Applying the Max operator further the entire inference occurs. After the inference, the COA (centroid of the area) is used for defuzzification. Suppose the output is R that is defined over membership A. So, the fuzzy set A is defined over aggregation of R. For continuous variable, it is given as

$$COA = \frac{\int \mu_A(r) \cdot r \, dr}{\int \mu_A(r) \cdot dr}$$

Another approach to this is mean of maxima. It is given as

$$r^* = \frac{\sum\limits_{r_i \in M} r_i}{|M|}$$

where, $M = \{r_i \,|\, \mu(r_i)\}$ is height of fuzzy set, $|M|$ is cardinality of M, r^* is mean of maxima and r_i is maxima.

Where can we use these systems? Today fuzzy rule-based systems are required for the diagnosis purposes. As said earlier, they also find a place in control systems.

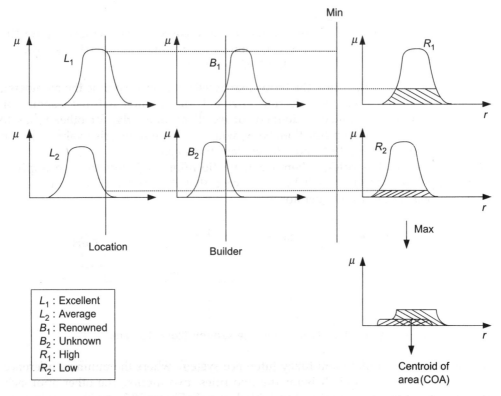

Figure 18.5 Fuzzy inference system: Two input, two rule.

Case Study for Determining Fuzzy Members

Let us take an example and study how this process works. Consider that a new employee is to be recruited in a sales company. The company needs to decide his salary range. We consider two parameters to decide the salary range of the new employee—communication skills and technical know-how. So, let us say these are the two inputs. The interviewer gives points/credits to him on the scale of 1–10 for this. Let us consider three rules that would be used in the evaluation process.

Rule 1: If the communication skills are excellent and technical know-how is over average then the salary is high.

Rule 2: If the communication skills are average and technical know-how is low then the salary is low.

Rule 3: If the communication skills are poor and technical know-how is good then the salary is average.

We are talking in linguistic terms yet. Let us narrow down on the linguistic terms to fuzzy linguistic sets:

Communication skills—excellent, average, poor
Technical know-how—over average, low, good

Now, we need to associate a membership function for them. Based on intuition, this can be given as below:

Say for triangular membership function, we may have

$$\mu_{\text{communication\_skill=average}} = \begin{cases} 1 & \text{if } cs \leq 6 \\ \dfrac{6.3 - cs}{0.3} & \text{if } 6 < cs < 6.8 \\ 0 & \text{if } cs \geq 6.3 \end{cases}$$

where *cs* denotes the communication skills. Similarly, for excellent and other fuzzy parameters and even for technical know-how, it can be defined.

Let us assume the following membership functions shown in Figure 18.6 (not upto scale) for the communication skills.

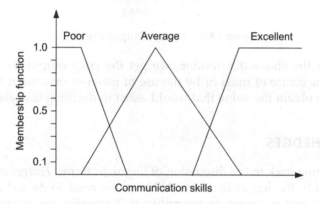

Figure 18.6 Membership function for communication skills.

Similarly, membership functions can be given for technical know-how. Assume that some input (say 9 points are given for communication skills and 6 for technical know-how) by the interviewer. Now, based on the membership functions, we can compute the memberships for it. We need to decide the salary front, where the output needs to be crisp. Now, for the given inputs, let us compute the rules. Remember that we have the memberships defined for communication skills and for technical know-how.

For Rule 1: If the communication skills are excellent and technical know-how is over average, then salary is high.

Now, for 'and', there are many ways of computing it. It can be simply the minimum of the two membership functions or the product rule. With product rule, we get

$$\mu_{Cs \cap T}(x) = \mu_{Cs=\text{excellent}}(9) * \mu_{T=\text{over-average}}(6)$$
$$= 0.7 * 0.4$$
$$= 0.28$$

That is, membership of salary to be high is 0.28.

In this way, we can compute the values for the other rules as well for the same set of inputs.

So, assume we get membership for salary to be low as 0.3 and average as 0.37. (The final output is shown in Figure 18.7 after computation of fuzzy membership values and *r* values of each rule.)

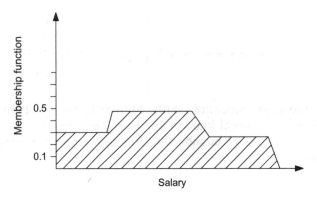

Figure 18.7   Salary: Output distribution.

Finally from the above distribution, we get the crisp output by defuzzification, i.e., by computing the centre of mass or by the use of mean of maximum technique. With this computation, we obtain the value that would assist in deciding the salary of the employee.

18.4   FUZZY HEDGES

We are now coming back to the discussion of linguistic terms. *Hedges* are special terms that are used to modify the linguistic terms. What is the need to do so? Assume we already have a fuzzy set and we want to exemplify it. Naturally, the fuzzy set is of linguistic terms. Suppose a fuzzy set of linguistic term 'bright' is defined. We can make it 'very bright', 'slightly bright', 'more bright' and so on. These words, i.e., very, slightly, more are fuzzy hedges. The fuzzy hedges modify the shape of the fuzzy set, rather than the membership function. Let 'The colour is bright' be a fuzzy predicate. Let us map it as '*x* is *B*'. The fuzzy set is *B*. A hedge *H* can be defined over *B* as follows:

$$\mu_{HB}(x) = h(\mu_B(x))$$

where *h* is the modifier.

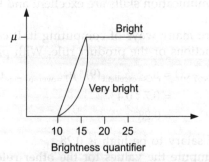

Figure 18.8   Hedges.

A few of the basic hedges are 'very', 'fairly' and 'a little'. 'Very' takes square of the membership. So, if we have 'The colour is bright' and $\mu_B(x) = 0.7$, then 'The colour is very bright' will have $\mu_B(x)^2 = 0.49$. 'Fairly' can take up the square root, i.e., $\sqrt{(\mu_B(x))}$. 'A little' can be $\mu_B(x)^{1.3}$ and so on. Figure 18.8 shows the hedge concept.

18.5 NEURO-FUZZY SYSTEMS

A neuro-fuzzy system is a form of hybrid system that is looked upon by the researchers. A *neuro-fuzzy system* or the *hybrid intelligent system* is the one that combines two or more techniques so that the limitations or individuals are overcome. Neural networks are good at pattern recognition, whereas fuzzy gives good reasoning capabilities. The hybrid system, thus, attempts to combine them to build better intelligent systems. Hybrid systems are gaining popularity with their requirement in control systems, credit evaluation and other applications.

Literature reports two models of neuro-fuzzy systems. First model shows that fuzzy inference gives the input to NN. The other model is multi-layered NN that governs the fuzzy inference mechanism. Figure 18.9 shows the two models.

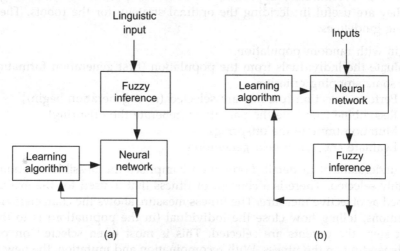

Figure 18.9 Models of neuro-fuzzy systems.

What does a neural network (NN) do? It is understood that the NN performs recognition. In fuzzy systems, NNs tune the membership functions of the fuzzy inference. Many versions and models in neuro-fuzzy systems have been developed till today. Let us define a hybrid neural network. It is a network that takes crisp signals as inputs and weights along with the transfer function. Unlike the normal neural network, the hybrid NN has fuzzy neuron. A sample fuzzy neuron for AND operation is given below in Figure 18.10.

In Figure 18.10, *T* and *S* stand for the T-norm and S-norm, respectively. The neuron is, thus, the realisation of the Min-Max composition. Don't you think the weights are the membership functions for the fuzzy systems? So, in neuro-fuzzy systems, the weights contribute the fuzzy sets and the transfer function takes up T-norm or S-norm. The hidden

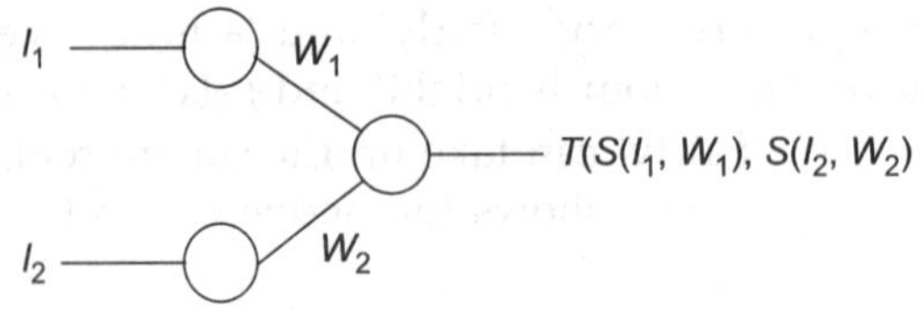

Figure 18.10 Fuzzy neuron (AND).

layers form the rule layers. An example of model is adpative neuro-fuzzy inference system (ANFIS). This system is used for Speech recognition, emotion recognition, load balancing, etc.

18.6 EVOLUTIONARY ALGORITHMS

Evolutionary algorithms aim at finding an optimal solution. Genetic algorithm and evolutionary programming are among the methods that belong to this class of algorithms. They make use of principles of evolution found in nature. What does an evolutionary algorithm do? In evolutionary approach, the solution space is searched to get the best solution. They are useful in deciding the optimal strategy for the robots. They work on the following guidelines:

1. Begin with random population.
2. Evaluate the individuals from the population (first generation formation)
3. Till some stopping criterion,
   (a) Perform selection [parents are selected (next generation begin)]
   (b) Recombine (combine the parents to generate the offspring)
   (c) Mutation (mutate the offspring)
   (d) Evaluate and select next generation

Let us understand it in detail. Population comprises the possible solutions. Initially, it is randomly selected. There is a concept of fitness that is used for the evaluation. This can be termed as objective measure. The fitness measure shows the characteristics required for the solutions, telling how close the individual (in the population) is to the solution. In the next step, the parents are selected. This is most often selected on probabilistic approach depending on the fitness. With recombination and mutation, the new population is generated. This process is carried out till a stopping criterion is reached, say fitness value. It could also be the number of iterations.

Let us look at the genetic algorithm in brief.

Genetic Algorithm (GA)

The genetic algorithm was introduced by J. Holland in 1975. Since then, genetic algorithm has seen many variations. In genetic algorithm, there are chromosomes, which we have referred to in the evolutionary algorithm. A chromosome consists of genes. Gene is said to be a part of the chromosome. In mutation, the gene is changed. The algorithm on similar lines of the basic evolutionary algorithm is given below:

1. Begin with the initial random population.

2. Generate fitness (evaluation).
3. Repeat until some stopping criterion is reached.
   (a) Select the parent.
   (b) Perform the cross-over and mutation.
   (c) Evaluate the new population.

Remember the chromosomes can be strings, bits, numbers, etc. The standard genetic approach uses binary numbers for the genes. Let us say for some problem, two parents are selected—11001 and 10011. Figure 18.11 depicts cross-over and mutation steps.

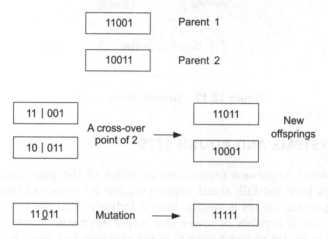

Figure 18.11 Cross-over and mutation.

When and where do we use this? As a simple example, if we want to find a polynomial of some degree (say 3) that fits to the given values of x and y, then we can have genetic approach where for the equation $y = ax^3 + bx^2 + cx + d$, random values for a, b, c, d are selected to form the initial population. The fitness is computed for them (Here, it would be the difference of expected and the actual y value) and further, on the basis of the fitness function, the solution can be obtained.

Fuzzy and Evolutionary Algorithm

Since we are discussing the fuzzy things, let us consider the combination of fuzzy and evolutionary approach (another hybrid approach!). There can be two cases of using the fuzzy systems in collaboration with the evolutionary algorithm—First is using the evolutionary approach for optimisation in fuzzy systems, thus building genetic fuzzy systems, and second is using fuzzy logic for modelling evolutionary algorithm components.

Genetic fuzzy systems (GFSs) are the ones that are most common in use even today. The main advantage of using these hybrid systems is that GA enables the exploration of the search space. Figure 18.12 shows the use of genetic algorithm for the fuzzy inference. It is generally used for tuning and learning the rules, thus building a better knowledge base of the rules.

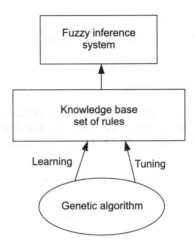

Figure 18.12 Genetic fuzzy system.

18.7 FUZZY SYSTEMS AND ROUGH SETS

Fuzzy sets talk about vagueness (vagueness in terms of the membership functions). In case of rough sets, they too talk about vagueness, but by means of boundary regions. If the boundary region for the set is empty, then it indicates that the set is crisp set, or else it forms a Rough set. It consists of lower and upper approximations. Let us understand them. Suppose U is the set of given objects in the universe and there is an indiscernibility relation R such that $R \subseteq U \times U$. Assume A to be subset of U. If A is to be characterised with respect to R, then the approximations are as follows:

1. **Lower approximation:** It is the set of objects that can be classified as A with respect to R.
2. **Upper approximation:** It is the set of objects that can be possibly classified as A with respect to R.
3. **Boundary region:** It is the set of objects which can neither be classified as A nor as $\sim A$ with respect to R. Thus, A forms a crisp set if the boundary is empty, else it forms a rough set.

How are fuzzy systems and rough sets used and where? At present, rough set-based neuro-fuzzy systems are worked on to build a hybrid system. The rough set theory is used for the dimensionality reduction. Rough set-based neuro-fuzzy systems (RNFSs) help in strengthening the interpretability of the fuzzy rules. Rough set-based approach along with fuzzy-NN is also preferred when the data is changing continuously. This helps in getting better learning capabilities for the network. In some systems for classification, it is not possible to have all the features available. In this case, to perform classification of data sets, where some features of the data set are missing, RNFSs are used.

SUMMARY

The chapter has introduced the preliminaries and related areas of work in the fuzzy systems. In real life, most of the time, things are fuzzy. We are uncertain about it. With the fuzzy logic and the membership functions, it is possible to have this inference under the uncertain circumstances. Fuzzy systems have taken up their place in control automation and finds huge demand in the medical domain too. Imagine an air conditioner whose temperature would be adjusted by the fuzzy logic depending on the people and the temperature of a room. Fuzzy logic and hybrid systems put forth the need and scope in the wide areas of decision support and classification systems. At present, fuzzy with NN and genetic algorithms is looked upon by the researchers. Researchers have suggested the use of fuzzy hybrid approach for scheduling buses and trains such that number of shifts for the driver can be appropriately determined. Rough set-based approach with neuro-fuzzy is also an upcoming area for research.

 KEYWORDS

1. **Crisp set:** It is a set in which an element is either a member of the set or it is not a member.

2. **Fuzzy set:** This is represented as a pair comprising the element and a membership value for a set.

3. **Membership function:** It is a function that maps value between 0 and 1 for an element indicating the degree of belongingness for that set.

4. **Fuzzy inference process:** The fuzzy inference process refers to the mapping of given input to an output using fuzzy logic. It comprises fuzzification, defuzzification and inference mechanism.

5. **Fuzzy hedges:** They modify the fuzzy membership and exemplify the fuzzy set.

6. **Neuro-fuzzy systems:** It is a form of hybrid intelligent system that helps in improved pattern recognition along with reasoning. This combines the approach to get benefits.

7. **Evolutionary algorithms:** These are the algorithms that are inspired by biological evolution; they help in getting optimal solutions.

8. **Genetic algorithm:** It is an evolutionary approach that helps in getting optimal solutions with the cross-over and mutations.

9. **Rough set theory:** It is a set theory that is based on vagueness but in terms of boundary conditions. This comprises approximations to have the boundary terms defined.

MULTIPLE CHOICE QUESTIONS

1. Which of the following statement is true about fuzzy sets?
   (a) Fuzzy sets are the subsets of crisp sets
   (b) Fuzzy sets are the subsets of rough sets
   (c) Crisp sets are the subsets of fuzzy sets
   (d) Rough sets and fuzzy sets are same

2. In which case we can say that the fuzzy set is normalised?
   (a) Core = empty, height = 1
   (b) Core = non-empty, height = Max value other than 1
   (c) Core = non-empty, height = 1
   (d) Core = non-empty, height = Min value

3. Which of the following statements are true for fuzzy logic?
   (i) It gives an exact answer which is considered.
   (ii) It gives an approximate value.
   (iii) It applies the logic the way humans apply.
   (a) All of them   (b) Only (i) and (iii)
   (c) Only (ii) and (iii)   (d) Only (iii)

CONCEPT REVIEW QUESTIONS

1. For the following fuzzy sets, $P = 0.3/0 + 0.4/1 + 0.32/2 + 1.0/3 + 0.86/4 + 0.22/5$ and $Q = 0.5/0 + 0.37/1 + 0.33/2 + 0.41/3 + 0.1/4 + 0.36.0/5$. Compute:
   (i) Union   (ii) Intersection   (iii) Compliment
   (iv) Core   (v) Height.

2. Write a note on evolutionary algorithms.

3. Compare fuzzy sets, crisp sets and rough sets with respect to grading system in school.

CRITICAL THINKING EXERCISE

1. What could be the possible advantages and disadvantages of combining neuro-fuzzy systems?

2. Is it possible to have fuzzy logic incorporated in a system following classical rules? Discuss.

3. Consider sentiment analysis for feedback forms. Assume a supervised learning approach is applied to it to determine classes (good/bad feedback). Can a fuzzy logic be helpful in such a system in some way to have additional output determination? Discuss.

4. How can fuzzy systems be used to regulate air-conditioning?

5. How can neuro-fuzzy system be used for accident prevention? Can you use evolutionary system to improve the performance.

⟨ PROJECT WORK ⟩

1. Implement a fuzzy inference system for a medical diagnosis system. Let us assume that we want to compute the risk for a person who is likely to be suffering from blood cancer. Assume that the input parameters are platelets count—low, sufficient, high; and sugar level—low, moderate, high. Take inputs from these parameters and design an inference system with three rules. Use different membership functions and defuzzification functions to compute the same.

2. Implement neuro-fuzzy system for speaker authentication for premises security.

CHAPTER **19**

Applications of Artificial Intelligence

Learning Objectives

❏ To identify and analyse AI-based approaches from product development
❏ To study and acquire knowledge about the various industry products from AI-baseline
❏ To have an overview of AI-based applications in business
❏ To study different case studies with AI methods to build intelligent systems
❏ To develop problem-solving skills using AI

INTRODUCTION

Today, in knowledge economy, we want all our appliances to outsmart other applications. Hence, we want them to exhibit intelligence. We expect them to behave intelligently, solve problem intelligently and understand our problems. Today, appliances have become our companions. We want our mobiles to be smart (i.e., should remind us without setting alarms), the text mining system to be intelligent (it should get context without specifically defining it) and even washing machine to be intelligent (it should understand the type of clothes without specifically setting the mode). It is not limited to these appliances, but we expect our car to be intelligent, homes to be intelligent, traffic signals to be intelligent and so on and so forth. Making these appliances intelligent, allowing them to learn and delivering right solutions to the user when required is what AI has been trying to do for the years. With increasing expectation from all the fields like automobile, machine tools, electrical, AI has a much bigger role to play in today's scenario. There are applications ranging from water purifiers to rocket launching and text matching to complex learning. The broad spectrum of these algorithms is discussed in detail in this chapter along with specific role played by AI in different industrial product building and processes.

430

Artificial intelligence can contribute to make any application more intelligent, thus it can overall optimise resources, relevance and can produce better results. Here, in this chapter, we discuss various applications of artificial intelligence.

19.1 RANGE OF APPLICATIONS

AI is needed everywhere to make the world more comfortable, to get optimal solutions and to get efficient output. To every gadget we have, household things and any luxury that we need, industries are striving hard to give the best. AI is the key role player in molding the things in the best possible way. We list a few of the application areas, where AI has become an inherent part.

1. Document management systems
2. Web innovations
3. Monitoring and control applications
4. Medical diagnosis systems
5. Intelligent transport systems
6. Planning and scheduling
7. Robotics
8. Image analysis and classification
9. Game playing
10. E-learning-based systems
11. Language processing and speech recognition
12. Sales analysis and forecasting
13. Warehouse optimisation
14. Agricultural industry
15. Space

The list goes on and on. Now, we would like to discuss some of the industry applications, where the use of AI techniques has improved and helped in building efficient and accurate systems. Figure 19.1 summarises a few of them.

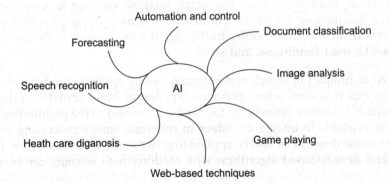

Figure 19.1 A few of the AI application domains.

19.2 WHICH AI TECHNIQUE TO USE?

There cannot be a thumb rule nor can one randomly take up any approach of AI for the problem at hand. Things are dependent on the application and the required results. It is obviously possible and appropriate too that for a specific application, multiple techniques can be the candidates. The selection of any specific methodology to build a system is based on the expected outcomes. Naturally, when it comes to classification tasks, one would go for the use of supervised/unsupervised techniques or probabilities and statistical methods. Pattern-based classification involves the use of neural networks most often. Robotics makes use of perception and image processing techniques along with machine learning. Searching is an approach used where the optimal solutions are required. Planning is the core task for an application to be successful. Fuzzy systems along with risks help in decision-making. In short, we cannot say specifically that one particular approach is the best, as it depends on what the application demands.

19.3 AI: APPLICATIONS AND EXAMPLES

In this section, we have an overview of the applications, where AI has contributed to a great extent in helping us to serve better. A few of them are described below:

Intelligent Transport System

Travel is inevitable to everyone nowadays. Whether it is for business or leisure, we need good roads, short distances, good restaurants to take halts and so on. An *intelligent transport system* is the one that can assist in the travel using AI. Imagine an intelligent transport system (GPS-based) of bus or train that would give the waiting time for the next coming bus/train to the user and that to in real time considering the possible issues that would arise in the travel. This type of system would not only be useful for the individuals but it would also help in maintaining the environment and making the travel safe. Another aspect for such a system would be making the user aware about the servicing and pollution details too for the vehicle.

Let us take an example of road transport. Imagine you are in your car and want to reach some destination. To travel within city, a route can be provided to reach the destination based on the road traffic, traffic signal time, timing (whether rush hours), impact of events, road conditions, and so on.

Role of AI: AI techniques of search and planning can be applied to get the shortest route. It can form an expert system, where previous experiences build knowledge that is used to draw conclusions. Uncertain knowledge too can be accounted in the pathfinding. If the road conditions are available in images or videos in real time, image processing techniques to determine the traffic density can also be applied to give the appropriate solution. Probabilistic approaches and density-based algorithms with reinforcement learning can be suited here.

Agricultural Systems

Uncertainty in the rain and weather changes affect the productivity of crops for the farmers. The farmers who generally follow the traditional pattern for agriculture, if wish to change the crop, then they can be given feasibility analysis for the same. An AI-based system can assist them in giving solutions regarding which crop to harvest to get the maximum benefit taking into account the environmental conditions and other factors. Agricultural domain demands appropriate tools and systems to handle the uncertainty. Use of robots for crop sowing and farm handling can reduce the burden of the farmers.

Role of AI: A simple rule-based system can even help in getting limited outcomes for the crop selection. Bayesian probability, search techniques and machine learning approaches are the ones that help in taking decisions. The crop selection problem can be formulated as a planning problem. Risk and uncertainty for decision-making are the other AI aspects that also affect the system outcomes and can be considered for the system development. Recent work in the field shows the use of evolutionary algorithms for optimal crop selection.

Automation Industry

In automation industry, robots are needed to do quality jobs with precision. Many's the time, the circumstances make it essential to have automation, as some jobs are difficult for humans to perform. In such cases, robots with high degree of intelligence and control are inevitable. One such industry based on providing automation is Precision Automation and Robotics India (PARI). The industry has contributed to automatic parking system and also to the building of robots to dispose of the scrap material. Another example is car assembling. In car manufacturing, the assembling of the parts is done by the use of robots. We already have discussed in previous chapters about robots performing cleaning operation. Not only this, but they can perform bomb disposal and many more. Adaptive nature to the changing environment is the need of the hour. Robots built for cleaning today work with respect to the changing environment.

What more can be done in automation? Imagine you sit in a car and it takes you on its own to the destination! We already have assistance in parking a car where guidance is provided intelligently.

Role of AI: Perception, imaging sensing and image processing along with the planning and learning and searching approaches are at work here to perform the task.

Forecasting Applications

Decision-making and forecasting are the most important aspects of one's life. Whether it is weather forecast or it is related to professional or personal decision, everyone is keen to know it. AI plays an important role in forecasting. It could also be in the application as identification of an employee, who would be committed to the company and would prove to be an asset. Further, forecasting can be for a business trend, share-market, real estate, flood/draught detection and even about who would win a match based on the statistical analysis.

We are highly influenced with movies. Just think of a system that would let us know about the forecast of a movie being hit or flop along with the inputs of the film's details.

Role of AI: Decision-making along with risk and planning becomes crucial for forecasting. Pattern recognition that analyses the previous pattern and notifies the changes can be applied here. Bayesian probability too can give significant information. Neural networks can also prove to be effective. Fuzzy systems and NN hybrid intelligent systems are also used.

Document Management Systems

Natural language processing is one of the highly looked upon area for text management. It is all about management and classification of data. The crux here is knowledge management. Often management and mining go hand in hand. Development of tools and learning scenarios for management need efficiency and accuracy. This is achieved by analysing the content, where the context also plays a very important role. Capturing of corporate knowledge base is made easy with the use of AI techniques; at the same time, even in heath care, biomedical tasks of retrieval and decision-making are taken care of. A document summarisation technique, where an abstract version is made available, is also an area of interest.

Role of AI: Since we are talking about NLP, information retrieval techniques and machine learning are bound to be a core part of the development of these systems. Statistical and probabilistic approaches like Bayes are found to be used widely. SVM and evolutionary approaches with fuzzy systems have too proved their worth.

Web-based Intelligent Systems

Why does one want the web services/portals to act intelligently? We cannot think of staying without using the internet for a day. If we need any sort of information or help, we use the web. What sort of intelligence does AI provide here? Some of the very recent ones are Animoto that creates a music video with its AI technology, where one gets a feel of real movie. Various parameters like the song, the instruments played and others are considered for making every video a new one. Other application could be where you are recommended movies that you should watch based on your personal choice. Such an application would be adaptive taking feedback from you to give a better service. Online shopping has now become a trend with various portals at your service. You become a privilege customer when their AI-based systems report them about your frequent purchases. You could be then given additional benefits and promo offers (which will give them better business forecasting here too!) Learning online is not new. An online learning tutor that adapts and personalises the way user wants has to exhibit intelligence; these systems are also gaining momentum in research. A web-based service for patient to manage his health issues is an asset and needs to be correct in diagnosis and provides essential guidelines.

Role of AI: Pattern analysis and recognition techniques play a significant role here. Neural networks and associative networks are also used.

Health-care Systems

AI and medical domain have been closely associated for years. Expert systems assist in diagnosis, and provide guidelines for medication. Though the intelligent system can be web-based, the expert system has often proved to be accurate in diagnosis. Medical practitioners even agree with the decisions provided by AI systems. It is not just about diagnosis, but even in the application of medical image categorisation and classification, AI techniques are used to a great extent. For cancer analysis, identification of genetic disorders and other diagnosis, AI is essential.

Role of AI: Genetic algorithms, Markov chaining and decision networks are used. Neural networks and Bayesian probability are used for the diagnosis/prediction purposes. Hybrid systems are also considered for the development of these systems.

Network Security

Everything comes to a standstill if the network is not there. With the network, there come various attacks that need to be recognised. AI plays an important role in the detection process. An intrusion detection system is the one that detects the attacks. Cyber crimes are on large increase nowadays, where AI techniques can act as guard. An AI-based firewall would be of immense use to protect the network. Such a system can be incremental where the knowledge is upgraded with the identification of any new attack.

Role of AI: Neural networks are most often preferred while building these systems. Many algorithms that help in mining like AdaBoost are also used. Self-organising maps too are used. Intelligent agents have proved their work in the detection process. Expert systems too are useful for the same.

Big Data and AI

Let us first understand about the big data before understanding the role of AI in it.

We can say that big data has become a current trend among researchers. It is said that almost 90% of the data that exists today is generated in the recent years. Due to the enormous growth in the data, analysis of data has become a challenging task. The data is unstructured here. By unstructured, we mean it is social media, satellite images, messages on the mobiles and so on. Often big data is defined on the basis of any kind of data source that has three characteristics, viz., large volume, high velocity, and a wide variety of data. Big data is often referred to as a technology, which is a combination of a variety of technologies that exist.

We are aware that it all started from a flat file to relational databases, and later on, to data warehouses. In this entire transition stage, there were some shortfalls that were identified and the next step was evolved. Now, in this process when we talk about big data, it is necessarily the data management for decision-making, i.e., big data analytics. This management was necessary's from the business intelligence's perspective, and moreover, the data handled was unstructured. The transactional analysis gave a new dimension to the business intelligence. Now, does this intelligence mean that we are to identify certain behaviour patterns or trends like the sell of goods and so on that would help in increasing the profits or is it something else? Till the evolution of big data, it remained and still will continue to be a requirement, but now the desired thing is the understanding of the useful patterns. This is required to have an insight into the future and that too at a high speed and from the huge data. Thus, the analysis and management of big data gets complicated. To add up, the factors that are key concern for big data management are speed, security, amount of real data analysis required and so on.

So, what sit at the heart of the big data are the technologies like distributed file systems, parallel processing with Hadoop and MapReduce. The requirement of big data actually geared up with the internet giants like Google and Facebook. So, there was a need to have approaches and methods that would be capable to execute and process the huge data sets in parallel with distribution. Thus, the concept of MapReduce was developed. It assigns some work to the nodes involved in the cluster. Hadoop is a framework that is based on the MapReduce. Thus, we have discussed about the basic concept of big data.

In which type of applications would big data technology be useful and what would be the role of AI in it? Let us take an example to understand this. For a country like India, where development and planning for future are very serious issues, big data analysis can be very much beneficial. The data collection with regard to population growth, Indian currency downfall, traffic scenario, urbanisation and many more will need the big data analysis. From the government's outlook, this will help in determining the future development plans. This is just one example, but as said earlier, from health domain to sports data, from blogs to social networking sites, everywhere there is need for having big data analysis. Now, in what way would AI be a key role player in the entire big data analysis? Still, we say that the big data is in nascent stage. Many companies are providing software solutions or services along with the infrastructure for it, and it altogether forms the big data market. Now, what AI can process and what sort of outcomes it can achieve are already known to us. Here, the role of AI would be in the form of intelligent agents, that would be used for pattern analysis for observing the environment changes in the data and recognising the drifts and hidden patterns. Do remember that the amount of data that AI can handle can be large and the analysis of big data for decision-making can definitely be an option that one would look at. Many AI techniques of machine learning are productive when put to work for this analysis. Mahout—an open source machine learning library from Apache includes a variety of clustering and classification algorithms. It is specially implemented from the perspective of scalability. It scales on the top of Hadoop. Still, in the development phase, it can be applied for decision-making and analysis depending on the nature of decisions required. These decisions can be anticipation of the decisions for business growth, cost reductions that would be required, increasing business revenues, identification of future traits, improving customer satisfactions and overall business process and so on.

19.4 CASE STUDIES

19.4.1 PARI

We would now have a detailed study of how an automation industry would work with AI with reference to Precision Automation and Robotics India (PARI). It is not an easy job to come up and build systems (robots) that are capable of handling highly complicated tasks which are difficult for humans to achieve. AI is the essence for this industry, which builds robots for automation and control.

What sort of AI techniques would be involved? Most often, when it comes to robotics and automation, you can guess that it is perception and action that takes place. Let us try to list out the activities (generalised) here.

1. Initial stage for a robot development is to capture the environment. With the sensors, the images are acquired. Thus, the current environment is perceived.
2. An agent (intelligent one) comes into picture at the next stage. The agent governs the entire synchronisation till the action takes place.
3. When images are available, image processing is bound to happen. Whatever is visualised must be captured and used effectively for the actions. (It could be also dependent on the other means or other sensors by which the objects are detected.) Image processing takes place to identify the objects and their details. Approaches for pre-processing, edge detection and recognition take place. Hence, pattern recognition techniques are employed to classify into some pre-learned knowledge.
4. Further, localisation and appropriate knowledge representation considering the uncertainty are very much important for path determination.
5. Path planning is essential to have the movement. We are very well aware that planning has a huge impact on the outcomes. This, in turn, decides the movement.
6. Finally, the ultimate task is acting on the environment by the means of effectors/actuators.

When we say that these methods are to be used, we cannot forget the support of the hardware like that of the sensors and the effectors to have the motion. *Degree of freedom* is the one that determines the direction of the movement for the effectors.

PARI's Innovation and Achievement

It provides robots to railways, automatic parking and other industries. With automatic parking provided by PARI, the energy cost is saved to a great extent. In railways, making worn-out blocks of the bogies usable by means of robots is the biggest achievement of the company, which results in large amount of cost saving by the railways.

19.4.2 Aquachill Systems India

Every industry today has a requirement of air conditioning. Aquachill Company provides air conditioning intelligently with the use of AI and machine learning.

What intelligence can be provided here that needs to just control the temperature? Let us have a generalised listing of how intelligence can be built here.

1. When it comes to temperature ranges, fuzzy systems have a role in the setting of the temperatures.
2. Pattern-based techniques are required that study the pattern in an industry and set the temperature. What sort of pattern would you think is required here? Say the number of employees that are moving in a particular cell or division. Besides, the leave pattern and the production pattern too are accounted in the temperature setting intelligently. Thus, the pattern recognition techniques are highly looked upon.
3. Hybrid systems with precise knowledge representation too can be made to use to make the cooling an intelligent one. With these techniques, considering the humidity and the intelligent absorption, the cooling can happen in a very effective and energy-saving mode.

Aquachill's Innovation and Achievement

With innovations in the system building and AI for having intelligent cooling that is based on the requirements of the customers and the environmental conditions, they have provided AI-based solutions. They have come up with intelligent cooling, where problems like waterlogging are avoided.

To conclude with the case studies, AI is evolving in every possible way, to have energy saving, cost cuttings, and of course, for profitability. What more can it help out with? Providing security through air conditioner, where an intruder is detected!

19.5   CASE STUDY: AGRICULTURAL DOMAIN—FARMER'S INTELLIGENT ASSISTANT

Problem

Today in India, farmers are facing hardships. Due to the natural calamities, sudden changes in the weather conditions and rainfall delay, their yield gets destroyed. Sometimes, owing to unavoidable circumstances or emergency, the yield does not reach the market. Most of the times, the in-between agents obtain maximum benefits, leaving a little for the farmer to survive. These factors and the uncertainty in the environment affect the overall agricultural development. Hence, same crop may not be suitable for different years and different seasons. One of the major problem the farmers are facing is selecting a right crop to maximise the yield. An intelligent system that can assist the farmers in various possible ways is needed today.

What Will the System Provide?

The system can provide a farmer with the selection of crop to plant, helpful fertilisers, appropriate price he would get and many other options. Here, we look at different AI approaches that can help in making these decisions with the availability of different input parameters.

Which Parameters are Involved in the Process?

Many parameters can be involved in this process such as soil type, temperature, rainfall, humidity, market in vicinity, land area, crops planted by adjoining farms, market trends and many more. The decision-making for the farmer and the parameters that influence this are depicted in Figure 19.2.

System and AI Role

With the revolution in mobile industry, almost every person owns a mobile. This intelligent assistant can be web-based, where the farmer can register and get the required information. The location of the farmer can be captured based on the latitude and longitude. Further, the images for soil type can be captured from the satellite to determine its type. The intelligent system can have the database available at prior. The basic architecture of this system is shown below in Figure 19.3.

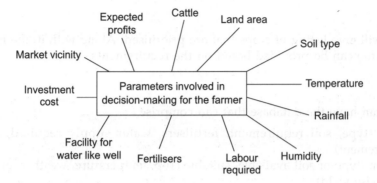

Figure 19.2 Parameters for crop selection.

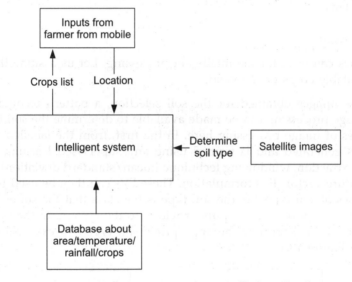

Figure 19.3 Architecture of an intelligent system.

Under such a scenario, the inputs/outputs and the processing details of the systems are given here. But first, let us summarise the list of techniques that can be employed showing the flow of systems with AI at different stages.

Inputs

1. Farmer's details including number of family members, earning members, his age, labour availability
2. Area/Region
3. Farm area
4. Expected benefits
5. Previous years' details about crop
6. Market availability

The farmer can get registered to the system, and in later stages, can avail all the benefits for decision-making.

Output

The system will give listing of crops that are prioritised. Along with it, the fertilisers and other details too can be provided based on the requirements.

Database

The system can have the database that can comprise

1. Crop (type, soil requirement, fertilisers, water supply required, temperature requirement)
2. Region (type of soil available, suitable crop, temperature, weather, market details, area-wise yield)
3. Farmer database (name, region, crops selected in the previous year, profits and other details)

Intelligent Processing

Many approaches can exist for the intelligent processing. Let us assume that we need to give just the suitable crops or the yield.

1. From the images obtained for the soil selection, a pattern recognition approach with image processing can be made available to determine the soil type. There are two cases of image processing here. In the first, from the labelled data, a feature vector is generated and is trained using any supervised learning approach. For feature extraction, windowing technique (mean/standard deviation) can be used to have feature vector (FV) formulation. These FVs can then be used to train and get the classes of soil type. So, the soil type is the class that the supervised approach learns. This is prior to the inputs provided to the system. In the operation phase, the system will determine the appropriate soil type. An example of the same is given in Figure 19.4.

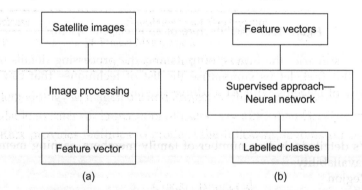

Figure 19.4   Image processing for soil type recognition.

2. Now comes the actual processing. The system can have multiple options, which are mentioned below:
   (i) The system can be a simple rule-based system that will give multiple choices of the crops. Extension to this is the use of weighted approach for the crops.

This would be based on initial learning experiences. Every crop will have some weight associated. This would be multiplied with the parameters obtained from the farmers. Finally, the decisions can be ranked. The outline of the approach is shown in Figure 19.5.

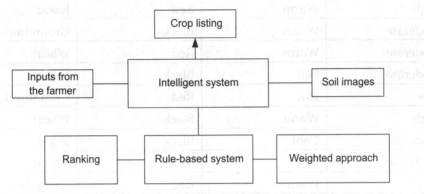

Figure 19.5 Building blocks for crop listing.

(ii) Bayesian probability and Markov chaining too can be useful for the process of crop determination, provided the prior probabilities are available. With every crop suitable for a region, the probability with the parameters given can be determined. Then, they can be ranked giving a list of the most suitable ones for plantation.

(iii) A system that would give the probability of good yield based on the crops can be looked at too. So, based on the past years' records, we can have a list of crops suitable for that particular region. On the current suggested crops, the intelligent system can suggest which would give a good yield.

EXAMPLE: Let us assume a sub-system for the crop suitability. Suppose we have some details available with us for crops. So, given some conditions, we want to determine which crop is suitable for the particular parameters. Using Naive Bayes, we can determine it.

Table 19.1 shows the available data for the classes to be determined (here the crops). So, we have some training set.

Let us use Naive Bayes. Assume we have classes—jowar, groundnut and wheat. In Naive Bayes, we are given a tuple X with some parameters and we want to predict a particular crop. Naive Bayes predicts a particular class C_i iff

$$P(C_i|X) > P(C_j|X)$$

where, $i \neq j$ and $1 \leq i, j \leq m$ (m is the number of classes)

In turn, we intend to maximise the posterior probability. We know according to the Bayes's theorem,

$$P(C_i|X) = \frac{P(X|C_i) * P(C_i)}{P(X)}$$

where $P(X)$ is constant, and hence, we consider the numerator only. Here, for the classes,

TABLE 19.1 Crop Production Parameters

Rainfall	Temperature	Soil	Crop
Low	Hot	Basalt	Jowar
High	Warm	Red	Jowar
Moderate	Warm	Black	Groundnut
Moderate	Warm	Red	Wheat
Moderate	Hot	Black	Jowar
Low	Hot	Red	Groundnut
High	Warm	Black	Wheat
Moderate	Cool	Black	Jowar
Moderate	Hot	Basalt	Wheat
Low	Warm	Red	Groundnut
High	Warm	Basalt	Jowar
High	Cool	Red	Groundnut

we have the probabilities, i.e., P(jowar), P(groundnut) and P(wheat) that can be computed from Table 19.1.

With Naive Bayes assumption of conditional independence, we compute

$$P(X|C_i) = \prod_{a=1}^{n} P(x_a|C_i) = P(x_1|C_i) * P(x_2|C_i) * \dots P(x_n|C_i)$$

All the attributes in the training set are categorical; if they were numeric, we would have to use Gaussian distribution with standard mean and deviations for computation of $P(x_a|C_i)$.

Let the query be {Rainfall=moderate, temperature=warm, soil=red}. This input is provided by the farmer who wants to know which crop is suitable. Now, with the available training data, we can compute the probabilities. Prior probability of each class (crop here) is computed as follows:

Probability = Number of tuples with x_a as the crop/Total number of tuples.

So, the probability that jowar is suitable is given as

$$P(\text{jowar}) = 5/12 = 0.4166.$$

Similarly, P(groundnut) = 4/12 = 0.333 and P(wheat) = 3/12 = 0.25
Let us begin with conditional probabilities computation.

Parameter 1   In the query of moderate rainfall,
P(rainfall = moderate | jowar) = 2/5 = 0.4
P(rainfall = moderate | groundnut) = 1/4 = 0.25
P(rainfall = moderate | wheat) = 2/3 = 0.666

Parameter 2   In the query of warm temperature,

P(temperature=warm | jowar) = 2/5 =0.4

P(temperature=warm | groundnut) = 2/4 =0.5

P(temperature=warm | wheat) = 2/3 = 0.666

Parameter 3   In the query of red soil,

P(soil=red | jowar) = 1/5 = 0.2

P(soil=red | groundnut) = 3/4 = 0.75

P(soil=red | wheat) = 1/3 = 0.333

$P(X \mid \text{jowar})$ = P(rainfall = moderate | jowar) * P(temperature = warm | jowar) * P(soil = red | jowar)

= 0.4 * 0.4 * 0.2 = 0.032

$P(X \mid \text{groundnut})$ = P(rainfall = moderate | groundnut) * P(temperature = warm | groundnut) * P(soil = red | groundnut)

= 0.25 * 0.5 * 0.75 = 0.0937

$P(X \mid \text{wheat})$ = P(rainfall = moderate | wheat) * P(temperature=warm | wheat) * P(soil=red | wheat)

= 0.666 * 0.666 * 0.333 = 0.1477

To predict the crop suitability, finally the posterior computations are done as follows:

$P(X \mid \text{jowar})$ * P(jowar) = 0.032 * 0.4166 = 0.0133

$P(X \mid \text{groundnut})$ * P(groundnut) = 0.0937 * 0.333 = 0.0312

$P(X \mid \text{wheat})$ * P(wheat) = 0.1477 * 0.25 = 0.0369

Since, wheat has higher probability, it predicts this crop suitability. Thus, we have discussed a simple example to understand how the approach can be useful on a larger scale.

A dynamic system for the problem is depicted in Figure 19.6. Owing to the dynamic nature of problem, as depicted in Figure 19.6, active learning can be used.

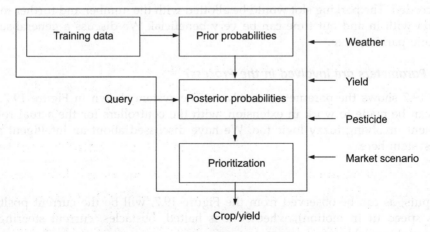

Figure 19.6   Dynamic crop selection.

Which other techniques can you adopt here? Can a simple feed-forward perceptron model of NN-based approach be appropriate here for final crop listing? With NN, the case is that given some inputs, it definitely belongs to one particular class. The network is trained to select only one class. For example, if we have 4 crops listing (4 classes), and we train the network with some parameters; it is bound to give single crop selection (one output) for a given input. When just a single crop would be sufficient for the farmer, only at that point of time, we could use such an approach. A hybrid system could possibly be an option that considers fuzzy logic.

19.6   CASE STUDY: AUTOMATIC CAR PARKING SYSTEM

Problem

Parking has always been a very big issue today with the immense rise in the number of vehicles. Imagine you have to reach to your friend's party and the venue is on an overcrowded street; you would be definitely looking for a system that would assist you in parking the car, providing you with the details of the available parking and how long possibly you would have to walk down to the party place after your car is parked! We discuss role of AI in solving this problem.

What will the System Provide?

The system will provide safe car parking option that would assist in the parking along with some details such as in what direction the car is required to be moved, rotation of the steering, gears, speed, lights required or not and so on.

There are two aspects of automatic car parking system. One is vision-based intelligent assistance that would assist the driver in parking. This would give the driver simple information about the empty slot available. Other is where the driver would simply leave the car at the parking entrance and an intelligent agent will drive through and park the car in the most appropriate slot for parking (without hitting anybody or damaging the car!). As an extension to these systems, the number plate image of the car would be captured and recorded. The parking slot would be allotted with the number and further maintaining this data with in and out time can be very beneficial. We discuss a generalised case for automatic parking here.

Which Parameters are Involved in the Process?

Figure 19.7 shows the parameters involved. The system shown in Figure 19.7, at a later stage, can be made to work in extension, with the controllers for the actual rotation and movement involving fuzzy logic too. We have discussed about an intelligent assistance-based system here.

Inputs

The inputs, as can be observed from the Figure 19.7, will be the current position of the car, its speed (if in motion), whether it is halted, obstacles, current steering position, parking slot available, etc.

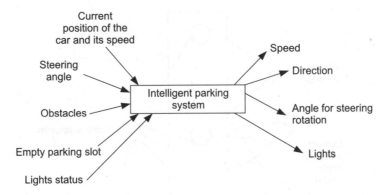

Figure 19.7   Parameters for the automatic parking system.

Outputs

The car would be parked appropriately with the details of what direction the movement should occur, angle for steering rotation and the speed.

Intelligent-parking Assistant

Let us consider a scenario for parking in forward direction (light factor is not considered at this instance). Before the system gets to work, the sensors would be required to capture the available empty parking slot and detect the obstacles in the movement. Let us brief the steps in the parking system.

1. ***Capturing of empty slot:***   Various sensors would capture the empty slots. This would involve basic image processing approach of segmentation and detection for the empty slot.

2. ***Selection of the nearest empty slot from the car position:***   Simple distance ranking—based calculation would be done to determine the nearest parking empty slot.

3. ***Communication of information:***   Assume that there exists a human computer interaction (HCI) and the display of the parking slot is given.

4. ***Automatic Parking system (APS) at work:***   This would include the following:
   (i) The entire motion for the parking would be planned.
   (ii) Target would be set and the search process would be evaluated.
   (iii) Based on the parameters at current position, angle of rotation would be computed. A supervised NN (Figure 19.8) can be used.
   (iv) Speed required would also be provided. Again, this can be any supervised machine learning approach that will provide the exact speed based on the current situation.
   (v) At the end, the system will notify to put the hand brake.

The supervised approach for selection of angle rotation can be based on Bayes's theory. . The entire system, thus, works as an intelligent agent to assist in the parking. It can be further enhanced by having a voice dialogue with the driver, and as said earlier, an entire automatic system with the controllers would be highly recommended nowadays.

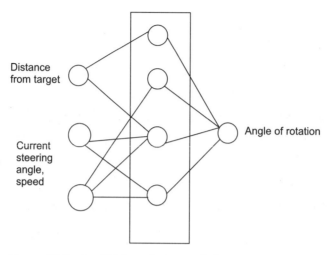

Figure 19.8 An NN-based approach for angle detection.

SUMMARY

The approaches and the case studies discussed have helped us in building a picture on how AI is making its position in every industry. AI is contributing towards industrial growth. Every time, every day new dimensions are added up to have better systems with huge contribution from AI. AI is now converging towards data mining, where the important information is mined using the machine learning approaches. To increase business productivity and profits, AI has the potential to mold the business environment, giving a new vision and prospective outcomes. The analysis gives directions for future decisions with reasoning.

It is very difficult to say that only specific industries are able to use AI, as almost everything that we wish to have, we feel it needs to possess intelligence. Text mining, data stream mining, web mining are the 'in' research areas. The core research in AI lies in improving and coming up with approaches and building systems that are capable of giving faster, effective, efficient and optimal outcomes for the tasks.

Last but not the least, we would like to give some more examples before we conclude. Imagine a scenario where you are driving a car and listening to radio. There are multiple radio stations. If intelligent agent is built in your car, then it would switch between the stations to tune in to your favourite song and based on your mood, you would just like it!

Let us take one more example. You get some SMS that you have won award for something. You are well aware that such SMSs are not valid. But even if you are in a critical meeting, the SMS alert is generated. If there is a built-in app in your mobile capable of recognising this and setting alerts based only on the context, won't it be useful?

And at the last, think of an intelligent system, which could take input as question papers, and the knowledge in the form of a book and give you the summarised answers for most frequently asked questions in the exam, it would be most interesting thing ever!

KEYWORDS

1. **Big data:** This is the collection of data sets that is too complex and large. Using standard tools for manipulation for such a data is difficult.

2. **MapReduce:** It is programming paradigm that enables the programmers to write programs to have parallel processing across the distributed cluster.

3. **Hadoop:** It is a framework that enables distributed computing environment. This is based on MapReduce.

4. **Mahout:** It is the library of machine learning algorithms implemented on Hadoop.

CONCEPT REVIEW QUESTIONS

1. How can intelligent learning agent concept be applied in traffic monitoring scenario? Explain in detail.

2. Consider a system where an employer needs to take up a decision regarding recruitment of an X person. From qualifications' perspective, he is eligible. If we want to employ HMM in some way for the decision, is it possible to use it? For what purpose the concept can be applied? Can Naive Bayes assist in the decision? Discuss.

3. Given a task of scheduling multiple sessions in a conference on two days, with some sessions sharing session chair and co-chair. How can searching technique be applied here? Explain the concept behind using it.

4. Can the concept of reinforcement learning be applicable for a game such as Temple run? Discuss.

CRITICAL THINKING EXERCISE

1. Consider an application to generate notes based on a presentation delivered by a teacher. Which AI tools and techniques would you use? Will there be any classifier involved? Detail the techniques.

2. There is an application that suggests a specific haircut which suits a person. Which AI models would it use in the background? Elaborate with features selection to the final decision.

3. Assume you are on the way to pick up your friend at around 11 am. You have started 1 hour before and you have a list of tasks to be carried out on the way. You complete your tasks and reach at 11 am. Which factors were considered by you from AI's perspective to reach by 11 am? Which techniques helped you to solve the tasks on the way? Elaborate.

4. Student's feedback is obtained by the HOD for the staff teaching them. The HOD needs to decide which staff needs improvement and which staff is the best among

them. How would an intelligent system assist the HOD to do this task? Which AI models can be applied to help in this decision-making? Will there be any pre-processing involved? Explain.

◁ PROJECT WORK ▷

1. Given some documents of text, build an intelligent PPT generator that would get the contents from the text appropriately for slides. Identify the title of the slide as well.

2. For a college, develop an intelligent time table generator. Some of the parameters to be considered are number of staff, number of subjects, number of batches—practical/theory (shift—yes/no), number of subjects the staff would teach, number of hours the staff has load, number of classrooms and laboratories. The system needs to tackle clashes as well.

3. Consider an image processing application that has a set of images of fruits. Develop an application that would detect if the fruit is raw or ripe. Try to detect if the fruit is decayed as well. A ripe or a raw fruit can have a decay also.

4. Build an intelligent desktop arranger that would arrange/create new folders based on the titles of the data/files saved or based on the contents. Only folders would exist on the desktop and no files.

5. For prioritising mobile messages based on the contents of the messages, develop an application to determine whether it is essential to generate an alert sound or not. For example, for a joke, there should not be an alert.

6. Given an essay on a particular topic that is handwritten by n number of persons. Perform an analysis on the basis of handwriting and the contents to determine the nature of that person.

7. Develop a lane-cutting identifier. The application would handle the traffic lanes and accurately identify the person who has violated the lane policy.

8. Suppose we have a person who has logged on someone else machine. The password, the intruder has entered is correct, but the way he is accessing the machine is different. Determine the intruder of a system using AI. Detect this behaviour along with the key stroke dynamics. Develop an application that can send an alert on mobile to determine this intruder.

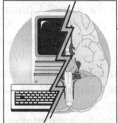

CHAPTER 20

Advance Topics in Artificial Intelligence

Learning Objectives

❑ To understand the concurrency aspect with the role of AI
❑ To understand the importance of intelligent agents in concurrency engineering
❑ To appreciate the role of AI in big data analytics and cloud computing
❑ To identify the role of AI in sentiment analysis
❑ To elaborate different aspects of AI with reference to recent technology trends

INTRODUCTION

Till this chapter, we have discussed and learnt about the different facets of AI. With time, many new technologies have evolved and they have impacted the way AI is used and can be applied. In this chapter, we will learn AI in association with new evolving technologies. Here, we will take a holistic look at AI and its relationships with new evolving trends and technologies. Social networking has made available tons and tons of data for processing. The big data and cloud computing have made it necessary to use AI on different dimensions for decision-making and knowledge building that led to many concurrency issues. The whole idea behind this chapter is to make the reader familiar with the new trends and appreciate the role of AI in each of the domains.

In this chapter, we would also highlight some of the aspects of pattern analytics and usefullness of AI in the learning contexts. Some aspects of sentiment analysis and deep learning are also covered to address the need of handling dynamic scenarios.

20.1 WHAT IS CONCURRENCY?

We believe that any complex task with large size and additional time constraints can be better resolved if the concurrency is employed. Applying concurrency will result in

449

betterment. But how would it be possible? From the definition of concurrency, it results in the execution of tasks simultaneously.

Are concurrency and parallelism the same? Concurrency is employed when the tasks in execution are moving towards a common goal. A concurrent task may be executed in serial or parallel. Concurrent execution together with parallel execution leads to the improvement in the performance of a given task. While parallelism with concurrency is the execution of concurrent tasks on multiple platforms.

Why and when is the concurrency required? As said earlier, a complex task could be solved with concurrency. Concurrency, actually, is not only about solving the task. It enables us to think and analyse with respect to the computation tasks being executed. Concurrency is needed in every environment. From simple browsing's perspective to database's services, we need concurrency. Let us look at AI's perspective towards concurrency.

20.1.1 AI and Concurrency

Today, though there is availability of multiple core systems, rarely we take the advantage of such a system. It is desired that the applications take fullest advantage of the system. Considering the complexity of the machine learning algorithms and techniques, a concurrent execution can definitely improve the process. This is, in fact, very crucial for the determination, especially for forecast applications. So, considering growth in data, say even in social media, the data needs to be mined for various purposes. An efficient concurrent approach can help in getting the desired results with complex machine learning techniques. Today, research has gradually shifted to concurrency, with the need of having parallelism too. Various programming languages have been proposed to handle the concurrent aspect like Go, ConGolog.

This was one point of view. Let us go to the other aspect. When we talk about concurrent programming, one would think of autonomous intelligent agents working to reach some goal. This can happen in distributed environment as well. So, a multi-agent system has risen to have intelligent modelling. Is just intelligent agent aspect a core concept for concurrent programming? In what other ways can AI techniques be applied to have concurrent execution as well? So, we are actually talking about two aspects— an agent who would carry the task, and AI techniques which would assign tasks to the agents. Building the agent to carry out the assigned task is known to us. The other aspect is determining the tasks that can actually happen concurrently. So, we need to identify intelligently which actions leading to different goals can be handled in concurrent. Co-ordination, co-operation and concurrency not only help in solving efficiency and resource management issues but also, with intelligence, can help in timely intelligent decision-making.

Let us look at another perspective of concurrency. Considering real-life actions, at present a lot of research has been undertaken to identify real-life actions that can be executed concurrently with AI. Various authors have worked on concurrent aspect for the identification of goal along with the set of actions that can have concurrent execution. The concept here is the identification of goal for even real-time videos. They include approaches of Bayes, skip-chain conditional random field, HMM and many more.

A simple diagram showing the non-concurrent and concurrent goal detection is given below in Figure 20.1.

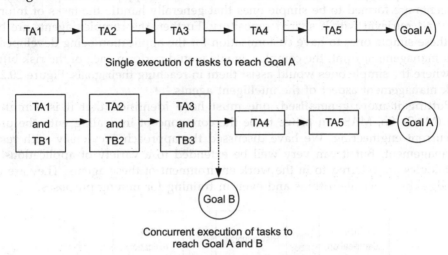

Single execution of tasks to reach Goal A

Concurrent execution of tasks to
reach Goal A and B

Figure 20.1   Single and concurrent task executions.

20.2   AGENT-BASED CONCURRENT ENGINEERING

Let us elaborate the role of agents in concurrent engineering by looking at the different applications. It is a well-known fact that an intelligent agent needs to behave rationally. While exhibiting this characteristic, the agent needs to adapt to the environment. There are different applications, where the intelligent agent can be proved very useful in concurrent engineering. Let us discuss them.

In any project development life cycle, there are multiple tasks that can occur concurrently. Large complexity issues exist in such projects, where there is an existence of data/resource sharing and co-ordination. Risk management in such concurrent engineering projects adds up with the complexities. The matter alleviates if the work operation involves multicite concurrency. So, this risk management is required throughout the building and development phase of the project life cycle. How can an agent help in such a scenario?

Approaches that lack the agent-based aspect have many shortfalls. In the absence of an intelligent agent, the risk management is wholly dependent on the sharing of the data and group decision support system. An intelligent agent in concurrent scenario helps in building an application independent interface for the communication. Assume a task of application development of aerospace engineering. In such an application, intelligent agents handle the tasks of risk identification, analysis, mitigation along with knowledge management. The agent helps in assisting the tasks of this risk management process. They are built on the belief–desire–intention (BDI) models. So, the agents need to progress based on beliefs (information that an agent has about itself and its environment), desires (the things an agent would have to satisfy) and intentions (knowledge or a sort of plan formed when an agent commits to achieve a particular target/goal). Each of the agents in such environment completes its intentions in co-ordination with each other. They are often built as pluggable members that can remove the application dependency aspect. Such agents are formed to be simple ones that generally handle the tasks of information storage and retrieval with a shared repository. Further, the complex agents are built on top of these simple ones to have customisation for the application being developed. From the risk management front, the complex agents would perform each of the risk-bifurcated tasks, where the simple ones would assist them in reaching their goals. Figure 20.2 shows the risk management aspect of the intelligent agents.

Putting it more generalised, one must have identified that it is a multi-agent system (MAS). So, MAS can prove to be the core concept in dealing with the problems of concurrent engineering. We have discussed the approach previously with respect to risk management. But it can very well be extended to a variety of applications. Often, the ontologies are referred to in the work environment of these agents. They are used in knowledge discovery algorithms and even in training for mining purposes.

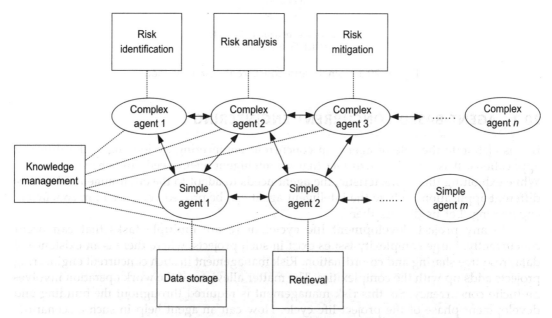

Figure 20.2 Intelligent agents: Communicating for risk management.

20.3 CLOUD COMPUTING AND INTELLIGENT AGENT

A very recent technology that provides computing as service without the need to purchase the resources is *cloud computing*. Cloud-based platform is always keen in providing improved business intelligence and services. An intelligent agent environment integrated with cloud can enable to achieve this task with increased flexibility, and at the same time, scalability and reliability too. There are different models of cloud—infrastructure as service (IaaS), Platform as service (PaaS) and software as service (SaaS). We can define the role of agent in each of them to exhibit betterment of the services.

In case of IaaS, an intelligent agent can assist in providing the basic resources required for the users. It can make use of ontologies for intelligent resource management and help in allocating the task to the most eligible and appropriate resource. In case of PaaS, the agents can assist in the development of environment, whereas the case of SaaS is all about the optimisation. If we take a simple application of health care services, then embedding agent architecture in such a system to build an e-medical service can help in many ways. A system that is essentially MAS will have each of the complex agent and simple agents working in co-ordination for the tasks like providing the services to allocation for services. These can as a whole, contribute in effective resource utilisation. These agents can tackle the tasks of emergency services, providing facilities to the patients and so on. They all co-ordinate and co-operate with each other. The entire scenario aims at providing efficient services with reduced costs.

There are numerous factors affecting the intelligence in AI. Till now, we have concentrated only from the intelligent agent front. Making it more generalised in terms of AI, the security factor, data integrity and confidentiality are some of the critical aspects of cloud computing.

20.4   PLANNING AND LOGIC IN INTELLIGENT AGENTS

From the current intelligent agent's perspective, we have always looked at the intelligent agent as the one who acts rationally. In the previous sections, we have discussed about the agent in concurrent programming as well as in cloud-based computing and MAS. We now put forth an aspect, where the agent involves not just the perception and action, but planning as well. To have this, there is a need of a strong logic-based programming to support the decisions of the agents. A typical *agent environment* is the one where the agent senses the environment and acts on it. In case of logic-based programming, planning needs to be involved. Often, it includes the following:

1. Agent environment and the expected outcomes from it
2. An interpreter that will analyze and have reasoning capabilities for the action

How is planning useful here?The logic programming involves planning of the actions. So, it tries to have stability in terms of planning and logical outcomes. The building blocks of these agents comprise fluents and situations, rather than the states and the simple actions. Naturally, this requires the history of the earlier actions and involves the use of situation calculus. Situations, thus, store the group of actions. Fluents include the objects, with the actions and situations. That is, they represent the characteristics of the objects in the situations or the results. Figure 20.3 shows its details.

A basic question arises here—where is this useful and why? These systems are looked upon for game playing. The decisions of actions from the opponent's viewpoint can be highly influenced with this in-built logic and can be proved useful as well. Thus, the systems are evolving from event-based intelligence to situation-based intelligence, and further, to system-based intelligence, where intelligent agent can sense the context, and accordingly, act in the given situation. The approaches can, thus, be useful in dynamic scenarios.

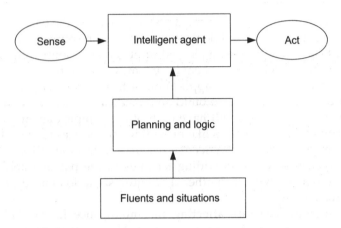

Figure 20.3 Logic and planning for intelligent agent.

20.5 BUSINESS INTELLIGENCE AND ANALYTICS

The field of business intelligence in relation with big data analytics is gaining importance day by day. Many companies have found out that rolling out an intelligence model results in significant growth in the business. The key behind this model is AI. Formally today, business intelligence deals with different areas of analytics, viz. mobile analytics, text analytics, big data analytics. Precisely, these all are clubbed under the title of business intelligence and analytics. So, the various techniques and facets discussed earlier are clubbed under this business intelligence in more comprehensive way.

Let us look at the different fields and get an overview of applications of them. We are already familiar that big data deals with the unstructured data, and the entire analysis becomes a complex task. Naturally, to handle this data, there comes the need for having distributed parallel processing. Here, comes the concept of Hadoop with MapReduce to deal with this data. What about the analytics? How is AI used here?

Since there is a tremendous data explosion, analytics in business intelligence has become the necessity today. Nowadays, artificial intelligence is being used on large scale for the governance tasks like draught estimation, population identification. With the tremendous growth in the population of the countries, AI-assisted technologies can always be looked upon by the governments for providing services.

The trend in big data basically emerged from the web and e-commerce applications and has been looked for analysis. The necessity of privacy concern has led to the development of mining activities in this context. AI context is not just looked at from this aspect, but for process mining as well to analyse the logs of the data. Another feature is text analytics. AI techniques find their place in information extraction, topic modelling, sentiment analysis and opinion mining. We are already familiar with cloud. It is basically web analytics that has emerged for deliverables as services. Business intelligence and AI also deal with mobile and network analytics. Mobile analytics carries the task of the analysis of the location of specific services, new apps promotion and even context-based services and management issues. Network analytics, still at very infant stage, is aimed at link mining and community detection activities.

To summarise, it is the pattern analytics that takes place with the discovery of the hidden patterns in the data. Today, it is moving towards the predictive analysis that is added to the identification of patterns; it possesses forecasting abilities.

EXAMPLE: Let us take an example of *kumbha mela* to understand how the analytics work. *Kumbha mela* is the event that produces large data. This big data can be used for analytics. But how can it be used? It is often observed that the management of such an event is a very difficult venture. There is a need for having large security, and at the same time, coordination with respect to the management of crowds. Many issues arise in this venture, even with relation to health. Analytics from the behaviour of the people, the background they are from, the health issues faced by them at particular events, the crowd gathering at specific locations, their need and entire details can be analysed and used for further decision-making. So, this entire data with intelligence can be used for addressing the problems and providing the people with improved security, appropriate health services and stay arrangements. IT can even open new opportunities for new businesses.

20.6   SENTIMENT ANALYSIS

We have already discussed about natural language processing and the related tasks. We divert towards the AI application for sentiment analysis. What is sentiment analysis? It is concerned with the polarity determination of the text, that is, to determine what the person wants to convey through his writing about any particular thing, whether it is positive/good or negative/bad or neutral. This is applicable in cases where one is getting reviews, say reviews of movies, opinions (opinion mining), feedback and so on. With the current trends, it deals with the data from the tweets and analyses them. From the comments, the analysis is done to have what the person feels about the subject he is commenting. It is indeed a need of the hour to extract, analyse and capture the viewer's opinions so as to have an improved decision-making.

What is the role of AI? The concept in this analysis is to use NLP techniques and machine learning algorithms to have outputs. Since it deals with the decisions of the data to predict a class, core concepts of machine learning are bound to have a role in it.

Sentiment analysis can be useful from business intelligence perspective also. For any product sale or for identifying the competitors strengths, reviews and opinions can be mined to get the answers. Yet determining the category of sentiment is a difficult task, as the words used to express the views could be interpreted is a wrong way.

20.7   BIG DATA AND SENSORY PROCESSING (SP) THEORY OF INTELLIGENCE

SP theory has been in the development stages for many years. The theory integrates and simplifies the concepts of AI, mainstream computing, cognitive modelling along with information compression. The theory states to have a brain-like system that can compress some of the information, learn and perceive new information and use it further for pattern recognition, reasoning and so on. The technique, thus, extends to overcome a variety of issues of big data, and attempts to be incremental in nature to address the velocity of the data streaming, and at the same time, targets the volume by making it smaller.

The principle of using this theory lies in the fact that the new information is perceived and the old one is represented in compressed form. The underline concept is of multiple alignment. An alignment determines the old data that needs to be compressed when a new data is perceived. This is based on probabilities, and sometimes, heuristic methods are also used. The theory is well-suited for partial pattern matching in the course when it is learning new patterns.

Though the theory has been established years ago, its application and exploitation are still in nascent stage and can definitely be an important and demanding branch in the coming years.

20.8 DEEP LEARNING

Before we conclude, just a glimpse on deep learning is mentioned here. It is a new field and at present, is termed as *cutting edge technology*. Deep learning aims at bringing the machine learning closer to artificial intelligence. By this, the learning process aims at mimicking the human brain. Especially, it aims at handling the unsupervised learning in an incremental way. In contrast to supervised machine learning algorithms, where massive amount of data is available, the learning can perform clustering based on some similarity factors. Deep learning aims to excel in this by achieving an incremental approach. Typical examples mentioned in literature include syllabus identification from some new language or face identification from videos—everything in real time and incremental way. So, the learning makes the data sense that can be in the form of image, text or sound. Deep learning comprises set of algorithms, which are based on distributed representations. It assumes that the observed data is made available by interactions at multiple levels for multiple factors. Hence, there exists a layered hierarchy that is exploited by these algorithms. The approach captures the features from this layered abstraction which are suitable for learning. At this time, it is difficult to state about the future of deep learning, since as of now, a handful of researchers are working on this learning.

SUMMARY

The chapter focuses on some on the emerging aspects of AI in solving real-world problems along with the research dimensions. It is aimed at getting broader views of the current trends with AI. A spectrum of opportunities lies open for all with AI and current technologies. Big data and cloud are the next things discussed here; AI has its impact and need everywhere. Analytics is what we need today and will continue to be the factor required for the future. It is all about business intelligence that demands more and more outcomes with AI. Lastly, we can say that AI will continue to be a necessary branch with huge potential in providing intelligent feature for every real-life situation to help in decision-making and analysis. Intelligent systems is the backbone of all modern systems and with this, new evolutions will help in coping up with the varied requirements of modern system.

KEYWORDS

1. **Cloud computing:** It is a technology that provides computing and other functionalities as services, avoiding the need to purchase them.
2. **Pattern analytics:** This refers to the discovery of meaningful patterns
3. **Sentiment analysis:** It determines the polarity based on the users' comments from the text data.
4. **Big data analytics:** It is the analysis of huge volume of unstructured data to discover the hidden patterns.
5. **Deep learning:** This deals with the approaches to built intelligent machines that exhibit human-like learning.

MULTIPLE CHOICE QUESTIONS

1. Pattern analytics intends to
   (a) Hide the meaningful patterns for processing
   (b) Select the useful patterns and study them
   (c) Discover the meaningful patterns
   (d) All of the above

2. Sentiment analysis is not about
   (a) Finding the opinion about the person on some product
   (b) Determining the polarity from the text
   (c) Feature-based sentiment classification
   (d) Finding sentiments in the text

3. Which of the statement is not true about big data?
   (i) It discovers hidden patterns from a variety of data
   (ii) Analytics of big data helps in better business decisions
   (iii) Hadoop, NoSQL and MapReduce are the technologies associated with it
   (iv) Social media activity, web logs are data sources for big data

   (a) (i), (iv)   (b) (iii)   (c) (ii)   (d) None of these

CONCEPT REVIEW QUESTIONS

1. What is pattern analytics? Explain with an example.
2. Explain the factors that an intelligent agent needs to handle in concurrent engineering.

CRITICAL THINKING EXERCISE

1. Is it possible for sentiment analysis to have multiclass classification? Discuss the validity and acceptability.

2. You are provided with some story. A tool needs to be developed to understand the gist of the story. Is it possible to have intelligence to achieve the required outcome? Explain your viewpoints.

PROJECT WORK

Try to develop a model using any machine learning technique to carry out sentiment analysis of one liner feedback. Assume a new hotel is opened and views on the same are obtained. Define your classes and use the pre-processing techniques to represent the data.

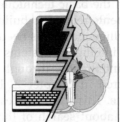

CHAPTER 21

Concluding Remarks: AI–Present and Future

Artificial Intelligence is the backbone of modern technologies. We want every application to behave more intelligently. We want our cars, washing machines, air conditioners and even homes to be intelligent. Right from the simple memorisation and rule-based decision-making, the machines are expected to infer, make context-based decisions and even compete with human being. AI has indeed revolutionised the world and offered new perspectives to the industries. AI, which was used to give a competitive edge to the organisations in the last decade, today has become an essential part of the organisations, appliances and education. AI has revolutionised mobile phones by making them smart. It has revolutionised televisions by making them intelligent. All this attracts more and more researchers towards the field of artificial intelligence.

Today, AI finds its roots in each and every domain, where one needs analysis and inference. Intelligence is needed in security, defence, traffic, network analysis and many other day-to-day applications and varied domains. Health care is one domain where AI has made huge impact. With intelligent image analysis, diagnostic help and assistance during operations along with intelligent appliances help in solving many problems. There are intelligent robots used by companies to deliver goods and pizzas, load trucks and park cars. The present AI systems, thus, have delivered value in all domains right from the mechanical engineering, e-commerce, banking, health care to the border security. With such a wide range of applications and delivered proven value by AI system, a question comes in mind of every professional, every researcher, and every student of AI course—what is the future of AI? This chapter tries to portray this picture with concluding remarks.

The following criterion should be kept in mind:

More intelligence → More data processing → More inference → Large dimensions → Increasing demand of intelligence → Complex problem

459

21.1 QUICK RECAP

In this book, we have gone through the basic techniques of AI and various algorithms. It is like a journey where all requirements related to building artificial intelligence or rather intelligent systems are covered. Intelligent systems need to exhibit intelligence, and hence, the introduction and evolution of intelligent systems have been explained at first. An intelligent system needs to exhibit intelligence through problem solving; hence, problem-solving techniques have been covered in Chapter 2. This is more about understanding problem and selecting right technique. This also includes implementation and measurement of performance. Problem solving is about search of the goal state. It is the journey from the start state to the goal state. Hence, searching is one of the major activities in solving problem. Even many problems can be solved using search-based techniques. Hence, in Chapter 3 we have covered search methods. Based on the availability of information, situation and context search can be informed or uninformed. Hence, Chapter 3 covers different uninformed and informed search techniques. The search methods evolved to cope up with complex problems and find out the solution for them. Different advanced search techniques have been learnt in Chapter 4. To behave intelligently, the problem solver needs to sense the environment, understand problem and respond appropriately. In Chapter 5, we have studied intelligent agent. Intelligent agents are the agents containing sensors and actuators and have an ability to respond to a situation intelligently. The problem that intelligent agents try to solve has constraints; rather there are constraints in all real-life scenarios. Hence, we have learnt about constraint satisfaction problems in Chapter 6. This has been studied with examples of some real life as well as some very well-known and standard constraint satisfaction problem.

Intelligent systems need to build knowledge and should apply reasoning in this entire process. In Chapter 7, we have covered knowledge and reasoning. This chapter covers different aspects of knowledge building including data mining, logic, reasoning and inference. The chapter gives us knowledge building aspects for intelligent agent. The uncertainty is part and parcel of all real-life scenarios, and hence, we need to build knowledge during dynamic real-life events, and hence, knowledge building should able to cope up with uncertainty. Chapter 8 covers uncertainty aspects of knowledge building. In this chapter, we have learnt about different probabilistic theories associated with uncertainty, conditional probability and handling complex decisions. To solve any problem, one needs to plan. Planning strategy needs to take into account all the aspects of problem. In Chapter 9, we have learnt about different planning strategies. We have discussed about hierarchical planning, partial ordered planning and conditional planning. These different aspects have not only showed the importance of planning to us but also allowed us to understand the role of planning as a component of intelligent system.

Learning is one of the basic aspects of intelligence. Intelligent systems should have an ability to learn. Hence, learning is the foundation of knowledge building and intelligent systems. In Chapter 10, we have understood the role of learning and also studied about different learning methods. This chapter offers us the guidance about different learning methods. Some of them are very basic, while some are very complex. In this chapter, we have learnt different statistical learning methods, neural network-based learning methods and paradigms like reinforcement learning. Then, in Chapter 11, we have studied different types of expert systems. Intelligent systems learn based on the text data. They need to understand speech; they are even expected to give directions. All this happens mainly in natural languages, and hence, it is important to understand the natural language and process the data in the form of natural languages. In Chapter 12, we have learnt natural language processing, where we have studied information extraction and machine translation as well.

Decision-making remains an important part of intelligence. We want the outcome of intelligence to be the most appropriate decision. Hence, decision theory is another important part of intelligent systems and artificial intelligence. Chapter 13, covers the decision theory. There are statistical problems and pattern recognition problems. The pattern recognition methods provide the ability to understand and process patterns efficiently and infer. In Chapter 14, we have learnt about these intelligent recognition systems. This chapter covers cognitive perspective and machine perception for pattern recognition. This equips us with the mandatory information along with the overall perspective of AI and building intelligent systems. But intelligence needs to handle some very dynamic scenarios. Think of game playing techniques, where a lot of dynamic aspects are taken into account. Game theory has offered another facet to the intelligent system. Hence, we have learnt about these techniques in Chapter 15, and about perception and actions in Chapter 16. Human beings learn dynamically and adaptively. It cannot be said that just one simple technique can help in concluding or solving a problem. To exhibit such a behaviour by intelligent systems, they need to have hybrid intelligence. Hence, we have gone through hybrid intelligent systems in Chapter 17. Based on the structure of our brain that informs us about the actions to be taken, neural networks show their ability in forecasting to classification domains. We have studied about them in Chapter 18. With all this information, we have gone through the process of building intelligent systems and studied some important industrial applications of AI and intelligent systems in Chapter 19. Chapter 20 discusses the concurrency aspect as well as the role of AI in big data analytics and cloud, sentiment analysis, and elaborates different aspects of AI with reference to new technology trends.

This journey has given us different facets of intelligent systems and details about their different aspects.

21.2 FUTURE OF INTELLIGENT SYSTEMS

The progress and journey of AI has opened the door for more possibilities and increased our expectations from every appliance. A home that can be intelligent and offer the required size of bedroom when one is there or change size of hall when the visitors come and that too without any mechanical arrangement done by human interventions is a definite possibility of tomorrow. Even it can be expected that in the same theatre one can watch his favourite star in the lead role while his wife can watch the same movie with the star of her choice in the lead role during the same time slot. The audience can interact with the characters playing roles in movies. One can play tennis with robot that can play exactly like their favourite tennis star, and many more intelligent problem solving opportunities are there. Future intelligent systems will not be constrained by technologies and will offer more thought for our imagination.

What AI delivered is more than what we could have imagined just three decades ago, and it has a potential to deliver many more applications with true intelligence. There are many problems in medical diagnostic system, road traffic and security system.

Future intelligent systems would need to solve them. In short, future intelligent systems should be dynamic and able to take systematic decisions and should have learning ability. This book is a platform to give pointers to build a real intelligent system and systematic perspective towards AI.

Figure 21.1 depicts intelligent systems as should have, ability to, need and exhibit (SANE) matrix. Future intelligent systems will be dynamic, agile, systemic and with great learning abilities.

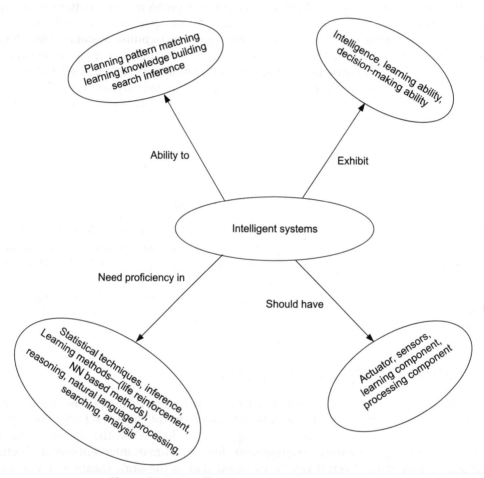

Figure 21.1 Intelligent systems as SANE matrix.

As Einstein has said, "We cannot solve the problems with the same level of thinking that created them". So, we need to change the level of thinking to solve problems. Future intelligent systems will have an ability to change the level of thinking to solve some of the very complex problems, which we could not imagine today.

Mathematical Background

This section discusses some of the mathematical aspects. We begin with the different distance measures, probabilities and some other important statistical concepts.

A.1 DISTANCE MEASURES

Measuring the similarity between the data points that are to be clustered or classified is based on the distance measures. The selection of a particular distance measure is dependent on what functionality (subjective) is to be carried out and what is the nature of the input data points. Let us look at the various distance measures along with their suitability for a particular type of data.

Minkowski Distance

$$\text{distance}(x, y) = \left(\sum_{i=1}^{n} \left| x_i - y_i \right|^q \right)^{1/q}$$

where x and y are two n-dimensional data objects and q is a positive integer. This distance is a generalised form of numeric data points.

Euclidean Distance

$$\text{distance}(x, y) = \sqrt{\left(\sum_{i=1}^{n} \left| x_i - y_i \right|^2 \right)}$$

As it can be observed from the formula, Euclidean distance is a case, where $q = 2$ for the Minkowski distance. This distance is often used for clustering and is the default one for the k-means.

Manhattan Distance

$$\text{distance } (x, y) = \left(\sum_{i=1}^{n} |x_i - y_i| \right)$$

For the Minkowski distance measure, when the value of $q = 1$, it results into Manhattan distance. What difference do we get from Euclidean and Manhattan? Manhattan computes the distance between the data points as if we are moving on a grid from one point to another. It is also known as *city block distance*. Whereas for Euclidean, it is the computation of hypotenuse of a triangle for two data points.

Maximum Distance: Infinity norm distance

$$\text{distance } (x, y) = \left(\max_{i=1}^{n} |x_i - y_i| \right)$$

It specifies the maximum distance between any components of the vectors.

Mahalanobis Distance

$$\text{distance } (x, y) = \sqrt{(x - y)' C^{-1} (x - y)}$$

The Mahalanobis distance measures the distance between the point x and the centre of mass y. C is the co-variance that is used. We know that the co-variance literal meaning is to measure the tendency of how two vectors vary. The co-variance, thus, is the average of the products of the deviations in the feature vectors from their mean values. The co-variance computation is done as follows:

$$\text{Cov} = \frac{\sum(x_i - \bar{x})(y_i - \bar{y})}{n - 1}$$

where x_i and y_i are the two variables, and $\bar{x}$ and $\bar{y}$ represent the mean of them, respectively.

This distance measure is often compared with Euclidean distance and people are often confused with the usage. Mahalanobis distance is concerned with the correlation of the data sets. It is useful for finding the outliers if they exist in the data sets. When the co-variance matrix becomes an identity matrix, it results into Euclidean distance.

Cosine Similarity

$$\cos \theta = \frac{v_1 \cdot v_2}{\|v_1\| \|v_2\|}$$

where v_1 and v_2 are the vectors. It is often used to compute similarity between the text documents. Cosine similarity is often used for high dimensional spaces.

A.2   PROBABILITY

We now proceed towards the probability computations. Let us begin with simple probability and conditional probabilities.

A.2.1 Simple Probability

Following terms are related to simple probability:

Sample Space and Events

A *sample space* is defined as a set of all possible outcomes. An *event* is defined as a subset of the sample space. Consider P to be the probability of outcome. In such a case, the probability of any event e, which is a subset of sample space S is given as follows:

$$P(e) = \frac{n(e)}{n(S)}$$

Here, $n(e)$ is the number of elements in the event e and $n(S)$ is the number of elements in the sample space S.

The types of event that can occur are categorised into

1. Independent events
2. Mutually exclusive events

Mutually Exclusive Events

When two or more events cannot take place or happen at the same time, they are mutually exclusive. Since they cannot occur simultaneously, they are dependent events. The probability for the mutually exclusive events always leads to 1. Let us consider events m and n which are mutually exclusive, then the probability is given as:

$$P(m \text{ or } n) = P(m) + P(n)$$

Independent Events

Independent events do not affect each other. There is no relation between the events and the cause of one event does not impact the other's outcome. For example, for the events m and n, if m and n are independent events, then the probabilities will be defined as:

$$P(m \text{ and } n) = P(m) * P(n)$$

Note: If we consider two events m and $\sim m$ which are mutually exclusive, then remember that they are not independent events.

A.2.2 Conditional Probability

A simple probability of any event (say x) is its occurrence under the absence of some additional information, which might impact that event's probability. *Conditional probability* is the one where occurrence of another event y might reflect change in x's probability. So, the conditional probability for this event is defined as the probability of event x, given event y (which has already occurred).

It is represented as $\qquad P(x \mid y)$

Let us consider two cases of independent and not independent events.

Not Independent Events

For events x and y that are not independent, and y is given (event occurred), then the probability computations will be

$$P(x \mid y) = P(x \text{ and } y)/P(y)$$

Similarly, the corollary can be given as:

$$P(x \text{ and } y) = P(x \mid y) * P(y)$$

Independent Events

For events that are independent, the conditional probability for x, given y, is defined as follows:

$$P(x \mid y) = P(y) * P(x)/P(y)$$

Hence, $P(x \mid y) = P(x)$

For events x and y
1. The product rule is $P(x \text{ and } y) = P(x \mid y) P(y) = P(y \mid x) P(x)$.
2. The sum rule is $P(x \vee y) = P(x) + P(y) - P(x \text{ and } y)$.

A.3   BAYESIAN PROBABILITY

We have studied Bayes's theorem and classification aspects earlier. Again, some mathematics and basics are covered here. So, we know that Bayesian classifier predicts membership of class depending on the probabilities. The Bayesian classifier is based on the Bayes's theorem and highlights the conditional probability (or most appropriately called *posterior probability*) that is based on the known prior probability. It addresses the classification problem to determine the best hypothesis, given some training data.

The parameters and the aspects involved in these probability value computations are explained below:

1. $P(h)$: This is initial probability (where h is some hypothesis). This is prior to the training data being available. It is also called *prior probability of h* or *marginal probability of h*.
2. $P(x)$: This is prior probability for the training data x. Here, knowledge about the hypothesis is unavailable. It is also known as *marginal probability of x*.
3. $P(x \mid h)$: It is the probability after observing the training data, given hypothesis.
4. $P(h \mid x)$: It is the posterior hypothesis. It is the probability that h holds, given some observed training data. It is given as

$$P(h \mid x) = \frac{P(x \mid h)\,P(h)}{P(x)}$$

The above formula is known as *Bayes's theorem*.

Let us look at how it is derived.

From the conditional probability, the probability of events x and y are given as the probability of x, given y.

$$P(x \mid y) = P(x \text{ and } y)/P(y)$$

whereas probability of y, given x is

$$P(y \mid x) = P(x \text{ and } y)/P(x)$$

Thus, we have

$$P(x \text{ and } y) = P(x \mid y) \, P(y) = P(y \mid x) \, P(x)$$

According to Bayes's theorem

$$P(x \mid y) = \frac{P(y \mid x) P(x)}{P(y)}$$

Naive Bayes

The classification approach that works on the Bayes's theorem is *Naive Bayes*. Here, the variables are considered to be independent. So, in any learning approach, we are familiar that there exists a training set. Let us consider T to be the training set comprising t_1 to t_n tuples, represented as

$$T = \{t_1, t_2, ..., t_n\}$$

Assume that the classes available are CL from 1 to m, where m is the number of classes. It is represented as

$$CL = \{C_1, C_2, ..., C_m\}$$

Now, given a new data ND, the job of the classifier is to predict the class for it. It can be represented as

$$ND = \{nd\_att_1, nd\_att_2, ..., nd\_att_n\}$$

where nd_att_1 to nd_att_n are the attributes or the parameters of the new data set.

The Bayes's classifier—Naive Bayes predicts a class for this new data on the basis of highest posterior probability. Let us say that the class predicted for this ND is C_i. This is done with the following rule:

$$P(C_i \mid ND) > P(C_j \mid ND)$$

such that $j \neq i$ and $1 \leq j \leq m$. Here, C_j is other class.

Thus, for this prediction and classification, we have to maximise $P(C_i \mid ND)$. This class C_i is at times referred to as *maximum posteriori hypothesis*. The Bayes's theorem gives us

$$P(C_i \mid ND) = \frac{P(ND \mid C_i) P(C_i)}{P(ND)}$$

To resolve this, the numerator value needs to be maximised. $P(ND)$ is a constant here. This is because it is independent of the value of C. So, we can infer that when the numerator value is maximised, so is the outcome.

If we assume that there is unavailability of the marginal probabilities, then the following holds true:

$$P(C_1) = P(C_2) = ... = P(C_m)$$

or else $P(C_i)$ = Number of training tuple of C_i/Number of tuples in the set.

With these two constraints, where $P(ND)$ and the probabilities of belongingness to classes are constant, we further infer that we have to maximise $P(ND|C_i)$.

According to the assumption of Naive Bayes, the parameters or the features of the data set are independent, given the class label. It is given as follows:

$$P(ND|C_i) = \prod_{p=1}^{n} P(nd\_att_p|C_i)$$

$$= P(nd\_att_1|C_i)P(nd\_att_2|C_i) \dots P(nd\_att_n|C_i)$$

Now, the attributes that are handled can belong to any of the following two categories:

1. Categorical
2. Continuous

Thus, for calculation of $P(ND|C_i)$ two cases are to be considered. In categorical, $P(nd\_att_p|C_i)$ refers to the number of tuples of class C_i, divided by $|C_i, T|$, which refers to the total number of tuples/sets in class C_i. Whereas in case of continuous valued, Gaussian distribution needs to be considered. Thus, we need to take into account the (∂) standard deviation (∂) and the mean (μ).

$$g(nd, \mu, \partial) = \frac{1}{\sqrt{2\pi}\partial} e^{-\frac{(nd\_att_p - \mu)^2}{2\partial^2}}$$

Then, we have

$$P(nd\_att_p | C_i) = g(nd\_att_p, \mu C_i, \partial C_i)$$

The posterior can be written as:

$$P(C_i|ND) = P(C_i) \prod_{p=1}^{n} P(nd\_att_p|C_i)$$

So, with the above rule, we label the new data ND to class C_i that will have highest posterior probability. Thus, we would predict the class that would satisfy the following condition:

$$P(ND|C_i)\,P(C_i) > P(ND)|C_j\,P(C_j)$$

where i is not equal to j and $i, j <$ total number of classes.

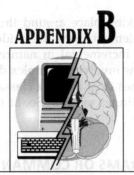

APPENDIX B

LISP Programming

B.1 WHAT IS LISP?

LISP stands for list processing. It is a language that was originated in 1950s by McCarthy, with an intention to be used for AI purposes. Today, it is available in varied forms and has been considered as a pioneer for functional languages. Currently Scheme, Clojure and Common LISP are the general purpose LISP dialects that are widely in use. Its main focus lies in processing everything in the form of lists. The main advantage of using it is that it allows the programmer to have a perfect picture that allows visualising the code in the way you have it in your mind. Moreover, the language supports incremental evolution in terms of coding as well.

B.2 AI APPLICATIONS

Since the language is originated as the requirement of AI, it supports a variety of applications even today. It finds place in pattern recognition applications. Robots and game playing too have used LISP. It also finds place in planning, scheduling and even in translation purposes. Not these, but there are many more applications where LISP can be used.

B.3 WHAT IS THE NEED OF LISP?

Is it not the case that this language has disappeared? That is a very relevant question that comes to your mind. LISP though has shown its presence earlier along with its competitors—Prolog and Python, it did receive a setback in the 1980s. It was in this period where applications received more concentration and AI was not looked upon. In the meantime, other languages like C, C++ and Java had started gaining momentum. But LISP survived and is widely in use.

With the current activities taking place around the open source community, today, Common LISP and Clojure implementations are widely used for applications. These are suited for problems that are incremental in nature, where new information can be accommodated. So, for applications involving complex data and evolving data, LISP is the option. Many LISP implementations exist for Java classes [1]. AutoLISP is too in practice. LISP is preferred in financial institutes as well. So, at the end, the fact is LISP is in use and would be used further too.

B.4 EXECUTING LISP PROGRAMS OR COMMANDS (USE OF COMMAND LINE)

With CLISP being installed on your machine, on the terminal you write 'clisp'. This will start the interpreter. On the prompt that would appear as '[1] >' you would type your LISP commands. To execute LISP programs, save them with .lisp extensions. To run them, write

> (load "first.lisp")

To execute function in the program, say we have written facto of a number, write

>(facto 4)
>24

B.5 SIMPLE LISP COMMANDS AND SYNTAX

Let us begin with basic primitives for the programming. First and foremost, let us understand that it follows prefix format.

So, on the LISP prompt, we could write

> (+ 1 10)
> 11

The solution 11 is displayed. So, the operator should occur first and then the arguments. Similarly, some of the sample examples for equation evaluation are

> (/ (+ 7 3) (+ 1 1))
> 5

LISP has concept of atoms and lists. Some of the examples of atoms are X, abc, q12, * . 23, 12.7 are numeric atoms. X, *abc*, q12 are referred to as *symbolic atoms*.

List consists of brackets ( ) that include atoms. It can be empty as well. Atoms and list together form expressions.

Some of the common functions in LISP are given below.

car

This gives the first atom of the given list. The list remains unchanged. For example,

> (car '(1 2 3))
> 1

cdr

This returns the rest of the list, excluding the first atom. Again, the list remains unchanged, only the remaining atoms are given. For example,

> (cdr '(1 2 3))
> (2 3)

setq

It is used to set the variables. For example,

> (setq x 12)
>12
or
> (setq str1 "Artificial")
> Artificial
or
> (setq x '(12 13 14))
> (12 13 14)

setf

This is similar to setq function. For example,

> (setf q(/ 10 2))
> 5

length

It gives the length of the list's arguments. If we have executed setq for *x* (previous example), then

> (length x)
> 3

eval

It evaluates the given expression. For example,

> (setq x 10)
>10
> (setq y '(+ x 3))
>(+ x 3)
> (eval y)
>13

atom

It returns true if the arguments in the list is atom. For example,

>(setq x (11 12 13))
>(11 12 13)

```
>(atom 'x)
>T
>(atom x)
>Nil
```

T indicates that the arguments are atoms, whereas Nil for x indicates it is not an atom.

listp

Except indicates whether the arguments are list or not. So,

```
>( listp 'x)
>Nil
>(listp x)
>T
```

cons

It adds element to the front of the list. For example,

```
> (cons '(a) '(b c d))
> ((A) BCD)
```

append

It simply concats of two or more lists. For example,

```
>(append '(1) '(2 3) (aaa))
> (1 2 3 AAA)
```

lambda

It is a temporary function. When one does not want to give any specific name to it, this function is used. For example,

```
> # '(lambda (z) (– z 3)
(LAMBDA (Z) (– Z 3)
> (funcall * 2)
> –1
```

Line no. 1 defines the function. We call the function with (funcall * argument). '*' indicates the last result. We get the output as –1.

B.6 CONDITIONAL STATEMENTS

If Statement

The if statement has following syntax:

```
(if (predicate)
    (execute this statement)
    (else execute this statement))
```

The above statement shows that in the if condition, only one statement can be executed. The else part is optional. If we want multiple statements, then we can have

```
(if (predicate)
(progn
    (execute statement1)
    (execute statement2)
    (execute statement n))
(else execute this statement))
```

Cond statement

The cond statement is used in following way:

```
(cond
    ((predicate 1) (statement 1))
    ((predicate 2) (statement 2))
    ((predicate n) (statement n))
    (t (else execute this statement)))
```

B.7 ITERATIONS

Loop

There are different variants of loop. A few of them are as follows:

1. (loop while(condition-statement)
   (execute this statement))
2. (loop do <statement> until <statement>)
3. (loop for x from 1 to n do <statements>)

Do

The do statement has following syntax:

```
(do (<variable initialisation-statements> <next-cycle-update statements>)
    (end condition statement)
    (<set of statements to be executed>))
```

B.8 INPUT/OUTPUT

In LISP, input/output is carried through the following commands:

read

This reads the input from the standard input device. For example,

```
>(n (read)
>4
>4
```

print

It prints the argument on the screen. The output is preceded by a new line. For example, if we have

>(print 5)

>5

>5

princ

This is similar to print, but does not consider a new line. For example,

> (princ "hi")
> hi
> "hi"

prin1

It is again one of the print commands, but with a difference. For example,

>(prin1 "hi")
> "hi"
> "hi"

format

This is somewhat similar to the printf statements we have in C. The syntax is

(format <destination><control-strings><arguments>)

For example, if we have to display a value of variable z, we can write it as

>(setq z 4)
>(format t "~d" z)
> 4
>Nil

t indicates the standard output, ~*d* is used for the integer output with base 10, ~*x*, ~0, ~*b* are for hexa, octal and binary number systems. ~$ is used for floating numbers.

B.9 FUNCTIONS

We use 'defun' to define functions that we want to use. The syntax for it is:

(defun function_name (parameters_optional)
    "optional – sentence for documentation"
    (function_steps))

Let us write a simple program that computes the average of two numbers.

(defun aveg(x y z)
    (/(+ x y z)3)
)

EXAMPLE: Let us write a program to print Fibonacci series. We will accept the limit from the user and display the series.

In LISP, a comment begins with ';' (semicolon).

```
; program to display Fibonacci series without recursion
(defun Fibonacci1()
; format t commands sends the srting to be printed on the standard output
  (format t "Enter end limit:")
  ;take input from user with read command
  (setf n(read))
  (if (eq n 1)
  (format t "0"))
  (if (eq n 2)
  (format t "0 1"))
  (if (> n 2)
    (progn
      (setf x 0)
      (setf y 1)
      (format t "0 1")
      (loop for i from 3 to n do
        (setq z (+ x y)
          x y
          y z)
      (format t " ~d" z))
    )
  )
)
```

The output for the program is

Enter end limit: 6
0 1 1 2 3 5

A recursive program for the same can be given as follows:

```
; program to display Fibonacci series with recursion
(defun Fibonacci1(n &optional (x 0) (y 1))
  (if (eq n 0)
    nil
  (progn
      (print x)
      (Fibonacci (- n 1) y (+ x y))
    )
  )
)
```

The output for the program will be

>(Fibonacci 6)
>0
>1
>1
>2
>3
>5

APPENDIX C

Prolog

C.1 WHAT IS PROLOG?

The key factor behind the invention of Prolog by Alain Colmerauer was to make use of logic in order to represent the knowledge. A language of 1970s, still has immense importance in AI for logic building. The motivation behind its usage was natural language processing. It gradually found way in other areas too. The core feature of this language is its ability to solve queries with the identification of relationships.

Today, many implementations of Prolog are available, most commonly ones are gprolog, SWI-Prolog and so on. Often used from research perspective is the SWI-Prolog that comes with a built-in IDE.

C.2 AI APPLICATIONS

For what sort of AI applications would we use Prolog? Since the language talks about queries that are resolved with relationships, the language has been most appropriate for building expert systems. We would find its importance in planning and reasoning applications as well. It suits for language parsing, databases and retrieval applications.

Embedded Prolog is also in use today, where the Prolog is embedded in C, C++, Java and so on. Thus, the main program is in other languages and Prolog supports them by providing them logic.

C.3 WHAT IS THE NEED OF PROLOG?

As discussed earlier, today Prolog is looked at from the perspective of embedding it with the other languages. Moreover, it spans a range of applications from web applications to expert systems and is still in use for research and commercial purposes.

C.4 EXECUTING PROLOG

Assume you have gprolog or SWI-Prolog installed in your machine. Simply by typing gprolog or swipl at the terminal, you can invoke it. Prolog programs are compiled with the following commands (Assume we have written prog.pl):

> consult(prog)
Or generally even the following is used:
> [prog].

Do remember the syntax varies with different prolog flavours. Once the program gets loaded, it is asked queries. As we study further, it will be clear.

C.5 SIMPLE PROLOG COMMANDS AND SYNTAX

Lists and Sequences
Lists in Prolog are represented as [...]. For example, a list can be [3, 4, 5] or [cat, bat, hat] or [p, q, [a, b, c]] and so on. A list has head and tail. The head of the list would be the first element, whereas the tail would comprise all the remaining elements.
Let us take as some examples with simple functions/built-in predicates for processing them.

1. **member:** It detects the members of the list.
   ?- member(X,[a,b,c]).
   The output we would get are-
   X=a;
   X=b;
   X=c;

2. **append:** This appends the members by generating the list.
   ?- append ([p,q],[r,s,t],Answer).
   Answer=[p,q,r,s,t]

3. **atom:** It checks if the argument is an atom or not.
   ?-atom(hello).
   yes
   ?-atom(has(book)).
   no

4. **atom_chars:** This separates the letters/individual items in the list or clubs them together.
   ?- atom_chars(hello,L).
   L=[h,e,l,l,o]
   yes
   ?-atom_chars(L,[h,e,l,l,o]).
   L= hello
   yes

C.6 SOME SIMPLE COMMANDS

1. **read(X):** This command reads the term given as input and stores in *X*.
2. **write(X):** This command writes the term in *X* to output port.
3. **nl:** It sets the cursor to a new line.
4. **get(X):** This command reads a character from the current input file
5. **put(X):** It writes character to the current output file.

Let us begin with the programming in Prolog.

A *prolog program* comprises facts and rules. We seek answers from this built knowledge. Let us write a simple program to understand the working.

We begin with the facts or clauses. They have to be in small letters and terminate with a period.

Sample Facts

1. subject(ai).
   Meaning: ai is subject
2. mother(Neha, Rohan).
   Meaning: Neha is mother of Rohan.

Rules

Rules are the ones that help us in defining more complex relations. For example, we have the following set of facts:

mother(Neha, Rohan)
father(Ram, Rohan)
wife(Riya, Rohan)

We define rules as follows:

parent(*X*,*Y*):   mother(*X*,*Y*); father(*X*,*Y*)
mother-in-law(*X*,*Y*):   mother(*X*,*Z*),wife(*Y*,*Z*)

The variables in Prolog begin with capital letters. Please note the difference in the first rule, *X* is said to be mother or father; hence, is separated by a semicolon';'. Whereas, in the second rule, we want both the conditions to be true, so a comma ',' is used.

While executing this code, we actually ask queries to get the answers. To get the parent of Rohan, the following query is typed and we get the answers:

|?- parent(X, Rohan).
X= Neha ? ;
X = Ram ? ;
no

(To get further answers, we would type a semicolon ';' as after getting Neha as answer, we have shown a semicolon.)

A sample Prolog code is given below:

Let us now look at a simple Prolog program. This is a sort of expert system that has rules. We invoke the program with rule_test.

```
rule_test1:-
    write('Did you have AI as elective?'),nl,
    read(Ans),
    (Ans = 'y' -> rule_test2;
     Ans = 'n' -> rule_test1_ans).

rule_test2:-
    write('Did you have Machine Learning/Pattern analytics as Elective?'),nl,
    read(Ans),
    (Ans = 'y' -> rule_test3;
     Ans = 'n' -> rule_test2_ans).

rule_test3:-
    write('Did you have Data Mining as elective?'),nl,
    read(Ans),
    (Ans = 'y' -> rule_test3_true_ans;
     Ans = 'n' -> rule_test3_fail_ans).

rule_test1_ans:-
    write('Take AI now').
rule_test2_ans:-
    write('Take basics of Machine learning now').
rule_test3_fail_ans:-
    write('Take AI and machine learning').
rule_test3_true_ans:-
    write('Take Business intelligence ........').
```

In the program, '->' invokes the corresponding rule and proceeds. Let us try to make a generalised version of the same code with some more additions.

```
question(quest1,'Did you have AI as elective?').
question(quest2,'Did you have Machine Learning/Pattern analytics as Elective?').
question(quest3,'Did you have Data Mining as elective?').

rule_test1:-
    ask(quest1,Ans),nl,
    (Ans = 'y' -> rule_test2;
     Ans = 'n' -> rule_test1_ans).

rule_test2:-
    ask(quest2,Ans),nl,
    (Ans = 'y' -> rule_test3;
     Ans = 'n' -> rule_test2_ans).
```

```
rule_test3:-
    ask(quest3,Ans),nl,
    (Ans = 'y' -> rule_test3_true_ans;
     Ans = 'n' -> rule_test3_fail_ans).

rule_test1_ans:-
    write('Take AI now').
rule_test2_ans:-
    write('Take basics of Machine learning now').
rule_test3_fail_ans:-
    write('Take AI and machine learning').
rule_test3_true_ans:-
    write('Take Business intelligence ........').

ask(Q,Ans):-  question(Q,Text),
        write(Text),
        write('(y/n) : '),
        read(Ans).
```

Lastly, we now look at some of the database or the knowledge base manipulation commands along with some more Prolog features. At the command prompt, if we write '?- listing.', we will get an output as yes.

The listing command actually specifies the predicates you have in the code or in the built-in interpreter. We can assert some facts by the use of assert command and remove with the use of retract command. How do we use it? Let us see.

1. *assert:* The assert command adds new facts to the knowledge base. For example, assert(plays(Rohan,cricket)).

Now, if you run listing, it will give you output as

```
?- listing.

:- dynamic plays/2.
plays(Rohan,cricket).
true.
```

The dynamic indicates that the facts are dynamically added in course of execution, unlike static facts that are pre-defined. Remember to add dynamically, it has to be with the use of assert. Similar to assert is asserta that adds the facts at the beginning and assertz that adds the facts at the end.

2. *retract:* The retract command removes the added facts from the database.
Suppose we have added three clauses using assert.

plays(Riya,tennis)
plays(Siya,basketball)

Then, retract(plays(Riya,tennis)) will remove the assertion. Even a command retract(plays(X,tennis)) will make you confirm that X=Riya and remove the assertion. retractall(plays(_,_)) will remove all the assertions with plays.

3. *Cuts:* A cut is given with a symbol '!'. These are used in the programs to avoid backtracking of the code. A tree generated during evaluation or applying rules results in pruning of the tree.

Consider the following piece of code without cuts. The program will be executed with 'go'. Now, on inputting 45, we will get both the outputs.

func(X):   ((X > 30 | X < 50) ->
               write('rule 1 invoked'),nl).

func(X):   (X > 40 ->
             write('rule 2 invoked'),nl).

go: write('Enter X:'),
      read(X),nl,
       func(X).

Now, rule 1 is modified with addition of cuts.

func(X):   ((X > 30 | X < 50) ->
               write('rule 1 invoked'),!).

func(X):   (X > 40 ->
             write('rule 2 invoked'),nl).

go: write('Enter X:'),
      read(X),nl,
       func(X).

The output that we will get is just rule 1 invoked on giving input of 45, even though the condition 2 is satisfied.

At the end, we will conclude with a simple expert system program that uses assert, retract and cuts. The system is built to suggest an elective. The intention of the code is to get the reader acquainted with the usage of assert and retract predicates.

```
elective(datamining):-
    prev_elective(ai),
    knowledge_about(machine_learning).

elective(wn_and_mobilecomputing):-
    prev_elective(adv_cn),
    knowledge_about(network_hardware).

prev_elective(X):-ask(previous_elective,X).
knowledge_about(X):-ask(knowldge_about,X).
```

% three rules for ask, the first two are used to check if the answer is learnt already

```
ask(Para,Option):-
    learnt(yes,Para,Option),    % cut if the answer is yes and learnt already
    !.
```

```
ask(Para,Option):-
    learnt(_,Para,Option),        % fail causes the rule to be failed.
        !,fail.                   % States that it is false

ask(Para,Option):-
    nl,write(Para:Option),
    write('(yes/no):'),
    read(Ans),                    % get the answer
    asserta(learnt(Ans,Para,Option)), % remember it
        Ans==yes.

run:-retractall(learnt(_,_,_)),   %forget/clear previously stored facts
        elective(X),
        nl,write('Suggested elective :'),
        write(X),nl.

run:- write('No elective suitable for you.'),nl.
```

We will invoke the program with run. The output suggests elective depending on the inputs. To conclude, we would say that the programming language Prolog is applicable to many domains, and specially suited for building expert systems and to provide a strong knowledge base.

APPENDIX D

Travelling Salesman Problem

D.1 PROBLEM

The problem of travelling salesman (TSP) states that given the number of cities and the distances between them, determine the shortest possible route such that all the cities are visited just once and the journey ends in the same city from where it started.

D.2 BRIEF HISTORY

In 1800, W.R. Hamilton and Thomas Kirkman formulated the TSP mathematically. Hamilton's Icosian game, which was based on Hamiltonian cycle, was the motivation of TSP. (Hamiltonian cycle can be defined as a cycle that visits each node in the graph cycle exactly once.) In 1930s, mathematician, Karl Menger studied the problem, defined it and presented brute-force approach. He noted the non-optimality feature in using the nearest neighbour with heuristic. The name *travelling salesman problem* was introduced by Hassler Whiteney to the problem. In 1950s to 1960s, the problem gained tremendous popularity. In 1972, Richard Karp proved Hamiltonian cycle problem to be NP-complete. After 1970s, researchers came up with techniques such as branch and bound to solve the problem. Till today, many approaches have been contributing to get the solution for the problem depending on the instances of the cities.

D.3 MODELLING THE PROBLEM

The problem can be modelled as graph—a graph which is weighted and undirected. The nodes represent the cities and the arcs represent the weights between them. In case of a symmetric graph, the distance between the connecting cities is same, whereas in case of asymmetric, it is different or even the route might not exist between the cities.

D.4 NP-HARD

The problem is an NP-hard problem. The problem remains to be NP-hard even though removal of the constraint to visit each city once takes place.

D.5 SAMPLE GRAPH

Given a graph, as shown in Figure D.1, mapping for a TSP in graph.

So, if the start city is P, the solution to the problem is to traverse all the cities and come back to P with minimum cost.

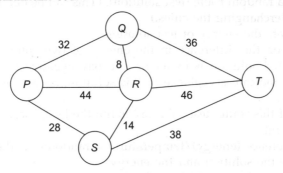

Figure D.1 Mapping for TSP.

D.6 SOLVING THE PROBLEM

Though there are many approaches to solve the TSP, the simplest one would be to explore all the options and then selecting the shortest route. Finding Hamiltonian cycles and having this approach is not effective at all when the number of nodes increases, as it increases the number of cycles. So, a simple brute force approach, which would yield time complexity of $O(n!)$, is not a approach to be looked at.

Many branch and bound techniques have been used till date to determine the path, which can give solutions to few thousands of cities. An exact solution was developed by Dantinz, Fulkerson and Johnson, which was based on linear programming. In 2005, Concorde TSP Solver solved the problem for 85,900 cities; developed by Applegate, Bixby, Chavatal and Cook. Heuristic and approximation approaches can be useful in finding the solutions for TSP.

Typically, lower and upper bounds are calculated to determine the estimates. An upper bound value suggests that this is not the best solution, but then the solution cost should be less than or equal to this upper bound. Similarly a lower bound value determines the minimum cost. To determine the upper bound, Prim's or Kruskal's or nearest neighbour approach is used, whereas in case of lower bound, it involves deletion of a node and then finding minimum spanning tree for the other remaining nodes.

Ant colony optimisation is another approach proposed by Marco Dorigo in 1997, that makes use to heuristic for getting good solutions.

What can you say about the techniques that we have studied throughout this book—A*, simulated annealing, genetic, etc. Are they all capable to solve and get the solution to this problem?

Simple algorithmic steps to solve the problem using simulated annealing are given below:

1. Begin with a random route (possible solution) from the set of tours that are valid.
2. Calculate the energy of this route.
3. Set initial temperature.
4. Till the temperature > cut-off temperature
   (i) Select a random route (test solution). (This can be obtained by minor changes, say interchanging the cities.)
   (ii) Calculate the energy of test solution.
   (iii) Based on the difference in the energy of two solutions, decide if this new generated solution is better or not. Say negative value—(global minimum) would indicate acceptance of this solution. So, update this solution and the energy.
   (iv) Even if this route (test solution) is not the best, it can be accepted with some probability.
   if (difference (energy)/temperature) > random(0,1) then
   update the solution and the energy.
   (v) Continue with step (i) by reducing the temperature.

The approach in each iteration lowers the temperature to assist in getting the solution.

Bibliography

Abbass, Hussein A., An Evolutionary Artificial Neural Networks Approach for Breast Cancer Diagnosis, *Artificial Intelligence in Medicine*, Vol. 25, No. 3, pp. 265–281, 2002.

Achler, Tsvi and Eyal Amir, Input feedback networks: Classification and inference based on network structure, *Frontiers in Artificial Intelligence and Applications*, 171, p. 15, 2008.

Ahmed, S., Tutorial on Natural Language Processing, Lecture notes, AI, 2009.

Alon, Shiri, and David Schmeidler, Purely Subjective Maxmin Expected Utility, Technical report, 2008.

Amarel, Saul, Problem-solving Procedures for Efficient Syntactic Analysis, Defense Technical Information Center, 1968.

Amarel, Saul, On Representations of Problems of Reasoning about Actions, *Machine Intelligence*, 3, No. 3, pp. 131–171, 1968.

Anusuya, M.A., and S.K. Katti, *Speech Recognition by Machine: A Review*, arXiv preprint arXiv:1001.2267, 2010.

Appelt, Douglas E., Introduction To information Extraction, *AI Communications*, Vol. 12, No. 3, pp. 161–172, 1999.

Arisha, Amr, Paul Young, and Mohie El Baradie, Job Shop Scheduling Problem: An Overview, 2001.

Bacchus, Fahiem, and Froduald Kabanza, Using Temporal Logics to Express Search Control Knowledge for Planning, *Artificial Intelligence*, Vol. 116, No. 1, pp. 123–191, 2000.

Balakrishnama, Suresh, and Aravind Ganapathiraju, Linear Discriminant Analysis—A Brief Tutorial, Institute for Signal and Information Processing, 1998.

Bennett, Casey C., and Kris Hauser, Artificial Intelligence Framework for Simulating Clinical Decision-making: A Markov Decision Process Approach, *Artificial Intelligence in Medicine*, 2012.

Bishop, Christopher M., *Pattern recognition and machine learning*, Vol. 1, Springer, New York, 2006.

Bradley, Derek, and Gerhard Roth, Adaptive Thresholding using the Integral Image, *Journal of Graphics*, GPU, and game tools, Vol. 2, Issue 2, pp. 13–21, 2007.

Brandenburger, Adam, Game Trees, 2007.

Brenner, Michael, Multiagent Planning with Partially Ordered Temporal Plans, International Joint Conference on Artificial Intelligence, Vol. 18, Lawrence Erlbaum Associates Ltd., 2003.

Brunelli, R., and Lucken, C. Von, Optimal Crop Selection using Multi-objective Evolutionary Algorithms, *AI Magazine*, pp. 96–105, 2009.

Canny, John, A Computational Approach to Edge Detection, Pattern Analysis and Machine Intelligence, *IEEE Transactions*, pp. 679–698, 6 November, 1986.

Chang, S. Grace, Bin Yu, and Martin Vetterli, Adaptive Wavelet Thresholding for Image Denoising and Compression, Image Processing, *IEEE Transactions*, pp. 1532–1546, 9 September, 2000.

Chapman, David, Nonlinear Planning: A Rigorous Reconstruction, *IJCAI*, pp. 1022–1024, 1985.

Chatterjee, Kalyan, and Hamid Sabourian, *Game Theory and Strategic Complexity*, pp. 1–36, 2008.

Chen, Dar-Ren, Ruey-Feng Chang, and Yu-Len Huang, Breast Cancer Diagnosis using Self-organizing Map for Sonography, *Ultrasound in Medicine and Biology*, Vol. 26, Issue 3, pp. 405–412, 2000.

Chen, Hsinchun, Roger HL Chiang, and Veda C. Storey, Business Intelligence and Analytics: from Big Data to Big Impact, *MIS quarterly*, Vol. 36, No. 4, pp. 1165–1188, 2012.

Chen, Hsinchun, Sherrilynne S. Fuller, Carol Friedman, and William Hersh, Knowledge Management, Data Mining, and Text Mining in Medical Informatics, *Medical Informatics*, pp. 3–33, Springer, US, 2005.

Chowdhury, Dilip Roy, et al., Neonatal Disease Diagnosis: AI Based Neuro-Genetic Hybrid Approach, 2012.

Clocksin, William F., Christopher S. Mellish, and W.F. Clocksin, *Programming in PROLOG*, Vol. 5, Springer, Berlin, 1987.

De Weerdt, Mathijs, Adriaan Ter Mors, and Cees Witteveen, Multi-agent Planning: An Introduction to Planning and Coordination, Handouts of the European Agent Summer, 2005.

De Saussure, Louis, Pragmatic Issues in Discourse Analysis, Critical Approaches to Discourse Analysis Across Disciplines, Vol. 1, Issue 1, pp. 179–195, 2007.

Dietterich, Thomas G., Machine Learning Research, *AI Magazine*, Vol. 18, No. 4, p. 97, 1997.

Dietterich, Thomas G., Ensemble Learning, *Handbook of Brain Theory and Neural Networks*, pp. 405–408, 2002.

Dubois, Didier J., *Fuzzy Sets and Systems: Theory and Applications*, Vol. 144, Academic Press, USA, 1980.

Duda, Richard O., Peter E. Hart, and David G. Stork, *Pattern Classification*, 2nd. ed., Wiley, New York, 2001.

Duda, Richard O., Peter E. Hart, and David G. Stork, *Pattern Classification*, Wiley-Interscience, USA, 2004.

Endriss, Ulle, Lecture Notes: An Introduction to Prolog Programming, 2007.

Esmael, Bilal, Arghad Arnaout, Rudolf K. Fruhwirth, and Gerhard Thonhauser, A Statistical Feature-Based Approach for Operations Recognition in Drilling Time Series, 2013.

Fainekos, Georgios E., Revising Temporal Logic Specifications for Motion Planning, Robotics and Automation (ICRA), *IEEE International Conference*, 2011.

Fern, Alan, Speedup Learning, pp. 907–911, 2010.

Fisher, Michael, and Michael Wooldridge, Distributed Problem-solving as Concurrent Theorem Proving, Multi-Agent Rationality, Springer Berlin Heidelberg, pp. 128–140, 1997.

Fox, Maria, and Derek Long, PDDL2.1: An Extension to PDDL for Expressing Temporal Planning Domains, *J. Artif. Intell. Res. (JAIR)*, Vol. 20, pp. 61–124, 2003.

Fullér, Robert, *Neural Fuzzy Systems*, Åbo Akademi, 1995.

Garibaldi, Jonathan M., and Robert I. John, Choosing Membership Functions of Linguistic Terms, Fuzzy Systems, FUZZ'03. *The 12th IEEE International Conference*, Vol. 1, IEEE, 2003.

Gonzales, Rafael C., and Richard E. Woods, *Digital Image Processing*, 1993.

Gordon, Andrew S., *Strategy Representation: An Analysis of Planning Knowledge*, Taylor & Francis, New Jersey, 2004.

Gorniak, Peter, and Ian Davis, SquadSmart: Hierarchical Planning and Coordinated Plan Execution for Squads of Characters, *AIIDE*, pp. 14–19, 2007.

Gu, Tao, Liang Wang, Zhanqing Wu, Xianping Tao, and Jian Lu., A Pattern Mining Approach to Sensor-based Human Activity Recognition, Knowledge and Data Engineering, *IEEE Transactions*, Vol. 23, No. 9, pp. 1359–1372, 2011.

Gupta, Megha, and Gaurav S. Sukhatme, Interactive Perception in Clutter, *Robotics: Science and Systems*, 2012.

Haazebroek, Pascal, Saskia van Dantzig, and Bernhard Hommel, A Computational Model of Perception and Action for Cognitive Robotics, Cognitive Processing, pp. 355–365, 2011.

Hastie, Trevor, Robert Tibshirani, Jerome Friedman, T. Hastie, J. Friedman, and R. Tibshirani, *The Elements of Statistical Learning*, Vol. 2, No. 1, Springer, New York, 2009.

Hayes, Philip J., and Jaime Guillermo Carbonell, *A Tutorial on Techniques and Applications for Natural Language Processing*, 1983.

He, Qiang, et al., Fuzzy Rough Set based Attribute Reduction for Information Systems with Fuzzy Decisions, *Knowledge-Based Systems*, Vol. 24, Issue 5, pp. 689–696, 2011.

Herrera, F., and M. Lozano, Fuzzy Evolutionary Algorithms and Genetic Fuzzy Systems: A Positive Collaboration between Evolutionary Algorithms and Fuzzy Systems, *Computational Intelligence*, Springer Berlin Heidelberg, New York, pp. 83–130, 2009.

Hinton, Geoffrey, Li Deng, Dong Yu, George E. Dahl, Abdel-rahman Mohamed, Navdeep Jaitly, Andrew Senior, et al., Deep Neural Networks for Acoustic Modeling in Speech Recognition: The Shared Views of Four Research Groups, Signal Processing Magazine, *IEEE*, Vol. 29, No. 6, pp. 82–97, 2012.

Holte, Robert C., *An Analytical Framework for Learning Systems*, 1988.

Horvitz, Eric J., John S. Breese, and Max Henrion, Decision Theory in Expert Systems and Artificial Intelligence, *International Journal of Approximate Reasoning*, Vol. 2, Issue 3, pp. 247–302, 1988.

Hu, Derek Hao, and Qiang Yang, CIGAR: Concurrent and Interleaving Goal and Activity Recognition, *AAAI*, Vol. 8, pp. 1363–1368, 2008.

Huang, Y., Chang C., Auto-parking System via Intelligent Computation Intelligence, World Academy of Science, Engineering and Technology, pp. 1060–1063, 2012.

Hulten, Geoff, David Maxwell Chickering, and David Heckerman, Learning Bayesian Networks from Dependency Networks: A Preliminary Study, *Proceedings of the Ninth International Workshop on Artificial Intelligence and Statistics*, 2003.

Hurwitz, Judith, Alan Nugent, Fern Halper, and Marcia Kaufman, Big Data for Dummies, 2013.

Hussain, Wan, Wan Ishak, and Fadzilah Siraj, *Artificial Intelligence in Medical Application: An Exploration*, 2008.

Jaeger, Herbert, Tutorial on training recurrent neural networks, covering BPPT, RTRL, EKF and the "echo state network" approach, GMD-Forschungszentrum Informationstechnik, 2002.

Jain, Ramesh, Rangachar Kasturi, and Brian G. Schunck, *Machine Vision*, Vol. 5, McGraw-Hill, New York, 1995.

Jang, J-SR, ANFIS: Adaptive-network-based Fuzzy Inference System, Systems, Man and Cybernetics, *IEEE Transactions*, Vol. 23, No. 3, pp. 665–685, 1993.

Jang, Jyh-Shing Roger, Chuen-Tsai Sun, and Eiji Mizutani, *Neuro-fuzzy and Soft Computing: A Computational Approach to Learning and Machine Intelligence*, PHI Learning, Delhi, 2010.

Jiawei, Han, and Micheline Kamber, Data Mining: Concepts and Techniques, San Francisco, CA, itd: Morgan Kaufmann, 5, 2001.

Johnson, Kyle, Introduction to Transformational Grammar, Lecture Notes, Ms. University of Massachusetts, Amherst, 2004.

Karlik, Bekir, and A. Vehbi Olgac, Performance Analysis of Various Activation Functions in Generalized MLP Architectures of Neural Networks, *Int. J. Artif Intell Expert Syst.*, Vol. 1, Issue 4, pp. 111–122, 2011.

Kaushik, Saroj, *Artificial Intelligence*, Cengage Learning, 2011, India.

Kemble, Kimberlee A., *An Introduction to Speech Recognition*, Voice Systems Middleware Education-IBM Corporation, 2001.

Kendal, Simon L., and Malcolm Creen, *An Introduction to Knowledge Engineering*, Springer, London, 2007.

Khoo, Yong Bing, Mingwei Zhou, Berman Kayis, Sule Savci, Ammar Ahmed, and Raden Kusumo, An Agent-based Risk Management Tool for Concurrent Engineering Projects, Complexity International, Vol. 12, pp. 1–9, 2004.

Klingbeil, Ellen, Ashutosh Saxena, and Andrew Y. Ng., Learning to Open New Doors, Intelligent Robots and Systems (IROS), *IEEE/RSJ International Conference*, 2010.

Knoblock, Graig A., *An Analysis of ABSTRIPS*, March 1992.

Konar, Amit, *Artificial Intelligence and Soft Computing: Behavioral and Cognitive Modeling of the Human Brain*, CRC press, USA, 1999.

Korf, Richard E., Toward a Model of Representation Changes, *Artificial Intelligence*, Vol. 14, No. 1, pp. 41–78, 1980.

Korytkowski, Marcin, Robert K. Nowicki, Rafal Scherer, and Leszek Rutkowski, MICOG Defuzzification Rough-neuro-fuzzy System Ensemble, Fuzzy Systems (FUZZ), *IEEE International Conference*, pp. 1–6, 2010.

Kulkarni, Parag, *Reinforcement and Systemic Machine Learning for Decision Making*, Vol. 1, John Wiley & Sons, USA, 2012.

Kusiak, A., and E. Szczerbicki, Artificial Intelligence in Concurrent Engineering, *CAD/CAM Robotics and Factories of the Future'90*, Springer Berlin Heidelberg, New York, pp. 39–48, 1991.

Lagoudakis, Michail G., *Planning and Intelligent Systems: An Introductory Overview*, 1996.

Larkin, Jill H., and Herbert A. Simon, Why a Diagram is (sometimes) Worth Ten Thousand Words, *Cognitive Science*, Vol. 11, No. 1, pp. 65–100, 1987.

Le, Quoc V., Ashutosh Saxena, and Andrew Y. Ng., Active Perception: Interactive Manipulation for Improving Object Detection, 2008.

Lee, Chul Min, and Shrikanth Narayanan, Emotion Recognition using a Data-driven Fuzzy Inference System, *Proc. Eurospeech*, 2003.

Lee, Sukhan, Summary of Perception Guided Navigation and Manipulation, *Recent Progress in Robotics: Viable Robotic Service to Human*, Springer Berlin Heidelberg, New York, pp. 109–111, 2008.

Levin, Jonatha, *Choice under Uncertainty*, 2006.

Li, Jingpeng, Fuzzy Evolutionary Approaches for Bus and Rail Driver Scheduling, University of Leeds, 2002.

Liao, Gwo-Ching, and Ta-Peng Tsao, Application of Fuzzy Neural Networks and Artificial Intelligence for Load Forecasting, *Electric Power Systems Research*, Vol. 70, Issue 3, pp. 237–244, 2004.

Lissner, Ingmar, and Philipp Urban, Toward a Unified Color Space for Perception-based Image Processing, Image Processing, *IEEE Transactions*, pp. 1153–1168, 2012.

Luger, George F., *Artificial Intelligence: Structures and Strategies for Complex Problem Solving*, Pearson Education, 2005, India.

Magoulas, George D., Vassilis P. Plagianakos, and Michael N. Vrahatis, Globally Convergent Algorithms with Local Learning Rates, Neural Networks, *IEEE Transactions*, pp. 774–779, 13 March 2002.

Maier, Edith, et al., SEMPER: A Web-based Support System for Patient Self-management, *Proceedings of the 23rd Bled eConference eTrust: Implications for the Individual, Enterprises and Society*, pp. 20–23, 2010.

Maini, Raman, and Himanshu Aggarwal, Study and Comparison of Various Image Edge Detection Techniques, *International Journal of Image Processing (IJIP)*, Vol. 3, Issue 1, pp. 1–11, 2009.

Mallach, Efrem G., *Decision Support and Data Warehouse Systems*, McGraw-Hill Higher Education, 2000.

Marshall, Kneale T., and Robert M. Oliver, *Decision Making and Forecasting: With Emphasis on Model Building and Policy Analysis*, McGraw-Hill, 1995.

McCarthy, John, Actions and Other Events in Situation Calculus, *KR*, pp. 615–628, 2002.

McCulloch, Warren S., and Walter Pitts, A Logical Calculus of the Ideas Immanent in Nervous Activity, *The Bulletin of Mathematical Biophysics*, Vol. 5, Issue 4, pp. 115–133, 1943.

Mehrotra, Kishan, Chilukur K. Mohan, and Sanjay Ranka, *Artificial Neural Networks*, MIT Press, 1997.

Miles, J.C., and A.J. Walker, The Potential Application of Artificial Intelligence in Transport, Intelligent Transport Systems, *IEE Proceedings*, Vol. 153, No. 3. IET, 2006.

Mirikitani, Derrick T., and Nikolay Nikolaev, Recursive Bayesian Recurrent Neural Networks for Time-series Modeling, Neural Networks, *IEEE Transactions*, pp. 262–274, 21 February, 2010.

Mitchell, Tom M., *Machine Learning*, WCB/McGraw-Hill, USA, 1997.

Mitkas, Pericles A., Andreas L. Symeonidis, Dionisis Kehagias, and Ioannis N. Athanasiadis, Application of Data Mining and Intelligent Agent Technologies to Concurrent Engineering, *ISPE CE*, pp. 11–18, 2003.

Mladenic, Dunja, and Marko Grobelnik, Artificial Intelligence Handling Text Data, *Informacijska Druzba 2012*, 2012.

Nau, Dana S., Tsz-Chiu Au, Okhtay Ilghami, Ugur Kuter, J. William Murdock, Dan Wu, and Fusun Yaman, SHOP2: An HTN Planning System, *J. Artif. Intell. Res. (JAIR)*, Vol. 20, pp. 379–404, 2003.

Navigli, Roberto, Word Sense Disambiguation: A Survey, ACM Computing Surveys (CSUR), Vol. 41, Issue 2, 2009.

Neumann, John von, and Oskar Morgenstern, *Theory of Games and Economic Behaviour*, Princeton University Press, 60th Anniversary Edition, NJ, 2007.

Newell, Allen and Herbert A., Simon, *Human Problem Solving*, Prentice Hall, Upper Saddle River, NJ, 1972.

Nowicki, Robert K., On Classification with Missing Data using Rough-neuro-fuzzy systems, *International Journal of Applied Mathematics and Computer Science*, Vol. 20, Issue 1, pp. 55–67, 2010.

Patterson, Dan, *Introduction to Artificial Intelligence and Expert Systems*, Prentice-Hall Inc., 1990.

Pawlak, Zdzislaw, Rough sets, *International Journal of Computer & Information Sciences*, Vol. 11, Issue 5, pp. 341–356, 1982.

Pednault, Edwin P.D., Generalizing Nonlinear Planning to Handle Complex Goals and Actions with Context-Dependent Effects, *IJCAI*, pp. 240–245, 1991.

Phuong, Nguyen Hoang, and Vladik Kreinovich, *Fuzzy Logic and Its Applications in Medicine*, 2000.

Plannerer, Bernd, *An Introduction to Speech Recognition*, Munich, Germany, 2005.

Plch, Tomáš, and Cyril Brom, Enhancements for Reactive Planning-tricks and Hacks, *Proceedings of SOFSEM*, 2010.

Polikar, R., Pattern Recognition, Wiley Encyclopedia of Biomedical Engineering, Copyright & 2006 John Wiley & Sons, Inc.

Popa, Cosmin, Adoption of Artificial Intelligence in Agriculture, *Proceedings of the 10th International Symposium*, "Prospects for the 3rd Millennium Agriculture", Sections: Agriculture, Environment Protection and Rural Development, Food Science and Technology, UASVM Cluj-Napoca, Romania, 29 September-1 October 2011, Vol. 68. No. 1, University of Agricultural Sciences and Veterinary Medicine, 2011.

Qadir, Ashequl, and Ellen Riloff, Classifying Sentences as Speech Acts in Message Board Posts, *Proceedings of the Conference on Empirical Methods in Natural Language Processing*, Association for Computational Linguistics, 2011.

Rajasekaran, S., and G.A. Vijayslakshmi Pai, *Neural Networks, Fuzzy Logic and Genetic Algorithms*, PHI Learning, Delhi, 2011.

Ramik, Jaroslav, Soft Computing: Overview and Recent Developments in Fuzzy Optimization, Ostravská univerzita, Listopad, pp. 33–42, 2001.

Rastgarpour, M., and J. Shanbehzadeh, Application of AI Techniques in Medical Image Segmentation and Novel Categorization of Available Methods and Tools, Lecture Notes in Engineering and Computer Science, 2188, pp. 519–523, 2011.

Rich, Elaine, Kevin Knight, and Shiv Shankar B. Nair, *Artificial Intelligence*, McGraw-Hill, India, 2010.

Rojas, Raúl, *Neural Networks: A Systematic Introduction*, Springer, Germany, 1996.

Rosenblatt, Frank, *Principles of Neurodynamics*, 1962.

Rossini, Peter, Using Expert Systems and Artificial Intelligence for Real Estate Forecasting, *Sixth Annual Pacific-Rim Real Estate Society Conference*, Sydney, Australia, 2000.

Russell, Stuart, and Peter Norvig, *Artificial Intelligence: A Modern Approach*, Prentice-Hall, Englewood Cliffs, 1995.

Sacerdoti, Earl D., A Structure for Plans and Behaviour, Sri International Menlo Park CA Artificial Intelligence Center, 1975.

Saliba, Elie, and Albert Dipanda, *An Overview of Pattern Recognition*, 2013.

Schaul, Tom, Sixin Zhang, and Yann LeCun, No More Pesky Learning Rates, *arXiv preprint arXiv:1206.1106*, 2012.

Schiffel, Stephan, and Michael Thielscher, Reconciling Situation Calculus and Fluent Calculus, *AAAI*, Vol. 6, pp. 287–292, 2006.

Seidenfeld, Teddy, When Normal and Extensive form Decisions Differ, *Studies in Logic and the Foundations of Mathematics*, Vol. 134, pp. 451–463, 1995.

Shank, R.C., Conceptual Dependency: A Theory of Natural Language Analysis, *Cognitive Psychology*, Vol. 3, 1972.

Smith, Lindsay I., *A Tutorial on Principal Components Analysis*, Cornell University, USA 51, Vol. 52, 2002.

Smith, Reid G., and Adam Farquhar, The Road Ahead for Knowledge Management: An AI Perspective, *AI Magazine*, Vol. 21, Issue 4, p.17, 2000.

Smith, Stephen L., Mac Schwager, and Daniela Rus, Persistent Robotic Tasks: Monitoring and Sweeping in Changing Environments, Robotics, *IEEE Transactions*, pp. 410–426, 28 February 2012.

Sossa, Humberto, et al., Automatic Design of Artificial Neural Networks and Associative Memories for Pattern Classification and Pattern Restoration, *Pattern Recognition*, Springer Berlin Heidelberg, New York, pp. 23–34, 2012.

Steele, Guy L., *Common LISP: The Language*, Digital Press, USA, 1990.

Talia, Domenico, Clouds Meet Agents: Toward Intelligent Cloud Services, *IEEE Internet Computing*, Vol. 16, No. 2, pp. 78–81, 2012.

Tennenholtz, Moshe, Game Theory and Artificial Intelligence, *Foundations and Applications of Multi-Agent Systems*, Springer Berlin Heidelberg, New York, pp. 49–58, 2002.

Thangarajah, John, Managing the Concurrent Execution of Goals in Intelligent Agents, Ph.D. dissertation, School of Computer Science and Information Technology, Faculty of Applied Science, Royal Melbourne Institute of Technology, Melbourne, 2005.

Thanh, Nguyen Duc, Wanqing Li, and Philip Ogunbona, An Improved Template Matching Method for Object Detection, *Computer Vision–ACCV 2009*, Springer Berlin Heidelberg, New York, pp. 193–202, 2010.

Tong, Simon, *Active Learning: Theory and Applications*, Stanford University, 2001.

Touretzky, David S., *Common Lisp: A Gentle Introduction to Symbolic Computation*, Courier Dover Publications, 2013.

Tyugu, Enn, Artificial Intelligence in Cyber Defense, *Cyber Conflict (ICCC), 2011 3rd International Conference on IEEE*, 2011.

Ultes-Nitsche, Ulrich, and I. Yoo, Steps toward an Intelligent Firewall—A Basic Model, *Proceedings of Conference on Information Security for South Africa (ISSA2003)*, 2003.

Valença, Ivna, and Teresa Ludermir, Hybrid Systems for River Flood Forecasting Using MLP, SOM and Fuzzy Systems, *Artificial Neural Networks–ICANN 2009,* Springer Berlin Heidelberg, New York, pp. 557–566, 2009.

Venable, K. Brent, and Neil Yorke-Smith, Disjunctive Temporal Planning with Uncertainty, *19th International Joint Conference on Artificial Intelligence (IJCAI 2005),* 2005.

Vinay S., Shridhar A., Prashanth D., An NLP based Requirements Analysis Tool, *IEEE International Advance Computing Conference,* pp. 2355–2360, 2009.

Von Neumann, John, and Oskar Morgenstern, *The Theory of Games and Economic Behaviour,* 1947.

Wilkins, David E., A Call for Knowledge-based Planning, *AI Magazine,* Vol. 22, Issue 1, p. 99, 2001.

Williams, Jason D., A Case Study of Applying Decision Theory in the Real World: POMDPs and Spoken Dialog Systems, Decision Theory Models for Applications in Artificial Intelligence: Concepts and Solutions, pp. 315–342, 2010.

Winston, Patrick Henry, *Artificial Intelligence,* Reading, Mass.: Addison-Wesley, 1984.

Witten, Ian H., and Eibe Frank, *Data Mining: Practical Machine Learning Tools and Techniques,* Morgan Kaufmann, India, 2005.

Wolff J., *Big Data and the SP Theory of Intelligence,* 2014.

Woods, Steven, and Qiang Yang, Program Understanding as Constraint Satisfaction: Representation and Reasoning Techniques, Automated Software Engineering, Vol. 5, No. 2, pp. 147–181, 1998.

Xiang, Wen-Jiang, et al., Camera Calibration by Hybrid Hopfield Network and Self-Adaptive Genetic Algorithm, pp. 302–308, 2012.

Yu, Ping-Fang, and Ernie Jia-li Du, Towards a Syntactic Structural Analysis and An Augmented Transition Explanation: A Comparative Study of the Globally Ambiguous Sentences and Garden Path Sentences, *Journal of Computers,* Vol. 7, No. 1, pp. 196–206, 2012.

Zheng, Lihong, and Xiangjian He., *Classification Techniques in Pattern Recognition,* 2005.

WEB LINKS

http://aitopics.org/sites/default/files/classic/Webber-Nilsson-Readings/Rdgs-NW-Buchanan-Feigenbaum.pdf visited on 02/10/2013

http://bits.blogs.nytimes.com/2013/06/19/handicapping-the-half-life-of-big-data visited on 27/09/2013

http://www.cs.bgu.ac.il/~sipper/courses/ecal051/lecon2.pdf visited on 02/10/2013

http://www.cse.iitd.ernet.in/~pkalra/csl783/canny.pdf visited on 15/03/3014

https://www.cs.purdue.edu/homes/suresh/390C-Spring2012/lectures/Lecture-1.pdf visited on 02/10/2013 http://www.fit.vutbr.cz/units/UIFS/grants/index.php?file=%2Fproj%2F533% 2Ffmnl03-atn.pdf&id=533 visited on 29/07/2013

http://www.horizons.gc.ca/eng/content/artificial-intelligence-data-analytics-might-manage-billions visited on 15/08/2013

http://www.inf.pucrs.br/felipe.meneguzzi/download/AAMAS_14/workshops/ AAMAS2014-W06/acan2014_6.pdf visited on 12/01/2014

http://www.lispworks.com/products/myths_and_legends.html visited on 01/01/2014

http://msl1.mit.edu/ESD10/block4/4.4_-_Game_Theory.pdf visited on 05/03/2014

http://www.newyorker.com/news/news-desk/is-deep-learning-a-revolution-in-artificial-intelligence visited on 21/08/2014

http://www.nouvo.ch/2013/04/des-drones-pour-sauver-des-vies visited on 05/03/2014

http://www.technologyreview.com/news/524026/is-google-cornering-the-market-on-deep-learning/ visited on 24/08/2014

http://web.eecs.utk.edu/~parker/Courses/CS594-spring06/handouts/Neural-net-notes. pdf visited on 12/03/2014

http://web.media.mit.edu/~hugo/publications/papers/BTTJ-ConceptNet.pdf visited on 05/03/2013

Index

497